PLAYFAIR
FOOTBALL
ANNUAL 1992-93

PLAYFAIR FOOTBALL ANNUAL 1992-93

EDITED BY JACK ROLLIN

HEADLINE

First published in 1992
by HEADLINE BOOK PUBLISHING PLC

10 9 8 7 6 5 4 3 2 1

Cover photograph Left: Shaun Teale (Aston Villa); right: Dean Saunders (Liverpool) (*Allsport*)

ISBN 0 7472 4032 9

Printed and bound in Great Britain by
HarperCollins Manufacturing, Glasgow

HEADLINE BOOK PUBLISHING PLC
Headline House,
79 Great Titchfield Street,
London W1P 7FN

CONTENTS

Other Football

Information and Records

EDITORIAL

The armchair fan has never had it so good, thanks to the £304 million deal with BSky B and BBC over five years for the Premier League for two games a week, ITV offering a limited selection of Football League matches and Channel 4 covering the Italian League. In addition comes the return of BBC highlights. But it will cost the viewer a satellite dish and probably more to watch the Premier League if extra pay-to-view is implemented.

On another front the England manager Graham Taylor was right when he said that once the League season ends and the FA Cup is out of the way, everyone expects the national side to be up and running for either of the major competitions, the European Championship and the World Cup. But averaging 12 games a season, the international fixture list is itself a formidable addition to the demands on players with clubs in the top echelon of the game.

This coming season will see a further attempt at the prevention of time-wasting with the introduction of a measure to prevent the goal-keeper being brought into action by his own players from up to half the length of the field, by restricting his right to handle the ball at all times. But it was the over-protection of the goalkeeper which caused the original problem. The penalty area has long since become a 'no-go' area when the goalkeeper is in possession.

Off the field, the implementation of the Taylor Report will cost top clubs millions of pounds as they shrink to all-seater capacities by 1994–95. They will claim increased prices of admission are necessary for this reason and that the income from television is insufficient to cover all outgoing costs. But the fans will see it in a different light.

The game is again at the crossroads and it will be a testing time for the FA Premier League. The new body and the Football League must bury their differences and act as neighbours, home and away, with both subject to paying the bill, as the cost of policing the game soars. While arrests at grounds were down last season for the third year in a row, with arrests and ejections at 8556 compared with 9190 the season before, the figures do not represent statistics outside stadia and for those who travel to matches by public transport, there remain too many instances of misbehaviour. Moreover that underlying current of unpleasantness which erupted in Sweden during the European Championship made it obvious that hooliganism is being contained over here, not eradicated. England fans who cause trouble abroad also watch games in England. Hosting the 1996 tournament will be an expensive experience as the FA has already noted.

ALDERSHOT TOWN   DIADORA DIV. 3

League Appearances: Baker, S. 9; Berry, G. 25; Bertschin, K. 17; Brown, K.B. 36; Burvill, G. 1(3); Cole, M.W. 1; Cooper, L.V. 20(1); Flower, J.G. 23(2); Granville, J. 30; Halbert, P.J. –(1); Heath, P. 15(10); Henry, C. 35; Hopkins, A. 20(4); Hucker, P.I. 1; Hutchinson, G.J. –(1); Joyce, A.J. 4; McDonald, I.C. 17(1); Ogley, M.A. 30(1); Osgood, S. 5; Parks, W.B. 3; Phillips, S.G. 5; Puckett, D.C. 29(3); Randall, A.J. 8(1); Rees, M. 19; Reinelt, R.S. 9(2); Stapleton, F. 1; Stewart, I.E. 6(5); Talbot, B. –(1); Terry, P.E. 14(2); Tomlinson, C. 1(1); Tucker, J.J. 4(2); Whitlock, M. 8(2).
League Goals (21): Puckett 7, Bertschin 2, Henry 2, Hopkins 2, Berry 1, Cooper 1, Heath 1, Joyce 1, Ogley 1, Rees 1, Stewart 1, own goals 1.
Rumbelows Cup (2): Bertschin 1, Puckett 1.
FA Cup (0).
Ground: Recreation Ground, High St, Aldershot GU11 1TW (0252 20211)
Manager: Steve Wignall   **Secretary:** P. Bridgeman
Colours: Red shirts (blue trim), white shorts (red flash), blue stockings (white trim)
Record home gate: 19,138 v Carlisle U, FA Cup 4th rd (replay), 28 January 1970
Honours – Nil

ARSENAL   FA PREMIER

Adams, Tony A.	Groves, Perry	Parlour, Raymond
Bacon, John P.G.	Heaney, Neil A.	Pates, Colin G.
Bould, Stephen A.	Hillier, David	Read, Paul C.
Campbell, Kevin J.	Lee, Justin D.	Rocastle, David C.
Carter, James W.C.	Limpar, Anders	Seaman, David A.
Clements, Steven	Linighan, Andrew	Selley, Ian
Cole, Andrew A.	Lydersen, Pal	Shaw, Paul
Davis, Paul V.	Marshall, Scott R.	Smith, Alan M.
Dickov, Paul	Merson, Paul C.	Webster, Kenneth D.
Dixon, Lee M.	Miller, Alan J.	Will, James A.
Flatts, Mark M.	Morrow, Stephen J.	Winterburn, Nigel
Gaunt, Craig	O'Leary, David A.	Wright, Ian E.

League Appearances: Adams, T.A. 35; Bould, S.A. 24(1); Campbell, K.J. 22(9); Carter, J.W.C. 5(1); Davis, P.V. 12; Dixon, L.M. 38; Groves, P. 5(8); Heaney, N.A. –(1); Hillier, D. 27; Limpar, A. 23(6); Linighan, A. 15(2); Lydersen, P. 5(2); Merson, P.C. 41(1); Morrow, S.J. –(2); O'Leary, D.A. 11(14); Parlour, R. 2(4); Pates, C.G. 9(2); Rocastle, D. 36(3); Seaman, D.A. 42; Smith, A.M. 33(6); Thomas, M.L. 6(4); Winterburn, N. 41; Wright, I.E. 30. ·
League Goals (81): Wright 24 (2 pens), Campbell 13, Merson 12, Smith 12, Dixon 4 (3 pens), Limpar 4, Rocastle 4, Adams 2, Bould 1, Groves 1, Hillier 1, Parlour 1, Thomas 1, Winterburn 1.
Rumbelows Cup (3): Wright 2, Merson 1.
FA Cup (1): Smith 1.
Ground: Arsenal Stadium, Highbury, London N5 (071-226 0304)
Manager: George Graham   **Secretary:** K. J. Friar
Colours: Red shirts with white sleeves, white shorts, red stockings

Record home gate: 73,295 v Sunderland, Div 1, 9 March 1935
Honours – Champions: Division 1: 1930–31, 1932–33, 1933–34, 1934–35, 1937–38, 1947–48, 1952–53, 1970–71, 1988–89, 1990–91
FA Cup winners: 1929–30, 1935–36, 1949–50, 1970–71, 1978–79
Football League Cup winners: 1986–87
Fairs Cup winners: 1969–70

ASTON VILLA   FA PREMIER

Atkinson, Dalian R.	Daley, Anthony M.	Parker, Garry S.
Barrett, Earl D.	Davis, Neil	Parrott, Mark A.
Beinlich, Stefan	Ehiogu, Ugochuku	Regis, Cyrille
Berry, Trevor J.	Farrell, David	Richardson, Kevin
Blake, Mark A.	Fenton, Graham A.	Sealey, Leslie J.
Boden, Christopher D.	Froggart, Stephen J.	Small, Bryan
Bosnich, Mark	Kubicki, Darisz	Spink, Nigel P.
Breitkreutz, Mattias	Livingstone, Glen	Staunton, Stephen
Carruthers, Martin G.	McGrath, Paul	Teale, Shaun
Cox, Neil J.	Oakes, Michael C.	Williams, Lee
Crisp, Richard I.	Olney, Ian D.	Yorke, Dwight

League Appearances: Atkinson, D.R. 11(3); Barrett, E.D. 13; Beinlich, S. –(2); Blake, M.A. 14; Bosnich, M. 1; Breitkreutz, M. 7(1); Carruthers, M.G. 2(1); Cowans, G.S. 10(2); Cox, N.J. 4(3); Daley, A.M. 29(5); Ehiogu, U. 4(4); Froggatt, S.J. 6(3); Kubicki, D. 23; McGrath, P. 41; Mortimer, P.H. 10(2); Mountfield, D.N. 2; Nielsen, K. 3(3); Olney, I.D. 14(6); Ormondroyd, I. –(1); Parker, G.S. 25; Penrice, G. 5(3); Price, C.J. 2(1); Regis, C. 39; Richardson, K. 42; Sealey, L.J. 18; Small, B. 8; Spink, N.P. 23; Staunton, S. 37; Teale, S. 42; Yorke, D. 27(5).
League Goals (48): Regis 11, Yorke 11, Daley 7, Richardson 6, Staunton 4 (1 pen), Blake 2, Olney 2, Atkinson 1, McGrath 1, Mortimer 1, Parker 1, Penrice 1.
Rumbelows Cup (1): Teale 1.
FA Cup (7): Yorke 5, Froggatt 1, Parker 1.
Ground: Villa Park, Trinity Rd, Birmingham B6 6HE (021-327 2299)
Manager: Ron Atkinson   **Secretary:** Steven Stride
Colours: Claret shirts, blue trim, white shorts, claret and blue trim, blue stockings, claret trim
Record home gate: 76,588 v Derby Co, FA Cup 6th rd, 2 March 1946
Honours – Champions: Division 1: 1893–94, 1895–96, 1896–97, 1898–99, 1899–1900, 1909–10, 1980–81; Division 2: 1937–38, 1959–60; Division 3: 1971–72
FA Cup winners: 1887, 1895, 1897, 1905, 1913, 1920, 1957
Football League Cup winners: 1961, 1975, 1977
European Cup winners: 1981–82
European Super Cup winners: 1982–83

BARNET   DIV. 3

Barnett, David	Bull, Gary W.	Evans, Nicholas J.
Bodley, Michael J.	Carter, Mark C.	Horton, Duncan

Lowe, Kenneth
Naylor, Dominic J.

Pape, Andrew M.
Showler, Paul

Tomlinson, David I.
Willis, Roger C.

League Appearances: Barnett, D. 3(1); Blackford, G.J. 2(4); Bodley, M.J. 36; Bull, G.W. 42; Carter, M.C. 32(4); Cawley, P.E. 3; Cooper, G.V. 13(1); Evans, N.J. 7(2); Hayrettin, H. –(4); Hoddle, C. 10(3); Horton, D. 24(5); Howell, D.C. 34; Hunt, J. 2(12); Johnson, R.S. 2; Joseph, F. 1; Lowe, K. 26(10); Lynch, A.J. 1(5); Morrow, S. 1; Murphy, F. 3(12); Naylor, D.J. 26; Nethercott, S. 3; Nugent, R. 2; Pape, A.M. 36; Payne, D.R. 13(1); Phillips, G.C. 6; Poole, G.J. 39(1); Showler, P. 39; Stein, E. –(1); Tomlinson, D.I. –(3); Willis, R.C. 33(5); Wilson, P. 23(2).
League Goals (81): Bull 20 (4 pens), Carter 19, Willis 12, Showler 7, Murphy 5, Horton 3, Howell 3, Lowe 3, Poole 2, Bodley 1, Cooper 1, Evans 1, Payne 1, Wilson 1, own goals 2.
Rumbelows Cup (6): Bull 2, Carter 2, Evans 2.
FA Cup (10): Carter 5, Bull 2, Evans 1, Naylor 1, Showler 1.
Ground: Underhill Stadium, Barnet Lane, Barnet, Herts EN5 2BE (081-441 6932)
Manager: Barry Fry   **Secretary:** Bryan Ayres
Colours: Amber shirts, black shorts, black stockings
Record home gate: 11,026 v Wycombe Wanderers. FA Amateur Cup 4th Round 1951–52
Honours – Nil

BARNSLEY DIV. 1

Archdeacon, Owen D.
Bishop, Darren C.
Bullimore, Wayne A.
Burton, Marc A.
Butler, Lee S.
Connelly, Dean
Currie, David N.
Davis, Steven P.

Eaden, Nicholas J.
Fleming, James G.
Graham, Deiniol W.T.
Gridelet, Philip R.
Hoyle, Colin R.
Liddell, Andrew M.
McCord, Brian J.
O'Connell, Brendan

Pearson, John S.
Rammell, Andrew V.
Redfern, Neil D.
Robinson, Mark J.
Smith, Mark C.
Taggart, Gerald P.
Whitehead, Philip M.
Williams, Gareth J.

League Appearances: Archdeacon, O.D. 40; Banks, I.F. 23(3); Bishop, C. 25(3); Bullimore, W.A. 17(1); Butler, L.S. 43; Connelly, D. 2(1); Currie, D.N. 30(7); Cross, P. 3; Davis, S.P. 8(1); Fleming, G.J. 40(2); Graham, D.W.T. 8(13); Liddell, A.M. –(1); McCord, B.J. 1(2); O'Connell, B.J. 34(2); Pearson, J.S. 8(2); Rammell, A.V. 31(6); Redfearn, N.D. 35(1); Robinson, M.J. 40(1); Saville, A.V. 14(8); Smith, M.C. 37(1); Taggart, G.P. 38; Whitehead, P.M. 3; Whitworth, N.A. 11; Williams, G. 15(2).
League Goals (46): Rammell 8, Currie 7, Archdeacon 6, Saville 6, O'Connell 4, Redfearn 4 (2 pens), Taggart 3, Banks 2, Robinson 2, Bullimore 1, Graham 1, Pearson 1, Smith 1.
Rumbelows Cup (2): O'Connell 1, Pearson 1.
FA Cup (0).
Ground: Oakwell Ground, Grove St, Barnsley (0226 295353)
Manager: Mel Machin   **Secretary:** Michael Spinks
Colours: Red shirts, white trim, white shorts, red stockings
Record home gate: 40,255 v Stoke C, FA Cup 5th rd, 15 February 1936
Honours – **Champions:** Division 3 (N): 1933–34, 1938–39, 1954–55
FA Cup winners: 1912

BIRMINGHAM CITY DIV. 1

Atkins, Ian L.
Beckford, Jason N.
Clarkson, Ian S.
Cooper, Mark N.
Donowa, Brian L.
Fox, Matthew C.
Foy, David L.
Frain, John W.
Gayle, John

Gleghorn, Nigel W.
Hicks, Martin
Hogan, Thomas E.
Jones, Paul T.
Mardon, Paul J.
Matthewson, Trevor
O'Neill, Alan
Peer, Dean
Rennie, David

Rodgerson, Ian
Rowbotham, Darren
Rutherford, Mark R.
Sale, Mark D.
Sturridge, Simon A.
Tait, Paul R.
Thomas, Martin R.

League Appearances: Atkins, I. 5(3); Aylott, T.K.C. 2; Beckford, J. 2(2); Carter, T.D. 2; Cheesewright, J.A. 1; Clarkson, I.S. 42; Cooper, M.N. 27(6); Dearden, K.C. 12; Dolan, E.J. 1(1); Donowa, B.L. 20(6); Drinkell, K. 5; Frain, J.W. 44; Francis, S.R. –(3); Gayle, J. 2(1); Gleghorn, N.W. 46; Hicks, M. 41(1); Hogan, T.E. –(1); Jones P.T. –(1); Mardon, P.J. 31(4); Matthewson, T. 35(1); Miller, A. 15; Okenla, F. 2(5); O'Neill, A. 2(2); Paskin, J. 8(2); Peer, D. 18(3); Rennie, D. 17; Rodgerson, I. 38(1); Rowbotham, D. 21(1); Sale, M.D. 2(4); Sturridge, S.A. 38(2); Tait, P.R. 10(2); Thomas, M.R. 16; Yates, M.J. 1(1).
League Goals (69): Gleghorn 17 (1 pen), Sturridge 10, Rodgerson 9, Matthewson 6, Frain 5 (5 pens), Cooper 4, Rowbotham 4, Paskin 3, Donowa 2, Drinkell 2, Rennie 2, Beckford 1, Gayle 1, Hicks 1, Okenla 1, Peer 1.
Rumbelows Cup (13): Gleghorn 5, Peer 3, Rodgerson 2, Hicks 1, Sturridge 1, Yates 1.
FA Cup (0).
Ground: St Andrews, Birmingham B9 4NH (021-772 0101/2689)
Manager: Terry Cooper **Secretary:** Alan G. Jones BA, MBA
Colours: Royal blue shirts, white shorts, blue stockings with white trim
Record home gate: 66,844 v Everton, FA Cup 5th rd, 11 February 1939
Honours – Champions: Division 2: 1892–93, 1920–21, 1947–48, 1954–55
Football League Cup winners: 1963
Associate Members Cup winners: 1991

BLACKBURN ROVERS FA PREMIER

Agnew, Stephen M.
Atkins, Mark N.
Brown, Richard A.
Collier, Darren
Cowans, Gordon S.
Dewhurst, Robert M.
Dickins, Matthew J.
Dobson, Anthony J.
Donnelly, Darren C.
Garner, Simon
Hendry, Edward C.J.

Hill, Keith J.
Livingstone, Stephen
May, David
Mimms, Robert A.
Moran, Kevin B.
Munro, Stuart
Newell, Michael C.
Price, Chistopher J.
Reid, Nicholas S.
Richardson, Lee J.
Sellars, Scott

Shearer, Duncan N.
Shepstone, Paul T.
Sherwood, Timothy A.
Skinner, Craig R.
Speedie, David R.
Sulley, Christopher S.
Tallon, Gary T.
Thorne, Peter L.
Wegerle, Roy C.
Wilcox, Jason M.
Wright, Alan G.

League Appearances: Agnew, S.M. 2; Atkins, M.N. 40(4); Baah, P.H. 1; Beardsmore, R.P. 1(1); Brown, R.A. 24(2); Cowans, G.S. 26; Dickins, M.J. 1; Dobson, A.J. 4(1); Duxbury, M. 5; Garner, S. 14(11); Gayle, H.A. 1(3); Hendry, E.C.J. 26(4); Hill, K.J. 31(1); Irvine, J.A. 4(2); Johnrose, L. 7; Livingstone, S. 6(4); May, D. 12; Mimms, R.A. 45; Moran, K.B. 37(4); Munro, S. 1; Newell, M.C. 18(2); Price, C.J. 11(2); Reid, N.S. 8(13); Richardson, L.J. 18(6); Sellars, S. 28(2); Shearer, D. 5(1); Shepstone, P.T.A. 1; Sherwood, T. 7(4); Skinner, C.R. 7(2); Speedie, D.R. 34(2); Sulley, C.S. 7; Wegerle, R.C. 9(3); Wilcox, J.M. 33(5); Wright, A. 32(1).
League Goals (70): Speedie 23 (1 pen), Sellars 7 (1 pen), Atkins 6, Newell 6 (2 pens), Garner 5, Hendry 4, Wilcox 4, Price 3, Moran 2, Wegerle 2, Cowans 1, Johnrose 1, Livingstone 1 (1 pen), Reid 1, Richardson 1, Shearer 1, Wright 1, own goals 1.
Rumbelows Cup (1); own goals 1.
FA Cup (5): Newell 3, Cowans 1, Speedie 1.
Ground: Ewood Park, Blackburn BB2 4JF (0254 55432)
Manager: Kenny Dalglish   **Secretary:** John W. Howarth FAAI
Colours: Blue and white halved shirts, white shorts, blue stockings
Record home gate: 61,783 v Bolton W, FA Cup 6th rd, 2 March, 1929
Honours – Champions: Division 1: 1911–12, 1913–14; Division 2: 1938–39; Division 3: 1974–75
FA Cup winners: 1884, 1885, 1886, 1890, 1891, 1928
Full Members' Cup winners: 1986–87

BLACKPOOL DIV. 2

Bamber, John D.
Bond, Richard
Briggs, Gary
Burgess, David J.
Cook, Mitchell
Davies, Michael J.
Eyres, David
Garner, Andrew
Gore, Ian G.
Gouck, Andrew S.
Groves, Paul
Horner, Philip M.
Leitch, Grant
McIlhargey, Stephen
Murphy, James A.
Murray, Mark
Rodwell, Anthony
Sinclair, Trevor L.
Stoneman, Paul

League Appearances: Bamber, J.D. 42; Bonner, M. 2(1); Briggs, G. 24; Brook, G. 1; Burgess, D.J. 16; Cook, M.C. 8; Davies, M.J. 26(3); Eyres, D. 41; Garner, A. 27(3); Gore, I.G. 41; Gouck, A.S. 20(4); Groves, P. 42; Hedworth, C. 4; Horner, P.M. 25(2); Kearton, J. 14; Kerr, D. 12; Leitch, G. 1(5); McIlhargey, S. 28; Mitchell, N.N. –(1); Murray, M. 2; Richards, C.L. –(3); Rodwell, A. 40; Sinclair, T.L. 15(12); Stoneman, P. 17(2); Taylor, P.M.R. 2(8); Wright, A.G. 12.
League Goals (71): Bamber 26, Eyres 9 (1 pen), Groves 9 (1 pen), Rodwell 8, Garner 5, Horner 4, Sinclair 3, Gouck 2, Taylor 2, Davies 1, Kerr 1, own goals 1.
Rumbelows Cup (8): Bamber 6, Groves 1, own goals 1.
FA Cup (2): Bamber 1, Groves 1.
Ground: Bloomfield Rd Ground, Blackpool FY1 6JJ (0253 404331)
Manager: Bill Ayre   **Secretary:** Jean Miskelly
Colours: Tangerine shirts with navy and white trim, white shorts, tangerine stockings with white tops

Record home gate: 38,098 v Wolverhampton W, Division 1, 17 September 1955
Honours – Champions: Division 2: 1929–30
FA Cup winners: 1953
Anglo-Italian Cup winners: 1971

BOLTON WANDERERS   DIV. 2

Brown, Michael A.
Brown, Phillip
Burke, David I.
Came, Mark R.
Darby, Julian T.
Felgate, David W.
Fisher, Neil J.
Green, Scott P.

Jeffrey, Michael R.
Kelly, Anthony G.
Lydiate, Jason L.
McAteer, Jason W.
Oliver, Darren
Patterson, Mark A.
Philliskirk, Anthony
Reeves, David

Roscoe, Andrew R.
Seagraves, Mark
Spooner, Nicholas M.
Storer, Stuart J.
Stubbs, Alan
Walker, Andrew
Winstanley, Mark A.

League Appearances: Brown, M.A. 23(4); Brown, P. 35(2); Burke, D.I. 37; Came, M.R. 18; Charnley, J. 3; Cowdrill, B.J. 1; Darby, J.T. 42(2); Dibble, A.G. 13; Felgate, D.W. 25; Fisher, N.J. 4(3); Green, S.P. 26(11); Jeffrey, M.R. 1(1); Kelly, A.G. 31; Kennedy, A.J. 1; Lydiate, J.L. 1; Maxwell, A. 3; Patterson, M.A. 36; Peyton, G.J. 1; Philliskirk, A. 42(1); Reeves, D. 24(11); Rose, K.P. 4; Seagraves, M. 39(1); Spooner, N. 14(1); Storer, S.J. 4(5); Stubbs, A. 26(6); Thompson, S.J. 2; Walker, A. 23(1); Winstanley, M.A. 27.
League Goals (57): Walker 15, Philliskirk 12 (4 pens), Reeves 8, Darby 6, Brown M 3, Brown P 2, Green 2, Kelly 2, Patterson 2 (1 pen), Fisher 1, Seagraves 1, Spooner 1, Stubbs 1, own goals 1.
Rumbelows Cup (6): Darby 3, Kelly 1, Patterson 1, Philliskirk 1.
FA Cup (12): Philliskirk 3 (2 pens), Reeves 3, Walker 3, Burke 1, Darby 1, Green 1.
Ground: Burnden Park, Bolton B13 2QR (0204 389200)
Manager: Bruce Rioch.   **Secretary:** Des McBain.
Colours: White shirts, navy blue shorts, red stockings, blue and white tops
Record home gate: 69,912 v Manchester C, FA Cup 5th rd, 18 February 1933
Honours – Champions: Division 2: 1908–09, 1977–78; Division 3: 1972–73
FA Cup winners: 1923, 1926, 1929, 1958
Associate Members Cup winners: 1989

AFC BOURNEMOUTH   DIV. 2

Bartram, Vincent L.
Brooks, Shaun
Cooke, Richard E.
Ekoku, Efan
Holmes, Matthew J.
McGorry, Brian P.

Mitchell, Paul R.
Morrell, Paul D.
Morris, Mark J.
Mundee, Denny W.J.
Puckett, David C.
Quinn, James M.

Rowland, Keith
Shearer, Peter A.
Watson, Alexander F.
Wood, Paul A.

League Appearances: Baker, S. 5(1); Bartram, V.L. 46; Bond, K.J. 38; Brooks, S. 6(1); Case, J.R. 38(2); Cooke, R.E. 20(11); Ekoku, E. 24(4); Fereday, W. 3(2); Holmes, M.J. 43(3); Jones, A.M. 6(1); Lawrence, G.R. 2(6); McGorry, B.P. 4(4); Mitchell, P.R. 1(4); Morrell, P.D.P. 23(1); Morris, M.J. 43; Mundee, D.W.J. 28(13); O'Driscoll, S.M. 40(4); Puckett, D.C. 1(3); Pulis, A.R. –(1); Quinn, J.M. 43; Rowland, K. 34(3); Shearer, P.A. 6(2); Statham, B. 2; Watson, A.F. 15; Wood, P.A. 35.

League Goals (52): Quinn 19 (3 pens), Ekoku 11, Wood 9, Holmes 3, Morris 3, Mundee 2, Bond 1, Case 1, Morrell 1, O'Driscoll 1, Shearer 1.

Rumbelows Cup (8): Jones 2, Quinn 2, Cooke 1, Lawrence 1, Morrell 1, Watson 1.

FA Cup (7): Bond 2, Mundee 2 (2 pens), Quinn 2, Wood 1.

Ground: Dean Court Ground, Bournemouth (0202 395381)

Manager: Tony Pulis   **Secretary:** Keith MacAlister

Colours: Red and black striped shirts, white shorts, white stockings

Record home gate: 28,799 v Manchester U, FA Cup 6th rd, 2 March 1957

Honours – Champions: Division 3: 1986–87

Associate Members' Cup winners: 1984

BRADFORD CITY DIV. 2

Babb, Philip A.	Jewell, Paul	Stuart, Mark R.
Bairstow, Scott	Lawford, Craig B.	Tinnon, Brian
Dowson, Alan P.	McCarthy, Sean C.	Tominson, Paul
Duxbury, Lee E.	McHugh, Michael B.	Torpey, Stephen D.J.
Duxbury, Michael	Oliver, Gavin R.	Treacy, Darren P.
James, Robert M.	Stapleton, Francis A.	Williams, Gary

League Appearances: Babb, P.A. 46; Blake, N. 6; Dowson, A.P. 16(2); Duxbury, L.E. 46; Duxbury, M. 16; Evans, M. 1; Gardner, S.G. 14; Howe, J. 3; James, R.M. 43; Jewell, P. 28(2); Leonard, M.A. 15(4); McCarthy, S.C. 27(2); McHugh, M.B. 5(4); Mitchell, C.B. 20; Morgan, D.J. 9(2); Oliver, G.R. 10; Reid, P.R. 7; Reid, W.A. 17(2); Richards, D.I. 5(2); Stapleton, F. 25(2); Stuart, M.R.N. 9(7); Tinnion, B. 21(5); Tomlinson, P. 45; Torpey, S. 41(2); Williams, G. 22; Willis, J.A. 9.

League Goals (62): McCarthy 16, Torpey 10, Tinnion 8 (2 pens), Jewell 6, Duxbury L 5, Babb 4, James 3 (3 pens), Reid W 3, Stuart 3, Richards 1, Willis 1, own goals 2.

Rumbelows Cup (5): Duxbury L 2 (1 pens), Leonard 1, Stuart 1, Tinnion 1 (1 pen).

FA Cup (2): Tinnion 2.

Ground: Valley Parade Ground, Bradford BD8 7DY (0274 306062)

Manager: Frank Stapleton   **Secretary:** Terry Newman

Colours: Amber and claret diamond shirts, black shorts, amber stockings

Record home gate: 39,146 v Burnley, FA Cup 4th rd, 11 March 1911

Honours – Champions: Division 2: 1907–08; Division 3: 1984–85; Division 3 (N): 1928–29

FA Cup winners: 1911 (first holders of the present trophy)

Bates, Jamie	Evans, Terence W.	Peters, Robert A.A.
Bayes, Ashley J.	Gayle, Marcus A.	Ratcliffe, Simon
Benstead, Graham M.	Godfrey, Kevin	Rostron, John W.
Birch, Paul A.	Holdsworth, Dean C.	Sealy, Anthony J.
Blissett, Gary P.	Luscombe, Lee J.	Smillie, Neil
Booker, Robert	Manuel, William A.J.	Statham, Brian
Buckle, Paul J.	Millen, Keith	

League Appearances: Bates, J. 41(1); Bayes, A.J. 1; Benstead, G.M. 37; Blissett, G.D. 31(6); Booker, R. 14(2); Buckle, P.J. 8(7); Cadette, R.R. 10(1); Driscoll, A. –(1); Evans, T.W. 44; Finnigan, A. 3; Gayle, M.A. 28(10); Godfrey, K. 26(5); Holdsworth, D.C. 40(1); Hughton, C. 12; Jones, K.A. 6; Kruszynski, Z. 8; Luscombe, L.J. 10(3); Manuel, W.A.J. 27(8); Millen, K. 34; Peters, R.A.G. 1(8); Ratcliffe, S. 31(3); Rostron, J.W. 15(3); Sealy, A.J. 9(9); Smillie, N. 44; Statham, B. 18; Suckling, P. 8.
League Goals (81): Holdsworth 24 (1 pen), Blissett 17 (1 pen), Evans 8, Smillie 7, Gayle 6, Godfrey 3, Luscombe 3, Booker 2, Ratcliffe 2, Bates 1, Buckle 1, Cadette 1, Jones 1, Millen 1, own goals 4.
Rumbelows Cup (15): Holdsworth 6, Cadette 4, Godfrey 3, Evans 1, Manuel 1.
FA Cup (7): Holdsworth 4, Bates 1, Blissett 1, Sealy 1.
Ground: Griffin Park, Braemar Rd, Brentford, Middlesex TW8 0NT (081-847 2511)
Manager: Phil Holder   **Secretary:** Polly Kates
Colours: Red and white striped shirts, black shorts, red stockings with black tops
Record home gate: 39,626 v Preston NE, FA Cup 6th rd, 5 March 1938
Honours – Champions: Division 2: 1934–35; Division 3: 1991–92; Division 3 (S) – 1932–33; Division 4: 1962–63

BRIGHTON & HOVE ALBION

DIV. 2

Beeney, Mark R.	Crumplin, John L.	Munday, Stuart C.
Bissett, Nicholas	Digweed, Perry M.	O'Reilly, Gary M.
Chapman, Ian R.	Farrington, Mark A.	Robinson, John R.C.
Chivers, Gay P.S.	Gall, Mark I.	Walker, Clive
Clarkson, David J.	Gallacher, Bernard	Wilkins, Dean M.
Codner, Robert A.G.	McCarthy, Paul J.	

League Appearances: Barham, M.F. 22(2); Beeney, M.R. 24(1); Bissett, N. 11(2); Briley, L. 11(4); Byrne, J.F. 13; Chapman, I.R. 35(2); Chivers, G.P.S. 36(2); Clarkson, D.J. 4(9); Codner, R.A.G. 44(1); Crumplin, J.L. 27(2); Digweed, P.M. 20; Farrington, M.A. 8(6); Funnell, S.P. –(1); Gall, M.I. 30(1); Gallacher, B. 31; Iovan, S. 4; McCarthy, P.J. 20; Meade, R.J. 35(5); Munday, S.C. 14; O'Dowd, G.H. –(1); O'Reilly, G.M. 28; Robinson, J.R.C. 34(2); Sommer, J.P. 1; Wade, B.A. 7; Walker, C. 23; Wilkins, D.M. 24(2).
League Goals (56): Gall 13, Meade 9, Codner 6, Robinson 6, Byrne 5, O'Reilly 3, Wade 3, Barham 2 (1 pen), Chapman 2, Walker 2, Bissett 1, Chivers 1, Farrington 1, Gallacher 1, Munday 1.

Rumbelows Cup (5): Byrne 2, Codner 1, Meade 1, Robinson 1.
FA Cup (6): Chapman 2 (1 pens), Meade 2, Gall 1, Walker 1.
Ground: Goldstone Ground, Old Shoreham Rd, Hove, Sussex BN3 7DE (0273 739535)
Manager: Barry Lloyd   **Secretary:** Steve Rooke
Colours: Blue and white vertical striped shirts, matching shorts with red trim, blue stockings
Record home gate: 36,747 v Fulham, Division 2, 27 December 1958
Honours – Champions: Division 3 (S): 1957–58; Division 4: 1964–65

BRISTOL CITY   DIV. 1

Aizlewood, Mark
Allison, Wayne
Atteveld, Raymond
Bent, Junior A.
Bryant, Matthew
Campbell, Gary
Clifford, Stephen A.
Connor, Terence F.
Dziekanowski, Dariusz P.
Edwards, Robert W.
Gavin, Mark W.
Harrison, Gerald R.
Leaning, Andrew J.
Llewellyn, Andrew D.
May, Andrew M.
McIntyre, James
Melon, Michael J.
Morgan, Nicholas
Osman, Russell C.
Paterson, Andrew
Rosenior, Leroy D.G.
Scott, Martin
Shelton, Gary
Vernon, Deion A.
Welch, Keith J.

League Appearances: Aizlewood, M. 34; Allison, W. 37(6); Atteveld, R. 4(3); Bent, J.A. 7(10); Bryant, M. 43; Caesar, G.C. 9(1); Cole, A. 12; Connor, T.F. 9(2); Dziekanowski, D.P. 16(1); Edwards, R.W. 12(8); Gavin, M.W. 12(2); Harrison, G.R. –(4); Leaning, A.J. 20; Llewellyn, A. 37; McIntyre, J. 1; May, A.M.P. 44(1); Mellon, M. 12(4); Morgan, N. 15(4); Osman, R. 30(1); Rennie, D. 27; Rosenior, L.D.G. 5(3); Scott, M. 46; Shelton, G. 18(1); Smith, D.A. 17(1); Taylor, R. 13(5); Welch, K.J. 26.
League Goals (55): Allison 10, Cole 8, Rosenior 5, Dziekanowski 4, Taylor 4, Morgan 3, Scott 3 (1 pen), Shelton 3, Bent 2, Bryant 2, Osman 2, Rennie 2, Aizlewood 1, Atteveld 1, Connor 1, Edwards 1, Gavin 1, May 1, Smith 1.
Rumbelows Cup (5): Morgan 2, Smith 2, Allison 1.
FA Cup (5): Dziekanowski 2, Bent 1, May 1, own goals 1.
Ground: Ashton Gate, Bristol BS3 2EJ (0272 632812)
Manager: Denis Smith   **Secretary:** Miss Jean Harrison.
Colours: Red shirts, white shorts, red and white stockings
Record home gate: 43,335 v Preston NE, FA Cup 5th rd, 16 February 1935
Honours – Champions: Division 2: 1905–06; Division 3 (S): 1922–23, 1926–27, 1954–55
Welsh Cup winners: 1934
Anglo-Scottish Cup winners: 1977–78
Associate Members Cup winners: 1985–86

BRISTOL ROVERS   DIV. 1

Alexander, Ian
Archer, Lee
Boothroyd, Adrian N.
Browning, Marcus T.
Chenoweth, Paul
Clark, William R.

Cross, Stephen C.
Evans, Richard W.
Hopkins, Jeffrey
Jones, Vaughan
Kelly, Gavin J.
Maddison, Lee R.
Mehew, David S.

Parkin, Brian.
Pounder, Antony M.
Purnell, Philip
Reece, Andrew J.
Saunders, Carl S.
Skinner, Justin
Stewart, Marcus P.

Taylor, Gareth K.
Taylor, John P.
Twentyman, Geoffrey
Wilson, David G.
Yates, Steven

League Appearances: Alexander, I. 41; Archer, L. 3(2); Bloomer, R. 4(5); Boothroyd, A. 8(5); Browning, M.T. 5(6); Clark, W.R. 22(2); Cross, S.C. 31(1); Evans, R.W. 2; Hopkins, J. 4(2); Jones, V. 1; Kelly, G. 3; Maddison, L.R. 8(2); Mehew, D.S. 37; Moore, K.T. 7; Parkin, B. 43; Pounder, A.M. 38(2); Purnell, P. 5(7); Reece, A.J. 42; Saunders, C.S. 31(5); Skinner, J. 41(1); Stewart, W.M.P. 17(16); Taylor, G.K. 1; Taylor, J.P. 8; Twentyman, G. 25; White, D.W. 35; Wilmott, I.M. 2; Wilson, D.G. 3; Yates, S. 39.
League Goals (60): Saunders 10 (1 pen), White 10, Mehew 9, Taylor 7, Stewart 5 (1 pen), Pounder 4, Reece 4, Skinner 3, Cross 2, Alexander 1, Clark 1, Evans 1, Twentyman 1, own goals 2.
Rumbelows Cup (5): Mehew 2, White 2, own goals 1.
FA Cup (7): Saunders 6, Alexander 1.
Ground: Twerton Park, Twerton, Bath. Telephone: 0272 352508. Training ground: 0272 861743. Match day ticket office: 0225 312327. Offices: 199 Two Mile Road, Kingswood, Bristol BS15 1AZ. (0272) 352303. Pirates Hotline 0898 338345.
Manager: Dennis Rofe   **Secretary:** R. C. Twyford
Colours: Blue and white quartered shirts, white shorts, blue stockings with two white rings on top
Record home gate: 9464 v Liverpool, FA Cup 4th rd, 8 February 1992 (Twerton Park). 38,472 v Preston NE, FA Cup 4th rd, 30 January 1960
Honours – Champions: Division 3 (S): 1952–53; Division 3: 1989–90

BURNLEY DIV. 2

Conroy, Michael K.
Davis, Stephen M.
Deary, John S.
Eli, Roger
Farrell, Andrew J.
Francis, John A.
Harper, Steven J.

Howarth, Neil
Jakub, Yanek
Lancashire, Graham
McKay, Paul W.
McKenzie, Paul
Measham, Ian
Monington, Mark D.

Painter, Peter R.
Pender, John P.
Randall, Adrian J.
Sonner, Daniel J.
Welch, Brian J.
Williams, David P.
Yates, Mark J.

League Appearances: Bray, I.M. 5(1); Conroy, M.K. 38; Davis, S.M. 40; Deary, J.S. 40; Eli, R. 29(4); Farrell, A.J. 38(1); France, M.P. 6; Francis, J.A. 36(1); Hamilton, D. 3(1); Hardy, J.P. 2(1); Harper, S.J. 31(4); Jakub, Y. 38(1); Kendall, M. 2; Lancashire, G. 9(16); McKenzie, P.A. 1(3); Marriott, A. 15; Measham, I. 27; Monington, M.D. 8(4); Mumby, P. 1; Painter, P.R. 9; Pearce, C.L. 14; Pender, J.P. 39; Randall, A.J. 11(7); Sonner, D.J. –(3); Walker, J.N. 6; Williams, D.P. 5; Yates, M.J. 9(8).

League Goals (79): Conroy 24 (5 pens), Eli 10, Francis 8, Lancashire 8, Davis 6 (1 pen), Deary 6, Farrell 3, Harper 3, Pender 3, Painter 2, Randall 2, Measham 1, Monington 1, Yates 1, own goals 1.
Rumbelows Cup (3): Conroy 1, Davis 1, own goals 1.
FA Cup (8): Harper 3, Eli 2, Conroy 1, Davis 1, Lancashire 1.
Ground: Turf Moor, Burnley BB10 4BX (0282 27777)
Manager: Jimmy Mullen **Secretary:** Mark Blackbourne
Colours: Claret shirts with sky blue sleeves, white shorts and stockings
Record home gate: 54,775 v Huddersfield T, FA Cup 3rd rd, 23 February 1924
Honours – Champions: Division 1: 1920–21, 1959–60; Division 2: 1897–98, 1972–73; Division 3: 1981–82; Division 4: 19 Record 30 consecutive 91–92
FA Cup winners: 1913–14

BURY   DIV. 3

Anderson, Lee C.	Knill, Alan R.	Stanislaus, Roger E.P.
Hughes, Ian	Mauge, Ronald C.	Stevens, Ian D.
Hulme, Kevin	Parkinson, Philip J.	Valentine, Peter
Jones (Quartey), David	Pollitt, Michael F.	Wilson, Darren A.
Kearney, Mark J.	Robertson, Paul	
Kelly, Gary A.	Robinson, Spencer L.	

League Appearances: Anderson, L.C. 3(2); Cullen, A. 4; Flitcroft, G.W. 12; Greenall, C.A. 37; Hulme, K. 21(9); Hughes, I. 13(4); Jones, D. –(9); Kearney, M.J. 43; Kelly, G.A. 46; Knill, A.R. 33(2); Lee, D. 2; Lyons, D.P. 9(1); Mauge, R.C. 15(7); Parkinson, P.J. 26(6); Robertson, P. 5; Robinson, S.L. 38(3); Smith, N.P. 30(4); Stanislaus, R. 36(4); Stevens, I.D. 44(1); Valentine, P. 38(1); Wilson, D.A. 30(2); Wilson, I. 21(3).
League Goals (55): Stevens 17, Robinson 10 (2 pens), Greenall 5 (1 pen), Hulme 4, Lyons 4, Smith 3, Stanislaus 3, Valentine 3, Kearney 1, Knill 1, Lee 1 (1 pen), Wilson D 1, Wilson I 1, own goals 1.
Rumbelows Cup (2): Mauge 1, Stanislaus 1.
FA Cup (0).
Ground: Gigg Lane, Bury B19 9HR (061-764 4881)
Manager: Mike Walsh **Assistant Secretary:** S. Atkinson.
Colours: White shirts, navy blue shorts, navy stockings
Record home gate: 35,000 v Bolton W, FA Cup 3rd rd, 9 January 1960
Honours – Champions: Division 2: 1894–95; Division 3: 1960–61
FA Cup winners: 1900, 1903

CAMBRIDGE UNITED   DIV. 1

Bailie, Colin J.	Dennis, John A.	Leadbitter, Christopher J.
Chapple, Philip R.	Dublin, Dion	Norbury, Michael
Cheetham, Michael M.	Fensome, Andrew B.	O'Shea, Daniel E.
Claridge, Stephen E.	Fowler, John A.	Parkhill, Philip R.B.
Clayton, Gary	Heathcote, Michael	Philpott, Lee
Daish, Liam S.	Kimble, Alan F.	Raynor, Paul J.

Robinson, David J. Smeeth, Jamie F. Wilkins, Richard J.
Rowett, Gary Vaughan, John
Sheffield, Jonathan White, Devan W.

League Appearances: Bailie, C.J. 23(5); Chapple, P.R. 29; Cheetham, M.M. 21(1); Claridge, S.E. 25(4); Clayton, G. 9(2); Daish, L.S. 22; Dennis, J.A. 36(4); Dublin, D. 40(3); Fensome, A.B. 34; Heaney, N. 9(4); Heathcote, M. 17(5); Kimble, A.F. 45; Leadbitter, C. 14(11); Norbury, M.S. 4(10); O'Shea, D.E. 30(1); Philpott, L. 29(2); Raynor, P.J. 5(3); Rowett, G. 10(3); Sheffield, J. 13; Taylor, J.P. 27(8); Vaughan, J. 33; White, D.W. 1(1); Wilkins, R. 30(2).
League Goals (65): Dublin 15, Claridge 12 (1 pen), Heathcote 5, Philpott 5, Taylor 5, Wilkins 4, Chapple 3, Cheetham 3, Dennis 2, Heaney 2, Norbury 2, Rowett 2, Fensome 1 (1 pen), Leadbitter 1, O'Shea 1, own goals 2.
Rumbelows Cup (5): Claridge 2, Dublin 2, Taylor 1.
FA Cup (2): Dublin 2.
Ground: Abbey Stadium, Newmarket Rd, Cambridge (0223 241237)
Manager: John Beck **Secretary:** Steve Greenall
Colours: Yellow shirts, black shorts, black and yellow stockings
Record home gate: 14,000 v Chelsea, Friendly, 1 May 1970
Honours – Champions: Division 3: 1990–91; Division 4: 1976–77

CARDIFF CITY DIV. 3

Abraham, Gareth J. Gill, Gary Pike, Christopher
Baddeley, Lee M. Griffith, Cohen Ramsey, Paul
Blake, Nathan A. Lewis, Allan Searle, Damon P.
Dale, Carl Millar, William P. Ward, Gavin J.
Gibbins, Roger G. Perry, Jason Williams, William J.

League Appearances: Abraham, G.J. 13(2); Baddeley, L.M. 14(4); Bellamy, G. 9; Blake, N.A. 27(4); Dale, C. 41; Gibbins, R.G. 41; Gill, G. 3(3); Gorman, A.D. 7(4); Griffith, C. 26(11); Hansbury, R. 18; Harrison, G. 10; Heard, T.P. 7(1); Jones, M. 13(1); Lewis, A. 8(4); Marriott, P.W. –(1); Matthews, N.P. 12(3); Millar, P. 8(7); Newton, E.J.I. 18; Perry, J. 35(1); Pike, C. 36(4); Ramsey, P. 39; Searle, D.P. 42; Semark, R.H. 4(2); Toshack, J.C. –(1); Unsworth, J.J. 1(2); Walsh, A. 1; Ward, G.J. 24; Williams, W.J. 5.
League Goals (66): Dale 22, Pike 21 (7 pens), Blake 6, Newton 4, Ramsey 3 (1 pen), Gibbins 1, Gill 1, Griffith 1, Harrison 1, Heard 1, Jones 1 (1 pen), Searle 1, own goals 3.
Rumbelows Cup (4): Gibbins 1, Jones 1 (1 pen), Millar 1, Searle 1.
FA Cup (1): Pike 1.
Ground: Ninian Park, Cardiff CF1 8SX (0222 398636)
First team coach: Eddie May **Secretary:**
Colours: All blue **Change colours:** Red shirts, white shorts, red stockings
Record home gate: 61,566, Wales v England, 14 October 1961. Club record: 57,893 v Arsenal, Division 1, 22 April 1953
Honours – Champions: Division 3 (S): 1946–47
FA Cup winners: 1926–27 (only occasion the Cup has been won by a club outside England)
Welsh Cup winners: 20 times

CARLISLE UNITED DIV. 3

Barnsley, Andrew	Holmes, Michael A.	Thorpe, Jeffrey R.
Dalziel, Ian	O'Hanlon, Kelham G.	Walling, Dean A.
Edmondson, Darren S.	Proudlock, Paul	Walsh, Derek
Holliday, John R.	Sendall, Richard A.	Watson, Andrew A.

League Appearances: Armstrong, K.W. 8(6); Barnsley, A. 28; Bennett, M. 5(2); Cranston, N.G. –(2); Deakin, J. 3; Edmondson, D.S. 26(1); Freeman, C.R. 4; Fyfe, T. 25(1); Gallimore, A. 16; Gorman, P.A. 5; Graham M.A. 37(1); Holliday, J.R. 16; Holmes, M. 15; Jeffels, S. 26; Lowery, A.W. 6(1); Miller, D.B. 25(1); Nevin, P.R. 2(6); O'Hanlon, K.G. 42; Potts, C. 3(3); Prins, J. 3(1); Proudlock, P. 26(8); Sendall, R. A. 1; Thomas, D.G. 35(2); Thorpe, J.R. 23(5); Walling, D.A. 33(4); Walsh, D. 14(1); Watson, A.A. 34(1); Wilkes, D.A. 1(3).
League Goals (41): Watson 14 (1 pen), Fyfe 5 (1 pen), Walling 5, Holmes M 4, Barnsley 3 (3 pens), Edmondson 2, Jeffels 2, Graham 1, Proudlock 1, Sendall 1, Thomas 1, Thorpe 1, own goals 1.
Rumbelows Cup (2): Barnsley 2.
FA Cup (4): Barnsley 2 (2 pens), Fyfe 1, Watson 1.
Ground: Brunton Park, Carlisle CA1 1LL (0228 26237)
Manager: Aidan McCaffery **Secretary:** Miss Alison Moore.
Colours: Blue shirts, white shorts, blue stockings
Record home gate: 27,500 v Birmingham C, FA Cup 3rd rd, 5 January 1957 and v Middlesbrough, FA Cup 5th rd, 7 February 1970
Honours – Champions: Division 3: 1964–65

CHARLTON ATHLETIC DIV. 1

Bacon, Paul D.	Dyer, Alexander C.	Minto, Scott C.
Balmer, Stuart M.	Gatting, Stephen P.	Nelson, Garry P.
Barness, Anthony	Gorman, Paul M.	Nguyen, The V.
Bolder, Robert	Grant, Kim T.	Pardew, Alan S.
Brown, Steven B.	Gritt, Stephen J.	Pitcher, Darren E.J.
Bumstead, John	Harrison, Lee D.	Salmon, Michael B.
Caton, Thomas	Leaburn, Carl W.	Walsh, Colin D.
Curbishley, Llewellyn	Lee, Robert M.	Webster, Simon P.

League Appearances: Bacon, P.D. 11(3); Balmer, S.M. 16(2); Barness, A. 16(6); Bolder, R.J. 46; Brown, S. B. –(1); Bumstead, J. 36; Curbishley, L.C. 1; Darlington, J.C. 1(1); Dyer, A.C. 3(10); Gatting, S.P. 30(2); Gorman, P.M. 5(3); Grant, K.T. –(4); Gritt, S.J. 4(10); Hendry, J. 1(4); Leaburn, C.W. 37(2); Lee, R. 39; Minto, S.C. 32(1); Nelson, G.P. 41; Pardew, A. 23(1); Peake, A.M. 20; Pitcher, D.E.J. 46; Rosenior, L. 3; Tivey, M.R. –(1); Walsh, C.D. 42; Webster, S.P. 44; Whyte, D.A. 7(1); Wilder, C.J. 2.
League Goals (54): Lee 12, Leaburn 11, Nelson 6, Webster 5, Walsh 4, Gorman 3, Pardew 2 (1 pen), Pitcher 2 (1 pen), Whyte 2, Barness 1, Gatting 1, Gritt 1, Hendry 1, Minto 1, own goals 2.
Rumbelows Cup (5): Leaburn 2, Minto 1, Peake 1, Walsh 1.
FA Cup (4): Gatting 2, Grant 1, Leaburn 1.

Ground: The Valley, Floyd Road, Charlton, London SE7 8BL (081-293-4567)
Player coaches: Alan Curbishley and Steve Gritt **Secretary:** Chris Parkes
Colours: Red shirts, white shorts, red stockings
Record home gate: 75,031 v Aston Villa, FA Cup 5th rd, 12 February 1938 (at The Valley)
Honours – Champions: Division 3 (S): 1928–29, 1934–35
FA Cup winners: 1947

CHELSEA   FA PREMIER

Allon, Joseph B.
Barnard, Darren S
Beasant, David
Burley, Craig W
Cascarino, Anthony G
Chatfield, Ian R.
Clarke, Stephen
Cundy, Jason V.
Dickens, Alan W.
Dicon, Kerry M.
Elliott, Paul M.
Hall, Gareth D.
Hitchcock, Kevin
Johnsen, Erland
Jones, Vincent P.
Le Saux, Graeme P.
Lee, David J.
Matthew, Damian
Monkou, Kenneth J.
Myers, Andrew
Newton, Edward J.I.
Pearce, Ian A.
Sinclair, Frank M.
Stuart, Graham C.
Townsend, Andrew D.
Wise, Dennis F.

League Appearances: Allen, C. 15(1); Allon, J.B. 2(9); Barnard, D.S. 1(3); Beasant, D.J. 21; Boyd, T. 22(1); Burley, C.W. 6(2); Cascarino, A.G. 11; Clarke, S. 31; Cundy, J.V. 12; Dickens, A.W. 6(4); Dixon, K.M. 32(3); Elliott, P. 35; Gilkes, M.E. –(1); Hall, G.D. 9(1); Hitchcock, K.J. 21; Johnsen, E. 6(1); Jones, V.P. 35; Lee, D.J. 1; Le Saux, Graeme P. 39(1); Matthew, D. 2(5); Monkou, K.J. 31; Myers, A. 9(2); Newton, E.J.I. –(1); Pearce, I.A. –(2); Sinclair, F.M. 8; Stuart, G.C. 20(7); Townsend, A.D. 35; Wilson, K. 15(7); Wise, D.F. 37(1).
League Goals (50): Wise 10 (2 pens), Allen C 7, Townsend 6, Dixon 5, Elliott 3, Jones 3, Le Saux 3, Wilson 3, Allon 2, Cascarino 2, Clarke 1, Cundy 1, Myers 1, Newton 1, Sinclair 1, own goals 1.
Rumbelows Cup (2): Townsend 1, Wise 1.
FA Cup (6): Allen 2, Wise 2, Jones 1, Stuart 1.
Ground: Stamford Bridge, London SW6 (071-385 5545)
Manager: Ian Porterfield **Secretary:** Yvonne Todd.
Colours: Royal blue shirts and shorts, white stockings
Record home gate: 82,905 v Arsenal, Division 1, 12 October 1935.
Honours – Champions: I>Football League: Division 1: 1954–55; Division 2: 1983–84, 1988–89 **Football League Cup winners:** 1964–65
Full Members' Cup winners: 1985–86
Full Members Cup winners: 1989–90 **European Cup-Winners' Cup winners:** 1970–71

CHESTER CITY   DIV. 2

Abel, Graham
Barrow, Graham
Bennett, Gary M.
Bishop, Edward M.
Butler, Barry G.
Comstive, Paul T.
Croft, Brian G.A.
Hinnigan, Joseph P.
Lightfoot, Christopher I.
Morton, Neil
Preece, Roger
Pugh, David
Rimmer, Stuart A.
Stewart, William I.
Whelan, Spencer R.

League Appearances: Abel, G. 40(4); Albiston, A.R. 44; Allen, A. –(1); Barrow, G. 40; Bennett, G.M. 40(2); Bishop, E.M. 21; Butler, B. 36(5); Comstive, P. 28; Croft, B.G.A. 18(14); Lightfoot, C. 44; McGuinness, P.E. 3(4); Morton, N. 12(22); Nolan, D.J. 1; Preece, R. 26(3); Pugh, D. 33(2); Rimmer, S.A. 44; Siddall, B. 9; Stewart, W.I. 37; Whelan, S. 30(2).
League Goals (56): Rimmer 13, Bennett 11, Abel 9 (5 pens), Butler 6, Lightfoot 5, Bishop 4, Comstive 3, Barrow 2, Morton 2, own goals 1.
Rumbelows Cup (5): Bennett 2, Rimmer 2, Barrow 1.
FA Cup (1): Barrow 1.
Ground: The Deva Stadium, Bumpers Lane, Chester. (0244 371376, 371809)
Manager: Harry McNally   **Secretary:** R. A. Allan
Colours: Royal blue shirts, white shorts, blue stockings, white trim
Record home gate: 20,500 v Chelsea, FA Cup 3rd rd (replay), 16 January, 1952
Honours – Welsh Cup winners: 1908, 1933, 1947
Debenhams Cup winners: 1977

CHESTERFIELD   DIV. 3

Brien, Anthony J.	Lemon, Paul A.	Rogers, Lee J.
Dyche, Sean M.	Leonard, Michael C.	Turnbull, Lee M.
Goldring, Mark	McGugan, Paul J.	Williams, Steven B.
Hebberd, Trevor N.	Morris, Andrew D.	
Lancaster, David	Norris, Stephen M.	

League Appearances: Benjamin, C. –(4); Brien, A.J. 40(1); Caldwell, D.W. 5(4); Cooke, J. 29(4); Dunn, I.G.W. 8(5); Dyche, S.M. 42; Evans, G.N. 1(4); Francis, L. 37(2); Goldring, M. 7; Grayson, N. 9(6); Gunn, B.C. 9; Hawke, W.R. 7; Hebberd, T.N. 22(2); Hewitt, J.R. 37; Lancaster, D. 27(2); Lemon, P.A. 13(2); Leonard, M.C. 35; McGugan, P.J. 37; Morris, A.D. 4(4); Norris, S.M. 21; Rogers, L.J. 13(5); Turnbull, L.M. 26(1); Whitehead, S.A. 3(2); Williams, S.B. 30(1).
League Goals (49): Norris 10, Cooke 7 (1 pen), Lancaster 7, Turnbull 7 (3 pens), Dyche 3, Hewitt 3, McGugan 3, Lemon 2, Morris 2, Williams 2, Dunn 1, Francis 1, Hawke 1.
Rumbelows Cup (1): Lancaster 1.
FA Cup (1): Cooke 1.
Ground: Recreation Ground, Chesterfield S40 4SX (0246 209765)
Manager: Chris McMenemy   **Secretary:** Nicola Hodgson
Colours: Blue shirts, white shorts, white stockings
Record home gate: 30,968 v Newcastle U, Division 2, 7 April 1939
Honours – Champions: Division 3 (N): 1930–31, 1935–36; Division 4: 1969–70, 1984–85
Anglo-Scottish Cup winners: 1980–81

COLCHESTER UNITED   DIV. 3

Ground: Layer Road Ground, Colchester. (0206 574042)
Manager: Roy McDonough   **Secretary:** Sue Smith
Colours: Royal blue and white striped shirts, royal blue shorts with white side panel, royal blue stockings with white hoops

---

COVENTRY CITY   FA PREMIER

Atherton, Peter
Billing, Peter G.
Booty, Martyn J.
Borrows, Brian
Busst, David J.
Drinkell, Kevin S.
Edwards, Paul R.
Fleming, Terry M.
Flynn, Sean

Furlong, Paul A.
Gallacher, Kevin W.
Greenman, Christopher
Gynn, Michael
Hurst, Lee J.
McGrath, Lloyd A.
Middleton, Craig D.
Ndlovu, Peter
Ogrizovic, Steven

Pearce, Andrew J.
Robson, Stewart I.
Rosario, Robert M.
Sansom, Kenneth G.
Sheridan, Anthony J.
Smith, David
Wilson, Carl N.
Woods, Raymond G.

League Appearances: Atherton, P. 35; Billing, P.G. 17(5); Booty, M.J. 2(1); Borrows, B. 34(1); Drinkell, K.S. 2(2); Edwards, P. 4(1); Emerson, D. 10(11); Flynn, S.M. 21(1); Furlong, P.A. 27(10); Gallacher, K.W. 33; Greenman, C. 4; Gynn, M. 21(2); Heald, P.A. 2; Hurst, L.J. 8(2); McGrath, L.A. 38(2); Middleton, C.D. 1; Ndlovu, P. 9(14); Ogrizovic, S. 38; Peake, T. 2; Pearce, A.J. 36; Robson, S.I. 37; Rosario, R.M. 26(3); Sansom, K.G. 21; Sealey, L.J. 2; Smith, D. 23(1); Woods, R.G. 9.
League Goals (35): Gallacher 8, Furlong 4, Rosario 4, Smith 4 (1 pen), Gynn 3 (1 pen), Robson 3, Flynn 2, Ndlovu 2, Pearce 2, Billing 1, McGrath 1, own goals 1.
Rumbelows Cup (6): Gallacher 2, Rosario 2, Furlong 1, McGrath 1.
FA Cup (1): Borrows 1 (1 pen).
Ground: Highfield Road Stadium, King Richard Street, Coventry CV2 4FW (0203 223535)
Manager: Bobby Gould   **Secretary:** Graham Hover
Colours: All sky blue
Record home gate: 51,455 v Wolverhampton W, Division 2, 29 April 1967
Honours – Champions: Division 2: 1966–67; Division 3: 1963–64; Division 3 (S): 1935–36
FA Cup winners: 1986–87

CREWE ALEXANDRA   DIV. 3

Annon, Richard
Callaghan, Aaron J.
Carr, Darren
Clarkson, Philip I.
Disley, Martin
Edwards, Robert
Evans, Stewart J.

Gardiner, Mark C.
Garvey, Stephen H.
Greygoose, Dean
Hignett, Craig
Lennon, Neil F.
Macauley, Steven R.
McKearney, David J.

Naylor, Anthony J.
Smart, Jason
Smith, Gareth S.
Sorvel, Neil S.
Walters, Steven P.
Wilson, Eugene

League Appearances: Bishop, E.M. 3; Callaghan, A.J. 36(1); Carr, D.J. 33(3); Clarkson, P.I. 18(10); Disley, M. –(1); Downes, C.B. 1(1); Edwards, P. 2; Edwards,

R. 22(6); Evans, S.J. 13(4); Futcher, R. 18(3); Gardiner, M.C. 37(1); Garvey, S.H. 8(3); Greygoose, D. 33; Hignett, C.J. 32(1); Jackson, M.J. 1; Jasper, D.W. 3(4); Jones, R. 8; Kelly, P.A. –(1); McKearney, D. 30(1); McPhillips, T. 5(1); Macauley, S.R. 9; Murphy, A.J. 1(6); Naylor, A.J. 34; Noble, D.W.T. 7; Payne, R. 3(3); Rose, C.J. 2(3); Rutherford, I. –(1); Smart, J. 10(1); Smith, G.S. 8(2); Sorvel, N.S. 5(4); Swain, K. 1; Walters, S. 34(1); Whitehurst, W. 4(6); Wilson, E. 41.
League Goals (66): Naylor 15, Hignett 13 (4 pens), Clarkson 6, Edwards R 6, Gardiner 5, Evans 4, Futcher 4, McKearney 4, Carr 3, Walters 3, Macauley 1, Murphy 1, own goals 1.
Rumbelows Cup (12): Naylor 3, Callaghan 2, Evans 2, Futcher 2, Edwards R 1, Gardiner 1, Hignett 1.
FA Cup (8): Naylor 3, Hignett 2, Gardiner 1, Walters 1, own goals 1.
Ground: Football Ground, Gresty Rd, Crewe (0270 213014)
Manager: Dario Gradi   **Secretary:** Mrs. G. Palin
Colours: Red shirts, white shorts, red stockings
Record home gate: 20,000 v Tottenham H, FA Cup 4th rd, 30 January 1960
Honours – Nil

CRYSTAL PALACE   FA PREMIER

Barnes, Andrew J.	Martyn, Antony N.	Sinnott, Lee
Bowry, Robert	McGoldrick, Eddie J.P.	Southgate, Gareth
Bright, Mark A.	Moralee, Jamie D.	Thomas, Geoffrey R.
Coleman, Christopher	Mortimer, Paul H.	Thorn, Andrew C.
Collymore, Stanley V.	Newman, Richard A.	Whyte, David A.
Glass, James R.	Osborn, Simon E.	Woodman, Andrew J.
Gordon, Dean D.	Rodger, Simon L.	Young, Eric
Gray, Andrew A.	Salako, John A.	
Humphrey, John	Shaw, Richard E.	

League Appearances: Barnes, A.J. –(1); Bodin, P. 3(1); Bright, M.A. 42; Coleman, C. 14(4); Collymore, S.V. 4(8); Gabbiadini, M. 15; Gordon, D.D. 2(2); Gray, A. 25; Hedman, R. –(3); Humphrey, J. 36(1); McGoldrick, E.J.P. 36; Martyn, A.N. 38; Moralee, J.D. 2(4); Mortimer, P.H. 17(4); Osborn, S.E. 13(1); Pardew, A.S. 3(5); Rodger, S.L. 20(2); Salako, J.A. 10; Shaw, R.E. 9(1); Sinnott, L. 35(1); Southgate, G. 26(4); Suckling, P.J. 3; Sullivan, N. 1; Thomas, G.R. 30; Thorn, A.C. 33; Whyte, D.A. 7(4); Wright, I.E. 8; Young, E. 30.
League Goals (53): Bright 17 (1 pen), Thomas 6, Gabbiadini 5, Wright 5, Coleman 4, McGoldrick 3, Gray 2 (2 pens), Mortimer 2, Osborn 2, Salako 2, Collymore 1, Whyte 1, Young 1, own goals 2.
Rumbelows Cup (15): Bright 4, Gray 4 (2 pens), Thorn 2, Collymore 1, Gabbiadini 1, Thomas 1, Whyte 1, own goals 1.
FA Cup (0).
Ground: Selhurst Park, London SE25 6PU (081-653 4462)
Manager: Steve Coppell   **Secretary:** Mike Hurst
Colours: Red and blue shirts, red shorts, red stockings
Record home gate: 51,482 v Burnley, Division 2, 11 May 1979
Honours – Champions: Division 2: 1978–79; Division 3 (S): 1920–21 **Full Members Cup winners:**

DARLINGTON DIV. 3

Cusack, Nicholas J.
Ellison, Anthony L.
Gaughen, Steven E.
Gregan, Sean M.
Hinchley, Gary

Isaacs, Anthony
Mardenborough,
Stephen A.
O'Shaughnessy, Stephen
Pickering, Nichol
Prudhoe, Mark

Smith, Kevan
Sunley, Mark
Swan, Adrian
Toman, James A.

League Appearances: Borthwick, J. 11(18); Clark, H.W. 5; Coatsworth, G. 9(1); Cook, M. 26(1); Cork, D. 22(8); Coverdale, D. 10(4); Cusack, N.J. 21; Dewhurst, R.M. 11; Ellison, A.L. 25(2); Gaughan, S. 20; Gill, G. 19(1); Gray, F.T. 6; Gregan, S.M. 17; Hamilton, G.J. 11; Hinchley, G. 6; Isaacs, A. 4(5); McCarrison, D. 5; McJannet, W.L. 19(1); Mardenborough, S. 21(8); O'Shaughnessy, S. 15; Pickering, N. 29; Prudhoe, M. 46; Reed, A.M. –(1); Shaw, S.R. –(1); Smith, K. 39; Sunley, M. 15; Tait, M.P. 34; Toman, J.A. 43; Trotter, M. 5; Tucker, L.D. –(5); Willis, J.A. 12.

League Goals (56): Ellison 10 (3 pens), Cusack 6, Mardenborough 6, Borthwick 5, Pickering 5, Toman 4, Cook 3, Cork 3, Hamilton 2, McCarrison 2, Willis 2, Coatsworth 1, Dewhurst 1, Gill 1, O'Shaughnessy 1, Smith 1, own goals 3.

Rumbelows Cup (1): Cook 1.

FA Cup (3): Ellison 1 (1 pen), Smith 1, Toman 1.

Ground: Feethams Ground, Darlington (0325 465097)

Manager: Billy McEwan. **Secretary:** Brian Anderson

Colours: Black and white

Record home gate: 21,023 v Bolton W, League Cup 3rd rd, 14 November 1960

Honours – Champions: Division 3 (N): 1924–25; Division 4 1990–91: Runners-up 1965–66

DERBY COUNTY DIV. 1

Chalk, Martyn P. G.
Clarke, Mark A.
Coleman, Simon
Comyn, Andrew J.
Curtis, Thomas
Davidson, Jonathan S.
Dunne, Simon A.P.
Forsyth, Michael E.
Gabbiadini, Marco
Hayward, Steve L.
Johnson, Thomas

Kavanagh, Jason C.
Kitson, Paul
McMinn, Kevin C.
Micklewhite, Gary
Nicholson, Shane M.
Patterson, Mark
Philips, Justin L.
Ramage, Craig D.
Round, Stephen
Sage, Melvyn
Simpson, Paul D.

Stallard, Mark
Straw, Robert G.
Sturridge, Dean C.
Sutton, Stephen J.
Taylor, Martin J.
Taylor, Stephen M.
Weston, Kinsley P.
Williams, David G.
Williams, Paul D.

League Appearances: Chalk, M.P.G. 4(3); Comyn, A.J. 46; Cross, S.C. –(4); Coleman, S. 43; Davidson, J.S. 1; Davison, R. 10; Forsyth, M.E. 43; Gabbiadini, M. 20; Gee, P.J. 17(2); Harford, M.G. 6; Hayward, S.L. 3(4); Johnson, T. 12; Kavanagh, J.C. 22(3); Kitson, P. 12; McMinn, K.C. 35(2); Micklewhite, G. 28(4); Ormondroyd, I. 25; Patterson, M. 8(4); Pickering, N. –(1); Ramage, C.D. 7;

Round, S.J. 2(1); Sage, M. 17; Shilton, P.L. 31; Simpson, P.D. 16; Stallard, M. 2(1); Sturridge, D.C. 1; Sutton, S. 10; Taylor, M.J. 5; Williams, D.G. 39; Williams, P.D. 41.
League Goals (69): Williams P 13 (6 pens), Davison 8, Ormondroyd 8, Simpson 7, Gabbiadini 6, Kitson 4, Harford 3, Coleman 2, Johnson T 2, McMinn 2, Micklewhite 2, Patterson 2, Ramage 2, Williams G 2, Chalk 1, Comyn 1, Forsyth 1, Gee 1, own goals 2.
Rumbelows Cup (3): Forsyth 1, Gee 1, Williams P 1 (1 pen).
FA Cup (7): Gee 2, Williams P 2, Chalk 1, Comyn 1, Ormondroyd 1.
Ground: Baseball Ground, Shaftesbury Crescent, Derby DE3 8NB (0332 40105)
Manager: Arthur Cox   **Secretary:** Michael Dunford
Colours: White shirts with black collar and red flash on sleeve, black shorts with red flash on one side, white stockings, black turnover
Record home gate: 41,826 v Tottenham H, Division 1, 20 September 1969
Honours – Champions: Division 1: 1971–72, 1974–75; Division 2: 1911–12, 1914–15, 1968–69, 1986–87; Division 3 (N) 1956–57
FA Cup winners: 1945–46

DONCASTER ROVERS DIV. 3

Bennett, Craig
Crichton, Paul A.
Crosby, Andrew K.
Cullen, David J.
Douglas, Colin F.
Gormley, Edward J.
Morrow, Grant R.
Reddish, Shane
Rowe, Brian
Samways, Mark
Tynan, Thomas E.

League Appearances: Ashurst, J. 37; Bennett, C. 3(2); Boyle, L.D. 2(1); Crichton, P.A. 16; Crosby, A.K. 15(7); Cullen, D.J. 7(1); Douglas, C.F. 33(1); Gallacher, B. 2; Gormley, E.J. 37; Harle, D. 13; Jeffrey, M.R. 11; Kerr, D. 7; Limber, N. 12; McKenzie, R.M. 7(10); Morris, N. –(1); Morrow, G.R. 19(1); Muir, J.G. 14(6); Nicholson, M. 21(3); Noteman, K.S. 34; Ormsby, B.T. 35; Penny, C.V. 1; Prindiville, S. 16; Rankine, S.M. 24; Raven, P. 7; Reddish, S. 15(2); Rowe, B. 18(7); Samways, M. 26; Stevenson, A.J. 1; Stiles, J.C. 9(1); Tynan, T.E. 5(6); Whitehurst, W. 9; Worboys, G.A. 6(1).
League Goals (40): Noteman 10, Jeffrey 6, Gormley 5, Ormsby 3 (1 pen), Rankine 3, Nicholson 2, Reddish 2, Worboys 2, Harle 1, Kerr 1, Limber 1, McKenzie 1, Muir 1, Tynan 1, own goals 1.
Rumbelows Cup (4): Whitehurst 2, Cullen 1, Noteman 1.
FA Cup (2): Rankine 1, Whitehurst 1.
Ground: Belle Vue Ground, Doncaster (0302 539441)
Manager: Steve Beaglehole   **Secretary:** Mrs K. J. Oldale
Colours: All red
Record home gate: 37,149 v Hull C, Division 3 (N), 2 October 1948
Honours – Champions: Division 3 (N) 1934–35, 1946–47, 1949–50; Division 4: 1965–66, 1968–69

EVERTON FA PREMIER

Ablett, Gary I.
Barlow, Stuart
Beagrie, Peter S.
Beardsley, Peter A.
Cottee, Antony R.
Ebbrell, John K.

Harper, Alan
Hinchcliffe, Andrew G.
Jackson, Matthew A.
Jenkins, Iain
Johnston, Maurice
Kearton, Jason B.

Keown, Martin R.
Moore, Neil
Nevin, Patrick K.F.
Peyton, Gerald J.
Quinlan, Philip E.
Snodin, Ian

Southall, Neville
Ward, Mark W.
Warzycha, Robert
Watson, David

League Appearances: Ablett, G.I. 17; Atteveld, R. 8(5); Barlow, S. 3(4); Beagrie, P.S. 20(7); Beardsley, P.A. 42; Cottee, A.R. 17(7); Ebbrell, J.K. 39; Harper, A. 29(4); Hinchcliffe, A.G. 15(3); Jackson, M.A. 30; Jenkins, I. 1(2); Johnston, M.T. 21; Keown, M.R. 39; McDonald, N.R. 1(4); Nevin, P.K.F. 7(10); Newell, M.C. 8(5); Ratcliffe, K. 8(1); Sheedy, K.M. 16; Southall, N. 42; Unsworth, D.G. 1(1); Ward, M.W. 37; Warzycha, R. 26(11); Watson, D. 35.

League Goals (52): Beardsley 15 (2 pens), Cottee 8 (2 pens), Johnston 7, Ward 4, Beagrie 3, Warzycha 3, Watson 3, Nevin 2, Ablett 1, Ebbrell 1, Jackson 1, Newell 1, Sheedy 1, Unsworth 1, own goals 1.

Rumbelows Cup (8): Beardsley 3, Beagrie 2, Atteveld 1, Cottee 1, Newell 1.

FA Cup (1): Beardsley 1.

Ground: Goodison Park, Liverpool L4 4EL (051-521 2020)

Manager: Howard Kendall   **Secretary:** Jim Greenwood

Colours: Royal blue shirts with white collar and white trim on sleeve, white shorts with blue trim, blue stockings

Record home gate: 78,299 v Liverpool, Division 1, 18 September 1948

Honours – Champions: Division 1: 1890–91, 1914–15, 1927–28, 1931–32, 1938–39, 1962–63, 1969–70, 1984–85, 1986–87; Division 2 1930–31

FA Cup winners: 1906, 1933, 1966, 1984

European Cup-Winners' Cup winners: 1984–85

EXETER CITY   DIV. 2

Brown, Jonathan
Chapman, Gary A.
Cook, Andrew C.
Cooper, David B.E.
Daniels, Scott
Dolan, Eammon J.

Harris, Andrew
Hiley, Scott P.
Hodge, John
Kelly, Thomas J.
Maloy, Kevin
Marshall, Gary

Miller, Kevin
Moran, Stephen J.
Thompstone, Ian P.
Whiston, Peter
Williams, Steven C.

League Appearances: Brown, J. 33(2); Chapman, G.A. 17(3); Cole, D.A. –(2); Cook, A.C. 38; Cooper, D.B.E. 9(4); Cooper, M.N. 3; Damerell, M. 1; Daniels, S.C. 43; Dolan, E.J. 5(2); Edwards, D. 4; Harris, A. 5(1); Hilaire, V.M. 24(9); Hiley, S.P. 33; Hobson, G. –(1); Hodge, J. 16(7); Humphrey, J.M. 2; Kelly, T.J. 32; Maloy, K. 4; Marshall, G. 17(11); Masefield, P.D. 1; Miller, K. 42; Moran, S.J. 31(3); Morris, A. 4(3); O'Doherty, K.B. 2; O'Donnell, C. 2; O'Shaughnessy, S. 1(2); Redwood, T.R.B. 1; Robson, M.A. 7(1); Rowbotham, D. 5; Thompstone, I.P. 15; Tonge, A.J. 1(2); Waters, G.J. 1(1); Whiston, P. 36; Williams, S.C. 36; Wimbleton, P.P. 35(1).

League Goals (57): Moran 19 (3 pens), Kelly 5 (2 pens), Chapman 4, Hilaire 4, Wimbleton 4, Daniels 3, Marshall 3, Thompstone 3, Whiston 3, Morris 2, Cooper 1, Hiley 1, Hodge 1, Robson 1, Rowbotham 1, own goals 2.

Rumbelows Cup (0).
FA Cup (3): Brown 1, Marshall 1, Moran 1.
Ground: St James Park, Exeter EX4 6PX (0392 54073)
Manager: Alan Ball **Secretary:** M. A. Holladay
Colours: Red and white striped shirts, black shorts, white stockings
Record home gate: 20,984 v Sunderland, FA Cup 6th rd (replay), 4 March 1931
Honours – Champions: Division 4: 1989–90
Division 3 (S) Cup winners: 1934

FULHAM DIV. 2

Brazil, Gary N.	Hails, Julian	North, Stacey S.
Cobb, Gary E.	Kelly, Mark D.	Onwere, Udo A.
Eckhardt, Jeffrey E.	Marshall, John P.	Pike, Martin R.
Farrell, Sean P.	Morgan, Simon C.	Stannard, James
Ferney, Martin J.	Nebbeling, Gavin M.	Thomas, Glen A.
Haag, Kelly J.	Newson, Mark J.	Tucker, Mark J.

League Appearances: Baker, G.E. 3(1); Brazil, G.N. 46; Browne, C.A. 1; Byrne, D. 5; Cobb, G.E. 4(7); Cole, A.A. 13; Eckhardt, J.E. 43; Farrell, S. 25; Finch, J. 5(1); Georgiou, G.J. 1(3); Haag, K. 18(16); Hails, J. 11(7); Kelly, M.D. 19(2); Kelly, P.L.M. 3; Marshall, J.P. 41; Milton, S. –(1); Morgan, S.C. 34(2); Nebbeling, G.M. 16; Newson, M. 25(1); Onwere, U.A. 19(8); Pike, M.R. 45; Scott, P.R. 37(2); Stannard, J. 46; Thomas, G.A. 45; Tucker, M.J. 1(1).
League Goals (57): Brazil 14 (2 pens), Farrell 10, Eckhardt 7, Haag 6, Cole 3, Morgan 3, Newson 3 (1 pen), Onwere 3, Thomas 3, Pike 2, Hails 1, Kelly M 1, Scott 1.
Rumbelows Cup (3): Brazil 2 (2 pens), Browne 1.
FA Cup (0).
Ground: Craven Cottage, Stevenage Rd, Fulham, London SW6 (071-736 6561)
Manager: Don Mackay **Secretary:** Mrs Janice O'Doherty
Colours: White shirts red and black trim, black shorts, white stockings red and black trim
Record home gate: 49,335 v Millwall, Division 2, 8 October 1938
Honours – Champions: Division 2: 1948–49; Division 3 (S): 1931–32

GILLINGHAM DIV. 3

Arnot, Andrew J.	Dempsey, Mark A.	Martin, Eliot J.
Beadle, Peter C.	Dunne, Joseph J.	O'Connor, Mark A.
Butler, Philip A.	Eeles, Anthony G.	Osborne, Lawrence W.
Carpenter, Richard	Hague, Paul	Palmer, Lee J.
Clark, Paul P.	Leahy, Mark A.	Smith, Neil J.
Clarke, Brian R.	Lim, Harvey C.	Walker, Alan
Crown, David I.	Lovell, Stephen J.	

League Appearances: Arnott, A.J. 7(12); Beadle, P.C. 25(8); Berkley, A.J. –(3); Branagan, K. 1; Butler, P.A. 5; Carpenter, R. 2(1); Clark, P.P. 42; Clarke, B.R. 9(2); Crown, D.I. 35(1); Dempsey, M.A.P. 18(12); Dunne, J. 7(4); Eeles, A.G. 14(3); Elsey, K.W. 25(2); Green, R.E. 12; Harrison, L.D. 2; Kim, H.C. 39; Lovell, S.J. 40(2); Martin, E.J. 22; O'Connor, M.A. 38(1); Osborne, L.W. 4(1); O'Shea, T.J. 30; Palmer, L.J. 5(6); Polston, A. 1(1); Smith, N.J. 26; Thomas, R.C. 8; Trusson, M.S. 6(4); Walker, A. 39(1).
League Goals (63): Crown 22, Lovell 16 (2 pens), Beadle 5, Green 4, Elsey 3, O'Connor 3, Arnott 2, Dempsey 2, Smith 2, Eeles 1, Thomas 1, Trusson 1 (1 pen), Walker 1.
Rumbelows Cup (4): Beadle 2, Lovell 1, Walker 1.
FA Cup (4): Walker 3, Smith 1.
Ground: Priestfield Stadium, Gillingham (0634 851854/8576828)
Manager: Damien Richardson   **Secretary:** Barrie Bright
Colours: Royal blue shirts, royal blue shorts, black stockings
Record home gate: 23,002 v QPR, FA Cup 3rd rd 10 January 1948
Honours – Champions: Division 4: 1963–64

GRIMSBY TOWN DIV. 1

Agnew, Paul	Futcher, Paul	Reece, Paul J.
Baraclough, Ian R.	Gilbert, David J.	Rees, Anthony A.
Childs, Gary P.C.	Hargreaves, Christian	Rodger, Graham
Cockerill, John	Jobling, Kevin A.	Sherwood, Stephen
Cunnington, Shaun G.	Jones, Murray L.	Smith, Mark C.
Dobbin, James	Lever, Mark	Watson, Thomas R.
Ford, Tony	McDermott, John	Woods, Neil S.

League Appearances: Agnew, P. 20(4); Birtles, G. 3(5); Childs, G.P.C. 29; Cockerill, J. 8(2); Cunnington, S.G. 33; Dobbin, J. 32; Ford, T. 17(5); Futcher, P. 29; Gilbert, D.J. 41; Hargreaves, C. 2(8); Jobling, K.A. 35(1); Jones, M.L. 14(14); Knight, I.J. 4; Lever, M. 35(1); McDermott, J. 39; Mendonca, C.P. 10; North, M. –(1); Reece, P.J. 25; Rees, A.A. 22(1); Rodger, G. 16; Sherwood, S. 21; Smith, M. 28(12); Watson, T.R. 13(4); Woods, N. 30(7).
League Goals (47): Woods 8, Dobbin 6, Cunnington 5, Rees 5, Smith 4, Childs 3, Jones 3, Mendonca 3, Gilbert 2, Jobling 2, Watson 2, Cockerill 1, Ford 1, McDermott 1, own goals 1.
Rumbelows Cup (5): Birtles 1, Dobbin 1, Gilbert 1 (1 pen), Jones 1, Rees 1.
FA Cup (1): Cunnington 1.
Ground: Blundell Park, Cleethorpes, South Humberside DN35 7PY (0472 697111)
Manager: Alan Buckley   **Secretary:** I. Fleming
Colours: Black and white vertical striped shirts, black shorts with red triangular panel on side, white stockings with red band on turnover
Record home gate: 31,651 v Wolverhampton W, FA Cup 5th rd, 20 February 1937
Honours – Champions: Division 2: 1900–01, 1933–34; Division 3 (N): 1925–26, 1955–56; Division 3: 1979–80; Division 4: 1971–72
League Group Cup winners: 1981–82

HALIFAX TOWN
DIV. 3

Abbott, Gregory S.
Barr, William J.
Bracey, Lee M.I.
Bradley, Russell
Brown, Nicholas J.

Evans, David G.
Griffiths, Neil
Hildersley, Ronald
Juryeff, Ian M.
Kamara, Alan

Lucketti, Christopher J.
Megson, Kevin C.
Paterson, Jamie R.
Richardson, Nicholas J.
Wilson, Paul A.

League Appearances: Abbott, G.S. 24(4); Barr, W.J. 34(1); Bracey, L.M.I. 32; Bradley, R. 25(1); Brown, N.J. 1; Cooper, G. 19(3); Donovan, K. 6; Ellis, M. 6(1); Evans, D. 26(5); German, D. 2(1); Gould, J.A. 9; Graham, T. 12(2); Gregory, A.G. 5; Griffiths, N. –(2); Hardy, J.P. –(4); Hildersley, R. 14(4); Hutchinson, I.N. 4(1); Juryeff, I.M. 37; Kamara, A. 34(1); Lewis, D.K. 11; Longley, S.E. 1; Lucketti, C.J. 31(5); Matthews, N. 3; Megson, K.C. 8(2); Norris, S.M. 17; Patterson, J.R. 13(2); Richards, S.C. 24(1); Richardson, N. 41; Wilson, P.A. 23.
League Goals (34): Richardson 8, Norris 5 (1 pen), Wilson 5 (1 pen), Juryeff 4, Barr 3 (1 pen), Cooper 3, Bradley 2, Patterson 2, Abbott 1, Hutchinson 1.
Rumbelows Cup (6): Barr 2, Cooper 1, Juryeff 1, Norris 1 (1 pen), Richardson 1.
FA Cup (2): Hildersley 1, Richardson 1.
Ground: Shay Ground, Halifax HX1 2YS. Offices: 7 Clare Road, Halifax HX1 2HX (0422 353423/366593)
Manager: John McGrath   **Secretary:** Bev Fielding
Colours: Royal blue shirts, white shorts, royal blue stockings
Record home gate: 36,885 v Tottenham H, FA Cup 5th rd, 15 February 1953
Honours – Nil

HARTLEPOOL UNITED
DIV. 2

Baker, David P.
Cross, Paul
Dalton, Paul
Fletcher, Steven M.
Garrett, Scott
Hodge, Martin J.

Honour, Brian
Johnrose, Leonard
Jones, Steven
Macphail, John
McGuckin, Thomas I.
Nobbs, Alan K.

Olsson, Paul
Saville, Andrew V.
Southall, Leslie N.
Thompson, Paul D.Z.

League Appearances: Baker, D.P. 29; Bennyworth, I.R. 12; Cross, P. 21; Dalton, P. 43; Davies, A.J. 2(1); Fletcher, S.M. 14(4); Gabbiadini, R. 1(8); Hodge, M. 40; Honour, B. 40; Johnrose, L. 15; Johnson, D.A. 7; Jones, S. 6; McCreery, D. 27(3); McGuckin, T.I. 7; McKinnon, R. 23; MacPhail, J. 40(1); Nesbitt, M.T. 1; Nobbs, A.K. 41; Olsson, P. 46; Peake, J.W. 5(1); Rush, D. 8; Saville, A.V. 1; Smith, A. 4(1); Smith, M. 7(1); Southall, N. 13(9); Thomas, J.W. 5(2); Tinkler, J. 31(8); Tupling, S. 17(4).
League Goals (57): Baker 13 (1 pen), Dalton 13 (1 pen), Olsson 6, Honour 4, Southall 3, Fletcher 2, Gabbiadini 2, Johnrose 2 (1 pen), Johnson 2, Rush 2, Bennyworth 1, MacPhail 1, McKinnon 1, Peake 1, Thomas 1, own goals 3.
Rumbelows Cup (5): Baker 1, Fletcher 1, Gabbiadini 1, Honour 1, Tinkler 1.
FA Cup (6): Baker 2 (1 pen), Dalton 1, Honour 1, Johnson 1, Tinkler 1.
Ground: The Victoria Ground, Clarence Road, Hartlepool (0429 272584)
Manager: Alan Murray   **Assistant Secretary:** Mrs. L. Charlton

Colours: Sky blue, navy blue and white squared shirts, navy blue shorts, sky blue stockings
Record home gate: 17,426 v Manchester U, FA Cup 3rd rd, 5 January 1957
Honours – Nil

HEREFORD UNITED   DIV. 3

Brain, Simon A.J.
Caffrey, Henry
Davies, Gareth M.
Devine, Stephen B.
Downs, Gregory
Fry, Christopher D.

Hall, Derek R.
Jennings, Kentoine
Jones, Richard J.
Judge, Alan G.
McIntyre, Stephen
Narbett, Jonathan V.

Robinson, Paul J.
Theodosiou, Andrew
Titterton, David S.J.
Wade, Psalms M.

League Appearances: Bradley, R. 3; Brain, S.A.J. 40(1); Burton, P.S. –(1); Caffrey, H. 12(5); Culpin, P. 1(1); Davies, G.M. 4; Devine, S.B. 35(2); Downs, G. 40; Elliott, A.R. 18; Fry, C.D. 33(4); Goddard, K.E. –(1); Hall, D.R. 15(5); Heritage, P.M. 38(1); Jennings, K. 9(2); Jones, R. 14(2); Jones, S.G. 3(2); Judge, A.G. 24; Lowndes, S.R. 29(3); McIntyre, S. 12; Morah, O.H. –(2); Narbett, J.V. 33; Nebbeling, G.M. 3; Pejic, M. 15; Robinson, P.J. 7(4); Russell, K.J. 3; Theodosiou, A. 33; Titterton, D.S.J. 20(5); Vaughan, N.M. 8(4); Wade, P.M. 10.
League Goals (44): Brain 10, Heritage 8, Narbett 8 (5 pens), Fry 3, Lowndes 3, Caffery 2, Downs 2 (1 pen), Devine 1, Jones R 1, Pejic 1, Russell 1, Theodosiou 1, Titterton 1, Vaughan 1, own goals 1.
Rumbelows Cup (2): Narbett 1 (1 pen), Theodosiou 1.
FA Cup (8): Brain 4, Fry 1, Heritage 1, Lowndes 1, Narbett 1.
Ground: Edgar Street, Hereford (0432 276666)
Manager: Greg Downs.   **Secretary:** David Vaughan
Colours: White shirts, black shorts, white stockings
Record home gate: 18,114 v Sheffield W, FA Cup 3rd rd, 4 January 1958
Honours – Champions: Division 3: 1975–76
Welsh Cup winners: , 1990

HUDDERSFIELD TOWN   DIV. 2

Barnett, Gary L.
Billy, Christopher A.
Charlton, Simon T.
Clarke, Timothy J.
Donovan, Kevin
Dyson, Jonathan P.

Haylock, Gary A.
Ireland, Simon P.
Jackson, Peter A.
Marsden, Christopher
Mitchell, Graham L.
O'Regan, Kieran

Onuora, Ifem
Parsley, Neil
Roberts, Iwan W.
Starbuck, Philip M.
Trevitt, Simon
Wright, Mark A.

League Appearances: Barnett, G.L. 27(4); Billy, C.A. 8(2); Booth, A.D. –(3); Butler, P.J.F. 7; Callaghan, N. 8; Campbell, D.M. 3; Charlton, S.T. 45; Clarke, T.J. 39; Donovan, K. 4(6); Haylock, G.A. 1; Ireland, S.P. 3(6); Jackson, P.A. 45; Kelly, J. 13(1); McNab, N. 11; Marsden, C. 23; Martin, L.B. 7; Mitchell, G.L. 43; O'Doherty, K.B. 1(1); Onuora, I. 38(3); O'Regan, K. 37(2); Parsley, N.R. 5;

Roberts, I.W. 46; Stapleton, F.A. 5; Starbuck, P.M. 42(2); Trevitt, S. 41; Walsh, A. –(4); Wright, M. 4(4).
League Goals (59): Roberts 24, Starbuck 14 (3 pens), Onuora 8, O'Regan 4 (1 pen), Barnett 3, Billy 2, Jackson 1, Marsden 1, Trevitt 1, own goals 1.
Rumbelows Cup (11): Roberts 3, Starbuck 3, Barnett 2, Onuora 2, Charlton 1.
FA Cup (9): Roberts 3, Donovan 2, Onuora 2, O'Regan 1, Stapleton 1.
Ground: Leeds Rd, Huddersfield HD1 6PE (0484 420335)
Manager: Ian Ross **Secretary:** C. D. Patzelt
Colours: Blue and white striped shirts, white shorts, white stockings
Record home gate: 67,037 v Arsenal, FA Cup 6th rd, 27 February 1932
Honours – Champions: Division 1: 1923–24, 1924–25, 1925–26; Division 2: 1969–70; Division 4: 1979–80
FA Cup winners: 1922

HULL CITY   DIV. 2

Atkinson, Graeme
Calvert, Mark R.
Cleminshaw, David C.
Fettis, Alan
France, Darren B.
Hobson, Gary
Hockaday, David
Hunter, Paul
Jacobs, Wayne G.
Jenkinson, Leigh
Mail, David
Matthews, Michael
Norton, David W.
Palin, Leigh G.
Stoker, Gareth
Warren, Lee A.
Wilcox, Russell
Windass, Dean
Young, Stuart R.

League Appearances: Allison, N.J. 5(2); Atkinson, G. 22(3); Brown, N.L. 25; Buckley, N.A. 4(1); Calvert, M.R. 7(4); Fettis, A. 43; France, D. 10(7); Hobson, G. 15(1); Hockaday, D. 12; Hunter, P. 11(4); Jacobs, W. G. 23(2); Jenkinson, L. 41(1); Kelly, A. 6; Mail, D. 36(1); Matthews, M. 10(6); Ngata, H. 7(4); Norton, D.W. 45; Palin, L. 13; Payton, A.P. 10; Pearson, J.S. 15; Shotton, M. 16(1); Stoker, G. 19(5); Walmsley, D.G. 4(5); Warren, L.A. 26(5); Wilcox, R. 40; Windass, D. 31(1); Wilson, S.L. 3; Young, S.R. 7(8).
League Goals (54): Atkinson 8, Jenkinson 8 (1 pen), Payton 7, Windass 6, France 4, Wilcox 4, Walmsley 3, Matthews 2, Norton 2, Stoker 2, Young 2, Brown 1, Calvert 1, Kelly 1, Mail 1, Palin 1, Warren 1.
Rumbelows Cup (3): Jenkinson 1, Payton 1, Young 1.
FA Cup (2): Hunter 1, Wilcox 1.
Ground: Boothferry Park, Hull HU4 6EU (0482 51119)
Manager: Terry Dolan **Secretary:** Tom Wilson.
Colours: Black and amber striped shirts, black shorts, amber stockings
Record home gate: 55,019 v Manchester U, FA Cup 6th rd, 26 February 1949
Honours – Champions: Division 3 (N): 1932–33, 1948–49; Division 3: 1965–66

IPSWICH TOWN   FA PREMIER

Bernal, Andrew
Dozzell, Jason A.W.
Fearon, Ronald T.
Forrest, Craig L.
Goddard, Paul
Gregory, David S.
Honeywood, Lee B.
Johnson, Gavin
Kiwomya, Christopher M.

Linighan, David Stockwell, Michael T. Winters, Jason
Lowe, David A. Thompson, G. M. Yallop, Frank W.
Milton, Simon C. Thompson, Neil Youds, Edward P.
Palmer, Stephen L. Whelan, Philip J. Zondervan, Romeo
Pennyfather, Glenn J. Whitton, Stephen P.

League Appearances: Dozzell, J.A.W. 45; Edmonds, D. –(2); Forrest, C.L. 46; Gayle, B.W. 5; Goddard, P. 19(5); Gregory, D.S. –(1); Humes, A. 5; Johnson, G. 33(9); Kiwomya, C.M. 43; Linighan, D. 36; Lowe, D.A. 7(7); Milton, S.C. 31(3); Moncur, J.F. 5(1); Palmer, S.L. 16(7); Pennyfather, G.J. 2(1); Stockwell, M.T. 46; Thompson, N. 45; Wark, J. 36(1); Whelan, P.J. 8; Whitton, S.P. 43; Yallop, F.W. 9(8); Youds, E.P. 1; Zondervan, R. 25(3).

League Goals (70): Kiwomya 16, Dozzell 11, Whitton 9 (4 pens), Milton 7, Thompson 6 (2 pens), Johnson 5, Goddard 4, Linighan 3, Wark 3 (1 pen), Stockwell 2, Whelan 2, Lowe 1, own goals 1.

Rumbelows Cup (0).

FA Cup (8): Dozzell 4, Johnson 1, Kiwomya 1, Milton 1, Whitton 1.

Ground: Portman Road, Ipswich, Suffolk IP1 2DA (0473 219211)

Manager: John Lyall   **Secretary:** David C. Rose

Colours: Blue shirts, white shorts, blue stockings

Record home gate: 38,010 v Leeds U, FA Cup 6th rd, 8 March 1975

Honours – Champions: Division 1: 1961–62; Division 2: 1960–61, 1967–68, 1991–92; Division 3 (S): 1953–54, 1956–57

UEFA Cup winners: 1980–81

LEEDS UNITED   FA PREMIER

Batty, David Hodge, Stephen B. Sterland, Melvyn
Cantona, Eric Kelly, Garry Strachan, Gordon D.
Chapman, Lee R. Kerr, Dylan Tinkler, Mark R.
Cousin, Scott Lukic, Jovan Varadi, Imre
Davison, Robert McAllister, Gary Wallace, Raymond G.
Day, Mervyn R. Newsome, Jon Wallace, Rodney S.
Dorigo, Anthony R. Nicholls, Ryan R. Wetherall, David
Fairclough, Courtney H. O'Connell, Patrick J. Whyte, Christopher A.
Haddock, Peter M. Shutt, Carl S. Wigley, Russell D.C.G.
Henderson, Damian M. Speed, Gary A.

League Appearances: Agana, P.A. 1(1); Batty, D. 40; Cantona, E. 6(9); Chapman, L.R. 38; Davison, R. –(2); Dorigo, A.R. 38; Fairclough, C.H. 30(1); Hodge, S.B. 12(11); Kamara, C. –(2); Kelly, G. –(2); Lukic, J. 42; McAllister, G. 41(1); McClelland, J. 16(2); Newsome, J. 7(3); Shutt, C.S. 6(8); Speed, G.A. 41; Sterland, M. 29(2); Strachan, G.D. 35(1); Varadi, I. 2(1); Wallace, R.S. 34; Wetherall, D. –(1); Whitlow, M. 3(7); Whyte, C. 41.

League Goals (74): Chapman 16, Wallace Rod 11, Hodge 7, Speed 7, Sterland 6 (2 pens), McAllister 5 (1 pen), Strachan 4 (4 pens), Cantona 3, Dorigo 3, Batty 2, Fairclough 2, Newsome 2, Shutt 1, Whitlow 1, Whyte 1, own goals 3.

Rumbelows Cup (11): Chapman 4, Speed 3, Wallace Rod 2, Shutt 1, Sterland 1 (1 pen).

FA Cup (0).

Ground: Elland Road, Leeds LS11 0ES (0532 716037)
Manager: Howard Wilkinson   **Secretary:** N. Pleasants
Colours: All white
Record home gate: 57,892 v Sunderland, FA Cup 5th rd (replay), 15 March 1967
Honours – Champions: Division 1: 1968–69, 1973–74, 1991–92; Division 2: 1923–24, 1963–64, 1989–90
FA Cup winners: 1972
European Fairs Cup winners: 1967–68, 1970–71

LEICESTER CITY   DIV. 1

Blyth, Ian	Mauchlen, Alister H.	Thompson, Stephen J.
Coatsworth, Gary	Mills, Gary R.	Trotter, Michael
Fitzpatrick, Paul J.	Muggleton, Carl D.	Walsh, Steven
Gee, Phillip	Oldfield, David C.	Ward, Ashley S.
Gibson, Colin J.	Ormondroyd, Ian	Whitlow, Michael
Gordon, Colin K.	Platnauer, Nicholas R.	Williams, Darren
Grayson, Simon N.	Poole, Kevin	Willis, James A.
Holden, Steven A.	Reid, Paul R.	Wright, Thomas E.
Hoult, Russell	Russell, Kevin J.	
James, Anthony C.	Smith, Richard G.	

League Appearances: Coatsworth, G. 2(1); Fitzpatrick, P.J. 21(5); Gee, P. 14; Gibson, C.J. 17; Gordon, C.K. 18(3); Grayson, S.N. 13; Hill, C.F. 10; Holden, S.A. 1; James, A.C. 12(1); Kelly, D.T.A. 12; Kitson, P. 29(1); Linton, D.M. –(1); Mauchlen, A.H. 14(6); Mills, G.R. 46; Muggleton, C.D. 4; Oakes, S.J. 1; Oldfield, D.C. 39(2); Ormondroyd, I. 14; Platnauer, N.R. 26(3); Poole, K. 42; Reid, P.R. 10(2); Russell, K.J. 7(13); Smith, R.G. 23(2); Thompson, S.J. 31(3); Trotter, M. –(2); Walsh, S. 43; Ward, A.S. 2(8); Whitlow, M. 4(1); Willis, J.A. 9(1); Wright, T.E. 42(2).
League Goals (62): Wright 12, Walsh 7, Kitson 6, Mills 6 (3 pens), Gordon 5, Russell 5, Fitzpatrick 4, Oldfield 4, Gibson 3, Thompson 3, Gee 2, Kelly 1, Mauchlen 1, Ormondroyd 1, Smith 1, own goals 1.
Rumbelows Cup (5): Kitson 2, Kelly 1, Mills 1, Walsh 1.
FA Cup (2): Kitson 1, Smith 1.
Ground: City Stadium, Filbert St, Leicester LE2 7FL (0533 555000)
Manager: Brian Little   **Secretary:** Alan Bennet
Colours: Blue shirts, white shorts, white stockings
Record home gate: 47,298 v Tottenham H, FA Cup 5th rd, 18 February 1928
Honours – Champions: Division 2: 1924–25, 1936–37, 1953–54, 1956–57, 1970–71, 1979–80
Football League Cup winners: 1964

LEYTON ORIENT   DIV. 2

Achampong, Kenneth	Burnett, Wayne	Castle, Stephen C.
Berry, Greg J.	Carter, Darren S.	Cobb, Paul

Cooper, Mark D.	Jones, Andrew M.	Taylor, Robert A.
Day, Keith	Newell, Paul C.	Tomlinson, Michael L.
Hackett, Warren J.	O'Neill, Mark A.	Turner, Christopher R.
Hales, Kevin P.	Ohanlon, George T.	Whitbread, Adrian R.
Harvey, Lee D.	Otto, Ricky	Zoricich, Chris V.
Heald, Paul A.	Patience, Brett J.	
Howard, Terence	Sharman, Keith E.	

League Appearances: Achampong, K. 20(4); Bart-Williams, C. 15; Berry, G.J. 30(6); Burnett, W. 33(3); Carter, D.S. 15(5); Castle, S.C. 35(2); Cobb, P. 1; Cooper, M.D. 11(7); Day, K. 31(2); Dickenson, K.J. 8; Hackett, W.J. 22; Hales, K.P. 6(4); Harvey, L.D. 5(8); Heald, P.A. 2; Hendon, I.M. 5(1); Howard, T. 45; Jones, A.M. 20(10); Newell, P.C. 10; Nugent, K.P. 36; Okai, S. 1; Otto, R. 23(9); Roeder, G.V. 6(2); Sayer, A. 8(1); Taylor, R.A. 6(5); Tomlinson, M.L. –(1); Turner, C.R. 34; Warren, M.W. –(1); Whitbread, A.R. 43; Wilder, C.J. 16; Zoricich, C. 19(3).

League Goals (62): Nugent 12, Castle 10, Berry 8, Cooper 6, Jones 5, Otto 5, Howard 4, Sayer 3, Achampong 2, Carter 2, Day 1, Okai 1, Taylor 1, Whitbread 1, Wilder 1.

Rumbelows Cup (6): Nugent 3, Berry 1, Burnett 1, Sayer 1.

FA Cup (9): Berry 2, Nugent 2, Castle 1 (1 pen), Cooper 1, Day 1, Harvey 1, Howard 1.

Ground: Leyton Stadium, Brisbane Road, Leyton, London E10 5NE (081-539 2223/4)

Manager: Peter Eustace   **Secretary:** Miss Carol Stokes

Colours: Red shirts with black and white bars, white shorts, red stockings

Record home gate: 34,345 v West Ham U, FA Cup 4th rd, 25 January 1964

Honours – Champions: Division 3: 1969–70; Division 3 (S): 1955–56

LINCOLN CITY DIV. 3

Bowling, Ian	Finney, Kevin	Smith, Paul M.
Bressington, Graham	Kabia, Jason	Ward, Paul T.
Brown, Grant A.	Lee, Jason B.	West, Dean
Carmichael, Matthew	Lormor, Anthony	West, Gary
Dobson, Paul	Puttnam, David P.	
Dunphy, Sean	Schofield, John D.	

League Appearances: Alexander, K. 5(10); Bowling, I. 20; Bressington, G. 2(1); Brown, G.A. 37; Carmichael, M. 36(4); Chapman, D. –(1); Clarke, D.A. 27(1); Costello, P. 3; Dickins, M. 20; Dixon, B. –(3); Dobson, P. 4(7); Dunphy, S. 5; Dye, D. –(2); Finney, K. 21(2); Hoult, R. 2; Kabia, J. 10(5); Lee, J.B. 33(2); Lormor, A. 33(2); Nicholson, S.M. 28(1); Puttnam, D.P. 37(2); Schofield, J.D. 39; Smith, N. –(1); Smith, P.M. 39; Ward, P. 28(1); West, D. 19(13); West, G. 14(4).

League Goals (50): Lormor 9, Carmichael 7 (4 pens), Lee 6, Puttnam 6, Dobson 4, Kabia 3, Smith P 3, West D 3, Finney 2, Alexander 1, Brown 1, Dunphy 1, Nicholson 1, Schofield 1, West G 1, own goals 1.

Rumbelows Cup (4): Schofield 2, Dobson 1, Ward 1.

FA Cup (1): Lee 1.

Ground: Sincil Bank, Lincoln LN5 8LD (0522 522224 & 510263)

Manager: Steve Thompson   **Secretary:** G. R. Davey
Colours: Red and white striped shirts, black shorts, red stockings with white trim
Record home gate: 23,196 v Derby Co, League Cup 4th rd, 15 November 1967
Honours – Champions: Division 3 (N): 1931–32, 1947–48, 1951–52; Division 4:
1975–76

LIVERPOOL FA PREMIER

Barnes, John C.B.
Burrows, David
Cousins, Anthony J.
Fowler, Robert B.
Grobbelaar, Bruce D.
Harkness, Steven
Hooper, Michael D.
Houghton, Raymond J.
Hutchinson, Donald
Johnston, Craig P.
Jones, Philip L.

Jones, Robert
Kenny, Marc V.
Kozma, Istvan
Marsh, Michael A.
McAree, Rodney J.
McManaman, Steven
Molby, Jan
Nicol, Stephen
Paterson, Scott
Redknapp, Jamie F.
Rosenthal, Ronny

Rush, Ian J.
Saunders, Dean N.
Tanner, Nicholas
Thomas, Michael L.
Venison, Barry
Walters, Mark
Whelan, Ronald A.
White, Tom
Wright, Mark

League Appearances: Ablett, G.I. 13(1); Barnes, J.C.B. 12; Burrows, D. 30;
Grobbelaar, B.D. 37; Harkness, S. 7(4); Hooper, M.D. 5; Houghton, R.J. 36;
Hutchison, D. –(3); Hysen, G. 3(2); Jones, R.M. 28; Kozma, I. 3(2); McMahon,
S. 15; McManaman, S. 26(4); Marsh, M.A. 19(15); Molby, J.25(1); Nicol, S. 34;
Redknapp, J.F. 5(1); Rosenthal, R. 7(13); Rush, I.J. 16(2); Saunders, D.N. 36;
Tanner, N. 32; Thomas, M.L. 16(1); Venison, B. 9(4); Walters, M.E. 18(7);
Whelan, R. A. 9(1); Wright, M. 21.
League Goals (47): Saunders 10, Houghton 8, McManaman 5, Molby 3 (1 pen),
Rosenthal 3, Rush 3, Thomas 3, Walters 3 (2 pens), Barnes 1, Burrows 1, Hysen
1, McMahon 1, Nicol 1, Redknapp 1, Tanner 1, Venison 1, own goals 1.
Rumbelows Cup (11): McManaman 3, Rush 3, Saunders 2, Walters 2, Houghton
1.
FA Cup (14): Barnes 3 (l pens), McManaman 3, Saunders 2, Thomas 2, Houghton
1, Molby 1, Rush 1, Whelan 1.
Ground: Anfield Road, Liverpool 4 (051-263 2361)
Manager: Graeme Souness   **Secretary:** Peter Robinson
Colours: All red with white markings
Record home gate: 61,905 v Wolverhampton W, FA Cup 4th rd, 2 February 1952
Honours – Champions: Division 1: 1900–01, 1905–06, 1921–22, 1922–23, 1946–47,
1963–64, 1965–66, 1972–73, 1975–76, 1976–77, 1978–79, 1979–80, 1981–82, 1982–
83, 1983–84, 1985–86, 1987–88, 1989–90 (Liverpool have a record number of 18
league Championship wins); Division 2: 1893–94, 1895–96, 1904–05, 1961–62
Runners-up 1977–78, 1986–87 **League Super Cup winners:** 1985–86

LUTON TOWN DIV. 1

Allpress, Tim J.
Campbell, Jamie

Chamberlain, Alec F.R.
Dreyer, John B.

Gillard, Kenneth J.
Gray, Philip

Greene, David M.	Linton, Desmond M.	Rees, Jason M.
Harford, Michael G.	Nogan, Kurt	Salton, Darren B.
Harvey, Richard G.	Oakes, Scott J.	Sommer, Juergen P.
Hughes, Ceri M.	Peake, Trevor	Telfer, Paul N.
James, Julian C.	Pembridge, Mark A.	Williams, Martin K.
Johnson, Marvin A.	Petterson, Andrew K.	
Kamara, Christopher	Preece, David W.	

League Appearances: Beaumont, D.A. 6(3); Black, K. 4; Campbell, J. 4(7); Chamberlain, A.F.R. 24; Day, M. 4; Dreyer, J.B. 42; Farrell, S.P. 3(1); Glover, E.L. 1; Gray, P. 9(5); Harvey, R.G. 31(1); Harford, M.G. 29; Holsgrove, P. 1; Hughes, C.M. 6(12); Jackson, M. 7(2); James, J.C. 28; Kamara, C. 28; Linton, D. 2(1); McDonough, D.K. 9; Nogan. K. 6(8); Oakes, S.J. 15(6); Peake, T. 38; Pembridge, M.A. 42; Preece, D.W. 34(4); Rees, J. 3(2); Rodger, G. 11(1); Salton, D.B. 2(1); Stein, B. 32(7); Sutton, S. 14; Telfer, P.N. 17(3); Thompson, S.J. 5; Varadi, I. 5(1); Williams, M.K. –(1).

League Goals (38): Harford 12, Pembridge 5 (2 pens), Gray 3, Preece 3, Stein 3, Dreyer 2 (1 pen), Harvey 2, James J 2, Oakes 2, Nogan 1, Telfer 1, Varadi 1, own goals 1.

Rumbelows Cup (4): Gray 3, Nogan 1.

FA Cup (0).

Ground: Kenilworth Road Stadium, 1 Maple Rd, Luton, Beds. LU4 8AW (0582 411622)

Manager: David Pleat   **Secretary:** J. K. Smylie.

Colours: White shirts, blue shorts, white stockings

Record home gate: 30,069 v Blackpool, FA Cup 6th rd replay, 4 March 1959

Honours – Champions: Division 2: 1981–82; Division 4: 1967–68; Division 3 (S): 1936–37

Football League Cup winners: 1987–88

MAIDSTONE UNITED   DIV. 3

Breen, Gary	Haylock, Paul	Sandeman, Bradley R.
Cuggy, Michael S.	Henry, Liburd A.	Smalley, Mark A.
Davis, Darren J.	Hesford, Iain	Sorrell, Antony C.
Donegal, Glenville P.	Lillis, Jason W.	Stebbing, Gary S.
Ellis, Neil J.	Oxbrow, Darren W.	Thompson, Leslie.

League Appearances: Breen, G. 19; Cuggy, M.S. 1(12); Davis, D. 20; Donegal, G.P. 9(5); Ellis, N.J. 22(6); Gall, M.I. 7(3); Haylock, P. 31(1); Hazel, I. 6(2); Henry, L. 36(1); Hesford, I. 42; Lillis, J.W. 21(2); Nethercott, S. 13; Newman, R. 9(1); Osborne, L.W. 16; Owers, A.R. 1; Oxbrow, D.W. 31; Painter, P.R. 27(3); Richards, C.L. 4; Rumble, P. 3(2); Rutter, S. –(1); Sandeman, B.R. 35(2); Sinclair, R.A. 1; Smalley, M.A. 33(1); Stebbing, G.S. 37; Thompson, L.A. 38; Tutton, A. –(4).

League Goals (45): Henry 7 (1 pen), Sandeman 7, Painter 5, Lillis 4, Osborne 4, Stebbing 3, Davis 2, Gall 2, Richards 2, Smalley 2, Cuggy 1 (1 pen), Donegal 1, Haylock 1, Hesford 1, Nethercott 1, Newman 1, Oxbrow 1.

Rumbelows Cup (0).

FA Cup (2): Henry 1, Thompson 1.

Ground: Ground: Watling Street, Dartford, Kent DA2 6EN. Club office: 1, Bower Terrace, Maidstone ME16 8RY. (0622 754403)
Manager: Clive Walker   **Secretary:** M. K. Mercer.
Colours: Gold shirts, black shorts, black stockings with gold trim
Record home gate: (at The Stadium, London Road, Maidstone): 10,591 v Charlton Ath., FA Cup 3rd rd replay, 15 January 1979
Honours – Nil

MANCHESTER CITY   FA PREMIER

Brennan, Mark R.	Kerr, David W.	Quinn, Niall J.
Brightwell, David J.	Lake, Paul A.	Redmond, Stephen
Brightwell, Ian R.	Limber, Nicholas	Reid, Peter
Coton, Anthony P.	Lomas, Stephen M.	Sheron, Michael N.
Curle, Keith	Margetson, Martyn W.	Simpson, Fitzroy
Dibble, Andrew	McMahon, Stephen	Sliney, Gary S.
Flitcroft, Gary W.	Megson, Gary J.	Thomas, Scott L.
Harkin, Sean C.	Owen, Phillip J.G.	Vonk, Michel C.
Hill, Andrew R.	Pointon, Neil G.	Wallace, Michael
Hughes, Michael E.	Quigley, Michael A.	White, David

League Appearances: Allen, C. –(3); Brennan, M.R. 13; Brightwell, D.J. 3(1); Brightwell, I. 36(4); Clarke, W. –(5); Coton, A.P. 37; Curle, K. 40; Dibble, A.G. 2; Heath, A.P. 20(8); Hendry, E.C.J. –(6); Hill, A.R. 36; Hoekman, D. –(1); Hughes, M.E. 24; McMahon, S. 18; Margetson, M.W. 3; Megson, G.J. 18(4); Mike, A.R. 2; Pointon, N. 39; Quigley, M.A. –(5); Quinn, N. 35; Redmond, S. 31; Reid, P. 29(2); Sheron, M.N. 20(9); Simpson, F. 9(2); Vonk, M.C. 8(1); White, D. 39
League Goals (61): White 18, Quinn 12, Sheron 7, Curle 5 (3 pens), Hill 4, Brennan 3 (2 pens), Allen C 2 (1 pen), Brightwell I 1, Clarke W 1, Heath 1, Hendry 1, Hughes 1, Mike 1, Pointon 1, Redmond 1 (1 pen), Simpson 1, own goals 1.
Rumbelows Cup (10): White 3, Heath 2, Quinn 2, Allen 1, Brennan 1, Sheron 1.
FA Cup (1): Reid 1.
Ground: Maine Road, Moss Side, Manchester M14 7WN (061-226 1191/2)
Manager: Peter Reid   **Secretary:** Bernard Halford
Colours: Sky blue shirts, dark blue collar, white shorts, navy blue stockings
Record home gate: 84,569 v Stoke C, FA Cup 6th rd, 3 March 1934 (British record for any game outside London or Glasgow)
Honours – Champions: Division 1: 1936–37, 1967–68; Division 2: 1898–99, 1902–03, 1909–10, 1927–28, 1946–47, 1965–66
FA Cup winners: 1904, 1934, 1956, 1969
Football League Cup winners: 1970, 1976
European Cup-Winners' Cup winners: 1969–70

MANCHESTER UNITED   FA PREMIER

Beardsmore, Russell P.	Brazil, Derek M.	Carey, Brian P.
Blackmore, Clayton G.	Bruce, Stephen R.	Doherty, Adrian J.

Donaghy, Malachy
Ferguson, Darren
Giggs, Ryan J.
Hughes, Leslie M.
Ince, Paul E.C.
Irwin, Dennis J.
Kanchelskis, Andrei
Lawton, Craig T.
Maiorana, Giuliano
Martin, Lee A.
McClair, Brian J.
McKee, Colin
Pallister, Garry A.
Parker, Paul A.
Phelan, Michael C.
Robins, Mark G.
Robson, Bryan
Schmeichel, Peter B.
Sharpe, Lee S.
Toal, Kiernan M.
Wallace, David L.
Walsh, Gary
Webb, Neil J.
Whitworth, Neil A.
Wilkinson, Ian M.

League Appearances: Blackmore, C.G. 19(14); Bruce, S.R. 37; Donaghy, M.M. 16(4); Ferguson, D. 2(2); Giggs, R.J. 32(6); Hughes, L.M. 38(1); Ince, P.E.C. 31(2); Irwin, D.J. 37(1); Kanchelskis, A. 28(6); McClair, B.J. 41(1); Martin, L.A. –(1); Pallister, G. A. 37(3); Parker, P.A. 24(2); Phelan, M.C. 14(4); Robins, M.G. 1(1); Robson, B. 26(1); Sharpe, L.S. 8(6); Schmeichel, P.D. 40; Walsh, G. 2; Webb, N.J. 29(2).

League Goals (63): McClair 18, Hughes 11, Bruce 5 (3 pens), Kanchelskis 5, Giggs 4, Irwin 4, Robson 4, Blackmore 3 (1 pen), Ince 3, Webb 3, Pallister 1, Sharpe 1, own goals 1.

Rumbelows Cup (15): McClair 4, Giggs 3, Kanchelskis 2, Robins 2, Blackmore 1, Bruce 1, Robson 1, Sharpe 1.

FA Cup (3): Hughes 1, Kanchelskis 1, McClair 1.

Ground: Old Trafford, Manchester M16 0RA (061-872 1661)

Manager: Alex Feguson   **Secretary:** Kenneth Merrett

Colours: Red shirts, white shorts, black stockings

Record home gate: 76,962 Wolverhampton W v Grimsby T, FA Cup semi-final. 25 March 1939. Club record: 70,504 v Aston Villa, Division 1, 27 December 1920

Honours – Champions: Division 1: 1907–8, 1910–11, 1951–52, 1955–56, 1956–57, 1964–65, 1966–67; Division 2: 1935–36, 1974–75

Football League Cup winners: 1991–92, 1982–83 (Runners-up), 1990–91 (Runners-up) **European Cup winners:** 1967–68

European Cup-Winners' Cup winners: 1990–91

MANSFIELD TOWN DIV. 2

Beasley, Andrew
Castledine, Gary J.
Charles, Stephen
Clark, Martin J.
Clarke, Nicholas J.
Davison, Wayne
Fairclough, Wayne R.
Fee, Gregory P.
Fleming, Paul
Ford, Gary
Foster, George W.
Gray, Kevin J.
Holland, Paul
McLoughlin, Paul B.
Noteman, Kevin S.
Pearcey, Jason
Roddis, Nicholas P.
Spooner, Stephen A.
Stant, Philip
Stringfellow, Ian R.
Wilkinson, Stephen J.
Withe, Christopher

League Appearances: Beasley, A. 9; Carr, C.P. 20; Castledine, G.J. 3(4); Charles, S. 40; Clark, M.J. 7(2); Clarke, N.J. 16; Fairclough, W.R. 18(7); Fee; G.P. 33(1); Fleming, P. 38; Ford, G. 39; Foster, G.W. 24; Gray, K.J. 11(7); Holland, P. 38; Kite, P.D. 11; McLoughlin, P.B. 10(2); Murray, M. –(1); Noteman, K.S. 6; Pearcey, J. 22; Spooner, S.A. 31; Stant, P.R. 39(1); Stringfellow, I.R. 7(10); Wilkinson, S.J. 30; Withe, C. 10.

League Goals (75): Stant 26, Wilkinson 14, Charles 6 (4 pens), Holland 6, Fee 4, Ford 4, Fairclough 3, McLoughlin 3, Spooner 2, Stringfellow 2, Clarke N 1, Withe 1, own goals 3.
Rumbelows Cup (2): Gray 1, Spooner 1.
FA Cup (0).
Ground: Field Mill Ground, Quarry Lane, Mansfield (0623 23567)
Manager: George Foster   **Secretary:** J. D. Eaton
Colours: Amber shirts with blue trim, blue shorts, amber stockings
Record home gate: 24,467 v Nottingham F, FA Cup 3rd rd, 10 January 1953
Honours – Champions: Division 3: 1976–77; Division 4: 1974–75
Associate Members Cup winners: 1986–87

MIDDLESBROUGH   FA PREMIER

Collett, Andrew A.	Mohan, Nicholas	Pollock, Jamie
Falconer, William H.	Moore, Alan	Proctor, Mark G.
Fleming, Curtis	Mustoe, Robbie	Ripley, Stuart E.
Gilchrist, Philip A.	Parkinson, Gary	Slaven, Bernard
Hendrie, John G.	Payton, Andrew P.	Todd, Andrew J.J.
Ironside, Ian	Peake, Andrew M.	Wilkinson, Paul
Kavanagh, Graham A.	Pears, Stephen	Young, Michael S.
Kernaghan, Alan N.	Peverell, Nicholas J.	
Lake, Robert M.	Phillips, James N.	

League Appearances: Arnold, I. –(1); Falconer, W.H. 25; Fleming, C. 23(5); Gittens, J. 9(3); Hendrie, J.G. 38; Hewitt, J. –(2); Ironside, I. 1; Kernaghan, A.N. 38; Marwood, B. 3; Mohan, N. 27; Mowbray, A.M. 17; Mustoe, R. 28(2); Parkinson, G.A. 23(4); Payton, A.P. 8(11); Peake, A.M. 20(3); Pears, S. 45; Phillips, J.N. 43; Pollock, J. 21(5); Proctor, M.G. 27(9); Ripley, S.E. 36(3); Shannon, R. –(1); Slaven, B. 28(10); Wilkinson, P. 46; Young, M.S. –(1).
League Goals (58): Slaven 16 (4 pens), Wilkinson 15, Falconer 5, Hendrie 3, Payton 3, Ripley 3, Kernaghan 2, Mohan 2, Mustoe 2, Phillips 2 (1 pen), Proctor 2, Gittens 1, Pollock 1, own goals 1.
Rumbelows Cup (8): Wilkinson 3, Hendrie 1, Mustoe 1, Parkinson 1 (1 pen), Ripley 1, Slaven 1.
FA Cup (7): Wilkinson 4, Kernaghan 2, Hendrie 1.
Ground: Ayresome Park, Middlesbrough, Cleveland TS1 4PB (0642 819659/ 815996)
Manager: Lennie Lawrence   **Secretary:** Keith Lamb
Colours: Red shirts, white shorts, red stockings
Record home gate: 53,596 v Newcastle U, Division 1, 27 December 1979
Honours – Champions: Division 2: 1926–27, 1928–29, 1973–74
Amateur Cup winners: 1895, 1898, *Anglo-Scottish Cup*

MILLWALL   DIV. 1

Allen, Malcolm	Barber, Phillip A.	Branagan, Keith G.
Armstrong, Christopher P.	Bogie, Ian	Colquhoun, John

Cooper, Colin T.	Goodman, Jonathan	McGlashan, John
Cunningham, Kenneth E.	Horne, Brian	McLeary, Alan T.
Davison, Aidan J.	Humphrey, John M.	Okyere-Darkoh, Joseph
Dawes, Ian R.	Keller, Kasey	Rae, Alex
Dolby, Tony C.	Kerr, Paul A.	Roberts, Andrew J.
Donegan, John	Lee, Brian R.	Stephenson, Paul
Emberson, Carl W.	Manning, Paul J.	Stevens, Keith H.
Falco, Mark P.	McCarthy, Michael	Thompson, David
Foran, Mark J.	McGinlay, John	Verveer, Etienne

League Appearances: Allen, M. 10(1); Armstrong, C.P. 8(17); Barber, P.A. 26(3); Bogie, I. 20(5); Branagan, K.G. 12; Colquhoun, J. 27; Cooper, C.T. 36; Cunningham, K.E. 15(2); Davison, H.J. 33; Dawes, I.R. 36; Falco, M.P. 19(2); Goodman, J. 15(2); Keller, K. 1; Kerr, P. 32(2); McCarthy, M.J. 14(3); McGinlay, J. 19(6); McGlashan, J. 5(3); McLeary, A.T. 28; Rae, A.S. 36(2); Roberts, A. 5(2); Stephenson, P. 26(2); Stevens, K.H. 24(3); Thompson, D. 29(4); Verveer, E. 24(1); Wood, S.A. 6(1).

League Goals (64): Kerr 12 (5 pens), Rae 11, McGinlay 8, Allen 5 (1 pen), Armstrong 4, Barber 4, Falco 4, Colquhoun 3, Goodman 3, Cooper 2, McCarthy 2, Stephenson 2, Verveer 2, own goals 2.

Rumbelows Cup (3): Armstrong 1, Colquhoun 1, Stephenson 1.

FA Cup (5): Rae 2, Kerr 1, Thompson 1, Verveer 1.

Ground: The Den, Cold Blow Lane, London SE14 5RH (071-639 3143, 071-639 4590)

Manager: Mick McCarthy   **Secretary:** G. I. S. Hortop

Colours: Blue shirts, white shorts, blue stockings

Record home gate: 48,672 v Derby Co, FA Cup 5th rd, 20 February 1937

Honours – Champions: Division 2: 1987–88; Division 3 (S): 1927–28, 1937–38; Division 4: 1961–62

Football League Cup winners: 1982–83

NEWCASTLE UNITED   DIV. 1

Appleby, Matthew W.	Kilcline, Brian	Roche, David
Brock, Kevin S.	Kristensen, Bjorn	Scott, Kevin W.
Carr, Franz A.	Makel, Lee R.	Sheedy, Kevin M.
Clark, Lee R.	Mason, Philip	Srnicek, Pavel
Elliot, Robert J.	McDonough, Darron K.	Stimson, Mark
Galvin, Anthony	Neilson, Alan B.	Thompson, Alan
Garland, Peter J.	O'Brien, Liam F.	Watson, John I.
Howey, Stephen N.	Peacock, Gavin K.	Watson, Stephen C.
Hunt, Andrew	Quinn, Michael	Wright, Thomas J.
Kelly, David T.	Ranson, Raymond	

League Appearances: Appleby, M.W. 16(2); Bodin, P. 6; Bradshaw, D.S. 17(2); Brock, K.S. 31(4); Carr, F.A. 12(3); Clark, L.R. 25(4); Elliott, R.J. 9; Garland, P.J. –(2); Howey, S.N. 13(8); Hunt, A. 21(6); Kelly, D.T. 25; Kilcline, B. 12; Kristensen, B. 1(1); McDonough, D. 2(1); Maguire, G. 3; Makel, L.R. 5(4); Neilson, A.B. 16; O'Brien, L.F. 40; Peacock, G. 46; Quinn, M. 18(4); Ranson, R. 5(1); Robinson, D.J. –(3); Roche, D. 18(8); Scott, K.W. 44; Sheedy, K.M. 13;

Srnicek, P. 13; Stimson, M. 23(1); Thompson, A. 12(2); Walker, A. 2; Watson, S.C. 23(5); Wilson, T. 2; Wright, T.J. 33..
League Goals (66): Peacock 16 (3 pens), Kelly 11, Hunt 9, Quinn 7 (1 pen), Clark 5, Brock 4, O'Brien 4, Carr 2, Howey 1, Makel 1, Neilson 1, Scott 1, Sheedy 1, Watson S 1, own goals 2.
Rumbelows Cup (5): Peacock 3, Howey 1, Hunt 1.
FA Cup (2): Hunt 2.
Ground: St James' Park, Newcastle-upon-Tyne NE1 4ST (091-232 8361)
Manager: Kevin Keegan **Secretary:** R. Cushing
Colours: Black and white striped shirts, black shorts, black stockings
Record home gate: 68,386 v Chelsea, Division 1, 3 Sept 1930
Honours – Champions: Division 1: 1904–05, 1906–07, 1908–09, 1926–27; Division 2: 1964–65
FA Cup winners: 1910, 1924, 1932, 1951, 1952, 1955
Texaco Cup winners: 1973–74, 1974–75
European Fairs Cup winners: 1968–69

NORTHAMPTON TOWN   DIV. 3

Angus, Terence N.	Brown, Stephen	Parker, Sean
Beavon, Michael S.	Burnham, Jason J.	Richardson, Barry
Bell, Michael	Chard, Phillip J.	Terry, Steve G.

League Appearances: Adams, C.J. –(1); Adcock, A.C. 14; Aldridge, M.J. 2(3); Angus, T.N. 37; Barnes, D.O. 18; Beavon, M.S. 33; Bell, M. 23(7); Benton, J. 4(1); Beresford, M. 15; Brown, S.F. 31(4); Bulzis, R.R.B. 1(3); Burnham, J.J. 36(4); Campbell, G. 12(10); Chard, P.J. 29; Colkin, K. 2(1); Edwards, D. 7; Farrell, S. 4; Gernon, F.A.J. 27(1); Johnson, D. 9(6); Kiernan, D.J. 6(3); McClean, C. 19; Parker, S. 5(1); Parsons, M.C. 13; Quow, T.S. 24(3); Richardson, B. 27; Scope, D.F. 1(4); Terry, S. 37; Thorpe, A. 11(1); Wilson, P.A. 14(2); Wood, D. 1.
League Goals (46): Adcock 7, Barnes 6, Bell 4, Beavon 3 (1 pen), Brown 3, Campbell 3, Chard 3, McClean 3, Terry 3, Angus 2, Burnham 2, Thorpe 2, Benton 1, Farrell 1 (1 pen), Scope 1, Wilson 1, own goals 1.
Rumbelows Cup (2): Barnes 2.
FA Cup (2): Adcock 1, Chard 1.
Ground: County Ground, Abington Avenue, Northampton NN1 4PS (0604 234100)
Manager: Phil Chard **Secretary:** Philip Mark Hough
Colours: White shirts, claret sleeves, claret shorts, claret stockings
Record home gate: 24,523 v Fulham, Division 1, 23 April 1966
Honours – Champions: Division 3: 1962–63; Division 4: 1986–87

NORWICH CITY   FA PREMIER

Beckford, Darren R.	Crook, Ian S.	Goss, Jeremy
Blades, Paul A.	Culverhouse, Ian B.	Gunn, Bryan J.
Bowen, Mark R.	Fleck, Robert	Johnson, Andrew J.
Butterworth, Ian S.	Fox, Ruel A.	Minett, Jason

Mortensen, Henrik
Newman, Robert N.
Pennock, Adrian B.
Phillips, David O.
Polston, John D.

Power, Lee M.
Smith, David C.
Sutch, Daryl
Sutton, Christopher R.
Ullathorne, Robert

Walton, Mark A.
Wooding, Timothy D.
Woodthorpe, Colin J.

League Appearances: Ball, S.J. –(2); Beckford, D.R. 25(5); Blades, P.A. 26; Bowen, M.R. 35(1); Butterworth, I.S. 31; Crook, I.S. 20(1); Culverhouse, I.B. 21; Fleck, R. 35(1); Fox, R.A. 27(10); Gordon, D.A. 15; Goss, J. 29(4); Gunn, B. 25; Johnson, A.J. 2; Newman, R.N. 41; Phillips, D.O. 34; Polston, J.D. 16(3); Power, L.M. 2(2); Sherwood, T.A. 7; Smith, D.C. 1; Sutch, D. 5(4); Sutton, C.R. 16(5); Ullathorne, R. 20; Walton, M. 17; Woodthorpe, C. 12(3).

League Goals (47): Fleck 11 (2 pens), Beckford 7, Newman 7, Gordon 4, Bowen 3 (1 pen), Ullathorne 3, Fox 2, Sutton 2, Butterworth 1, Crook 1, Goss 1, Phillips 1, Polston 1, Power 1, Woodthorpe 1, own goals 1.

Rumbelows Cup (12): Fleck 6, Beckford 3, Fox 1, Gordon 1, Newman 1.

FA Cup (8): Sutton 3, Fleck 2 (1 pen), Bowen 1, Newman 1, Phillips 1.

Ground: Carrow Road, Norwich NR1 1JE (0603 612131)

Manager: Mike Walker. **Secretary:** A. R. W. Neville

Colours: Yellow shirts green trim, green shorts yellow trim, yellow stockings

Record home gate: 43,984 v Leicester C, FA Cup 6th rd, 30 March 1963

Honours – Champions: Division 2: 1971–72, 1985–86; Division 3 (S): 1933–34

Football League Cup winners: 1962, 1985

NOTTINGHAM FOREST   FA PREMIER

Black, Kingsley
Boardman, Craig G.
Bowyer, Gary D.
Byrne, Raymond
Charles, Gary A.
Chettle, Stephen
Clough, Nigel H.
Crosby, Gary
Crossley, Mark G.
Davies, Christian A.
Forrest, Cuan F.
Gaynor, Tommy

Gemmill, Scot
Glasser, Neil R.
Glover, Edward L.
Hope, Christopher J.
Howe, Stephen
Kaminsky, Jason M.G.
Keane, Roy M.
Kilford, Ian A.
Laws, Brian
Marriott, Andrew
McGregor, Paul A.
Orlygsson, Thorvaldur

Pearce, Stuart
Sheringham, Edward P.
Smith, Mark A.
Stone, Stephen B.
Tiler, Carl
Walker, Desmond S.
Warner, Vance
Wassall, Darren P.
Williams, Brett
Wilson, Terry
Woan, Ian S.
Wright, Dale C.

League Appearances: Black, K. 25; Charles, G.A. 30; Chettle, S. 17(5); Clough, N.H. 33(1); Crosby, G. 31(2); Crossley, M.G. 36; Gaynor, T. 3(1); Gemmill, S. 39; Glover, E.L. 12(4); Jemson, N.B. 6; Kaminsky, J.M.G.S. –(1); Keane, R. 39; Laws, B. 10(5); Marriott, A. 6; Orlygsson, T. 5; Parker, G.S. 5(1); Pearce, S. 30; Sheringham, E.P. 39; Stone, S.B. –(1); Tiler, C. 24(2); Walker, D.S. 32(1); Wassall, D.P. 10(4); Williams, B. 9; Wilson, T. 1; Woan, I.S. 20(1).

League Goals (60): Sheringham 13 (2 pens), Gemmill 8, Keane 8, Clough 5, Pearce 5 (1 pen), Woan 5, Black 4, Crosby 3, Charles 1, Chettle 1, Jemson 1, Parker 1, Tiler 1, Walker 1, own goals 3.

Rumbelows Cup (20): Sheringham 5, Keane 4, Gaynor 3, Black 2, Gemmill 2, Glover 2, Clough 1, Pearce 1.

FA Cup (7): Clough 2, Pearce 2, Sheringham 2 (1 pen), own goals 1.
Ground: City Ground, Nottingham NG2 5FJ (0602 822202)
Manager: Brian Clough OBE, MA.   **Secretary:** P. White
Colours: Red shirts, white shorts, red stockings
Record home gate: 49,946 v Manchester U, Division 1, 28 October 1967
Honours – Champions: Division 1: 1977–78; Division 2: 1906–07, 1921–22; Division 3 (S): 1950–51
Full Members Cup winners: 1989

NOTTS COUNTY — DIV. 1

Agana, Patrick A.O.	Lund, Gary J.	Thomas, Dean R.
Bartlett, Kevin F.	O'Riordan, Donald J.	Turner, Philip
Blackwell, Kevin P.	Palmer, Charles A.	Walker, James B.
Cherry, Steven R.	Paris, Alan D.	Walker, Richard N.
Devlin, Paul J.	Patterson, Gary	Wells, Mark A.
Dolan, Kenneth P.	Robinson, Philip J.	Williams, Andrew
Draper, Mark A.	Short, Christian M.	Wilson, Kevin J.
Dryden, Richard A.	Short, Craig J.	Worboys, Gavin
Harding, Paul	Slawson, Stephen M.	Yates, Dean R.
Johnson, Michael O.	Snook, Edward K.	

League Appearances: Agana, P.A. 11(2); Bartlett, K.F. 24(5); Cherry, S.R. 42; Cox, P.R. –(1); Devlin, P.J. 1(1); Draper, M.A. 32(3); Dryden, R. 28(1); Farina, F. 1(2); Harding, P. 25(4); Johnson, M.O. 5; Johnson, T. 31; Lund, G.J. 10(3); McClelland, J. 6; Matthews, R. 1(4); O'Riordan, D.J. 1; Palmer, C.A. 40(1); Paris, A.D. 26(1); Regis, D. 5(4); Rideout, P.D. 9(2); Robinson, P.J. 1; Short, C.M. 20(7); Short, J.C. 38; Slawson, S.M. 3(10); Thomas, D.R. 34(2); Turner, P. 22(7); Wells, M.A. –(1); Williams, A. 14(1); Wilson, K.J. 8; Yates, D.R. 24(1).
League Goals (40): Johnson T 9 (3 pens), Bartlett 7, Matthews 3, Rideout 3, Short Craig 3, Lund 2, Yates 2, Agana 1, Draper 1, Dryden 1, Harding 1, Slawson 1, Thomas 1, Turner 1, Williams 1, Wilson 1, own goals 2.
Rumbelows Cup (4): Bartlett 2, Johnson T 2 (1 pen).
FA Cup (4): Draper 1, Johnson T 1, Lund 1, Turner 1.
Ground: County Ground, Meadow Lane, Nottingham NG2 3HJ (0602 861155)
Manager: Neil Warnock   **Secretary:** N. E. Hook MCIM, AMID
Colours: Black and white broad striped shirts, amber sleeve and neck trim, black shorts with white side flash, black stockings with white and amber trim
Record home gate: 47,310 v York C, FA Cup 6th rd, 12 March 1955
Honours – Champions: Division 2: 1896–97, 1913–14, 1922–23; Division 3 (S): 1930–31, 1949–50; Division 4: 1970–71
FA Cup winners: 1893–94

OLDHAM ATHLETIC — FA PREMIER

Adams, Neil J.	Bernard, Paul R.J.	Donachie, William
Barlow, Andrew J.	Bunn, Frankie S.	Fleming, Craig

Gerrard, Paul W.
Halle, Guner
Hallworth, Jonathan G.
Harriott, Marvin L.
Henry, Nicholas I.
Holden, Andrew I.
Holden, Richard W.
Jobson, Richard I.
Keeley, John H.
Makin, Christopher
Marshall, Ian P.
McDonald, Neil R.
Miller, Robert J.
Milligan, Michael J.
Moulden, Paul A.
Palmer, Roger N.
Ritchie, Andrew T.
Sharp, Graeme M.
Tolson, Neil
Wilson, Gregory J.

League Appearances: Adams, N.J. 21(5); Barlow, A.J. 28; Barrett, E.D. 29; Bernard, P.R.J. 16(5); Currie, D.N. 1(3); Fleming, C. 28(4); Halle. G. 10; Hallworth, J.G. 41; Henry, N.I. 42; Holden, R.W. 38(4); Jobson, R.I. 36; Kane, P. 1(3); Keeley, J.H. 1; Kilcline, B. 8; McDonald, N. 14(3); Marshall, I.P. 41; Milligan, M. 36; Moulden, P. –(2); Palmer, R.N. 14(7); Ritchie, A.T. 7(7); Sharp, G.M. 42; Snodin, G. 8.
League Goals (63): Sharp 12 (1 pen), Marshall 10 (1 pen), Henry 6, Bernard 5, Holden 5, Adams 4, Milligan 3, Palmer 3, Ritchie 3, Barlow 2, Barrett 2, Jobson 2, Currie 1, Fleming 1, McDonald 1, Moulden 1, Snodin 1, own goals 1.
Rumbelows Cup (11): Ritchie 4, Sharp 2, Henry 1, Holden 1, Jobson 1, Milligan 1, Palmer 1.
FA Cup (3): Adams 1, Palmer 1, Sharp 1.
Ground: Boundary Park, Oldham (061-624 4972)
Manager: Joe Royle   **Secretary:** Terry Cale
Colours: All blue with red piping
Record home gate: 47,671 v Sheffield W, FA Cup 4th rd. 25 January 1930
Honours – Champions: Division 2: 1990–91; Division 3 (N): 1952–53; Division 3: 1973–74

OXFORD UNITED DIV. 1

Allen, Christopher A.
Beauchamp, Joseph D.
Druce, Mark A.
Durnin, John
Evans, Ceri L.
Ford, Michael P.
Jackson, Darren W.
Kee, Paul V.
Keeble, Matthew E.
Lewis, Michael
Magilton, James
McClaren, Stephen
McDonnell, Matthew T.
Melville, Andrew R.
Penney, David M.
Phillips, Leslie M.
Robinson, Leslie
Smart, Garry J.
Veysey, Kenneth J.
Wanless, Paul S.

League Appearances: Allen, C.A. 13(1); Aylott, T.K.C. 35(2); Bannister, G. 7(3); Beauchamp, J.D. 24(3); Byrne, P.P. –(1); Druce, M.A. –(2); Durnin, J. 28(9); Evans, C.L. 27(2); Ford, M.P. 9; Foster, S.B. 22; Harris, A. 1; Jackson, D.W. 4(1); Kee, P.V. 8; Keeley, J.H. 6; Lewis, M. 40; McClaren, S. 4; Magilton, J. 44; Melville, A.R. 45; Nogan, L.M. 22; Penney, D.M. 17(6); Phillips, L.M. 7; Robinson, L. 27; Simpson, P.D. 30(1); Smart, G. 38(1); Stein, E.M.S. 6(1); Veysey, K.J. 32; Wanless, P.S. 3(3); Williams, B. 7.
League Goals (66): Magilton 12 (2 pens), Simpson 9, Durnin 8, Beauchamp 7, Aylott 6, Nogan 5, Lewis 4, Melville 4, Penney 4, Bannister 2, Foster 2, Allen 1, Ford 1, Stein 1.
Rumbelows Cup (0).
FA Cup (5): Beauchamp 1, Magilton 1 (1 pen), Penney 1, Simpson 1, own goals 1.
Ground: Manor Ground, Headdington, Oxford (0865 61503)

Manager: Brian Horton   **Secretary:** Mick Brown
Colours: Gold, navy blue trim, navy blue shorts, navy stockings
Record home gate: 22,750 v Preston NE, FA Cup 6th rd, 29 February 1964
Honours – Champions: Division 2: 1984–85; Division 3: 1967–68, 1983–84
Football League Cup winners: 1985–86

PETERBOROUGH UNITED   DIV. 1

Adcock, Anthony C.
Barber, Frederick
Barnes, David O.
Charlery, Kenneth

Cooper, Gary
Costello, Peter
Halsall, Michael
Luke, Noel E.

Robinson, David A.
Robinson, Ronald
Sterling, Worrel R.
Welsh, Stephen

League Appearances: Adcock, A.C. 23(1); Barber, F. 39; Barnes, D.O. 15; Bennett, I.M. 7; Butterworth, G.J. 14(5); Charlery, K.L. 33(4); Cooper, G. 33; Cooper, S.B. 2(7); Costello, P. –(1); Culpin, P. –(7); Ebdon, M. 12(3); Gavin, P.J. 8(3); Halsall, M. 45; Howarth, L. 6(1); Johnson, P.E. 11; Kimble, G.L. 30; Luke, N.E. 42(1); McInerney, I. 3(7); Riley, D. 23(5); Robinson, D.A. 43; Robinson, R. 24(3); Salman, D.M.M. 1; Sterling, W.R. 43(2); Welsh, S.G. 42; White, C.J. 7(1).
League Goals (65): Charlery 16 (1 pen), Riley 9, Adcock 7, Barnes 5, Halsall 5 (1 pen), Cooper G 4 (3 pens), Kimble 4, Sterling 4, Robinson D 3, Culpin 2, Ebdon 2 (1 pen), Butterworth 1, McInerney 1, own goals 2.
Rumbelows Cup (11): Gavin 4, Charlery 2, Kimble 2, Halsall 1, Riley 1, Sterling 1.
FA Cup (7): Cooper G 2 (1 pens), Charlery 1, Culpin 1, Halsall 1, Riley 1, Sterling 1.
Ground: London Road Ground, Peterborough PE2 8AL (0733 63947)
Manager: Chris Turner   **Secretary:** Arnold V. Blades
Colours: Royal blue shirts, white shorts, blue stockings   **Change colours:** Green shirts, white shorts, green stockings
Record home gate: 30,096 v Swansea T, FA Cup 5th rd, 20 February 1965
Honours – Champions: Division 4: 1960–61, 1973–74

PLYMOUTH ARGYLE   DIV. 2

Adcock, Paul M.
Barlow, Martin D.
Burrows, Adrian M.
Clode, Mark J.
Cross, Ryan
Edworthy, Marc
Evans, Michael J.

Fiore, Mark J.
Garner, Darren J.
Hodges, Kevin
Marker, Nicholas R.T.
Marshall, Dwight W.
McCall, Stephen H.
Morgan, Stephen A.

Morrison, Andrew C.
Nugent, Kevin P.
Regis, David
Smith, David A.
Spearing, Anthony
Turner, Robert P.
Wilmot, Rhys J.

League Appearances: Barlow, M.D. 23(5); Burrows, A. 14(1); Clement, A.D. 20(6); Cross, R. 12; Damerell, M.A. –(1); Edworthy, M. 7(8); Evans, M.J. 11(2);

Fiore, M.J. 25(7); Garner, D.J. 8(2); Hodges, K. 11(3); Hopkins, J. 8; Jones, S.A. –(1); Lee, D.J. 9; McCall, S.H. 9; Marker, N.R.T. 44; Marshall, D.W. 44; Meaker, M.J. 4; Morgan, S.A. 45; Morrison, A.C. 29(1); Nugent, K. 2(2); Pickard, O. –(2); Quamina, M.E. 4(1); Regis, D. 21(3); Salman, D.M.M. 26(2); Scott, M.J. 3(3); Shilton, P.L. 7; Smith, D.A. 14(4); Spearing, A. 30; Turner, R.P. 25; Van Rossum, J.C. 9; Walter, D.W. 5; Wilmot, R.J. 34; Witter, A. 3.
League Goals (42): Marshall 14, Fiore 4, Barlow 3, Burrows 3, Morrison 3, Turner 3 (1 pen), Morgan 2, Regis 2, Smith 2, Lee 1, Marker 1, McCall 1, Salman 1, Witter 1, own goals 1.
Rumbelows Cup (3): Barlow 1, Morrison 1, Turner 1.
FA Cup (0).
Ground: Home Park, Plymouth, Devon P12 3DQ (0752 562561-2-3)
Manager: Peter Shilton.   **Secretary:** Liz Baker
Colours: Green and white striped shirts, black shorts, black stockings
Record home gate: 43,596 v Aston Villa, Division 2, 10 October 1936
Honours – Champions: Division 3 (S): 1929–30, 1951–52; Division 3: 1958–59

PORTSMOUTH   DIV. 1

Anderton, Darren R.	Doling, Stuart J.	Neill, Warren A.
Aspinall, Warren	Gale, Shaun M.	Powell, Darryl A.
Awford, Andrew T.	Gosney, Andrew R.	Ross, Michael P.
Beresford, John	Kelly, Mark J.	Russell, Lee
Burns, Christopher	Knight, Alan E.	Stevens, Gary A.
Butters, Guy	Kuhl, Martin	Symons, Christopher J.
Chamberlain, Mark V.	Maguire, Gavin T.	Whittingham, Guy
Clarke, Colin J.	McLoughlin, Alan F.	Wigley, Steven
Daniel, Raymond C.	Murray, Shaun	

League Appearances: Anderton, D.R. 40(2); Aspinall, W. 9(15); Awford, A.T. 45; Beresford, J. 35; Burns, C. 42(4); Butters, G. 32(1); Chamberlain, M.V. 10(6); Clarke, C.J. 19(5); Daniel, R.C. 7(1); Doling, S.J. 7(6); Gosney, A.R. 1; Hebberd, T.N. 1(3); Hendon, I.M. 1(3); Knight, A.E. 45; Kuhl, M. 41; McFarlane, A.A. –(2); McLoughlin, A.F. 14; Murray, S. 2; Neill, W.A. 38; Powell, D.A. 26(10); Ross, M.P. –(3); Russell, L. 7(2); Symons, C.J. 46; Whittingham, G. 30(5); Wigley, S. 8(15).
League Goals (65): Whittingham 11, Burns 8, Anderton 7, Beresford 6 (4 pens), Powell 6, Aspinall 4, Clarke 4, Kuhl 3, Wigley 3, Butters 2, Doling 2, McLoughlin 2, Chamberlain 1, Symons 1, own goals 5.
Rumbelows Cup (8): Beresford 2 (1 pen), Anderton 1, Aspinall 1, Burns 1, Butters 1, Clarke 1, Kuhl 1.
FA Cup (11): Anderton 5, Clarke 2, Whittingham 2, Aspinall 1, McLoughlin 1.
Ground: Fratton Park, Frogmore Rd, Portsmouth PO4 8RA (0705 731204)
Manager: Jim Smith   **Secretary:** P. Weld
Colours: Blue shirts, white shorts, red stockings
Record home gate: 51,385 v Derby Co, FA Cup 6th rd, 26 February 1949
Honours – Champions: Division 1: 1948–49, 1949–50; Division 3 (S): 1923–24; Division 3: 1961–62, 1982–83
FA Cup winners: 1939

PORT VALE DIV. 2

Aspin, Neil	Hughes, Darren J.	Swan, Peter H.
Cross, Nicholas J.R.	Jeffers, John J.	Van Der Laan, Robertus P.
Foyle, Martin J.	Kent, Kevin J.	Walker, Raymond
Glover, Dean V.	Mills, Brian	Webb, Alan R.
Harrison, Michael	Mills, Simon A.	Wood, Trevor J.
Houchen, Keith M.	Porter, Andrew M.	

League Appearances: Allon, J. 2(4); Aspin, N. 42; Beckford, J.N. 4(1); Cross, N.J.R. 7(1); Foyle, M.J. 43; Glover, D.V. 46; Grew, M.S. 46; Houchen, K.M. 18(3); Hughes, D.J. 42; Jalink, N. 20(8); Jeffers, J.J. 27(6); Kent, K.J. 13(10); Kidd, R.A. 1; Lowe, D.A. 8(1); Mills, B. 13(8); Mills, S. 31(2); Parkin, T.J. 4(3); Porter, A.M. 30(2); Swan, P.H. 27(6); Van der Laan, R.P. 43; Walker, R. 26; Webb, A.R. 3; West, C. 5; Williams, A. 5.

League Goals (42): Foyle 11, Van der Laan 5, Houchen 4, Jeffers 3, Swan 3, Hughes 2, Lowe 2, Mills B 2, Mills S 2, Walker 2 (2 pens), Beckford 1, Glover 1 (1 pen), Jalink 1, Porter 1, West 1, own goals 1.

Rumbelows Cup (7): Foyle 4, Houchen 1, Mills B 1, Van der Laan 1.

FA Cup (0).

Ground: Vale Park, Burslem, Stoke-on-Trent (0782 814134)

Manager: John Rudge   **Secretary:** Eddie Harrison.

Colours: White shirts, black shorts, black and white stockings

Record home gate: 50,000 v Aston Villa, FA Cup 5th rd, 20 February 1960

Honours – Champions: Division 3 (N): 1929–30, 1953–54; Division 4: 1958–59

PRESTON NORTH END DIV. 2

Ashcroft, Lee	Flitcroft, David J.	Kell, Alan T.
Cartwright, Lee	Flynn, Michael A.	Kerfoot, Jason J.T.
Christie, David	Greenall, Colin A.	Moylon, Craig J.
Eaves, David M.C.	James, Martin J.	Shaw, Graham P.
Farnworth, Simon	Jepson, Ronald F.	
Finney, Stephen K.	Joyce, Warren G.	

League Appearances: Ainsworth, G. 2(3); Allpress, T.J. 7(2); Ashcroft, L. 35(3); Berry, G.F. 4; Cartwright, L. 31(2); Christie, D. –(2); Cross, P. 5; Farnworth, S. 23; Finney, S.K. –(2); Flynn, M.A. 43; Greenall, C. 9; Greenwood, N.P. 16(4); Hughes, A.F.S. 14(1); James, J.C. 6; James, M.J. 36; Jepson, R.F. 23(1); Johnrose, L. 1(2); Joyce, W.G. 28(1); Kelly, A.T. 23; Kerfoot, J.J.T. –(3); Lambert, M.R. 7(4); Senior, S. 35; Shaw, G.P. 45(1); Swann, G. 28(1); Thomas, J.W. 8(3); Thompson, D.S. 18(7); Whitworth, N.A. 6; Williams, N.J.F. 17(9); Wrightson, J.G. 36(1).

League Goals (61): Shaw 14 (1 pen), Ashcroft 5, Jepson 5, Joyce 5 (3 pens), Swann 5, Cartwright 4, James M 4, Flynn 3, Greenwood 3, Lambert 2, Thomas 2, Thompson 2, Finney 1, Greenall 1, Johnrose 1, Senior 1, Williams 1, Wrightson 1, own goals 1.

Rumbelows Cup (6): Joyce 2 (1 pen), Swann 2, Shaw 1, Wrightson 1.

FA Cup (6): Flynn 1, Greenwood 1, Senior 1, Shaw 1, Swann 1, Thomas 1.

Ground: Deepdale, Preston PR1 6RU (0772 795919)
Manager: Les Chapman **Secretary:** D. J. Allan
Colours: White shirts, navy blue shorts, navy blue stockings
Record home gate: 42,684 v Arsenal, Division 1, 23 April 1938
Honours – Champions: Division 1: 1888–89 (first champions), 1889–90; Division 2: 1903–04, 1912–13, 1950–51; Division 3: 1970–71
FA Cup winners: 1889, 1938

QUEENS PARK RANGERS   FA PREMIER

Allen, Bradley J.	Gallen, Stephen J.	Penrice, Gary K.
Bailey, Dennis L.	Herrera, Roberto	Ready, Karl
Bardsley, David J.	Holloway, Ian S.	Roberts, Anthony M.
Barker, Simon	Impey, Andrew R.	Sinton, Andrew
Brevett, Rufus E.	Law, Brian J.	Stejskal, Jan
Caldwell, Peter J.	Maddix, Danny S.	Thompson, Garry L.
Channing, Justin A.	McCarthy, Alan J.	Tillson, Andrew
Doyle, Maurice	McDonald, Alan	Waddock, Gary P.
Ferdinand, Leslie	McEnroe, David J.	Wilkins, Raymond C.
Finlay, Darren J.	Meaker, Michael J.	Wilson, Clive
Freedman, Douglas A.	Peacock, Darren	Witter, Anthony J.

League Appearances: Allen, B.J. 10(1); Bailey, D. 19(5); Bardsley, D.J. 41; Barker, S. 31(3); Brevett, R.E. 6(1); Ferdinand, L. 21(2); Holloway, I.S. 34(6); Impey, A.R. 13; Iorfa, D. –(1); McCarthy, A.J. 3; McDonald, A. 27(1); Maddix, D.S. 19; Meaker, M.J. –(1); Peacock, D. 39; Penrice, G. 13(6); Ready, K. 1; Roberts, A.M. 1; Sinton, A. 38; Stejskal, J. 41; Thompson, G.L. 10(5); Tillson, A. 9(1); Walsh, P. 2; Wegerle, R.C. 18(3); Wilkins, R.C. 26(1); Wilson, C. 40.
League Goals (48): Ferdinand 10, Bailey 9, Barker 6, Allen 5, Wegerle 5 (1 pen), Penrice 3, Sinton 3, Wilson 3 (2 pens), Peacock 1, Thompson 1, Wilkins 1, own goals 1.
Rumbelows Cup (9): Thompson 3, Bailey 2, Barker 2, Bardsley 1, Penrice 1.
FA Cup (0).
Ground: South Africa Road, W12 7PA (081-743 0262)
Manager: Gerry Francis **Secretary:** Miss S. F. Marson
Colours: Blue and white hooped shirts, white shorts, white stockings
Record home gate: 35,353 v Leeds U, Division 1, 27 April 1974
Honours – Champions: Division 2: 1982–83; Division 3 (S): 1947–48; Division 3: 1966–67
Football League Cup winners: 1966–67

READING   DIV. 2

Bailey, Danny S.	Holzman, Stephen P.	Richardson, Steven E.
Dillon, Kevin P.	Honey, Daniel W.	Taylor, Scott D.
Francis, Stephen S.	Lovell, Stuart A.	Williams, Adrian
Gilkes, Earl G.M.	Maskell, Craig D.	
Gooding, Michael C.	McPherson, Keith A.	

League Appearances: Archibald, S. 1; Bailey, D.S. 23(1); Barkus, L.P. 4(2); Bass, D. 2(1); Britton, G.J. –(2) Byrne, D.S. 7; Cockram, A.C. 2(4); Cooper, N.J. 6(1); Dillon, K.P. 29; Fealey, N.J. 1; Francis, S.S. 32; Giamattei, A.P. –(2); Gilkes, M.E. 19(1); Gooding, M.C. 39(1); Gray, A. –(1); Holzman, M.R. 11(5); Jones, L. 28(1); Keeley, J. 6; Lee, D.J. 5; Leighton, J. 8; Leworthy, D.J. 3(3); Lovell, S.A. 16(8); McGhee, M. 23(9); McPherson, K.A. 44; Maskell, C.D. 29(5); Morrow, S. 3; Richardson, S. E. 38; Robinson, D. 8; Senior, T.J. 20(5); Seymour, C. 3(1); Streete, F.A. 34; Taylor, S.D. 22(7); Williams, A. 40.
League Goals (59): Maskell 16 (3 pens), Senior 7, Lee 5, McGhee 5, Lovell 4, Williams 4, Dillon 3 (1 pen), Gooding 3, Byrne 2, Taylor 2, Barkus 1, Cockram 1, Holzman 1, McPherson 1, Richardson 1, own goals 3.
Rumbelows Cup (0).
FA Cup (6): Lovell 2, Williams 2, Gooding 1, Taylor 1.
Ground: Elm Park, Norfolk Road, Reading (0734 507878)
Manager: Mark McGhee **Secretary:** Jayne E. Hill
Colours: Navy and white hooped shirts, navy blue shorts, navy blue stockings
Record home gate: 33,042 v Brentford, FA Cup 5th rd, 19 February 1927
Honours – Champions: Division 3: 1985–86; Division 3 (S): 1925–26; Division 4: 1978–79
Full Members Cup winners: 1987–88

ROCHDALE DIV. 3

Bowden, Jon L.	Flounders, Andrew J.	Payne, Mark R.C.
Brown, Anthony J.	Graham, James	Reeves, Alan
Butler, Paul J.	Leonard, Mark A.	Rose, Kevin P.
Chapman, Vincent J.	Milner, Andrew J.	Ryan, John B.
Doyle, Stephen C.	Parker, Carl	Whitehall, Steven C.

League Appearances: Bowden, J.L. 25(6); Brown, A.J. 40; Brown, M. 18; Butler, P.J. 22(3); Cowdrill, B.J. 15; Dearden, K.C. 2; Doyle, S.C. 27; Flounders, A.J. 42; Graham, J. 29(2); Gray, G. 6; Halpin, J.W. 22(9); Hilditch, M. –(2); Jones, A. 12(1); Kilner, A.W. 3; Kinsey, S. 3(3); Leonard, M. 9; Milner, A.J. 28(5); Morgan, S.J. 1(11); Palin, L.G. 3; Parker, C. 5(1); Payne, M.C. 32(2); Reeves, A. 33(1); Rose, K. 28; Ryan, J.B. 29(3); Stiles, J.C. 2(2); Whitehall, S.C. 20(14); Williams, D.P. 6.
League Goals (57): Flounders 17 (5 pens), Milner 10, Whitehall 8, Bowden 6, Reeves 3, Payne 2, Ryan 2, Brown M 1, Cowdrill 1, Halpin 1, Kinsey 1, Leonard 1, Parker 1, own goals 3.
Rumbelows Cup (7): Milner 3, Ryan 2, Whitehall 2.
FA Cup (4): Flounders 1, Halpin 1, Jones 1, Milner 1.
Ground: Spotland, Willbutts Lane, Rochdale OL11 5DA (0706 44648)
Manager: Dave Sutton **Secretary:** Mrs Anne Pettifor.
Colours: Blue/white trim
Record home gate: 24,231 v Notts Co, FA Cup 2nd rd, 10 December 1949
Honours – Nil

ROTHERHAM UNITED   DIV. 2

Barrick, Dean
Cunningham, Anthony E.
Goater, Leonardo S.
Goodwin, Shaun L.
Hathaway, Ian A.
Hazel, Desmond L.
Hodges, Mark

Howard, Jonathan
Hutchings, Christopher
Johnson, Nigel M.
Law, Nicholas
Mercer, William
Page, Donald R.
Pickering, Albert G.

Richardson, Neil T.
Ridenton, Michael
Rockett, Jason
Russell, William
Taylor, Andrew
Todd, Mark K.

League Appearances: Barrick, D. 32(2); Cunningham, A.E. 34(2); Ford, S.T. 4; Goater, L.S. 17(7); Goodwin, S.L. 39; Hathaway, I.A. 2(6); Hazel, D.L. 34(4); Howard, J. 9(1); Hutchings, C. 41; Johnson, N.M. 35; Law, N. 42; McKnight, A.D. 3; Mercer, W. 35; Page, D.R. 29(2); Pickering, A.G. 27; Richardson, N.T. 18; Robinson, R. 5; Russell, W. 6; Snodin, G. 3; Taylor, A. 6; Todd, M.K. 23; Watts, J. 7(3); Wilson, R.J. 11(3).

League Goals (70): Cunningham 18, Page 11, Goater 9, Hazel 8, Goodwin 5, Hutchings 4 (1 pen), Howard 3, Wilson 3, Johnson 2, Richardson 2, Todd 2, Barrick 1, Robinson R 1, Watts 1.

Rumbelows Cup (1): Robinson 1.

FA Cup (4): Page 2, Cunningham 1, Goodwin 1.

Ground: Millmoor Ground, Rotherham (0709 562434)

Manager: Phil Henson   **Secretary:** N. Darnill

Colours: Red shirts, white shorts, red stockings

Record home gate: 25,000 v Sheffield U, Division 2, 13 December 1952 and v Sheffield W, Division 2, 26 January 1952

Honours – Champions: Division 3: 1980–81; Division 3 (N) – 1950–51; Division 4: 1988–89

SCARBOROUGH   DIV. 3

Ashdjian, John A.
Carter, Stephen G.
Foreman, Darren
Himsworth, Gary P.

Hirst, Lee W.
Jules, Mark A.
Lee, Christopher
Meyer, Adrian M.

Mockler, Andrew J.
Mooney, Thomas J.
Mudd, Paul A.
Thompson, Simon L.

League Appearances: Ash, M.C. 16(3); Ashdjian, J.A. 18(14); Carter, S.G. 2(1); Curran, C. 8; Fletcher, A.M. 14(7); Ford, S. 6; Foreman, D. 12(12); Gabbiadini, R. 3(4); Hewitt, S. 2; Himsworth, G.P. 33(3); Hirst, L. 30; Holmes, D.J. 3(6); Hughes, P. 17; Ironside, I. 7; James, C. 12(1); Jules, M.A. 30(11); Lee, C. 41; Logan, D. 21; McGee, O.E. 8; Manderson, D.A. –(1); Marshall, C. 4; Meyer, A.M. 30; Mockler, A.J. 20(4); Mooney, T.J. 40; Moore, J. 3(4); Mudd, P.A. 36; Price, M.A.R.J. 2(1); Priestley, J.A. 9; Reed, J.P. 5(1); Rocca, J.C. 3; Swales, S.C. 4; Taylor, I. 1; Thompson, S. 22(1).

League Goals (64): Ashdjian 9, Jules 8, Mooney 8, Fletcher 5, Meyer 5, Himsworth 4 (2 pens), Mockler 4 (4 pens), Thompson 3, Curran 2, Foreman 2, Hirst 2, Lee 2, Gabbiadini 1, Holmes 1, Marshall 1, Moore 1, Mudd 1, Price 1, own goals 4.

Rumbelows Cup (10): Mooney 3, Foreman 2 (1 pen), Ashdjian 1, Himsworth 1, Hirst 1, Jules 1, Mockler 1 (1 pen).
FA Cup (0).
Ground: The McCain Stadium, Seamer Road, Scarborough YO12 4HF (0723 375094)
Manager: Ray McHale   **Secretary:** K. E. Sheppard MISM, MLIA.
Colours: Red shirts, white shorts, red stockings
Record home gate: 11,130 v Luton T, FA Cup 3rd rd, 8 January 1938. Football League: 7314 v Wolverhampton W, Division 4, 15 August 1987
Honours – Nil

SCUNTHORPE UNITED DIV. 3

Alexander, Graham
Buckley, John W.
Daws, Anthony
Goodacre, Samuel D.
Hamilton, Ian R.
Helliwell, Ian

Hicks, Stuart J.
Hill, David M.
Hine, Mark
Humphries, Glenn
Joyce, Joseph P.
Longden, David P.

Martin, Dean S.
Musselwhite, Paul S.
Stevenson, Andrew J.
White, Jason G.

League Appearances: Alexander, G. 30(6); Batch, N.A. 1; Buckley, J.W. 26(2); Daws, A. 32(4); Elliott, M.S. 8; Hamilton, I.R. 41; Helliwell, I. 38(1); Hicks, S.J. 21; Hill, D.M. 36(1); Hine, M. 7(3); Humphries, G. 32; Hyde, G.S. 1(7); Joyce, J.P. 40; Lister, S.H. 16(3); Longden, D.P. 40(1); Marples, C. 1; Martin, D.S. 36(1); Musselwhite, P.S. 24; Samways, M. 8; Stevenson, A.J. 1(1); White, J.G. 15(7); Whitehead, P.M. 8.
League Goals (64): White 11, Hamilton 9 (4 pens), Helliwell 9, Daws 7 (1 pen), Buckley 6, Alexander 5, Hill 5, Humphries 3, Joyce 2, Martin 2, Elliott 1, Lister 1, own goals 3.
Rumbelows Cup (3): Alexander 1, Helliwell 1, Humphries 1.
FA Cup (4): Helliwell 2, Daws 1, White 1.
Ground: Glanford Park, Scunthorpe, South Humberside (0724 848077)
Manager: Bill Green   **Secretary:** A. D. Rowing
Colours: Sky blue shirts with two claret rings on sleeves, white collor, white shorts with claret stripe, white stockings with claret and blue bar
Record home gate: Old Showground: 23,935 v Portsmouth, FA Cup 4th rd, 30 January 1954. Glanford Park: 8775 v Rotherham U, Division 4, 1 May 1989
Honours – Champions: Division 3 (N): 1957–58

SHEFFIELD UNITED FA PREMIER

Barnes, David
Beesley, Paul
Bradshaw, Carl
Bryson, James I.C.
Cork, Alan G.

Cowan, Thomas
Deane, Brian C.
Duffield, Peter
Fickling, Ashley
Gage, Kevin W.

Gannon, John S.
Gayle, Brian W.
Hartfield, Charles J.
Hill, Colin F.
Hodges, Glyn P.

Hoyland, Jamie W.	Mendonca, Clive P.	Tracey, Simon P.
Kite, Philip D.	Peel, Nathan J.	Walton, David L.
Lake, Michael C.	Pemberton, John M.	Ward, Mitchum D.
Littlejohn, Adrian S.	Reed, John P.	Whitehouse, Dane L.
Lucas, Richard	Rees, Melvyn J.	Wilder, Christopher J.
Marwood, Brian	Rogers, Paul A.	

League Appearances: Agana, P.A.O. 13; Barnes, D. 15; Beesley, P. 38(2); Booker, R. 8(4); Bradshaw, C. 15(3); Bryson, J.I.C. 29(5); Cork, A.G. 7(1); Cowan, T. 20; Davison, R. 6(5); Day, M. 1; Deane, B.C. 30; Duffield, P. –(2); Gage, K. 22; Gannon, J.S. 32; Gayle, B.W. 33; Hartfield, C.J. 6(1); Hill, C.F. 11(4); Hodges, G.P. 22(4); Hoyland, J.W. 23(3); Jones, V. 4; Kite, P.D. 4; Lake, M.C. 8(10); Littlejohn, A.S. 5(2); Lucas, R. –(1); Marwood, B. 1(4); Mendonca, C.P. 4(6); Peel, N.J. –(1); Pemberton, J.M. 19(1); Reed, J.P. –(1); Rees, M. 8; Rogers, P.A. 13; Tracey, S.P. 29; Ward, M.D. 4(2); Whitehouse, D.L. 25(9); Wilder, C.J. 4; Wood, P.A. 3(1).

League Goals (65): Deane 12, Bryson 9, Whitehouse 7, Agana 4, Davison 4, Hoyland 4, Lake 4, Gayle 3, Beesley 2, Bradshaw 2, Cork 2, Gage 2, Hodges 2, Ward 2, Gannon 1, Hill 1, Marwood 1, Mendonca 1, own goals 2.

Rumbelows Cup (3): Deane 2, Hoyland 1.

FA Cup (7): Deane 2, Bradshaw 1, Gayle 1, Hodges 1, Lake 1, Whitehouse 1.

Ground: Bramall Lane Ground, Sheffield S2 4SU (0742 738955)

Manager: Dave Bassett **Secretary:** D. Capper AFA

Colours: Colours: Narrow red and white striped shirts with thin black stripe, black shorts, black stockings with red and white trim

Record home gate: 68,287 v Leeds U, FA Cup 5th rd, 15 February 1936

Honours – Champions: Division 1: 1897–98; Division 2: 1952–53; Division 4: 1981–82

FA Cup winners: 1899, 1902, 1915, 1925

SHEFFIELD WEDNESDAY   FA PREMIER

Anderson, Vivian A.	Johnson, David A.	Shirtliff, Peter A.
Bart-Williams,	Jones, Ryan A.	Warhurst, Paul
Christopher G.	Key, Lance	Watson, Gordon W.G.
Beresford, Marlon	King, Philip G.	Watts, Julian
Chambers, Leroy D.	Nilsson, Nils L.R.	Williams, Michael A.
Harkes, John A.	Palmer, Carlton L.	Williams, Paul A.
Hirst, David E.	Pearson, Nigel G.	Wilson, Daniel J.
Hyde, Graham	Pressman, Kevin P.	Woods, Christopher C.
Jemson, Nigel B.	Sheridan, John J.	Worthington, Nigel

League Appearances: Anderson, V.A. 15(7); Bart-Williams, C.G. 12(3); Francis, T.J. –(20); Harkes, J.A. 14(15); Hirst, D.E. 33; Hyde, G. 9(4); Jemson, N.B. 11(9); Johnson, D.A. 5(1); King, P.G. 38(1); MacKenzie, S. –(3); Nilsson, N.L.R. 39; Palmer, C.L. 42; Pearson, N.G. 31; Pressman, K.P. 1; Sheridan, J.J. 24; Shirtliff, P.A. 12; Warhurst, P. 31(2); Watson, G. 4; Williams, P.A. 31(9); Wilson, D.J. 35(1); Woods, C.C.E. 41; Worthington, N. 34.

League Goals (62): Hirst 18, Williams 9, Sheridan 6 (1 pen), Palmer 5, Worthington 5, Jemson 4, Anderson 3, Harkes 3, Wilson 3, Pearson 2, Francis 1, King 1, Nilsson 1, own goals 1.
Rumbelows Cup (5): Francis 2, Anderson 1, Hirst 1, Williams 1.
FA Cup (3): Bart-Williams 1, Hirst 1, Sheridan 1.
Ground: Hillsborough, Sheffield, S6 1SW (0742 343122)
Manager: Trevor Francis   **Secretary:** G. H. Mackrell FCCA
Colours: Blue and white striped shirts, black shorts, black stockings
Record home gate: 72,841 v Manchester C, FA Cup 5th rd, 17 February 1934
Honours – Champions: Division 1: 1902–03, 1903–04, 1928–29, 1929–30; Division 2: 1899–1900, 1925–26, 1951–52, 1955–56, 1958–59
FA Cup winners: 1896, 1907, 1935 **Football League Cup winners:** 1990–91

SHREWSBURY TOWN   DIV. 3

Blake, Mark C.	Hopkins, Robert A.	Smith, Mark A.
Clark, Howard W.	Lynch, Thomas	Spink, Dean P.
Donaldson, O'Neill M.	Lyne, Neil G.F.	Summerfield, Kevin
Griffiths, Carl B.	MacKenzie, Stephen	Taylor, Robert M.
Harmon, Darren J.	O'Toole, Christopher P.	Worsley, Graeme

League Appearances: Barton, M. 1; Bennett, D. 2; Blake, M.C. 39; Bremner, K. 7; Carr, C.P. 1; Cash, S. 8; Clark, H.W. 21(2); Donaldson, O.M. 9(10); Evans, P.S. 1(1); Gorman, P.A. 14(1); Griffiths, C.B. 20(7); Harmon, D. 1(4); Heathcote, M. 5; Henry, A. 39(1); Hopkins, R.A. 18(9); Hughes, K.D. 23; Lynch, T.M. 37(3); Lyne, N.G.F. 43(1); McKeown, G. 8; MacKenzie, S. 13; O'Toole, C. 13(14); Parkin, T.J. 5; Paskin, J. 1; Perks, S.J. 22; Ryan, D.T. 2; Smith, M.A. 19(3); Spink, D.P. 34(6); Summerfield, K. 44; Taylor, R.M. 29; Walsh, A. 2; Williams, M. –(1); Williams, M.S. 2(1); Worsley, G. 23(2).
League Goals (53): Griffiths 8, Lyne 8, Henry 7 (2 pens), Summerfield 7, Hopkins 3, Bennett 2, Bremner 2, Donaldson 2, Harmon 2, Lynch 2, Taylor 2, Carr 1, Cash 1, MacKenzie 1, McKeown 1, Smith 1, Spink 1, Worsley 1, own goals 1.
Rumbelows Cup (7): Summerfield 4, Lyne 2, Carr 1.
FA Cup (2): Lyne 1, Smith 1.
Ground: Gay Meadow, Shrewsbury (0743 360111)
Manager: John Bond   **Secretary:** M. J. Starkey
Colours: Amber/blue trim shirts, blue trim, blue shorts, amber stockings, blue trim
Record home gate: 18,917 v Walsall, Division 3, 26 April 1961
Honours – Champions: Division 3: 1978–79
Welsh Cup winners: 1891, 1938, 1977, 1979, 1984, 1985

SOUTHAMPTON   FA PREMIER

Adams, Michael R.	Bound, Matthew T.	Dowie, Iain
Andrews, Ian E.	Cherednik, Aleksey	Flowers, Timothy D.
Banger, Nicholas L.	Cockerill, Glenn	Gittens, Jon
Benali, Francis V.	Dodd, Jason R.	Gray, Stuart

Hall, Richard A.
Horne, Barry
Hughes, David R.
Hurlock, Terence A.
Kenna, Jeffrey J.
Le Tissier, Matthew P.

Lee, David
Macdonald, Callum
Madddison, Neil S.
Moody, Paul
Moore, Kevin T.
Powell, Lee

Roast, Stephen
Ruddock, Neil
Shearer, Alan
Tisdale, Paul R.
Widdrington, Thomas
Wood, Stephen A.

League Appearances: Adams, M.R. 34; Andrews, I.E. 1; Banger, N.L. –(4); Benali, F.V. 19(3); Bound, M.T. –(1); Cockerill, G. 36(1); Dodd, J.R. 26(2); Dowie, I. 25(5); Flowers, T.D. 41; Gilkes, M.E. 4(2); Gittens, J. 9(2); Gray, S. 10(2); Hall, R.A. 21(5); Horne, B. 34; Hurlock, T.A. 27(2); Kenna, J.J. 14; Le Tissier, M. P. 31(1); Lee, D. 11(8); McLoughlin, A.F. –(2); Maddison, N.S. 4(2); Moody, P. 2(2); Moore, T.K. 15(1); Osman, R.C. 5; Powell, L. 1(3); Rideout, P.D. 4; Ruddock, N. 30; Shearer, A. 41; Widdrington, T. 2(1); Wood, S. 15.
League Goals (39): Shearer 13 (1 pen), Dowie 9, Le Tissier 6 (2 pens), Cockerill 4, Adams 3, Hall 3, Horne 1.
Rumbelows Cup (6): Shearer 3, Cockerill 2, Le Tissier 1.
FA Cup (10): Hall 2, Horne 2, Shearer 2, Gray 1, Le Tissier 1, Ruddock 1, Wood 1.
Ground: The Dell, Milton Road, Southampton SO9 4XX (0703 220505)
Manager: Ian Branfoot   **Secretary:** Brian Truscott
Colours: Red and white striped shirts, black shorts, white stockings, red trim
Record home gate: 31,044 v Manchester U, Division 1, 8 October 1969
Honours – Champions: Division 3 (S). 1921–22; Division 3: 1959–60
FA Cup winners: 1975–76

SOUTHEND UNITED   DIV. 1

Angell, Brett
Ansah, Andrew
Austin, Dean B.
Benjamin, Ian T.
Butler, Peter J.
Cagigao, Francisco
Cornwell, John A.
Edwards, Andrew D.

Hall, Mark A.
Heffer, Steven P.
Hyslop, Christian T.
Jones, Keith A.
Locke, Adam S.
Martin, David
O'Callaghan, Kevin
Powell, Christopher G.R.

Prior, Spencer J.
Royce, Simon
Sansome, Paul E.
Scully, Patrick J.
Smith, Paul W.
Sussex, Andrew R.
Tilson, Stephen B.

League Appearances: Angell, B. 42(1); Ansah, A. 40; Austin, D.B. 45; Benjamin, I. 45; Butler, P.J. 4(5); Cornwell, J.A. 43; Edwards, A.D. 7(2); Hall, M.A. 1(2); Hyslop, C. 2; Jones, K. 33(1); Locke, A.S. 5(5); Martin, D. 5; O'Callaghan, K. 2(6); Powell, C.G. 44; Prior, S.J. 42; Royce, S. 1; Sansome, P.E. 45; Scully, P.J. 44; Sussex, A. 12(3); Tilson, S.B. 44(2).
League Goals (63): Angell 21, Ansah 9, Benjamin 9, Tilson 7. Jones 5, Scully 3, Sussex 3, Austin 2 (1 pen), Martin 1, Prior 1, own goals 2.
Rumbelows Cup (1): Angell 1.
FA Cup (0).
Ground: Roots Hall Football Ground, Victoria Avenue, Southend-on-Sea SS2 6NQ (0702 340707)
Manager: Colin Murphy.   **Secretary:** J. W. Adams

STOCKPORT COUNTY   DIV. 2

Barras, Anthony
Beaumont, Christopher P.
Carstairs, James W.
Edwards, Neil R.
Finley, Alan J.
Frain, David
Francis, Kevin D.M.
Gannon, James P.
Knowles, Darren T.
Matthews, Neil
Miller, David B.
Moore, Christian
Muir, Johnny G.
Preece, Andrew P.
Redfern, David
Todd, Lee
Ward, Peter
Wheeler, Paul
Williams, Paul R.C.
Williams, William R.

League Appearances: Barras, A. 42; Beaumont, C. 33(1); Carstairs, J.W. 20; Edwards, N.R. 39; Finley, A. 15(3); Frain, D. 37(2); Francis, K. 34(1); Gannon, J.P. 43; Kilner, A.W. 13(5); Knowles, D.T. 28(3); Loram, M. 1(3); Lillis, M.A. 9(2); Matthews, N. 4(5); Miller, D.B. –(3); Moore, C. –(1); Muir, J.G. 3(1); Paskin, W.J. 3(2); Preece, A. 23(2); Redfern, D. 7; Thorpe, A. 33(1); Todd, L. 17(2); Ward, P. 44; Wheeler, P. 13(9); Williams, P.R.C. 12(1); Williams, W.R. 33(2).
League Goals (75): Gannon 16 (4 pens), Francis 15, Preece 13, Barras 5 (1 pen), Wheeler 5, Frain 4 (1 pen), Kilner 3 (2 pens), Beaumont 2, Lillis 2, Williams B 2, Finley 1, Matthews 1, Paskin 1, Ward 1, Williams P 1, own goals 3.
Rumbelows Cup (2): Francis 1, Wheeler 1.
FA Cup (3): Francis 1, Gannon 1, own goals 1.
Ground: Edgeley Park, Hardcastle Road, Stockport, Cheshire SK3 9DD (061-480 8888)
Manager: Danny Bergara   **Secretary:** John Simpson.
Colours: Blue with red and white flecked shirts, royal blue shorts, white stockings
Record home gate: 27,833 v Liverpool, FA Cup 5th rd, 11 February 1950
Honours – Champions: Division 3 (N): 1921–22, 1936–37; Division 4 – 1966–67

STOKE CITY   DIV. 2

Barnes, Paul L.
Beeston, Carl F.
Biggins, Wayne
Brunton, Robert A.M.
Butler, John E.
Cranson, Ian
Devlin, Mark A.
Ellis, Anthony J.
Foley, Steven
Fowler, Lee
Fox, Peter D.
Gallimore, Anthony
Kelly, Anthony O.N.
Kevan, David J.
Long, Keith D.
Male, Christopher
Overson, Vincent D.
Percival, Jason C.
Reid, Mark
Rennie, Paul A.
Sandford, Lee R.
Sinclair, Ronald M.
Stein, Earl M.S.
Ware, Paul D.
Wright, Ian M.

League Appearances: Barnes, P.L. 3(10); Beeston, C.F. 42(1); Bent, J. 1; Biggins, W. 41; Blake, N.L.G. 12(1); Butler, J.E. 42; Cranson, I. 41; Ellis, A.J. 9(6); Foley, S. 20; Fowler, L.E. 15(1); Gallimore, A.M. 2(1); Grimes, A.A. 4(6); Heath, A.P.

5(1); Keaton, J. 16; Kelly, A. 10(3); Kennedy, M.F. 19(1); Kevan, D.J. 43;
Overson, V.D. 34(1); Pressman, K.P. 4; Rennie, P.A. 1; Russell, K. 5; Sandford,
L.R. 37(1); Scott, I. 6(3); Sinclair, R. 26; Steele, T.W. 7; Stein, M.E.S. 36; Ware,
P.D. 22(2) Wright, I.M. 3.
League Goals (69): Biggins 22 (4 pens), Stein 16, Ellis 4, Barnes 3, Beeston 3,
Butler 3, Overson 3, Ware 3, Cranson 2, Kelly 2, Foley 1, Grimes 1, Kevan 1,
Russell 1, Scott 1, Steele 1, own goals 2.
Rumbelows Cup (7): Biggins 2 (1 pens), Kelly 2, Beeston 1, Cranson 1, Ellis 1.
FA Cup (1): Beeston 1.
Ground: Victoria Ground, Stoke-on-Trent (0782 413511)
Manager: Lou Macari   **Secretary:** M. J. Potts
Colours: Red and white striped shirts, white shorts, red stockings
Record home gate: 51,380 v Arsenal, Division 1, 29 March 1937
Honours – Champions: Division 2: 1932–33, 1962–63; Division 3 (N): 1926–27
Football League Cup winners: 1971–72 **Autoglass Cup winners:** 1992

SUNDERLAND   DIV. 1

Armstrong, Gordon I.	Goodman, Donald R.	Pascoe, Colin J.
Atkinson, Brian	Gray, Martin D.	Patterson, Ian D.
Ball, Kevin A.	Hardyman, Paul G.T.	Rogan, Anthony G.P.
Bennett, Gary E.	Hauser, Thomas	Rush, David
Bracewell, Paul W.	Hawke, Warren R.	Sampson, Ian
Brady, Kieron	Kay, John	Smith, Anthony
Brodie, Stephen E.	Mooney, Brian J.	Walls, Wayne M.
Byrne, John F.	Norman, Anthony J.	Williams, Paul L.
Carter, Timothy D.	Ord, Richard J.	
Davenport, Peter	Owers, Gary	

League Appearances: Agboola, R.O.F. 1; Armstrong, G.T. 40; Atkinson, B. 29(1);
Ball, K.A. 31(2); Beagrie, P. 5; Bennett, G.E. 38(1); Bracewell, P.W. 39; Brady,
K. 4(4); Byrne, J.F. 27; Carter, T.D. 2; Cullen, A. 1; Davenport, P. 25(11);
Gabbiadini, M. 9; Goodman, D.R. 20(2); Gray, M. –(1); Hardyman, P.G. 29(3);
Hauser, T. 5(7); Hawke, W. R. 2(2); Kay, J. 41; Mooney, B.J. 6(3); Norman, A.J.
44; Ord, R.J. 5(1); Owers, G. 24(6); Pascoe, C.J. 12(8); Rogan, A.G.P. 33; Rush,
D. 20(5); Russell, C.S. 1(3); Sampson, I. 7(1); Smith, A. 2; Williams, P.L. 4(3).
League Goals (61): Goodman 11, Armstrong 10, Byrne 7 (1 pen), Gabbiadini 5,
Davenport 4, Owers 4 (2 pens), Rush 4, Bennett 3, Brady 3, Atkinson 2, Hardyman
2, Pascoe 2, Ball 1, Beagrie 1, Rogan 1, own goals 1.
Rumbelows Cup (1): Hauser 1.
FA Cup (14): Byrne 7, Atkinson 2, Davenport 2, Armstrong 1, Hardyman 1, Rush
1.
Ground: Roker Park Ground, Sunderland (091-514 0332)
Manager: Malcolm Crosby.   **Secretary:** G. Davidson FCA
Colours: Red and white striped shirts, black shorts, red stockings, white turnover
Record home gate: 75,118 v Derby Co, FA Cup 6th rd replay, 8 March 1933
Honours – Champions: Division 1: 1891–92, 1892–93, 1894–95, 1901–02, 1912–13,
1935–36; Division 2: 1975–76; Division 3: 1987–88
FA Cup winners: 1937, 1973

SWANSEA CITY   DIV. 2

Agboola, Reuben O.F.   Ford, Jonathan S.   Jenkins, Stephen R.
Bowen, Jason P.   Freestone, Roger   Kendall, Mark
Chalmers, Paul   Gilligan, James M.   Legg, Andrew
Chapell, Shaun R.   Harris, Mark A.   McMahon, Steven
Cornforth, John M.   Heeps, James A.   Walker, Keith C.
Coughlin, Russell   Hough, David J.   Williams, John

League Appearances: Agboola, R. 20(1); Barnhouse, D.J. –(1); Beauchamp, J.D. 5; Bowen, J. 5(6); Bracey, L.M.I. 3; Brazil, D.M. 12; Chalmers, P. 14(7); Chapple, S. 17(4); Connor, T.F. 6; Cornforth, J.M. 17; Coughlin, R.J. 32(1); Davey, S. 3(2); Davies, A. 6(2); Davies, M. 1; Freeman, C.R. 8(4); Freestone, R. 42; Ford, J.S. 42(2); Gilligan, J.M. 24(1); Harris, M.A. 44; Hodgson, D. 1(2); Hough, D.J. 5; Jenkins, S.J. 31(3); Kendall, M. 1; Legg, A. 46; McClean, C.A. 4; Purnell, P. 5; Raynor, P.J. 18(8); Thornber, S.J. 26(7); Walker, K.C. 30(2); Wallace, R. 2; Williams, J. 36(3).
League Goals (55): Williams 11, Legg 9, Chalmers 7, Gilligan 7, Thornber 4, Harris 3, Beauchamp 2, Chapple 2, Raynor 2, Brazil 1, Connor 1, Coughlin 1, Davies A 1, Purnell 1, Walker 1, own goals 2.
Rumbelows Cup (5): Thornber 2, Chalmers 1, Chapple 1, Gilligan 1.
FA Cup (3): Gilligan 1, Harris 1, Walker 1.
Ground: Vetch Field, Swansea SA1 3SU (0792 474114)
Manager: Frank Burrows   **Secretary:** George Taylor
Colours: White shirts, white shorts, black stockings
Record home gate: 32,796 v Arsenal, FA Cup 4th rd, 17 February 1968
Honours – Champions: Division 3 (S): 1924–25, 1948–49
Welsh Cup winners: 9 times

SWINDON TOWN   DIV. 1

Bennett, David   Hoddle, Glenn   Moncur, John
Bodin, Paul J.   Hunt, Paul C.   Murray, Edwin J.
Calderwood, Colin   Jones, Tom   Summerbee, Nicholas J.
Close, Shaun C.   Kerslake, David   Taylor, Shaun
Digby, Fraser C.   Ling, Martin   Viveash, Adrian L.
Hall, Darren M.   Lorenzo, Nestar G.   White, Stephen J.
Hammond, Nicholas D.   McLaren, Ross
Hazard, Michael   Mitchell, David S.

League Appearances: Bodin, P. 21; Calderwood, C. 46; Close, S.C. 4(8); Digby, F.C. 21; Foley, S. 5(4); Gibson, T.B. 8(1); Hammond, N.D. 25; Hazard, M. 44; Hoddle, G. 22; Jones, T. 37(4); Kerslake, D. 38(1); Ling, M. 17(4); Lorenzo, N.G. 2(2); MacLaren, R. 32; Mitchell, D.S. 24(3); Moncur, J. 1(2); Shearer, D.N. 37; Simpson, F. 29(1); Summerbee, N.J. 16(11); Taylor, S. 42; Viveash, A.L. 9(1); Waddock, G.P. 5(1); White, S.J. 21(2).
League Goals (69): Shearer 22, White 10, Hazard 6 (3 pens), Calderwood 5, Mitchell 5, Jones 4, Simpson 4, Taylor 4, Ling 3, Bodin 2 (1 pen), Close 1, Gibson 1, Kerslake 1, MacLaren 1.

Rumbelows Cup (13): Shearer 6, White 3, Hazard 1, Mitchell 1, Summerbee 1, Taylor 1.
FA Cup (7): Shearer 4, Mitchell 2, Calderwood 1.
Ground: County Ground, Swindon, Wiltshire SN1 2ED. (0793 430430)
Manager: Glenn Hoddle   **Secretary:** Jon Pollard
Colours: Red shirts, red shorts, red stockings
Record home gate: 32,000 v Arsenal, FA Cup 3rd rd, 15 January 1972
Honours – Champions: Division 4: 1985–86 (with record 102 points)
Football League Cup winners: 1968–69
Anglo-Italian Cup winners: 1970

TORQUAY UNITED DIV. 3

Bastow, Ian J.
Colcombe, Scott
Curran, Christopher
Davis, Arron
Elliott, Matthew S.
Fashanu, Justinus S.
Hall, Paul A.
Holmes, Paul
Joyce, Sean W.
Loram, Mark J.
Myers, Christopher
Sang, Neil
Saunders, Wesley

League Appearances: Bennellick, J.A. –(1); Colcombe, S. 21(7); Compton, P.D. 19; Curran, C. 15(2); Darby, D.A. 6(8); Davis, A. 9(3); Dobie, M.W.G. 18(2); Dobbins, W.L. 18(3); Edwards, D.S. 7; Elliott, M.S. 33; Fashanu, J. 21; Fillery, M. 4; Franklin, J.T. 1(1); Hall, P.A. 34(4); Herrera, R. 11; Hodges, D. 3(3); Hodges, K. 3; Holmes, M.A. 18; Holmes, P. 36; Howells, G. 38; Joyce, S.W. 29(6); Lange, A.S. 1; Lloyd, P.R. 13; Loram, M.J. 30(1); Lowe, M.I. 7; McNichol, J.A. 2; Moore, D.M. 5; Myers, C. 36(3); Rowbotham, D. 14; Rowland, A.J. 5(2); Sang, N. 8(6); Saunders, W. 17(1); Smith, P. –(1); Trollope, P. 10; Uzzell, J.E. 10; Whiston, P.M. 4.
League Goals (42): Fashanu 10 (3 pens), Elliott 5, Loram 5 (3 pens), Myers 4, Rowbotham 3 (2 pens), Saunders 3, Darby 2, Dobie 2, Dobbins 1, Hall 1, Holmes M 1, Holmes P 1, Joyce 1, Moore 1, Rowland 1, own goals 1.
Rumbelows Cup (4): Elliott 2, Hodges 1, Loram 1 (1 pen).
FA Cup (7): Loram 3, Hall 2, Colcombe 1, Holmes M 1.
Ground: Plainmoor Ground, Torquay, Devon TQ1 3PS (0803 328666/7)
Manager: Paul Compton   **Secretary:** C. Olney
Colours: Yellow and white striped shirts, navy shorts, navy stockings
Record home gate: 21,908 v Huddersfield T, FA Cup 4th rd, 29 January 1955
Honours – Nil

TOTTENHAM HOTSPUR FA PREMIER

Allen, Paul K.
Amar, Mohamed A.
Barmby, Nicholas J.
Bergsson, Gudni
Caskey, Darren M.
Culverhouse, David P.
Dearden, Kevin C.
Durie, Gordon
Edinburgh, Justin C.
Fenwick, Terence W.
Gascoigne, Paul J.
Hendon, Ian M.
Hendry, John
Hodges, Lee L.
Houghton, Scott A.
Howells, David
Lineker, Gary W.
Mabbutt, Gary V.

Mahorn, Paul G.	Samways, Vincent	Tuttle, David P.
Marlowe, Andrew D.	Sedgley, Stephen P.	Van Denhauwe, Patrick W.
McDonald, David H.	Stewart, Paul A.	Walker, Ian M.
Morah, Olisa H.	Thompson-Minton,	Walsh, Paul A.
Moran, Paul	Jeffrey S.	Watson, Kevin E.
Nethercott, Stuart	Thorstvedt, Erik	Young, Neil A.
Potts, Anthony J.	Turner, Andrew P.	

League Appearances: Allen, P.K. 38(1); Amar, M.A. (Nayim) 22(9); Bergsson, G. 17(11); Cundy, J.V. 10; Durie, G.S. 31; Edinburgh, J.V. 22(1); Fenwick, T.W. 22(1); Gray, A.A. 14; Hendon, I.M. –(2); Hendry, J. 1(4); Houghton, S.A. –(10); Howells, D. 27(4); Lineker, G.W. 35; Mabbutt, G.V. 40; Samways, V. 26(1); Sedgley, S.P. 21(13); Stewart, P.A. 38; Thompson-Minton, J.S. 2; Thorstvedt, E. 24; Tuttle, D. 2; Van Den Hauwe, P.W.R. 35; Walker, I.M. 18; Walsh, P.A. 17(12).
League Goals (58): Lineker 28 (2 pens), Durie 7, Stewart 5, Allen 3, Walsh 3, Houghton 2, Mabbutt 2, Bergsson 1, Gray 1, Hendry 1, Howells 1, Minton 1, Nayim 1, Samways 1, own goals 1.
Rumbelows Cup (14): Lineker 5 (2 pens), Allen 2, Durie 2, Howells 1, Samways 1, Stewart 1, Walsh 1, own goals 1.
FA Cup (0).
Ground: 748 High Rd, Tottenham, London N17 0AP (081-808 6666)
First team coach: Doug Livermore   **Secretary:** Peter Barnes
Colours: White shirts, navy blue shorts, navy stockings with white turnover
Record home gate: 75,038 v Sunderland, FA Cup 6th rd, 5 March 1938
Honours – Champions: Division 1: 1950–51, 1960–61; Division 2: 1919–20, 1949–50
FA Cup winners: 1901 (as non-League club), 1921, 1961, 1962, 1967, 1981, 1982, 1991 (8 wins stands as the record)
Football League Cup winners: 1970–71, 1972–73
European Cup-Winners' Cup winners: 1962–63
UEFA Cup winners: 1971–72, 1983–84

TRANMERE ROVERS   DIV. 1

Aldridge, John W.	Hughes, Mark	Mungall, Steven H.
Branch, Graham	Irons, Kenneth	Nixon, Eric W.
Brannon, Gerald D.	Malkin, Christopher G.	Nolan, Iain R.
Cooper, Stephen B.	Martindale, David	Smith, Michael
Coyne, Daniel	McGreal, John	Steel, William J.
Draper, Anthony J.	McNab, Neil	Thomas, Ton
Foster, Michael G.	Morgan, Alan M.	Vickers, Stephen
Garnett, Shaun M.	Morrissey, John J.	
Higgins, David A.	Muir, Ian J.	

League Appearances: Aldridge, J.W. 43; Branch, G. –(4); Brannan, G.D. 18; Cooper, S.B. 4(5); Garnett, S.M. 8; Harvey, J. 19(5); Higgins, D.A. 33; Hughes, M. 33; Irons, K. 43; McGreal, J. 3; McNab, N. 3(9); Malkin, C.G. 23(12); Martindale, D. 29(2); Morrissey, J.J. 40; Muir, I.J. 13(7); Mungall, S.H. 17(1);

Nevin, P.K.F. 8; Nixon, E.W. 46; Nolan, I.R. 34; Steel, W.J. 16(5); Thomas, T. 30; Vickers, S.H. 43.

League Goals (56): Aldridge 22 (5 pens), Irons 7, Morrissey 5, Muir 5, Steel 4, Malkin 3, Thomas 3, Brannan 1, Cooper S 1, Harvey 1, Higgins 1, Hughes 1, Nolan 1, Vickers 1.
Rumbelows Cup (13): Aldridge 8 (2 pens), Steel 3, Irons 1, Malkin 1.
FA Cup (7): Aldridge 3, Irons 2, Malkin 1, Morrissey 1.
Ground: Prenton Park, Prenton Road West, Birkenhead (051-608 3677)
Manager: John King **Secretary:** Norman Wilson FAAI
Colours: All white
Record home gate: 24,424 v Stoke C, FA Cup 4th rd, 5 February 1972
Honours – Champions: Division 3 (N): 1937–38 **Welsh Cup winners:** 1935 **Associate Members Cup winners:** 1990

WALSALL DIV. 3

Cecere, Michele J.	Knight, Richard	Ntamark, Charles
Chine, Athumani	Macdonald, Kevin D.	O'Hara, Stephen
Edwards, David J.	Marsh, Christopher J.	Smith, Dean
Gayle, Mark S.R.	May, Leroy A.	Statham, Derek J.
Goldsmith, Martin	McDonald, Rodney	Williams, Wayne
Jackson, Robert G.	Methven, Colin J.	Winter, Steven D.

League Appearances: Anderson, C.R. 25(1); Brown, R.C. 6(3); Cecere, M.J. 29(6); Chine, A.A. 4(1); Edwards, D.J. 13(9); Essers, P. 1; Gayle, M.S.R. 24; Grealish, A.P. 3(2); Hobson, G. 3; Jackson, R.G. 7(2); Lane, M.J. 6(4); MacDonald, K.D. 20; McDonald, R. 38(1); McLoughlin, P.B. 9; McKnight, A.D. 8; Marsh, C.J. 34(3); May, L.A. 1(3); Methven, C.J. 42; Musker, R. 3; Ntamark, C. 41; O'Hara, S. 35(2); Robinson, S. –(1); Sinclair, R. 10; Smith, D. 9; Statham, D.J. 29; Tolson, N. 3(6); Walsh, A. 4; Williams, W. 42; Winter, S.D. 13(3).
League Goals (48): McDonald 18, Cecere 8, McLoughlin 4, MacDonald 3, Ntamark 3, O'Hara 3, Anderson 2, Methven 2, Edwards 1, Marsh 1, Tolson 1, own goals 2.
Rumbelows Cup (2): MacDonald 1 (1 pen), Ntamark 1.
FA Cup (1): Tolson 1.
Ground: Bescot Staum, Bescot Cresent, Walsall ES1 4SA (0922 22791)
Manager: Kenny Hibbitt **Secretary:** Roy Whalley
Colours: Red shirts, white shorts, red stockings
Record home gate: 10,628 B International, England v Switzerland, 20 May 1991.
Honours – Champions: Division 4: 1959–60

WATFORD DIV. 1

Alsford, Julian	Butler, Stephen	Gallen, Joseph M.
Ashby, Barry J.	Byrne, David S.	Gibbs, Nigel J.
Bazeley, Darren S.	Drysdale, Jason	Hessenthaler, Andrew
Blissett, Luther L.	Dublin, Keith B.L.	Holdsworth, David G.

Inglethorpe, Alex M.
James, David
Johnson, Richard M.
Kennedy, Andrew J.
Lavin, Gerard
McLaughlin, Joseph

Meara, James S.
Nicholas, Peter
Nogan, Lee M.
Nwaokolo, Daniel N.
Porter, Gary
Putney, Trevor A.

Sheppard, Simon
Soloman, Jason R.
Thomas, Roderick C.
Waugh, Keith

League Appearances: Ashby, B.J. 18(3); Bazeley, D.S. 25(9); Blissett, L.L. 34(8); Butler, S. 28(15); Devonshire, A.E. –(1); Drysdale, J. 36(1); Dublin, K.B.L. 46; Gibbs, N.J. 43; Hessenthaler, A. 35; Holdsworth, D.G. 33; Inglethorpe, A.M. –(2); James, D. 43; Johnson, R.M. 1(1); Kennedy, A.J. 4(3); Lavin, G. –(1); McLaughlin, J. 22; Morrow, S.J. 7(1); Nicholas, P. 25; Nogan, L.M. 23; Porter, G.M. 34(10); Putney, T.A. 26(2); Soloman, J.R. 19(10); Thomas, R.C. 1(4); Waugh, K. 3.
League Goals (51): Blissett 10, Butler 8, Porter 8 (4 pens), Bazeley 6, Drysdale 5 (1 pen), Nogan 5, Holdsworth 2, Putney 2, Gibbs 1, Hessenthaler 1, Kennedy 1, McLaughlin 1, Nicholas 1.
Rumbelows Cup (4): Bazeley 1, Blissett 1, Kennedy 1, Porter 1.
FA Cup (2): Blissett 2.
Ground: Vicarage Road Stadium, Watford WD1 8ER (0923 230933)
Manager: Steve Perryman MBE   **Chief Executive:** Eddie Plumley FAAI
Colours: Yellow shirts (black/red striped band), red shorts, yellow trim, red stockings (yellow/black tops)
Record home gate: 34,099 v Manchester U, FA Cup 4th rd (replay), 3 February 1969
Honours – Champions: Division 3: 1968–69; Division 4: 1977–78

WEST BROMWICH ALBION   DIV. 2

Ampadu, Kwame
Bannister, Gary
Bradley, Darren M.
Burgess, Daryl
Cartwright, Neil A.
Coldicott, Stacy
Fereday, Wayne
Gould, Jonathan A.

Hackett, Gary S.
Harbey, Graham K.
Heggs, Carl S.
Hodson, Simeon P.
Hunter, Roy I.
McNaly, Bernard A.
Naylor, Stuart W.
Piggott, Gary D.

Raven, Paul
Robson, Gary
Shakespeare, Craig R.
Strodder, Gary J.
Taylor, Robert
White, Eric W.
Williams, Paul A.

League Appearances: Ampadu, P.K. 15(6); Bannister, G. 11(4); Bowen, S.A. 8; Bradley, D.M. 35(2); Burgess, D. 36; Cartwright, N.A. 3; Dibble, A.G. 9; Fereday, W. 19(3); Ford, T. 15; Foster, A.M. 4(4); Goodman, D.R. 11; Hackett, G.S. 13(2); Harbey, G.K. 46; Hodson, S.P. 25; Heggs, C. 3; Hunter, R.I. 2(4); McNally, B.A. 17(4); Miller, A. 3; Naylor, S. 34; Palmer, L.J. –(1); Parkin, S. 8(1); Piggott, G.D. 3(2); Pritchard, D.M. 1(4); Raven, P.D. 6(1); Roberts, G.P. 12; Robson, G. 29(3); Rogers, D. 4(6); Shakespeare, C.R. 42(2); Sinclair, F.M. 6; Strodder, G.J. 37; Taylor, R. 19; West, C. 5(2); White, E.W. 9(1); Williams, P.A. 16(18).
League Goals (64): Robson 9, Shakespeare 8 (5 pens), Taylor 8, Goodman 7, Williams 5, Ampadu 3, Bannister 3, Strodder 3, Bradley 2, Burgess 2, Fereday 2, Roberts 2 (1 pen), West 2, Bowen 1, Foster 1, Harbey 1, Hunter 1, McNally 1, Raven 1, Rogers 1, Sinclair 1.

Rumbelows Cup (2): Goodman 1, Shakespeare 1 (1 pen).
FA Cup (7): Shakespeare 2 (1 pens), Goodman 1, McNally 1, Robson 1, Strodder 1, Williams 1.
Ground: The Hawthorns, West Bromwich B71 4LF (021-525 8888)
Manager: Ossie Ardiles   **Secretary:** Dr J. J. Evans BA, PHD. (Wales).
Colours: Navy blue and white striped shirts, white shorts, blue and white stockings
Record home gate: 64,815 v Arsenal, FA Cup 6th rd, 6 March 1937
Honours – Champions: Division 1: 1919–20; Division 2: 1901–02, 1910–11
FA Cup winners: 1888, 1892, 1931, 1954, 1968
Football League Cup winners: 1965–66

WEST HAM UNITED　　　　　　　　　　DIV. 1

Allen, Clive D.	Foster, Colin J.	Parks, Anthony
Allen, Martin J.	Gale, Anthony P.	Parris, George
Banks, Steven	Horlock, Kevin	Potts, Steven J.
Bishop, Ian W.	Keen, Kevin I.	Purdie, John D.
Breacker, Timothy S.	Marquis, Paul R.	Rush, Matthew J.
Brown, Kenneth J.	Martin, Dean	Slater, Stuart I.
Clarke, Simon N.	Miklosko, Ludek	Small, Michael A.
Dicks, Julian A.	Morley, Trevor W.	Thomas, Mitchell A.

League Appearances: Allen, C.D. 4; Allen, M.J. 14(5); Atteveld, R. 1; Bishop, I.W. 41; Breacker, T.S. 33(1); Brown, K.J. 25(2); Clarke, S.N. –(1); Dicks, J.A. 23; Foster, C.J. 24; Gale, A.P. 24(1); Hughton, C.W.G. –(1); Keen, K.I. 20(9); McAvennie, F. 16(4); Martin, A.E. 7; Martin, D.E. 1(1); Miklosko, L. 36; Morley, T.W. 13(11); Parks, A. 6; Parris, G.M.R. 20(1); Potts, S.J. 34; Rosenior, L.D.G. 5(4); Rush, M.J. 3(7); Slater, S.I. 41; Small, M.A. 37(3); Thomas, M.A. 34(1) .
League Goals (37): Small 13 (1 pen), McAvennie 6, Brown 3, Dicks 3 (3 pens), Thomas 3, Breacker 2, Morley 2, Rush 2, Allen C 1, Bishop 1, Rosenior 1.
Rumbelows Cup (8): Small 4 (1 pen), Keen 1, McAvennie 1, Morley 1, Parris 1.
FA Cup (8): Allen 2, Dicks 2, Morley 2, Foster 1, Small 1.
Ground: Boleyn Ground, Green Street, Upton Park, London E13 (081-472 2740)
Manager: Billy Bonds MBE   **Secretary:** T. M. Finn
Colours: Claret and blue shirts, white shorts, white stockings
Record home gate: 42,322 v Tottenham H, Division 1, 17 October 1970
Honours – Champions: Division 2: 1957–58, 1980–81
FA Cup winners: 1964, 1975, 1980
European Cup-Winners' Cup winners: 1964–65

WIGAN ATHLETIC　　　　　　　　　　DIV. 2

Adkins, Nigel H.	Jones, Philip A.	Powell, Gary
Appleton, Stephen	Langley, Kevin J.	Rimmer, Neill
Daley, Phillip	Nugent, Stephen	Sharratt, Christopher M.
Doolan, John	Parkinson, Joseph S.	Tankard, Allen J.
Gray, Robert P.	Patterson, Darren J.	Worthington, Gary L.
Griffiths, Bryan K.	Pennock, Anthony	
Johnson, Alan K.	Pilling, Andrew J.	

League Appearances: Adkins, N.H. 46; Appleton, S. 4(5); Atherton, P. 1; Carberry, J. 1(4); Collins, D.D. 9; Connelly, D. 12; Daley, P. 37(1); Doolan, J. 2; Edwardson, B.J. –(1); Gray, R.P. 2(3); Griffiths, B. 26(2); Johnson, A.K. 41(3); Jones, P.A. 40(1); Langley, K.J. 45; Nugent, S. 2; Parkinson, J.S. 36; Patterson, D.J. 39(1); Pilling, A.J. 21(6); Powell, G. 22(12); Rimmer, N. 9; Sharratt, C.M. –(4); Skipper, P.D. 15(3); Smith, J. –(6); Smyth, J.M. 2(6); Tankard, A.J. 44; Taylor, C.D. 7; Widdrington, T. 5(1); Williams, W.J. 4; Worthington, G. 34(7).
League Goals (58): Worthington 15 (2 pens), Daley 14, Powell 7, Griffiths 4 (1 pen), Johnson 4, Parkinson 3, Connelly 2, Langley 2, Pilling 2, Taylor 2, Jones 1, Patterson 1, own goals 1.
Rumbelows Cup (8): Patterson 3, Worthington 2, Griffiths 1 (1 pen), Jones 1, Rimmer 1.
FA Cup (4): Griffiths 1, Pilling 1, Powell 1, Worthington 1.
Ground: Springfield Park, Wigan (0942 44433)
Manager: Bryan Hamilton **Secretary:** W. Kenyon.
Colours: Blue shirts red and white trim, blue shorts with red and white trim, blue stockings
Record home gate: 27,500 v Hereford U, 12 December 1953
Honours – Associate Members Cup winners: 1984–85

WIMBLEDON   FA PREMIER

Anthrobus, Stephen A.	Fairweather, Carlton	Perry, Christopher J.
Ardley, Neal C.	Fashanu, John	Phelan, Terry
Barton, Warren D.	Fitzgerald, Scott B.	Ryan, Vaughan W.
Bennett, Michael R.	Gibson, Terence B.	Sanchez, Lawrence P.
Blackwell, Dean R.	Joseph, Roger	Scales, John R.
Castledine, Stewart M.	Kruszynski, Zbigniew	Segers, Johannes C.
Clarke, Andrew W.	McAllister, Brian	Skinner, Justin J.
Cotterill, Stephen	McCarthy, Jamie	Sullivan, Neil
Dobbs, Gerald F.	McGee, Paul	Talboys, Steven
Earle, Robert	Miller, Paul A.	
Elkins, Gary	Newhouse, Aidan R.	

League Appearances: Anthrobus, S.A. 10; Ardley, N.C. 7(1); Barton, W. 42; Bennett, M.R. 5; Blackwell, D.R. 1(3); Castledine, S.M. –(2); Clarke, A.W. 13(21); Cork, A.G. 12(7); Dobbs, G.F. 2(2); Earle, R. 40; Elkins, G. 15(3); Fairweather, C. 6; Fashanu, J. 38; Fitzgerald, S. 34(2); Gibson, T.B. 7; Hayes, M. 1(1); Joseph, R.A. 25(1); Kruszynski, Z. 1; McAllister, B. 9(1); McGee, P. 15(1); Miller, P.A. 22; Newhouse, A. 5(7); Phelan, T.M. 37; Ryan, V.W. 16(5); Sanchez, L.P. 16; Scales, J.R. 41; Segers, N. 41; Sullivan, N. 1.
League Goals (53): Fashanu 18 (5 pens), Earle 14, Clarke 3, Sanchez 3, Cork 2, McGee 2, Miller 2, Ryan 2, Barton 1, Bennett 1, Blackwell 1, Elkins 1, Fitzgerald 1, Newhouse 1, Phelan 1.
Rumbelows Cup (3): Clarke 1, Fashanu 1 (1 pen), McGee 1.
FA Cup (1): Fashanu 1.
Ground: Selhurst Park, South Norwood, London E5. Telephone: 081-771 2233
Manager: Joe Kinnear. **Secretary:** Adrian Cook
Colours: Blue shirts yellow trim, blue shorts yellow trim, blue stockings yellow trim

Record home gate: 18,000 v HMS Victory, FA Amateur Cup 3rd rd, 1934–35 (at Plough Lane)
Honours – Champions: Division 4: 1982–83

WOLVERHAMPTON WANDERERS   DIV. 1

Ashley, Kevin M.	Hindmarch, Robert	Steele, Timothy W.
Bellamy, Gary	Jones, Paul S.	Stowell, Michael
Bennett, Thomas M.	Kelly, James	Taylor, Colin D.
Birch, Paul	Madden, Lawrence D.	Thompson, Andrew R.
Bull, Stephen G.	Mountfield, Derek N.	Turner, Graham M.
Burke, Mark S.	Mutch, Andrew T.	Venus, Mark
Cook, Paul A.	Rankine, Simon M.	Westley, Shane L.M.
Dennison, Robert	Roberts, Darren A.	
Downing, Keith G.	Simkin, Darren S.	

League Appearances: Ashley, K.M. 44; Bellamy, G. 1(3); Bennett, T.M. 37(1); Birch, P. 43(2); Bull, S.G. 43; Burke, M.S. 13(5); Clarke, N.J. 1; Clarke, W. 1; Cook, P.A. 43; Dennison, R. 12(10); Downing, K.G. 30(2); Kelly, J. –(3); McLoughlin, P.B. 3; Madden, L.D. 43; Mountfield, D. 28; Mutch, A. 35(2); Paskin, W.J. 1(1); Rankine, S.M. 10(5); Steele, T.W. 10(7); Stowell, M. 46; Taylor, C.D. 1(2); Thompson, A.R. 15(2); Venus, M. 46.
League Goals (61): Bull 20, Mutch 10, Birch 8 (1 pen), Cook 8 (2 pens), Steele 3, Bennett 2, Burke 2, Ashley 1, Dennison 1, Madden 1, Mountfield 1, Rankine 1, Venus 1, own goals 2.
Rumbelows Cup (8): Bull 3, Birch 2, Steele 2, Burke 1.
FA Cup (0).
Ground: Molineux Grounds, Wolverhampton WV1 4QR (0902 712181)
Manager: Graham Turner   **Secretary:** Keith Pearson ACIS
Colours: Gold shirts, black shorts, gold stockings
Record home gate: 61,315 v Liverpool, FA Cup 5th rd, 11 February 1939
Honours – Champions: Division 1: 1953–54, 1957–58, 1958–59; Division 2: 1931–32, 1976–77; Division 3 (N): 1923–24; Division 3: 1988–89; Division 4: 1987–88
FA Cup winners: 1893, 1908, 1949, 1960
Football League Cup winners: 1973–74, 1979–80
Associate Members Cup winners: 1988

WREXHAM   DIV. 3

Connolly, Karl	Paskin, William J.	Thackeray, Andrew J.
Hardy, Philip	Pejic, Melvyn	Thomas, Reginald M.
Humes, Anthony	Phillips, Wayne	Watkin, Stephen
Morris, Mark	Sertori, Mark A.	
Owen, Gareth	Taylor, Peter M.R.	

League Appearances: Beaumont, N. 13(1); Bowden, J.L. 6; Carey, B.P. 13; Connolly, K. 33(3); Cross, J.N. 3(3); Davies, G.J. 21(1); Durkan, K.J. –(1); Flynn, B. 6; Griffiths, I.J. 3; Hardy, P. 42; Humes, A. 8; Ireland, S.P. 2(3); Jones, D. –(1); Jones, J.P. 11; Jones, K.R. –(1); Jones, P.K. 11(10); Kelly, J. 9; Knight, C. 1; Lewis, D.K. 8(1); Lunt, R.J. –(1); Marshall, C. 3; Morris, M. 8; O'Keefe, V.J. 34; Owen, G. 33(3); Paskin, W.J. 14(3); Pejic, M. 6(1); Phillips, S.G. 1(1); Phillips, W. 28(2); Preece, A.P. 9(1); Sertori, M.A. 36; Skipper, P.D. 2; Taylor, P.M. 6(3); Thackeray, A.J. 42; Thomas, M.R. 26; Watkin, S. 24(4).
League Goals (52): Connolly 8, Watkin 8, Owen 7, Jones L 5, Davies 4, Bowden 3 (2 pens), Paskin 3, Phillips W 3, Thackeray 3, Preece 2, Carey 1, Phillips S 1, Thomas 1, own goals 3.
Rumbelows Cup (1): Thackeray 1.
FA Cup (10): Watkin 5, Thomas 2, Connolly 1, Jones L 1, Phillips W 1.
Ground: Racecourse Ground, Mold Road, Wrexam (0978 262129)
Manager: Brian Flynn   **Secretary:** D. L. Rhodes
Colours: Red shirts, white shorts, red stockings
Record home gate: 34,445 v Manchester U, FA Cup 4th rd, 26 January 1957
Honours – Champions: Division 3: 1977–78
Welsh Cup winners: 21 times

YORK CITY DIV. 3

Atkin, Paul A.	Hall, Wayne	Pepper, Colin N.
Barratt, Anthony	Kiely, Dean L.	Stancliffe, Paul I.
Blackstone, Ian K.	Marples, Christopher	Tilley, Darren J.
Bushell, Stephen	McCarthy, Jonathan D.	Tutill, Stephen A.
Canham, Anthony	McMillan, Lyndon A.	Warburton, Raymond
Crosby, Philip A.	Naylor, Glenn	

League Appearances: Atkin, P.A. 29(4); Barratt, A. 15(6); Blackstone, I.K. 26(4); Bushell, S.P. 15(1); Canham, A. 28(3); Crosby, P. 25; Curtis, A. 4(3); Gosney, A. 5; Hall, W. 36(1); Kiely, D. 21; McCarthy, J.D. 42; McLoughlin, P. 1; McMillan, L.A. 41; Marples, C. 16; Naylor, G. 14(7); Osborne, S. 6(3); Pepper, N. 33(2); Reid, S. 28; Shepstone, P.T.A. 2; Stancliffe, P. 16(2); Tilley, D.J. 13(2); Tutill, S.A. 39; Warburton, R. 7(2).
League Goals (42): Blackstone 8, Naylor 8, McCarthy 6, Canham 5, Pepper 4 (1 pen), Barratt 3, Hall 3, Atkin 1, McMillan 1, Reid 1, Stancliffe 1, Tutill 1.
Rumbelows Cup (3): Blackstone 1, Canham 1, McCarthy 1.
FA Cup (4): Blackstone 2, Hall 1, McCarthy 1.
Ground: Bootham Crescent, York (0904 624447)
Manager: John Ward.   **Secretary:** Keith Usher
Colours: Red shirts, blue shorts, red stockings
Record home gate: 28,123 v Huddersfield T, FA Cup 6th rd, 5 March 1938
Honours – Champions: Division 4: 1983–84

LEAGUE REVIEW

With a week to go in an exciting race for the championship, there was a sudden anti-climax when Leeds United scrambled to a 3-2 win at Sheffield United during a midday kick-off and Manchester United lost 2-0 at Liverpool a few hours later to give Leeds their first title since 1974.

Manchester United had seemed well on the way to success for most of the season. Indeed Alex Ferguson's team were well in command from September 7 until losing to the bottom club West Ham on April 22 by a single goal. There had been good omens for them winning the championship. They were unbeaten until losing 3-2 at Sheffield Wednesday on October 26, but it proved to be an unlucky 13. However in 1974-75 after nine unbeaten games at the start they went on to win the Second Division title and in 1956-57 they survived a dozen matches without loss and took the League championship itself. So when United were again the last team in the Football League to suffer defeat, it appeared that it was to be third time lucky once more.

Leeds were worthy champions nonetheless and if there was some consolation for Manchester United, they were able to win the Rumbelows Cup at the expense of Nottingham Forest, whose minor reward was to capture the Zenith Data Systems Cup.

Arsenal never looked capable of retaining the League crown until it was too late. After a surprise defeat in the FA Cup when Wrexham beat them 2-1 in the third round, they finished strongly but to no avail. And for Liverpool with problems of on-the-field injuries and off-the-field illness to manager Graeme Souness, who underwent successful heart surgery, they had one of their poorest seasons for decades. But Anfield did manage one trophy.

The last Football League season before the introduction of the Premier League almost caused an embarrassing situation for the new competition's image from the FA Cup. There was a strong possibility that the finalists would be both from the Second Division, but Liverpool just edged out Portsmouth in a penalty shoot-out and went on to beat Sunderland 2-0 in the final.

The play-offs again helped to stimulate interest throughout the divisions but though attendances reached the 20 million mark for the first time in ten years, the increase was due in no small measure to the fact that more games were played in the First Division and both this section and Division Two showed a drop on average. But the lower two divisions both showed an increase despite the financial problems affecting many clubs, which culminated in Aldershot becoming the first League club since Accrington Stanley in 1962 to fail to complete their programme.

The new FA Premier League starts with expectations high for the richer clubs at least, but there must be considerable concern that many of the smaller teams will fall by the wayside.

THE LEAGUE – DIVISION I

HOME TEAM	Arsenal	Aston Villa	Chelsea	Coventry C.	Crystal Palace	Everton	Leeds U.	Liverpool
Arsenal	—	0–0	3–2	1–2	4–1	4–2	1–1	4–0
Aston Villa	3–1	—	3–1	2–0	0–1	0–0	1–4	1–0
Chelsea	1–1	2–0	—	0–1	1–1	2–2	0–1	2–2
Coventry C.	0–1	1–0	0–1	—	1–2	0–1	0–0	0–0
Crystal Palace	1–4	0–0	0–0	0–1	—	2–0	1–0	1–0
Everton	3–1	0–2	2–1	3–0	2–2	—	1–1	1–1
Leeds U.	2–2	0–0	3–0	2–0	1–1	1–0	—	1–0
Liverpool	2–0	1–1	1–2	1–0	1–2	3–1	0–0	—
Luton T.	1–0	2–0	2–0	1–0	1–1	0–1	0–2	0–0
Manchester C.	1–0	2–0	0–0	1–0	3–2	0–1	4–0	2–1
Manchester U.	1–1	1–0	1–1	4–0	2–0	1–0	1–1	0–0
Norwich C.	1–3	2–1	0–1	3–2	3–3	4–3	2–2	3–0
Nottingham F.	3–2	2–0	1–1	1–0	5–1	2–1	0–0	1–1
Notts Co.	0–1	0–0	2–0	1–0	2–3	0–0	2–4	1–2
Oldham Ath.	1–1	3–2	3–0	2–1	2–3	2–2	2–0	2–3
Q.P.R.	0–0	0–1	2–2	1–1	1–0	3–1	4–1	0–0
Sheffield U.	1–1	2–0	0–1	0–3	1–1	2–1	2–3	2–0
Sheffield W.	1–1	2–3	3–0	1–1	4–1	2–1	1–6	0–0
Southampton	0–4	1–1	1–0	0–0	1–0	1–2	0–4	1–1
Tottenham H.	1–1	2–5	1–3	4–3	0–1	3–3	1–3	1–2
West Ham U.	0–2	3–1	1–1	0–1	0–2	0–2	1–3	0–0
Wimbledon	1–3	2–0	1–2	1–1	1–1	0–0	0–0	0–0

1991–92 RESULTS

Luton T.	Manchester C.	Manchester U.	Norwich C.	Nottingham F.	Notts Co.	Oldham Ath.	Q.P.R.	Sheffield U.	Sheffield W.	Southampton	Tottenham H.	West Ham U.	Wimbledon
2–0	2–1	1–1	1–1	3–3	2–0	2–1	1–1	5–2	7–1	5–1	2–0	0–1	1–1
4–0	3–1	0–1	1–0	3–1	1–0	1–0	0–1	1–1	0–1	2–1	0–0	3–1	2–1
4–1	1–1	1–3	0–3	1–0	2–2	4–2	2–1	1–2	0–3	1–1	2–0	2–1	2–2
5–0	0–1	0–0	0–0	0–2	1–0	1–1	2–2	3–1	0–0	2–0	1–2	1–0	0–1
1–1	1–1	1–3	3–4	0–0	1–0	0–0	2–2	2–1	1–1	1–0	1–2	2–3	3–2
1–1	1–2	0–0	1–1	1–1	1–0	2–1	0–0	0–2	0–1	0–1	3–1	4–0	2–0
2–0	3–0	1–1	1–0	1–0	3–0	1–0	2–0	4–3	1–1	3–3	1–1	0–0	5–1
2–1	2–2	2–0	2–1	2–0	4–0	2–1	1–0	2–1	1–1	0–0	2–1	1–0	2–3
—	2–2	1–1	2–0	2–1	1–1	2–1	0–1	2–1	2–2	2–1	0–0	0–1	2–1
4–0	—	0–0	2–1	2–1	2–0	1–2	2–2	3–2	0–1	0–1	1–0	2–0	0–0
5–0	1–1	—	3–0	1–2	2–0	1–0	1–4	2–0	1–1	1–0	3–1	2–1	0–0
1–0	0–0	1–3	—	0–0	0–1	1–2	0–1	2–2	1–0	2–1	0–1	2–1	1–1
1–1	2–0	1–0	2–0	—	1–1	3–1	1–1	2–5	0–2	1–3	1–3	2–2	4–2
2–1	1–3	1–1	2–2	0–4	—	2–0	0–1	1–3	2–1	1–0	0–2	3–0	1–1
5–1	2–5	3–6	2–2	2–1	4–3	—	2–1	2–1	3–0	1–1	1–0	2–2	0–1
2–1	4–0	0–0	0–2	0–2	1–1	1–3	—	1–0	1–1	2–2	1–2	0–0	1–1
1–1	4–2	1–2	1–0	4–2	1–3	2–0	0–0	—	2–0	0–2	2–0	1–1	0–0
3–2	2–0	3–2	2–0	2–1	1–0	1–1	4–1	1–3	—	2–0	0–0	2–1	2–0
2–1	0–3	0–1	0–0	0–1	1–1	1–0	2–1	2–4	0–1	—	2–3	1–0	1–0
4–1	0–1	1–2	3–0	1–2	2–1	0–0	2–0	0–1	0–2	1–2	—	3–0	3–2
0–0	1–2	1–0	4–0	3–0	0–2	1–0	2–2	1–1	1–2	0–1	2–1	—	1–1
3–0	2–1	1–2	3–1	3–0	2–0	2–1	0–1	3–0	2–1	0–1	3–5	2–0	—

THE LEAGUE – DIVISION II

HOME TEAM	Barnsley	Blackburn R.	Brighton & H.A.	Bristol C.	Bristol R.	Cambridge U.	Charlton Ath.	Derby Co.	Grimsby T.
Barnsley	—	2–1	1–2	1–2	0–1	0–0	1–0	0–3	4–1
Blackburn R.	3–0	—	1–0	4–0	3–0	2–1	0–2	2–0	2–1
Brighton & H.A.	3–1	0–3	—	0–0	3–1	1–1	1–2	1–2	3–0
Bristol C.	0–2	1–0	2–1	—	1–0	1–2	0–2	1–2	1–1
Bristol R.	0–0	3–0	4–1	3–2	—	2–2	1–0	2–3	2–3
Cambridge U.	2–1	2–1	0–0	0–0	6–1	—	1–0	0–0	0–1
Charlton Ath.	1–1	0–2	2–0	2–1	1–0	1–2	—	0–2	1–3
Derby Co.	1–1	0–2	3–1	4–1	1–0	0–0	1–2	—	0–0
Grimsby T.	0–1	2–3	0–1	3–1	0–1	3–4	1–0	0–1	—
Ipswich T.	2–0	2–1	3–1	4–2	1–0	1–2	2–0	2–1	0–0
Leicester C.	3–1	3–0	2–1	2–1	1–1	2–1	0–2	1–2	2–0
Middlesbrough	0–1	0–0	4–0	3–1	2–1	1–1	2–0	1–1	2–0
Millwall	1–1	1–3	1–2	2–3	0–1	1–2	1–0	1–2	1–1
Newcastle U.	1–1	0–0	0–1	3–0	2–1	1–1	3–4	2–2	2–0
Oxford U.	0–1	1–3	3–1	1–1	2–2	1–0	1–2	2–0	1–2
Plymouth Arg.	2–1	1–3	1–1	1–0	0–0	0–1	0–2	1–1	1–2
Portsmouth	2–0	2–2	0–0	1–0	2–0	3–0	1–2	0–1	2–0
Port Vale	0–0	2–0	2–1	1–1	0–1	1–0	1–1	1–0	0–1
Southend U.	2–1	3–0	2–1	1–1	2–0	1–1	1–1	1–0	3–1
Sunderland	2–0	1–1	4–2	1–3	1–1	2–2	1–2	1–1	1–2
Swindon T.	3–1	2–1	2–1	2–0	1–0	0–2	1–2	1–2	1–1
Tranmere R.	2–1	2–2	1–1	2–2	2–2	1–2	2–2	4–3	1–1
Watford	1–1	2–1	0–1	5–2	1–0	1–3	2–0	1–2	2–0
Wolverhampton W.	1–2	0–0	2–0	1–1	2–3	2–1	1–1	2–3	2–1

1991–92 RESULTS

Ipswich T.	Leicester C.	Middlesbrough	Millwall	Newcastle U.	Oxford U.	Plymouth Arg.	Portsmouth	Port Vale	Southend	Sunderland	Swindon T.	Tranmere R.	Watford	Wolverhampton W.
1–0	3–1	2–1	0–2	3–0	1–0	1–3	2–0	0–0	1–0	0–3	1–1	1–1	0–3	2–0
1–2	0–1	2–1	2–1	3–1	1–1	5–2	1–1	1–0	2–2	2–2	2–1	0–0	1–0	1–2
2–2	1–2	1–1	3–4	2–2	1–2	1–0	2–1	3–1	3–2	2–2	0–2	0–2	0–1	3–3
2–1	2–1	1–1	2–2	1–1	1–1	2–0	0–2	3–0	2–2	1–0	1–1	2–2	1–0	2–0
3–3	1–1	2–1	3–2	1–2	2–1	0–0	1–0	3–3	4–1	2–1	1–1	1–0	1–1	1–1
1–1	5–1	0–0	1–0	0–2	1–1	1–1	2–2	4–2	0–1	3–0	3–2	0–0	0–1	2–1
1–1	2–0	0–0	1–0	2–1	2–2	0–0	3–0	2–0	2–0	1–4	0–0	0–1	1–1	0–2
1–0	1–2	2–0	0–2	4–1	2–2	2–0	2–0	3–1	1–2	1–2	2–1	0–1	3–1	1–2
1–2	0–1	1–0	1–1	1–1	1–0	2–1	1–1	1–2	3–2	2–0	0–0	2–2	0–1	0–2
—	0–0	2–1	0–0	3–2	2–1	2–0	5–2	2–1	1–0	0–1	1–4	4–0	1–2	2–1
2–2	—	2–1	1–1	1–2	2–1	2–0	2–2	0–1	2–0	3–2	3–1	1–0	1–2	3–0
1–0	3–0	—	1–0	3–0	2–1	2–1	2–0	1–0	1–1	2–1	2–2	1–0	1–2	0–0
2–3	2–0	2–0	—	2–1	2–1	2–1	1–1	1–0	2–0	4–1	1–1	0–3	0–4	2–1
1–1	2–0	0–1	0–1	—	4–3	2–2	1–0	2–2	3–2	1–0	3–1	2–3	2–2	1–2
1–1	1–2	1–2	2–2	5–2	—	3–2	2–1	2–2	0–1	3–0	5–3	1–0	0–0	1–0
1–0	2–2	1–1	3–2	2–0	3–1	—	3–2	1–0	0–2	1–0	0–4	1–0	0–1	1–0
1–1	1–0	4–0	6–1	3–1	2–1	4–1	—	1–0	1–1	1–0	1–1	2–0	0–0	1–0
1–2	1–2	1–2	0–2	0–1	2–1	1–0	0–2	—	0–0	3–3	2–2	1–1	2–1	1–1
1–2	1–2	0–1	2–3	4–0	2–3	2–1	2–3	0–0	—	2–0	3–2	1–1	1–0	0–2
3–0	1–0	1–0	6–2	1–1	2–0	0–1	1–0	1–1	1–2	—	0–0	1–1	3–1	1–0
0–0	0–0	0–1	3–1	2–1	2–1	1–0	2–3	1–0	3–1	5–3	—	2–0	3–1	1–0
0–1	1–2	1–2	2–1	3–2	1–2	1–0	2–0	2–1	1–1	1–0	0–0	—	1–1	4–3
0–1	0–1	1–2	0–2	2–2	2–0	1–0	2–1	0–0	1–2	1–0	0–0	0–0	—	0–2
1–2	1–0	1–2	0–0	6–2	3–1	1–0	0–0	0–2	3–1	1–0	2–1	1–1	3–0	—

THE LEAGUE – DIVISION III

HOME TEAM	Birmingham C.	Bolton W.	Bournemouth	Bradford C.	Brentford	Bury	Chester C.	Darlington	Exeter C.
Birmingham C.	—	2–1	0–1	2–0	1–0	3–2	3–2	1–0	1–0
Bolton W.	1–1	—	0–2	1–1	1–2	2–1	0–0	2–0	1–2
Bournemouth	2–1	1–2	—	1–3	0–0	4–0	2–0	1–2	1–0
Bradford C.	1–2	4–4	3–1	—	0–1	1–1	1–1	0–1	1–1
Brentford	2–2	3–2	2–2	3–4	—	0–3	2–0	4–1	3–0
Bury	1–0	1–1	0–1	0–1	0–3	—	1–2	1–0	3–1
Chester C.	0–1	0–1	0–1	0–0	1–1	3–1	—	2–5	5–2
Darlington	1–1	3–2	0–0	1–3	1–2	0–2	1–1	—	5–2
Exeter C.	2–1	2–2	0–3	1–0	1–2	5–2	0–0	4–1	—
Fulham	0–1	1–1	2–0	2–1	0–1	4–2	2–2	4–0	0–0
Hartlepool U.	1–0	0–4	1–0	1–0	1–0	0–0	1–0	2–0	3–1
Huddersfield T.	3–2	1–0	0–0	1–0	2–1	3–0	2–0	2–1	0–0
Hull C.	1–2	2–0	0–1	0–0	0–3	0–1	1–0	5–2	1–2
Leyton Orient	0–0	2–1	1–1	1–1	4–2	4–0	1–0	2–1	1–0
Peterborough U.	2–3	1–0	2–0	2–1	0–1	0–0	2–0	1–1	1–1
Preston N.E.	3–2	2–1	2–2	1–1	3–2	2–0	0–3	2–1	1–3
Reading	1–1	1–0	0–0	1–2	0–0	3–2	0–0	2–2	1–0
Shrewsbury T.	1–1	1–3	1–2	3–2	1–0	1–1	2–2	0–2	6–1
Stockport Co.	2–0	2–2	5–0	4–1	2–1	2–0	0–4	2–0	4–1
Stoke C.	2–1	2–0	1–1	0–0	2–1	1–2	0–1	3–0	5–2
Swansea C.	0–2	1–1	3–1	2–2	1–1	2–1	3–0	4–2	1–0
Torquay U.	1–2	2–0	1–0	1–1	1–1	0–2	3–2	3–0	1–0
W.B.A.	0–1	2–2	4–0	1–1	2–0	1–1	1–1	3–1	6–3
Wigan Ath.	3–0	1–1	2–0	2–1	2–1	2–0	2–1	1–2	4–1

1991–92 RESULTS

	Fulham	Hartlepool U.	Huddersfield T.	Hull C.	Leyton Orient	Peterborough U.	Preston N.E.	Reading	Shrewsbury T.	Stockport Co.	Stoke C.	Swansea C.	Torquay U.	W.B.A.	Wigan Ath.
	3–1	2–1	2–0	2–2	2–2	1–1	3–1	2–0	1–0	3–0	1–1	1–1	3–0	0–3	3–3
	0–3	2–2	1–1	1–0	1–0	2–1	1–0	1–1	1–0	0–0	3–1	0–0	1–0	3–0	1–1
	0–0	2–0	1–1	0–0	0–1	1–2	1–0	3–2	1–0	1–0	1–2	3–0	2–1	2–1	3–0
	3–4	1–1	1–1	2–1	1–1	2–1	1–1	1–0	3–0	1–0	1–0	4–6	2–0	1–1	1–1
	4–0	1–0	2–3	4–1	4–3	2–1	1–0	1–0	2–0	2–1	2–0	3–2	3–2	1–2	4–0
	3–1	1–1	4–4	3–2	4–2	3–0	2–3	0–1	0–0	0–0	1–3	1–0	0–0	1–1	1–4
	2–0	2–0	0–0	1–1	1–0	2–4	3–2	2–2	1–4	3–2	0–0	2–0	2–0	1–2	1–0
	3–1	4–0	1–3	0–1	0–1	1–2	0–2	2–4	3–3	1–3	0–1	1–1	3–2	0–1	0–1
	1–1	1–1	0–1	0–3	2–0	2–2	4–1	2–1	1–0	2–1	0–0	2–1	1–0	1–1	0–1
	—	1–0	1–0	0–0	2–1	0–1	1–0	1–0	0–1	1–2	1–1	3–0	2–1	0–0	1–1
	2–0	—	0–0	2–3	2–3	0–1	2–0	2–0	4–2	0–1	1–1	0–1	1–1	0–0	4–3
	3–1	1–0	—	1–1	1–0	0–0	1–2	1–2	2–1	0–1	1–2	1–0	4–0	3–0	3–1
	0–0	0–2	1–0	—	1–0	1–2	2–2	0–1	4–0	0–2	0–1	3–0	4–1	1–0	1–1
	0–1	4–0	1–0	1–0	—	1–2	0–0	1–1	2–0	3–3	0–1	1–2	2–0	1–1	3–1
	4–1	3–2	2–0	3–0	0–2	—	1–0	5–3	1–0	3–2	1–1	3–1	1–1	0–0	0–0
	1–2	1–4	1–0	3–1	2–1	1–1	—	1–1	2–2	3–2	2–2	1–1	3–0	2–0	3–0
	0–2	0–1	1–0	0–1	3–2	1–1	2–2	—	2–1	1–1	3–4	1–0	6–1	1–2	3–2
	0–0	1–4	1–1	2–3	0–1	2–0	2–0	1–2	—	0–1	1–0	0–0	2–2	1–3	1–0
	2–0	0–1	0–0	1–1	1–0	3–0	2–0	1–0	1–4	—	0–0	5–0	2–1	3–0	3–3
	2–2	3–2	0–2	2–3	2–0	3–3	2–1	3–0	1–0	2–2	—	2–1	3–0	1–0	3–0
	2–2	1–1	0–1	0–0	2–2	1–0	2–2	1–2	1–2	2–1	2–1	—	1–0	0–0	3–0
	0–1	3–1	0–1	2–1	1–0	2–2	1–0	1–2	1–2	2–0	1–0	1–0	—	1–0	0–1
	2–3	1–2	2–1	1–0	1–3	4–0	3–0	2–0	2–0	1–0	2–2	2–3	1–0	—	1–1
	0–2	1–1	1–3	0–1	1–1	3–0	3–0	1–1	1–1	1–3	1–0	1–0	0–0	0–1	—

THE LEAGUE – DIVISION IV

HOME TEAM	Barnet	Blackpool	Burnley	Cardiff C.	Carlisle U.	Chesterfield	Crewe Alex.	Doncaster R.
Barnet	—	3–0	0–0	3–1	4–2	1–2	4–7	1–0
Blackpool	4–2	—	5–2	1–1	1–0	3–1	0–2	1–0
Burnley	3–0	1–1	—	3–1	2–0	3–0	1–1	2–1
Cardiff C.	3–1	1–1	0–2	—	1–0	4–0	1–1	2–1
Carlisle U.	1–3	1–2	1–1	2–2	—	1–2	2–1	1–0
Chesterfield	3–2	1–1	0–2	2–2	0–0	—	2–1	0–0
Crewe Alex.	3–0	1–0	1–0	1–1	2–1	3–1	—	1–0
Doncaster R.	1–0	0–2	1–4	1–2	0–3	0–1	1–3	—
Gillingham	3–3	3–2	3–0	0–0	1–2	0–1	0–1	2–1
Halifax T.	3–1	1–2	0–2	1–1	3–2	2–0	2–1	0–0
Hereford U.	2–2	1–2	2–0	2–2	1–0	1–0	1–2	0–1
Lincoln C.	0–6	2–0	0–3	0–0	1–0	1–2	2–2	2–0
Maidstone U.	1–1	0–0	0–1	1–1	5–1	0–1	2–0	2–2
Mansfield T.	1–2	1–1	0–1	3–0	2–1	2–1	4–3	2–2
Northampton T.	1–1	1–1	1–2	0–0	2–2	1–1	0–1	3–1
Rochdale	1–0	4–2	1–3	2–0	3–1	3–3	1–0	1–1
Rotherham U.	3–0	2–0	2–1	1–2	1–0	1–1	1–2	3–1
Scarborough	0–4	1–2	3–1	2–2	2–2	3–2	2–1	1–0
Scunthorpe U.	1–1	2–1	2–2	1–0	4–0	2–0	1–0	3–2
Walsall	2–0	4–2	2–2	0–0	0–0	2–2	2–3	1–3
Wrexham	1–0	1–1	2–6	0–3	3–0	0–1	1–0	1–2
York C.	1–4	1–0	1–2	1–3	2–0	0–1	1–1	1–1

1991–92 RESULTS

Gillingham	Halifax T.	Hereford U.	Lincoln C.	Maidstone U.	Mansfield T.	Northampton T.	Rochdale	Rotherham U.	Scarborough	Scunthorpe U.	Walsall	Wrexham	York C.
2–0	3–0	1–0	1–0	3–2	2–0	3–0	3–0	2–5	5–1	3–2	0–1	2–0	2–0
2–0	3–0	2–0	3–0	1–1	2–1	1–0	3–0	3–0	1–1	2–1	3–0	4–0	3–1
4–1	1–0	2–0	1–0	2–1	3–2	5–0	0–1	1–2	1–1	1–1	2–0	1–2	3–1
2–3	4–0	1–0	1–2	0–5	3–2	3–2	1–2	1–0	2–1	2–2	2–1	5–0	3–0
0–0	1–1	1–0	0–2	3–0	1–2	2–1	0–0	1–3	2–2	0–0	3–3	0–1	1–1
3–3	4–0	2–0	1–5	3–0	0–2	1–2	0–1	1–1	1–0	0–1	0–1	1–1	1–3
2–1	3–2	4–2	1–0	1–1	1–2	1–1	1–1	0–1	3–3	1–1	0–1	2–1	1–0
1–1	0–2	2–0	1–5	3–0	0–1	0–3	2–0	1–1	3–2	1–2	0–1	3–1	0–1
—	2–0	2–1	1–3	1–1	2–0	3–1	0–0	5–1	2–0	4–0	4–0	2–1	1–1
0–3	—	0–2	1–4	1–1	1–3	0–1	1–1	0–4	1–0	1–4	1–0	4–3	0–0
2–0	0–2	—	3–0	2–2	0–1	1–2	1–1	1–0	4–1	1–2	1–2	3–1	2–1
1–0	0–0	3–0	—	1–0	2–0	1–2	0–3	0–2	0–2	4–2	1–0	0–0	0–0
1–1	0–1	3–2	0–2	—	0–0	1–1	1–1	0–0	2–1	0–1	2–1	2–4	1–0
4–3	3–2	1–1	0–0	2–0	—	2–0	2–1	1–0	1–2	1–3	3–1	3–0	5–2
0–0	4–0	0–1	1–0	1–0	1–2	—	2–2	1–2	3–2	0–1	0–1	1–1	2–2
2–1	1–0	3–1	1–0	1–2	0–2	1–0	—	1–1	2–2	2–0	1–1	2–1	1–1
1–1	1–0	0–0	1–1	3–3	1–1	1–0	2–0	—	0–2	5–0	2–1	3–0	4–0
2–1	3–0	1–1	1–1	2–0	0–0	2–1	3–2	0–3	—	4–1	2–3	4–1	1–0
2–0	1–0	1–1	0–2	2–0	1–4	3–0	6–2	1–0	1–1	—	1–1	3–1	1–0
0–1	3–0	3–0	0–0	1–1	3–3	1–2	1–3	0–2	0–0	2–1	—	0–0	1–1
2–1	2–0	0–1	1–1	0–0	3–2	2–2	2–1	0–3	2–0	4–0	2–1	—	2–1
1–1	1–1	1–0	1–1	1–1	1–2	0–0	0–1	1–1	4–1	3–0	2–0	2–2	—

BARCLAYS LEAGUE FINAL TABLES 1991–92

First Division

			Home		Goals		Away			Goals			
	P	W	D	L	F	A	W	D	L	F	A	Pts	GD
1 Leeds U	42	13	8	0	38	13	9	8	4	36	24	82	+37
2 Manchester U	42	12	7	2	34	13	9	8	4	29	20	78	+30
3 Sheffield W	42	13	5	3	39	24	8	7	6	23	25	75	+13
4 Arsenal	42	12	7	2	51	22	7	8	6	30	24	72	+35
5 Manchester C	42	13	4	4	32	14	7	6	8	29	34	70	+13
6 Liverpool	42	13	5	3	34	17	3	11	7	13	23	64	+7
7 Aston Villa	42	13	3	5	31	16	4	6	11	17	28	60	+4
8 Nottingham F	42	10	7	4	36	27	6	4	11	24	31	59	+2
9 Sheffield U	42	9	6	6	29	23	7	3	11	36	40	57	+2
10 Crystal Palace	42	7	8	6	24	25	7	7	7	29	36	57	−8
11 QPR	42	6	10	5	25	21	6	8	7	23	26	54	+1
12 Everton	42	8	8	5	28	19	5	6	10	24	32	53	+1
13 Wimbledon	42	10	5	6	32	20	3	9	9	21	33	53	0
14 Chelsea	42	7	8	6	31	30	6	6	9	19	30	53	−10
15 Tottenham H	42	7	3	11	33	35	8	4	9	25	28	52	−5
16 Southampton	42	7	5	9	17	28	7	5	9	22	27	52	−16
17 Oldham Ath	42	11	5	5	46	36	3	4	14	17	31	51	−4
18 Norwich C	42	8	6	7	29	28	3	6	12	18	35	45	−16
19 Coventry C	42	6	7	8	18	15	5	4	12	17	29	44	−9
20 Luton T	42	10	7	4	25	17	0	5	16	13	54	42	−33
21 Notts Co	42	7	5	9	24	29	3	5	13	16	33	40	−22
22 West Ham U	42	6	6	9	22	24	3	5	13	15	35	38	−22

LEADING GOALSCORERS 1991–92

DIVISION 1	League	FA Cup	Rumbelows League Cup	Other Cups	Total
Ian Wright (Arsenal) (Including 5 for Crystal Palace)	29	0	2	0	31
Gary Lineker (Tottenham H)	28	0	5	2	35
Brian McClair (Manchester U)	18	1	4	2	25
David White (Manchester C)	18	0	3	0	21
David Hirst (Sheffield W)	18	1	1	1	21
John Fashanu (Wimbledon)	18	1	1	0	20
Mark Bright (Crystal Palace)	17	0	4	1	22
Lee Chapman (Leeds U)	16	0	4	0	20
Peter Beardsley (Everton)	15	1	3	1	20
Robert Fleck (Norwich C)	11	2	6	0	19
Mick Harford (Luton T) (Including 3 for Derby Co)	15	0	0	0	15
Robbie Earle (Wimbledon)	14	0	0	1	15
Teddy Sheringham (Nottingham F)	13	2	5	2	22
Alan Shearer (Southampton)	13	2	3	3	21
Mike Small (West Ham U)	13	1	4	0	18
Kevin Campbell (Arsenal)	13	0	0	1	14
Alan Smith (Arsenal)	12	1	4	0	17
Graeme Sharp (Oldham Ath)	12	1	2	0	15
Paul Merson (Arsenal)	12	0	1	0	13

Second Division		Home			Goals		Away			Goals			
	P	W	D	L	F	A	W	D	L	F	A	Pts	GD
1 Ipswich T	46	16	3	4	42	22	8	9	6	28	28	84	+20
2 Middlesbrough	46	15	6	2	37	13	8	5	10	21	28	80	+17
3 Derby Co	46	11	4	8	35	24	12	5	6	34	27	78	+18
4 Leicester C	46	14	4	5	41	24	9	4	10	21	31	77	+7
5 Cambridge U	46	10	9	4	34	19	9	8	6	31	28	74	+18
6 Blackburn R	46	14	5	4	41	21	7	6	10	29	32	74	+17
7 Charlton Ath	46	9	7	7	25	23	11	4	8	29	25	71	+6
8 Swindon T	46	15	3	5	38	22	3	12	8	31	33	69	+14
9 Portsmouth	46	15	6	2	41	12	4	6	13	24	39	69	+14
10 Watford	46	9	5	9	25	23	9	6	8	26	25	65	+3
11 Wolverhampton W	46	11	6	6	36	24	7	4	12	25	30	64	+7
12 Southend U	46	11	5	7	37	26	6	6	11	26	37	62	0
13 Bristol R	46	11	9	3	43	29	5	5	13	17	34	62	−3
14 Tranmere R	46	9	9	5	37	32	5	10	8	19	24	61	0
15 Millwall	46	10	4	9	32	32	7	6	10	32	39	61	−7
16 Barnsley	46	11	4	8	27	25	5	7	11	19	32	59	−11
17 Bristol C	46	10	8	5	30	24	3	7	13	25	47	54	−16
18 Sunderland	46	10	8	5	36	23	4	3	16	25	42	53	−4
19 Grimsby T	46	7	5	11	25	28	7	6	10	22	34	53	−15
20 Newcastle U	46	9	8	6	38	30	4	5	14	28	54	52	−18
21 Oxford U	46	10	6	7	39	30	3	5	15	27	43	50	−7
22 Plymouth Arg	46	11	5	7	26	26	2	4	17	16	38	48	−22
23 Brighton & HA	46	7	7	9	36	37	5	4	14	20	40	47	−21
24 Port Vale	46	7	8	8	23	25	3	7	13	19	34	45	−17

DIVISION 2	League	FA Cup	Rumbelows League Cup	Other Cups	Total
Duncan Shearer *(Blackburn R)* *(Including 32 for Swindon T)*	23	4	6	0	**33**
David Speedie *(Blackburn R)*	23	1	0	2	**26**
John Aldridge *(Tranmere R)*	22	3	8	7	**40**
Brett Angell *(Southend U)*	21	0	1	1	**23**
Steve Bull *(Wolverhampton W)*	20	0	3	0	**23**
Don Goodman *(Sunderland) (Including 9 for WBA)*	18	1	1	0	**20**
Gavin Peacock *(Newcastle U)*	16	1	3	2	**22**
Marco Gabbiadini *(Derby Co) (Including 5 for Sunderland, 7 for Crystal Palace)*	16	0	1	2	**19**
Paul Simpson *(Derby Co) (Including 12 for Oxford U)*	16	1	0	2	**19**
Chris Kiwomya *(Ipswich T)*	16	1	0	2	**19**
Bernie Slaven *(Middlesbrough)*	16	0	1	1	**18**
Paul Wilkinson *(Middlesbrough)*	15	4	3	2	**24**
Dion Dublin *(Cambridge U)*	15	1	3	0	**19**
Mark Gall *(Brighton & HA) (Including 3 for Maidstone U)*	15	1	0	1	**17**
Dwight Marshall *(Plymouth Arg)*	14	0	0	1	**15**

Third Division		Home			Goals		Away			Goals			
	P	W	D	L	F	A	W	D	L	F	A	Pts	GD
1 Brentford	46	17	2	4	55	29	8	5	10	26	26	82	+26
2 Birmingham C	46	15	6	2	42	22	8	6	9	27	30	81	+17
3 Huddersfield T	46	15	4	4	36	15	7	8	8	23	23	78	+21
4 Stoke C	46	14	5	4	45	24	7	9	7	24	25	77	+20
5 Stockport Co	46	15	5	3	47	19	7	5	11	28	32	76	+24
6 Peterborough U	46	13	7	3	38	20	7	7	9	27	38	74	+7
7 WBA	46	12	6	5	45	25	7	8	8	19	24	71	+15
8 Bournemouth	46	13	4	6	33	18	7	7	9	19	30	71	+4
9 Fulham	46	11	7	5	29	16	8	6	9	28	37	70	+4
10 Leyton Orient	46	12	7	4	36	18	6	4	13	26	34	65	+10
11 Hartlepool U	46	12	5	6	30	21	6	6	11	27	36	65	0
12 Reading	46	9	8	6	33	27	7	5	11	26	35	61	−3
13 Bolton W	46	10	9	4	26	19	4	8	11	31	37	59	+1
14 Hull C	46	9	4	10	28	23	7	7	9	26	31	59	0
15 Wigan Ath	46	11	6	6	33	21	4	8	11	25	43	59	−6
16 Bradford C	46	8	10	5	36	30	5	9	9	26	31	58	+1
17 Preston NE	46	12	7	4	42	32	3	5	15	19	40	57	−11
18 Chester C	46	10	6	7	34	29	4	8	11	22	30	56	−3
19 Swansea C	46	10	9	4	35	24	4	5	14	20	41	56	−10
20 Exeter C	46	11	7	5	34	25	3	4	16	23	55	53	−23
21 Bury	46	8	7	8	31	31	5	5	13	24	43	51	−19
22 Shrewsbury T	46	7	7	9	30	31	5	4	14	23	37	47	−15
23 Torquay U	46	13	3	7	29	19	0	5	18	13	49	47	−26
24 Darlington	46	5	5	13	31	39	5	2	16	25	51	37	−34

DIVISION 3	League	FA Cup	Rumbelows League Cup	Other Cups	Total
Dean Holdsworth *(Brentford)*	24	4	6	4	38
Iwan Roberts *(Huddersfield T)*	24	3	3	4	34
Wayne Biggins *(Stoke C)*	22	0	2	4	28
Jimmy Quinn *(Bournemouth)*	19	2	2	1	24
Steve Moran *(Exeter C)*	19	1	0	1	21
Mark Stein *(Stoke C) (Including 1 for Oxford U)*	17	0	0	6	23
Nigel Gleghorn *(Birmingham C)*	17	0	5	0	22
Gary Blissett *(Brentford)*	17	1	0	0	18
Ian Stevens *(Bury)*	17	0	0	1	18
Ken Charlery *(Peterborough U)*	16	1	2	7	26
Jim Gannon *(Stockport Co)*	16	1	0	4	21
Kevin Francis *(Stockport Co)*	15	1	1	9	26
Andy Walker *(Bolton W)*	15	3	0	0	18
Gary Worthington *(Wigan Ath)*	15	1	2	0	18

Fourth Division				Home			Away			Goals			
	P	W	D	L	F	A	W	D	L	F	A	Pts	GD
1 Burnley	42	14	4	3	42	16	11	4	6	37	27	83	+36
2 Rotherham U	42	12	6	3	38	16	10	5	6	32	21	77	+33
3 Mansfield T	42	13	4	4	43	26	10	4	7	32	27	77	+22
4 Blackpool	42	17	3	1	48	13	5	7	9	23	32	76	+26
5 Scunthorpe U	42	14	5	2	39	18	7	4	10	25	41	72	+5
6 Crewe Alex	42	12	6	3	33	20	8	4	9	33	31	70	+15
7 Barnet	42	16	1	4	48	23	5	5	11	33	38	69	+20
8 Rochdale	42	12	6	3	34	22	6	7	8	23	31	67	+4
9 Cardiff C	42	13	3	5	42	26	4	12	5	24	27	66	+13
10 Lincoln C	42	9	5	7	21	24	8	6	7	29	20	62	+6
11 Gillingham	42	12	5	4	41	19	3	7	11	22	34	57	+10
12 Scarborough	42	12	5	4	39	28	3	7	11	25	40	57	-4
13 Chesterfield	42	6	7	8	26	28	8	4	9	23	33	53	-12
14 Wrexham	42	11	4	6	31	26	3	5	13	21	47	51	-21
15 Walsall	42	5	10	6	28	26	7	3	11	20	32	49	-10
16 Northampton T	42	5	9	7	25	23	6	4	11	21	34	46	-11
17 Hereford U	42	9	4	8	31	24	3	4	14	13	33	44	-13
18 Maidstone U	42	6	9	6	24	22	2	9	10	21	34	42	-11
19 York C	42	6	9	6	26	23	2	7	12	16	35	40	-16
20 Halifax T	42	7	5	9	23	35	3	3	15	11	40	38	-41
21 Doncaster R	42	6	2	13	21	35	3	6	12	19	30	35	-25
22 Carlisle U	42	5	9	7	24	27	2	4	15	17	40	34	-26

Aldershot's record expunged from the table.

DIVISION 4	League	FA Cup	Rumbelows League Cup	Other Cups	Total
Dave Bamber *(Blackpool)*	26	1	6	2	35
Phil Stant *(Mansfield T)*	26	0	0	0	26
Mike Conroy *(Burnley)*	24	1	2	2	29
Carl Dale *(Cardiff C)*	22	0	0	2	24
Dave Crown *(Gillingham)*	22	0	0	1	23
Chris Pike *(Cardiff C)*	21	1	0	1	23
Gary Bull *(Barnet)*	20	2	2	2	26
Tony Cunningham *(Rotherham U)*	18	1	0	0	19
Rod McDonald *(Walsall)*	18	0	0	0	18
Andy Flounders *(Rochdale)*	17	1	0	0	18
Steve Lovell *(Gillingham)*	16	0	1	0	17
Tony Naylor *(Crewe Alex)*	15	3	3	2	23
Steve Norris *(Chesterfield) (Including 5 for Halifax T)*	15	1	0	0	16
Craig Hignett *(Crewe Alex)*	13	2	1	3	19

N.B. Other Cups: European Cup, Cup-Winners' Cup, UEFA Cup, Zenith Data Systems Cup and Autoglass Trophy plus play-offs.

DIVISION ONE LEAGUE POSITIONS 1966–67 TO 1990–91

	1990–91	1989–90	1988–89	1987–88	1986–87	1985–86	1984–85	1983–84	1982–83	1981–82	1980–81	1979–80	1978–79
Arsenal	1	4	1	6	4	7	7	6	10	5	3	4	7
Aston Villa	17	2	17	–	22	16	10	10	6	11	1	7	8
Birmingham C	–	–	–	–	–	21	–	20	17	16	13	–	21
Blackpool	–	–	–	–	–	–	–	–	–	–	–	–	–
Bolton W	–	–	–	–	–	–	–	–	–	–	–	22	17
Brighton & HA	–	–	–	–	–	–	–	–	22	13	19	16	–
Bristol C	–	–	–	–	–	–	–	–	–	–	–	20	13
Burnley	–	–	–	–	–	–	–	–	–	–	–	–	–
Carlisle U	–	–	–	–	–	–	–	–	–	–	–	–	–
Charlton Ath	–	19	14	17	19	–	–	–	–	–	–	–	–
Chelsea	11	5	–	18	14	6	6	–	–	–	–	–	22
Coventry C	16	12	7	10	10	17	18	19	19	14	16	15	10
Crystal Palace	3	15	–	–	–	–	–	–	–	–	22	13	–
Derby Co	20	16	5	15	–	–	–	–	–	–	–	21	19
Everton	9	6	8	4	1	2	1	7	7	8	15	19	4
Fulham	–	–	–	–	–	–	–	–	–	–	–	–	–
Huddersfield T	–	–	–	–	–	–	–	–	–	–	–	–	–
Ipswich T	–	–	–	–	–	20	17	12	9	2	2	3	6
Leeds U	4	–	–	–	–	–	–	–	–	20	9	11	5
Leicester C	–	–	–	–	20	19	15	15	–	–	21	–	–
Liverpool	2	1	2	1	2	1	2	1	1	1	5	1	1
Luton T	18	17	16	9	7	9	13	16	18	–	–	–	–
Manchester C	5	14	–	–	21	15	–	–	20	10	12	17	15
Manchester U	6	13	11	2	11	4	4	4	3	3	8	2	9
Middlesbrough	–	–	18	–	–	–	–	–	–	22	14	9	12
Millwall	–	20	10	–	–	–	–	–	–	–	–	–	–
Newcastle U	–	–	20	8	17	11	14	–	–	–	–	–	–
Norwich C	15	10	4	14	5	–	20	14	14	–	20	12	16
Nottingham F	8	9	3	3	8	8	9	3	5	12	7	5	2
Notts Co	–	–	–	–	–	–	–	21	15	15	–	–	–
Oxford U	–	–	–	21	18	18	–	–	–	–	–	–	–
Portsmouth	–	–	–	19	–	–	–	–	–	–	–	–	–
QPR	12	11	9	5	16	13	19	5	–	–	–	–	20
Sheffield U	13	–	–	–	–	–	–	–	–	–	–	–	–
Sheffield W	–	18	15	11	13	5	8	–	–	–	–	–	–
Southampton	14	7	13	12	12	14	5	2	12	7	6	8	14
Stoke C	–	–	–	–	–	–	22	18	13	18	11	18	–
Sunderland	19	–	–	–	–	–	21	13	16	19	17	–	–
Swansea City	–	–	–	–	–	–	–	–	21	6	–	–	–
Tottenham H	10	3	6	13	3	10	3	8	4	4	10	14	11
Watford	–	–	–	20	9	12	11	11	2	–	–	–	–
WBA	–	–	–	–	–	22	12	17	11	17	4	10	3
West Ham U	–	–	19	16	15	3	16	9	8	9	–	–	–
Wimbledon	7	8	12	7	6	–	–	–	–	–	–	–	–
Wolv'hampton W	–	–	–	–	–	–	–	22	–	21	18	6	18

Team	1977–78	1976–77	1975–76	1974–75	1973–74	1972–73	1971–72	1970–71	1969–70	1968–69	1967–68	1966–67
Arsenal	5	8	17	16	10	2	5	1	12	4	9	7
Aston Villa	8	4	16	–	–	–	–	–	–	–	–	21
Birmingham C	11	13	19	17	19	10	–	–	–	–	–	–
Blackpool	–	–	–	–	–	–	–	22	–	–	–	22
Bolton W	–	–	–	–	–	–	–	–	–	–	–	–
Brighton & HA	–	–	–	–	–	–	–	–	–	–	–	–
Bristol C	17	18	–	–	–	–	–	–	–	–	–	–
Burnley	–	–	21	10	6	–	–	21	14	14	14	14
Carlisle	–	–	–	22	–	–	–	–	–	–	–	–
Charlton Ath	–	–	–	–	–	–	–	–	–	–	–	–
Chelsea	16	–	–	21	17	12	7	6	3	5	6	9
Coventry C	7	19	14	14	16	19	18	10	6	20	20	–
Crystal Palace	–	–	–	–	–	21	20	18	20	–	–	–
Derby Co	12	15	4	1	3	7	1	9	4	–	–	–
Everton	3	9	11	4	7	17	15	14	1	3	5	6
Fulham	–	–	–	–	–	–	–	–	–	–	22	18
Huddersfield T	–	–	–	–	–	–	22	15	–	–	–	–
Ipswich T	18	3	6	3	4	4	13	19	18	12	–	–
Leeds U	9	10	5	9	1	3	2	2	2	1	4	4
Leicester C	22	11	7	18	9	16	12	–	–	21	13	8
Liverpool	2	1	1	2	2	1	3	5	5	2	3	5
Luton T	–	–	–	20	–	–	–	–	–	–	–	–
Manchester C	4	2	8	8	14	11	4	11	10	13	1	15
Manchester U	10	6	3	–	21	18	8	8	8	11	2	1
Middlesbrough	14	12	13	7	–	–	–	–	–	–	–	–
Millwall	–	–	–	–	–	–	–	–	–	–	–	–
Newcastle U	21	5	15	15	15	9	11	12	7	9	10	20
Norwich C	13	16	10	–	22	20	–	–	–	–	–	–
Nottingham F	1	–	–	–	–	–	21	16	15	18	11	2
Notts Co	–	–	–	–	–	–	–	–	–	–	–	–
Oxford U	–	–	–	–	–	–	–	–	–	–	–	–
Portsmouth	–	–	–	–	–	–	–	–	–	–	–	–
QPR	19	14	2	11	8	–	–	–	–	22	–	–
Sheffield U	–	–	22	6	13	14	10	–	–	–	21	10
Sheffield W	–	–	–	–	–	–	–	–	22	15	19	11
Southampton	–	–	–	–	20	13	19	7	19	7	16	19
Stoke C	–	21	12	5	5	15	17	13	9	19	18	12
Sunderland	–	20	–	–	–	–	–	–	21	17	15	17
Swansea City	–	–	–	–	–	–	–	–	–	–	–	–
Tottenham H	–	22	9	19	11	8	6	3	11	6	7	3
Watford	–	–	–	–	–	–	–	–	–	–	–	–
WBA	6	7	–	–	–	22	16	17	16	10	8	13
West Ham U	20	17	18	13	18	6	14	20	17	8	12	16
Wimbledon	–	–	–	–	–	–	–	–	–	–	–	–
Wolv'hampton W	15	–	20	12	12	5	9	4	13	16	17	–

DIVISION TWO LEAGUE POSITIONS 1966–67 TO 1990–91

	1990–91	1989–90	1988–89	1987–88	1986–87	1985–86	1984–85	1983–84	1982–83	1981–82	1980–81	1979–80	1978–79
Aston Villa	–	–	–	2	–	–	–	–	–	–	–	–	–
Barnsley	8	19	7	14	11	12	11	14	10	6	–	–	–
Birmingham C	–	–	23	19	19	–	2	–	–	–	–	3	–
Blackburn R	19	5	5	5	12	19	5	6	11	10	4	–	22
Blackpool	–	–	–	–	–	–	–	–	–	–	–	–	–
Bolton W	–	–	–	–	–	–	–	–	22	19	18	–	–
Bournemouth	–	22	12	17	–	–	–	–	–	–	–	–	–
Bradford C	–	23	14	4	10	13	–	–	–	–	–	–	–
Brighton & HA	6	18	19	–	22	11	6	9	–	–	–	–	2
Bristol C	9	–	–	–	–	–	–	–	–	–	21	–	–
Bristol R	13	–	–	–	–	–	–	–	–	–	22	19	16
Burnley	–	–	–	–	–	–	–	–	21	–	–	21	13
Bury	–	–	–	–	–	–	–	–	–	–	–	–	–
Cambridge U	–	–	–	–	–	–	–	22	12	14	13	8	12
Cardiff C	–	–	–	–	–	–	21	15	–	20	19	15	9
Carlisle U	–	–	–	–	–	20	16	7	14	–	–	–	–
Charlton Ath	16	–	–	–	–	2	17	13	17	13	–	22	19
Chelsea	–	–	1	–	–	–	–	1	18	12	12	4	–
Coventry C	–	–	–	–	–	–	–	–	–	–	–	–	–
Crystal Palace	–	–	3	6	6	5	15	18	15	5	–	–	1
Derby Co	–	–	–	–	1	–	–	20	13	16	6	–	–
Fulham	–	–	–	–	–	22	9	11	4	–	–	20	10
Grimsby T	–	–	–	–	21	15	10	5	19	17	7	–	–
Hereford U	–	–	–	–	–	–	–	–	–	–	–	–	–
Huddersfield T	–	–	–	23	17	16	13	12	–	–	–	–	–
Hull C	24	14	21	15	14	6	–	–	–	–	–	–	–
Ipswich T	14	9	8	8	5	–	–	–	–	–	–	–	–
Leeds U	–	1	10	7	4	14	7	10	8	–	–	–	–
Leicester C	22	13	15	13	–	–	–	–	3	8	–	1	17
Leyton Orient	–	–	–	–	–	–	–	–	–	22	17	14	11
Luton T	–	–	–	–	–	–	–	–	–	1	5	6	18
Manchester C	–	–	2	9	–	–	3	4	–	–	–	–	–
Manchester U	–	–	–	–	–	–	–	–	–	–	–	–	–
Mansfield T	–	–	–	–	–	–	–	–	–	–	–	–	–
Middlesbrough	7	21	–	3	–	21	19	17	16	–	–	–	–
Millwall	5	–	–	1	16	9	–	–	–	–	–	–	21.
Newcastle U	11	3	–	–	–	–	–	3	5	9	11	9	8
Northampton T	–	–	–	–	–	–	–	–	–	–	–	–	–
Norwich C	–	–	–	–	–	1	–	–	–	3	–	–	–
Nottingham F	–	–	–	–	–	–	–	–	–	–	–	–	–
Notts Co	4	–	–	–	–	–	20	–	–	–	2	17	6
Oldham Ath	1	8	16	10	3	8	14	19	7	11	15	11	14
Oxford U	10	17	17	–	–	–	1	–	–	–	–	–	–
Plymouth Arg	18	16	18	16	7	–	–	–	–	–	–	–	–
Port Vale	15	11	–	–	–	–	–	–	–	–	–	–	–
Portsmouth	17	12	20	–	2	4	4	16	–	–	–	–	–
Preston NE	–	–	–	–	–	–	–	–	–	–	20	10	7

1977–78	1976–77	1975–76	1974–75	1973–74	1972–73	1971–72	1970–71	1969–70	1968–69	1967–68	1966–67	
–	–	–	2	14	3	–	–	21	18	16	–	Aston Villa
–	–	–	–	–	–	–	–	–	–	–	–	Barnsley
–	–	–	–	–	–	2	9	18	7	4	10	Birmingham C
5	12	15	–	–	–	–	21	8	19	8	4	Blackburn R
20	5	10	7	5	7	6	–	2	8	3	–	Blackpool
1	4	4	10	11	–	–	22	16	17	12	9	Bolton W
–	–	–	–	–	–	–	–	–	–	–	–	Bournemouth
–	–	–	–	–	–	–	–	–	–	–	–	Bradford C
4	–	–	–	–	22	–	–	–	–	–	–	Brighton & HA
–	–	2	5	16	5	8	19	14	16	19	15	Bristol C
18	15	18	19	–	–	–	–	–	–	–	–	Bristol R
11	16	–	–	–	1	7	–	–	–	–	–	Burnley
–	–	–	–	–	–	–	–	–	21	–	22	Bury
–	–	–	–	–	–	–	–	–	–	–	–	Cambridge U
19	18	–	21	17	20	19	3	7	5	13	20	Cardiff C
–	20	19	–	3	18	10	4	12	12	10	3	Carlisle U
17	7	9	–	–	–	21	20	20	3	15	19	Charlton Ath
–	2	11	–	–	–	–	–	–	–	–	–	Chelsea
–	–	–	–	–	–	–	–	–	–	–	1	Coventry C
9	–	–	–	20	–	–	–	–	2	11	7	Crystal Palace
–	–	–	–	–	–	–	–	–	1	18	17	Derby Co
10	17	12	9	13	9	20	–	–	22	–	–	Fulham
–	–	–	–	–	–	–	–	–	–	–	–	Grimsby T
–	22	–	–	–	–	–	–	–	–	–	–	Hereford U
–	–	–	–	–	21	–	–	1	6	14	6	Huddersfield T
22	14	14	8	9	13	12	5	13	11	17	12	Hull C
–	–	–	–	–	–	–	–	–	–	1	5	Ipswich T
–	–	–	–	–	–	–	–	–	–	–	–	Leeds U
–	–	–	–	–	–	–	1	3	–	–	–	Leicester C
14	19	13	12	4	15	17	17	–	–	–	–	Leyton Orient
13	6	7	–	2	12	13	6	–	–	–	–	Luton T
–	–	–	–	–	–	–	–	–	–	–	–	Manchester C
–	–	–	1	–	–	–	–	–	–	–	–	Manchester U
21	–	–	–	–	–	–	–	–	–	–	–	Mansfield T
–	–	–	–	1	4	9	7	4	4	6	–	Middlesbrough
16	10	–	20	12	11	3	8	10	10	7	8	Millwall
–	–	–	–	–	–	–	–	–	–	–	–	Newcastle U
–	–	–	–	–	–	–	–	–	–	–	21	Northampton T
–	–	–	3	–	–	1	10	11	13	9	11	Norwich C
–	3	8	16	7	14	–	–	–	–	–	–	Nottingham F
15	8	5	14	10	–	–	–	–	–	–	–	Notts Co
8	13	17	18	–	–	–	–	–	–	–	–	Oldham Ath
–	–	20	11	18	8	15	14	15	20	–	–	Oxford U
–	21	16	–	–	–	–	–	–	–	22	16	Plymouth Arg
–	–	–	–	–	–	–	–	–	–	–	–	Port Vale
–	–	22	17	15	17	16	16	17	15	5	14	Portsmouth
–	–	–	–	21	19	18	–	22	14	20	13	Preston NE

DIVISION TWO LEAGUE POSITIONS 1966–67 TO 1990–91

	1990–91	1989–90	1988–89	1987–88	1986–87	1985–86	1984–85	1983–84	1982–83	1981–82	1980–81	1979–80	1978–79
QPR	–	–	–	–	–	–	–	–	1	5	8	5	–
Reading	–	–	–	22	13	–	–	–	–	–	–	–	–
Rotherham U	–	–	–	–	–	–	–	–	20	7	–	–	–
Sheffield U	–	2	–	21	9	7	18	–	–	–	–	–	20
Sheffield W	3	–	–	–	–	–	–	2	6	4	10	–	–
Shrewsbury T	–	–	22	18	18	17	8	8	9	18	14	13	–
Southampton	–	–	–	–	–	–	–	–	–	–	–	–	–
Stoke C	–	24	13	11	8	10	–	–	–	–	–	–	3
Sunderland	–	6	11	–	20	18	–	–	–	–	–	2	4
Swansea C	–	–	–	–	–	–	–	21	–	–	3	12	–
Swindon T	21	4	6	12	–	–	–	–	–	–	–	–	–
Tottenham H	–	–	–	–	–	–	–	–	–	–	–	–	–
Walsall	–	–	24	–	–	–	–	–	–	–	–	–	–
Watford	20	15	4	–	–	–	–	–	–	2	9	18	–
WBA	23	20	9	20	15	–	–	–	–	–	–	–	–
West Ham U	2	7	–	–	–	–	–	–	–	–	1	7	5
Wimbledon	–	–	–	–	–	3	12	–	–	–	–	–	–
Wolv'hampton W	12	10	–	–	–	–	22	–	2	–	–	–	–
Wrexham	–	–	–	–	–	–	–	–	–	21	16	16	15
York C	–	–	–	–	–	–	–	–	–	–	–	–	–

DIVISION THREE LEAGUE POSITIONS 1966–67 TO 1990–91

	1990–91	1989–90	1988–89	1987–88	1986–87	1985–86	1984–85	1983–84	1982–83	1981–82	1980–81	1979–80	1978–79
Aldershot	–	–	24	20	–	–	–	–	–	–	–	–	–
Aston Villa	–	–	–	–	–	–	–	–	–	–	–	–	–
Barnsley	–	–	–	–	–	–	–	–	–	–	2	11	–
Barrow	–	–	–	–	–	–	–	–	–	–	–	–	–
Birmingham C	12	7	–	–	–	–	–	–	–	–	–	–	–
Blackburn R	–	–	–	–	–	–	–	–	–	–	–	2	–
Blackpool	–	23	19	10	9	12	–	–	–	–	23	18	12
Bolton W	4	6	10	–	21	18	17	10	–	–	–	–	–
Bournemouth	9	–	–	–	1	15	10	17	14	–	–	–	–
Bradford C	8	–	–	–	–	–	1	7	12	–	–	–	–
Brentford	6	13	7	12	11	10	13	20	9	8	9	19	10
Brighton & HA	–	–	–	2	–	–	–	–	–	–	–	–	–
Bristol C	–	2	11	5	6	9	5	–	–	23	–	–	–
Bristol R	–	1	5	8	19	16	6	5	7	15	–	–	–
Burnley	–	–	–	–	–	–	21	12	–	1	8	–	–
Bury	7	5	13	14	16	20	–	–	–	–	–	21	19

1977–78	1976–77	1975–76	1974–75	1973–74	1972–73	1971–72	1970–71	1969–70	1968–69	1967–68	1966–67	
–	–	–	–	–	2	4	11	9	–	2	–	QPR
–	–	–	–	–	–	–	–	–	–	–	–	Reading
–	–	–	–	–	–	–	–	–	–	21	18	Rotherham U
12	11	–	–	–	–	–	2	6	9	–	–	Sheffield U
–	–	–	22	19	10	14	15	–	–	–	–	Sheffield W
–	–	–	–	–	–	–	–	–	–	–	–	Shrewsbury T
2	9	6	13	–	–	–	–	–	–	–	–	Southampton
7	–	–	–	–	–	–	–	–	–	–	–	Stoke C
6	–	1	4	6	6	5	13	–	–	–	–	Sunderland
–	–	–	–	–	–	–	–	–	–	–	–	Swansea C
–	–	–	–	22	16	11	12	5	–	–	–	Swindon T
3	–	–	–	–	–	–	–	–	–	–	–	Tottenham H
–	–	–	–	–	–	–	–	–	–	–	–	Walsall
–	–	–	–	–	–	22	18	19	–	–	–	Watford
–	–	3	6	8	–	–	–	–	–	–	–	WBA
–	–	–	–	–	–	–	–	–	–	–	–	West Ham U
–	–	–	–	–	–	–	–	–	–	–	–	Wimbledon
–	1	–	–	–	–	–	–	–	–	–	2	Wolv'hampton W
–	–	–	–	–	–	–	–	–	–	–	–	Wrexham
–	–	21	15	–	–	–	–	–	–	–	–	York C

1977–78	1976–77	1975–76	1974–75	1973–74	1972–73	1971–72	1970–71	1969–70	1968–69	1967–68	1966–67	
–	–	21	20	8	–	–	–	–	–	–	–	Aldershot
–	–	–	–	–	–	1	4	–	–	–	–	Aston Villa
–	–	–	–	–	–	22	12	7	10	–	–	Barnsley
–	–	–	–	–	–	–	–	23	19	8	–	Barrow
–	–	–	–	–	–	–	–	–	–	–	–	Birmingham C
–	–	–	1	13	3	10	–	–	–	–	–	Blackburn R
–	–	–	–	–	–	–	–	–	–	–	–	Blackpool
–	–	–	–	–	1	7	–	–	–	–	–	Bolton W
–	–	–	21	11	7	3	–	21	4	12	20	Bournemouth
22	–	–	–	–	–	24	19	10	–	–	–	Bradford C
–	–	–	–	–	22	–	–	–	–	–	–	Brentford
–	2	4	19	19	–	2	14	5	12	10	19	Brighton & HA
–	–	–	–	–	–	–	–	–	–	–	–	Bristol C
–	–	–	–	2	5	6	6	3	16	15	5	Bristol R
–	–	–	–	–	–	–	–	–	–	–	–	Burnley
15	7	13	14	–	–	–	22	19	–	2	–	Bury

	1990-91	1989-90	1988-89	1987-88	1986-87	1985-86	1984-85	1983-84	1982-83	1981-82	1980-81	1979-80	1978-79
Cambridge U	1	–	–	–	–	–	24	–	–	–	–	–	–
Cardiff C	–	21	16	–	–	22	–	–	2	–	–	–	–
Carlisle U	–	–	–	–	21	–	–	–	–	2	19	6	6
Charlton Ath	–	–	–	–	–	–	–	–	–	–	3	–	–
Chester C	19	16	8	15	15	–	–	–	–	24	18	9	16
Chesterfield	–	–	22	18	17	17	–	–	24	11	5	4	20
Colchester U	–	–	–	–	–	–	–	–	–	–	22	5	7
Crewe Alex	22	12	–	–	–	–	–	–	–	–	–	–	–
Crystal Palace	–	–	–	–	–	–	–	–	–	–	–	–	–
Darlington	–	–	–	–	22	13	–	–	–	–	–	–	–
Derby Co	–	–	–	–	–	3	7	–	–	–	–	–	–
Doncaster R	–	–	–	24	13	11	14	–	23	19	–	–	–
Exeter C	16	–	–	–	–	–	–	24	19	18	11	8	9
Fulham	21	20	4	9	18	–	–	–	–	3	13	–	–
Gillingham	–	–	23	13	5	5	4	8	13	6	15	16	4
Grimsby T	3	–	–	22	–	–	–	–	–	–	–	1	–
Halifax T	–	–	–	–	–	–	–	–	–	–	–	–	–
Hartlepool U	–	–	–	–	–	–	–	–	–	–	–	–	–
Hereford U	–	–	–	–	–	–	–	–	–	–	–	–	–
Huddersfield T	11	8	14	–	–	–	–	–	3	17	4	–	–
Hull C	–	–	–	–	–	–	3	4	–	–	24	20	8
Leyton Orient	13	14	–	–	–	–	22	11	20	–	–	–	–
Lincoln C	–	–	–	–	–	21	19	14	6	4	–	–	24
Luton T	–	–	–	–	–	–	–	–	–	–	–	–	–
Mansfield T	24	15	15	19	10	–	–	–	–	–	–	23	18
Middlesbrough	–	–	–	–	2	–	–	–	–	–	–	–	–
Millwall	–	–	–	–	–	–	2	9	17	9	16	14	–
Newport Co	–	–	–	–	23	19	18	13	4	16	12	–	–
Northampton T	–	22	20	6	–	–	–	–	–	–	–	–	–
Notts Co	–	3	9	4	7	8	–	–	–	–	–	–	–
Oldham Ath	–	–	–	–	–	–	–	–	–	–	–	–	–
Oxford U	–	–	–	–	–	–	–	1	5	5	14	17	11
Peterborough U	–	–	–	–	–	–	–	–	–	–	–	–	21
Plymouth Arg	–	–	–	–	–	2	15	19	8	10	7	15	15
Portsmouth	–	–	–	–	–	–	–	–	1	13	6	–	–
Port Vale	–	–	3	11	12	–	–	23	–	–	–	–	–
Preston NE	17	19	6	16	–	–	23	16	16	14	–	–	–
QPR	–	–	–	–	–	–	–	–	–	–	–	–	–
Reading	15	10	18	–	–	1	9	–	21	12	10	7	–
Rochdale	–	–	–	–	–	–	–	–	–	–	–	–	–
Rotherham U	23	9	–	21	14	14	12	18	–	–	1	13	17
Scunthorpe U	–	–	–	–	–	–	–	21	–	–	–	–	–
Sheffield U	–	–	2	–	–	–	–	3	11	–	21	12	–
Sheffield W	–	–	–	–	–	–	–	–	–	–	–	3	14
Shrewsbury T	18	11	–	–	–	–	–	–	–	–	–	–	1
Southend U	2	–	21	17	–	–	–	22	15	7	–	22	13
Southport	–	–	–	–	–	–	–	–	–	–	–	–	–
Stockport Co	–	–	–	–	–	–	–	–	–	–	–	–	–
Stoke C	14	–	–	–	–	–	–	–	–	–	–	–	–
Sunderland	–	–	–	1	–	–	–	–	–	–	–	–	–

	1977-78	1976-77	1975-76	1974-75	1973-74	1972-73	1971-72	1970-71	1969-70	1968-69	1967-68	1966-67
Cambridge U	2	–	–	–	21	–	–	–	–	–	–	–
Cardiff C	–	–	2	–	–	–	–	–	–	–	–	–
Carlisle U	13	–	–	–	–	–	–	–	–	–	–	–
Charlton Ath	–	–	–	3	14	11	–	–	–	–	–	–
Chester C	5	13	17	–	–	–	–	–	–	–	–	–
Chesterfield	9	18	15	15	5	16	13	5	–	–	–	–
Colchester U	8	–	22	11	–	–	–	–	–	–	22	13
Crewe Alex	–	–	–	–	–	–	–	–	–	23	–	–
Crystal Palace	–	3	5	5	–	–	–	–	–	–	–	–
Darlington	–	–	–	–	–	–	–	–	–	–	–	22
Derby C	–	–	–	–	–	–	–	–	–	–	–	–
Doncaster R	–	–	–	–	–	–	–	23	11	–	–	23
Exeter C	17	–	–	–	–	–	–	–	–	–	–	–
Fulham	–	–	–	–	–	–	–	2	4	–	–	–
Gillingham	7	12	14	10	–	–	–	24	20	20	11	11
Grimsby T	–	23	18	16	6	9	–	–	–	–	21	17
Halifax T	–	–	24	17	9	20	17	3	18	–	–	–
Hartlepool U	–	–	–	–	–	–	–	–	–	22	–	–
Hereford U	23	–	1	12	18	–	–	–	–	–	–	–
Huddersfield T	–	–	–	24	10	–	–	–	–	–	–	–
Hull C	–	–	–	–	–	–	–	–	–	–	–	–
Leyton Orient	–	–	–	–	–	–	–	–	1	18	18	14
Lincoln C	16	9	–	–	–	–	–	–	–	–	–	–
Luton T	–	–	–	–	–	–	–	–	2	3	–	–
Mansfield T	–	1	11	–	–	–	21	7	6	15	20	9
Middlesbrough	–	–	–	–	–	–	–	–	–	–	–	2
Millwall	–	–	3	–	–	–	–	–	–	–	–	–
Newport Co	–	–	–	–	–	–	–	–	–	–	–	–
Northampton T	–	22	–	–	–	–	–	–	–	21	17	–
Notts Co	–	–	–	–	2	4	–	–	–	–	–	–
Oldham Ath	–	–	–	–	1	4	11	–	–	24	16	10
Oxford U	18	17	–	–	–	–	–	–	–	–	1	16
Peterborough U	4	16	10	7	–	–	–	–	–	–	24	15
Plymouth Arg	19	–	–	2	17	8	8	15	17	5	–	–
Portsmouth	24	20	–	–	–	–	–	–	–	–	–	–
Port Vale	21	19	12	6	20	6	15	17	–	–	–	–
Preston NE	3	6	8	9	–	–	–	1	–	–	–	–
QPR	–	–	–	–	–	–	–	–	–	–	–	1
Reading	–	21	–	–	–	–	–	21	8	14	5	4
Rochdale	–	–	–	–	24	13	18	16	9	–	–	–
Rotherham U	20	4	16	–	–	21	5	8	14	11	–	–
Scunthorpe U	–	–	–	–	–	24	–	–	–	–	23	18
Sheffield U	–	–	–	–	–	–	–	–	–	–	–	–
Sheffield W	14	8	20	–	–	–	–	–	–	–	–	–
Shrewsbury T	11	10	9	–	22	15	12	13	15	17	3	6
Southend U	–	–	23	18	12	14	–	–	–	–	–	–
Southport	–	–	–	–	23	–	–	–	22	8	14	–
Stockport Co	–	–	–	–	–	–	–	–	24	9	13	–
Stoke C	–	–	–	–	–	–	–	–	–	–	–	–
Sunderland	–	–	–	–	–	–	–	–	–	–	–	–

DIVISION THREE LEAGUE POSITIONS 1966–67 TO 1990–91

	1990–91	1989–90	1988–89	1987–88	1986–87	1985–86	1984–85	1983–84	1982–83	1981–82	1980–81	1979–80	1978–79
Swansea C	20	17	12	–	–	24	20	–	–	–	–	–	3
Swindon T	–	–	–	–	3	–	–	–	–	22	17	10	5
Torquay U	–	–	–	–	–	–	–	–	–	–	–	–	–
Tranmere R	5	4	–	–	–	–	–	–	–	–	–	–	23
Walsall	–	24	–	3	8	6	11	6	10	20	20	–	22
Watford	–	–	–	–	–	–	–	–	–	–	–	–	2
Wigan Ath	10	18	17	7	4	4	16	15	18	–	–	–	–
Wimbledon	–	–	–	–	–	–	–	2	–	21	–	24	–
Wolv'hampton W	–	–	1	–	–	23	–	–	–	–	–	–	–
Workington	–	–	–	–	–	–	–	–	–	–	–	–	–
Wrexham	–	–	–	–	–	–	–	–	22	–	–	–	–
York City	–	–	–	23	20	7	8	–	–	–	–	–	–

DIVISION FOUR LEAGUE POSITIONS 1966–67 TO 1990–91

	1990–91	1989–90	1988–89	1987–88	1986–87	1985–86	1984–85	1983–84	1982–83	1981–82	1980–81	1979–80	1978–79
Aldershot	23	22	–	–	6	16	13	5	18	16	6	10	5
Barnsley	–	–	–	–	–	–	–	–	–	–	–	–	4
Barrow	–	–	–	–	–	–	–	–	–	–	–	–	–
Blackpool	5	–	–	–	–	–	2	6	21	12	–	–	–
Bolton W	–	–	–	3	–	–	–	–	–	–	–	–	–
Bournemouth	–	–	–	–	–	–	–	–	–	4	13	11	18
Bradford C	–	–	–	–	–	–	–	–	–	2	14	5	15
Bradford PA	–	–	–	–	–	–	–	–	–	–	–	–	–
Brentford	–	–	–	–	–	–	–	–	–	–	–	–	–
Bristol C	–	–	–	–	–	–	–	4	14	–	–	–	–
Burnley	6	16	16	10	22	14	–	–	–	–	–	–	–
Bury	–	–	–	–	–	–	4	15	5	9	12	–	–
Cambridge U	–	6	8	15	11	22	–	–	–	–	–	–	–
Cardiff C	13	–	–	2	13	–	–	–	–	–	–	–	–
Carlisle U	20	8	12	23	–	–	–	–	–	–	–	–	–
Chester C	–	–	–	–	–	2	16	24	13	–	–	–	–
Chesterfield	18	7	–	–	–	–	1	13	–	–	–	–	–
Colchester U	–	24	22	9	5	6	7	8	6	6	–	–	–
Crewe Alex	–	–	3	17	17	12	10	16	23	24	18	23	24
Darlington	1	–	24	13	–	–	3	14	17	13	8	22	21
Doncaster R	11	20	23	–	–	–	–	2	–	–	3	12	22
Exeter C	–	1	13	22	14	21	18	–	–	–	–	–	–
Gillingham	15	14	–	–	–	–	–	–	–	–	–	–	–
Grimsby T	–	2	9	–	–	–	–	–	–	–	–	–	2
Halifax T	22	23	21	18	15	20	21	21	11	19	23	18	23
Hartlepool U	3	19	19	16	18	7	19	23	22	14	9	19	13
Hereford U	17	17	15	19	16	10	5	11	24	10	22	21	14
Huddersfield T	–	–	–	–	–	–	–	–	–	–	–	1	9

1977-78	1976-77	1975-76	1974-75	1973-74	1972-73	1971-72	1970-71	1969-70	1968-69	1967-68	1966-67	
–	–	–	–	–	23	14	11	–	–	–	21	Swansea C
10	11	19	4	–	–	–	–	–	2	9	8	Swindon T
–	–	–	–	–	–	23	10	13	6	4	7	Torquay U
12	14	–	22	16	10	20	18	16	7	19	–	Tranmere R
6	15	7	8	15	17	9	20	12	13	7	12	Walsall
–	–	–	23	7	19	–	–	–	1	6	3	Watford
–	–	–	–	–	–	–	–	–	–	–	–	Wigan Ath
–	–	–	–	–	–	–	–	–	–	–	–	Wimbledon
–	–	–	–	–	–	–	–	–	–	–	–	Wolv'hampton W
–	–	–	–	–	–	–	–	–	–	–	24	Workington
1	5	6	13	4	12	16	9	–	–	–	–	Wrexham
–	24	–	–	3	18	19	–	–	–	–	–	York City

1977-78	1976-77	1975-76	1974-75	1973-74	1972-73	1971-72	1970-71	1969-70	1968-69	1967-68	1966-67	
5	17	–	–	–	4	17	13	6	15	9	10	Aldershot
7	6	12	15	13	14	–	–	–	–	2	16	Barnsley
–	–	–	–	–	–	22	24	–	–	–	3	Barrow
–	–	–	–	–	–	–	–	–	–	–	–	Blackpool
–	–	–	–	–	–	–	–	–	–	–	–	Bolton W
17	13	6	–	–	–	–	2	–	–	–	–	Bournemouth
–	4	17	10	8	16	–	–	–	4	5	11	Bradford C
–	–	–	–	–	–	–	–	24	24	24	23	Bradford PA
4	15	18	8	19	–	3	14	5	11	14	9	Brentford
–	–	–	–	–	–	–	–	–	–	–	–	Bristol C
–	–	–	–	–	–	–	–	–	–	–	–	Burnley
–	–	–	–	4	12	9	–	–	–	–	–	Bury
–	1	13	6	–	3	10	20	–	–	–	–	Cambridge U
–	–	–	–	–	–	–	–	–	–	–	–	Cardiff C
–	–	–	–	–	–	–	–	–	–	–	–	Carlisle U
–	–	–	4	7	15	20	5	11	14	22	19	Chester C
–	–	–	–	–	–	–	–	1	20	7	15	Chesterfield
–	3	–	–	3	22	11	6	10	6	–	–	Colchester U
15	12	16	18	21	21	24	15	15	–	4	5	Crewe Alex
19	11	20	21	20	24	19	12	22	5	16	–	Darlington
12	8	10	17	22	17	12	–	–	1	10	–	Doncaster R
–	2	7	9	10	8	15	9	18	17	20	14	Exeter C
–	–	–	–	2	9	13	–	–	–	–	–	Gillingham
6	–	–	–	–	–	1	19	16	23	–	–	Grimsby T
20	21	–	–	–	–	–	–	–	2	11	12	Halifax T
21	22	14	13	11	20	18	23	23	–	3	8	Hartlepool U
–	–	–	–	–	2	–	–	–	–	–	–	Hereford U
11	9	5	–	–	–	–	–	–	–	–	–	Huddersfield T

	1990–91	1989–90	1988–89	1987–88	1986–87	1985–86	1984–85	1983–84	1982–83	1981–82	1980–81	1979–80	1978–79
Hull C	–	–	–	–	–	–	–	–	2	8	–	–	–
Leyton Orient	–	–	6	8	7	5	–	–	–	–	–	–	–
Lincoln C	14	10	10	–	24	–	–	–	–	–	2	7	–
Luton T	–	–	–	–	–	–	–	–	–	–	–	–	–
Maidstone U	19	5	–	–	–	–	–	–	–	–	–	–	–
Mansfield T	–	–	–	–	–	3	14	19	10	20	7	–	–
Newport Co	–	–	–	24	–	–	–	–	–	–	–	3	8
Northampton T	10	–	–	–	1	8	23	18	15	22	10	13	19
Notts Co	–	–	–	–	–	–	–	–	–	–	–	–	–
Oldham Ath	–	–	–	–	–	–	–	–	–	–	–	–	–
Peterborough U	4	9	7	7	10	17	11	7	9	5	5	8	–
Portsmouth	–	–	–	–	–	–	–	–	–	–	–	4	7
Port Vale	–	–	–	–	–	4	12	–	3	7	19	20	16
Preston NE	–	–	–	–	2	23	–	–	–	–	–	–	–
Reading	–	–	–	–	–	–	–	3	–	–	–	–	1
Rochdale	12	12	18	21	21	18	17	22	20	21	15	24	20
Rotherham U	–	–	1	–	–	–	–	–	–	–	–	–	–
Scarborough	9	18	5	12	–	–	–	–	–	–	–	–	–
Scunthorpe U	8	11	4	4	8	15	9	–	4	23	16	14	12
Sheffield U	–	–	–	–	–	–	–	–	–	1	–	–	–
Shrewsbury T	–	–	–	–	–	–	–	–	–	–	–	–	–
Southend U	–	3	–	–	3	9	20	–	–	–	1	–	–
Southport	–	–	–	–	–	–	–	–	–	–	–	–	–
Stockport Co	2	4	20	20	19	11	22	12	16	18	20	16	17
Swansea C	–	–	–	6	12	–	–	–	–	–	–	–	–
Swindon T	–	–	–	–	–	1	8	17	8	–	–	–	–
Torquay U	7	15	14	5	23	24	24	9	12	15	17	9	11
Tranmere R	–	–	2	14	20	19	6	10	19	11	21	15	–
Walsall	16	–	–	–	–	–	–	–	–	–	–	2	–
Watford	–	–	–	–	–	–	–	–	–	–	–	–	–
Wigan Ath	–	–	–	–	–	–	–	–	–	3	11	6	6
Wimbledon	–	–	–	–	–	–	–	–	1	–	4	–	3
Wolv'hampton W	–	–	–	1	4	–	–	–	–	–	–	–	–
Workington	–	–	–	–	–	–	–	–	–	–	–	–	–
Wrexham	24	21	7	11	9	13	15	20	–	–	–	–	–
York C	21	13	11	–	–	–	–	1	7	17	24	17	10

1977–78	1976–77	1975–76	1974–75	1973–74	1972–73	1971–72	1970–71	1969–70	1968–69	1967–68	1966–67	
–	–	–	–	–	–	–	–	–	–	–	–	Hull C
–	–	–	–	–	–	–	–	–	–	–	–	Leyton Orient
–	–	1	5	12	10	5	21	8	8	13	24	Lincoln C
–	–	–	–	–	–	–	–	–	–	1	17	Luton T
–	–	–	–	–	–	–	–	–	–	–	–	Maidstone U
–	–	–	1	17	6	–	–	–	–	–	–	Mansfield T
16	19	22	12	9	5	14	22	21	22	12	18	Newport C
10	–	2	16	5	23	21	7	14	–	–	–	Northampton T
–	–	–	–	–	–	–	1	7	19	17	20	Notts Co
–	–	–	–	–	–	–	3	19	–	–	–	Oldham Ath
–	–	–	–	1	19	8	16	9	18	–	–	Peterborough U
–	–	–	–	–	–	–	–	–	–	–	–	Portsmouth
–	–	–	–	–	–	–	–	4	13	18	13	Port Vale
–	–	–	–	–	–	–	–	–	–	–	–	Preston NE
8	–	3	7	6	7	16	–	–	–	–	–	Reading
24	18	15	19	–	–	–	–	–	3	19	21	Rochdale
–	–	–	3	15	–	–	–	–	–	–	–	Rotherham U
–	–	–	–	–	–	–	–	–	–	–	–	Scarborough
14	20	19	24	18	–	4	17	12	16	–	–	Scunthorpe U
–	–	–	–	–	–	–	–	–	–	–	–	Sheffield U
–	–	–	2	–	–	–	–	–	–	–	–	Shrewsbury T
2	10	–	–	–	–	2	18	17	7	6	6	Southend U
23	23	23	11	–	1	7	8	–	–	–	2	Southport
18	14	21	20	24	11	23	11	–	–	–	1	Stockport Co
3	5	11	22	14	–	–	–	3	10	15	–	Swansea C
–	–	–	–	–	–	–	–	–	–	–	–	Swindon T
9	16	9	14	16	18	–	–	–	–	–	–	Torquay U
–	–	4	–	–	–	–	–	–	–	–	4	Tranmere R
–	–	–	–	–	–	–	–	–	–	–	–	Walsall
1	7	8	–	–	–	–	–	–	–	–	–	Watford
–	–	–	–	–	–	–	–	–	–	–	–	Wigan Ath
13	–	–	–	–	–	–	–	–	–	–	–	Wimbledon
–	–	–	–	–	–	–	–	–	–	–	–	Wolv'hampton W
–	24	24	23	23	13	6	10	20	12	23	–	Workington
–	–	–	–	–	–	–	–	2	9	8	7	Wrexham
22	–	–	–	–	–	–	4	13	21	21	22	York C

LEAGUE CHAMPIONSHIP HONOURS

**Won on goal average. †won on goal difference.*
No championships during WWI and WWII.

First Division

	First	Pts	Second	Pts	Third	Pts
1888–9 *a*	Preston NE	40	Aston Villa	29	Wolverhampton W	28
1889–90	Preston NE	33	Everton	31	Blackburn R	27
1890–1	Everton	29	Preston NE	27	Wolverhampton / Notts Co	26
1891–2 *b*	Sunderland	42	Preston NE	37	Bolton W	36
1892–3 *c*	Sunderland	48	Preston NE	37	Everton	36
1893–4	Aston Villa	44	Sunderland	38	Derby Co	36
1894–5	Sunderland	47	Everton	42	Aston Villa	39
1895–6	Aston Villa	45	Derby Co	41	Everton	39
1896–7	Aston Villa	47	Sheffield U	36	Derby Co	36
1897–8	Sheffield U	42	Sunderland	37	Wolverhampton W	35
1898–9 *d*	Aston Villa	45	Liverpool	43	Burnley	39
1899–1900	Aston Villa	50	Sheffield U	48	Sunderland	41
1900–1	Liverpool	45	Sunderland	43	Notts Co	40
1901–2	Sunderland	44	Everton	41	Newcastle U	37
1902–3	The Wednesday	42	Aston Villa	41	Sunderland	41
1903–4	The Wednesday	47	Manchester C	44	Everton	43
1904–5	Newcastle U	48	Everton	47	Manchester C	46
1905–6 *e*	Liverpool	51	Preston NE	47	The Wednesday	44
1906–7	Newcastle U	51	Bristol C	48	Everton	45
1907–8	Manchester U	52	Aston Villa	43	Manchester C	43
1908–9	Newcastle U	53	Everton	46	Sunderland	44
1909–10	Aston Villa	53	Liverpool	48	Blackburn R	45
1910–11	Manchester U	52	Aston Villa	51	Sunderland	45
1911–12	Blackburn R	49	Everton	46	Newcastle U	44
1912–13	Sunderland	54	Aston Villa	50	Sheffield W	49
1913–14	Blackburn R	51	Aston Villa	44	Middlesbrough	43
1914–15	Everton	46	Oldham Ath	45	Blackburn R	43
1919–20 *f*	WBA	60	Burnley	51	Chelsea	49
1920–1	Burnley	59	Manchester C	54	Bolton W	52
1921–2	Liverpool	57	Tottenham H	51	Burnley	49
1922–3	Liverpool	60	Sunderland	54	Huddersfield T	53
1923–4	*Huddersfield T	57	Cardiff C	57	Sunderland	53
1924–5	Huddersfield T	58	WBA	56	Bolton W	55
1925–6	Huddersfield T	57	Arsenal	52	Sunderland	48
1926–7	Newcastle U	56	Huddersfield T	51	Sunderland	49
1927–8	Everton	53	Huddersfield T	51	Leicester C	48
1928–9	Sheffield W	52	Leicester C	51	Aston Villa	50
1929–30	Sheffield W	60	Derby Co	50	Manchester C	47
1930–1	Arsenal	66	Aston Villa	59	Sheffield W	52
1931–2	Everton	56	Arsenal	54	Sheffield W	50
1932–3	Arsenal	58	Aston Villa	54	Sheffield W	51
1933–4	Arsenal	59	Huddersfield T	56	Tottenham H	49
1934–5	Arsenal	58	Sunderland	54	Sheffield W	49
1935–6	Sunderland	56	Derby Co	48	Huddersfield T	48
1936–7	Manchester C	57	Charlton Ath	54	Arsenal	52
1937–8	Arsenal	52	Wolverhampton W	51	Preston NE	49
1938–9	Everton	59	Wolverhampton W	55	Charlton Ath	50
1946–7	Liverpool	57	Manchester U	56	Wolverhampton W	56
1947–8	Arsenal	59	Manchester U	52	Burnley	52

1948–9	Portsmouth	58	Manchester U	53	Derby Co	53
1949–50	*Portsmouth	53	Wolverhampton W	53	Sunderland	52
1950–1	Tottenham H	60	Manchester U	56	Blackpool	50
1951–2	Manchester U	57	Tottenham H	53	Arsenal	53
1952–3	*Arsenal	54	Preston NE	54	Wolverhampton W	51
1953–4	Wolverhampton W	57	WBA	53	Huddersfield T	51
1954–5	Chelsea	52	Wolverhampton W	48	Portsmouth	48
1955–6	Manchester U	60	Blackpool	49	Wolverhampton W	49
1956–7	Manchester U	64	Tottenham H	56	Preston NE	56
1957–8	Wolverhampton W	64	Preston NE	59	Tottenham H	51
1958–9	Wolverhampton W	61	Manchester U	55	Arsenal	50
1959–60	Burnley	55	Wolverhampton W	54	Tottenham H	53
1960–1	Tottenham H	66	Sheffield W	58	Wolverhampton W	57
1961–2	Ipswich T	56	Burnley	53	Tottenham H	52
1962–3	Everton	61	Tottenham H	55	Burnley	54
1963–4	Liverpool	57	Manchester U	53	Everton	52
1964–5	*Manchester U	61	Leeds U	61	Chelsea	56
1965–6	Liverpool	61	Leeds U	55	Burnley	55
1966–7	Manchester U	60	Nottingham F	56	Tottenham H	56
1967–8	Manchester C	58	Manchester U	56	Liverpool	55
1968–9	Leeds U	67	Liverpool	61	Everton	57
1969–70	Everton	66	Leeds U	57	Chelsea	55
1970–1	Arsenal	65	Leeds U	64	Tottenham H	52
1971–2	Derby Co	58	Leeds U	57	Liverpool	57
1972–3	Liverpool	60	Arsenal	57	Leeds U	53
1973–4	Leeds U	62	Liverpool	57	Derby Co	48
1974–5	Derby Co	53	Liverpool	51	Ipswich T	57
1975–6	Liverpool	60	QPR	59	Manchester U	56
1976–7	Liverpool	57	Manchester C	56	Ipswich T	52
1977–8	Nottingham F	64	Liverpool	57	Everton	55
1978–9	Liverpool	68	Nottingham F	60	WBA	59
1979–80	Liverpool	60	Manchester U	58	Ipswich T	53
1980–1	Aston Villa	60	Ipswich T	56	Arsenal	53
1981–2 g	Liverpool	87	Ipswich T	83	Manchester U	78
1982–3	Liverpool	82	Watford	71	Manchester U	70
1983–4	Liverpool	80	Southampton	77	Nottingham F	74
1984–5	Everton	90	Liverpool	77	Tottenham H	77
1985–6	Liverpool	88	Everton	86	West Ham	84
1986–7	Everton	86	Liverpool	77	Tottenham H	71
1987–8 h	Liverpool	90	Manchester U	81	Nottingham F	73
1988–9 i†	Arsenal	76	Liverpool	76	Nottingham F	64
1989–90 i	Liverpool	79	Aston Villa	70	Tottenham H	63
1990–1	Arsenal‡	83	Liverpool	76	Crystal Palace	69
1991–2 g	Leeds U	82	Manchester U	78	Sheffield W	75

Maximum points: *a* 44; *b* 56; *c* 60; *d* 58; *e* 76; *f* 84; *g* 126; *h* 120; *i* 114.
‡ Two points deducted.

Second Division

1892–3 a	Small Heath	36	Sheffield U	35	Darwen	30
1893–4 b	Liverpool	50	Small Heath	42	Notts Co	39
1894–5 c	Bury	48	Notts Co	39	Newton Heath	38
1895–6	*Liverpool	46	Manchester C	46	Grimsby T	42
1896–7	Notts Co	42	Newton Heath	39	Grimsby T	38
1897–8	Burnley	48	Newcastle U	45	Manchester C	39
1898–9 d	Manchester C	52	Glossop NE	46	Leicester Fosse	45
1899–1900	The Wednesday	54	Bolton W	52	Small Heath	46
1900–1	Grimsby T	49	Small Heath	48	Burnley	44

1901–2	WBA	55	Middlesbrough	51	Preston NE	42
1902–3	Manchester C	54	Small Heath	51	Woolwich A	48
1903–4	Preston NE	50	Woolwich A	49	Manchester U	48
1904–5	Liverpool	58	Bolton W	56	Manchester U	53
1905–6 e	Bristol C	66	Manchester U	62	Chelsea	53
1906–7	Nottingham F	60	Chelsea	57	Leicester Fosse	48
1907–8	Bradford C	54	Leicester Fosse	52	Oldham Ath	50
1908–9	Bolton W	52	Tottenham H	51	WBA	51
1909–10	Manchester C	54	Oldham Ath	53	Hull C	53
1910–11	WBA	53	Bolton W	51	Chelsea	49
1911–12	*Derby Co	54	Chelsea	54	Burnley	52
1912–13	Preston NE	53	Burnley	50	Birmingham	46
1913–14	Notts Co	53	Bradford PA	49	Woolwich A	49
1914–15	Derby Co	53	Preston NE	50	Barnsley	47
1919–20 f	Tottenham H	70	Huddersfield T	64	Birmingham	56
1920–1	*Birmingham	58	Cardiff C	58	Bristol C	51
1921–2	Nottingham F	56	Stoke C	52	Barnsley	52
1922–3	Notts Co	53	West Ham U	51	Leicester C	51
1923–4	Leeds U	54	Bury	51	Derby Co	51
1924–5	Leicester C	59	Manchester U	57	Derby Co	55
1925–6	Sheffield W	60	Derby Co	57	Chelsea	52
1926–7	Middlesbrough	62	Portsmouth	54	Manchester C	54
1927–8	Manchester C	59	Leeds U	57	Chelsea	54
1928–9	Middlesbrough	55	Grimsby T	53	Bradford	48
1929–30	Blackpool	58	Chelsea	55	Oldham Ath	53
1930–1	Everton	61	WBA	54	Tottenham H	51
1931–2	Wolverhampton W	56	Leeds U	54	Stoke C	52
1932–3	Stoke C	56	Tottenham H	55	Fulham	50
1933–4	Grimsby T	59	Preston NE	52	Bolton W	51
1934–5	Brentford	61	Bolton W	56	West Ham U	56
1935–6	Manchester U	56	Charlton Ath	55	Sheffield U	52
1936–7	Leicester C	56	Blackpool	55	Bury	52
1937–8	Aston Villa	57	Manchester U	53	Sheffield U	53
1938–9	Blackburn R	55	Sheffield U	54	Sheffield W	53
1946–7	Manchester C	62	Burnley	58	Birmingham C	55
1947–8	Birmingham C	59	Newcastle U	56	Southampton	52
1948–9	Fulham	57	WBA	56	Southampton	55
1949–50	Tottenham H	61	Sheffield W	52	Sheffield U	52
1950–1	Preston NE	57	Manchester C	52	Cardiff C	50
1951–2	Sheffield W	53	Cardiff C	51	Birmingham C	51
1952–3	Sheffield U	60	Huddersfield T	58	Luton T	52
1953–4	*Leicester C	56	Everton	56	Blackburn R	55
1954–5	*Birmingham C	54	Luton T	54	Rotherham U	54
1955–6	Sheffield W	55	Leeds U	52	Liverpool	48
1956–7	Leicester C	61	Nottingham F	54	Liverpool	53
1957–8	West Ham U	57	Blackburn R	56	Charlton Ath	55
1958–9	Sheffield W	62	Fulham	60	Sheffield U	53
1959–60	Aston Villa	59	Cardiff C	58	Liverpool	50
1960–1	Ipswich T	59	Sheffield U	58	Liverpool	52
1961–2	Liverpool	62	Leyton O	54	Sunderland	53
1962–3	Stoke C	53	Chelsea	52	Sunderland	52
1963–4	Leeds U	63	Sunderland	61	Preston NE	56
1964–5	Newcastle U	57	Northampton T	56	Bolton W	50
1965–6	Manchester C	59	Southampton	54	Coventry C	53
1966–7	Coventry C	59	Wolverhampton W	58	Carlisle U	52
1967–8	Ipswich T	59	QPR	58	Blackpool	58
1968–9	Derby Co	63	Crystal Palace	56	Charlton Ath	50

1969–70	Huddersfield T	60	Blackpool	53	Leicester C	51
1970–1	Leicester C	59	Sheffield U	56	Cardiff C	53
1971–2	Norwich C	57	Birmingham C	56	Millwall	55
1972–3	Burnley	62	QPR	61	Aston Villa	50
1973–4	Middlesbrough	65	Luton T	50	Carlisle U	49
1974–5	Manchester U	61	Aston Villa	58	Norwich C	53
1975–6	Sunderland	56	Bristol C	53	WBA	53
1976–7	Wolverhampton W	57	Chelsea	55	Nottingham F	52
1977–8	Bolton W	58	Southampton	57	Tottenham H	56
1978–9	Crystal Palace	57	Brighton	56	Stoke C	56
1979–80	Leicester C	55	Sunderland	54	Birmingham C	53
1980–1	West Ham U	66	Notts Co	53	Swansea C	50
1981–2 *g*	Luton T	88	Watford	80	Norwich C	71
1982–3	QPR	85	Wolverhampton W	75	Leicester C	70
1983–4 †	Chelsea	88	Sheffield W	88	Newcastle U	80
1984–5	Oxford U	84	Birmingham C	82	Manchester C	74
1985–6	Norwich C	84	Charlton Ath	77	Wimbledon	76
1986–7	Derby Co	84	Portsmouth	78	Oldham Ath	75
1987–8 *h*	Millwall	82	Aston Villa	78	Middlesbrough	78
1988–9 *i*	Chelsea	99	Manchester C	82	Crystal Palace	81
1989–90 †	Leeds U	85	Sheffield U	85	Newcastle U	80
1990–1	Oldham Ath	88	West Ham U	87	Sheffield W	82
1991–2	Ipswich T	84	Middlesbrough	80	Derby Co	78

Maximum points: *a* 44; *b* 56; *c* 60; *d* 58; *e* 76; *f* 84; *g* 126; *h* 132; *i* 138.

Third Division

1958–9 *a*	Plymouth Arg	62	Hull C	61	Brentford	57
1959–60	Southampton	61	Norwich C	59	Shrewsbury T	52
1960–1	Bury	68	Walsall	62	QPR	60
1961–2	Portsmouth	65	Grimsby T	62	Bournemouth	59
1962–3	Northampton T	62	Swindon T	58	Port Vale	54
1963–4	*Coventry C	60	Crystal Palace	60	Watford	58
1964–5	Carlisle U	60	Bristol C	59	Mansfield T	59
1965–6	Hull C	69	Millwall	65	QPR	57
1966–7	QPR	67	Middlesbrough	55	Watford	54
1967–8	Oxford U	57	Bury	56	Shrewsbury T	55
1968–9	*Watford	64	Swindon T	64	Luton T	61
1969–70	Orient	62	Luton T	60	Bristol R	56
1970–1	Preston NE	61	Fulham	60	Halifax T	56
1971–2	Aston Villa	70	Brighton	65	Bournemouth	62
1972–3	Bolton W	61	Notts Co	57	Blackburn R	55
1973–4	Oldham Ath	62	Bristol R	61	York C	61
1974–5	Blackburn R	60	Plymouth Arg	59	Charlton Ath	55
1975–6	Hereford U	63	Cardiff C	57	Millwall	56
1976–7	Mansfield T	64	Brighton & HA	61	Crystal Palace	59
1977–8	Wrexham	61	Cambridge U	58	Preston NE	56
1978–9	Shrewsbury T	61	Watford	60	Swansea C	60
1979–80	Grimsby T	62	Blackburn R	59	Sheffield W	58
1980–1	Rotherham U	61	Barnsley	59	Charlton Ath	59
1981–2 *b*†	Burnley	80	Carlisle U	80	Fulham	78
1982–3	Portsmouth	91	Cardiff C	86	Huddersfield T	82
1983–4	Oxford U	95	Wimbledon	87	Sheffield U	83
1984–5	Bradford C	94	Millwall	90	Hull C	87
1985–6	Reading	94	Plymouth Arg	87	Derby Co	84
1986–7	Bournemouth	97	Middlesbrough	94	Swindon T	87
1987–8	Sunderland	93	Brighton & HA	84	Walsall	82

1988–9	Wolverhampton W	92	Sheffield U	84	Port Vale	84
1989–90	Bristol R	93	Bristol C	91	Notts Co	87
1990–91	Cambridge U	86	Southend U	85	Grimsby T	83
1991–92	Brentford	82	Birmingham C	81	Huddersfield T	78

Maximum points: *a* 92; *b* 138.

Third Division (Southern Section)

1920–1 *a*	Crystal Palace	59	Southampton	54	QPR	53
1921–2	*Southampton	61	Plymouth Arg	61	Portsmouth	53
1922–3	Bristol C	59	Plymouth Arg	53	Swansea T	53
1923–4	Portsmouth	59	Plymouth Arg	55	Millwall	54
1924–5	Swansea T	57	Plymouth Arg	56	Bristol C	53
1925–6	Reading	57	Plymouth Arg	56	Millwall	53
1926–7	Bristol C	62	Plymouth Arg	60	Millwall	56
1927–8	Millwall	65	Northampton T	55	Plymouth Arg	53
1928–9	*Charlton Ath	54	Crystal Palace	54	Northampton T	52
1929–30	Plymouth Arg	68	Brentford	61	QPR	51
1930–1	Notts Co	59	Crystal Palace	51	Brentford	50
1931–2	Fulham	57	Reading	55	Southend U	53
1932–3	Brentford	62	Exeter C	58	Norwich C	57
1933–4	Norwich C	61	Coventry C	54	Reading	54
1934–5	Charlton Ath	61	Reading	53	Coventry C	51
1935–6	Coventry C	57	Luton T	56	Reading	54
1936–7	Luton T	58	Notts Co	56	Brighton	53
1937–8	Millwall	56	Bristol C	55	QPR	53
1938–9	Newport Co	55	Crystal Palace	52	Brighton	49
1946–7	Cardiff C	66	QPR	57	Bristol C	51
1947–8	QPR	61	Bournemouth	57	Walsall	51
1948–9	Swansea T	62	Reading	55	Bournemouth	52
1949–50	Notts Co	58	Northampton T	51	Southend U	51
1950–1 *b*	Nottingham F	70	Norwich C	64	Reading	57
1951–2	Plymouth Arg	66	Reading	61	Norwich C	61
1952–3	Bristol R	64	Millwall	62	Northampton T	62
1953–4	Ipswich T	64	Brighton	61	Bristol C	56
1954–5	Bristol C	70	Leyton O	61	Southampton	59
1955–6	Leyton O	66	Brighton	65	Ipswich T	64
1956–7	*Ipswich T	59	Torquay U	59	Colchester U	58
1957–8	Brighton	60	Brentford	58	Plymouth Arg	58

Maximum points: *a* 84; *b* 92.

Third Division (Northern Section)

1921–2 *a*	Stockport Co	56	Darlington	50	Grimsby T	50
1922–3	Nelson	51	Bradford PA	47	Walsall	46
1923–4 *b*	Wolverhampton W	63	Rochdale	62	Chesterfield	54
1924–5	Darlington	58	Nelson	53	New Brighton	53
1925–6	Grimsby T	61	Bradford PA	60	Rochdale	59
1926–7	Stoke C	63	Rochdale	58	Bradford PA	55
1927–8	Bradford PA	63	Lincoln C	55	Stockport Co	54
1928–9	Bradford C	63	Stockport Co	62	Wrexham	52
1929–30	Port Vale	67	Stockport Co	63	Darlington	50
1930–1	Chesterfield	58	Lincoln C	57	Wrexham	54
1931–2 *c*	*Lincoln C	57	Gateshead	57	Chester	50
1932–3 *b*	Hull C	59	Wrexham	57	Stockport Co	54
1933–4	Barnsley	62	Chesterfield	61	Stockport Co	59

1934–5	Doncaster R	57	Halifax T	55	Chester	54
1935–6	Chesterfield	60	Chester	55	Tranmere R	55
1936–7	Stockport Co	60	Lincoln C	57	Chester	53
1937–8	Tranmere R	56	Doncaster R	54	Hull C	53
1938–9	Barnsley	67	Doncaster R	56	Bradford C	52
1946–7	Doncaster R	72	Rotherham U	64	Chester	56
1947–8	Lincoln C	60	Rotherham U	59	Wrexham	50
1948–9	Hull C	65	Rotherham U	62	Doncaster R	50
1949–50	Doncaster R	55	Gateshead	53	Rochdale	51
1950–1 *d*	Rotherham U	71	Mansfield T	64	Carlisle U	62
1951–2	Lincoln C	69	Grimsby T	66	Stockport Co	59
1952–3	Oldham Ath	59	Port Vale	58	Wrexham	56
1953–4	Port Vale	69	Barnsley	58	Scunthorpe U	57
1954–5	Barnsley	65	Accrington S	61	Scunthorpe U	58
1955–6	Grimsby T	68	Derby Co	63	Accrington S	59
1956–7	Derby Co	63	Hartlepool U	59	Accrington S	58
1957–8	Scunthorpe U	66	Accrington S	59	Bradford C	57

Maximum points: *a* 70; *b* 84; *c* 80; *d*, 92.

Fourth Division

1958–9 *a*	Port Vale	64	Coventry C	60	York C	60
1959–60	Walsall	65	Notts Co	60	Torquay U	60
1960–1	Peterborough U	66	Crystal Palace	64	Northampton T	60
1961–2†	Millwall	56	Colchester U	55	Wrexham	53
1962–3	Brentford	62	Oldham Ath	59	Crewe Alex	59
1963–4	*Gillingham	60	Carlisle U	60	Workington T	59
1964–5	Brighton	63	Millwall	62	York C	62
1965–6	*Doncaster R	59	Darlington	59	Torquay U	58
1966–7	Stockport Co	64	Southport	59	Barrow	59
1967–8	Luton T	66	Barnsley	61	Hartlepools U	60
1968–9	Doncaster R	59	Halifax T	57	Rochdale	56
1969–70	Chesterfield	64	Wrexham	61	Swansea C	60
1970–1	Notts Co	69	Bournemouth	60	Oldham Ath	59
1971–2	Grimsby T	63	Southend U	60	Brentford	59
1972–3	Southport	62	Hereford U	58	Cambridge U	57
1973–4	Peterborough U	65	Gillingham	62	Colchester U	59
1974–5	Mansfield T	68	Shrewsbury T	62	Rotherham U	59
1975–6	Lincoln C	74	Northampton T	68	Reading	60
1976–7	Cambridge U	65	Exeter C	62	Colchester U	59
1977–8	Watford	71	Southend U	60	Swansea C	56
1978–9	Reading	65	Grimsby T	61	Wimbledon	61
1979–80	Huddersfield T	66	Walsall	64	Newport Co	61
1980–1	Southend U	67	Lincoln C	65	Doncaster R	56
1981–2 *b*	Sheffield U	96	Bradford C	91	Wigan Ath	91
1982–3	Wimbledon	98	Hull C	90	Port Vale	88
1983–4	York C	101	Doncaster R	85	Reading	82
1984–5	Chesterfield	91	Blackpool	86	Darlington	85
1985–6	Swindon T	102	Chester C	84	Mansfield T	81
1986–7	Northampton T	99	Preston NE	90	Southend U	80
1987–8	Wolverhampton W	90	Cardiff C	85	Bolton W	78
1988–9	Rotherham U	82	Tranmere R	80	Crewe Alex	78
1989–90	Exeter C	89	Grimsby T	79	Southend U	75
1990–1	Darlington	83	Stockport Co	82	Hartlepool U	82
1991–2 †	Burnley	80	Rotherham U	77	Mansfield T	77

Maximum points: *a* 92; *b* 138.

† Maximum points 88 owing to Accrington Stanley's resignation.

‡ Maximum points 126 owing to Aldershot being expelled.

RELEGATED CLUBS

(Since inception of automatic promotion and relegation in 1898–9)
* *Subsequently re-elected to Division 1 when League was extended after the War.*
** *Relegated after playoffs*

Division I to Division II

1898–99 Bolton W and Sheffield W
1899–1900 Burnley and Glossop
1900–01 Preston NE and WBA
1901–02 Small Heath and Manchester C
1902–03 Grimsby T and Bolton W
1903–04 Liverpool and WBA
1904–05 League extended. Bury and Notts Co, two bottom clubs in First Division, re-elected.
1905–06 Nottingham F and Wolverhampton W
1906–07 Derby Co and Stoke C
1907–08 Bolton W and Birmingham C
1908–09 Manchester C and Leicester Fosse
1909–10 Bolton W and Chelsea
1910–11 Bristol C and Nottingham F
1911–12 Preston NE and Bury
1912–13 Notts Co and Woolwich Arsenal
1913–14 Preston NE and Derby Co
1914–15 Tottenham H and Chelsea*
1919–20 Notts Co and Sheffield W
1920–21 Derby Co and Bradford PA
1921–22 Bradford C and Manchester U
1922–23 Stoke C and Oldham Ath
1923–24 Chelsea and Middlesbrough
1924–25 Preston NE and Nottingham F
1925–26 Manchester C and Notts Co
1926–27 Leeds U and WBA
1927–28 Tottenham H and Middlesbrough
1928–29 Bury and Cardiff C
1929–30 Burnley and Everton
1930–31 Leeds U and Manchester U
1931–32 Grimsby T and West Ham U
1932–33 Bolton W and Blackpool
1933–34 Newcastle U and Sheffield U
1934–35 Leicester C and Tottenham H
1935–36 Aston Villa and Blackburn R
1936–37 Manchester U and Sheffield W
1937–38 Manchester C and WBA
1938–39 Birmingham C and Leicester C
1946–47 Brentford and Leeds U
1947–48 Blackburn R and Grimsby T
1948–49 Preston NE and Sheffield U
1949–50 Manchester C and Birmingham C
1950–51 Sheffield W and Everton
1951–52 Huddersfield and Fulham
1952–53 Stoke C and Derby Co
1953–54 Middlesbrough and Liverpool
1954–55 Leicester C and Sheffield W
1955–56 Huddersfield and Sheffield U
1956–57 Charlton Ath and Cardiff C
1957–58 Sheffield W and Sunderland
1958–59 Portsmouth and Aston Villa
1959–60 Luton T and Leeds U
1960–61 Preston NE and Newcastle U
1961–62 Chelsea and Cardiff C
1962–63 Manchester C and Leyton O
1963–64 Bolton W and Ipswich T
1964–65 Wolverhampton W and Birmingham C
1965–66 Northampton T and Blackburn R
1966–67 Aston Villa and Blackpool
1967–68 Fulham and Sheffield U
1968–69 Leicester C and QPR
1969–70 Sunderland and Sheffield W
1970–71 Burnley and Blackpool
1971–72 Huddersfield T and Nottingham F
1972–73 Crystal Palace and WBA
1973–74 Southampton, Manchester U, Norwich C
1974–75 Luton T, Chelsea, Carlisle U
1975–76 Wolverhampton W, Burnley, Sheffield U
1976–77 Sunderland, Stoke C, Tottenham H
1977–78 West Ham U, Newcastle U, Leicester C
1978–79 QPR, Birmingham C, Chelsea
1979–80 Bristol C, Derby Co, Bolton W
1980–81 Norwich C, Leicester C, Crystal Palace
1981–82 Leeds U, Wolverhampton W, Middlesbrough
1982–83 Manchester C, Swansea C, Brighton & HA

1983–84 Birmingham C, Notts Co,
Wolverhampton W
1984–85 Norwich C, Sunderland, Stoke
C
1985–86 Ipswich T, Birmingham C,
WBA
1986–87 Leicester C, Manchester C,
Aston Villa
1987–88 Chelsea**, Portsmouth,
Watford, Oxford U

1988–89 Middlesbrough,West Ham U,
Newcastle U
1989–90 Sheffield W, Charlton Ath,
Millwall
1990–91 Sunderland and Derby Co
1991–92 Luton T, Notts Co,
West Ham U

Division II to Division III

1920–21 Stockport Co
1921–22 Bradford and Bristol C
1922–23 Rotherham C and
Wolverhampton W
1923–24 Nelson and Bristol C
1924–25 Crystal Palace and
Coventry C
1925–26 Stoke C and Stockport Co
1926–27 Darlington and Bradford C
1927–28 Fulham and South Shields
1928–29 Port Vale and Clapton O
1929–30 Hull C and Notts Co
1930–31 Reading and Cardiff C
1931–32 Barnsley and Bristol C
1932–33 Chesterfield and Charlton Ath
1933–34 Millwall and Lincoln C
1934–35 Oldham Ath and Notts Co
1935–36 Port Vale and Hull C
1936–37 Doncaster R and Bradford C
1937–38 Barnsley and Stockport Co
1938–39 Norwich C and Tranmere R
1946–47 Swansea T and Newport Co
1947–48 Doncaster R and Millwall
1948–49 Nottingham F and Lincoln C
1949–50 Plymouth Arg and Bradford
1950–51 Grimsby T and Chesterfield
1951–52 Coventry C and QPR
1952–53 Southampton and Barnsley
1953–54 Brentford and Oldham Ath
1954–55 Ipswich T and Derby Co
1955–56 Plymouth Arg and Hull C
1956–57 Port Vale and Bury
1957–58 Doncaster R and Notts Co
1958–59 Barnsley and Grimsby T
1959–60 Bristol C and Hull C
1960–61 Lincoln C and Portsmouth
1961–62 Brighton & HA and Bristol R
1962–63 Walsall and Luton T
1963–64 Grimsby T and Scunthorpe U
1964–65 Swindon T and Swansea T
1965–66 Middlesbrough and Leyton O
1966–67 Northampton T and Bury
1967–68 Plymouth Arg and Rotherham
U

1968–69 Fulham and Bury
1969–70 Preston NE and Aston Villa
1970–71 Blackburn R and Bolton W
1971–72 Charlton Ath and Watford
1972–73 Huddersfield T and Brighton
& HA
1973–74 Crystal Palace, Preston NE,
Swindon T
1974–75 Millwall, Cardiff C, Sheffield
W
1975–76 Oxford U, York C,
Portsmouth
1976–77 Carlisle U, Plymouth Arg,
Hereford U
1977–78 Blackpool, Mansfield T, Hull
C
1978–79 Sheffield U, Millwall,
Blackburn R
1979–80 Fulham, Burnley, Charlton
Ath
1980–81 Preston NE, Bristol C,
Bristol R
1981–82 Cardiff C, Wrexham, Orient
1982–83 Rotherham U, Burnley,
Bolton W
1983–84 Derby Co, Swansea C,
Cambridge U
1984–85 Notts Co, Cardiff C,
Wolverhampton W
1985–86 Carlisle U, Middlesbrough,
Fulham
1986–87 Sunderland**, Grimsby T,
Brighton & HA
1987–88 Huddersfield T, Reading,
Sheffield U**
1988–89 Shrewsbury T, Birmingham
C, Walsall
1989–90 Bournemouth, Bradford,
Stoke C
1990–91 WBA and Hull C
1991–92 Plymouth Arg, Brighton &
HA, Port Vale

Division III to Division IV

1958–59 Rochdale, Notts Co, Doncaster R and Stockport
1959–60 Accrington S, Wrexham, Mansfield T and York C
1960–61 Chesterfield, Colchester U, Bradford C and Tranmere R
1961–62 Newport Co, Brentford, Lincoln C and Torquay U
1962–63 Bradford PA, Brighton, Carlisle U and Halifax T
1963–64 Millwall, Crewe Alex, Wrexham and Notts Co
1964–65 Luton T, Port Vale, Colchester U and Barnsley
1965–66 Southend U, Exeter C, Brentford and York C
1966–67 Doncaster R, Workington, Darlington and Swansea T
1967–68 Scunthorpe U, Colchester U, Grimsby T and Peterborough U (demoted)
1968–69 Oldham Ath, Crewe Alex, Hartlepool and Northampton
1969–70 Bournemouth, Southport, Barrow, Stockport Co
1970–71 Reading, Bury, Doncaster R, Gillingham
1971–72 Mansfield T, Barnsley, Torquay U, Bradford C
1972–73 Rotherham U, Brentford, Swansea C, Scunthorpe U
1973–74 Cambridge U, Shrewsbury T, Southport, Rochdale
1974–75 AFC Bournemouth, Tranmere R, Watford, Huddersfield T

1975–76 Aldershot, Colchester U, Southend U, Halifax T
1976–77 Reading, Northampton T, Grimsby T, York C
1977–78 Port Vale, Bradford C, Hereford U, Portsmouth
1978–79 Peterborough U, Walsall, Tranmere R, Lincoln C
1979–80 Bury, Southend U, Mansfield T, Wimbledon .
1980–81 Sheffield U, Colchester U, Blackpool, Hull C
1981–82 Wimbledon, Swindon T, Bristol C, Chester
1982–83 Reading, Wrexham, Doncaster R, Chesterfield
1983–84 Scunthorpe U, Southend U, Port Vale, Exeter C
1984–85 Burnley, Orient, Preston NE, Cambridge U
1985–86 Lincoln C, Cardiff C, Wolverhampton W, Swansea C
1986–87 Bolton W**, Carlisle U, Darlington, Newport Co
1987–88 Doncaster R, York C, Grimsby T, Rotherham U**
1988–89 Southend U, Chesterfield, Gillingham, Aldershot
1989–90 Cardiff C, Northampton T, Blackpool, Walsall
1990–91 Crewe Alex, Rotherham U, Mansfield T
1991–92 Bury, Shrewsbury T, Torquay U, Darlington

*** Relegated after playoffs.*

APPLICATIONS FOR RE-ELECTION TO THIRD DIVISION UNTIL 1957–58

Seven: Walsall.
Six: Exeter C, Halifax T, Newport Co.
Five: Accrington S, Barrow, Gillingham, New Brighton, Southport.
Four: Rochdale, Norwich C.
Three: Crystal Palace, Crewe Alex, Darlington, Hartlepools U, Merthyr T, Swindon T.
Two: Aberdare Ath, Aldershot, Ashington, Bournemouth, Brentford, Chester, Colchester U, Durham C, Millwall, Nelson, QPR, Rotherham U, Southend U, Tranmere R, Watford, Workington.
One: Bradford C, Bradford PA, Brighton, Bristol R, Cardiff C, Carlisle U, Charlton Ath, Gateshead, Grimsby T, Mansfield T, Shrewsbury T, Torquay U, York C.

APPLICATIONS FOR RE-ELECTION TO FOURTH DIVISION UNTIL 1985–86

Eleven: Hartlepool U.
Seven: Crewe Alex.
Six: Barrow (lost League place to Hereford U 1972), Halifax T, Rochdale, Southport (lost League place to Wigan Ath 1978), York C.
Five: Chester C, Darlington, Lincoln C, Stockport Co, Workington (lost League place to Wimbledon 1977).
Four: Bradford PA (lost League place to Cambridge U 1970), Newport Co, Northampton T.
Three: Doncaster R, Hereford U.
Two: Bradford C, Exeter C, Oldham Ath, Scunthorpe U, Torquay U.
One: Aldershot, Colchester U, Gateshead (lost League place to Peterborough U 1960), Grimsby T, Swansea C, Tranmere R, Wrexham, Blackpool, Cambridge U, Preston NE.
Accrington S resigned and Oxford U were elected 1962.
Port Vale were forced to re-apply following expulsion in 1968.

Gateshead not re-elected, their place being taken by Peterborough in the 1960–1 season.
Accrington resigned March 1962, and Oxford U elected to replace them in 1962–3 season.
Bradford not re-elected, their place being taken by Cambridge U in the 1970–1 season.
Barrow not re-elected, their place being taken by Hereford U in the 1972–3 season.
Workington not re-elected, their place being taken by Wimbledon in the 1977–8 season.
Southport not re-elected, their place being taken by Wigan in the 1978–9 season.
Aldershot forced to withdraw March 1992.

LEAGUE STATUS FROM 1986–87

1986–87 *Relegated:* Lincoln C *Promoted:* Scarborough
1987–88 *Relegated:* Newport Co *Promoted:* Lincoln C
1988–89 *Relegated:* Darlington *Promoted:* Maidstone U
1989–90 *Relegated:* Colchester U *Promoted:* Darlington
1990–91 *Relegated:* (no club) *Promoted:* Barnet
1991–92 *Relegated:* (no club) *Promoted:* Colchester U

Promoted after play-offs

1986–87 Aldershot to Division 3
1987–88 Swansea C to Division 3
1988–89 Leyton O to Division 3
1989–90 Cambridge U to Division 3; Sunderland to Division 1
1990–91 Notts Co to Division 1; Tranmere R to Division 2; Torquay U to Division 3
1991–92 Blackburn R to Division 1; Peterborough U to Division 2; Blackpool to Division 3 (divisions to be FA Premier League and First and Second Division for 1992–93)

LEAGUE TITLE WINS

League Division I–18–Liverpool; 10–Arsenal, Everton; 7–Aston Villa, Manchester U; 6–Sunderland; 4–Newcastle, Sheffield Wednesday; 3–Huddersfield, Leeds, Wolves; 2–Blackburn R, Burnley, Derby Co, Manchester C, Portsmouth, Preston NE, Tottenham; 1–Chelsea, Ipswich, Nottingham F, Sheffield U, West Bromwich Albion.

League Division II–6–Manchester C, Leicester C; 5–Sheffield Wednesday; 4–*Birmingham, Derby Co, Ipswich, Liverpool; 3–Middlesbrough, Notts Co, Preston; 2–Aston Villa, Bolton, Burnley, Chelsea, Grimsby, Leeds, Manchester U, Norwich C, Nottingham F, Stoke, Tottenham, West Bromwich, West Ham U, Wolverhampton W; 1–Blackburn R, Blackpool, Bradford C, Brentford, Bristol C, Bury, Coventry, Crystal P, Everton, Fulham, Huddersfield, Leeds U, Luton, Millwall, Newcastle, Oldham Ath, Oxford U, QPR, Sheffield U, Sunderland.
  Once as Small Heath.

League Division III–2–Oxford U, Portsmouth; 1–Aston Villa, Blackburn R, Bolton, Bournemouth, Bradford C, Brentford, Bristol R, Burnley, Bury, Cambridge U, Carlisle, Coventry, Grimsby T, Hereford U, Hull, Mansfield, Northampton, Oldham Ath, Orient, Plymouth, Preston NE, Queen's Park Rangers, Reading, Rotherham U, Shrewsbury T, Southampton, Sunderland, Watford, Wolverhampton W, Wrexham.

League Division IV–2–Chesterfield, Doncaster R, Peterborough U; 1–Brentford, Brighton, Burnley, Cambridge, Darlington, Exeter C, Gillingham, Grimsby, Huddersfield T, Lincoln C, Luton, Mansfield T, Millwall, Northampton T, Notts Co, Port Vale, Reading, Rotherham U, Sheffield U, Southend U, Southport, Swindon T, Walsall, Watford, Wimbledon, Wolverhampton W, York C.

To 1957–58
Division III (South): Bristol C; 2 Charlton, Ipswich, Millwall, Notts Co, Plymouth, Swansea; 1 Brentford, Brighton, Bristol R, Cardiff, Coventry, Crystal P, Fulham, Leyton Orient, Luton, Newport, Nottingham F, Norwich, Portsmouth, Queen's Park Rangers, Reading, Southampton.
Division III (North): 3 Barnsley, Doncaster, Lincoln; 2 Chesterfield, Grimsby, Hull, Port Vale, Stockport; 1 Bradford, Bradford C, Darlington, Derby, Nelson, Oldham, Rotherham, Scunthorpe, Stoke, Tranmere, Wolverhampton.

LEAGUE ATTENDANCES SINCE 1946–47

Season	Matches	Total	Season	Matches	Total
1946–47	1848	35,604,606	1969–70	2028	29,600,972
1947–48	1848	40,259,130	1970–71	2028	28,194,146
1948–49	1848	41,271,414	1971–72	2028	28,700,729
1949–50	1848	40,517,865	1972–73	2028	25,448,642
1950–51	2028	39,584,967	1973–74	2028	24,982,203
1951–52	2028	39,015,866	1974–75	2028	25,577,977
1952–53	2028	37,149,966	1975–76	2028	24,896,053
1953–54	2028	36,174,590	1976–77	2028	26,182,800
1954–55	2028	34,133,103	1977–78	2028	25,392,872
1955–56	2028	33,150,809	1978–79	2028	24,540,627
1956–57	2028	32,744,405	1979–80	2028	24,623,975
1957–58	2028	33,562,208	1980–81	2028	21,907,569
1958–59	2028	33,610,985	1981–82	2028	20,006,961
1959–60	2028	32,538,611	1982–83	2028	18,766,158
1960–61	2028	28,619,754	1983–84	2028	18,358,631
1961–62	2015	27,979,902	1984–85	2028	17,849,835
1962–63	2028	28,885,852	1985–86	2028	16,488,577
1963–64	2028	28,535,022	1986–87	2028	17,379,218
1964–55	2028	27,641,168	1987–88	2030	17,959,732
1965–66	2028	27,206,980	1988–89	2036	18,464,192
1966–67	2028	28,902,596	1989–90	2036	19,445,442
1967–68	2028	30,107,298	1990–91	2036	19,508,202
1968–69	2028	29,382,172	1991–92	2064	20,487,273

This is the first time since the war that attendances have risen for six consecutive seasons.

	TOTAL ATTENDANCES	AVERAGE ATTENDANCES
DIVISION 1	9,989,160	21,622
DIVISION 2	5,809,787	10,525
DIVISION 3	2,993,352	5,423
DIVISION 4	1,694,974	3,404
TOTAL	20,487,273	9,926

(Division 4 figures include matches played by Aldershot)

BARCLAYS LEAGUE ATTENDANCES 1991–92

DIVISION ONE STATISTICS

	Average gate		+/−%	Season 1991/92	
	1990/91	*1991/92*		*Highest*	*Lowest*
Arsenal	36,864	31,905	−13.5	42,073	22,096
Aston Villa	25,663	24,818	−3.3	39,995	15,745
Chelsea	20,738	18,684	−9.9	30,230	7148
Coventry City	13,794	13,876	+0.6	23,962	8454
Crystal Palace	19,660	17,618	−10.4	29,017	12,109
Everton	25,028	23,148	−7.5	37,681	14,783
Leeds United	28,946	29,459	+1.8	33,020	26,220
Liverpool	36,038	34,799	−3.4	39,072	25,457
Luton Town	10,274	9715	−5.4	13,410	7533
Manchester City	27,874	27,690	−0.7	38,180	21,437
Manchester United	43,218	44,984	+4.1	47,576	38,554
Norwich City	15,468	13,858	−10.4	20,411	10,514
Nottingham Forest	22,137	23,721	+7.2	30,168	19,707
Notts County	8164	10,987	+34.6	21,055	6198
Oldham Athletic	13,247	15,087	+13.9	18,952	12,125
Queens Park Rangers	13,524	13,592	+0.5	22,603	8495
Sheffield United	21,461	22,097	+3.0	31,832	16,062
Sheffield Wednesday	26,605	29,560	+11.1	40,327	20,574
Southampton	15,413	14,070	−8.7	18,581	8658
Tottenham Hotspur	30,632	27,761	−9.4	35,087	19,834
West Ham United	22,551	21,342	−5.4	25,678	16,896
Wimbledon	7631	6905	−9.5	15,009	3121

DIVISION TWO STATISTICS

	Average gate		+/−%	Season 1991/92	
	1990/91	*1991/92*		*Highest*	*Lowest*
Barnsley	8937	7508	−16.0	13,337	5328
Blackburn Rovers	8126	13,251	+63.1	19,511	8898
Brighton & Hove A	8386	8002	−4.6	11,647	4420
Bristol City	13,495	11,479	−14.9	20,183	7735
Bristol Rovers	5929	5850	−1.3	7622	3547
Cambridge United	5503	7078	+28.6	9741	4810
Charlton Athletic	6548	6786	+3.6	15,357	3658
Derby County	16,257	14,664	−9.8	22,608	10,559
Grimsby Town	7237	6921	−4.4	11,613	4583
Ipswich Town	11,772	14,274	+21.3	26,467	8646
Leicester City	11,546	15,202	+31.7	21,894	10,950
Middlesbrough	17,023	14,703	−13.6	19,424	9685
Millwall	10,846	7921	−27.0	12,882	5703
Newcastle United	16,834	21,148	+25.6	30,261	13,136
Oxford United	5780	5671	−1.9	10,528	3420
Plymouth Argyle	6851	6739	−1.6	17,459	4090
Portsmouth	9689	11,789	+21.7	20,133	7147
Port Vale	8092	7382	−8.8	10,384	5310
Southend United	6174	6733	+9.1	10,003	4462
Sunderland	22,577	18,390	−18.5	29,224	12,790
Swindon Town	9805	10,009	+2.1	13,238	7261
Tranmere Rovers	6740	8845	+31.2	13,705	5797
Watford	9576	8511	−11.1	13,547	4785
Wolverhampton W	15,837	13,743	−13.2	19,123	8536

DIVISION THREE STATISTICS

| | Average gate | | +/−% | Season 1991/92 | |
	1990/91	1991/92		Highest	Lowest
AFC Bournemouth	6017	5471	−9.1	7721	3558
Birmingham City	7030	12,400	+76.4	27,508	8154
Bolton Wanderers	7277	6030	−17.1	10,000	3535
Bradford City	6644	6115	−8.0	10,050	4170
Brentford	6144	7156	+16.5	12,071	4586
Bury	3572	2901	−18.8	5886	1663
Chester City	1564	1857	+18.7	4895	871
Darlington	4021	2904	−27.8	5658	1223
Exeter City	4243	3627	−14.5	5830	2214
Fulham	4057	4492	+10.7	8671	2465
Hartlepool United	3180	3201	+0.7	5413	2140
Huddersfield Town	5351	7540	+40.9	11,884	4674
Hull City	6165	4115	−33.3	5310	3093
Leyton Orient	4194	4460	+6.3	7347	2795
Peterborough United	5211	6279	+20.5	14,539	2810
Preston North End	5214	4722	−9.4	7740	2932
Reading	4079	3841	−5.8	6649	2535
Shrewsbury Town	3442	3456	+0.4	8557	1866
Stockport County	3562	4896	+37.5	8129	2745
Stoke City	11,565	13,007	+12.5	23,626	8527
Swansea City	3665	3367	−8.1	5629	2081
Torquay United	2986	2734	−8.4	5696	1884
West Bromwich Albion	11,993	12,711	+6.0	26,168	8439
Wigan Athletic	2889	2862	−0.9	5950	1787

DIVISION FOUR STATISTICS

	Average gate		+/-%	Season 1991/92	
	1990/91	*1991/92*		*Highest*	*Lowest*
Barnet	2918	3643	+24.8	5090	2038
Blackpool	4059	4335	+6.8	8007	2842
Burnley	7882	10,521	+33.5	21,218	5876
Cardiff City	2946	6195	+110.3	16,030	2356
Carlisle United	3006	2554	−15.0	9051	1672
Chesterfield	3712	3439	−7.4	7789	1802
Crewe Alexandra	3748	3733	−0.4	5530	2476
Doncaster Rovers	2831	2058	−27.3	3507	1247
Gillingham	3523	3135	−11.0	6717	2322
Halifax Town	1699	1633	−3.9	4291	881
Hereford United	2599	2735	+5.2	5744	1294
Lincoln City	2967	2822	−4.9	7884	1737
Maidstone United	1854	1429	−22.9	3264	842
Mansfield Town	2683	3803	+41.7	8333	1966
Northampton Town	3710	2789	−24.8	4344	1784
Rochdale	2238	2784	+24.4	8175	1691
Rotherham United	4600	4750	+3.3	8930	3137
Scarborough	1597	1677	+5.0	2604	935
Scunthorpe United	3114	3189	+2.4	5303	2224
Walsall	4149	3367	−18.8	5287	2045
Wrexham	1885	2608	+38.4	4053	1266
York City	2516	2506	−0.4	7620	1605

** The above figures include games played by Aldershot before termination of their League membership.*

TRANSFER TRAIL 1991–92
(*from May 1991 to May 1992*)

	From	To
May 1991		
28 Cook, Mitchell	Halifax Town	Darlington
31 Smalley, Mark A.	Mansfield Town	Maidstone United
30 Tiler, Carl	Barnsley	Nottingham Forest
June 1991		
25 Agnew, Stephen M.	Barnsley	Blackburn Rovers
14 Beckford, Darren R.	Port Vale	Norwich City
27 Boyd, Thomas	Motherwell	Chelsea
13 Carr, Franz A.	Nottingham Forest	Newcastle United
6 Dorigo, Anthony R.	Chelsea	Leeds United
25 Foyle, Martin J.	Oxford United	Port Vale
24 Jones, Alexander	Carlisle United	Rochdale
14 Manuel, William A. J.	Gillingham	Brentford
11 Newsome, Jon	Sheffield Wednesday	Leeds United
28 Payne, Mark C.	Stockport County	Rochdale
5 Pennock, Anthony	Stockport County	Wigan Athletic
18 Robinson, Paul J.	Plymouth Argyle	Hereford United
7 Wallace, Rodney S.	Southampton	Leeds United
6 Ward, Peter	Rochdale	Stockport County
3 Wilson, Darren A.	Manchester City	Bury
July 1991		
22 Abbott, Gregory S.	Bradford City	Halifax Town
2 Bailey, Dennis	Birmingham City	Queens Park Rangers
31 Baird, Ian J.	Middlesbrough	Heart of Midlothian
25 Barber, Philip A.	Crystal Palace	Millwall
24 Bartram, Vincent L.	Wolverhampton Wdrs.	AFC Bournemouth
24 Bishop, Darren C.	Bury	Barnsley
22 Butler, Lee S.	Aston Villa	Barnsley
19 Cascarino, Tony G.	Aston Villa	Celtic
22 Clarke, Timothy J.	Coventry City	Huddersfield Town
19 Coleman, Christopher J.	Swansea City	Crystal Palace
16 Conroy, Michael K.	Reading	Burnley
25 Cooper, Colin T.	Middlesbrough	Millwall
26 Davis, Steven P.	Burnley	Barnsley
15 Dobbin, James	Barnsley	Grimsby Town
16 Dobbins, Wayne L.	West Bromwich Albion	Torquay United
19 Earle, Robert	Port Vale	Wimbledon
17 Elliott, Paul	Celtic	Chelsea
15 Ellis, Neil J.	Chester City	Maidstone United
4 Fitzpatrick, Paul J.	Carlisle United	Leicester City
4 Fleming, Paul	Halifax Town	Mansfield Town
25 Hodge, Stephen B	Nottingham Forest	Leeds United
15 Jones, Murray L.	Exeter City	Grimsby Town
15 Ling, Martin	Southend United	Swindon Town
11 Lyne, Neil G.F.	Nottingham Forest	Shrewsbury Town
17 Milligan, Michael J.	Everton	Oldham Athletic
26 Mitchell, David S.	Chelsea	Swindon Town
31 Morris, Mark J.	Sheffield United	AFC Bournemouth
24 Mortimer, Paul H.	Charlton Athletic	Aston Villa
15 Newman, Robert N.	Bristol City	Norwich City

		From	*To*
25	O'Shaughnessy, S.	Rochdale	Exeter City
8	Pearson, John S.	Leeds United	Barnsley
11	Peyton, Gerald J.	AFC Bournemouth	Everton
30	Poole, Kevin	Middlesbrough	Leicester City
29	Richards, Stephen C.	Scarborough	Halifax Town
1	Ryan, John B.	Chesterfield	Rochdale
31	Sale, Mark D.	Stoke City	Cambridge United
19	Saunders, Dean N	Derby County	Liverpool
17	Sharp, Graeme M.	Everton	Oldham Athletic
31	Sheffield, Jonathan	Norwich City	Cambridge United
1	Shepherd, Anthony	Carlisle United	Motherwell
23	Sheringham, Edward P.	Millwall	Nottingham Forest
1	Spearing, Anthony	Leicester City	Plymouth Argyle
4	Sussex, Andy	Crewe Alexandra	Southend United
26	Taylor, Shaun	Exeter City	Swindon Town
25	Teale, Shaun	AFC Bournemouth	Aston Villa
30	Ward, Ashley S.	Manchester City	Leicester City
17	Warhurst, Paul	Oldham Athletic	Sheffield Wednesday
8	Wallace, Raymond G.	Southampton	Leeds United
25	Welch, Keith	Rochdale	Bristol City
15	Wetherall, David	Sheffield Wednesday	Leeds United
15	Wright, Mark	Derby County	Liverpool

August 1991

23	Aitken, Robert S.	Newcastle United	St Mirren
14	Allon, Joseph B.	Hartlepool United	Chelsea
16	Armstrong, C. P.	Wrexham	Millwall
23	Atherton, Peter	Wigan Athletic	Coventry City
15	Barber, Frederick	Walsall	Peterborough United
16	Bogie, Ian	Preston North End	Millwall
5	Beardsley, Peter	Liverpool	Everton
14	Blissett, Luther L.	AFC Bournemouth	Watford
22	Brown, Malcolm	Stockport County	Rochdale
15	Brown, Michael A.	Shrewsbury Town	Bolton Wanderers
6	Buckley, John W.	Partick Thistle	Scunthorpe United
15	Coleman, Simon	Middlesbrough	Derby County
17	Colquhoun, John	Heart of Midlothian	Millwall
8	Comyn, Andrew J.	Aston Villa	Derby County
2	Cornforth, John M.	Sunderland	Swansea City
1	Cowan, Thomas	Rangers	Sheffield United
5	Crosby, Phil	Peterborough United	York City
14	Cunningham, A. E.	Bolton Wanderers	Rotherham United
14	Curle, Keith	Wimbledon	Manchester City
17	Davis, Stephen M.	Southampton	Burnley
14	Dobie, Mark W. G.	Cambridge United	Torquay United
30	Donowa, Brian L.	Bristol City	Birmingham City
9	Dryden, Richard	Exeter City	Notts County
16	Durie, Gordon S.	Chelsea	Tottenham Hotspur
16	Falco, Mark P.	Queens Park Rangers	Millwall
16	Falconer, William H.	Watford	Middlesbrough
15	Fleming, Craig	Halifax Town	Oldham Athletic
16	Fleming, Curtis	St Patricks	Middlesbrough
15	Gillespie, Gary T.	Liverpool	Celtic
8	Graham, Deiniol W. T.	Manchester United	Barnsley
16	Gray, Phillip	Tottenham Hotspur	Luton Town
12	Harper, Alan	Manchester City	Everton

		From	*To*
16	Helliwell, Ian	York City	Scunthorpe United
16	Hogan, Thomas E.	Cobh Ramblers	Birmingham City
23	Hogg, Graeme J.	Portsmouth	Heart of Midlothian
12	Holloway, Ian S.	Bristol Rovers	Queens Park Rangers
14	Honor, Christian	Bristol City	Airdrieonians
9	Houchen, Keith M.	Hibernian	Port Vale
15	Ironside, Ian	Scarborough	Middlesbrough
30	Jones, Vincent P.	Sheffield United	Chelsea
9	Kamara, Alan	Scarborough	Halifax Town
15	Kelly, Anthony G.	Shrewsbury Town	Bolton Wanderers
1	Kilcline, Brian	Coventry City	Oldham Athletic
27	Lancaster, David	Blackpool	Chesterfield
27	Lee, David	Bury	Southampton
13	McAllister, Kevin	Chelsea	Falkirk
15	McCall, Stuart	Everton	Rangers
16	Mardon, Paul J.	Bristol City	Birmingham City
1	Mendonca, Clive P.	Rotherham United	Sheffield United
21	Millar, Paul	Port Vale	Cardiff City
12	Munro, Stuart	Rangers	Blackburn Rovers
16	Nelson, Garry P.	Brighton & Hove Albion	Charlton Athletic
16	Norton, David W.	Notts County	Hull City
5	O'Hanlon, Kelham G.	Rotherham United	Carlisle United
29	Overson, Vincent D.	Birmingham City	Stoke City
16	Page, Donald R.	Wigan Athletic	Rotherham United
16	Painter, Peter R.	Chester City	Maidstone United
8	Parker, Paul A.	Queens Park Rangers	Manchester United
27	Peake, Trevor	Coventry City	Luton Town
1	Peel, Nathan J.	Preston North End	Sheffield United
16	Putney, Trevor A.	Middlesbrough	Watford
16	Quamina, Mark E.	Wimbledon	Plymouth Argyle
5	Quinn, James M.	West Ham United	AFC Bournemouth
23	Ramsey, Paul	Leicester City	Cardiff City
9	Rice, Brian	Nottingham Forest	Falkirk
15	Rimmer, Stuart A.	Barnsley	Chester City
8	Sinnott, Lee	Bradford City	Crystal Palace
27	Skinner, Justin	Fulham	Bristol Rovers
16	Small, Michael A.	Brighton & Hove Albion	West Ham United
16	Speedie, David R.	Liverpool	Blackburn Rovers
1	Stant, Philip R.	Fulham	Mansfield Town
17	Starbuck, Phillip M.	Nottingham Forest	Huddersfield Town
7	Staunton, Stephen	Liverpool	Aston Villa
16	Swan, Peter H.	Hull City	Port Vale
7	Thomas, Mitchell A.	Tottenham Hotspur	West Ham United
19	Thompson, Gary L.	Crystal Palace	Queens Park Rangers
13	Thompson, Steven J.	Bolton Wanderers	Luton Town
13	Walters, Mark E.	Rangers	Liverpool
12	Ward, Mark W.	Manchester City	Everton
16	West, Gary	Port Vale	Lincoln City
16	Wilkinson, Paul	Watford	Middlesbrough
6	Williams, Gareth	Aston Villa	Barnsley
19	Witter, Anthony J.	Crystal Palace	Queens Park Rangers
15	Woods, Christopher	Rangers	Sheffield Wednesday
30	Yates, Mark J.	Birmingham City	Burnley

Temporary Transfers

15	Beresford, Marlon	Sheffield Wednesday	Northampton Town

	From	*To*
2 Brown, Kenneth J.	Plymouth Argyle	West Ham United
23 Byrne, Brian	Huddersfield Town	Shelbourne
21 Byrne, David S.	Watford	Reading
19 Dale, Carl	Chester City	Cardiff City
27 Hoult, Russell	Leicester City	Lincoln City
13 Keaton, Jason	Everton	Stoke City
22 Kerr, Dylan	Leeds United	Doncaster Rovers
29 Marriott, Andrew	Nottingham Forest	Burnley
15 Miller, Alan	Arsenal	West Bromwich Albion
14 Morrow, Stephen	Arsenal	Watford
29 O'Doherty, Kenneth B.	Huddersfield Town	Exeter City
15 Priestley, Jason A.	Carlisle United	Scarborough
15 Rush, David	Sunderland	Hartlepool United
13 Smith, Mark A.	Nottingham Forest	Shrewsbury Town

September 1991

2 Black, Kingsley	Luton Town	Nottingham Forest
18 Bowden, Jon L.	Wrexham	Rochdale
6 Bradley, Russell	Hereford United	Halifax Town
3 Brown, Kenneth J.	Plymouth Argyle	West Ham United
6 Caesar, Gus C.	Cambridge United	Bristol City
5 Chapman, Gary A.	Notts County	Exeter City
13 Cook, Andrew C.	Southampton	Exeter City
21 Connor, Terence F.	Swansea City	Bristol City
5 Cooper, Mark N.	Exeter City	Birmingham City
12 Cross, Stephen C.	Derby County	Bristol Rovers
5 Currie, David N.	Oldham Athletic	Barnsley
2 Dale, Carl	Chester City	Cardiff City
6 Dolan, Eamonn J.	Birmingham City	Exeter City
3 Dowie, Iain	West Ham United	Southampton
19 Evans, Stewart J.	Rotherham United	Crewe Alexandra
25 Freestone, Roger	Chelsea	Swansea City
17 Gayle, Brian W.	Ipswich Town	Sheffield United
23 Gray, Stuart	Aston Villa	Southampton
12 Harford, Michael G.	Derby County	Luton Town
12 Heathcote, Michael	Shrewsbury Town	Cambridge United
4 Hill, David M.	Ipswich Town	Scunthorpe United
9 Hurlock, Terry A.	Rangers	Southampton
17 Jemson, Nigel B.	Nottingham Forest	Sheffield Wednesday
16 Rideout, Paul D.	Southampton	Notts County
13 Rowbotham, Darren	Exeter City	Torquay United
20 Smith, Mark A.	Nottingham Forest	Shrewsbury Town
13 Taylor, Robert M.	Sheffield Wednesday	Shrewsbury Town
12 Titterton, David S.J.	Coventry City	Hereford United
13 Whiston, Peter M.	Torquay United	Exeter City
6 Wimbleton, Paul P.	Shrewsbury Town	Exeter City
24 Wright, Ian E.	Crystal Palace	Arsenal

Temporary Transfers

12 Aylott, Trevor K. C.	Birmingham City	Oxford United
26 Beagrie, Peter	Everton	Sunderland
26 Beckford, Jason N.	Manchester City	Port Vale
11 Berry, George F.	Preston North End	Aldershot
12 Brazil, Derek M.	Manchester United	Swansea City
9 Byrne, Brian	Shelbourne	Huddersfield T. (Tr. back)
12 Cash, Stuart	Nottingham Forest	Shrewsbury Town

		From	*To*
19	Clark, Howard W.	Coventry City	Darlington
26	Clarke, Wayne	Manchester City	Wolverhampton Wdrs.
5	Cole, Andrew A.	Arsenal	Fulham
12	Costello, Peter	Peterborough United	Lincoln City
26	Cross, Paul	Barnsley	Preston North End
19	Davison, Robert	Leeds United	Derby County
6	Dibble, Andrew G.	Manchester City	Bolton Wanderers
27	Dibble, Andrew G.	Bolton Wanderers	Manchester City (Tr. back)
19	Dickinson, Stephen	Bradford City	Blackpool
3	Edwards, Neil R.	Leeds United	Stockport County
13	Farrell, Sean	Luton Town	Northampton Town
26	Fillery, Michael	Oldham Athletic	Torquay United
5	Freestone, Roger	Chelsea	Swansea City
2	Glover, Edward I.	Nottingham Forest	Luton Town
19	Hamilton, Gary J.	Middlesbrough	Darlington
26	Hawke, Warren R.	Sunderland	Chesterfield
23	Hayes, Martin	Celtic	Coventry City
27	Hewitt, John	Celtic	Middlesbrough
12	James, Julian C.	Luton Town	Preston North End
12	Lange, Anthony S.	Wolverhampton Wdrs.	Torquay United
30	McLoughlin, Alan	Southampton	Aston Villa
5	McLoughlin, Paul B.	Wolverhampton Wdrs.	Walsall
25	Matthews, Neil	Stockport County	Halifax Town
26	Marshall, Colin	Barnsley	Wrexham
26	Mauge, Ronald C.	Bury	Manchester City
5	Nethercott, Stuart	Tottenham Hotspur	Maidstone United
19	Ormondroyd, Ian	Aston Villa	Derby County
19	Parkin, Timothy J.	Port Vale	Shrewsbury Town
11	Paskin, William J.	Wolverhampton Wdrs.	Stockport County
5	Redfearn, Neil D.	Oldham Athletic	Barnsley
26	Reed, John P.	Sheffield United	Scarborough
27	Rush, David	Hartlepool United	Sunderland (Tr. back)
18	Shannon, Robert	Dundee	Middlesbrough
5	Sinclair, Ronald	Bristol City	Walsall
15	Stein, Mark E. S.	Oxford United	Stoke City
11	Todd, Mark	Sheffield United	Rotherham United
20	Walker, Andrew	Celtic	Newcastle United
16	Walsh, Paul	Tottenham Hotspur	Queens Park Rangers
19	Watson, Andrew A.	Swansea City	Carlisle United
12	Widdrington, Thomas	Southampton	Wigan Athletic
2	Williams, David P.	Burnley	Rochdale

October 1991

4	Aylott, Trevor K.C.	Birmingham City	Oxford United
17	Beaumont, David	Luton Town	Hibernian
23	Byrne, John F.	Brighton & Hove Albion	Sunderland
8	Carter, James W. C.	Liverpool	Arsenal
31	Coatsworth, Gary	Darlington	Leicester City
2	Edwards, Neil R.	Leeds United	Stockport County
1	Gabbiadini, Marco	Sunderland	Crystal Palace
24	Gall, Mark I.	Maidstone United	Brighton & Hove Albion
18	Jackson, Matthew A.	Luton Town	Everton
1	Jones, Andrew M.	AFC Bournemouth	Leyton Orient
21	Jones, Keith A.	Brentford	Southend United
4	Jones, Robert M.	Crewe Alexandra	Liverpool
22	Linton, Desmond	Leicester City	Luton Town

<table>
<tr><th></th><th>*From*</th><th>*To*</th></tr>
<tr><td>1 McDonald, Neil</td><td>Everton</td><td>Oldham Athletic</td></tr>
<tr><td>18 Mortimer, Paul H.</td><td>Aston Villa</td><td>Crystal Palace</td></tr>
<tr><td>22 Oakes, Scott J.</td><td>Leicester City</td><td>Luton Town</td></tr>
<tr><td>29 Penrice, Gary</td><td>Aston Villa</td><td>Queens Park Rangers</td></tr>
<tr><td>10 Redfearn, Neil D.</td><td>Oldham Athletic</td><td>Barnsley</td></tr>
<tr><td>4 Rogan, Anthony G. P.</td><td>Celtic</td><td>Sunderland</td></tr>
<tr><td>22 Thompson, Stephen J.</td><td>Luton Town</td><td>Leicester City</td></tr>
<tr><td>9 Wood, Stephen</td><td>Millwall</td><td>Southampton</td></tr>
<tr><td>25 Wright, Alan</td><td>Blackpool</td><td>Blackburn Rovers</td></tr>
</table>

Temporary Transfers

<table>
<tr><td>30 Allpress, Timothy J.</td><td>Luton Town</td><td>Preston North End</td></tr>
<tr><td>30 Beauchamp, Joseph D.</td><td>Oxford United</td><td>Swansea City</td></tr>
<tr><td>17 Bracey, Lee M. I.</td><td>Swansea City</td><td>Halifax Town</td></tr>
<tr><td>1 Branagan, Keith</td><td>Millwall</td><td>Gillingham</td></tr>
<tr><td>28 Branagan, Keith</td><td>Gillingham</td><td>Millwall (Tr. back)</td></tr>
<tr><td>9 Connelly, Dean</td><td>Barnsley</td><td>Wigan Athletic</td></tr>
<tr><td>31 Cullen, Anthony</td><td>Sunderland</td><td>Bury</td></tr>
<tr><td>4 Dibble, Andrew G.</td><td>Manchester City</td><td>Bolton Wanderers</td></tr>
<tr><td>10 Drinkell, Kevin</td><td>Coventry City</td><td>Birmingham City</td></tr>
<tr><td>3 Gallimore, Anthony</td><td>Stoke City</td><td>Carlisle United</td></tr>
<tr><td>17 Gosney, Andrew</td><td>Portsmouth</td><td>York City</td></tr>
<tr><td>3 Gray, Brian</td><td>Birmingham City</td><td>Shelbourne</td></tr>
<tr><td>17 Harris, Andrew</td><td>Birmingham City</td><td>Oxford United</td></tr>
<tr><td>31 Haylock, Garry</td><td>Huddersfield Town</td><td>Shelbourne</td></tr>
<tr><td>24 Hopkins, Jeffrey</td><td>Crystal Palace</td><td>Plymouth Argyle</td></tr>
<tr><td>17 James, Julian</td><td>Preston North End</td><td>Luton Town (Tr. back)</td></tr>
<tr><td>31 Johnson, David A.</td><td>Sheffield Wednesday</td><td>Hartlepool United</td></tr>
<tr><td>24 Kennedy, Andrew J.</td><td>Watford</td><td>Bolton Wanderers</td></tr>
<tr><td>11 Key, Lance</td><td>Sheffield Wednesday</td><td>York City</td></tr>
<tr><td>15 Kinnaird, Paul</td><td>St Mirren</td><td>Leyton Orient</td></tr>
<tr><td>24 Lewis, Dudley K.</td><td>Huddersfield Town</td><td>Halifax Town</td></tr>
<tr><td>31 McCarrison, Dugald</td><td>Celtic</td><td>Darlington</td></tr>
<tr><td>10 Maguire, Gavin</td><td>Portsmouth</td><td>Newcastle United</td></tr>
<tr><td>18 Marwood, Brian</td><td>Sheffield United</td><td>Middlesbrough</td></tr>
<tr><td>24 Matthews, Neil</td><td>Halifax Town</td><td>Stockport Co (Tr. back)</td></tr>
<tr><td>25 Maxwell, Alastair</td><td>Motherwell</td><td>Liverpool</td></tr>
<tr><td>24 Moncur, John F.</td><td>Tottenham Hotspur</td><td>Ipswich Town</td></tr>
<tr><td>30 Morrow, Stephen</td><td>Arsenal</td><td>Reading</td></tr>
<tr><td>10 Osman, Russell</td><td>Southampton</td><td>Bristol City</td></tr>
<tr><td>24 Palin, Leigh</td><td>Hull City</td><td>Rochdale</td></tr>
<tr><td>3 Payne, Russell</td><td>Liverpool</td><td>Crewe Alexandra</td></tr>
<tr><td>17 Richards, Carroll L.</td><td>Blackpool</td><td>Maidstone United</td></tr>
<tr><td>3 Rutherford, Mark</td><td>Birmingham City</td><td>Shelbourne</td></tr>
<tr><td>17 Smith, Neil J.</td><td>Tottenham Hotspur</td><td>Gillingham</td></tr>
<tr><td>11 Suckling, Perry</td><td>Crystal Palace</td><td>Brentford</td></tr>
<tr><td>25 Turner, Christopher R.</td><td>Sheffield Wednesday</td><td>Leyton Orient</td></tr>
<tr><td>17 Walker, Andrew F,</td><td>Celtic</td><td>Newcastle Utd (Tr. back)</td></tr>
<tr><td>17 Williams, William J.</td><td>AFC Bournemouth</td><td>Wigan Athletic</td></tr>
<tr><td>3 Wood, Paul A.</td><td>Sheffield United</td><td>AFC Bournemouth</td></tr>
</table>

November 1991

<table>
<tr><td>12 Agana, Patrick A.</td><td>Sheffield United</td><td>Notts County</td></tr>
<tr><td>8 Agboola, Reuben</td><td>Sunderland</td><td>Swansea City</td></tr>
<tr><td>21 Bart-Williams, C. G.</td><td>Leyton Orient</td><td>Sheffield Wednesday</td></tr>
<tr><td>22 Booker, Robert</td><td>Sheffield United</td><td>Brentford</td></tr>
</table>

	From	*To*
27 Comstive, Paul	Bolton Wanderers	Chester City
29 Cooper, Neale	Reading	Dunfermline Athletic
28 Cowans, Gordon S.	Aston Villa	Blackburn Rovers
21 Ford, Tony	West Bromwich Albion	Grimsby Town
8 Gordon, Dale A.	Norwich City	Rangers
28 Harris, Andrew	Birmingham City	Exeter City
8 Hendry, Edward C. J.	Manchester City	Blackburn Rovers
20 Johnston, Maurice T.	Rangers	Everton
1 Kamara, Christopher	Leeds United	Luton Town
22 Kane, Paul	Oldham Athletic	Aberdeen
8 Mowbray, Anthony M.	Middlesbrough	Celtic
15 Newell, Michael C.	Everton	Blackburn Rovers
15 Osman, Russell	Southampton	Bristol City
21 Pardew, Alan	Crystal Palace	Charlton Athletic
29 Parker, Garry S.	Nottingham Forest	Aston Villa
22 Payton, Andrew P.	Hull City	Middlesbrough
7 Regis, David	Notts County	Plymouth Argyle
28 Peake, Andrew M.	Charlton Athletic	Middlesbrough
8 Sloan, Scott	Newcastle United	Falkirk
25 Smith, Neil J.	Tottenham Hotspur	Gillingham
7 Stein, Mark E. S.	Oxford United	Stoke City
27 Tallon, Gary T.	Drogheda United	Blackburn Rovers
15 Todd, Mark	Sheffield United	Rotherham United
21 Turner, Christopher R.	Sheffield Wednesday	Leyton Orient
1 Watson, Andrew A.	Swansea City	Carlisle United
7 Wood, Paul A.	Sheffield United	AFC Bournemouth
15 Youds, Edward P.	Everton	Ipswich Town

Temporary Transfers

	From	*To*
21 Bennett, David	Swindon Town	Shrewsbury Town
28 Britton, Gerard J.	Celtic	Reading
1 Carstairs, James W.	Cambridge United	Stockport County
21 Carter, Timothy D.	Sunderland	Birmingham City
15 Gage, Kevin	Aston Villa	Sheffield United
15 Gosney, Andrew R.	York City	Portsmouth (Tr. back)
18 Harrison, Lee	Charlton Athletic	Fulham
22 Hewitt, John	Middlesbrough	Celtic (Tr. back)
5 Keeley, John H.	Oldham Athletic	Oxford United
26 Kennedy, Andrew J.	Bolton Wanderers	Watford (Tr. back)
21 Kite, Philip D.	Sheffield United	Mansfield Town
29 Leighton, James	Manchester United	Reading
1 Livingstone, Glen	Aston Villa	Omagh Town
1 McInerney, Ian	Peterborough United	Derry City
4 McLoughlin, Paul	Walsall	Wolverhampton Wdrs. (Tr. back)
20 Meaker, Michael	Queens Park Rangers	Plymouth Argyle
20 Morah, Olisa H.	Tottenham Hotspur	Hereford United
29 Morrow, Stephen	Reading	Arsenal (Tr. back)
7 Mountfield, Derek	Aston Villa	Wolverhampton Wdrs.
6 Narbett, Jonathan V.	Hereford United	Leicester City
21 Paskin, John	Wolverhampton Wdrs.	Birmingham City
18 Polston, Andrew	Tottenham Hotspur	Gillingham
27 Raven, Paul	West Bromwich Albion	Doncaster Rovers
23 Reed, John	Scarborough	Sheffield United (Tr. back)
21 Rose, Kevin	Bolton Wanderers	Rochdale
28 Rosenior, Leroy	West Ham United	Charlton Athletic

<table>
<tr><td></td><td>From</td><td>To</td></tr>
<tr><td>7 Russell, Kevin J.</td><td>Leicester City</td><td>Hereford United</td></tr>
<tr><td>21 Sinclair, Ronald</td><td>Bristol City</td><td>Stoke City</td></tr>
<tr><td>13 Sommer, Juergen P.</td><td>Luton Town</td><td>Brighton & Hove Albion</td></tr>
<tr><td>20 Statham, Brian</td><td>Tottenham Hotspur</td><td>AFC Bournemouth</td></tr>
<tr><td>28 Sutton, Steven</td><td>Nottingham Forest</td><td>Luton Town</td></tr>
<tr><td>1 West, Colin</td><td>West Bromwich Albion</td><td>Port Vale</td></tr>
<tr><td>29 Whitehead, Philip M.</td><td>Barnsley</td><td>Scunthorpe United</td></tr>
<tr><td>28 Wilder, Christopher J.</td><td>Sheffield United</td><td>Charlton Athletic</td></tr>
<tr><td>21 Will, James</td><td>Arsenal</td><td>Sheffield United</td></tr>
<tr><td>12 Witter, Tony</td><td>Queens Park Rangers</td><td>Millwall</td></tr>
</table>

December 1991

<table>
<tr><td>6 Allen, Clive</td><td>Manchester City</td><td>Chelsea</td></tr>
<tr><td>5 Clarke, Nicholas J.</td><td>Wolverhampton Wdrs.</td><td>Mansfield Town</td></tr>
<tr><td>6 Gavin, Mark W.</td><td>Watford</td><td>Bristol City</td></tr>
<tr><td>6 Goodman, Donald R.</td><td>West Bromwich Albion</td><td>Sunderland</td></tr>
<tr><td>4 Kelly, David T.</td><td>Leicester City</td><td>Newcastle United</td></tr>
<tr><td>24 McMahon, Steve</td><td>Liverpool</td><td>Manchester City</td></tr>
<tr><td>12 Nogan, Lee M.</td><td>Oxford United</td><td>Watford</td></tr>
<tr><td>18 Ormondroyd, Ian</td><td>Aston Villa</td><td>Derby County</td></tr>
<tr><td>12 Osborne, Lawrence W.</td><td>Maidstone United</td><td>Gillingham</td></tr>
<tr><td>18 Preece, Andrew</td><td>Wrexham</td><td>Stockport County</td></tr>
<tr><td>12 Randall, Adrian J.</td><td>Aldershot</td><td>Burnley</td></tr>
<tr><td>6 Rose, Kevin P.</td><td>Bolton Wanderers</td><td>Rochdale</td></tr>
<tr><td>19 Smith, David A.</td><td>Bristol City</td><td>Plymouth Argyle</td></tr>
<tr><td>16 Thomas, Michael L.</td><td>Arsenal</td><td>Liverpool</td></tr>
<tr><td>24 Thompson, Simon</td><td>Rotherham United</td><td>Scarborough</td></tr>
<tr><td>20 Trotter, Michael</td><td>Darlington</td><td>Leicester City</td></tr>
<tr><td>20 Willis, James A.</td><td>Darlington</td><td>Leicester City</td></tr>
<tr><td>19 Wilson, Paul A.</td><td>Northampton Town</td><td>Halifax Town</td></tr>
</table>

Temporary Transfers

<table>
<tr><td>30 Adcock, Anthony C.</td><td>Northampton Town</td><td>Peterborough United</td></tr>
<tr><td>19 Beardsmore, Russell P.</td><td>Manchester United</td><td>Blackburn Rovers</td></tr>
<tr><td>5 Bodin, Paul</td><td>Crystal Palace</td><td>Newcastle United</td></tr>
<tr><td>24 Carey, Brian P.</td><td>Manchester United</td><td>Wrexham</td></tr>
<tr><td>10 Davison, Robert</td><td>Derby County</td><td>Leeds United (Tr. back)</td></tr>
<tr><td>20 Dewhurst, Robert M.</td><td>Blackburn Rovers</td><td>Darlington</td></tr>
<tr><td>19 Farrell, Sean</td><td>Luton Town</td><td>Fulham</td></tr>
<tr><td>12 Fereday, Wayne</td><td>AFC Bournemouth</td><td>West Bromwich Albion</td></tr>
<tr><td>19 Humphrey, John M.</td><td>Millwall</td><td>Exeter City</td></tr>
<tr><td>26 Kendall, Mark</td><td>Swansea City</td><td>Burnley</td></tr>
<tr><td>31 Kerr, Dylan</td><td>Leeds United</td><td>Blackpool</td></tr>
<tr><td>12 MacKenzie, Stephen</td><td>Sheffield Wednesday</td><td>Shrewsbury Town</td></tr>
<tr><td>19 Miller, Alan</td><td>Arsenal</td><td>Birmingham City</td></tr>
<tr><td>12 Nebbeling, Gavin M.</td><td>Fulham</td><td>Hereford United</td></tr>
<tr><td>12 Purnell, Philip</td><td>Bristol Rovers</td><td>Swansea City</td></tr>
<tr><td>10 Robinson, Ronald</td><td>Rotherham United</td><td>Peterborough United</td></tr>
<tr><td>12 Sinclair, Frank M.</td><td>Chelsea</td><td>West Bromwich Albion</td></tr>
<tr><td>11 Williams, Andrew</td><td>Leeds United</td><td>Port Vale</td></tr>
<tr><td>12 Williams, William J.</td><td>AFC Bournemouth</td><td>Cardiff City</td></tr>
</table>

January 1992

<table>
<tr><td>14 Ablett, Gary I.</td><td>Liverpool</td><td>Everton</td></tr>
<tr><td>2 Beckford, Jason</td><td>Manchester City</td><td>Birmingham City</td></tr>
<tr><td>10 Bodin, Paul</td><td>Crystal Palace</td><td>Swindon Town</td></tr>
<tr><td>16 Bracey, Lee M. I.</td><td>Swansea City</td><td>Halifax Town</td></tr>
</table>

		From	*To*
9	Cadette, Richard R.	Brentford	Falkirk
31	Caesar, Gus C.	Bristol City	Airdrieonians
24	Cross, Paul	Barnsley	Hartlepool United
24	Cusack, Nicholas J.	Motherwell	Darlington
17	Dziekanowski, D. P.	Celtic	Bristol City
15	Farrell, Sean	Luton Town	Fulham
31	Gabbiadini, Marco	Crystal Palace	Derby County
21	Gaughan, Stephen	Sunderland	Darlington
31	Jones, Alexander	Rochdale	Motherwell
28	Jones, David	Aston Villa	Wrexham
24	Limber, Nicholas	Doncaster Rovers	Manchester City
8	McKinnon, Robert	Hartlepool United	Motherwell
17	McLoughlin, Paul B.	Wolverhampton Wdrs.	Mansfield Town
9	Pejic, Melvyn	Hereford United	Wrexham
31	Rankine, Simon M.	Doncaster Rovers	Wolverhampton Wdrs.
10	Rideout, Paul D.	Notts County	Glasgow Rangers
2	Rowbotham, Darren	Torquay United	Birmingham City
9	Sinclair, Ronald M.	Bristol City	Stoke City
31	Taylor, Robert	Bristol City	West Bromwich Albion
23	Thompstone, Ian P.	Oldham Athletic	Exeter City
24	Williams, William J.	AFC Bournemouth	Cardiff City

Temporary Transfers

25	Bacon, John	Arsenal	Shamrock Rovers
10	Barlow, Stuart	Everton	Rotherham United
15	Byrne, David	Watford	Fulham
23	Callaghan, Nigel	Aston Villa	Huddersfield Town
9	Collins, David D.	Liverpool	Wigan Athletic
9	Duxbury, Michael	Blackburn Rovers	Bradford City
16	Foley, Steven	Swindon Town	Stoke City
10	Foy, David L.	Birmingham City	Cobh Ramblers
22	Freeman, Clive R.	Swansea City	Carlisle United
28	Gilkes, Michael E.	Reading	Chelsea
30	Hardy, Jason P.	Burnley	Halifax Town
24	Harrison, Gerald	Bristol City	Cardiff City
30	Harrison, Lee D.	Fulham	Charlton Athletic (Tr. back)
9	Heaney, Neil	Arsenal	Cambridge United
16	Hendon, Ian M.	Tottenham Hotspur	Portsmouth
21	Hodges, Kevin	Plymouth Argyle	Torquay United
21	Johnrose, Leonard	Blackburn Rovers	Preston North End
9	Kearton, Jason	Everton	Blackpool
30	Kelly, Anthony	Stoke City	Hull City
22	Kilner, Andrew W.	Stockport County	Rochdale
30	Lee, David J.	Chelsea	Reading
16	McLoughlin, Paul	York City	Wolverhampton Wdrs. (Tr. back)
26	McNab, Neil	Tranmere Rovers	Huddersfield Town
9	Mendonca, Clive P.	Sheffield United	Grimsby Town
9	Moore, Kevin T.	Southampton	Bristol Rovers
13	Mountfield, Derek	Aston Villa	Wolverhampton Wdrs.
23	Newton, Edward J. I.	Chelsea	Cardiff City
16	Norris, Stephen M.	Halifax Town	Chesterfield
9	Pearson, John S.	Barnsley	Hull City
29	Rees, Melvyn	West Bromwich Albion	Norwich City
3	Robson, Mark A.	Tottenham Hotspur	Exeter City

<table>
<tr><td></td><td>From</td><td>To</td></tr>
<tr><td>8 Rodger, Graham</td><td>Luton Town</td><td>Grimsby Town</td></tr>
<tr><td>2 Russell, Kevin</td><td>Leicester City</td><td>Stoke City</td></tr>
<tr><td>30 Scott, Morrys J.</td><td>Plymouth Argyle</td><td>St Patricks</td></tr>
<tr><td>13 Sheffield, Jonathan</td><td>Cambridge United</td><td>Sheffield United</td></tr>
<tr><td>21 Sinclair, Frank M.</td><td>West Bromwich Albion</td><td>Chelsea (Tr. back)</td></tr>
<tr><td>6 Smith, Anthony</td><td>Sunderland</td><td>Hartlepool United</td></tr>
<tr><td>16 Smith, Jeremy</td><td>Wigan Athletic</td><td>Derry City</td></tr>
<tr><td>16 Statham, Brian</td><td>Tottenham Hotspur</td><td>Brentford</td></tr>
<tr><td>30 Stevenson, Andrew J.</td><td>Scunthorpe United</td><td>Doncaster Rovers</td></tr>
<tr><td>22 Taylor, Colin</td><td>Wolverhampton Wdrs.</td><td>Wigan Athletic</td></tr>
<tr><td>9 Walker, Andrew</td><td>Glasgow Celtic</td><td>Bolton Wanderers</td></tr>
<tr><td>9 Witter, Anthony</td><td>Queens Park Rangers</td><td>Plymouth Argyle</td></tr>
<tr><td>15 Whitehurst, William</td><td>Doncaster Rovers</td><td>Crewe Alexandra</td></tr>
<tr><td>16 Whitworth, Neil A.</td><td>Manchester United</td><td>Preston North End</td></tr>
<tr><td>11 Williams, Andrew</td><td>Port Vale</td><td>Leeds United (Tr. back)</td></tr>
<tr><td>30 Wilson, Terry</td><td>Nottingham Forest</td><td>Newcastle United</td></tr>
</table>

February 1992

<table>
<tr><td>7 Adcock, Anthony C.</td><td>Northampton Town</td><td>Peterborough United</td></tr>
<tr><td>7 Barnes, David O.</td><td>Northampton Town</td><td>Peterborough United</td></tr>
<tr><td>25 Barrett, Earl D.</td><td>Oldham Athletic</td><td>Aston Villa</td></tr>
<tr><td>6 Boyd, Thomas</td><td>Chelsea</td><td>Celtic</td></tr>
<tr><td>19 Carstairs, James</td><td>Cambridge United</td><td>Stockport County</td></tr>
<tr><td>7 Cascarino, Anthony</td><td>Celtic</td><td>Chelsea</td></tr>
<tr><td>14 Fereday, Wayne</td><td>AFC Bournemouth</td><td>*West Bromwich Albion</td></tr>
<tr><td>28 Foley, Steven</td><td>Swindon Town</td><td>Stoke City</td></tr>
<tr><td>21 Gage, Kevin W.</td><td>Aston Villa</td><td>Sheffield United</td></tr>
<tr><td>21 Harmon, Darren</td><td>Notts County</td><td>Shrewsbury Town</td></tr>
<tr><td>21 Holmes, Michael</td><td>Torquay United</td><td>Carlisle United</td></tr>
<tr><td>28 Johnrose, Leonard</td><td>Blackburn Rovers</td><td>Hartlepool United</td></tr>
<tr><td>21 Kelly, James</td><td>Wrexham</td><td>Wolverhampton Wdrs.</td></tr>
<tr><td>28 Kelly, Paul A.</td><td>Manchester City</td><td>Crewe Alexandra</td></tr>
<tr><td>8 Kozma, Istvan</td><td>Dunfermline Athletic</td><td>Liverpool</td></tr>
<tr><td>7 Leighton, James</td><td>Manchester United</td><td>Dundee</td></tr>
<tr><td>3 Mountfield, Derek</td><td>Aston Villa</td><td>Wolverhampton Wdrs.</td></tr>
<tr><td>28 Muir, Johnny G.</td><td>Doncaster Rovers</td><td>Stockport County</td></tr>
<tr><td>26 Norris, Stephen M.</td><td>Halifax Town</td><td>Chesterfield</td></tr>
<tr><td>28 O'Neill, Alan</td><td>Cobh Ramblers</td><td>Birmingham City</td></tr>
<tr><td>21 Paskin, William J.</td><td>Wolverhampton Wdrs.</td><td>Wrexham</td></tr>
<tr><td>7 Price, Christopher J.</td><td>Aston Villa</td><td>Blackburn Rovers</td></tr>
<tr><td>13 Rodger, Graham</td><td>Luton Town</td><td>Grimsby Town</td></tr>
<tr><td>28 Sherwood, Timothy A.</td><td>Norwich City</td><td>Blackburn Rovers</td></tr>
<tr><td>20 Simpson, Paul D.</td><td>Oxford United</td><td>Derby County</td></tr>
<tr><td>28 Statham, Brian</td><td>Tottenham Hotspur</td><td>Brentford</td></tr>
<tr><td>11 Walker, Andrew F.</td><td>Celtic</td><td>Bolton Wanderers</td></tr>
</table>

Temporary Transfers

<table>
<tr><td>27 Agana, Patrick A.</td><td>Notts County</td><td>Leeds United</td></tr>
<tr><td>27 Allon, Joseph</td><td>Chelsea</td><td>Port Vale</td></tr>
<tr><td>7 Atteveld, Raymond</td><td>Everton</td><td>West Ham United</td></tr>
<tr><td>27 Blake, Noel</td><td>Stoke City</td><td>Bradford City</td></tr>
<tr><td>6 Branagan, Keith</td><td>Millwall</td><td>Fulham</td></tr>
<tr><td>13 Cowdrill, Barry J.</td><td>Bolton Wanderers</td><td>Rochdale</td></tr>
<tr><td>21 Dewhurst, Robert</td><td>Darlington</td><td>Blackburn R. (Tr. back)</td></tr>
<tr><td>27 Dibble, Andrew G.</td><td>Manchester City</td><td>West Bromwich Albion</td></tr>
<tr><td>13 Donovan, Kevin</td><td>Huddersfield Town</td><td>Halifax Town</td></tr>
</table>

		From	*To*
26	Gallimore, Anthony	Stoke City	Carlisle United
19	Gittens, Jon	Southampton	Middlesbrough
27	Gray, Andrew A.	Crystal Palace	Tottenham Hotspur
22	Hayes, Martin	Celtic	Wimbledon
27	Hendry, John	Tottenham Hotspur	Charlton Athletic
21	Hogan, Thomas E.	Birmingham City	Cobh Ramblers
6	Keeley, John	Oldham Athletic	Reading
19	Kilcline, Brian	Oldham Athletic	Newcastle United
14	Kite, Phillip	Mansfield Town	Sheffield United (Tr. back)
6	Leighton, James	Reading	Manchester Utd. (Tr. back)
17	McLoughlin, Alan F.	Southampton	Portsmouth
14	Marples, Christopher	York City	Scunthorpe United
18	Moncur, John F.	Tottenham Hotspur	Nottingham Forest
27	Moore, Kevin	Bristol Rovers	Southampton (Tr. back)
13	Nethercott, Stuart	Tottenham Hotspur	Barnet
28	Newman, Richard	Crystal Palace	Maidstone United
13	Paskin, William J.	Wolverhampton Wdrs.	Shrewsbury Town
20	Paskin, William J.	Shrewsbury Town	Wolverhampton Wdrs. (Tr. back)
13	Peake, Jason W.	Leicester City	Hartlepool United
21	Peyton, Gerard J.	Everton	Bolton Wanderers
20	Rennie, David	Bristol City	Birmingham City
12	Sherwood, Timothy A.	Norwich City	Blackburn Rovers
20	Steele, Timothy L.	Wolverhampton Wdrs.	Stoke City
21	Walker, Joseph N.	Heart of Midlothian	Burnley
20	Whitworth, Neil A.	Manchester United	Barnsley
27	Wilder, Christopher J.	Sheffield United	Leyton Orient
4	Williams, Andrew	Leeds United	Notts County
27	Williams, Brett	Nottingham Forest	Oxford United

March 1992

		From	*To*
27	Allen, Clive D.	Chelsea	West Ham United
26	Atteveld, Raymond	Everton	Bristol City
26	Cook, Mitchell C.	Darlington	Blackpool
9	Cork, Alan G.	Wimbledon	Sheffield United
27	Cowdrill, Barry J.	Bolton Wanderers	Rochdale
26	Curran, Christopher	Crewe Alexandra	Scarborough
27	Dickins, Matthew J.	Lincoln City	Blackburn Rovers
6	Duxbury, Michael	Blackburn Rovers	Bradford City
24	Garland, Peter J.	Tottenham Hotspur	Newcastle United
11	Gee, Phillip	Derby County	Leicester City
13	Grayson, Simon N.	Leeds United	Leicester City
27	Greenall, Colin	Bury	Preston North End
27	Heath, Adrian P.	Manchester City	Stoke City
2	Hughton, C. W. G.	West Ham United	Brentford
27	Humes, Anthony	Ipswich Town	Wrexham
23	Johnson, Thomas	Notts County	Derby County
12	Jones, Phillip L.	Wrexham	Liverpool
20	Kilcline, Brian	Oldham Athletic	Newcastle United
11	Kitson, Paul	Leicester City	Derby County
27	Leonard, Mark	Bradford City	Rochdale
19	Lydiate, Jason L.	Manchester United	Bolton Wanderers
26	McCall, Stephen H.	Sheffield Wednesday	Plymouth Argyle
20	McDonough, Darron K.	Luton Town	Newcastle United
27	McLoughlin, Alan F.	Southampton	Portsmouth
23	Mahood, Alan S.	Nottingham Forest	Morton

		From	*To*
31	Miller, David	Carlisle United	Stockport County
30	Moncur, John	Tottenham Hotspur	Swindon Town
27	Noteman, Kevin S.	Doncaster Rovers	Mansfield Town
23	Nugent, Kevin	Leyton Orient	Plymouth Argyle
11	Ormondroyd, Ian	Derby County	Leicester City
27	Painter, Peter R.	Maidstone United	Burnley
10	Raynor, Paul J.	Swansea City	Cambridge United
26	Rees, Melvyn	West Bromwich Albion	Sheffield United
20	Reid, Wesley	Bradford City	Airdrieonians
19	Rennie, David	Bristol City	Birmingham City
20	Robinson, Ronald	Rotherham United	Peterborough United
26	Sale, Mark	Cambridge United	Birmingham City
13	Saville, Andrew V.	Barnsley	Hartlepool United
27	Shearer, Duncan	Swindon Town	Blackburn Rovers
6	Simpson, Fitzroy	Swindon Town	Manchester City
6	Sutton, Stephen J.	Nottingham Forest	Derby County
28	Taylor, John P.	Cambridge United	Bristol Rovers
24	Taylor, Peter M.	Blackpool	Wrexham
24	Tolson, Neil	Walsall	Oldham Athletic
13	Watts, Julian	Rotherham United	Sheffield Wednesday
6	Wegerle, Roy C.	Queens Park Rangers	Blackburn Rovers
28	White, Devan W.	Bristol Rovers	Cambridge United
27	Whitlow, Michael	Leeds United	Leicester Clty
27	Williams, Andrew	Leeds United	Notts County
27	Wilson, Kevin J.	Chelsea	Notts County

Temporary Transfers

19	Bannister, Gary	West Bromwich Albion	Oxford United
18	Bellamy, Gary	Wolverhampton Wdrs.	Cardiff City
26	Bent, Junior A.	Bristol City	Stoke City
19	Bishop, Edwards M.	Chester City	Crewe Alexandra
27	Bremner, Kevin	Dundee	Shrewsbury Town
24	Butler, Peter J. F.	Southend United	Huddersfield Town
4	Callaghan, Nigel	Huddersfield Town	Aston Villa (Tr. back)
26	Charnley, James	St Mirren	Bolton Wanderers
12	Cole, Andrew A.	Arsenal	Bristol City
26	Cooper, Stephen B.	Tranmere Rovers	Peterborough United
26	Cundy, Jason V.	Chelsea	Tottenham Hotspur
6	Davison, Robert	Leeds United	Sheffield United
5	Day, Mervyn R.	Leeds United	Luton Town
19	Dearden, Kevin C.	Tottenham Hotspur	Birmingham City
26	Elliott, Matthew S.	Torquay United	Scunthorpe United
5	Flitcroft, Garry W.	Manchester City	Bury
26	Ford, Stuart	Rotherham United	Scarborough
26	Gibson, Terrence B.	Wimbledon	Swindon Town
4	Gilkes, Michael E.	Reading	Southampton
26	Gough, Alan T.	Portsmouth	Fulham
6	Green, Richard E.	Swindon Town	Gillingham
24	Harrison, Lee D.	Charlton Athletic	Gillingham
13	Harrison, Gerald	Cardiff City	Bristol City (Tr. back)
10	Heald, Paul A.	Leyton Orient	Coventry City
26	Hendon, Ian M.	Tottenham Hotspur	Leyton Orient
17	Herrera, Roberto	Queens Park Rangers	Torquay United
26	Hill, Colin F.	Sheffield United	Leicester City
26	Horne, Brian	Millwall	Watford
25	Hoult, Russell	Leicester City	Blackpool

		From	To
11	Ireland, Simon P.	Huddersfield Town	Wrexham
5	Ironside, Ian	Middlesbrough	Scarborough
5	Jeffrey, Michael R.	Bolton Wanderers	Doncaster Rovers
12	Johnson, Thomas	Notts County	Derby County
25	Kerr, Dylan	Blackpool	Leeds United (Tr. back)
25	Kruszynski, Zbigniew	Wimbledon	Brentford
26	Lange, Anthony S.	Wolverhampton Wdrs.	Portsmouth
26	Lee, David J.	Chelsea	Plymouth Argyle
26	Loram, Mark J.	Torquay United	Stockport County
19	Lowe, David A.	Ipswich Town	Port Vale
5	McClelland, John	Leeds United	Notts County
5	McKeown, Gary J.	Arsenal	Shrewsbury Town
26	Marshall, Colin	Barnsley	Scarborough
12	Mauchlen, Alistair H.	Leicester City	Leeds United
16	Maxwell, Alistair	Motherwell	Bolton Wanderers
19	Mendonca, Clive P.	Sheffield United	Grimsby Town
4	Morris, Andrew D.	Chesterfield	Exeter City
4	Morrow, Stephen J.	Arsenal	Barnet
4	Nevin, Patrick K. F.	Everton	Tranmere Rovers
26	Petterson, Andrew K.	Luton Town	Ipswich Town
7	Peyton, Gerry J.	Bolton Wanderers	Everton (Tr. back)
26	Peyton, Gerry J.	Everton	Norwich City
26	Pollitt, Michael F.	Bury	Lincoln City
10	Pressman, Kevin P.	Sheffield Wednesday	Stoke City
26	Rees, Melvyn	Norwich City	West Bromwich Albion (Tr. back)
19	Reid, Paul R.	Leicester City	Bradford City
26	Salman, Danis M. M.	Plymouth Argyle	Peterborough United
26	Samways, Mark	Doncaster Rovers	Scunthorpe United
25	Sealey, Leslie J.	Aston Villa	Coventry City
5	Shepstone, Paul T.	Blackburn Rovers	York City
26	Stiles, John C.	Doncaster Rovers	Rochdale
27	Thomas, Roderick C.	Watford	Gillingham
26	Trollope, Paul J.	Swindon Town	Torquay United
26	Varadi, Imre	Leeds United	Luton Town
19	Waddock, Gary P.	Queens Park Rangers	Swindon Town
26	Whyte, David A.	Crystal Palace	Charlton Athletic
5	Williams, Andrew	Leeds United	Notts County
26	Willis, James A.	Leicester City	Bradford City

April 1992

22	Nicholson, Shane M.	Lincoln City	Derby County

Temporary Transfers

1	Brown, Kevan	Aldershot	Portsmouth
15	Day, Mervyn R.	Luton Town	Leeds United (Tr. back)
2	Gilkes, Earl G.M.	Southampton	Reading (Tr. back)
1	Hoult, Matthew J.	Blackburn Rovers	Aston Villa
28	Hoult, Russell	Blackpool	Leicester City (Tr. back)
10	Key, Lance	Sheffield Wednesday	York City
21	Whitworth, Neil A.	Barnsley	Manchester Utd. (Tr. back)

May 1992

Temporary Transfer

6	Varadi, Imre	Luton Town	Leeds United (Tr. back)

LIST OF REFEREES FOR SEASON 1992–93

Paul Alcock (S. Merstham, Surrey)
David Allison (Lancaster)
Gerald Ashby, (Worcester)
David Axcell, (Southend)
Mike Bailey, (Impington, Cambridge)
Keren Barrett, (Coventry)
Steven Bell, (Huddersfield)
Ray Bigger, (Croydon)
Martin Bodenham, (Looe, Cornwall)
Jim Borrett, (Harleston, Norfolk)
John Brandwood, (Lichfield, Staffs.)
Kevin Breen, (Liverpool)
Alf Buksh, (London)
Keith Burge, (Tonypandy)
Billy Burns, (Scarborough)
Vic Callow, (Solihull)
John Carter, (Christchurch)
Brian Coddington, (Sheffield)
Keith Cooper, (Pontypridd)
Keith Cooper, (Swindon)
Ian Cruikshanks, (Hartlepool)
Paul Danson, (Leicester)
Alan Dawson, (Jarrowe)
Roger Dilkes, (Mossley, Lancs.)
Phil Don, (Hanworth Park, Middlesex)
Steve Dunn, (Bristol)
Paul Durkin, (Portland, Dorset)
David Elleray, (Harrow)
Tom Fitzharris, (Bolton)
Alan Flood, (Stockport)
Peter Foakes, (Clacton-on-Sea)
David Frampton, (Poole, Dorset)
Dermot Gallagher, (Banbury, Oxon.)
Rodger Gifford, (Llanbradach, Mid. Glam.)
Ron Groves, (Weston-Super-Mare)
Allan Gunn, (South Chailey, Sussex)
Keith Hackett, (Sheffield)
Bob Hamer, (Bristol)
Paul Harrison, (Oldham)
Robert Hart, (Darlington)
Ian Hemley, (Ampthill, Beds.)
Ian Hendrick, (Preston)
Brian Hill, (Kettering)
Terry Holbrook, (Walsall)
Mike James, (Horsham)
Peter Jones, (Loughborough)

John Key, (Sheffield)
Howard King, (Merthyr Tydfil)
John Kirkby, (Sheffield)
Ken Leach, (Wolverhampton)
Ray Lewis, (Gt. Bookham, Surrey)
John Lloyd, (Wrexham)
Stephen Lodge, (Barnsley)
Terry Lunt, (Ashton-in-Makerfield, Lancs)
Ken Lupton, (Stockton-on-Tees)
Kevin Lynch, (Lincoln)
John Martin, (Nr. Alton, Hants.)
Roger Milford, (Bristol)
Kelvin Morton, (Bury St. Edmunds)
John Moules, (Erith, Kent)
Bob Nixon, (West Kirkby, Wirrall)
Jim Parker, (Preston)
Roger Pawley, (Cambridge)
Mike Peck, (Kendal)
David Phillips, (Barnsley)
Micky Pierce, (Portsmouth)
Graham Poll, (Berkhamsted)
Graham Pooley, (Bishops Stortford)
Richard Poulain, (Huddersfield)
Ken Redfern, (Whitley Bay)
Mike Reed, (Birmingham)
Jim Rushton, (Stoke-on-Trent)
Paul Scoble, (Portsmouth)
Dave Shadwell, (Bromsgrove)
Ray Shepherd, (Leeds)
Gurnam Singh, (Wolverhampton)
Arthur Smith, (Rubery, Birmingham)
Paul Taylor, (Waltham Cross, Herts.)
Colin Trussell, (Liverpool)
Paul Vanes, (Warley, West Midlands)
Tony Ward, (London)
John Watson, (Whitley Bay)
Trevor West, (Hull)
Clive Wilkes, (Gloucester)
Alan Wilkie, (Chester-le-Street)
Gary Willard, (Worthing, W. Sussex)
Jeff Winter, (Middlesbrough)
Roger Wiseman (Borehamwood, Herts.)
Eddie Wolstenholme, (Blackburn)
Joe Worrall, (Warrington)
Philip Wright, (Northwich)

WORLD CLUB CHAMPIONSHIP

Played annually up to 1974 and intermittently until 1979 between the winners of
the European Cup and the winners of the South American Champions Cup —
known as the Copa Libertadores. In 1980 the winners were decided by one match
arranged in Tokyo in February 1981 and the venue has been the same since.

1960 Real Madrid beat Penarol 0-0, 5-1
1961 Penarol beat Benfica 0-1, 5-0, 2-1
1962 Santos beat Benfica 3-2, 5-2
1963 Santos beat AC Milan 2-4, 4-2, 1-0
1964 Inter-Milan beat Independiente 0-1, 2-0, 1-0
1965 Inter-Milan beat Independiente 3-0, 0-0
1966 Penarol beat Real Madrid 2-0, 2-0
1967 Racing Club beat Celtic 0-1, 2-1, 1-0
1968 Estudiantes beat Manchester United 1-0, 1-1
1969 AC Milan beat Estudiantes 3-0, 1-2
1970 Feyenoord beat Estudiantes 2-2, 1-0
1971 Nacional beat Panathinaikos* 1-1, 2-1
1972 Ajax beat Independiente 1-1, 3-0
1973 Independiente beat Juventus* 1-0
1974 Atletico Madrid* beat Independiente 0-1, 2-0
1975 Independiente and Bayern Munich could not agree dates; no matches.
1976 Bayern Munich beat Cruzeiro 2-0, 0-0
1977 Boca Juniors beat Borussia Moenchengladbach* 2-2, 3-0
1978 Not played
1979 Olimpia beat Malmo* 1-0, 2-1
1980 Nacional beat Nottingham Forest 1-0
1981 Flamengo beat Liverpool 3-0
1982 Penarol beat Aston Villa 2-0
1983 Gremio Porto Alegre beat SV Hamburg 2-1
1984 Independiente beat Liverpool 1-0
1985 Juventus beat Argentinos Juniors 4-2 on penalties after a 2-2 draw
1986 River Plate beat Steaua Bucharest 1-0
1987 FC Porto beat Penarol 2-1 after extra time
1988 Nacional (Uru) beat PSV Eindhoven 7-6 on penalties after 1-1 draw
1989 AC Milan beat Atletico Nacional (Col) 1-0 after extra time
1990 AC Milan beat Olimpia 3-0

* European Cup runners-up; winners declined to take part.

1991

8 December in Tokyo

Red Star Belgrade (1) 3 *(Jugovic 19, 58, Pancev 72)*

Colo Colo (0) 0 60,000

Red Star Belgrade: Milojevic; Radinovic, Vasilijevic, Belodedic, Najdoski, Jugovic,
Stosic, Ratkovic, Savicevic, Mihajlovic, Pancev.
Colo Colo: Moron; Garrido, Margas, Miguel Ramirez, Salvatierra (Dabrowski 65)
Mendoza, Vilches, Barticciotto, Pizarro, Yanez, Martinez (Rubio 60).
Referee: Rothlisberger (Switzerland).

FA CUP REVIEW

Liverpool, the odds-on favourites, dispatched Sunderland 2-0 in a final memorable for an electrifying second half performance by Steve McManaman on the right flank. He made the first goal for Michael Thomas by sheer skill and persistence, before continuing to torment the Sunderland defence with his weaving runs.

Yet until he was switched from the left side just before half-time, Sunderland had had an equal share of the play. Indeed they contributed the miss of the match when John Byrne snatched at a clear chance and miscued completely. But had Thomas not squandered an even earlier opening, the outcome might have been known well before the break.

Both sides claimed to have been denied a penalty, Rob Jones on Sunderland's Peter Davenport appearing to be the less obvious infringement compared with Paul Bracewell's upending of McManaman. Then two minutes after the interval, McManaman wriggled on the touchline, shrugged off the opposition and flicked the ball invitingly into space for Thomas. The Liverpool midfield player let it bounce once and volleyed over Tony Norman in the Sunderland goal. Sunderland's contribution virtually ended with that goal. Dean Saunders hit the bar and then in the 68th minute, Ian Rush finished off a move involving Ray Houghton, Saunders and Thomas to set a cup record with his fifth goal in three finals.

Sunderland's victims in the cup had been Port Vale, Oxford United then both West Ham and Chelsea after replays before they beat Norwich City 1-0 in the semi-final, Byrne thus scoring in every round. Liverpool accounted for Crewe, Bristol Rovers after a replay, Ipswich also at the second attempt and Aston Villa. In their semi-final they drew 1-1 with Portsmouth but survived to the final after a penalty shoot-out in the replay. The outcry against this ludicrously unfair lottery might well have been louder had the Anfield side failed to reach Wembley, providing an all-Second Division final for the first time in the competition's history.

FINAL at Wembley
9 MAY

Liverpool (0) 2 *(Thomas, Rush)*

Sunderland (0) 0   79,544

Liverpool: Grobbelaar; Jones, Burrows, Nicol, Molby, Wright, Saunders, Houghton, Rush, McManaman, Thomas.

Sunderland: Norman; Owers, Ball, Bennett, Rogan, Rush (Hardyman), Bracewell, Davenport, Armstrong, Byrne, Atkinson (Hawke).
Referee: P. Don (Middlesex).

FA CUP 1991–92

FIRST ROUND
Aldershot (0) 0 Enfield (0) 1
Atherstone (0) 0 Hereford U (0) 0
Barnet (2) 5 Tiverton (0) 0
Blackpool (1) 2 Grimsby T (0) 1
Bournemouth (0) 3 Bromsgrove (1) 1
Brentford (2) 3 Gillingham (1) 3
Bridlington (0) 1 York C (0) 2
Burnley (0) 1 Doncaster R (0) 1
Bury (0) 0 Bradford C (0) 1
Carlisle U (0) 1 Crewe Alex (1) 1
Chester C (1) 1 Guiseley (0) 0
Colchester U (0) 0 Exeter C (0) 0
Crawley (2) 4 Northampton T (2) 2
Darlington (1) 2 Chesterfield (1) 1
Emley (0) 0 Bolton W (1) 3
Fulham (0) 0 Hayes (0) 2
Gretna (0) 0 Rochdale (0) 0
Halesowen (2) 2 Farnborough (2)
Hartlepool U (1) 3 Shrewsbury T (1) 2
Huddersfield T (3) 7 Lincoln U (0) 0
Kettering (0) 1 Wycombe (0) 1
Kidderminster (0) 0 Aylesbury (0) 1
Leyton Orient (0) 2 Welling (1) 1
Maidstone U (1) 1 Sutton U (0) 0
Mansfield T (0) 0 Preston NE (0) 1
Morecambe (0) 0 Hull C (1) 1
Peterborough U (6) 7 Harlow (0) 0
Runcorn (0) 0 Tranmere R (1) 3
Scarborough (0) 0 Wigan Ath (1) 2
Scunthorpe U (0) 1 Rotherham U (1) 1
Slough (1) 3 Reading (0) 3
Stockport Co (0) 3 Lincoln C (0) 1
Stoke C (0) 0 Telford (0) 0
Swansea C (1) 2 Cardiff C (1) 1
Torquay U (2) 3 Birmingham C (0) 0
WBA (3) 6 Marlow (0) 0
Windsor (2) 2 Woking (1) 4
Witton (1) 1 Halifax T (0) 1
Wrexham (1) 5 Winsford (1) 2
Yeovil (0) 1 Walsall (0) 1

FIRST ROUND REPLAYS
Crewe Alex (2) 5 Carlisle U (0) 3 *aet*
Doncaster R (1) 1 Burnley (1) 3
Exeter C (0) 0 Colchester U (0) 0

Farnborough (0) 4 Halesowen (0) 0
Gillingham (0) 1 Brentford (1) 3
Halifax T (0) 1 Witton (0) 2 *aet*
Hereford U (1) 3 Atherstone (0) 0
Reading (2) 2 Slough (0) 1
Rochdale (3) 3 Gretna (0) 1
Rotherham U (1) 3 Scunthorpe (0) 3
aet; Rotherham U won 7-6 on penalties
Telford (1) 2 Stoke C (0) 1
Walsall (0) 0 Yeovil (0) 1 *aet*
Wycombe (0) 0 Kettering (0) 2

SECOND ROUND
Aylesbury (1) 2 Hereford U (2) 3
Blackpool (0) 0 Hull C (0) 1
Bolton W (2) 3 Bradford C (0) 1
Bournemouth (0) 2 Brentford (0) 1
Burnley (0) 2 Rotherham U (0) 0
Crewe Alex (0) 2 Chester C (0) 0
Darlington (0) 1 Hartlepool U (2) 2
Enfield (0) 1 Barnet (1) 4
Exeter C (0) 0 Swansea (0) 0
Hayes (0) 0 Crawley (1) 2
Leyton Orient (1) 2 WBA (0) 1
Maidstone U (1) 1 Kettering (1) 2
Peterborough U (0) 0 Reading (0) 0
Preston NE (3) 5 Witton (0) 1
Rochdale (1) 1 Huddersfield T (0) 2
Torquay U (0) 1 Farnborough (1) 1
Wigan Ath (1) 2 Stockport Co (0) 0
Woking (1) 3 Yeovil (0) 0
Wrexham (0) 1 Telford (0) 0
York C (0) 1 Tranmere R (1) 1

SECOND ROUND REPLAYS
Farnborough (2) 4 Torquay U (0) 3
Reading (0) 1 Peterborough U (0) 0
Swansea C (0) 1 Exeter C (1) 2
Tranmere R (1) 2 York C (0) 1

THIRD ROUND
Aston Villa (0) 0 Tottenham H (0) 0
Blackburn R (1) 4 Kettering (0) 1
Bolton W (0) 2 Reading (0) 0
Bournemouth (0) 0 Newcastle U (0) 0
Brighton & HA (3) 5 Crawley (0) 0
Bristol C (0) 1 Wimbledon (1) 1
Bristol R (2) 5 Plymouth Arg (0) 0
Burnley (1) 2 Derby Co (1) 2
Charlton Ath (1) 3 Barnet (1) 1

Coventry C (0) 1 Cambridge U (1) 1
Crewe Alex (0) 0 Liverpool (3) 4
Everton (1) 1 Southend U (0) 0
Exeter C (0) 1 Portsmouth (1) 2
Farnborough (0) 1 West Ham U (0) 1
Huddersfield T (0) 0 Millwall (4) 4
Hull C (0) 0 Chelsea (1) 2
Ipswich T (0) 1 Hartlepool U (1) 1
Leeds U (0) 0 Manchester U (1) 1
Leicester C (0) 1 Crystal Palace (0) 0
Middlesbrough (0) 2 Manchester C (1) 1
Norwich C (0) 1 Barnsley (0) 0
Nottingham F (0) 1 Wolverhampton W (0)
Notts Co (0) 2 Wigan Ath (0) 0
Oldham Ath (0) 1 Leyton Orient (1) 1
Oxford U (2) 3 Tranmere R (0) 1
Preston NE (0) 0 Sheffield W (0) 2
Sheffield U (1) 4 Luton T (0) 0
Southampton (2) 2 QPR (0) 0
Sunderland (2) 3 Port Vale (0) 0
Swindon T (2) 3 Watford (1) 2
Woking (0) 0 Hereford U (0) 0
Wrexham (0) 2 Arsenal (1) 1

THIRD ROUND REPLAYS
Cambridge U (0) 1 Coventry C (0) 0
Derby Co (0) 2 Burnley (0) 0
Hartlepool U (0) 0 Ipswich T (1) 2
Hereford U (1) 2 Woking (0) 1 *aet*
Leyton Orient (0) 4 Oldham Ath (1) 2
Newcastle U (1) 2 Bournemouth (0) 2
aet; Bournemouth won 4-3 on penalties
Tottenham H (0) 0 Aston Villa (1) 1
West Ham U (0) 1 Farnborough (0) 0
Wimbledon (0) 0 Bristol C (1) 1

FOURTH ROUND
Bolton W (0) 2 Brighton & HA (0) 1
Bristol R (0) 1 Liverpool (1) 1
Cambridge U (0) 0 Swindon T (1) 3
Charlton Ath (0) 0 Sheffield U (0) 0
Chelsea (0) 1 Everton (0) 0
Derby Co (2) 3 Aston Villa (4) 4
Ipswich T (2) 3 Bournemouth (0) 0
Leicester C (0) 1 Bristol C (1) 2
Norwich C (1) 2 Millwall (0) 1
Nottingham F (1) 2 Hereford U (0) 0
Notts Co (1) 2 Blackburn R (0) 1
Oxford U (0) 2 Sunderland (2) 3
Portsmouth (0) 2 Leyton Orient (0) 0

Sheffield W (1) 1 Middlesbrough (1) 2
Southampton (0) 0 Manchester U (0) 0
West Ham U (1) 2 Wrexham (0) 2

FOURTH ROUND REPLAYS
Liverpool (0) 2 Bristol R (1) 1
Manchester U (1) 2 Southampton (2) 2
aet; Southampton won 4-2 on penalties
Sheffield U (3) 3 Charlton Ath (0) 1
Wrexham (0) 0 West Ham U (1) 1

FIFTH ROUND
Bolton W (0) 2 Southampton (2) 2
Chelsea (1) 1 Sheffield U (0) 0
Ipswich T (0) 0 Liverpool (0) 0
Norwich C (2) 3 Notts Co (0) 0
Nottingham F (1) 4 Bristol C (0) 1
Portsmouth (0) 1 Middlesbrough (0) 1
Sunderland (0) 1 West Ham U (0) 1
Swindon T (0) 1 Aston Villa (1) 2

FIFTH ROUND REPLAYS
Liverpool (1) 3 Ipswich T (0) 2 *aet*
Middlesbrough (2) 2 Portsmouth (2) 4
Southampton (1) 3 Bolton W (1) 2 *aet*
West Ham U (1) 2 Sunderland (2) 3

SIXTH ROUND
Chelsea (1) 1 Sunderland (0) 1
Liverpool (0) 1 Aston Villa (0) 0
Portsmouth (1) 1 Nottingham F (0) 0
Southampton (0) 0 Norwich C (0) 0

SIXTH ROUND REPLAYS
Norwich C (0) 2 Southampton (1) 1 *aet*
Sunderland (1) 2 Chelsea (0) 1

SEMI-FINALS
Liverpool (0) 1 Portsmouth (0) 1 *aet*
Sunderland (1) 1 Norwich C (0) 0

SEMI-FINAL REPLAY
Portsmouth (0) 0 Liverpool (0) 0
aet; Liverpool won 3-1 on penalties

FINAL at Wembley
9 MAY
Liverpool (0) 2 *(Thomas, Rush)*
Sunderland (0) 0   79,544

PAST FA CUP FINALS

Details of some goalscorers are not available for the early years

1872	The Wanderers .... 1 *Betts*	Royal Engineers 0	
1873	The Wanderers .... 2 *Kinnaird, Wollaston*	Oxford University 0	
1874	Oxford University .... 2 *Mackarness, Patton*	Royal Engineers 0	
1875	Royal Engineers .... 1 *Renny-Tailyour*	Old Etonians .... 1* *Bonsor*	
Replay	Royal Engineers .... 2 *Renny-Tailyour, Stafford*	Old Etonians 0	
1876	The Wanderers .... 1 *Edwards*	Old Etonians .... 1* *Bonsor*	
Replay	The Wanderers .... 3 *Wollaston, Hughes 2*	Old Etonians 0	
1877	The Wanderers .... 2 *Kenrick, Heron*	Oxford University .... 1* *Kinnaird (og)*	
1878	The Wanderers .... 3 *Kenrick 2, unknown*	Royal Engineers .... 1 *Unknown*	
1879	Old Etonians .... 1 *Clerke*	Clapham Rovers 0	
1880	Clapham Rovers .... 1 *Lloyd-Jones*	Oxford University 0	
1881	Old Carthusians .... 3 *Wyngard, Parry, Todd*	Old Etonians 0	
1882	Old Etonians .... 1 *Anderson*	Blackburn Rovers 0	
1883	Blackburn Olympic .... 2 *Costley, Matthews*	Old Etonians .... 1* *Goodhart*	
1884	Blackburn Rovers .... 2 *Brown, Forrest*	Queen's Park, Glasgow .... 1 *Christie*	
1885	Blackburn Rovers .... 2 *Forrest, Brown*	Queen's Park, Glasgow 0	
1886	Blackburn Rovers 0	West Bromwich Albion 0	
Replay	Blackburn Rovers .... 2 *Brown, Sowerbutts*	West Bromwich Albion 0	
1887	Aston Villa .... 2 *Hunter, Hodgetts*	West Bromwich Albion 0	
1888	West Bromwich Albion . 2 *Woodhall, Bayliss*	Preston NE .... 1 *Goodall*	
1889	Preston NE .... 3 *Dewhurst, Ross, Thompson*	Wolverhampton W 0	
1890	Blackburn Rovers .... 6 *Dewar, John, Southworth, Lofthouse, Townley 3*	Sheffield W .... 1 *Bennett*	

1891	Blackburn Rovers......... 3	Notts Co.....................................1
	Dewar, John Southworth, Townley	*Oswald*
1892	West Bromwich Albion . 3	Aston Villa 0
	Geddes, Nicholls, Reynolds	
1893	Wolverhampton W 1	Everton 0
	Allen	
1894	Notts Co..................... 4	Bolton W...................................1
	Watson, Logan 3	*Cassidy*
1895	Aston Villa 1	West Bromwich Albion 0
	Devey	
1896	Sheffield W 2	Wolverhampton W 1
	Spiksley 2	*Black*
1897	Aston Villa 3	Everton 2
	Campbell, Wheldon, Crabtree	*Boyle, Bell*
1898	Nottingham F 3	Derby Co 1
	Capes 2, McPherson	*Bloomer*
1899	Sheffield U................... 4	Derby Co 1
	Bennett, Beers, Almond, Priest	*Boag*
1900	Bury 4	Southampton 0
	McLuckie 2, Wood, Plant	
1901	Tottenham H................ 2	Sheffield U...............................2
	Brown 2	*Bennett, Priest*
Replay	Tottenham H................ 3	Sheffield U...............................1
	Cameron, Smith, Brown	*Priest*
1902	Sheffield U................... 1	Southampton 1
	Common	*Wood*
Replay	Sheffield U................... 2	Southampton 1
	Hedley, Barnes	*Brown*
1903	Bury 6	Derby Co 0
	Ross, Sagar, Leeming 2, Wood, Plant	
1904	Manchester C 1	Bolton W...................................0
	Meredith	
1905	Aston Villa 2	Newcastle U..............................0
	Hampton 2	
1906	Everton 1	Newcastle U..............................0
	Young	
1907	Sheffield W 2	Everton 1
	Stewart, Simpson	*Sharp*
1908	Wolverhampton W 3	Newcastle U..............................1
	Hunt, Hedley, Harrison	*Howie*
1909	Manchester U 1	Bristol C...................................0
	A. Turnbull	
1910	Newcastle U................ 1	Barnsley 1
	Rutherford	*Tuffnell*
Replay	Newcastle U................ 2	Barnsley 0
	Shepherd 2 (1 pen)	

1911	Bradford C 0	Newcastle U 0
Replay	Bradford C 1	Newcastle U 0
	Spiers	
1912	Barnsley 0	West Bromwich Albion 0
Replay	Barnsley 1	West Bromwich Albion 0*
	Tuffnell	
1913	Aston Villa 1	Sunderland............0
	Barber	
1914	Burnley 1	Liverpool............0
	Freeman	
1915	Sheffield U 3	Chelsea 0
	Simmons, Fazackerley, Kitchen	
1920	Aston Villa 1	Huddersfield T............0*
	Kirton	
1921	Tottenham H................1	Wolverhampton W 0
	Dimmock	
1922	Huddersfield T............1	Preston NE 0
	Smith (pen)	
1923	Bolton W................2	West Ham U 0
	Jack, J.R. Smith	
1924	Newcastle U 2	Aston Villa 0
	Harris, Seymour	
1925	Sheffield U 1	Cardiff C 0
	Tunstall	
1926	Bolton W................1	Manchester C 0
	Jack	
1927	Cardiff C 1	Arsenal 0
	Ferguson	
1928	Blackburn Rovers............3	Huddersfield T............1
	Roscamp 2, McLean	*A. Jackson*
1929	Bolton W................2	Portsmouth 0
	Butler, Blackmore	
1930	Arsenal 2	Huddersfield T............0
	James, Lambert	
1931	West Bromwich Albion .2	Birmingham 1
	W.G. Richardson 2	*Bradford*
1932	Newcastle U 2	Arsenal 1
	Allen 2	*John*
1933	Everton 3	Manchester C 0
	Stein, Dean, Dunn	
1934	Manchester C 2	Portsmouth 1
	Tilson 2	*Rutherford*
1935	Sheffield W 4	West Bromwich Albion 2
	Rimmer 2, Palethorpe, Hooper	*Boyes, Sandford*
1936	Arsenal 1	Sheffield U............0
	Drake	
1937	Sunderland................3	Preston NE 1
	Gurney, Carter, Burbanks	*F. O'Donnell*

1938	Preston NE 1	Huddersfield T 0*
	Mutch (pen)	
1939	Portsmouth 4	Wolverhampton W 1
	Parker 2, Barlow,	*Dorsett*
	Anderson	
1946	Derby Co 4	Charlton Ath 1*
	H. Turner (og), Doherty,	*H. Turner*
	Stamps 2	
1947	Charlton Ath 1	Burnley 0*
	Duffy	
1948	Manchester U 4	Blackpool 2
	Rowley 2, Pearson,	*Shimwell (pen), Mortensen*
	Anderson	
1949	Wolverhampton W 3	Leicester C 1
	Pye 2, Smyth,	*Griffiths*
1950	Arsenal 2	Liverpool...................................0
	Lewis 2	
1951	Newcastle U 2	Blackpool 0
	Milburn 2	
1952	Newcastle U 1	Arsenal 0
	G. Robledo	
1953	Blackpool 4	Bolton W...................................3
	Mortensen 3, Perry	*Lofthouse, Moir, Bell*
1954	West Bromwich Albion ...	Preston NE 2
	Allen 2 (1 pen), Griffin	*Morrison, Wayman*
1955	Newcastle U 3	Manchester C 1
	Milburn, Mitchell,	*Johnstone*
	Hannah	
1956	Manchester C 3	Birmingham C 1
	Hayes, Dyson, Johnstone	*Kinsey*
1957	Aston Villa 2	Manchester U............................1
	McParland 2	*T. Taylor*
1958	Bolton W..................... 2	Manchester U............................0
	Lofthouse 2	
1959	Nottingham F 2	Luton T.....................................1
	Dwight, Wilson	*Pacey*
1960	Wolverhampton W 3	Blackburn Rovers.......................0
	McGrath (og), Deeley 2	
1961	Tottenham H................ 2	Leicester C 0
	Smith, Dyson	
1962	Tottenham H................ 3	Burnley 1
	Greaves, Smith,	*Robson*
	Blanchflower (pen)	
1963	Manchester U 3	Leicester C 1
	Herd 2, Law	*Keyworth*
1964	West Ham U 3	Preston NE 2
	Sissons, Hurst, Boyce	*Holden, Dawson*
1965	Liverpool..................... 2	Leeds U 1*
	Hunt, St John	*Bremner*

1966	Everton .... 3 *Trebilcock 2, Temple*	Sheffield W ....2 *McCalliog, Ford*
1967	Tottenham H.................. 2 *Robertson, Saul*	Chelsea ....1 *Tambling*
1968	West Bromwich Albion . 1 *Astle*	Everton 0*
1969	Manchester C .... 1 *Young*	Leicester C 0
1970	Chelsea .... 2 *Houseman, Hutchinson*	Leeds U ....2* *Charlton, Jones*
Replay	Chelsea .... 2 *Osgood, Webb*	Leeds U ....1* *Jones*
1971	Arsenal .... 2 *Kelly, George*	Liverpool................................1* *Heighway*
1972	Leeds U .... 1 *Clarke*	Arsenal 0
1973	Sunderland.................... 1 *Porterfield*	Leeds U 0
1974	Liverpool...................... 3 *Keegan 2, Heighway*	Newcastle 0
1975	West Ham U .... 2 *A. Taylor 2*	Fulham..................................0
1976	Southampton .... 1 *Stokes*	Manchester U.........................0
1977	Manchester U .... 2 *Pearson, J. Greenhoff*	Liverpool................................1 *Case*
1978	Ipswich T...................... 1 *Osborne*	Arsenal 0
1979	Arsenal .... 3 *Talbot, Stapleton, Sunderland*	Manchester U.........................2 *McQueen, McIlroy*
1980	West Ham U .... 1 *Brooking*	Arsenal 0
1981	Tottenham H................. 1 *Hutchison (og)*	Manchester C.........................1* *Hutchison*
Replay	Tottenham H................. 3 *Villa 2, Crooks*	Manchester C.........................2 *Mackenzie, Reeves (pen)*
1982	Tottenham H................. 1 *Hoddle*	QPR......................................1* *Fenwick*
Replay	Tottenham H................. 1 *Hoddle (pen)*	QPR......................................0
1983	Manchester U .... 2 *Stapleton, Wilkins*	Brighton & HA ....2* *Smith, Stevens*
Replay	Manchester U .... 4 *Robson 2, Whiteside, Muhren*	Brighton & HA ....0 *(pen)*
1984	Everton .... 2 *Sharp, Gray*	Watford.................................0
1985	Manchester U .... 1 *Whiteside*	Everton 0*

1986	Liverpool 3	Everton 1
	Rush 2, Johnston	*Lineker*
1987	Coventry C 3	Tottenham H...........................2*
	Bennett, Houchen,	*C. Allen, Kilcline (og)*
	Mabbutt (og)	
1988	Wimbledon 1	Liverpool..................................0
	Sanchez	
1989	Liverpool..................... 3	Everton...................................2*
	Aldridge, Rush 2	*McCall 2*
1990	Manchester U 3	Crystal Palace.........................3*
	Robson, Hughes 2	*O'Reilly, Wright 2*
Replay	Manchester U 1	Crystal P 0
	Martin	
1991	Tottenham H............... 2	Nottingham F 1*
	Stewart, Walker (og)	*Pearce*
1992	Liverpool.................... 2	Sunderland..............................0
	Thomas, Rush	

**After extra-time*

FA CUP WINNERS SINCE 1871

Tottenham Hotspur	8	Barnsley	1
Aston Villa	7	Blackburn Olympic	1
Manchester United	7	Blackpool	1
Blackburn Rovers	6	Bradford City	1
Newcastle United	6	Burnley	1
Arsenal	5	Cardiff City	1
Liverpool	5	Charlton Athletic	1
The Wanderers	5	Chelsea	1
West Bromwich Albion	5	Clapham Rovers	1
Bolton Wanderers	4	Coventry City	1
Everton	4	Derby County	1
Manchester City	4	Huddersfield Town	1
Sheffield United	4	Ipswich Town	1
Wolverhampton Wanderers	4	Leeds United	1
Sheffield Wednesday	3	Notts County	1
West Ham United	3	Old Carthusians	1
Bury	2	Oxford University	1
Nottingham Forest	2	Portsmouth	1
Old Etonians	2	Royal Engineers	1
Preston North End	2	Southampton	1
Sunderland	2	Wimbledon	1

APPEARANCES IN FA CUP FINAL

Arsenal	11	Burnley	3
Everton	11	Chelsea	3
Manchester United	11	Nottingham Forest	3
Newcastle United	11	Portsmouth	3
Liverpool	10	Southampton	3
West Bromwich Albion	10	Barnsley	2
Aston Villa	9	Birmingham City	2
Tottenham Hotspur	9	Bury	2
Blackburn Rovers	8	Cardiff City	2
Manchester City	8	Charlton Athletic	2
Wolverhampton Wanderers	8	Clapham Rovers	2
Bolton Wanderers	7	Notts County	2
Preston North End	7	Queen's Park (Glasgow)	2
Old Etonians	6	Blackburn Olympic	1
Sheffield United	6	Bradford City	1
Huddersfield Town	5	Brighton & Hove Albion	1
Sheffield Wednesday	5	Bristol City	1
The Wanderers	5	Coventry City	1
Derby County	4	Crystal Palace	1
Leeds United	4	Fulham	1
Leicester City	4	Ipswich Town	1
Oxford University	4	Luton Town	1
Royal Engineers	4	Old Carthusians	1
Sunderland	4	Queen's Park Rangers	1
West Ham United	4	Watford	1
Blackpool	3	Wimbledon	1

RUMBELOWS CUP REVIEW

Although one set of statistics presented after the Rumbelows Cup Final put Manchester United, the winners, and Nottingham Forest, the losers, having each gained possession 31 times and lost it on 84 occasions, United appeared more in control and deserved their 1-0 success. Forest looked jaded after six League and Cup games in two weeks, though United, their own League form unimpressive at the time, functioned well only spasmodically in a disappointing match.

Thus Forest were deprived of a record fifth League Cup success and United became the first beaten finalists to return triumphant the following season after losing 1-0 to Sheffield Wednesday in 1991.

Interest was sustained through the 1992 final because of the slender lead taken by United through Brian McClair in the 14th minute. Gary Pallister found McClair inside the Forest half, but the Scottish international was only able to touch the ball on for Ryan Giggs. The Welsh teenager made ground and drew the opposition to him before squaring to the unmarked McClair, who hit a left foot shot across Andy Marriott in the Forest goal from about 12 yards, a split second before being tackled. McClair had a second half effort cleared off the line by Brian Laws.

In the run up to the final, United had had the more impressive record, finding only Middlesbrough a real problem in the semi-final before winning in extra time. Forest struggled after the third round and needed replays to overcome Southampton and Crystal Palace. They also found Tottenham Hotspur in determined mood in the semi-final which also required the extra period to settle matters.

The competition began with a rare 5-5 draw involving Barnet and Brentford, one of several high scoring matches in the first round which did not produce a single goalless draw. But it was the second round which provided the highest score by a single team, when Oldham Athletic beat Torquay United 7-1, Andy Ritchie scoring four times. Appropriately it was Manchester United who put Oldham out in the fourth round by 2-0.

FINAL at Wembley

12 APR

Manchester U (1) 1 *(McClair)*

Nottingham F (0) 0   76,810

Manchester U: Schmeichel; Parker, Irwin, Bruce, Phelan, Pallister, Kanchelskis (Sharpe), Ince, McClair, Hughes, Giggs.
Nottingham F: Marriott; Charles (Laws), Williams, Walker, Wassall, Keane, Crosby, Gemmill, Clough, Sheringham, Black.
Referee: G. Courtney (Spennymoor).

RUMBELOWS CUP 1991–92

FIRST ROUND, FIRST LEG
Barnet (2) 5 Brentford (2) 5
Blackburn R (1) 1 Hull C (0) 1
Bolton W (1) 2 York C (0) 2
Chester C (0) 1 Lincoln C (0) 0
Crewe Alex (3) 5 Doncaster R (1) 2
Darlington (1) 1 Huddersfield T (0) 0
Halifax T (3) 3 Tranmere R (2) 4
Hartlepool U (1) 1 Bury (0) 0
Leyton Orient (3) 5 Northampton T (0) 0
Mansfield T (0) 0 Blackpool (2) 3
Peterborough U (1) 3 Aldershot (0) 1
Portsmouth (1) 2 Gillingham (0) 1
Preston NE (2) 5 Scarborough (2) 4
Rochdale (2) 5 Carlisle U (1) 1
Rotherham U (0) 1 Grimsby T (2) 3
Shrewsbury T (1) 1 Plymouth Arg (0) 1
Stockport Co (0) 1 Bradford C (1) 1
Swansea C (1) 2 Walsall (0) 2
Swindon T (2) 2 WBA (0) 0
Torquay U (1) 2 Hereford U (0) 0
Watford (2) 2 Southend U (0) 0
Wigan Ath (1) 3 Burnley (1) 1
Wrexham (0) 1 Scunthorpe U (0) 0
Cambridge U (0) 1 Reading (0) 0
Cardiff C (1) 3 Bournemouth (1) 2
Charlton Ath (2) 4 Fulham (0) 2
Exeter C (0) 0 Birmingham C (1) 1
Leicester C (1) 3 Maidstone U (0) 0
Stoke C (1) 1 Chesterfield (0) 0

FIRST ROUND, SECOND LEG
Aldershot (0) 1 Peterborough U (1) 2
Birmingham C (2) 4 Exeter C (0) 0
Blackpool (1) 4 Mansfield T (1) 2
Bournemouth (1) 4 Cardiff C (1) 1
Brentford (3) 3 Barnet (0) 1
Burnley (0) 2 Wigan Ath (0) 3
Bury (0) 2 Hartlepool U (0) 2
Carlisle U (0) 1 Rochdale (0) 1
Chesterfield (0) 1 Stoke C (1) 2
Doncaster R (1) 2 Crewe Alex (0) 4
Fulham (1) 1 Charlton Ath (1) 1
Gillingham (1) 3 Portsmouth (2) 4
Grimsby T (1) 1 Rotherham U (0) 0
Hull C (0) 1 Blackburn R (0) 0

Plymouth Arg (1) 2 Shrewsbury T* (0) 2 *aet*
Scunthorpe U (0) 3 Wrexham (0) 0
Tranmere R (1) 4 Halifax T (2) 3
Walsall (0) 0 Swansea C (1) 1
York C (1) 1 Bolton W (1) 2
Bradford C (1) 3 Stockport Co (0) 1 *aet*
Hereford U (1) 2 Torquay U (1) 1
Huddersfield T (1) 4 Darlington (0) 0
Lincoln C (1) 4 Chester C* (1) 3 *aet*
Maidstone U (0) 0 Leicester C (0) 1
Reading (0) 0 Cambridge U (2) 3
Scarborough (0) 3 Preston NE (1) 1 *aet*
Southend U (1) 1 Watford (1) 1
WBA (1) 2 Swindon T (0) 2
Northampton T (1) 2 Leyton Orient (0) 0

SECOND ROUND, FIRST LEG
Blackpool (0) 1 Barnsley (0) 0
Bradford C (1) 1 West Ham U (1) 1
Brentford (3) 4 Brighton & HA (0) 1
Crewe Alex (3) 3 Newcastle U (2) 4
Everton (0) 1 Watford (0) 0
Hull C (0) 0 QPR (1) 3
Leyton Orient (0) 0 Sheffield W (0) 0
Middlesbrough (0) 1 Bournemouth (0) 1
Oldham Ath (1) 7 Torquay U (0) 1
Portsmouth (0) 0 Oxford U (0) 0
Port Vale (1) 2 Notts Co (0) 1
Scarborough (1) 1 Southampton (2) 3
Scunthorpe U (0) 0 Leeds U (0) 0
Sunderland (0) 1 Huddersfield T (1) 2
Wigan Ath (2) 2 Sheffield U (1) 2
Wimbledon (1) 1 Peterborough U (2) 2
Wolverhampton W (4) 6 Shrewsbury T (1) 1
Bristol R (1) 1 Bristol C (2) 3
Charlton Ath (0) 0 Norwich C (1) 2
Chelsea (0) 1 Tranmere R (0) 1
Coventry C (2) 4 Rochdale (0) 0
Derby Co (0) 0 Ipswich T (0) 0
Grimsby T (0) 0 Aston Villa (0) 0
Hartlepool U (0) 1 Crystal Palace (1) 1
Leicester C (0) 1 Arsenal (1) 1
Liverpool (1) 2 Stoke C (1) 2
Luton T (0) 2 Birmingham C (1) 2
Manchester C (0) 3 Chester C (0) 1
Manchester U (1) 3 Cambridge U (0) 0
Millwall (1) 2 Swindon T (2) 2
Nottingham F (2) 4 Bolton W (0) 0
Swansea C (0) 1 Tottenham H (0) 0

SECOND ROUND, SECOND LEG
Arsenal (0) 2 Leicester C (0) 0
Barnsley (1) 2 Blackpool (0) 0 *aet*
Birmingham C (1) 3 Luton T (0) 2
Bolton W (2) 2 Nottingham F (3) 5
Bournemouth (0) 1 Middlesbrough (1) 2 *aet*
Bristol C (1) 2 Bristol R* (1) 4 *aet*
Chester C (0) 0 Manchester C (1) 3
Crystal Palace (2) 6 Hartlepool U (0) 1
Ipswich T (0) 0 Derby Co (2) 2
Leeds U (0) 3 Scunthorpe U (0) 0
Peterborough U (1) 2 Wimbledon (0) 2
Rochdale (0) 1 Coventry C (0) 0
Sheffield U (0) 1 Wigan Ath (0) 0
Shrewsbury T (1) 3 Wolverhampton W (1) 1
Swindon T (0) 3 Millwall (1) 1
Tranmere R (1) 3 Chelsea (0) 1 *aet*
Watford (0) 1 Everton (0) 2
Aston Villa (0) 1 Grimsby T* (0) 1 *aet*
Brighton & HA (3) 4 Brentford (1) 2 *aet*
Cambridge U (0) 1 Manchester U (1) 1
Huddersfield T (0) 4 Sunderland (0) 0
Newcastle U (0) 1 Crewe Alex (0) 0
Norwich C (2) 3 Charlton Ath (0) 0
Notts Co (0) 3 Port Vale* (1) 2 *aet*
Oxford U (0) 0 Portsmouth (1) 1
QPR (3) 5 Hull C (1) 1
Sheffield W (0) 4 Leyton Orient (1) 1
Southampton (2) 2 Scarborough (0) 2
Stoke C (0) 2 Liverpool (1) 3
Torquay U (0) 0 Oldham Ath (1) 2
Tottenham H (1) 5 Swansea C (0) 1
West Ham U (2) 4 Bradford C (0) 0

THIRD ROUND
Birmingham C (0) 1 Crystal Palace (0) 1
Grimsby T (0) 0 Tottenham H (1) 3
Huddersfield T (0) 1 Swindon T (2) 4
Leeds U (0) 3 Tranmere R (0) 1
Liverpool (1) 2 Port Vale (1) 2
Manchester C (0) 0 QPR (0) 0
Middlesbrough (1) 1 Barnsley (0) 0
Oldham Ath (0) 2 Derby Co (1) 1
Peterborough U (0) 1 Newcastle U (0) 0
Sheffield U (0) 0 West Ham U (1) 2
Coventry C (1) 1 Arsenal (0) 0
Everton (2) 4 Wolverhampton W (1) 1
Manchester U (0) 3 Portsmouth (0) 1
Norwich C (0) 4 Brentford (0) 1

Nottingham F (1) 2 Bristol R (0) 0
Sheffield W (1) 1 Southampton (0) 1

THIRD ROUND REPLAYS
Crystal Palace (0) 1 Birmingham C (0) 1 *aet*
Port Vale (1) 1 Liverpool (3) 4
QPR (1) 1 Manchester C (1) 3
Southampton (0) 1 Sheffield W (0) 0

THIRD ROUND SECOND REPLAY
Crystal Palace (2) 2 Birmingham C (1) 1

FOURTH ROUND
Middlesbrough (0) 2 Manchester C (0) 1
Peterborough U (1) 1 Liverpool (0) 0
Coventry C (0) 1 Tottenham H (1) 2
Everton (1) 1 Leeds U (2) 4
Manchester U (2) 2 Oldham Ath (0) 0
Norwich C (0) 2 West Ham U (0) 1
Nottingham F (0) 0 Southampton (0) 0
Swindon T (0) 0 Crystal Palace (1) 1

FOURTH ROUND REPLAY
Southampton (0) 0 Nottingham F (1) 1

FIFTH ROUND
Crystal Palace (0) 1 Nottingham F (0) 1
Leeds U (1) 1 Manchester U (1) 3
Peterborough U (0) 0 Middlesbrough (0) 0
Tottenham H (0) 2 Norwich C (1) 1

FIFTH ROUND REPLAYS
Nottingham F (3) 4 Crystal Palace (1) 2
Middlesbrough (0) 1 Peterborough (0) 0

SEMI-FINALS, FIRST LEG
Nottingham F (0) 1 Tottenham H (1) 1
Middlesbrough (0) 0 Manchester U (0) 0

SEMI-FINALS, SECOND LEG
Tottenham H (1) 1 Nottingham F (1) 2 *aet*
Manchester U (1) 2 Middlesbrough (0) 1 *aet*

FINAL at Wembley
12 APR
Manchester U (1) 1 *(McClair)*
Nottingham F (0) 0 76,810

* *Won on away goals*

PAST LEAGUE CUP FINALS

Played as two legs up to 1966

1961	Rotherham U 2	Aston Villa 0	
	Webster, Kirkman		
	Aston Villa 3	Rotherham U 0*	
	O'Neill, Burrows, McParland		
1962	Rochdale 0	Norwich C 3	
		Lythgoe 2, Punton	
	Norwich C 1	Rochdale 0	
	Hill		
1963	Birmingham C 3	Aston Villa 1	
	Leek 2, Bloomfield	*Thomson*	
	Aston Villa 0	Birmingham C 0	
1964	Stoke C 1	Leicester C 1	
	Bebbington	*Gibson*	
	Leicester C 3	Stoke C 2	
	Stringfellow, Gibson, Riley	*Viollet, Kinnell*	
1965	Chelsea 3	Leicester C 2	
	Tambling, Venables (pen), McCreadie	*Appleton, Goodfellow*	
	Leicester C 0	Chelsea 0	
1966	West Ham U 2	WBA 1	
	Moore, Byrne	*Astle*	
	WBA 4	West Ham U 1	
	Kaye, Brown, Clark, Williams	*Peters*	
1967	QPR 3	WBA 2	
	Morgan R, Marsh, Lazarus	*Clark C 2*	
1968	Leeds U 1	Arsenal 0	
	Cooper		
1969	Swindon T 3	Arsenal 1	
	Smart, Rogers 2	*Gould*	
1970	Manchester C 2	WBA 1	
	Doyle, Pardoe	*Astle*	
1971	Tottenham H 2	Aston Villa 0	
	Chivers 2		
1972	Chelsea 1	Stoke C 2	
	Osgood	*Conroy, Eastham*	
1973	Tottenham H 1	Norwich C 0	
	Coates		
1974	Wolverhampton W 2	Manchester C 1	
	Hibbitt, Richards	*Bell*	
1975	Aston Villa 1	Norwich C 0	
	Graydon		
1976	Manchester C 2	Newcastle U 1	
	Barnes, Tueart	*Gowling*	

1977	Aston Villa 0	Everton 0
Replay	Aston Villa 1	Everton 1*
	Kenyon (og)	*Latchford*
Replay	Aston Villa 3	Everton 2*
	Little 2, Nicholl	*Latchford, Lyons*
1978	Nottingham F 0	Liverpool...............................0*
Replay	Nottingham F 1	Liverpool...............................0
	Robertson (pen)	
1979	Nottingham F 3	Southampton 2
	Birtles 2, Woodcock	*Peach, Holmes*
1980	Wolverhampton W 1	Nottingham F 0
	Gray	
1981	Liverpool.................... 1	West Ham U 1*
	Kennedy, A	*Stewart (pen)*
Replay	Liverpool.................... 2	West Ham U 1
	Dalglish, Hansen	*Goddard*
1982	Liverpool.................... 3	Tottenham H...........................1*
	Whelan 2, Rush	*Archibald*
1983	Liverpool.................... 2	Manchester U..........................1*
	Kennedy, Whelan	*Whiteside*
1984	Liverpool.................... 0	Everton 0*
Replay	Liverpool.................... 1	Everton 0
	Souness	
1985	Norwich C 1	Sunderland.............................0
	Chisholm (og)	
1986	Oxford U.................... 3	QPR....................................0
	Hebberd, Houghton, Charles	
1987	Arsenal 2	Liverpool...............................1
	Nicholas 2	*Rush*
1988	Luton T..................... 3	Arsenal 2
	Stein B 2, Wilson	*Hayes, Smith*
1989	Nottingham F 3	Luton T................................1
	Clough 2, Webb	*Harford*
1990	Nottingham F 1	Oldham Ath............................0
	Jemson	
1991	Sheffield W 1	Manchester U..........................0
	Sheridan	

After extra time

ZENITH DATA SYSTEMS CUP 1991–92

FIRST ROUND
Grimsby T (1) 1 Wolverhampton W (0) 0
Port Vale (1) 1 Blackburn R (0) 0
Tranmere R (2) 6 Newcastle U (2) 6
aet; Tranmere R won 3–2 on penalties
Plymouth Arg (1) 1 Portsmouth (0) 0
Swindon T (0) 3 Oxford U (0) 3
aet; Swindon T won 4–3 on penalties
Leicester C (3) 4 Barnsley (0) 3 *aet*
Bristol R (1) 1 Ipswich T (1) 3
Cambridge U (1) 1 Charlton Ath (1) 1
aet; Cambridge U won 4–2 on penalties
Watford (0) 0 Southend U (1) 1

SECOND ROUND
Everton (1) 3 Oldham Ath (1) 2
Leeds U (0) 1 Nottingham F (2) 3
Middlesbrough (0) 4 Derby Co (2) 2 *aet*
Sheffield U (0) 3 Notts Co (1) 3
aet; Notts Co won 2–1 on penalties
Tranmere R (2) 5 Grimsby T (1) 1
Bristol C (1) 1 Southampton (0) 2
Crystal Palace (0) 4 Southend U (1) 2 *aet*
Ipswich T (0) 1 Luton T (0) 1
aet; Ipswich T won 2–1 on penalties
Plymouth Arg (2) 4 Millwall (0) 0
West Ham U (1) 2 Cambridge U (0) 1
Coventry C (0) 0 Aston Villa (1) 2
Leicester C (0) 4 Port Vale (0) 0
Sheffield W (1) 3 Manchester C (1) 2
Brighton & HA (2) 3 Wimbledon (1) 2
Chelsea (0) 1 Swindon T (0) 0
Norwich C (1) 1 QPR (1) 2

QUARTER-FINALS
Aston Villa (0) 0 Nottingham F (1) 2
Middlesbrough (0) 0 Tranmere R (0) 1
Notts Co (0) 1 Sheffield W (0) 0
Chelsea (1) 2 Ipswich T (1) 2
aet; Chelsea won 4–3 on penalties
Plymouth Arg (0) 0 Southampton (0) 1
QPR (0) 2 Crystal Palace (2) 3
West Ham U (2) Brighton & HA (0) 0
Leicester C (2) 2 Everton (0) 1

NORTHERN SEMI-FINALS
Tranmere R (0) 0 Nottingham F (1) 2
Notts Co (1) 1 Leicester C (0) 2 *aet*

SOUTHERN SEMI-FINALS
Crystal Palace (0) 0 Chelsea (1) 1
Southampton (0) 2 West Ham (1) 1

SOUTHERN FINAL First Leg
Southampton (1) 2 Chelsea (0) 0

SOUTHERN FINAL Second Leg
Chelsea (1) 1 Southampton (2) 3

NORTHERN FINAL First Leg
Leicester C (0) 1 Nottingham F (0) 1

NORTHERN FINAL Second Leg
Nottingham F (1) 2 Leicester C (0) 0

FINAL (at Wembley)
29 MAR
Nottingham F (2) 3 *(Gemmill 2, Black)*
Southampton (0) 2 *(Le Tissier, Moore)* aet 67,688
Nottingham F: Marriott; Charles, Pearce (Chettle), Walker, Wassall, Keane,
Crosby, Gemmill, Clough, Sheringham, Black.
Southampton: Flowers; Kenna, Benali, Horne, Moore, Ruddock, Le Tissier,
Cockerill, Shearer, Dowie, Hurlock.
Referee: K. Hackett (Sheffield).

AUTOGLASS TROPHY 1991–92

Rotherham U and Chesterfield given byes to First Round

PRELIMINARY ROUND
Wrexham (0) 1 Mansfield T (0) 0
Aldershot (0) 0 Brentford (1) 2
Blackpool (1) 1 Burnley (3) 3
Bournemouth (2) 3 Swansea C (0) 0
Darlington (2) 2 Crewe Alex (0) 2
Hull C (2) 2 Bradford C (1) 1
Leyton Orient (1) 1 Reading (0) 0
Peterborough U (0) 2 Wrexham (0) 0
Rochdale (0) 1 Preston NE (0) 1
Scunthorpe U (0) 1 Bury (1) 3
Walsall (0) 0 Stoke C (0) 2
Wigan Ath (0) 0 Huddersfield T (1) 1
WBA (2) 4 Shrewsbury T (0) 0
York C (0) 1 Carlisle U (1) 1
Exeter C (2) 2 Torquay U (1) 1

Maidstone U (1) 2 Fulham (2) 6
Barnet (1) 3 Aldershot (0) 0
Bradford C (2) 3 Hartlepool U (2) 3
Burnley (2) 2 Doncaster R (0) 0
Bury (2) 2 Halifax T (1) 2
Carlisle U (3) 4 Stockport Co (0) 0
Crewe Alex (1) 2 Chester C (0) 1
Huddersfield T (0) 1 Scarborough (0) 1
Preston NE (1) 2 Bolton W (0) 1
Shrewsbury T (0) 1 Lincoln C (0) 0
Torquay U (0) 0 Hereford U (1) 1
Swansea C (0) 0 Cardiff C (0) 0
Fulham (1) 2 Gillingham (0) 0
Reading (0) 0 Northampton T (2) 2
Northampton T (1) 1 Leyton Orient (1) 2
Lincoln C (0) 1 WBA (0) 2
Bolton W (0) 4 Rochdale (0) 1
Cardiff C (3) 3 Bournemouth (2) 3
Gillingham (2) 4 Maidstone U (0) 2
Brentford (1) 3 Barnet (1) 6
Doncaster R (0) 2 Blackpool (0) 2
Stoke C (2) 3 Birmingham C (1) 1
Birmingham C (0) 0 Walsall (0) 1
Chester C (2) 2 Darlington (0) 1
Halifax T (0) 0 Scunthorpe U (0) 2
Hartlepool U (2) 2 Hull C (0) 0
Hereford U (1) 2 Exeter C (0) 1
Stockport Co (2) 3 York C (0) 0
Scarborough (0) 1 Wigan Ath (0) 1
Mansfield T (2) 2 Peterborough U (1) 1 *abandoned 69 mins; fog*
Mansfield T (0) 0 Peterborough U (2) 3

FIRST ROUND
Barnet (2) 3 Northampton T (1) 2
Bury (0) 2 Chesterfield (0) 1
Carlisle U (0) 1 Stockport Co (3) 3
Crewe Alex (1) 2 Bolton W (0) 0
Fulham (1) 2 Gillingham (0) 0
Huddersfield T (1) Blackpool (0) *abandoned half-time; fog*
Preston NE (1) 2 Hull C (1) 3 *aet*
Rotherham U (2) 2 Chester C (0) 0 *abandoned 66 mins; fog*
Stoke C (1) 3 Cardiff C (0) 0
WBA (0) 0 Exeter C (1) 1
Burnley (0) 0 Scarborough (0) 0 *abandoned 90 mins; frost*
Hartlepool U (1) 2 Scunthorpe U (1) 1
Hereford U (0) 0 Walsall (0) 1 *aet*
Huddersfield T (1) 1 Blackpool (1) 1
aet; Huddersfield T won 3–1 on penalties
Leyton Orient (2) 3 Brentford (0) 2

Rotherham U (2) 3 Chester C (0) 0
Burnley (0) 3 Scarborough (0) 1
Bournemouth (0) 1 Wrexham (0) 2
Peterborough U (0) 1 Shrewsbury T (0) 0

QUARTER-FINALS
Northern Section
Bury (1) 1 Huddersfield T (0) 2
Crewe Alex (0) 1 Hull C (0) 0
Stockport Co (1) 3 Hartlepool U (0) 0
Rotherham U (0) 1 Burnley (0) 1

Southern Section
Barnet (0) 0 Leyton Orient (1) 1
Stoke C (3) 3 Walsall (0) 1
Fulham (0) 0 Wrexham (0) 2
Peterborough U (0) 1 Exeter C (0) 0

SEMI-FINALS
Northern Section
Burnley (2) 2 Huddersfield T (0) 0
Crewe Alex (0) 1 Stockport Co (2) 2

Southern Section
Leyton Orient (0) 0 Stoke C (1) 1
Peterborough U (2) 3 Wrexham (0) 1

Northern Section Final First Leg
Burnley (0) 0 Stockport Co (1) 1

Southern Section Final First Leg
Stoke C (2) 3 Peterborough U (1) 3

Northern Section Final Second Leg
Stockport Co (1) 2 Burnley (1) 1

Southern Section Final Second Leg
Peterborough U (0) 0 Stoke C (0) 1

FINAL (at Wembley)
16 MAY
Stoke C (0) 1 *(Stein)*
Stockport Co (0) 0 48,339
Stoke C: Fox; Butler, Kevan, Cranson, Overson, Sandford, Kelly, Foley, Stein, Biggins, Heath.
Stockport Co: Edwards; Knowles, Todd, Frain (Thorpe), Barras, Williams B, Gannon, Ward, Francis, Beaumont, Wheeler (Williams P).
Referee: R. Hart (Darlington).

FA CHARITY SHIELD WINNERS 1908-91

1908	Manchester U v QPR	4-0 after 1-1 draw
1909	Newcastle U v Northampton T	2-0
1910	Brighton v Aston Villa	1-0
1911	Manchester U v Swindon T	8-4
1912	Blackburn R v QPR	2-1
1913	Professionals v Amateurs	7-2
1919	WBA v Tottenham H	2-0
1920	Tottenham H v Burnley	2-0
1921	Huddersfield T v Liverpool	1-0
1922	Not played	
1923	Professionals v Amateurs	2-0
1924	Professionals v Amateurs	3-1
1925	Amateurs v Professionals	6-1
1926	Amateurs v Professionals	6-3
1927	Cardiff C v Corinthians	2-1
1928	Everton v Blackburn R	2-1
1929	Professionals v Amateurs	3-0
1930	Arsenal v Sheffield W	2-1
1931	Arsenal v WBA	1-0
1932	Everton v Newcastle U	5-3
1933	Arsenal v Everton	3-0
1934	Arsenal v Manchester C	4-0
1935	Sheffield W v Arsenal	1-0
1936	Sunderland v Arsenal	2-1
1937	Manchester C v Sunderland	2-0
1938	Arsenal v Preston NE	2-1
1948	Arsenal v Manchester U	4-3
1949	Portsmouth v Wolverhampton W	1-1*
1950	World Cup Team v Canadian Touring Team	4-2
1951	Tottenham H v Newcastle U	2-1
1952	Manchester U v Newcastle U	4-2
1953	Arsenal v Blackpool	3-1
1954	Wolverhampton W v WBA	4-4*
1955	Chelsea v Newcastle U	3-0
1956	Manchester U v Manchester C	1-0
1957	Manchester U v Aston Villa	4-0
1958	Bolton W v Wolverhampton W	4-1
1959	Wolverhampton W v Nottingham F	3-1
1960	Burnley v Wolverhampton W	2-2*
1961	Tottenham H v FA XI	3-2
1962	Tottenham H v Ipswich T	5-1
1963	Everton v Manchester U	4-0
1964	Liverpool v West Ham U	2-2*
1965	Manchester U v Liverpool	2-2*
1966	Liverpool v Everton	1-0
1967	Manchester U v Tottenham H	3-3*
1968	Manchester C v WBA	6-1
1969	Leeds U v Manchester C	2-1
1970	Everton v Chelsea	2-1

1971	Leicester C v Liverpool	1-0
1972	Manchester C v Aston Villa	1-0
1973	Burnley v Manchester C	1-0
1974	Liverpool† v Leeds U	1-1
1975	Derby Co v West Ham U	2-0
1976	Liverpool v Southampton	1-0
1977	Liverpool v Manchester U	0-0*
1978	Nottingham F v Ipswich T	5-0
1979	Liverpool v Arsenal	3-1
1980	Liverpool v West Ham U	1-0
1981	Aston Villa v Tottenham H	2-2*
1982	Liverpool v Tottenham H	1-0
1983	Manchester U v Liverpool	2-0
1984	Everton v Liverpool	1-0
1985	Everton v Manchester U	2-0
1986	Everton v Liverpool	1-1*
1987	Everton v Coventry C	1-0
1988	Liverpool v Wimbledon	2-1
1989	Liverpool v Arsenal	1-0
1990	Liverpool v Manchester U	1-1*

* Each club retained shield for six months. † Won on penalties.

FA CHARITY SHIELD 1991

Arsenal (0) 0, Tottenham H (0) 0

at Wembley, 10 August 1991, attendance 65,483

Arsenal: Seaman; Dixon, Winterburn, Hillier, O'Leary, Adams, Rocastle (Thomas), Davis, Smith, Merson, Campbell (Cole).

Tottenham H: Thorstvedt; Fenwick, Van Den Hauwe, Sedgley, Howells, Mabbutt, Stewart, Nayim, Samways, Lineker, Allen.

Referee: T. Holbrook (Staffs).

SCOTTISH CLUBS

ABERDEEN   PREM. DIV.

Ground: Pittodrie Stadium, Aberdeen AB2 1QH (0224 632328)
Colours: All red with white trim.
Year formed: 1903. **Manager:** Willie Miller.
League appearances: Bett, J. 38; Booth, S. 21(12); Cameron, I. 4(2); Connor, R. 11; Ferguson, G. (4); Gibson, A. 2(3); Gillhaus, H. 24(5); Grant, B. 33; Humphries, M. 2; Irvine, B. 41; Jess, E. 33(6); Kane, P. 22(3); McKimmie, S. 39; McLeish, A. 7; Mason, P. 28(3); Paatelainen, M. 6; Roddie, A. 1(9); Smith, G. 15(1); Snelders, T. 42; Ten Caat, T. 28(2); Van der Ark, W. 7(11); Van de Ven, P. 20(3); Watson, Graham 4(5); Watson, Gregg 4(6); Watt, M. 2; Winnie, D. 27(1); Wright, S. 23.
Goals–League: (55): Jess 12, Mason 7, Grant 6, Booth 5, Gillhaus 5 (1 pen), Ten Caat 5, Irvine 4, Kane 2, Roddie 2, Van de Ven 2, Bett 1, Paatelainen 1, Smith 1, Winnie 1, own goal 1.
Scottish Cup: (0).   **Skol Cup:** (4): Booth 1, Grant 1, Van de Ven 1, Winnie 1.

AIRDRIEONIANS   PREM. DIV.

Ground: Broomfield Park, Gartlea Road, Airdrie ML6 9JL (0236 62067)
Colours: White shirts with red diamond, white shorts.
Year formed: 1878. **Manager:** Alex MacDonald.
League appearances: Abercromby, M. 1(3); Balfour, E. 40(1); Black, K. 33; Boyle, J. 36(1); Butler, J. 1; Caesar, A. 12; Conn, S. 26(1); Coyle, O. 40(3); Crainie, D. (3); Gray, S. (2); Harvey, G. (2); Honor, C. 30; Jack, P. 17(7); Kidd, W. 32; Kirkwood, D. 27(9); Lawrence, A. 26(5); McCulloch, W. 1; McKenna, A. (2); McKnight, A. 2; McPhee, I. (1); Martin, J. 41; Reid, W. 5(2); Sandison, J. 40; Smith, A. 22(6); Smith, J. 1; Stewart, A. 41; Watson, J. 10(12).
Goals–League: (50): Coyle 11, Kirkwood 9 (4 pens), Lawrence 7 (1 pen), Conn 5, Smith A 4; Watson 4, Boyle 3, Balfour 2, Black 2 (1 pen), Gray 1, Jack 1, Stewart 1.
Scottish Cup: (9): Smith A 5, Black 1, Boyle 1, Conn 1, Coyle 1.
Skol Cup: (4): Coyle 2, Crainie 1 (pen), Watson 1.

ALBION ROVERS   DIV. 2

Ground: Cliftonhill Stadium, Main Street, Coatbridge ML5 3RB (0236 432350)
Colours: Yellow shirts with red and white trim, red shorts with yellow stripes.
Year formed: 1882. **Manager:** Michael Oliver.
League appearances: Anderson, R. 15; Archer, S. 15; Bulloch, S. 1; Cadden, S. 28; Clark, R. 36; Connelly, S. 7; Cougan, C. 1(5); Cousin, J. 1; Cranmer, C. 12(1); Easton, S. 12(4); Edgar, D. 5(3); Ferguson, W. 16(5); Gallagher, B. 11; Gallagher, J. 13(4); Green, J. 5(12); Henderson, J. 4(3); Hendry, A. 6; Hinchcliffe, C. 1; Horne, J. 12(9); Jackson, D. 3; Jackson, S. 15; Kelly, J. 13(3); McAnenay, M. 5; McBride, M. 1; McConnachie, R. 4; McCoy, G. 22; McCulloch, R. 5; McKenzie, T. 11; McKeown, D. 32; McLafferty, M. 19; McTeague, G. 12; Maxwell, D. 1; Meechan, J. 1; Millar, G. 18(3); Miller, J. 8(4); Moore, S. 17(3); Pryce, J. 7(3); Quinton, I. 2(4); Riley, D. 1; Stalker, I. 6(1); Thomson, R. 1; Troup, W. 8(6); Walsh, R. 14; Watson, E. 2(1).
Goals–League: (42): McCoy 11, Clark 5 (2 pens), Moore 5, Edgar 3, Henderson 3, Anderson 2, Ferguson 2, Cadden 1, Hendry 1, Jackson S 1, McAnenay 1, McKenzie 1, McKeown 1, McTeague 1, Quinton 1, Stalker 1, Thomson 1, own goal 1.
Scottish Cup: (0).
Skol Cup: (4): McAnenay 2, Stalker 1, Watson 1.
B & Q Cup: (5): Archer 1, Cadden 1, Ferguson 1, Henderson 1, Troup 1.

ALLOA   DIV. 2

Ground: Recreation Park, Alloa FK10 1RR (0259 722695)
Colours: Gold shirts with black trim, black shorts.
Year formed: 1883. **Manager:** Hugh McCann.
League appearances: Bennett, N. 10(2); Binnie, N. 1; Black, I. 1(10); Butter, J. 38; Campbell, C. 36; Campbell, K. 3(1); Conroy, J. (1); Gibson, J. 20(3); Hendry, M. 29; Henry, S. 12(3); Irvine, J. 3(11); Lee, R. 35; McAvoy, N. 19(11); McCallum, M. 8(2); McCormick, S. (5); McCulloch, K. 29; Moffat, B. 24(14); Newbigging, W. 35; Ramsay, S. 28; Romaines, S. 35; Smith, S. 34(1); Thomson, J. 6(1); Wilcox, D. 23(5).
Goals–League: (58): Hendry 12, Newbigging 10 (4 pens), Smith 7, Moffat 6, Wilcox 4, Henry 3, McAvoy 3, McCallum 3, Ramsay 3, Gibson 2, McCulloch 2, Lee 1, McCormick 1, Romaines 1.
Scottish Cup: (7): McAvoy 2, Moffat 2, Newbigging 2 (1 pen), Hendry 1.
Skol Cup: (1): McCallum 1.
B & Q Cup: (1): Henry 1.

ARBROATH   DIV. 2

Ground: Gayfield Park, Arbroath DD11 1QB (0241 72157)
Colours: Maroon shirts, white shorts.
Year formed: 1878. **Manager:** Mike Lawson.
League appearances: Adam, C. 21; Balfour, D. 11; Boyd, W. 25(1); Brown, S. 4; Carlin, G. 11; Farnan, C. 37; Florence, S. 11(2); Gallagher, J. 8; Gray, B. (2); Hamilton, J. 36(1); Harkness, M. 28; Holmes, W. 15(10); Hunter, M. (2); Joyce, B. 4(4); McKenna, A. 25(7); McNaughton, B. 24(1); Martin, C. 33; Mitchell, B. 32; Morton, J. 15 (12); Roberts, P. 7 (3); Smith, Raymond 2(11); Smith, Richard 2; Sneddon, H. 12(1); Sorbie, S. 36; Strachan, A. 16(2); Tindal, K. 11(1); Tosh, P. 3(6).
Goals–League: (49): Sorbie 12, McKenna 10, McNaughton 7, Morton 4, Adam 3, Holmes 3, Farnan 2, Roberts 2, Boyd 1, Carlin 1, Tosh 1, own goals 3.
Scottish Cup: (2): Adam 1, McNaughton 1.
Skol Cup: (0).
B & Q Cup: (2): Holmes 1, Hunter 1.

AYR UNITED   DIV. 1

Ground: Somerset Park, Ayr KA8 9NB (0292 263435)
Colours: White shirts with black trim, black shorts.
Year formed: 1910. **Manager:** George Burley.
League appearances: Agnew, G. 36; Archibald, S. 1; Auld, S. 22(1); Brown, R. (1); Bryce, T. 39(2); Burley, G. 9; Duncan, C. 16; Evans, S. 6(2); Fraser, A. 8(1); Furphy, W. 39; Gardner, L. 16; George, D. 34; Graham, A. 40; Hood, G. 2(3); Howard, N. 21; Kennedy, D. 38(4); McAllister, I. 4(3); McLean, P. 29(1); McTurk, A. 11(5); McVie, G. 5; Purdie, D. 27; Robertson, M. 1; Shaw, G. 16(24); Smith, M. 11(8); Traynor, J. 26; Walker, T. 20(4); Weir, P. 7(3).
Goals–League: (63): Graham 14, Shaw 10 (1 pen), Bryce 9 (2 pens), Agnew 5, Smith 5, Walker 5, Traynor 4, Fraser 3, McLean 3, McAllister 2, Auld 1, George 1, McTurk 1.
Scottish Cup: (2): George 1, Graham 1.
Skol Cup: (6): Shaw 3, Graham 2, Bryce 1 (pen).
B & Q Cup: (9): Smith 3, Graham 2, Auld 1, Fraser 1, McLean 1, Shaw 1.

BERWICK RANGERS   DIV. 2

Ground: Shielfield Park, Berwick-on-Tweed TD15 2EF (0289 307424)
Colours: Black and gold striped shirts, black shorts.
Year formed: 1881. **Manager:** John Anderson.
League appearances: Bickmore, S. 27(2); Callachan, R. 12(5); Cass, M. 22(3); Clinging, I. 2; Davidson, G. 34; Egan, J. 10; Garner, W. 27; Graham, T. 13(5); Irvine, M. 1; Leitch, G. 27(1); Locke, S. 9(2); McGovern, J. 15(9); McLaren, P. 10(6); Malcolm, D. 1(1); Marshall, B. 1; Neil, M. 14(1); Neilson, D. 29; O'Donnell, J. 35(1); Purves, S. 2(2); Rae, R. (2); Ross, A. 17(3); Scally, D. 6(3); Sneddon, M. 1(3); Tait, G. 13(5); Thorpe, B. 31; Todd, K. 37; Wilson, W. 32; Wojtowycz, M. 1(1).
Goals—League: (50): Bickmore 12, Todd 8, Thorpe 7, Ross 6 (1 pen), Tait 6, Graham 3 (1 pen), Davidson 2 (1 pen), Cass 1, Leitch 1, McGovern 1, O'Donnell 1, Scally 1, own goal 1.
Scottish Cup: (7): Bickmore 2, Neil 2, Graham 1, Locke 1, Todd 1.
Skol Cup: (0).
B & Q Cup: (4): Ross 2, Thorpe 1, Todd 1.

BRECHIN CITY   DIV. 2

Ground: Glebe Park, Brechin DD9 6BJ (0356 622856)
Colours: All red.
Year formed: 1906. **Manager:** John Ritchie.
League appearances: Ainslie, C. 3; Allan, R. 26; Baillie, R. 24; Brand, R. 15(11); Brown, R. 37; Cairney, H. 13; Clark, J. 1(2); Conway, F. 19(1); Dow, R. 6(2); Fisher, D. 5(8); Garden, S. 5; Gibson, J. 9; Heggie, A. 3; Hill, H. 14(6); Hutchinson, W. (1); Hutt, G. 15(2); Lawrie, D. 4; Lees, G. 29(3); Lorimer, R. 23; McKillop, A. 19; McLaren, P. 6; Miller, M. 12(5); Nicolson, K. 16; Paterson, I. G. 16(8); Pryde, I. 2; Ritchie, P. 24; Ross, A. 19; Scott, D. 28; Thomson, N. 19(4); Thomson, S. 11; Traynor, R. 1; Wardell, S. 5(4).
Goals—League: (54): Ritchie 12 (1 pen), Lees 8, Brand 7, Ross 7 (1 pen), Brown 3, Conway 3, Thomson S 3, Lorimer 2, Nicolson 2, Paterson 2, Hutt 1, McKillop 1, Miller 1, Scott 1, Thomson N 1.
Scottish Cup: (1): Ritchie 1.
Skol Cup: (3): Ritchie 2 (1 pen), Pryde 1.
B & Q Cup: (2): Ritchie 2.

CELTIC   PREM. DIV.

Ground: Celtic Park, Glasgow G40 3RE (041-556 2611)
Colours: Green and white hooped shirts, white shorts.
Year formed: 1888. **Manager:** Liam Brady.
League appearances: Bonner, P. 19; Boyd, T. 12(1); Cascarino, A. 13(11); Collins, J. 36(2); Coyne, T. 32(7); Creaney, G. 21(11); Dziekanowski, D. (1); Fulton, S. 18(12); Galloway, M. 26(8); Gillespie, G. 24; Grant, P. 20(2); McNally, M. 22(3); McStay, P. 31; Marshall, G. 25; Miller, J. 23(3); Morris, C. 29(3); Mowbray, T. 14(1); Nicholas, C. 32(5); O'Neil, B. 25(3); Rogan, A. 5; Smith, B. 1(2); Walker, A. (1); Wdowczyk, D. 18(1); Whyte, D. 38(2).
Goals—League: (88): Nicholas 21 (3 pens), Coyne 15, Creaney 14, Collins 11, McStay 7, Cascarino 4, Fulton 2, Galloway 2, Gillespie 2, Miller 2, Mowbray 2, Boyd 1, McNally 1, Morris 1, O'Neil 1, Whyte 1, own goal 1.
Scottish Cup: (11): Creaney 6, Coyne 4, Collins 1.
Skol Cup: (7): Creaney 3, Nicholas 2, Fulton 1, Miller 1.

CLYDE DIV. 2

Ground: Douglas Park, Hamilton ML3 0DF (Mon-Fri: 041-248 7953)
(Match days: 0698 286103)
Colours: White shirts with red and black trim, black shorts.
Year formed: 1878. **Manager:** Alex Smith.
League appearances: Archibald, S. 4; Burke, P. 4; Clarke, S. 28; Gaughan, M. 3; Haggerty, N. 1; Howie, S. 15; Knox, K. 35; McAulay, J. 10(4); McCoy, G. 4(1); McFarlane, R. 28; McGarvey, F. 12; MacIver, S. 6(1); McVie, G. 2; Mallan, S. 14(9); Malone, P. (1); Morrison, S. 18(16); O'Hara, F. 4(1); Quinn, K. 3(2); Roberts, P. (1); Ronald, P. 25(4); Ross, S. 2; Scott, M. 12(7); Speirs, C. 23(3); Stevenson, H. 22; Tennant, S. 34; Tierney, P. 1(6); Thompson, D. 31; Thomson, J. 23(3); Watson, E. 6(4); Wilson, K. 29(3); Wylde, G. 30(1).
Goals—League: (61): Thompson 16 (1 pen), Clarke 7, Morrison 7 (1 pen), McGarvey 6, Mallan 5, Wilson 3, Archibald 2, McAulay 2, McCoy 2, Quinn 2, Ronald 2, Scott 2, Thomson 2, Speirs 1, Tennant 1, Watson 1.
Scottish Cup: (3): Morrison 1, Scott 1, Wilson 1.
Skol Cup: (0).
B & Q Cup: (0).

CLYDEBANK DIV. 1

Ground: Kilbowie Park, Clydebank G81 2PB (041-952 2887)
Colours: Red, black and white design, white shorts.
Year formed: 1965. **Manager:** John Steedman.
League appearances: Crawford, J. 35(1); Curry, T. 1(1); Dickson, Joe 12(1); Dickson, John 14(10); Duncanson, J. 9; Eadie, K. 39; Flannigan, C. 8; Gallacher, J. 2; Goldie, P. 8(2); Harvey, P. 38(3); Henry, J. 32(3); Kelly, P. 7(9); King, T. 16(5); Lansdowne, A. 11(3); McIntosh, M. 25(2); Maher, J. 38(1); Mair, G. 28(3); Rossiter, B. 7(1); Rowe, G. 30(3); Sermanni, P. 4(1); Smith, B. 10; Spence, W. 37; Sweeney, S. 18; Templeton, H. 2(2); Traynor, J. 12(3); Woods, S. 5; Wright, B. 36(1).
Goals—League: (59): Eadie 22 (2 pens), Henry 8, McIntosh 5, Rowe 5, Dickson John 4, Harvey 4, Wright 4, Mair 2, Flannigan 1, King 1, Templeton 1 (pen), Traynor 1, own goal 1.
Scottish Cup: (4): Eadie 2, Harvey 1, Henry 1.
Skol Cup: (0).
B & Q Cup: (5): Dickson John 2, Eadie 1, Henry 1, McIntosh 1.

COWDENBEATH DIV. 1

Ground: Central Park, Cowdenbeath KY4 9EY (0383 511205)
Colours: Royal blue shirts with white stripes, white shorts.
Year formed: 1881. **Manager:** Andy Harrow.
League appearances: Archibald, E. 36; Bennett, W. 3; Buckley, G. 33(2); Douglas, H. 14(4); Ferguson, S. 7(4); Fraser, S. 19(10); Hamill, K. 2(2); Irvine, N. 31; Irving, A. 14(16); Johnston, P. (3); Lamont, P. 36(1); Lamont, W. 26; McGovern, D. 28(1); McMahon, B. 1(4); Malone, G. 31; O'Hanlon, S. 10; Robertson, A. 37; Robertson, C. 3; Scott, C. 15(1); Syme, W. 20(12); Thomson, K. (1); Watt, D. 37; Wright, J. 26(1).
Goals—League: (74): Buckley 21, Lamont P 18 (1 pen), Malone 8 (3 pens), Syme 5, Irving 4, Wright 4, Robertson 3, Scott 3, Archibald 2, Fraser 2, Douglas 1, Irvine 1, McGovern 1, McMahon 1.
Scottish Cup: (8): Lamont P 3, Malone 2 (1 pen), Archibald 1, Irving 1, own goal 1.
Skol Cup: (1): Robertson 1.
B & Q Cup: (2): Fraser 1, Robertson 1.

DUMBARTON

DIV. 1

Ground: Boghead Park, Dumbarton G82 2JA (0389 62569 and 67864)
Colours: Gold with white band, gold shorts.
Year formed: 1872. **Manager:** Billy Lamont.
League appearances: Boyd, J. 34(2); Carson, T. 6; Cowell, J. 1(7); Dempsey, J. 28(2); Edgar, D. (1); Foster, A. 1(4); Gibson, C. 37; Gilmour, J. 36(1); Gow, S. 34; Hughes, J. 3(3); McConville, R. 21(3); McCracken, D. 3(3); McFarlane, I. 33; McGarvey, M. 3(5); MacIver, S. (3); McNair, C. (1); McQuade, J. 32(1); Marsland, J. 29(4); Martin, P. 38; Meechan, J. 33(3); Melvin, M. 38; Millar, S. 1(1); Nelson, M. 6(2); Willock, A. 12(18).
Goals–League: (65): Gilmour 19 (7 pens), McQuade 13, Gibson 9, Meechan 9, Willock 7, McConville 3, Martin 2, MacIver 1, Marsland 1, Melvin 1.
Scottish Cup: (4): Boyd 1, Dempsey 1, Gilmour 1 (pen), McQuade 1.
Skol Cup: (2): Gibson 2.
B & Q Cup: (1): Gibson 1.

DUNDEE

PREM. DIV.

Ground: Dens Park, Dundee DD3 7JY (0382 826104)
Colours: Dark blue shirts with red and white trim, white shorts.
Year formed: 1893. **Manager:** Simon Stainrod.
League appearances: Beedie, S. 40; Bremner, K. 15(9); Campbell, D. 12(3); Campbell, S. 29(1); Chisholm, G. 37(2); Christie, M. 1; Craib, M. 19; Craig, A. 23(2); Dinnie, A. 24(5); Dodds, W. 42; Dow, A. (4); Forbes, G. 3; Forsyth, S. 11(4); Frail, S. 2(1); Fraser, C. 12; Gallagher, E. 13(9); Jamieson, W. 38; Leighton, J. 13; McCall, I. 26(1); McLeod, G. 12(3); McMartin, G. 17(8); McQuillan, J. 39(1); Mathers, P. 31; Ritchie, P. 3(3); Shannon, R. 4; Stainrod, S. 11(2); West, C. 7(2).
Goals–League: (80): Dodds 19 (2 pens), Gallagher 11, McCall 9, Craig 7, Bremner 6, Chishold 5, Beedie 4, Jamieson 4, Campbell S 3 (2 pens), McQuillan 3, West 3, Campbell D 2 (1 pen), Stainrod 2, McMartin 1, Ritchie 1.
Scottish Cup: (2): Dinnie 1, McMartin 1.
Skol Cup: (2): Craig 2.
B & Q Cup: (0).

DUNDEE UNITED

PREM. DIV.

Ground: Tannadice Park, Dundee DD3 7JW (0382 833166)
Colours: Tangerine shirts with black trim, black shorts.
Year formed: 1909 as Dundee Hibernians, Dundee United from 1923. **Manager:** Jim McLean.
League appearances: Bollan, G. 8(2); Bowman, D. 37(4); Clark, J. 31(4); Cleland, A. 24(7); Connolly, P. 1(4); Dailly, C. 5(3); Ferguson, D. 37(1); Ferreyra, V. 20(3); French, H. 5(1); Jackson, D. 24(4); Johnson, G. 10; McInally, J. 32; McKinlay, W. 22; McKinnon, R. 21(4); McLaren, A. 7(6); Main, A. 17; Malpas, M. 44; Muller, J. 4(1); Narey, D. 24; O'Neil, J. 11(1); O'Neill, M. 5(3); Paatelainen, M. 15(15); Pochettino, J. (2); Preston, A. 2; Van der Hoorn, F. 41; Van der Kamp, G. 27; Welsh, B. 10(1).
Goals–League: (66): Ferguson 15, Jackson 11 (2 pens), Paatelainen 6, Cleland 4, Ferreyra 4, McInally 4, McKinnon 4, O'Neill 4 (2 pens), Bowman 3, Malpas 3 (1 pen), Bollan 1, Clark 1, French 1, Johnson 1, McKinlay 1, Van der Hoorn 1, Welsh 1, own goal 1.
Scottish Cup: (7): Ferguson 2, Ferreyra 1, Malpas 1, O'Neil 1, Paatelainen 1, own goal, 1.
Skol Cup: (5): Paatelainen 2, Clark 1, French 1, O'Neill 1.

DUNFERMLINE ATHLETIC DIV. 1

Ground: East End Park, Dunfermline KY12 7RB (0383 724295)
Colours: Black and white striped shirts, black shorts.
Year formed: 1885. **Manager:** Jocky Scott.
League appearances: Bowes, M. 12(2); Cooper, N, 21; Cunnington, E. 35(1); Davies, W. 22(11); Drizic, M. 1; Farningham, R. 4; French, H. 31; Gallagher, E. 3(1); Grant, A. (1); Haro, M. 7(3); Irons, D. 1(1); Kelly, N. 8; Kozma, I. 18(5); Laing, D. (3); Leitch, S. 29(4); McAllister, P. 2(2); McCall, I. 9; McCathie, N. 38(2); McParland, I. 11(5); McWilliams, D. 21(3); Moyes, D. 39; O'Boyle, G. 12(4); Reilly, J. 1(4); Rhodes, A. 44; Robertson, C. 31(2); Shannon, R. 27; Sharp, R. 25; Sinclair, C. 10(7); Williamson, A. 6(1); Wilson, T. 16.
Goals–League: (22): Moyes 5, Leitch 4, McWilliams 3, French 2, McParland 2, Farningham 1, McCall 1, McCathie 1, O'Boyle 1, Robertson 1, Sinclair 1.
Scottish Cup: (4): Cunnington 1, Davies 1, French 1, McParland 1.
Skol Cup: (9): Leitch 2, O'Boyle 2, Kozma 1, McParland 1, McWilliams 1 (pen), Moyes 1, Robertson 1.

EAST FIFE DIV. 2

Ground: Bayview Park, Methil, Fife KY8 3AG (0333 26323)
Colours: Black and gold striped shirts, black shorts.
Year formed: 1903. **Manager:** Gavin Murray.
League appearances: Allan, G. 2(1); Beaton, D. 38; Bell, G. 3; Blyth, A. (1); Brown, I. 3(6); Brown, W. 14(3); Burns, W. 31; Callaghan, T. 4; Charles, R. 37; Cowell, J. 4; Hall, A. (1); Hamilton, R. 2; Hayton, G. 4(13); Herd, W. 16(2); Hope, D. 29(3); McBride, J. 38(1); McCracken, D. 12(4); Moffat, J. 2; Prior, S. 10(1); Rogerson, S. (1); Scott, R. 33(4); Skelligan, R. 3(3); Sludden, J. 39; Smith, P. 9(1); Speirs, A. 7(8); Spence, T. 33; Taylor, P. H. 28(3); Wilson, S. 28(4).
Goals–League: (72): Sludden 21, Scott 16, Beaton 9 (3 pens), McBride 8, Brown W 5, Hayton 4, Hope 3, Brown I 1, Herd 1, McCracken 1, Spence 1, Wilson 1, own goal 1.
Scottish Cup: (11): Beaton 4, Skelligan 3, Sludden 2, Brown W 1, Scott 1.
Skol Cup: (2): Hope 2.
B & Q Cup: (6): Sludden 2, Hayton 1, Scott 1, Spence 1, Wilson 1.

EAST STIRLING DIV. 2

Ground: Firs Park, Falkirk FK2 7AY (0324 23583)
Colours: Black and white hoops, black shorts.
Year formed: 1880. **Manager:** Dom Sullivan.
League appearances: Barclay, S. 12(11); Brannigan, K. 5; Craig, D. 34; Crawford, P. 5(5); Diver, D. 35; Ferguson, S. 4(2); Friar, P. 11; Gardiner, F. 4; Griffen, J. (1); Houston, P. 28; Kennedy, H. 11(2); Lawson, O. 4; Lytwyn, C. 19(1); McAleer, E. 16(2); McConville, A. 24(3); McKinnon, C. 37; McMillan, C. 13; McNally, J. 6(6); Mitchell, B. 2; Roberts, P. 1; Rooney, J. 19(3); Ross, B. 13(2); Russell, G. 21; Speirs, G. 19; Thomson, S. 27(5); Walker, D. 1(5); Watson, G. 35; Watson, T. 13(6); Workman, J. 10.
Goals–League: (61): Diver 18, Lytwyn 11 (1 pen), McKinnon 9, McConville 4, Crawford 3, McNally 3, Barclay 2, Friar 2, Rose 2, Speirs 2 (1 pen), Rooney 1, Workman 1, own goals 3.
Scottish Cup: (0).
Skol Cup: (2): Diver 1, Lytwyn 1.
B & Q Cup: (2): McKinnon 1, Ross 1.

FALKIRK PREM. DIV.

FALKIRK — PREM. DIV.

Ground: Brockville Park, Falkirk FK1 5AX (0324 24121 and 32487)
Colours: Dark blue shirts with white trim, white shorts.
Year formed: 1876. **Manager:** Jim Jefferies.
League appearances: Baptie, C. 34(4); Cadette, R. 11(3); Cody, S. 2(3); Duffy, N. 39; Godfrey, P. 15(1); Hamilton, G. 2(1); Hughes, J. 38; Johnston, F. 10(2); Lennox, G. 15(10); McAllister, K. 42; McDougall, G. 4; McGivern, S. 23(7); McKenzie, S. (2); McQueen, T. 26; May, E. 33(3); Mooney, M. (4); Oliver, N. 34(1); Rice, B. 14(2); Rutherford, P. 2(4); Simpson, M. (1); Sloan, S. 20(3); Smith, P. 31(1); Stainrod, S. 22(1); Taggart, C. (8); Taylor, A. 21(1); Westwater, I. 40; Whittaker, B. 6.
Goals–League: (54): McAllister 9, May 9, Baptie 7, Stainrod 5, Sloan 4, Cadette 3, McGivern 3, Duffy 2, Godfrey 2, Hughes 2, Smith 2, Cody 1, McQueen 1, Rice 1 (pen), Taylor 1, own goals 2.
Scottish Cup: (3): Sloan 2, McGivern 1.
Skol Cup: (3): McAllister 2, Taylor 1.

FORFAR ATHLETIC DIV. 2

FORFAR ATHLETIC — DIV. 2

Ground: Station Park, Forfar, Angus DD8 3BT (0307 63576)
Colours: Sky blue shirts, navy shorts.
Year formed: 1885. **Manager:** Tommy Campbell.
League appearances: Adam, C. 9; Brazil, A. 22(3); Byrne, J. 9(1); Campbell, A. 7(5); Dolan, S. 2(3); Glass, S. 1; Hamill, A. 39; Hegarty, P. 8; Holt, J. 36; Hutton, G. 2(1); Johnston, C. 7(7); McAulay, A. 12(13); McKenna, I. 18(5); MacKinnon, D. 27(1); McPhee, I. 16; Mearns, G. 11(6); Morris, R. 40; Paterson, I. 2(4); Paton, P. 18(1); Peters, S. 3; Petrie, S. 36(5); Price, G. 11(8); Pryde, I. 27(8); Ramsay, A. 3; Smith, P. (1); Thomson, S. 44; Whyte, G. 38; Winter, G. 36(5).
Goals–League: (36): Winter 8 (2 pens), Petrie 7, Adam 3 (1 pen), Campbell 3, Paton 3, Pryde 3, McAulay 2, Whyte 2, Hegarty 1, Johnston 1, McKenna 1, Mearns 1, Price 1.
Scottish Cup: (1): Brazil 1.
Skol Cup: (0).
B & Q Cup: (2): Whyte 2.

HAMILTON ACADEMICAL DIV. 1

HAMILTON ACADEMICAL — DIV. 1

Ground: Douglas Park, Hamilton ML3 0DF (0698 286103)
Colours: Red and white hooped shirts, white shorts.
Year formed: 1875. **Manager:** Iain Munro.
League appearances: Burns, H. 7(2); Clark, G. 24(8); Cramb, C. 2(10); Ferguson, A. 16; Harris, C. 27(5); Hillcoat, C. 24(3); McAnenay, M. 4(4); McCluskey, G. 29(3); McCulloch, R. 15; McDonald, P. 34(4); McGuigan, R. 9(1); McKee, K. 34; McKenzie, P. 29; McLean, S. (1); Millen, A. 39; Miller, C. 43; Monaghan, M. 13; Moore, S. (3); Napier, C. 18(4); Reid, W. 34(1); Smith, T. 25(4); Stark, W. 6(8); Ward, K. 12; Weir, J. 40.
Goals–League: (72): Clark 14, Smith 13, McCluskey 12, Harris 8 (4 pens), McDonald 5 (2 pens), Ward 5, Reid 4, Hillcoat 2, Napier 2, Cramb 1, McAnenay 1, McGuigan 1, McKee 1, Millen 1, Miller 1, Weir 1.
Scottish Cup: (0).
Skol Cup: (2): Burns H 1, Clark 1.
B & Q Cup: (13): McCluskey 3, Smith 3, Napier 2, Harris 1, Millen 1, Miller 1, Reid 1, Weir 1.

HEART OF MIDLOTHIAN — PREM. DIV.

Ground: Tynecastle Park, Gorgie Road, Edinburgh EH11 2NL (031-337 6132)
Colours: Maroon shirts, white shorts.
Year formed: 1874. **Manager:** Joe Jordan.
League appearances: Baird, I. 30; Bannon, E. 10(3); Crabbe, S. 37(4); Ferguson, D. 37(1); Ferguson, I. 12(18); Foster, W. 1(6); Harrison, T. (1); Hogg, G. 13(5); Levein, C. 36; Mackay, G. 41(2); McKinlay, T. 37(2); McLaren, A. 38; McPherson, D. 44; Millar, J. 40(1); Penney, S. 3(6); Robertson, J. 42; Smith, H. 44; Snodin, G. 4(3); Wright, G. 15(9).
Goals—League: (60): Crabbe 15 (3 pens), Robertson 14 (3 pens), Millar 7, Baird 6, Ferguson I 4, Bannon 2, Levein 2, McKinlay 2, McPherson 2, Ferguson D 1, Hogg 1, Mackay 1, McLaren 1, Wright 1, own goal 1.
Scottish Cup: (9): Robertson 4 (1 pen), Crabbe 1, Ferguson I 1, Hogg 1, Mackay 1, McLaren 1.
Skol Cup: (5): Baird 2, Crabbe 2, Robertson 1 (pen).

HIBERNIAN — PREM. DIV.

Ground: Easter Road Stadium, Edinburgh EH7 5QG (031-661 2159)
Colours: Green shirts with white sleeves and collar, white shorts.
Year formed: 1875. **Manager:** Alex Miller.
League appearances: Bailey, L. 1; Beaumont, D. 17(4); Burridge, J. 35; Donald, G. 3(2); Evans, G. 26(15); Farrell, D. 3(3); Fellenger, D. 4(2); Findlay, W. 8(1); Hamilton, B. 37(3); Hunter, G. 37; Lennon, D. 3(8); Love, G. 1; MacLeod, M. 22; McGinlay, P. 43; McGraw, M. 14(10); McIntyre, T. 37; Miller, W. 29(1); Milne, C. 7(1); Mitchell, G. 26(1); Nicholls, D. 5; Orr, N. 21(7); Raynes, S. (1); Reid, C. 9; Sneddon, A. 3(2); Tortolano, J. 22(3); Tweed, S. 1; Weir, M. 30(1); Wright, K. 40.
Goals—League: (53): Weir 11, McGinlay 9, Wright 9, Evans 6, McIntyre 6 (2 pens), Donald 3, Hamilton 3, Hunter 2, Lennon 1, McGraw 1, Tortolano 1, own goal 1.
Scottish Cup: (7): Wright 3 (1 pen), Evans 1, McGinlay 1, McIntyre 1, Weir 1.
Skol Cup: (11): Wright 5, McGinlay 2, McIntyre 2 (1 pen), Evans 1, MacLeod 1.

KILMARNOCK — DIV. 1

Ground: Rugby Park, Kilmarnock KA1 2DP (0563 25184)
Colours: Blue and white striped shirts, blue shorts.
Year formed: 1869. **Manager:** Tommy Burns.
League appearances: Black, T. 23; Brayshaw, A. (1); Burgess, S. 1; Burns, H. 29(3); Burns, T. 40; Callaghan, T. 6(1); Campbell, C. 35(3); Clark, C. 1; Elliott, D. (2); Flexney, P. 27; Geddes, R. 33; Graham, A. 11; Jack, R. 27(10); Jenkins, E. (2); MacPherson, A. 42(1); McQuilter, R. (1); McSkimming, S. 23(7); McStay, W. 5(4); Mitchell, A. 42; Montgomerie, R. 26(4); Paterson, C. 28; Porteous, I. 16(9); Reid, D. 1; Reilly, M. 15(4); Roberts, M. (1); Skilling, M. (1); Stark, W. 1; Stephen, R. 1; Tait, T. 18(5); Williamson, R. 33(3).
Goals—League: (59): Campbell 10, Mitchell 10, Williamson 9 (1 pen), Jack 8, Burns H 4; Black 3 (2 pens), Burns T 3, MacPherson 3, Tait 3, McSkimming 1, Montgomerie 1, Porteous 1, own goals 3.
Scottish Cup: (2): Burns H 1, Mitchell 1.
Skol Cup: (2): Campbell 1, McSkimming 1.
B & Q Cup: (1): Burns H 1.

MEADOWBANK THISTLE　　　　　　　　　DIV. 1

Ground: Meadowbank Stadium, Edinburgh EH7 6AE (031-661 5351)
Colours: Amber with black trim, black shorts.
Year formed: 1943 as Ferranti Thistle, Meadowbank Thistle from 1974.
Manager: Donald Park.
League appearances: Armstrong, G. 44; Banks, A. 32(3); Boyd, W. (3); Christie, M. 34; Cormack, P. (1); Coughlin, J. 30(1); Duthie, M. 1(3); Graham, T. 4(2); Grant, D. 31; Hutchison, M. 1(1); Irvine, W. 16(12); Kane, K. 26(12); Little, I. 37(1); Logan, S. 18; McNaughton, B. (5); McNeill, W. 7(10); McQueen, J. 44; Murray, M. 1; Neil, C. 1; Nicol, A. 33(1); Perry, J. 11(4); Roseburgh, D. 30; Ryrie, B. 2(1); Scott, S. 2; Sprott, A. 24(3); Williamson, S. 42; Young, J. 13(3).
Goals–League: (37): Roseburgh 8 (2 pens), Irvine 5 (1 pen), Logan 5, Kane 4, Perry 3, Little 2, Young 2, Christie 1, Coughlin 1, Graham 1, Grant 1, McNaughton 1, Nicol 1, Sprott 1, Williamson 1.
Scottish Cup: (6): Little 2, Perry 2, Roseburgh 1, Williamson 1.
Skol Cup: (0).
B & Q Cup: (1): Logan 1.

MONTROSE　　　　　　　　　　　　　　DIV. 2

Ground: Links Park, Montrose DD10 8QD (0674 73200)
Colours: Blue with white trim, white shorts.
Year formed: 1879. **Manager:** Jim Leishman.
League appearances: Allan, M. 28(10); Callaghan, W. 11; Chalmers, C. 16(2); Craib, S. 13(6); Den Bieman, I. 37(5); Dolan, A. 7(1); Dornan, A. 24; Fleming, J. 35(2); Forbes, G. 9; Fotheringham, J. 4(19); Fraser, C. 8; Houghton, G. 1(1); Kerr, B. 18(4); King, S. 30; Larter, D. 43; Locke, A. 1; Lyons, A. 1(1); Mackay, H. 14(6); McCarron, F. 11; McGachie, J. 28(1); Masson, P. 2; Maver, C. 39; Morrison, B. 40; Robertson, I. 23(1); Rougvie, D. 17; Smith, J. 11; Thomson, M. 2; Wolecki, E. 11(5).
Goals–League: (45): McGachie 9, Mackay 8, Den Bieman 6, King 6, Allan 4 (2 pens), Maver 4, Kerr 2 (1 pen), Robertson 2, Craib 1, Fotheringham 1, Smith 1, Wolecki 1.
Scottish Cup: (0).
Skol Cup: (2): Rougvie 1, Wolecki 1.
B & Q Cup: (8): King 3, Den Bieman 1, Kerr 1, McGachie 1, Maver 1, Rougvie 1.

MORTON　　　　　　　　　　　　　　　DIV. 1

Ground: Cappielow Park, Greenock PA15 2TY (0475 23571)
Colours: Blue and white hooped shirts, white shorts.
Year formed: 1874. **Manager:** Allan McGraw.
League appearances: Alexander, R. 30; Boag, J. 19; Brown, C. 5(6); Collins, D. 44; Deeney, M. 4(5); Doak, M. 43; Fowler, J. 5(4); Gahagan, J. 6(2); Graham, P. 2; Hopkin, D. 17(4); Hunter, J. 3; Johnstone, D. 18; Kelly, G. 2; Lilley, D. 13(12); McArthur, S. 29(4); MacCabe, D. 4(8); McDonald, I. 11(6); McGoldrick, K. 1(6); McInnes, D. 38(4); Mahood, A. 4(1); Mathie, A. 42; Ogg, G. 17(2); Pickering, M. 34; Rafferty, S. 37(6); Tolmie, J. 14; Wylie, D. 42.
Goals–League: (66): Mathie 18 (2 pens), Alexander 10, Doak 9, McInnes 7 (1 pen), Hopkin 3, Lilley 3, McArthur 3, Rafferty 3, Tolmie 3, Gahagan 2, Collins 1, Deeney 1, Johnstone 1, Pickering 1, own goal 1.
Scottish Cup: (9): Alexander 3, Mathie 3 (2 pens), Hopkin 1, McArthur 1, Rafferty 1.
Skol Cup: (2): McInnes 1, Ogg 1.
B & Q Cup: (4): Mathie 2, Doak 1, McArthur 1.

MOTHERWELL PREM. DIV.

Ground: Fir Park, Motherwell ML1 2QN (0698 61437/8)
Colours: Amber shirts with claret band, claret shorts.
Year formed: 1886. **Manager:** Tommy McLean.
League appearances: Angus, I. 23(2); Arnott, D. 26; Bryce, S. 2(3); Cooper, D. 38(1); Cusack, N. 17; Dolan, J. 28(4); Dykstra, S. 1; Ferguson, I. 9(11); Gardner, J. 6(6); Gourlay, A. (1); Griffin, J. 22; Jones, A. 12; Kirk. S. 28(10); McCart, C. 22; McGrillen, P. 5(11); McKinnon, R. 16; McLeod, J. 9(5); Maaskrant, R. 12; Martin, B. 25; Nijholt, L. 39; O'Donnell, P. 42; Philliben, J. 30(2); Russell, R. 7(9); Shepherd, A. 1(4); Simpson, N. 20(1); Thomson, W. 43; Verheul, B. 1(2).
Goals—League: (43): Arnott 8, Kirk 6, Nijholt 5 (3 pens), O'Donnell 4, Angus 3, Cooper 3 (1 pen), Cusack 2, Dolan 2, McCart 2, Russell 2, Griffin 1, Jones 1, McKinnon 1, Philliben 1, own goals 2.
Scottish Cup: (6): Arnott 1, Ferguson 1, Kirk 1, Martin 1, Nijholt 1 (pen), O'Donnell 1.
Skol Cup: (1): Kirk 1.

PARTICK THISTLE PREM. DIV.

Ground: Firhill Park, Glasgow G20 7AL (041-943 4811)
Colours: Amber shirts with red trim, red shorts.
Year formed: 1876. **Manager:** John Lambie.
League appearances: Annand, E. (1); Bell, D. 8(4); Duffy, J. 37(1); English, I. 12(14); Farningham, R. 33; Flood, J. 4(2); Friar, P. 1; Harvie, S. 7(2); Irons, D. 40(1); Johnston, S. 19(1); Kennedy, A. 9; Kinnaird, P. 13; Law, R. 25(6); Lowrie, R. 1; McGlashan, C. 43(1); McGovern, P. 1(4); McLaughlin, P. 30(3); McWalter, M. 5(2); McVicar, D. 10; Magee, K. (6); Murdoch, A. 32; Murray, M. 23; Nelson, C. 11; Peebles, G. 1(1); Rae, G. 36(2); Robertson, G. 33(3); Roche, D. 1(1); Shaw, G. 40(3); Tierney, G. 9(4).
Goals—League: (62): McGlashan 18 (4 pens), Shaw 9, Irons 8, Farningham 7, English 5, Rae 3, Duffy 2 (1 pen), Johnston 2, Kinnaird 2, Law 2, Kennedy 1, Tierney 1, own goals 2.
Scottish Cup: (0).
Skol Cup: (2): McGlashan 1, own goal 1.
B & Q Cup: (4): McGlashan 2, Rae 1, Shaw 1.

QUEEN OF THE SOUTH DIV. 2

Ground: Palmerston Park, Dumfries DG2 9BA (0387 54853)
Colours: Royal blue shirts, white shorts.
Year formed: 1919. **Manager:** —.
League appearances: Bell, A. 31; Campbell, K. 4; Davidson, A. 23; Fraser, G. 3(7); Gillespie, A. 20; Gordon, S. 36; Hetherington, K. 17(1); Leslie, S. 2(1); McFarlane, A. 23(2); McGhie, W. 27(1); McGuire, D. 17(8); McGuire, J. 36(1); McKeown, B. 16; Mills, D. 8(1); Moffat, I. 1(5); Robertson, J. 27(2); Sim, W. 13(3); Smyth, D. 9; Templeton, H. 27; Thomson, A. 39; Thomson, I. 34; Thomson, M. 16.
Goals—League: (71): Thomson A 26, McGuire J 13, Thomson I 10 (1 pen), Templeton 7, Bell 2, Gordon 2, McGhie 2, McKeown 2, Robertson 2, Hetherington 1, McFarlane 1, Moffat 1, Smyth 1, own goal 1.
Scottish Cup: (1): Thomson A 1.
Skol Cup: (0).
B & Q Cup: (12): Thomson A 6, McGuire J 4, Robertson 1, own goal 1.

QUEEN'S PARK   DIV. 2

Ground: Hampden Park, Glasgow G42 9BA (041-632 1275)
Colours: Black and white hooped shirts, white shorts.
Year formed: 1867. **Coach:** Eddie Hunter.
League appearances: Callan, D. 8; Caven, R. 35; Chalmers, J. 29; Elder, G. 34; Flannigan, M. 6(8); Graham, D. 18(1); Greig, D. (2); Houston, J. 1; Jack, S. 37(2); Jackson, D. 22(7); MacColl, A. 13(1); Mackay, M. 25(2); McArthur, P. 2(3); McCormick, S. 31(1); McEntegart, S. 23(3); McFadyen, James 6(3); McFadyen, Joe 3(4); McKeever, R. (1); Mackenzie, K. 13(1); McLean, S. 10; Moonie, D. 9; O'Brien, J. 30(1); O'Neill, J. 12(13); Orr, G. 13(3); Orr, J. 11; Rodden, J. 21; Stevenson, C. 17(2).
Goals–League: (59): McCormick 17, Caven 6, O'Neill 6 (1 pen), Rodden 6, O'Brien 5, McEntegart 4, Jackson 3, Mackay 3, McFadyen James 2, Elder 1, Flannigan 1, Jack 1, MacColl 1, McFadyen Joe 1, McLean 1, Stevenson 1.
Scottish Cup: (0).
Skol Cup: (4): Mackay 2, Mackenzie 2.
B & Q Cup: (1): O'Brien 1.

RAITH ROVERS   DIV. 1

Ground: Stark's Park, Pratt Street, Kirkcaldy KY1 1SA (0592 263514)
Colours: Navy blue shirts, white shorts.
Year formed: 1883. **Manager:** Jimmy Nicholl.
League appearances: Arthur, G. 44; Brewster, C. 40(2); Burn, P. 11(4); Coyle, R. 27(2); Dair, J. (4); Dalziel, G. 38(1); Dennis, S. 42; Dunleavy, D. 6(5); Ferguson, I. 7(2); Hetherston, P. 31; McGeachie, G. 18; MacKenzie, A. 18(4); MacLeod, I. 44; McStay, J. 34; Nelson, M. 32(2); Nicholl, J. 32; Quinn, S. 1(1); Raeside, R. 12(1); Sinclair, D. 19(3); Strang, S. 6(7); Williamson, T. 18(7); Young, D. 4(5).
Goals–League: (59): Dalziel 26 (1 pen), Brewster 12, MacKenzie 3, Nelson 3, Strang 3, McStay 2, Williamson 2, Dunleavy 1, Ferguson 1, Hetherston 1, MacLeod 1, Nicholl 1, Sinclair 1, own goals 2.
Scottish Cup: (0).
Skol Cup: (5): Brewster 2, MacKenzie 2, Nelson 1.
B & Q Cup: (5): Dalziel 5 (1 pen).

RANGERS   PREM. DIV.

Ground: Ibrox Stadium, Glasgow G51 2XD (041-427 8500)
Colours: Royal blue shirts, white shorts.
Year formed: 1873. **Manager:** Walter Smith.
League appearances: Brown, J. 18(7); Durrant, I. 9(4); Ferguson, I. 12(4); Goram, A. 44; Gordon, D. 23; Gough, R. 33; Hateley, M. 29; Huistra, P. 25(7); Johnston, M. 10(1); Kuznetsov, O. 16(2); McCall, S. 35(1); McCoist, A. 37(1); McGregor, J. 1; McSwegan, G. (4); Mikhailichenko, A. 24(3); Morrow, J. 3; Nisbet, S. 20; Pressley, S. (1); Rideout, P. 7(4); Robertson, A. 3(4); Robertson, D. 42; Robertson, L. 1; Spackman, N. 42; Spencer, J. 4(4); Steven, T. 2; Stevens, G. 43; Vinnicombe, C. 1(1).
Goals–League: (101): McCoist 34 (1 pen), Hateley 21 (3 pens), Mikhailichenko 10, Gordon 5, Huistra 5, Johnston 5 (2 pens), Nisbet 5, Brown 4, Gough 2, Stevens 2, Ferguson 1, McCall 1, Rideout 1, Robertson D 1, Spencer 1, Steven 1, own goals 2.
Scottish Cup: (9): McCoist 4, Hateley 2, Mikhailichenko 2, Gough 1.
Skol Cup: (9): Johnston 5, Durrant 1, McCoist 1, Robertson D 1, Spackman 1.

ST JOHNSTONE PREM. DIV.

Ground: McDiarmid Park, Crieff Road, Perth PH1 2SJ (0738 26961)
Colours: Royal blue shirts with white trim, white shorts.
Year formed: 1884. **Manager:** Alex Totten.
League appearances: Arkins, V. 14(7); Baltacha, S. 30(1); Barron, D. 1(3); Bingham, D. 7(2); Cherry, P. 24; Curran, H. 36(3); Davies, J. 37(3); Deas, P. 17(1); Dunne, L. 9(8); Grant, R. 17(8); Hamilton, L. 43; Inglis, J. 39(1); Kennedy, S. 1; McGinnis, G. 28(1); McVicar, D. 3(1); Maskrey, S. 12(12); Moore, A. 18(3); Redford, I. 28; Stewart, R. 17; Treanor, M. 31(2); Turner, T. 31(2); Ward, K. 2(10); Wright, P. 39(2).
Goals–League: (52): Wright 18, Curran 8, Arkins 5, Redford 3, Stewart 3, Turner 3, Grant 2, Maskrey 2, Treanor 2 (2 pens), Baltacha 1, Bingham 1, Cherry 1, Moore 1, Ward 1, own goal 1.
Scottish Cup: (7): Moore 3, Wright 3, McGinnis 1.
Skol Cup: (2): Redford 1, Ward 1.

ST MIRREN DIV. 1

Ground: St Mirren Park, Paisley PA3 2EJ (041-889 2558 and 041-840 1337)
Colours: White shirts with black vertical stripes, black shorts.
Year formed: 1877. **Manager:** Jimmy Bone.
League appearances: Aitken, R. 34; Baillie, A. 17(1); Baker, M. 1; Beattie, J. 24; Black, T. 9; Broddle, J. 35; Charnley, J. 23(3); Dawson, R. 5(2); Elliot, D. 21(7); Fridge, L. 14; Fullarton, J. (1); Hewitt, J. 14; Irvine, A. 25(3); Kinnaird, P. 1(2); Kinsey, S. 1(5); Lambert, P. 36(4); Lavety, B. 3(2); McDonald, A. (3); McDowall, K. 19(10); McEwan, A. (1); McGill, D. 3(10); McGowne, K. 31(5); McIntyre, P. 20(3); McWhirter, N. 9(2); Manley, R. 32; Martin, B. 17; Money, C. 30; Reid, M. 11(4); Stickroth, T. 13(4); Torfason, G. 27(2); Wishart, F. 9.
Goals–League: (33): Torfason 8, Charnley 4, Hewitt 3, Irvine 3, Broddle 2, Lambert 2, Lavety 2, McDowall 2, Martin 2, Aitken 1, Black 1 (pen), Elliot 1, McGowne 1, Stickroth 1.
Scottish Cup: (0).
Skol Cup: (4): Kinnaird 1, Lambert 1, McWhirter 1, own goal 1.

STENHOUSEMUIR DIV. 2

Ground: Ochilview Park, Stenhousemuir FK5 5QL (0324 562992)
Colours: Maroon shirts with white trim, white shorts.
Year formed: 1884. **Manager:** Dennis Lawson.
League appearances: Aitken, N. 27(2); Anderson, P. 30; Anderson, R. 1; Bainbridge, S. 6(6); Barnstaple, K. 13; Barr, R. 20; Bell, A. 1; Bullen, L. 1; Cairney, H. 18; Clouston, B. 36; Conroy, J. 10(11); Donalds, G. 11(12); Fallon, M. 1; Ferguson, N. 1; Fisher, J. 17; Gardiner, J. 1(1); Girasoli, C. 7(9); Guthrie, F. 1; Haddon, L. 7(2); Hallford, E. 20; Hulme, M. 1; Hutchinson, T. 2; Irvine, J. 3; Kemp, B. 20; Kelly, C. 26; Livingstone, J. 1; McAvoy, M. 1; McCallum, M. 7; McCormick, S. 26; McKenzie, T. 1; McLafferty, W. 15(1); Mann, G. (2); Mathieson, M. 18; Murdoch, S. 1; Nelson, M. 7(1); Prior, S. 18; Quinton, I. 16; Robertson, M. 1(3); Speirs, A. 9(3); Tracey, K. 17(2); Walker, C. 3(1); Wilson, C. 7(3).
Goals–League: (46): Mathieson 6, McCallum 5, Donald 4, Girasoli 4, McCormick 4, Bainbridge 3, Conroy 3, Speirs 3 (1 pen), Anderson 2, McLafferty 2, Prior 2, Cairney 1, Clouston 1, Fisher 1, Haddon 1, Kemp 1, Nelson 1, Quinton 1, Wilson 1.
Scottish Cup: (1): McLafferty 1.
Skol Cup: (2): Bainbridge 1, McCormick 1.
B & Q Cup: (3): Bainbridge 1, Conroy 1, Speirs 1.

STIRLING ALBION DIV. 1

Ground: Annfield Park, Stirling FK8 2HE (0786 50399)
Colours: Red shirts with white sleeves, white shorts.
Year formed: 1945. **Manager:** John Brogan.
League appearances: Armstrong, P. 29(3); Brogan, J. (1); Conway, M. 7(6); Docherty, A. 2(9); Docherty, R. 23(5); Hay, G. 10(3); Hendry, M. 8; Kerr, J. 40; Lawrie, D. 40; Lloyd, D. 9(1); McCormack, J. 18(2); McGeown, M. 43; McInnes, I. 40(3); Mitchell, C. 41(1); Moore, V. 27(10); O'Neill, T. 5; Pew, D. 2(6); Picken, J. 1; Reid, J. 7(13); Reilly, R. 30; Robertson, S. 25(5); Shanks, D. 32(2); Smith, J. (1); Watson, P. 10; Watters, W. 35(3).
Goals–League: (50): Watters 17, Moore 7 (1 pen), Armstrong 4, McInnes 4, Reilly 4, Hendry 3, Lawrie 3, Mitchell 3 (3 pens), Lloyd 2, Pew 2, Shanks 1.
Scottish Cup: (1): Reilly 1.
Skol Cup: (0).
B & Q Cup: (3): Moore 1, Reilly 1, Watters 1.

STRANRAER DIV. 2

Ground: Stair Park, Stranraer DG9 8BS (0776 3271)
Colours: Royal blue shirts with amber band, blue shorts.
Year formed: 1870. **Manager:** Alex McAnespie.
League appearances: Brannigan, K. 21; Cook, D. 16(10); Duffy, B. 36; Duncan, G. 27(4); Elliot, D. (1); Evans, S. 9; Ewing, A. 19(5); Gallagher, A. 22; Geraghty, M. 2(11); Grant, A. 28(3); Harkness, C. 20(9); Henderson, D. 32(1); Holland, B. 3; Hughes, J. 36; Love, J. 21(8); Lowe, L. 2(1); McCann, J. 25(1); McDowall, P. 14; McNiven, J. 19(3); Scott, R. 1; Shirkie, S. 12; Sloan, T. 35(1); Spittal, I. 27(1); Walker, D. 2.
Goals–League: (46): Sloan 14, Henderson 7, Cook 5, Grant 5, Ewing 4, Harkness 4 (1 pen), Gallagher 2, Geraghty 1, McDowall 1, McNiven 1, Spittal 1, own goal 1.
Scottish Cup: (7): Harkness 3, Sloan 3, Gallagher 1.
Skol Cup: (0).
B & Q Cup: (5): Cook 1, Gallagher 1, Harkness 1, Henderson 1, McCann 1.

SCOTTISH REVIEW

Rangers duly won the championship, the turning point probably coming as early as 23 November when they were surprisingly beaten 1-0 at Ibrox by struggling St Mirren. The champions lost only one other match 2-0 at home to Celtic on 21 March.

Runners-up Hearts kept in the hunt and had a purple patch from late October to early January when they were unbeaten in 15 outings. They finished one point ahead of Celtic who could have overhauled them on the last day of the season but were beaten 2-1 by Hibernian at Parkhead. This after 16 games without defeat.

At the bottom half of the table, there was not much doubt concerning the relegation favourites. Despite St Mirren's day of euphoria at Ibrox, they were ten points adrift of the next club above them and Dunfermline Athletic six points worse off than St Mirren.

Dunfermline had to wait until 20 November for their first win and managed only three others during the entire season. They scored only 22 goals in the 44 games. However the Fifers did much better in the Skol Cup and reached the final where they were beaten 2-0 by Hibernian. who had their moments during the League season as well.

Airdrie were the surprise team in the Scottish Cup, but were beaten 2-1 by Rangers in the final. Rangers Ally McCoist, who started the season unsure of a regular place, not only topped the League marksmen in Scotland with 34 goals, but in the whole of Europe.

Back in the Premier League came Dundee and Partick Thistle. Dundee were never lower than second all season, but Partick only just edged out Hamilton on goal difference. Montrose and Forfar were relegated to the First Division but there was a closer race to take their places.

Only three points separated Dumbarton, Cowdenbeath, Alloa and East Fife in the Second Division promotion race. Dumbarton finished a point ahead of Cowden who managed a goalless draw on the last day of the season at Alloa to pip their rivals by a point.

Super-super-league talk was again in the air. It would mean extending an arm of friendship to top English clubs to really make it work and there are far too many obstacles involving entry into Europe and even problems for the national team if this idea went much further.

SCOTTISH LEAGUE – PREMIER DIVISION RESULTS 1991–92

	Aberdeen	Airdrie	Celtic	Dundee U	Dunfermline Ath	Falkirk	Hearts	Hibernian	Motherwell	Rangers	St Johnstone	St Mirren
Aberdeen	—	3–1	1–0	0–1	3–0	1–1	0–2	1–1	3–1	2–3	1–2	4–1
		1–0	2–2	0–2	1–1	1–1	2–0	0–1	2–0	0–2	4–1	0–0
Airdrie	1–2	—	0–3	1–3	3–1	0–0	2–3	0–1	0–1	0–4	1–2	4–1
	2–0		0–0	1–0	3–2	2–2	2–1	0–3	2–0	0–0	0–3	1–1
Celtic	2–1	3–1	—	4–1	1–0	4–1	3–1	0–0	2–2	0–2	4–0	0–0
	1–0	2–0		3–1	2–0	2–0	1–2	1–2	4–1	1–3	3–2	4–0
Dundee U	0–0	0–0	3–4	—	3–0	2–1	0–1	1–1	2–2	3–2	1–2	4–1
	4–0	2–1	1–1		0–0	2–1	2–0	1–0	2–2	1–2	2–1	1–3
Dunfermline Ath	0–0	1–2	1–3	1–2	—	0–4	1–2	1–2	0–0	0–5	0–0	1–4
	0–0	0–0	0–1	0–1		1–0	0–2	0–0	3–1	1–3	0–3	0–0
Falkirk	0–1	3–2	4–3	0–4	0–1	—	1–2	3–2	1–1	0–2	2–3	3–0
	2–2	0–3	0–3	1–3	2–0		1–2	2–3	0–1	1–3	2–0	1–0
Hearts	1–0	1–0	3–1	1–1	1–0	1–1	—	0–0	2–0	1–0	2–1	0–0
	0–4	2–2	1–2	1–0	1–0	2–0		1–1	3–1	0–1	2–0	0–0
Hibernian	1–0	2–2	1–1	1–0	3–0	2–2	1–1	—	0–0	0–3	2–1	4–1
	1–1	0–2	0–2	3–2	5–0	0–1	1–2		0–0	1–3	0–1	0–0
Motherwell	0–1	1–2	0–2	1–1	3–0	4–2	0–1	1–1	—	0–2	1–1	1–0
	3–3	0–3	0–0	1–2	1–2	0–1	0–1	1–1		1–2	3–1	3–0
Rangers	0–2	4–0	1–1	1–1	4–0	1–1	2–0	4–2	2–0	—	6–0	0–1
	0–0	5–0	0–2	2–0	2–1	4–1	1–1	2–0	2–0		3–1	4–0
St Johnstone	1–4	1–0	1–0	1–1	3–2	2–3	0–1	0–1	0–1	2–3	—	1–0
	0–0	1–1	2–4	1–1	1–0	1–1	0–5	1–1	0–0	1–2		1–2
St Mirren	0–1	1–2	0–5	1–1	0–0	0–0	2–3	0–1	1–2	1–2	1–1	—
	0–2	4–1	1–1	0–1	3–1	0–1	0–1	0–1	1–2	1–2	1–5	

SCOTTISH LEAGUE – DIVISION I RESULTS 1991–92

	Ayr U	Clydebank	Dundee	Forfar Ath	Hamilton A	Kilmarnock	Meadowbank T	Montrose	Morton	Partick T	Raith R	Stirling A
Ayr U	—	3–0	4–1	4–0	0–2	0–3	7–0	2–0	3–2	1–3	1–0	1–2
	—	3–1	0–0	1–0	2–0	0–2	0–0	0–0	1–0	0–2	1–1	1–2
Clydebank	3–2	—	1–2	3–3	1–1	1–1	1–1	4–1	3–1	0–0	0–2	0–1
	1–0	—	2–2	2–0	1–3	0–3	1–1	4–2	2–3	1–2	1–1	2–1
Dundee	3–1	4–0	—	4–0	4–0	2–1	3–1	1–0	0–1	1–2	1–1	0–0
	1–1	3–0	—	3–1	1–2	1–1	2–1	1–2	2–2	1–0	3–2	5–0
Forfar Ath	2–3	2–1	2–4	—	0–0	0–1	0–0	2–2	1–4	0–3	0–1	1–1
	0–1	1–3	0–3	—	1–3	0–0	1–0	2–0	1–5	0–0	1–2	1–1
Hamilton A	3–1	0–0	1–3	4–0	—	2–2	3–1	2–0	1–1	1–1	4–1	3–1
	2–1	2–3	1–1	2–1	—	0–1	2–0	4–1	0–0	0–2	1–0	1–0
Kilmarnock	1–1	2–1	1–2	4–2	1–2	—	1–0	0–0	1–0	2–3	1–0	0–0
	1–1	1–0	2–0	2–0	0–2	—	2–1	5–1	0–1	1–3	1–0	2–0
Meadowbank T	1–1	1–1	1–2	0–0	3–3	2–3	—	0–0	0–1	0–1	2–0	0–1
	0–1	2–0	0–0	2–0	1–2	1–0	—	0–1	1–2	0–0	0–1	0–0
Montrose	1–3	1–3	1–2	2–1	2–2	2–2	2–2	—	1–1	0–2	0–3	4–1
	0–0	2–2	2–3	2–1	0–1	0–1	2–2	—	1–1	0–1	2–2	0–0
Morton	3–4	1–7	3–0	1–3	1–0	0–1	2–1	1–1	—	2–1	0–2	2–1
	2–0	5–0	0–0	1–1	1–1	0–0	3–1	2–2	—	0–1	0–1	2–0
Partick T	3–0	0–3	2–6	1–1	1–1	1–0	0–2	1–0	3–4	—	5–0	1–0
	4–1	2–1	2–0	0–0	0–0	2–1	1–2	3–0	1–0	—	0–1	0–1
Raith R	0–0	4–0	0–1	2–0	1–3	1–1	1–1	2–1	1–1	1–0	—	1–0
	2–4	0–0	1–0	2–0	2–1	1–1	3–0	5–0	2–0	0–0	—	1–2
Stirling A	0–0	3–0	1–1	1–3	0–1	0–3	2–3	2–2	2–1	1–1	1–3	—
	1–2	2–0	1–1	4–1	3–0	1–0	0–0	4–1	4–3	1–1	1–2	—

SCOTTISH LEAGUE – DIVISION II RESULTS 1991–92

	Albion R	Alloa	Arbroath	Berwick R	Brechin R	Clyde	Cowdenbeath	Dumbarton	East Fife	East Stirling	Queen of South	Queen's Park	Stenhousemuir	Stranraer
Albion R	—	2–1 1–3	0–1	1–2	0–3 1–2	2–2 0–2	0–4 1–2	0–3 1–1	0–1	1–1 1–3	1–1	1–1 3–4	1–1	2–1
Alloa	1–0	—	0–0	2–1	1–0 6–1	4–2	4–2 0–0	1–2	1–1 1–2	0–1 1–0	3–1 3–1	1–0 2–1	1–0	3–1 0–0
Arbroath	2–1 1–1	2–2 1–3	—	1–1	3–2	0–0 3–0	2–1 1–0	1–0	0–0	3–3	2–3 0–3	2–2 2–1	2–0	1–0
Berwick R	3–1 1–1	0–1 0–1	0–0 3–2	—	1–1	2–1	1–3	2–2 1–5	1–2 1–4	1–0	1–1	1–3	0–1 0–1	0–0 1–2
Brechin C	1–2	0–2	1–1 1–0	2–2 1–2	—	1–0 1–2	0–1	0–4	4–4 0–1	0–0	7–1 1–1	2–0 1–0	1–0 0–0	2–1
Clyde	6–2	2–0 0–1	1–1	2–0 0–1	0–0	—	4–0	0–1	1–0 4–0	2–1	2–3 2–1	3–1	0–0 4–0	4–2 1–1
Cowdenbeath	1–0	1–1	3–1	2–0 4–1	2–1 2–1	0–3 3–1	—	2–1	3–3 3–1	3–2 4–0	0–1 3–1	0–2	2–0	2–0
Dumbarton	4–3	2–2 1–1	2–1 1–1	1–1	3–0 1–3	0–0 2–1	0–0 2–1	—	1–2 0–1	1–1	3–1	3–1	1–0	1–0 0–0
East Fife	3–2 3–1	0–0	2–2 3–1	3–1	2–1	1–2	1–0	2–2 0–2	—	2–2 0–2	4–1 5–1	2–0 1–1	4–4	2–1
East Stirling	2–1	2–1	1–1 0–5	4–1 0–4	3–3 0–0	2–1 2–1	2–3	1–2	4–2	—	2–1	2–1	2–1 0–3	2–2 1–0
Queen of the South	2–4 3–0	1–3	0–2	0–3 0–3	4–2	1–2	3–3	2–4 1–2	3–1	5–1 2–3	—	2–2 5–3	2–1 1–3	0–2
Queen's Park	1–1	2–1	1–0	3–2 4–1	0–1	0–1 1–0	2–3 1–2	0–3 0–0	1–0	4–2 1–1	1–4	—	2–1 2–0	0–1 5–2
Stenhousemuir	1–1 4–0	4–0 1–1	2–1 1–0	0–2	0–2	1–2	3–3 2–4	1–0 0–1	2–1 1–2	2–1 1–2	1–3	1–3	—	0–1
Stranraer	1–2 2–0	1–0	2–0 1–0	2–2	1–3 1–1	2–0	2–2	2–1 1–0	0–2 1–2	3–5	0–2 1–3	2–1	3–2 1–1	—

B & Q SCOTTISH LEAGUE FINAL TABLES 1991–92

Premier Division	P	Home W	D	L	Goals F	A	Away W	D	L	Goals F	A	GD	Pts
Rangers	44	14	5	3	50	14	19	1	2	51	17	+70	72
Hearts	44	12	7	3	26	15	15	2	5	34	22	+23	63
Celtic	44	15	3	4	47	20	11	7	4	41	22	+46	62
Dundee U	44	10	7	5	37	25	9	6	7	29	25	+16	51
Hibernian	44	7	8	7	28	25	9	9	4	25	20	+8	49
Aberdeen	44	9	6	7	32	23	8	8	6	23	19	+13	48
Airdrieonians	44	7	5	10	25	33	6	5	11	25	37	−20	36
St Johnstone	44	5	7	10	21	32	8	3	11	31	41	−21	36
Falkirk	44	7	2	13	29	41	5	9	8	25	32	−19	35
Motherwell	44	5	6	11	25	29	5	8	9	18	32	−18	34
St Mirren	44	2	5	15	18	36	4	7	11	15	37	−40	24
Dunfermline Ath	44	2	7	13	11	35	2	3	17	11	45	−58	18

First Division	P	Home W	D	L	Goals F	A	Away W	D	L	Goals F	A	GD	Pts
Dundee	44	13	5	4	46	20	10	7	5	34	28	+32	58
Partick T	44	11	4	7	33	24	12	7	3	19	12	+26	57
Hamilton A	44	12	6	4	39	21	10	7	5	33	27	+24	57
Kilmarnock	44	12	4	6	31	20	9	8	5	28	17	+22	54
Raith R	44	11	7	4	33	16	10	4	8	26	26	+17	53
Ayr U	44	11	4	7	35	21	7	7	8	28	34	+8	47
Morton	44	9	6	7	32	28	8	6	8	34	31	+7	46
Stirling Albion	44	8	7	7	35	29	6	6	10	15	28	−7	41
Clydebank	44	7	8	7	33	33	5	4	13	26	44	−18	36
Meadowbank T	44	4	8	10	17	20	3	8	11	20	39	−22	30
Montrose	44	3	10	9	28	38	2	7	13	17	47	−40	27
Forfar Ath	44	3	7	12	18	38	2	5	15	18	47	−49	22

Second Division	P	Home W	D	L	Goals F	A	Away W	D	L	Goals F	A	GD	Pts
Dumbarton	39	9	8	3	29	20	11	4	4	36	17	+28	52
Cowdenbeath	39	14	2	3	40	20	8	5	7	34	32	+22	51
Alloa	39	13	4	3	34	15	7	6	6	24	23	+20	50
East Fife	39	10	7	2	42	26	9	4	7	30	31	+15	49
Clyde	39	11	4	4	38	15	7	3	10	23	28	+18	43
East Stirling	39	10	4	5	32	33	5	7	8	29	37	−9	41
Arbroath	39	9	7	3	29	23	3	7	10	20	25	+1	38
Brechin C	39	7	7	6	27	24	6	5	8	27	31	−1	38
Queen's Park	39	10	3	7	31	26	4	4	11	28	37	−4	35
Stranraer	39	9	4	7	29	29	4	5	10	17	27	−10	35
Queen of the S	39	6	2	11	37	44	8	3	9	34	42	−15	33
Berwick R	39	4	6	10	20	32	6	5	8	30	33	−15	31
Stenhousemuir	39	7	3	9	27	28	4	5	11	19	29	−11	30
Albion R	39	2	6	12	19	39	3	4	12	23	42	−39	20

Scottish League Leading Scorers 1991–92

Listed in order of League goals

Premier Division	League	Scottish Cup	Skol Cup	B & Q	Total
Ally McCoist (Rangers)	34	4	1	0	**39**
Charlie Nicholas (Celtic)	21	0	2	0	**23**
Paul Wright (St Johnstone)	18	3	0	0	**21**
Tommy Coyne (Celtic)	15	4	0	0	**19**
Scott Crabbe (Hearts)	15	1	2	0	**18**
Duncan Ferguson (Dundee U)	15	2	0	0	**17**
First Division					
Gordon Dalziel (Raith R)	26	0	0	5	**31**
Ken Eadie (Clydebank)	22	2	0	1	**25**
Billy Dodds (Dundee)	19	0	0	0	**19**
Alex Mathie (Morton)	18	3	0	2	**23**
Colin McGlashan (Partick T)	18	0	1	2	**21**
Willie Watters (Stirling A)	17	0	0	1	**18**
Second Division					
Andy Thomson (Queen of Sth)	26	1	0	6	**33**
John Sludden (East Fife)	21	2	0	2	**25**
Graham Buckley (Cowdenbeath)	21	0	0	0	**21**
Jim Gilmour (Dumbarton)	19	1	0	0	**20**
Danny Diver (East Stirling)	18	0	1	0	**19**
Steve McCormick (Queen's Park)	17	0	0	0	**17**

Scottish League and Cup Honours

Championship wins
42 – Rangers (including one shared); 35 – Celtic; 4 – Aberdeen, Hearts, Hibernian; 2 – Dumbarton (including one shared); 1 – Dundee, Dundee U, Kilmarnock, Motherwell, Third Lanark.

Scottish FA Cup
29 – Celtic; 25 – Rangers; 10 – Queen's Park; 7 – Aberdeen; 5 – Hearts; 3 – Clyde, St Mirren, Vale of Leven; 2 – Dunfermline Ath, Falkirk, Hibernian, Kilmarnock, Motherwell, Renton, Third Lanark; 1 – Airdrieonians, Dumbarton, Dundee, East Fife, Morton, Partick Th, St Bernard's.

Scottish League/Skol Cup
16 – Rangers; 9 – Celtic; 5 – Aberdeen, Hearts; 3 – Dundee, East Fife; 2 – Dundee U, Hibernian; 1 – Motherwell, Partick Th.

SCOTTISH LEAGUE HONOURS LIST

Premier Division (maximum points: *a*, 72; *b*, 88)

	First	Pts	Second	Pts	Third	Pts
1975–76*a*	Rangers	54	Celtic	48	Hibernian	43
1976–77*a*	Celtic	55	Rangers	46	Aberdeen	43
1977–78*a*	Rangers	55	Aberdeen	53	Dundee U	40
1978–79*a*	Celtic	48	Rangers	45	Dundee U	44
1979–80*a*	Aberdeen	48	Celtic	47	St Mirren	42
1980–81*a*	Celtic	56	Aberdeen	49	Rangers	44
1981–82*a*	Celtic	55	Aberdeen	53	Rangers	43
1982–83*a*	Dundee U	56	Celtic	55	Aberdeen	55
1983–84*a*	Aberdeen	57	Celtic	50	Dundee U	47
1984–85*a*	Aberdeen	59	Celtic	52	Dundee U	47
1985–86*a*	Celtic	50	Hearts	50	Dundee U	47
1986–87*b*	Rangers	69	Celtic	63	Dundee U	60
1987–88*b*	Celtic	72	Hearts	62	Rangers	60
1988–89*a*	Rangers	56	Aberdeen	50	Celtic	46
1989–90*a*	Rangers	51	Aberdeen	44	Hearts	44
1990–91*a*	Rangers	55	Aberdeen	53	*Celtic	41
1991–92*a*	Rangers	72	Hearts	63	Celtic	62

First Division (Maximum points: *a*, 52; *b*, 78; *c*, 88)

	First	Pts	Second	Pts	Third	Pts
1975–76*a*	Partick T	41	Kilmarnock	35	Montrose	30
1976–77*b*	St Mirren	62	Clydebank	58	Dundee	51
1977–78*b*	*Morton	58	Hearts	58	Dundee	57
1978–79*b*	Dundee	55	*Kilmarnock	54	Clydebank	54
1979–80*b*	Hearts	53	Airdrieonians	51	Ayr U	44
1980–81*b*	Hibernian	57	Dundee	52	St Johnstone	51
1981–82*b*	Motherwell	61	Kilmarnock	51	Hearts	50
1982–83*b*	St Johnstone	55	Hearts	54	Clydebank	50
1983–84*b*	Morton	54	Dumbarton	51	Partick T	46
1984–85*b*	Motherwell	50	Clydebank	48	Falkirk	45
1985–86*b*	Hamilton A	56	Falkirk	45	Kilmarnock	44
1986–87*c*	Morton	57	Dunfermline Ath	56	Dumbarton	53
1987–88*c*	Hamilton A	56	Meadowbank T	52	Clydebank	49
1988–89*b*	Dunfermline Ath	54	Falkirk	52	Clydebank	48
1989–90*b*	St Johnstone	58	Airdrieonians	54	Clydebank	44
1990–91*b*	Falkirk	54	Airdrieonians	53	Dundee	52
1991–92*c*	Dundee	58	*Partick T	57	Hamilton A	57

Second Division (maximum points: *a*, 52; *b*, 78)

	First	Pts	Second	Pts	Third	Pts
1975–77*a*	*Clydebank	40	Raith R	40	Alloa	35
1976–77*b*	Stirling A	55	Alloa	51	Dunfermline Ath	50
1977–78*b*	*Clyde	53	Raith R	53	Dunfermline Ath	48
1978–79*b*	Berwick R	54	Dunfermline Ath	52	Falkirk	50
1979–80*b*	Falkirk	50	East Stirling	49	Forfar Ath	46
1980–81*b*	Queen's Park	50	Queen of the S	46	Cowdenbeath	45
1981–82*b*	Clyde	59	Alloa	50	Arbroath	50

1982–83b	Brechin C	55	Meadowbank T	54	Arbroath	49
1983–84b	Forfar Ath	63	East Fife	47	Berwick R	43
1984–85b	Montrose	53	Alloa	50	Dunfermline Ath	49
1985–86b	Dunfermline Ath	57	Queen of the S	55	Meadowbank T	49
1986–87b	Meadowbank T	55	*Raith R	52	Stirling A	52
1987–88b	Ayr U	61	St Johnstone	59	Queen's Park	51
1988–89b	Albion R	50	Alloa	45	Brechin C	43
1989–90b	Brechin C	49	Kilmarnock	48	Stirling A	47
1990–91b	Stirling A	54	Montrose	46	Cowdenbeath	45
1991–92b	Dumbarton	52	Cowdenbeath	51	Alloa	50

First Division to 1974–75 (maximum points: a, 36; b, 44; c, 40; d, 52; e, 60; f, 68; g, 76; h, 84)

	First	Pts	Second	Pts	Third	Pts
1890–91a‡	‡Dumbarton	29	Rangers	29	Celtic	24
1891–92b	Dumbarton	37	Celtic	35	Hearts	30
1892–93a	Celtic	29	Rangers	28	St Mirren	23
1893–94a	Celtic	29	Hearts	26	St Bernard's	22
1894–95a	Hearts	31	Celtic	26	Rangers	21
1895–96a	Celtic	30	Rangers	26	Hibernian	24
1896–97a	Hearts	28	Hibernian	26	Rangers	25
1897–98a	Celtic	33	Rangers	29	Hibernian	22
1898–99a	Rangers	36	Hearts	26	Celtic	24
1899–1900a	Rangers	32	Celtic	25	Hibernian	24
1900–01c	Rangers	35	Celtic	29	Hibernian	25
1901–02a	Rangers	28	Celtic	26	Hearts	22
1902–03b	Hibernian	37	Dundee	31	Rangers	29
1903–04d	Third Lanark	43	Hearts	39	Rangers	38
1904–05d	Celtic	41	Rangers	41	Third Lanark	35
1905–06e	Celtic	49	Hearts	43	Airdrieonians	38
1906–07f	Celtic	55	Dundee	48	Rangers	45
1907–08f	Celtic	55	Falkirk	51	Rangers	50
1908–09f	Celtic	51	Dundee	50	Clyde	48
1909–10f	Celtic	54	Falkirk	52	Rangers	46
1910–11f	Rangers	52	Aberdeen	48	Falkirk	44
1911–12f	Rangers	51	Celtic	45	Clyde	42
1912–13f	Rangers	53	Celtic	49	Hearts	41
1913–14g	Celtic	65	Rangers	59	Hearts	54
1914–15g	Celtic	65	Hearts	61	Rangers	50
1915–16g	Celtic	67	Rangers	56	Morton	51
1916–17g	Celtic	64	Morton	54	Rangers	53
1917–18f	Rangers	56	Celtic	55	Kilmarnock	43
1918–19f	Celtic	58	Rangers	57	Morton	47
1919–20h	Rangers	71	Celtic	68	Motherwell	57
1920–21h	Rangers	76	Celtic	66	Hearts	56
1921–22h	Celtic	67	Rangers	66	Raith R	56
1922–23g	Rangers	55	Airdrieonians	50	Celtic	46
1923–24g	Rangers	59	Airdrieonians	50	Celtic	41
1924–25g	Rangers	60	Airdrieonians	57	Hibernian	52
1925–26g	Celtic	58	*Airdrieonians	50	Hearts	50

1926–27g	Rangers	56	Motherwell	51	Celtic	49
1927–28g	Rangers	60	*Celtic	55	Motherwell	55
1928–29g	Rangers	67	Celtic	51	Motherwell	50
1929–30g	Rangers	60	Motherwell	55	Aberdeen	53
1930–31g	Rangers	60	Celtic	58	Motherwell	56
1931–32g	Motherwell	66	Rangers	61	Celtic	48
1932–33g	Rangers	62	Motherwell	59	Hearts	50
1933–34g	Rangers	66	Motherwell	62	Celtic	47
1934–35g	Rangers	55	Celtic	52	Hearts	50
1935–36g	Celtic	66	*Rangers	61	Aberdeen	61
1936–37g	Rangers	61	Aberdeen	54	Celtic	52
1937–38g	Celtic	61	Hearts	58	Rangers	49
1938–39g	Rangers	59	Celtic	48	Aberdeen	46
1946–47e	Rangers	46	Hibernian	44	Aberdeen	39
1947–48e	Hibernian	48	Rangers	46	Partick T	36
1948–49e	Rangers	46	Dundee	45	Hibernian	39
1949–50e	Rangers	50	Hibernian	49	Hearts	43
1950–51e	Hibernian	48	Rangers	38	Dundee	38
1951–52e	Hibernian	45	Rangers	41	East Fife	37
1952–53e	*Rangers	43	Hibernian	43	East Fife	39
1953–54e	Celtic	43	Hearts	38	Partick T	35
1954–55e	Aberdeen	49	Celtic	46	Rangers	41
1955–56f	Rangers	52	Aberdeen	46	*Hearts	45
1956–57f	Rangers	55	Hearts	53	Kilmarnock	42
1957–58f	Hearts	62	Rangers	49	Celtic	46
1958–59f	Rangers	50	Hearts	48	Motherwell	44
1959–60f	Hearts	54	Kilmarnock	50	*Rangers	42
1960–61f	Rangers	51	Kilmarnock	50	Third Lanark	42
1961–62f	Dundee	54	Rangers	51	Celtic	46
1962–63f	Rangers	57	Kilmarnock	48	Partick T	46
1963–64f	Rangers	55	Kilmarnock	49	*Celtic	47
1964–65f	*Kilmarnock	50	Hearts	50	Dunfermline Ath	49
1965–66f	Celtic	57	Rangers	55	Kilmarnock	45
1966–67f	Celtic	58	Rangers	55	Clyde	46
1967–68f	Celtic	63	Rangers	61	Hibernian	45
1968–69f	Celtic	54	Rangers	49	Dunfermline Ath	45
1969–70f	Celtic	57	Rangers	45	Hibernian	44
1970–71f	Celtic	56	Aberdeen	54	St Johnstone	44
1971–72f	Celtic	60	Aberdeen	50	Rangers	44
1972–73f	Celtic	57	Rangers	56	Hibernian	45
1973–74f	Celtic	53	Hibernian	49	Rangers	48
1974–75f	Rangers	56	Hibernian	49	Celtic	45

Second Division to 1974–75 from 1921–22 (maximum points: *a*, 76; *b*, 72; *c*, 68; *d*, 52; *e*, 60)

	First	*Pts*	*Second*	*Pts*	*Third*	*Pts*
1921–22a	Alloa	60	Cowdenbeath	47	Armadale	45
1922–23a	Queen's Park	57	Clydebank	**50	St Johnstone	**45
1923–24a	St Johnstone	56	Cowdenbeath	55	Bathgate	44

Season						
1924–25a	Dundee U	50	Clydebank	48	Clyde	47
1925–26a	Dunfermline Ath	59	Clyde	53	Ayr U	52
1926–27a	Bo'ness	56	Raith R	49	Clydebank	45
1927–28a	Ayr U	54	Third Lanark	45	King's Park	44
1928–29b	Dundee U	51	Morton	50	Arbroath	47
1929–30a	*Leith Ath	57	East Fife	57	Albion R	54
1930–31a	Third Lanark	61	Dundee U	50	Dunfermline Ath	47
1931–32a	*East Stirling	55	St Johnstone	55	*Raith Rovers	46
1932–33c	Hibernian	54	Queen of the S	49	Dunfermline Ath	47
1933–34c	Albion R	45	Dunfermline Ath	44	Arbroath	44
1934–35c	Third Lanark	52	Arbroath	50	St Bernard's	47
1935–36c	Falkirk	59	St Mirren	52	Morton	48
1936–37c	Ayr U	54	Morton	51	St Bernard's	48
1937–38c	*Raith R	59	Albion R	48	Airdrieonians	47
1938–39c	Cowdenbeath	60	*Alloa	48	East Fife	48
1946–47d	Dundee	45	Airdrieonians	42	East Fife	31
1947–48e	East Fife	53	Albion R	42	Hamilton A	40
1948–49e	Raith R	42	Stirling Albion	42	*Airdrieonians	41
1949–50e	Morton	47	Airdrieonians	44	*St Johnstone	36
1950–51e	*Queen of the S	45	Stirling Albion	45	*Ayr U	36
1951–52e	Clyde	44	Falkirk	43	Ayr U	39
1952–53e	Stirling Albion	44	Hamilton A	43	Queen's Park	37
1953–54e	Motherwell	45	Kilmarnock	42	*Third Lanark	36
1954–55e	Airdrieonians	46	Dunfermline Ath	42	Hamilton A	39
1955–56b	Queen's Park	54	Ayr U	51	St Johnstone	49
1956–57b	Clyde	64	Third Lanark	51	Cowdenbeath	45
1957–58b	Stirling Albion	55	Dunfermline Ath	53	Arbroath	47
1958–59zb	Ayr U	60	Arbroath	51	Stenhousemuir	40
1959–60b	St Johnstone	53	Dundee U	50	Queen of the S	49
1960–61b	Stirling Albion	55	Falkirk	54	Stenhousemuir	50
1961–62b	Clyde	54	Queen of the S	53	Morton	44
1962–63b	St Johnstone	55	East Stirling	49	Morton	48
1963–64b	Morton	67	Clyde	53	Arbroath	46
1964–65b	Stirling Albion	59	Hamilton A	50	Queen of the S	45
1965–66b	Ayr U	53	Airdrieonians	50	Queen of the S	49
1966–67b	Morton	69	Raith R	58	Arbroath	57
1967–68b	St Mirren	62	Arbroath	53	*East Fife	40
1968–69b	Motherwell	64	Ayr U	53	East Fife	47
1969–70b	Falkirk	56	Cowdenbeath	55	Queen of the S	50
1970–71b	Partick T	56	East Fife	51	Arbroath	46
1971–72b	*Dumbarton	52	Arbroath	52	Stirling Albion	50
1972–73b	Clyde	56	Dumfermline Ath	52	*Raith R	47
1973–74b	Airdrieonians	60	Kilmarnock	59	Hamilton A	55
1974–75b	Falkirk	54	*Queen of the S	53	Montrose	53

*On goal average/difference. †Held jointly after indecisive play-off. ‡Won on deciding match. ‡‡Held jointly. **Two points deducted for fielding ineligible player. Competition suspended 1940–45.*

RELEGATED CLUBS

From Premier Division

1975–76 Dundee, St Johnstone
1976–77 Hearts, Kilmarnock
1977–78 Ayr U, Clydebank
1978–79 Hearts, Motherwell
1979–80 Dundee, Hibernian
1980–81 Kilmarnock, Hearts
1981–82 Partick T, Airdrieonians
1982–83 Morton, Kilmarnock
1983–84 St Johnstone, Motherwell
1984–85 Dumbarton, Morton
1985–86 *No relegation due to League reorganisation*
1986–87 Clydebank, Hamilton A
1987–88 Falkirk, Dunfermline Ath, Morton
1988–89 Hamilton A
1989–90 Dundee
1990–91 None
1991–92 St Mirren, Dunfermline Ath

From First Division

1975–76 Dunfermline Ath, Clyde
1976–77 Raith R, Falkirk
1977–78 Alloa Ath, East Fife
1978–79 Montrose, Queen of the S
1979–80 Arbroath, Clyde
1980–81 Stirling A, Berwick R
1981–82 East Stirling, Queen of the S
1982–83 Dunfermline Ath, Queen's Park
1983–84 Raith R, Alloa
1984–85 Meadowbank T, St Johnstone
1985–86 Ayr U, Alloa
1986–87 Brechin C, Montrose
1987–88 East Fife, Dumbarton
1988–89 Kilmarnock, Queen of the S
1989–90 Albion R, Alloa
1990–91 Clyde, Brechin C
1991–92 Montrose, Forfar Ath

Relegated from First Division to 1973–74

1921–22 *Queen's Park, Dumbarton, Clydebank
1922–23 Albion R, Alloa Ath
1923–24 Clyde, Clydebank
1924–25 Third Lanark, Ayr U
1925–26 Raith R, Clydebank
1926–27 Morton, Dundee U
1927–28 Dunfermline Ath, Bo'ness
1928–29 Third Lanark, Raith R
1929–30 St Johnstone, Dundee U
1930–31 Hibernian, East Fife
1931–32 Dundee U, Leith Ath
1932–33 Morton, East Stirling
1933–34 Third Lanark, Cowdenbeath
1934–35 St Mirren, Falkirk
1935–36 Airdrieonians, Ayr U
1936–37 Dunfermline Ath, Albion R
1937–38 Dundee, Morton
1938–39 Queen's Park, Raith R
1946–47 Kilmarnock, Hamilton A
1947–48 Airdrieonians, Queen's Park
1948–49 Morton, Albion R
1949–50 Queen of the S, Stirling Alb
1950–51 Clyde, Falkirk
1951–52 Morton, Stirling Albion

1952–53 Motherwell, Third Lanark
1953–54 Airdrieonians, Hamilton A
1954–55 No clubs relegated
1955–56 Stirling Albion, Clyde
1956–57 Dunfermline Ath, Ayr U
1957–58 East Fife, Queen's Park
1958–59 Queen of the S, Falkirk
1959–60 Arbroath, Stirling Albion
1960–61 Ayr U, Clyde
1961–62 St Johnstone, Stirling Albion
1962–63 Clyde, Raith R
1963–64 Queen of the S, East Stirling
1964–65 Airdrieonians, Third Lanark
1965–66 Morton, Hamilton A
1966–67 St Mirren, Ayr U
1967–68 Motherwell, Stirling Albion
1968–69 Falkirk, Arbroath
1969–70 Raith R, Partick T
1970–71 St Mirren, Cowdenbeath
1971–72 Clyde, Dunfermline Ath
1972–73 Kilmarnock, Airdrieonians
1973–74 East Fife, Falkirk
1974–75 *League reorganised at end of season*

*Season 1921–22—only 1 club promoted, 3 clubs relegated.

SKOL CUP 1991–92

First Round
Alloa 0, Stranraer 0*
 Stranraer won 8-7 on penalties
East Fife 2, East Stirling 2*
 East Stirling won 4-2 on penalties
Queen of the S 0, Albion R 4
Queen's Park 4, Stenhousemuir 2
Berwick R 0, Dumbarton 1
Cowdenbeath 1, Arbroath 0

Second Round
Brechin C 3, St Mirren 3*
 St Mirren won 5-4 on penalties
Dumbarton 1, Airdrieonians 2*
Dundee U 3, Montrose 2
Dunfermline Ath 4, Alloa 1
Falkirk 3, East Stirling 0
Hamilton A 2, Forfar Ath 0*
Hearts 3, Clydebank 0
Partick T 2, Albion R 0
Raith R 4, Motherwell 1
Rangers 6, Queen's Park 0
Stirling Albion 0, Hibernian 3
Clyde 0, Aberdeen 4
Dundee 2, Ayr U 4
Meadowbank T 0, St Johnstone 2
Morton 2, Celtic 4
Cowdenbeath 0, Kilmarnock 1

Third Round
Ayr U 2, St Johnstone 0
Celtic 3, Raith R 1
Dundee U 1, Falkirk 0
Aberdeen 0, Airdrieonians 1
Dunfermline Ath 1, St Mirren 1*
 Dunfermline Ath won 3-2 on penalties
Hamilton A 0, Hearts 2
Kilmarnock 2, Hibernian 3
Partick T 0, Rangers 2

Quarter-finals
Airdrieonians 0, Celtic 0*
 Airdrieonians won 4-2 on penalties
Ayr U 0, Hibernian 2
Dunfermline Ath 3, Dundee U 1
Hearts 0, Rangers 1

Semi-finals – at Tynecastle Park
Dunfermline Ath 1, Airdrieonians 1*
 Dunfermline Ath won 3-2 on penalties
Rangers 0, Hibernian 1

Final – at Hampden Park, att. 40,377
Hibernian 2, Dunfermline Ath 0

* *After extra time*

PAST SCOTTISH LEAGUE CUP FINALS

Season	Winner		Runner-up	
1946–47	Rangers	4	Aberdeen	0
1947–48	East Fife	0 4	Falkirk	0 1
1948–49	Rangers	2	Raith Rovers	0
1949–50	East Fife	3	Dunfermline	0
1950–51	Motherwell	3	Hibernian	0
1951–52	Dundee	3	Rangers	2
1952–53	Dundee	2	Kilmarnock	0
1953–54	East Fife	3	Partick Thistle	2
1954–55	Hearts	4	Motherwell	2
1955–56	Aberdeen	2	St Mirren	1
1956–57	Celtic	0 3	Partick Thistle	0 0
1957–58	Celtic	7	Rangers	1
1958–59	Hearts	5	Partick Thistle	1
1959–60	Hearts	2	Third Lanark	1
1960–61	Rangers	2	Kilmarnock	0
1961–62	Rangers	1 3	Hearts	1 1
1962–63	Hearts	1	Kilmarnock	0
1963–64	Rangers	5	Morton	0
1964–65	Rangers	2	Celtic	1
1965–66	Celtic	2	Rangers	1
1966–67	Celtic	1	Rangers	0
1967–68	Celtic	5	Dundee	3
1968–69	Celtic	6	Hibernian	2
1969–70	Celtic	1	St Johnstone	0
1970–71	Rangers	1	Celtic	0
1971–72	Partick Thistle	4	Celtic	1
1972–73	Hibernian	2	Celtic	1
1973–74	Dundee	1	Celtic	0
1974–75	Celtic	6	Hibernian	3
1975–76	Rangers	1	Celtic	0
1976–77	Aberdeen	2	Celtic	1
1977–78	Rangers	2	Celtic	1
1978–79	Rangers	2	Aberdeen	1
1979–80	Aberdeen	0 0	Dundee U	0 3
1980–81	Dundee	0	Dundee U	3
1981–82	Rangers	2	Dundee U	1
1982–83	Celtic	2	Rangers	1
1983–84	Rangers	3	Celtic	2
1984–85	Rangers	1	Dundee U	0
1985–86	Aberdeen	3	Hibernian	0
1986–87	Rangers	2	Celtic	1
1987–88	Rangers†	3	Aberdeen	3
1988–89	Aberdeen	2	Rangers	3
1989–90	Aberdeen	2	Rangers	1
1990–91	Rangers	2	Celtic	1

†*Won on penalties*

B & Q CUP 1991–92

First Round
Berwick R 3, East Stirling 2
Brechin C 2, Albion R 4
Clydebank 4, Clyde 0
Cowdenbeath 2, Partick T 3
Dundee 0, Ayr U 2
Forfar Ath 2, Stranraer 2
Hamilton A 5, Alloa 1
Montrose 2, Dumbarton 1
Stenhousemuir 3, Arbroath 2
Meadowbank T 1, East Fife 2

Second Round
Clydebank 1, Raith R 1*
  Raith R won 4-3 on penalties
Montrose 2, Albion R 1
Morton 2, Kilmarnock 1
Partick T 1, Hamilton A 2
Queen of the S 3, Stirling Albion 3*
  Queen of the S won 5-4 on penalties
Queen's Park 1, East Fife 2
Stenhousemuir 0, Ayr U 2
Stranraer 3, Berwick R 1

Quarter-finals
Ayr U 2, Stranraer 0
East Fife 2, Hamilton A 3
Montrose 4, Queen of the S 7*
Morton 2, Raith R 3

Semi-finals
Ayr U 3, Queen of the S 2
Hamilton A 2, Raith R 1

Final – at Fir Park, att. 9633
Hamilton A (1) 1 *(Harris)*
Ayr U (0) 0

* *After extra time*

SCOTTISH CUP 1991–92

FIRST ROUND
Albion R (0) 0 Arbroath (1) 2
Alloa (3) 7 Hawick Royal Albert (0) 1
East Fife (2) 6 Queen's Park (0) 0
East Stirling (0) 0 Dumbarton (2) 2
Vale of Leithen (1) 1 Stranraer (1) 2
Gala Fairydean (1) 2 Ross County (1) 2

FIRST ROUND REPLAYS
Ross County (3) 3 Gala Fairydean (0) 0

SECOND ROUND
Alloa (0) 0 Dumbarton (0) 2
Berwick R (3) 7 Ross County (2) 4
Brechin C (0) 0 East Fife (0) 0
Huntly (0) 4 Civil Service Strollers (2) 2
Peterhead (1) 1 Cowdenbeath (0) 1
Stenhousemuir (1) 1 Caledonian (0) 4
Stranraer (2) 4 Queen of the S (0) 1
Clyde (1) 2 Arbroath (0) 0

SECOND ROUND REPLAYS
Cowdenbeath (4) 6 Peterhead (0) 1
East Fife (1) 3 Brechin C (1) 1

THIRD ROUND
Aberdeen (0) 0 Rangers (1) 1
Airdrieonians (0) 2 Stranraer (0) 1
Ayr U (0) 1 Motherwell (0) 1
Caledonian (1) 3 Clyde (1) 1
Celtic (3) 6 Montrose (0) 0
Clydebank (1) 3 Cowdenbeath (1) 1
Dumbarton (0) 0 Huntly (0) 2
Forfar Ath (0) 0 Dunfermline Ath (0) 0
Hamilton A (0) 0 Falkirk (0) 1
Hibernian (1) 2 Partick T (0) 0
Meadowbank T (0) 1 Kilmarnock (0) 1
Morton (1) 4 East Fife (2) 2
Raith R (0) 0 St Johnstone (0) 2
St Mirren (0) 0 Hearts (0) 0
Dundee U (4) 6 Berwick R (0) 0
Dundee (0) 1 Stirling Albion (0) 1

THIRD ROUND REPLAYS
Kilmarnock (0) 1 Meadowbank T (1) 1
aet; Meadowbank T won 4-3 on penalties
Motherwell (4) 4 Ayr U (0) 1
Dunfermline Ath (0) 3 Forfar Ath (0) 1
Hearts (0) 3 St Mirren (0) 0
Stirling Albion (0) 0 Dundee (1) 1

FOURTH ROUND
Celtic (1) 2 Dundee U (1) 1
Caledonian (0) 2 St Johnstone (1) 2
Clydebank (0) 1 Hibernian (2) 5
Dunfermline Ath (1) 1 Hearts (1) 2
Falkirk (0) 0 Dundee (0) 0
Huntly (0) 1 Airdrieonians (0) 3
Morton (1) 2 Meadowbank T (0) 2
Rangers (0) 2 Motherwell (1) 1

FOURTH ROUND REPLAYS
Dundee (0) 0 Falkirk (0) 1
Meadowbank T (2) 2 Morton (0) 3
St Johnstone (1) 3 Caledonian (0) 0

QUARTER-FINALS
St Johnstone (0) 0 Rangers (2) 3
Celtic (2) 3 Morton (0) 0
Hibernian (0) 0 Airdrieonians (0) 2
Hearts (2) 3 Falkirk (1) 1

SEMI-FINALS
Celtic (0) 0 Rangers (1) 1
Airdrieonians (0) 0 Hearts (0) 0

SEMI-FINAL REPLAY
Airdrieonians (1) 1 Hearts (0) 1
aet; Airdrieonians won 4-2 on penalties

FINAL
Rangers (2) 2 *(Hateley, McCoist)*
Airdrieonians (0) 1 *(Smith)*, 44,045

SCOTTISH CUP PAST FINALS

1974 Queens Park 2   Clydesdale 0
1875 Queen's Park 3   Renton 0
1876 Queen's Park 1 2   Third Lanark 1 0
1877 Vale of Leven 0 1 3   Rangers 0 1 2
1878 Vale of Leven 1   Third Lanark 0
1879 Vale of Leven 1   Rangers 1
Vale of Leven awarded, Rangers did not appear for replay
1880 Queen's Park 3 Thornlibank 0
1881 Queen's Park 2 3   Dumbarton 1 1
Replayed because of protest
1882 Queen's Park 2 4   Dumbarton 2 1
1883 Dumbarton 2 2   Vale of Leven 2 1
1884 *Queen's Park awarded cup when Vale of Leven did not appear for the final*
1885 Renton 0 3   Vale of Leven 0 1
1886 Queen's Park 3   Renton 1
1887 Hibernian 2   Dumbarton 1
1888 Renton 6   Cambuslang 1
1889 Third Lanark 3 2   Celtic 0 1
Replayed because of protest
1890 Queen's Park 1 2   Vale of Leven 1 1
1891 Hearts 1   Dumbarton 0
1892 Celtic 1 5   Queen's Park 0 1
Replayed because of protest
1893 Queen's Park 2   Celtic 1
1894 Rangers 3   Celtic 1
1895 St Bernards 3   Renton 1
1896 Hearts 3   Hibernian 1
1897 Rangers 5   Dumbarton 1
1898 Rangers 2   Kilmarnock 0
1899 Celtic 2   Rangers 0
1900 Celtic 4   Queen's Park 3
1901 Hearts 4   Celtic 3
1902 Hibernian 1   Celtic 0
1903 Rangers 1 0 2   Hearts 1 0 0
1904 Celtic 3   Rangers 2
1905 Third Lanark 0 3   Rangers 0 1
1906 Hearts 1   Third Lanark 0
1907 Celtic 3   Hearts 0
1908 Celtic 5   St Mirren 1
1909 *After two drawn games between Celtic and Rangers, 2–2, 1–1,*
there was a riot and the cup was withheld
1910 Dundee 2 0 2   Clyde 2 0 1
1911 Celtic 0 2   Hamilton Acad 0 0
1912 Celtic 2   Clyde 0
1913 Falkirk 2   Raith R 0
1914 Celtic 0 4   Hibernian 0 1
1920 Kilmarnock 3 Albion R 2
1921 Partick Th 1   Rangers 0
1922 Morton 1   Rangers 0
1923 Celtic 1   Hibernian 0
1924 Airdrieonians 2   Hibernian 0
1925 Celtic 2   Dundee 1
1926 St Mirren 2   Celtic 0
1927 Celtic 3   East Fife 1
1928 Rangers 4   Celtic 0
1929 Kilmarnock 2   Rangers 0
1930 Rangers 0 2   Partick Th 0 1
1931 Celtic 2 4   Motherwell 2 2
1932 Rangers 1 3   Kilmarnock 1 0
1933 Celtic 1   Motherwell 0

1934 Rangers 5   St Mirren 0
1935 Rangers 2   Hamilton Acad 1
1936 Rangers 1   Third Lanark 0
1937 Celtic 2   Aberdeen 1
1938 East Fife 1 4   Kilmarnock 1 2
1939 Clyde 4   Motherwell 0
1947 Aberdeen 2   Hibernian 1
1948 Rangers 1 1   Morton 1 0
1949 Rangers 4   Clyde 1
1950 Rangers 3   East Fife 0
1951 Celtic 1   Motherwell 0
1952 Motherwell 4   Dundee 0
1953 Rangers 1 1   Aberdeen 1 0
1954 Celtic 2   Aberdeen 1
1955 Clyde 1 1   Celtic 1 0
1956 Hearts 3   Celtic 1
1957 Falkirk 1 2   Kilmarnock 1 1
1958 Clyde 1   Hibernian 0
1959 St Mirren 3   Aberdeen 1
1960 Rangers 2   Kilmarnock 0
1961 Dunfermline Ath 0 2   Celtic 0 0
1962 Rangers 2   St Mirren 0
1963 Rangers 1 3   Celtic 1 0
1964 Rangers 3   Dundee 1
1965 Celtic 3   Dunfermline Ath 2
1966 Rangers 0 1   Celtic 0 0
1967 Celtic 2   Aberdeen 0
1968 Dunfermline Ath 3   Hearts 1
1969 Celtic 4   Rangers 0
1970 Aberdeen 3   Celtic 1
1971 Celtic 1 2   Rangers 1 1
1972 Celtic 6   Hibernian 1
1973 Rangers 3   Celtic 2
1974 Celtic 3   Dundee U 0
1975 Celtic 3   Airdrieonians 1
1976 Rangers 3   Hearts 1
1977 Celtic 1   Rangers 0
1978 Rangers 2   Aberdeen 1
1979 Rangers 0 0 3   Hibernian 0 0 2
1980 Celtic 1   Rangers 0
1981 Rangers 0 4   Dundee U 0 1
1982 Aberdeen 4   Rangers 1 (aet)
1983 Aberdeen 1   Rangers 0 (aet)
1984 Aberdeen 2   Celtic 1 (aet)
1985 Celtic 2   Dundee U 1
1986 Aberdeen 3   Hearts 0
1987 St Mirren 1   Dundee U 0 (aet)
1988 Celtic 2   Dundee U 1
1989 Celtic 1   Rangers 0
1990 Aberdeen† 0   Celtic 0
1991 Rangers 2   Airdrieonians 1

†*won on penalties*

WELSH FOOTBALL 1991–92

THE ABACUS LEAGUE

National Division

	P	W	D	L	F	A	Pts
Abergavenny Thursdays	30	23	5	2	64	24	74
Briton Ferry Athletic	30	23	1	6	76	43	70
Aberystwyth Town	30	18	6	6	65	35	60
Haverfordwest County	30	16	7	7	61	41	55
Ton Pentre	30	16	6	8	51	53	54
Maesteg Park Athletic	30	15	6	9	57	37	51
Cwmbran Town	30	11	12	7	50	42	45
Afan Lido	30	12	7	11	54	47	43
Pembroke	30	10	7	13	50	48	37
Llanelli	30	9	6	15	43	61	33
Ebbw Vale	30	8	8	14	38	61	32
Inter Cardiff	30	7	8	15	32	45	29
Caldicot	30	6	6	18	36	60	24
Brecon Corries	30	6	5	19	36	61	23
Bridgend Town	30	4	8	18	35	58	20
Ferndale	30	4	6	20	31	63	18

Division One

	P	W	D	L	F	A	Pts
Blaenrhondda	32	18	8	6	76	47	62
Morriston	32	18	3	11	58	47	57
Ammanford	32	16	9	7	55	35	57
Port Talbot	32	15	9	8	57	41	54
Caerleon	32	15	8	9	58	34	53
Pontypridd/Ynys	32	15	4	13	57	53	49
Aberaman	32	14	6	12	52	48	48
Cardiff Civil Service	32	13	9	10	51	48	48
Taffs Well	32	13	7	12	42	41	46
Risca United	32	12	6	14	51	52	42
Llanwern	32	10	9	13	44	44	39
BP	32	11	5	16	47	54	38
Newport YMCA	32	11	5	16	41	54	38
Cardiff Corries	32	9	9	14	54	60	36
Pontllanfraith	32	8	10	14	38	57	34
Seven Sisters	32	8	7	17	37	62	31
Garw	32	5	8	19	30	73	23

Division Two

	P	W	D	L	F	A	Pts
AFC Porth	32	28	3	1	79	20	87
Carmarthen	32	22	6	4	61	19	72
Skewen	32	18	7	7	51	33	61
Tonyrefail	32	16	8	8	54	36	56
Caerau	32	16	8	8	52	39	56
SW Police	32	15	8	9	54	39	53
Pontyclun	32	13	9	10	51	39	48
Treharris	32	12	7	13	51	54	43
Pontardawe	32	12	5	15	43	52	41
Pontlottyn	32	10	9	13	42	42	39
Goytre United	32	10	8	14	44	47	38
Milford United	32	11	5	16	48	68	38
Panteg	32	8	5	19	37	63	29

	P	W	D	L	F	A	Pts
Cardiff Institute	32	7	7	18	41	67	28
AFC Tondu	32	5	9	18	39	61	24
Abercynon	32	6	6	20	38	69	24
Trelewis	32	4	8	20	26	65	20

Abacus Youth Trophy: Cwmbran Town 1, Afan Lido 0.

IRISH FOOTBALL 1991–92

SMIRNOFF IRISH LEAGUE CHAMPIONSHIP

Final Table

	P	W	D	L	F	A	Pts
Glentoran	30	24	5	1	78	26	77
Portadown	30	21	2	7	59	19	65
Linfield	30	17	9	4	58	23	60
Larne	30	16	7	7	54	31	55
Glenavon	30	16	4	10	54	36	52
Crusaders	30	14	5	11	55	37	47
Ards	30	10	11	9	50	46	41
Bangor	30	11	6	13	45	52	36
Omagh Town	30	10	6	14	51	58	36
Ballymena United	30	8	11	11	37	50	35
Ballyclare Comrades	30	8	8	14	37	64	32
Cliftonville	30	7	10	13	27	34	31
Cliftonville	30	7	10	13	27	34	31
Coleraine	39	7	8	15	35	57	29
Newry Town	30	8	5	17	28	57	29
Distillery	30	5	7	18	31	55	22
Carrick Rangers	30	2	8	20	24	78	14

NB: Bangor penalised three points – ineligible player.

REPUBLIC OF IRELAND 1991–92

Final League Table

	P	W	D	L	F	A	Pts
Shelbourne	33	21	7	5	57	29	49
Derry City	33	17	10	6	49	21	44
Cork City	33	16	11	6	47	30	43
Dundalk	33	14	12	7	44	31	40
Bohemians	33	14	9	10	45	34	37
Shamrock Rovers	33	9	15	9	33	30	33
St Patrick's Ath	33	9	11	13	38	46	29
Sligo Rovers	33	7	11	15	33	42	25
Drogheda United	33	7	13	13	24	45	25
Bray Wanders	33	7	10	16	16	38	24
Athlone Town*	33	6	11	16	31	50	23
Galway United*	33	7	8	18	37	58	22

EUROPEAN CUPS REVIEW

British clubs had a disappointing season in Europe, only Liverpool managing to survive until the quarter-final of the UEFA Cup. The Anfield club had an erratic time of it, mirroring their performances in the Football League.

After a comfortable first round draw on paper, they were flattered by the margin of their aggregate win over the Finnish side Kuusysi, but showed more of their powers of resource and determination against Auxerre. Two goals down on the away leg in France, Liverpool retrieved the deficit by half-time and snatched the winning goal in the 84th minute through Mark Walters. Tirol proved only token opposition in the third round, but Genoa were a different proposition in round four.

This quarter-final found them up against a typical Italian side adequately suited to the demands of European football, yet surprisingly making their first appearance in one of the three major competitions on the continent. Liverpool had little answer to the swift counter-attacking and clinically efficient finishing, well though they played for long periods in both legs. But Genoa deserved this success and it was all the more surprising when the Italians lost to Ajax in the semi-finals.

Ajax met Torino in the final. These other Italians had accounted for Real Madrid in the semi-final and were considered firm favourites to maintain their country's reputation in the UEFA Cup. But Ajax drew 2-2 in Turin and rode their luck in the return game in Amsterdam, where the Italians dominated and hit the woodwork three times. Ajax thus emulated the feat of Juventus in winning all three European tournaments.

In the European Cup, Barcelona at last achieved the prize which has long eluded them. Again there was a strong Dutch and Ajax connection with coach Johan Cruyff masterminding Barcelona's performance. But it needed extra time before Ronald Koeman, the Dutch sweeper, rammed in a free-kick in the 112th minute to overcome Sampdoria, the other Genoese side.

French hopes in the Cup-Winners' Cup rested on Monaco, but there was to be no trophy for them. Werder Bremen beat the team from the principality 2-0 in Lisbon. It was their first such honour.

EUROPEAN CUP 1991–92

First Round, First Leg

Anderlecht	(1) 1	Grasshoppers	(0) 1
Arsenal	(1) 6	FK Austria	(0) 1
Barcelona	(1) 3	Hansa Rostock	(0) 0
Besiktas	(0) 1	PSV Eindhoven	(1) 1
Brondby	(0) 3	Zaglebie Lubin	(0) 0
Fram	(0) 2	Panathinaikos	(1) 2
Hamrun Spartans	(0) 0	Benfica	(4) 6
HJK Helsinki	(0) 0	Kiev Dynamo	(0) 1
IFK Gothenburg	(0) 0	Flamurtari	(0) 0
Kaiserslautern	(1) 2	Etur	(0) 0
Kispest Honved	(0) 1	Dundalk	(1) 1
Red Star Belgrade	(2) 4	Portadown	(0) 0
Sampdoria	(2) 5	Rosenborg	(0) 0
Sparta Prague	(1) 1	Rangers	(0) 0
Uni Craiova	(1) 2	Apollon	(0) 0
Union Luxembourg	(0) 0	Marseille	(4) 5

First Round, Second Leg

Apollon	(1) 3	Uni Craiova	(0) 0
Benfica	(0) 4	Hamrun Spartans	(0) 0
Dundalk	(0) 0	Kispest Honved	(2) 2
Etur	(1) 1	Kaiserslautern	(0) 1
FK Austria	(0) 1	Arsenal	(0) 0
Flamurtari	(1) 1	IFK Gothenburg	(0) 1
Grasshoppers	(0) 0	Anderlecht	(2) 3
Hansa Rostock	(0) 1	Barcelona	(0) 0
Kiev Dynamo	(1) 3	HJK Helsinki	(0) 0
Marseille	(1) 5	Union Luxembourg	(0) 0
Panathinaikos	(0) 0	Fram	(0) 0
Portadown	(0) 0	Red Star Belgrade	(2) 4
PSV Eindhoven	(1) 2	Besiktas	(1) 1
Rangers	(0) 2	Sparta Prague	(0) 1
Rosenborg	(0) 1	Sampdoria	(0) 2
Zaglebie Lubin	(0) 2	Brondby	(1) 1

Second Round, First Leg

Barcelona	(1) 2	Kaiserslautern	(0) 0
Benfica	(1) 1	Arsenal	(1) 1
Kiev Dynamo	(0) 1	Brondby	(1) 1
Kispest Honved	(0) 2	Sampdoria	(0) 1
Marseille	(1) 3	Sparta Prague	(0) 2
Panathinaikos	(1) 2	IFK Gothenburg	(0) 0
PSV Eindhoven	(0) 0	Anderlecht	(0) 0
Red Star Belgrade	(1) 3	Apollon	(1) 1

Second Round, Second Leg

Anderlecht	(1) 2	PSV Eindhoven	(0) 0
Apollon	(0) 0	Red Star Belgrade	(0) 2
Arsenal	(1) 1	Benfica	(1) 3
Brondby	(0) 0	Kiev Dynamo	(1) 1
IFK Gothenburg	(2) 2	Panathinaikos	(0) 2
Kaiserslautern	(1) 3	Barcelona	(0) 1
Sampdoria	(2) 3	Kispest Honved	(0) 1
Sparta Prague	(1) 2	Marseille	(0) 1

Semi-finals (League system)
Group A

Anderlecht	(0) 0	Panathinaikos	(0) 0
Sampdoria	(1) 2	Red Star Belgrade	(0) 0
Panathinaikos	(0) 0	Sampdoria	(0) 0
Red Star Belgrade	(1) 3	Anderlecht	(1) 2
Anderlecht	(0) 3	Sampdoria	(1) 2
Panathinaikos	(0) 0	Red Star Belgrade	(0) 2
Red Star Belgrade	(0) 1	Panathinaikos	(0) 0
Sampdoria	(2) 2	Anderlecht	(0) 0
Panathinaikos	(0) 0	Anderlecht	(0) 0
Red Star Belgrade	(1) 1	Sampdoria	(2) 3
Anderlecht	(2) 3	Red Star Belgrade	(1) 2
Sampdoria	(1) 1	Panathinaikos	(1) 1

Final table

	P	W	D	L	F	A	Pts
Sampdoria	6	3	2	1	10	5	8
Red Star Belgrade	6	3	0	3	9	10	6
Anderlecht	6	2	2	2	8	9	6
Panathinaikos	6	0	4	2	1	4	4

Group B

Barcelona	(2) 3	Sparta Prague	(1) 2
Kiev Dynamo	(1) 1	Benfica	(0) 0
Benfica	(0) 0	Barcelona	(0) 0
Sparta Prague	(2) 2	Kiev Dynamo	(0) 1
Benfica	(0) 1	Sparta Prague	(1) 1
Kiev Dynamo	(0) 0	Barcelona	(1) 2
Barcelona	(0) 3	Kiev Dynamo	(0) 0
Sparta Prague	(1) 1	Benfica	(1) 1
Benfica	(1) 5	Kiev Dynamo	(0) 0
Sparta Prague	(0) 1	Barcelona	(0) 0
Barcelona	(2) 2	Benfica	(1) 1
Kiev Dynamo	(0) 1	Sparta Prague	(0) 0

Final table

	P	W	D	L	F	A	Pts
Barcelona	6	4	1	1	10	4	9
Sparta Prague	6	2	2	2	7	7	6
Benfica	6	1	3	2	8	5	5
Kiev Dynamo	6	2	0	4	3	12	4

Final: Barcelona (0) 1, Sampdoria (0) 0 *aet*

(at Wembley, 20 May 1992, 70,827)

Barcelona: Zubizarreta; Nando, Ferrer, Koeman, Juan Carlos, Bakero, Salinas (Goicoechea 64), Stoichkov, Laudrup, Guardiola (Alexanco 113), Eusebio. *Scorer:* Koeman 111.
Sampdoria: Pagliuca; Mannini, Katanec, Pari, Vierchowod, Lanna, Lombardo, Cerezo, Vialli (Buso 100), Mancini, Bonetti I (Invernizzi 72).
Referee: Schmidhuber (Germany).

EUROPEAN SUPER CUP

Played annually between the winners of the European Champions' Cup and the European Cup-Winners' Cup.

Previous Matches

1972 Ajax beat Rangers 3-1, 3-2
1973 Ajax beat AC Milan 0-1, 6-0
1974 Not contested
1975 Dynamo Kiev beat Bayern Munich 1-0, 2-0
1976 Anderlecht beat Bayern Munich 4-1, 1-2
1977 Liverpool beat Hamburg 1-1, 6-0
1978 Anderlecht beat Liverpool 3-1, 1-2
1979 Nottingham F beat Barcelona 1-0, 1-1
1980 Valencia beat Nottingham F 1-0, 1-2
1981 Not contested
1982 Aston Villa beat Barcelona 0-1, 3-0
1983 Aberdeen beat Hamburg 0-0, 2-0
1984 Juventus beat Liverpool 2-0
1985 Juventus v Everton not contested due to UEFA ban on English clubs
1986 Steaua Bucharest beat Dynamo Kiev 1-0
1987 FC Porto beat Ajax 1-0, 1-0
1988 KV Mechelen beat PSV Eindhoven 3-0, 0-1
1989 AC Milan beat Barcelona 1-1, 1-0
1990 AC Milan beat Sampdoria 1-1, 2-0

Old Trafford, 19 November 1991, 22,110

Manchester U (0) 1 *(McClair 67)*

Red Star Belgrade (0) 0

Manchester U: Schmeichel; Martin (Giggs 71), Irwin, Bruce, Webb, Pallister, Kanchelskis, Ince, McClair, Hughes, Blackmore.
Red Star Belgrade: Milojevic; Radinovic, Vasilijevic, Belodedic, Najdoski, Tanjga, Stosic, Jugovic, Pancev, Savicevic (Ivic 82), Mihajlovic
Referee: Van der Ende (Holland).

EUROPEAN CUP-WINNERS' CUP 1991–92

Preliminary Round, First Leg

Galway	(0) 0	Odense	(1) 3
Stockerau	(0) 0	Tottenham H	(1) 1

Preliminary Round, Second Leg

Odense	(1) 4	Galway	(0) 0
Tottenham H	(1) 1	Stockerau	(0) 0

First Round, First Leg

Athinaikos	(0) 0	Manchester U	(0) 0
Bacau	(0) 0	Werder Bremen	(3) 6
CSKA Moscow	(0) 1	Roma	(0) 2
Fyllingen	(0) 0	Atletico Madrid	(1) 1
Glenavon	(1) 3	Ilves	(1) 2
Hajduk Split	(0) 1	Tottenham H	(0) 0
Katowice	(1) 2	Motherwell	(0) 0
Levski	(1) 2	Ferencvaros	(1) 3
Norrkoping	(1) 4	Jeunesse Esch	(0) 0
Odense	(0) 0	Banik Ostrava	(1) 2
Omonia	(0) 0	FC Brugge	(0) 0
Partizani	(0) 0	Feyenoord	(0) 0
Stahl Eisenhuttenstadt	(1) 1	Galatasaray	(1) 2
Swansea C	(0) 1	Monaco	(2) 2
Valletta	(0) 0	Porto	(2) 3
Valur	(0) 0	Sion	(0) 1

First Round, Second Leg

Atletico Madrid	(4) 7	Fyllingen	(0) 2
Banik Ostrava	(0) 2	Odense	(1) 1
FC Brugge	(0) 2	Omonia	(0) 0
Ferencvaros	(2) 4	Levski	(0) 1
Feyenoord	(0) 1	Partizani	(0) 0
Galatasaray	(1) 3	Stahl Eisenhuttenstadt	(0) 0
Ilves	(1) 2	Glenavon	(0) 1
Jeunesse Esch	(0) 1	Norrkoping	(2) 2
Manchester U	(0) 2	Athinaikos	(0) 0
Monaco	(5) 8	Swansea C	(0) 0
Motherwell	(1) 3	Katowice	(0) 1
Porto	(0) 1	Valletta	(0) 0
Roma	(0) 0	CSKA Moscow	(1) 1
Sion	(0) 1	Valur	(0) 1
Tottenham H	(2) 2	Hajduk Split	(0) 0
Werder Bremen	(3) 5	Bacau	(0) 0

Second Round, First leg

Atletico Madrid	(1) 3	Manchester U	(0) 0
Galatasaray	(0) 0	Banik Ostrava	(0) 1
Ilves	(0) 1	Roma	(1) 1

Katowice	(0) 0	FC Brugge	(1) 1
Norrkoping	(1) 1	Monaco	(1) 2
Sion	(0) 0	Feyenoord	(0) 0
Tottenham H	(2) 3	Porto	(0) 1
Werder Bremen	(3) 3	Ferencvaros	(1) 2

Second Round, Second Leg

Banik Ostrava	(1) 1	Galatasaray	(2) 2
FC Brugge	(0) 3	Katowice	(0) 0
Ferencvaros	(0) 0	Werder Bremen	(0) 1
Feyenoord	(0) 0	Sion	(0) 0

(Feyenoord won 5-3 on penalties)

Manchester U	(1) 1	Atletico Madrid	(0) 1
Monaco	(1) 1	Norrkoping	(0) 0
Porto	(0) 0	Tottenham H	(0) 0
Roma	(3) 5	Ilves	(0) 2

Quarter-finals, First Leg

Atletico Madrid	(1) 3	FC Brugge	(2) 2
Feyenoord	(0) 1	Tottenham H	(0) 0
Roma	(0) 0	Monaco	(0) 0
Werder Bremen	(0) 2	Galatasaray	(1) 1

Quarter-finals, Second Leg

FC Brugge	(1) 2	Atletico Madrid	(1) 1
Galatasaray	(0) 0	Werder Bremen	(0) 0
Monaco	(1) 1	Roma	(0) 0
Tottenham H	(0) 0	Feyenoord	(0) 0

Semi-finals, First Leg

| FC Brugge | (1) 1 | Werder Bremen | (0) 0 |
| Monaco | (1) 1 | Feyenoord | (1) 1 |

Semi-finals, Second Leg

| Feyenoord | (0) 2 | Monaco | (1) 2 |
| Werder Bremen | (1) 2 | FC Brugge | (0) 0 |

Final: Werder Bremen (1) 2, Monaco (0) 0

(in Lisbon, 6 May 1992, 16,000)

Werder Bremen: Rollmann; Wolter (Schaaf 34), Borowka, Bratseth, Bode, Bockenfeld, Eilts, Votova, Neubarth (Kohn 75), Allofs, Rufer. *Scorers:* Allofs 41, Rufer 54.
Monaco: Ettori; Valery (Djorkaeff 62), Petis, Mendy, Sonor, Dib, Gnako, Passi, Rui Barros, Weah, Fofana (Clement 59).
Referee: D'Elia (Italy).

UEFA CUP 1991–92

First Round, First leg

Aberdeen	(0) 0	B 1903 Copenhagen	(0) 1
Ajax	(0) 3	Orebro	(0) 0
Anorthosis	(0) 1	Steaua	(1) 2
Bangor	(0) 0	Olomouc	(1) 3
Boavista	(1) 2	Internazionale	(0) 1
Celtic	(2) 2	Ekeren	(0) 0
Cork C	(1) 1	Bayern Munich	(1) 1
CSKA Sofia	(0) 0	Parma	(0) 0
Eintracht Frankfurt	(4) 6	Spora	(1) 1
Gent	(0) 0	Lausanne	(1) 1
Gijon	(0) 2	Partizan	(0) 0
Groningen	(0) 0	Erfurt	(1) 1
Halle	(0) 2	Moscow Torpedo	(0) 1
Hamburg	(0) 1	Gornik Zabrze	(0) 1
HASK Gradjanski	(0) 2	Trabzonspor	(2) 3
Ikast	(0) 0	Auxerre	(0) 1
KR Reykjavik	(0) 0	Torino	(1) 2
Liverpool	(2) 6	Kuusysi	(1) 1
Lyon	(1) 1	Osters	(0) 0
MP Mikkeli	(0) 0	Moscow Spartak	(1) 2
Neuchatel Xamax	(1) 2	Floriana	(0) 0
Oviedo	(1) 1	Genoa	(0) 0
PAOK Salonika	(1) 1	Mechelen	(0) 1
Salgueiros	(0) 1	Cannes	(0) 0
Slavia Sofia	(1) 1	Osasuna	(0) 0
Slovan Bratislava	(0) 1	Real Madrid	(1) 2
Sporting Lisbon	(0) 1	Dinamo Bucharest	(0) 0
Sturm Graz	(0) 0	Utrecht	(0) 1
Stuttgart	(4) 4	Pecs	(0) 1
Tirol	(0) 2	Tromso	(0) 1
Vac Izzo	(0) 1	Moscow Dynamo	(0) 0
Vllaznia	(0) 0	AEK Athens	(0) 1

First Round, Second Leg

AEK Athens	(1) 2	Vllaznia	(0) 0
Auxerre	(2) 5	Ikast	(0) 1
B 1903 Copenhagen	(0) 2	Aberdeen	(0) 0
Bayern Munich	(0) 2	Cork C	(0) 0
Cannes	(0) 1	Salgueiros	(0) 0

(Cannes won 4-2 on penalties)

Dinamo Bucharest	(1) 2	Sporting Lisbon	(0) 0
Ekeren	(1) 1	Celtic	(1) 1
Erfurt	(0) 1	Groningen	(0) 0
Floriana	(0) 0	Neuchatel Xamax	(0) 0
Genoa	(1) 3	Oviedo	(1) 1
Gornik Zabrze	(0) 0	Hamburg	(0) 3
Internazionale	(0) 0	Boavista	(0) 0
Kuusysi	(0) 1	Liverpool	(0) 0
Lausanne	(0) 0	Gent	(0) 1

(Gent won 4-1 on penalties)

Mechelen	(0) 0	PAOK Salonika	(0) 1
Moscow Dynamo	(2) 4	Vac Izzo	(1) 1
Moscow Spartak	(1) 3	MP Mikkeli	(1) 1
Moscow Torpedo	(2) 3	Halle	(0) 0
Olomouc	(1) 3	Bangor	(0) 0
Orebro	(0) 0	Ajax	(0) 1
Osasuna	(2) 4	Slavia Sofia	(0) 0
Osters	(1) 1	Lyon	(0) 1
Parma	(0) 1	CSKA Sofia	(0) 1
Partizan	(0) 2	Gijon	(0) 0

(Gijon won 3-2 on penalties)

Pecs	(1) 2	Stuttgart .	(0) 2
Real Madrid	(1) 1	Slovan Bratislava	(0) 1
Spora	(0) 0	Eintracht Frankfurt	(2) 5
Steaua	(0) 2	Anorthosis	(0) 2
Torino	(2) 6	KR Reykjavik	(1) 1
Trabzonspor	(0) 1	HASK Gradjanski	(1) 1
Tromso	(1) 1	Tirol	(1) 1
Utrecht	(0) 3	Sturm Graz	(0) 1

Second Round, First Leg

Auxerre	(1) 2	Liverpool	(0) 0
B 1903 Copenhagen	(1) 6	Bayern Munich	(1) 2
Cannes	(0) 0	Moscow Dynamo	(1) 1
Erfurt	(1) 1	Ajax	(0) 2
Genoa	(2) 3	Dinamo Bucharest	(0) 1
Gent	(0) 0	Eintracht Frankfurt	(0) 0
Gijon	(1) 2	Steaua	(1) 2
Hamburg	(1) 2	CSKA Sofia	(0) 0
Lyon	(0) 3	Trabzonspor	(0) 4
Moscow Spartak	(0) 0	AEK Athens	(0) 0
Neuchatel Xamax	(3) 5	Celtic	(0) 1
Olomouc	(0) 2	Moscow Torpedo	(0) 0
Osasuna	(0) 0	Stuttgart	(0) 0
PAOK Salonika	(0) 0	Tirol	(0) 2
Torino	(1) 2	Boavista	(0) 0
Utrecht	(1) 1	Real Madrid	(1) 3

Second Round, Second Leg

Ajax	(1) 3	Erfurt	(0) 0
Bayern Munich	(0) 1	B 1903 Copenhagen	(0) 0
Boavista	(0) 0	Torino	(0) 0
Celtic	(0) 1	Neuchatel Xamax	(0) 0
CSKA Sofia	(1) 1	Hamburg	(1) 4
AEK Athens	(0) 2	Moscow Spartak	(1) 1
Dinamo Bucharest	(0) 2	Genoa	(1) 2
Eintracht Frankfurt	(0) 0	Gent	(1) 1
Liverpool	(2) 3	Auxerre	(0) 0
Moscow Dynamo	(1) 1	Cannes	(1) 1
Moscow Torpedo	(0) 0	Olomouc	(0) 0

Real Madrid	(1) 1	Utrecht	(0) 0
Steaua	(0) 1	Gijon	(0) 0
Stuttgart	(0) 2	Osasuna	(2) 3
Tirol	(1) 2	PAOK Salonika	(0) 0
Trabzonspor	(3) 4	Lyon	(1) 1

Third Round, First Leg

AEK Athens	(1) 2	Torino	(2) 2
B 1903 Copenhagen	(1) 1	Trabzonspor	(0) 0
Gent	(1) 2	Moscow Dynamo	(0) 0
Hamburg	(1) 1	Olomouc	(2) 2
Neuchatel Xamax	(1) 1	Real Madrid	(0) 0
Osasuna	(0) 0	Ajax	(0) 1
Steaua	(0) 0	Genoa	(1) 1
Tirol	(0) 0	Liverpool	(0) 2

Third Round, Second Leg

Ajax	(1) 1	Osasuna	(0) 0
Genoa	(0) 1	Steaua	(0) 0
Liverpool	(1) 4	Tirol	(0) 0
Moscow Dynamo	(0) 0	Gent	(0) 0
Olomouc	(1) 4	Hamburg	(0) 1
Real Madrid	(0) 4	Neuchatel Xamax	(0) 0
Torino	(0) 1	AEK Athens	(0) 0
Trabzonspor	(0) 0	B 1903 Copenhagen	(0) 0

Quarter-finals, First Leg

B 1903 Copenhagen	(0) 0	Torino	(1) 2
Genoa	(1) 2	Liverpool	(0) 0
Gent	(0) 0	Ajax	(0) 0
Olomouc	(1) 1	Real Madrid	(1) 1

Quarter-finals, Second Leg

Ajax	(2) 3	Gent	(0) 0
Liverpool	(0) 1	Genoa	(1) 2
Real Madrid	(0) 1	Olomouc	(0) 0
Torino	(1) 1	B 1903 Copenhagen	(0) 0

Semi-finals, First Leg

| Genoa | (0) 2 | Ajax | (1) 3 |
| Real Madrid | (0) 2 | Torino | (0) 1 |

Semi-finals, Second Leg

| Ajax | (0) 1 | Genoa | (1) 1 |
| Torino | (1) 2 | Real Madrid | (0) 0 |

Final
First Leg: Torino (0) 2, Ajax (1) 2
(in Turin, 29 April 1992, 65,377)

Torino: Marchegiani; Cravero (Bresciani 80), Bruno, Annoni, Benedetti, Venturin, Martin Vazquez, Scifo, Mussi (Sordo 83), Lentini, Casagrande.
Scorer: Casagrande 61, 83.
Ajax: Menzo; Blind, Silooy, Jonk, De Boer, Van't Schip, Winter, Bergkamp, Kreek, Pettersson, Roy (Gronendijk 82).
Scorers: Jonk 44, Pettersson 74 (pen).
Referee: Worrall (England).

Second Leg: Ajax (0) 0, Torino (0) 0
(in Amsterdam, 13 May 1992, 40,000)

Ajax: Menzo; Silooy, Blind, Jonk, De Boer, Winter, Kreek (Vink 80), Alflen, Van't Schip, Pettersson, Roy (Van Loen 65).
Torino: Marchegiani; Mussi, Cravero (Sordo 58), Benedetti, Fusi, Policano, Martin Vazquez, Scifo (Bresciani 62), Venturin, Casagrande, Lentini.
Referee: Petrovic (Yugoslavia).

UEFA CUP PAST FINALS

Year					
1972	Tottenham H	2 1	Wolverhampton W	1 1
1973	Liverpool	3 0	Borussia Moenchengladbach	0 2
1974	Feyenoord	2 2	Tottenham H	2 0
1975	Borussia Moenchengladbach	0 5	Twente Enschede	0 1
1976	Liverpool	3 1	FC Brugge	2 1
1977	Juventus**	1 1	Athletic Bilbao	0 2
1978	PSV Eindhoven	0 3	Bastia	0 0
1979	Borussia Moenchengladbach	1 1	Red Star Belgrade	1 0
1980	Borussia Moenchengladbach	3 0	Eintracht Frankfurt**	2 1
1981	Ipswich T	3 2	AZ 67 Alkmaar	0 4
1982	IFK Gothenburg	1 3	Hamburg	0 0
1983	Anderlecht	1 1	Benfica	0 1
1984	Tottenham H†	1 1	Anderlecht	1 1
1985	Real Madrid	3 0	Videoton	0 1
1986	Real Madrid	5 0	Cologne	1 2
1987	IFK Gothenburg	1 1	Dundee U	0 1
1988	Bayer Leverkusen†	0 3	Espanol	0 3
1989	Napoli	2 3	Stuttgart	1 3
1990	Juventus	3 0	Fiorentina	1 0
1991	Internazionale	2 0	AS Roma	0 1

*After extra time **Won on away goals †Won on penalties aet ‡Aggregate score*

EUROPEAN CUP PAST FINALS

Year				
1956	Real Madrid	4	Stade de Rheims	3
1957	Real Madrid	2	Fiorentina	0
1958	Real Madrid	3	AC Milan	2*
1959	Real Madrid	2	Stade de Rheims	0
1960	Real Madrid	7	Eintracht Frankfurt	3
1961	Benfica	3	Barcelona	2
1962	Benfica	5	Real Madrid	3
1963	AC Milan	2	Benfica	1
1964	Internazionale	3	Real Madrid	1
1965	Internazionale	1	Benfica	0
1966	Real Madrid	2	Partizan Belgrade	1
1967	Celtic	2	Internazionale	1
1968	Manchester U	4	Benfica	1*
1969	AC Milan	4	Ajax	1
1970	Feyenoord	2	Celtic	1*
1971	Ajax	2	Panathinaikos	0
1972	Ajax	2	Internazionale	0
1973	Ajax	1	Juventus	0
1974	Bayern Munich	1 4	Atletico Madrid	1 0
1975	Bayern Munich	2	Leeds U	0
1976	Bayern Munich	1	St Etienne	0
1977	Liverpool	3	Borussia Moenchengladbach	1
1978	Liverpool	1	FC Brugge	0
1979	Nottingham F	1	Malmö	0
1980	Nottingham F	1	Hamburg	0
1981	Liverpool	1	Real Madrid	0
1982	Aston Villa	1	Bayern Munich	0
1983	Hamburg	1	Juventus	0
1984	Liverpool†	1	AS Roma	1
1985	Juventus	1	Liverpool	0
1986	Steaua Bucharest†	0	Barcelona	0

1987	Porto	2	Bayern Munich	1
1988	PSV Eindhoven†	0	Benfica	0
1989	AC Milan	4	Steaua Bucharest	0
1990	AC Milan	1	Benfica	0
1991	Red Star Belgrade†	0	Marseille	0

EUROPEAN CUP-WINNERS' CUP PAST FINALS

1961	Fiorentina	4	Rangers	1‡
1962	Atletico Madrid	1 3	Fiorentina	1 0
1963	Tottenham H	5	Atletico Madrid	1
1964	Sporting Lisbon	3 1	MTK Budapest	3* 0
1965	West Ham U	2	Munich 1860	0
1966	Borussia Dortmund	2	Liverpool	1*
1967	Bayern Munich	1	Rangers	0*
1968	AC Milan	2	Hamburg	0
1969	Slovan Bratislava	3	Barcelona	2
1970	Manchester C	2	Gornik Zabrze	1
1971	Chelsea	1 2	Real Madrid	1* 1*
1972	Rangers	3	Dynamo Moscow	2
1973	AC Milan	1	Leeds U	0
1974	Magdeburg	2	AC Milan	0
1975	Dynamo Kiev	3	Ferencvaros	0
1976	Anderlecht	4	West Ham U	2
1977	Hamburg	2	Anderlecht	0
1978	Anderlecht	4	Austria Vienna	0
1979	Barcelona	4	Fortuna Dusseldorf	3*
1980	Valencia†	0	Arsenal	0
1981	Dynamo Tbilisi	2	Carl Zeiss Jena	1
1982	Barcelona	2	Standard Liege	1
1983	Aberdeen	2	Real Madrid	1*
1984	Juventus	2	Porto	1
1985	Everton	3	Rapid Vienna	1
1986	Dynamo Kiev	3	Atletico Madrid	0
1987	Ajax	1	Lokomotiv Leipzig	0
1988	Mechelen	1	Ajax	0
1989	Barcelona	2	Sampdoria	0
1990	Sampdoria	2	Anderlecht	0
1991	Manchester U	2	Barcelona	1

FAIRS CUP FINALS

1958	Barcelona	8	London	2‡
1960	Barcelona	4	Birmingham C	1‡
1961	AS Roma	4	Birmingham C	2‡
1962	Valencia	7	Barcelona	3‡
1963	Valencia	4	Dynamo Zagreb	1‡
1964	Real Zaragoza	2	Valencia	1
1965	Ferencvaros	1	Juventus	0
1966	Barcelona	4	Real Zaragoza	3‡
1967	Dynamo Zagreb	2	Leeds U	0‡
1968	Leeds U	1	Ferencvaros	0‡
1969	Newcastle U	6	Ujpest Dozsa	2‡
1970	Arsenal	4	Anderlecht	3‡
1971	Leeds U	3**	Juventus	3‡

EUROPEAN CHAMPIONSHIP
PAST FINALS

Paris, 10 July 1960 USSR 2, YUGOSLAVIA 1*
USSR: Yachin; Tchekeli, Kroutikov, Voinov, Maslenkin, Netto, Metreveli, Ivanov, Ponedelnik, Bubukin, Meshki. **Scorers:** Metreveli, Ponedelnik.
Yugoslavia: Vidinic; Durkovic, Jusufi, Zanetic, Miladinovic, Perusic, Sekularac, Jerkovic, Galic, Matus, Kostic. **Scorer:** Netto (og)

Madrid, 21 June 1964 SPAIN 2, USSR 1
Spain: Iribar; Rivilla, Calleja, Fuste, Olivella, Zoco, Amancio, Pereda, Marcellino, Suarez, Lapetra. **Scorers:** Perede, Marcellino.
USSR: Yachin; Chustikov, Mudrik, Voronin, Shesternjev, Anitchkin, Chislenko, Ivanov, Ponedelnik, Kornaev, Khusainov. **Scorer:** Khusainov.

Rome, 8 June 1968 ITALY 1, YUGOSLAVIA 1
Italy: Zoff; Burgnich, Facchetti, Ferrini, Guarneri, Castano, Domenghini, Juliano, Anastasi, Lodetti, Prati. **Scorer:** Domenghini.
Yugoslavia: Pandelic; Fazlagic, Damjanovic, Pavlovic, Paunovic, Holcer, Petkovic, Acimovic, Musemic, Trivic, Dzajic, **Scorer:** Dzajic.

Replay: Rome, 10 June 1968 ITALY 2, YUGLOSLAVIA 0
Italy: Zoff; Burgnich, Facchetti, Rosato, Guarneri, Salvadore, Domenghini, Mazzola, Anastasi, De Sista, Riva. **Scorers:** Riva, Anastasi.
Yugoslavia: Pantelic; Fazlagic, Damjanovic, Pavlovic, Paunovic, Holcer, Hosic, Acimovic, Musemic, Trivic, Dzajic.

Brussels, 18 June 1972 WEST GERMANY 3, USSR 0
West Germany: Maier; Hottges, Schwarzenbeck, Beckenbauer, Breitner, Hoeness, Wimmer, Netzer, Heynckes, Muller, Kremers. **Scorers:** Muller 2, Wimmer.
USSR: Rudakov; Dzodzuashvili, Khurtsilava, Kaplichny, Istomin, Troshkin, Kolotov, Baidachni, Konkov (Dolmatov), Banishevski (Konzinkievits), Onishenko.

Belgrade, 20 June 1976 CZECHOSLOVAKIA 2, WEST GERMANY 2*
Czechoslovakia: Viktor; Dobias (Vesely F), Pivarnik, Ondrus, Capkovic, Gogh, Moder, Panenka, Svehlik (Jurkemik), Masny, Nehoda. **Scorers:** Svehlik, Dobias.
West Germany: Maier; Vogts, Beckenbauer, Schwarzenbeck, Dietz, Bonhof, Wimmer (Flohe), Müller D, Beer (Bongartz), Hoeness, Holzenbein. **Scorers:** Müller, Holzenbein.
Czechoslovakia won 5-3 on penalties.

Rome, 22 June 1980 WEST GERMANY 2, BELGIUM 1
West Germany: Schumacher; Briegel, Forster K, Dietz, Schuster, Rummenigge, Hrubesch, Müller, Allofs, Stielike, Kalz. **Scorers:** Hrubesch 2.
Belgium: Pfaff; Gerets, Millecamps, Meeuws, Renquin, Cools, Van der Eycken, Van Moer, Mommens, Van der Elst, Ceulemans. **Scorer:** Van der Eycken.

Paris, 27 June 1984 FRANCE 2, SPAIN 0
France: Bats; Battiston (Amoros), Le Roux, Bossis, Domergue, Giresse, Platini, Tigana, Fernandez, Lacombe (Genghini), Bellone. **Scorers:** Platini, Bellone.
Spain: Arconada; Urquiaga, Salva (Roberto), Gallego, Camacho, Francisco, Julio Alberto (Sarabia), Senor, Victor, Carrasco, Santilana.

Munich, 25 June 1988 HOLLAND 2, USSR 0
Holland: Van Breukelen; Van Aerle, Van Tiggelen, Wouters, Koeman R, Rijkaard, Vanenburg, Gullit, Van Basten, Muhren, Koeman E. **Scorers:** Gullit, Van Basten.
USSR: Dassayev; Khidiatulin, Aleinikov, Mikhailichenko, Litovchenko, Demianenko, Belanov, Gotsmanov (Baltacha), Protasov (Pasulko), Zavarov, Rats.

** After extra time*

EUROPEAN CUP 1992–93

Qualifying Round

Shelbourne v Tavria Simferopol; Klaksvikar v Skonto Riga; Olimpija Ljubljana v Norma Tallinn; Valetta v Maccabi Tel Aviv.

First Round

Glentoran v Marseille; Rangers v Lyngby; Sion v Shelbourne or Tavria Simferopol; Stuttgart v Leeds U; AEK Athens v Apoel; Barcelona v Viking; FC Brugge v Valetta or Maccabi; FK Austria v CSKA Sofia; IFK Gothenburg v Besiktas; Kuusysi v Dinamo Bucharest; Lech Poznan v Klaksvikar or Skonto Riga; AC Milan v Olimpija Ljubljana or Norma Tallinn; PSV Eindhoven v Zalgiris Vilnius; Slovan Bratislava v Ferencvaros; Union Luxembourg v Porto; Vikingur v CSKA Moscow.

CUP-WINNERS' CUP 1992–93

Qualifying Round

Avenir Beggen v B36 Thorshavn; Branik Maribor v Hamrun Spartans; Hapoel Petah Tikva v Stromsgodset Drammen; Vaduz v Chernomorets Odessa.

First Round

Admira Wacker v Cardiff C; Airdrieonians v Sparta Prague; Glenavon v Antwerp; Liverpool v Apollon Limassol; Steaua Bucharest v Bohemians Dublin; AIK Stockholm v Aarhus; Boavista v Valur; Branik Maribor or Hamrun Spartans v Atletico Madrid; Levski v Lucerne; Feyenoord v Stromsgodset Drammen or Hapoel Petah Tikva; Monaco v Miedz Legnica; Moscow Spartak v B36 Thorshavn or Avenir Beggen; Olympiakos v Vaduz or Chernomorets Odessa; Parma v Ujpest Dozsa; Trabzonspor v Turku; Werder Bremen v Hannover.

UEFA CUP 1992–93

First Round

Cologne v Celtic; Hibernian v Anderlecht; Manchester U v Moscow Torpedo; Sheffield W v Spora; Slavia Prague v Hearts; Standard Liege v Portadown; Vitesse v Derry City; Austria Salzburg v Ajax; Benfica v Belvedur Izola; Caen v Zaragoza; Electroputere Craiova v Panathinaikos; FC Copenhagen v Mikkelin; Fenerbahce v Botev Plovdiv; Floriana v Dortmund; Fram v Kaiserslautern; Grasshoppers v Sporting Lisbon; Guimaraes v Real Sociedad; Juventus v Anorthosis; Katowice v Galatasaray; Kiev Dynamo v Rapid Vienna; Lokomotiv Plovdiv v Auxerre; Mechelen v Orebro; Moscow Dynamo v Rosenborg; Norrkoping v Torino; Paris St Germain v PAOK Salonika; Real Madrid v Politehnica Timisoara; Sigma Olomouc; Tirol v Roma; VAC Izzo v Groningen; Valencia v Napoli; Widzew Lodz v Eintracht Frankfurt; Neuchatel Xamax v Fram.

Qualifying round ties on August 19 and September 2, first round September 16 and 30.

EUROPEAN CHAMPIONSHIP 1990–92

Qualifying Tournament

Group 1

Reykjavik, 30 May 1990, 5250
Iceland (1) 2 *(Gudjohnsen 42, Edvaldsson 88)*
Albania (0) 0
Iceland: Kristinsson B; Thordarson, Edvaldsson, Orlygsson T (Jonsson K 46), Gretarsson, Jonsson Saevar, Berg, Ormslev, Torfarson (Orlygsson O 67), Petursson, Gudjohnsen.
Albania: Strakosha; Noga (Illiadhe 75), Lekbello, Kovi, Vapa, Jeri, Shehu (Arbete 46), Josa, Millo, Abazi, Demollari.

Reykjavik, 5 September 1990, 8388
Iceland (0) 1 *(Edvaldsson 85)*
France (1) 2 *(Papin 12, Cantona 74)*
Iceland: Sigurdsson; Thrainsson, Edvaldsson, Bergsson, Jonsson Saevar, Orlygsson T (Margeirsson 63), Gretarsson, Thordarson, Ormslev (Kristinsson R 63), Gudjohnsen, Petursson.
France: Martini; Amoros, Boli, Sauzee, Casoni, Blanc (Durand 75), Pardo, Deschamps, Perez, Papin, Cantona (Fernandez 83).

Kosice, 26 September 1990, 30,184
Czechoslovakia (1) 1 *(Danek 43)*
Iceland (0) 0
Czechoslovakia: Stejskal; Kadlec, Kocian, Hipp, Hasek, Bilek (Weiss 67), Kubik, Kula, Moravcik, Skuhravy, Danek.
Iceland: Sirgurdsson; Thrainsson, Bergsson, Edvaldsson, Jonsson Saevar, Kristinsson R (Jonsson K 61), Gretarsson, Thordarson, Jonsson Siggi, Gudjohnsen, Margeirsson (Ormslev 76).

Seville, 10 October 1990, 18,399
Spain (1) 2 *(Butragueno 63, Munoz 66)*
Iceland (0) 1 *(Jonsson Siggi 66)*
Spain: Zubizarreta; Nando, Serna, Rafa Paz (Beguiristain 62), Sanchis, Fernando, Goicoechea, Michel, Butragueno, Martin Vazquez, Carlos (Valverde 71).
Iceland: Sigurdsson; Thrainsson, Edvaldsson, Jonsson K (Gregory 80), Gretarsson, Jonsson Saevar, Bergsson, Jonsson Siggi (Ormslev 72), Gudjohnsen, Thordarson, Margeirsson.

Paris, 13 October 1990, 38,249
France (0) 2 *(Papin 60, 83)*
Czechoslovakia (0) 1 *(Skuhravy 89)*
France: Martini; Boli, Blanc, Casoni, Angloma (Fernandez 52), Deschamps, Sauzee, Durand, Papin, Cantona, Vahirua (Silvestre 85).
Czechoslovakia: Stejskal; Kula, Kadlec, Kocian, Hipp, Moravcik, Chovanec, Kubik (Tittel 85), Bilek (Pecko 82), Skuhravy, Knoflicek.

Prague, 14 November 1990, 21,980
Czechoslovakia (1) 3 *(Danek 16, 67, Moravcik 77)*
Spain (1) 2 *(Roberto 30, Carlos 54)*
Czechoslovakia: Miklosko; Kocian, Kadlec, Hipp, Hasek, Tittel, Moravcik, Kula, Bilek (Belak 80), Danek (Kuka 89), Skuhravy.
Spain: Zubizarreta; Quique, Sanchis, Nando, Serna, Michel (Amor 85), Martin Vazquez, Roberto, Goicoechea, Butragueno, Carlos (Bakero 62).

Tirana, 17 November 1990, 12,972
Albania (0) 0
France (1) 1 *(Boli 25)*
Albania: Arapi; Leskaj (Ferko 46), Stafa, Ibro, Hodja, Lekbello, Zmijani, Demollari, Josa, Kushta, Majaci (Kacaci 56).
France: Martini; Boli, Durand, Casoni, Blanc, Pardo, Deschamps, Sauzee, Tibeuf (Ginola 66), Ferreri, Vahirua (Angloma 82).

Seville, 19 December 1990, 12,625
Spain (4) 9 *(Amor 21, Carlos 24, 65, Butragueno 31, 57, 68, 88, Hierro 40, Bakero 76)*
Albania (0) 0
Spain: Zubizarreta; Sanchis, Alcorta, Goicoechea (Bakero 75), Amor, Hierro, Manolo, Michel (Quique 62), Butragueno, Martin Vazquez, Carlos.
Albania: Arapi; Ibro, Lekbello, Stafa, Kola (Demollari 39), Kushta, Millo, Zmijani, Ferko (Josa 55), Dema, Tahiri.

Paris, 20 February 1991, 45,000
France (1) 3 *(Sauzee 15, Papin 58, Blanc 77)*
Spain (1) 1 *(Bakero 11)*
France: Martini; Amoros, Boli, Casoni, Blanc, Pardo (Fernandez 50), Durand, Sauzee, Papin, Cantona, Vahirua (Deschamps 83).
Spain: Zubizarreta; Quique, Nando, Juanito, Sanchis, Michel, Amor, Vizcaino (Soler 61), Goicoechea, Bakero, Butragueno (Manolo 75).

Paris, 30 March 1991, 25,000
France (4) 5 *(Sauzee 1, 19, Papin 34 (pen), 43, Lekbello 79 (og))*
Albania (0) 0
France: Martini; Amoros, Boli, Blanc, Durand, Fernandez, Sauzee (Deschamps 73), Cocard, Cantona, Papin, Vahirua (Baills 57).
Albania: Nallbani; Zmijani, Lekbello, Vata, Gjergi, Ocelli, Dume, Canaj, Demollari, Tahiri, Kepa.

Tirana, 1 May 1991, 10,000
Albania (0) 0
Czechoslovakia (0) 2 *(Kubik 47, Kuka 67)*
Albania: Nallbani; Zmijani, Dema (Kola 73), Daja, Ocelli, Shpuza, Kushta, Memushi, Barbullushi (Dosti 63), Dume (Kole 70), Milori.
Czechoslovakia: Miklosko; Kula, Kadlec, Hasek (Hapal 19), Grussmann, Tittel, Nemec, Kubik, Kuka, Kukleta (Chylek 84), Moravcik.

Tirana, 26 May 1991, 5000
Albania (0) 1 *(Abazi 56)*
Iceland (0) 0
Albania: Nallbani; Memushi (Josa 17), Ocelli, Lekbello, Shpuza, Daja, Millo, Demollari, Milori, Kushta, Abazi.
Iceland: Sigurdsson; Jonsson Saevar, Bergsson, Gislason, Kristiansson, Kristinsson R (Stefansson 62), Orlygsson T, Thordarson, Gretarsson, Sverrisson, Gregory (Marteinsson 75).

Reykjavik, 5 June 1991, 5000
Iceland (0) 0
Czechoslovakia (1) 1 *(Hasek 15)*
Iceland: Sigurdsson; Jonsson Saevar, Bergsson, Edvaldsson, Gislason, Thordarson, Gretarsson, Orlygsson T, Kristinsson R, Gudjohnsen, Sverrisson (Stefansson 70).
Czechoslovakia: Miklosko; Grussmann, Kocian, Tittel, Hasek, Hapal, Kubik, Kula, Nemec, Danek (Pecko 89), Skuhravy (Kuka 41).

Bratislava, 4 September 1991, 50,000
Czechoslovakia (1) 1 *(Nemecek 21)*
France (0) 2 *(Papin 53, 89)*
Czechoslovakia: Miklosko; Kocian, Tittel, Novotny, Knoflicek (Hapal 80), Kristofik (Frydek 22), Nemecek, Moravcik, Nemec, Pecko, Kuka.
France: Martini; Amoros, Blanc, Angloma (Durand 76), Boli, Casoni, Deschamps, Sauzee, Papin, Cocard (Perez 46), Vahirua.

Reykjavik, 25 September 1991, 8900
Iceland (0) 2 *(Orlygsson T 71, Sverrisson 78)*
Spain (0) 0
Iceland: Kristinsson B; Valsson (Marteinsson 46), Ormslev, Bergsson, Jonsson Saevar, Jonsson K, Jonsson Siggi, Gretarsson, Sverrisson, Thordarson, Orlygsson T, Bjarnason (Magnusson 73).
Spain: Zubizarreta; Abelardo, Eusebio, Sanchis, Solozabal, Michel, Vizcaino, Martin Vazquez (Hierro 67), Goicoechea, Manolo, Butragueno.

Seville, 12 October 1991, 27,500
Spain (1) 1 *(Abelardo 33)*
France (2) 2 *(Fernandez 12, Papin 15)*
Spain: Zubizarreta; Cristobal, Solozabal (Eusebio 46), Abelardo, Sanchis, Vizcaino, Manolo, Bango, Butragueno, Martin Vazquez (Alvaro 73), Hierro.
France: Martini; Amoros, Blanc, Boli, Casoni, Deschamps, Angloma, Fernandez (Durand 82), Perez (Garde 62), Cantona, Papin.

Olomouc, 16 October 1991, 2366
Czechoslovakia (2) 2 *(Kula 35, Lancz 39)*
Albania (0) 1 *(Zmijani 62)*
Czechoslovakia: Miklosko; Jurasko, Tittel, Nemecek, Hapal, Moravcik, Lancz (Sedlacek 64), Frydek, Kula, Danek (Pecko 72), Kuka.
Albania: Strakosha; Zmijani, Lekbello, Kacaj, Cipi, Josa, Milori, Kola (Daja 53), Gjondeda, Abazi, Barbullushi.

Seville, 13 November 1991, 24,500
Spain (1) 2 *(Abelardo 10, Michel 79 (pen))*
Czechoslovakia (0) 1 *(Nemecek 59)*
Spain: Zubizarreta; Abelardo, Soler, Solozabal, Sanchis, Hierro, Moya (Conte 59), Michel, Butragueno, Martin Vazquez (Nadal 46), Vizcaino.
Czechoslovakia: Stejskal; Suchoparek, Glonek, Vlk (Grussmann 65), Kristov, Nemecek, Nemec, Novotny, Pecko, Kula, Dubovsky (Latal 79).

Paris, 20 November 1991, 35,000
France (1) 3 *(Simba 42, Cantona 60, 68)*
Iceland (0) 1 *(Sverrisson 71)*
France: Martini; Amoros, Blanc, Angloma, Casoni (Boli 46), Deschamps, Fernandez, Perez, Cantona, Simba, Vahirua.
Iceland: Kristinsson B; Valsson, Bergsson (Jonsson Saevar 81), Jonsson K, Ormslev, Bjarnason, Orlygsson T, Jonsson Kn, Gudjohnsen, Torfason (Sverrisson 56), Gretarsson.
Albania v Spain, 18 December 1991 not played

	P	W	D	L	F	A	Pts
France	8	8	0	0	20	6	16
Czechoslovakia	8	5	0	3	12	9	10
Spain	7	3	0	4	17	12	6
Iceland	8	2	0	6	7	10	4
Albania	7	1	0	6	2	21	2

France qualified

Group 2

Geneva, 12 September 1990, 12,000
Switzerland (1) 2 *(Hottiger 19, Bickel 63)*
Bulgaria (0) 0
Switzerland: Walker; Geiger, Herr, Schepull, Hottiger, Koller, Bickel, Hermann, Sutter A (Piffaretti 88), Knup (Chapuisat 64), Turkyilmaz.
Bulgaria: Valov; Dochev, Zhelev, Iliev, Ivanov, Vasev (Bankov 14), Yanchev, Yordanov, Balakov (Todorov 65), Kostadinov E, Stoichkov.

Hampden Park, 12 September 1990, 12,081
Scotland (1) 2 *(Robertson 37, McCoist 76)*
Romania (1) 1 *(Camataru 13)*
Scotland: Goram; McKimmie, Malpas, McAllister (Nevin 73), Irvine, McLeish, Robertson, McStay, McCoist, MacLeod, Connor (Boyd 59).
Romania: Lung; Petrescu, Klein, Sandoi, Rotariu, Popescu G, Lacatus, Mateut (Sabau 79), Camataru (Raducioiu 62), Hagi, Lupescu.

Bucharest, 17 October 1990, 15,350
Romania (0) 0
Bulgaria (1) 3 *(Sirakov 28, Todorov 48, 76)*
Romania: Stelea; Petrescu, Klein (Sandoi 46), Andone, Rotariu, Popescu G, Lacatus, Sabau, Raducioiu (Balint 46), Hagi, Lupescu.
Bulgaria: Mikhailov; Dochev, Ivanov, Vasev, Iliev, Yankov, Yanchev, Stoichkov, Balakov, Sirakov (Kostadinov E 75), Yordanov (Todorov 46).

Hampden Park, 17 October 1990, 20,740
Scotland (1) 2 *(Robertson 34, McAllister 53)*
Switzerland (0) 1 *(Knup 66)*
Scotland: Goram; McKimmie, Nicol, McCall, McPherson, McLeish, Robertson, McAllister (Collins 79), McCoist, MacLeod, Boyd (Durie 68).
Switzerland: Walker; Piffaretti (Sutter B 80), Schepull (Chassot 73), Herr, Egli, Bickel, Knup, Hermann, Turkyilmaz, Sutter A, Chapuisat.

Sofia, 14 November 1990, 40,000
Bulgaria (0) 1 *(Todorov 74)*
Scotland (1) 1 *(McCoist 9)*
Bulgaria: Mikhailov; Dochev, Mladenov, Yankov, Bankov, Yanchev (Todorov 52), Yordanov, Stoichkov, Penev, Sirakov, Balakov (Kostadinov E 80).
Scotland: Goram; McKimmie, Malpas, McInally, McPherson, Gillespie, Durie (Nevin 67), McAllister, McCoist, McClair, Boyd.

Serravalle, 14 November 1990, 931
San Marino (0) 0
Switzerland (3) 4 *(Sutter A 7, Chapuisat 27, Knup 43, Chassot 87)*
San Marino: Benedettini; Montironi, Guerra, Gobbi, Muccioli (Toccacieli 46), Bonini (Matteoni 46), Zanotti L, Francini, Ceccoli, Pasolini, Macina.
Switzerland: Walker; Hottiger, Geiger, Herr, Sutter B, Bickel (Piffaretti 59), Chapuisat, Hermann, Sutter A, Turkyilmaz (Chassot 46), Knup.

Bucharest, 5 December 1990, 6380
Romania (3) 6 *(Sabau 2, Mateut 18, Raducioiu 43, Lupescu 56, Badea 77, Petrescu 85)*
San Marino (0) 0
Romania: Prunea; Petrescu, Iovan, Popescu G, Rednic, Sabau, Mateut, Lupescu (Stanici 65), Dumitrescu (Badea 46), Lacatus, Raducioiu.
San Marino: Benedettini; Montironi, Conti, Guerra, Zanotti L, Toccacieli, Matteoni, Ceccoli, Francini, Pasolini (Zanotti P 72), Macina (Bacciocchi 46).

Hampden Park, 27 March 1991, 33,119
Scotland (0) 1 *(Collins 84)*
Bulgaria (0) 1 *(Kostadinov 89)*
Scotland: Goram; McPherson, Malpas, McInally, Gough, McLeish, Strachan (Collins 80), McClair, McCoist, McStay, Durie (Robertson 80).
Bulgaria: Mikhailov; Dochev, Ivanov, Kiriakov, Iliev, Yankov, Kostadinov E, Yordanov, Penev, Sirakov (Alexandrov 86), Balakov (Tanev 86).

Serravalle, 27 March 1991, 745
San Marino (1) 1 *(Pasolini 30 (pen))*
Romania (2) 3 *(Hagi 17 (pen), Raducioiu 45, Matteoni (og) 86)*
San Marino: Benedettini; Canti, Guerra, Gobbi (Toccacieli 74), Muccioli, Matteoni, Francini, Pasolini (Mularoni 89), Ceccoli, Mazza M, Mazza P.
Romania: Prunea; Petrescu, Popescu G (Timofte D 46), Lupescu, Klein, Sandoi, Sabau, Mateut (Timofte I 65), Hagi, Lacatus, Raducioiu.

Neuchatel, 3 April 1991, 15,700
Switzerland (0) 0
Romania (0) 0
Switzerland: Huber; Geiger, Hottiger, Ohrel, Herr, Koller, Bonvin (Bickel 33), Hermann, Aeby, Turkyilmaz (Sutter B 75), Knup.
Romania: Prunea; Petrescu, Klein, Sandoi, Lupescu, Popescu G, Sabau, Hagi (Mateut 85), Lacatus, Radiciolu (Timofte I 89), Timofte D.

Sofia, 1 May 1991, 40,000
Bulgaria (2) 2 *(Kostadinov 11, Sirakov 25)*
Switzerland (0) 3 *(Knup 58, 85, Turkyilmaz 90)*
Bulgaria: Mikhailov; Dochev (Todorov 75), Kiriakov, Yankov, Iliev, Ivanov, Yordanov, Penev, Sirakov (Tanev 65), Balakov, Kostadinov E.
Switzerland: Huber; Egli, Herr, Hottiger, Ohrel, Bonvin, Hermann, Knup (Schepull 87), Koller (Chapuisat 75), Sutter B, Turkyilmaz.

Serravalle, 1 May 1991, 3512
San Marino (0) 0
Scotland (0) 2 *(Strachan 63 (pen), Durie 66)*
San Marino: Benedettini; Canti, Muccioli, Zanotti (Toccacieli 60), Gobbi, Guerra, Ceccoli, Mazza M, Mazza P, Francini, Pasolini (Matteoni 79).
Scotland: Goram; McKimmie, Nicol (Robertson 74), McCall, McPherson, Malpas, Gallacher, Strachan, McClair (Nevin 57), McAllister, Durie.

Serrevalle, 22 May 1991, 612
San Marino (0) 0
Bulgaria (2) 3 *(Ivanov 12, Sirakov 19, Penev 59)*
San Marino: Benedettini; Canti, Montironi, Muccioli, Gobbi, Guerra, Ceccoli (Matteoni 82), Mazza M, Mazza P, Francini, Pasolini (Bacciocchi 64).
Bulgaria: Mikhailov; Dimitrov, Ivanov, Kiriakov, Yankov, Anghelov (Todorov 76), Kostadinov E, Gheorghiev, Penev, Sirakov, Yotov (Metkov 56).

St Gallen, 5 June 1991, 12,000
Switzerland (3) 7 *(Knup 2, 86, Hottiger 12, Sutter B 28, Hermann 54, Ohrel 77, Turkyilmaz 89)*
San Marino (0) 0
Switzerland: Huber; Egli (Schepull 74), Herr, Hottiger (Ohrel 74), Hermann, Koller, Sutter A, Sutter B, Turkyilmaz, Knup, Chapuisat.
San Marino: Benedettini; Muccioli, Guerra, Gobbi, Canti, Matteoni (Valentini 46), Mazza M, Francini, Zanotti, Pasolini, Bacciocchi (Malaroni 65).

Berne, 11 September 1991, 48,000
Switzerland (2) 2 *(Chapuisat 30, Hermann 39)*
Scotland (0) 2 *(Durie 47, McCoist 83)*
Switzerland: Huber; Hottiger, Ohrel, Herr, Sforza, Heldmann (Sutter B 64), Knup, Hermann, Turkyilmaz, Sutter A (Bickel 60), Chapuisat.
Scotland: Goram; McKimmie (McClair 66), Boyd, McPherson, Malpas, Strachan, McCall, Nicol, Johnston (McAllister 40), Durie, McCoist.

Sofia, 16 October 1991, 8000
Bulgaria (3) 4 *(Valentini (og) 20, Stoichkov 39 (pen), Yankov 41, Iliev 85)*
San Marino (0) 0
Bulgaria: Mikhailov; Kiriakov, Rakov, Vidov, Iliev, Yankov, Kostadinov E, Stoichkov (Lechkov 69), Penev, Kolev (Yordanov 46), Balakov.
San Marino: Benedettini; Toccacieli, Valentini, Matteoni, Gobbi, Guerra, Mannzaroli, De la Valle, Mazza P, Francini, Pasolini.

Bucharest, 16 October 1991, 30,000
Romania (0) 1 *(Hagi 73 (pen))*
Scotland (0) 0
Romania: Lung; Petrescu, Klein, Sandoi, Lupescu, Popescu G, Lacatus, Timofte D (Timofte I 60), Raducioiu (Dumitrescu 75), Hagi, Munteanu.
Scotland: Goram; McKimmie, Malpas, McCall, McPherson, Levein, Strachan, Galloway (Aitken 70), McClair, Durie, Boyd (Gallacher 59).

Bucharest, 13 November 1991, 35,000
Romania (0) 1 *(Mateut 72)*
Switzerland (0) 0
Romania: Lung; Popescu A, Popescu G, Sandoi, Klein (Munteanu 3), Lupescu, Timofte D (Sabau 46), Hagi, Mateut, Lacatus, Raducioiu.
Switzerland: Huber; Hottiger, Sforza, Herr, Schepull, Ohrel, Sutter B (Bonvin 63), Hermann (Bickel 77), Sutter A, Turkyilmaz, Chapuisat.

Hampden Park, 13 November 1991, 35,170
Scotland (3) 4 *(McStay 10, Gough 31, Durie 37, McCoist 62)*
San Marino (0) 0
Scotland: Goram; McPherson (Johnston 46), Malpas, McAllister, Gough, Levein (Gallacher 60), McCall, Robertson, McCoist, McStay, Durie.
San Marino; Benedettini; Conti, Muccioli, Mazza M, Gobbi, Guerra, Zanotti, Bonini, Mazza P, Francini, Pasolini (Mannzaroli 67).

Sofia, 20 November 1991, 20,000
Bulgaria (0) 1 *(Sirakov 56)*
Romania (1) 1 *(Popescu A 30)*
Bulgaria: Mikhailov; Khubchev, Rakov, Kiriakov, Iliev (Mladenov 57), Yankov, Kostadinov E (Yordanov 69), Stoichkov, Penev, Sirakov, Balakov.
Romania: Lung; Popescu A, Munteanu, Sandoi (Timofte I 68), Lupescu, Popescu G, Lacatus (Dumitrescu 60), Sabau, Raducioiu, Hagi, Mateut.

	P	W	D	L	F	A	Pts
Scotland	8	4	3	1	14	7	11
Switzerland	8	4	2	2	19	7	10
Romania	8	4	2	2	13	7	10
Bulgaria	8	3	3	2	15	8	9
San Marino	8	0	0	8	1	33	0

Scotland qualified

Group 3

Moscow, 12 September 1990, 23,000
USSR (1) 2 *(Kanchelskis 22, Kuznetsov 60)*
Norway (0) 0
USSR: Uvarov; Chernishov, Gorlukovich, Kuznetsov O, Tishenko (Kulkov 79), Shalimov, Mikhailichenko, Kanchelskis, Getsko (Kolivanov 70), Protasov, Dobrovolski.
Norway: Thorstvedt; Lydersen, Pedersen T, Bratseth, Halle, Berg (Pedersen E 61), Ahlsen, Gulbrandsen, Jakobsen, Andersen, Fjortoft (Dahlum 66).

Bergen, 10 October 1990, 6300
Norway 0 (0)
Hungary 0 (0)
Norway: Thorstvedt; Halle, Pedersen T, Bratseth, Lydersen, Pedersen E, Ahlsen, Brandhaug, Jakobsen (Andersen 72), Sorloth, Fjortoft (Dahlum 76).
Hungary: Petry; Monos, Pinter, Szalma, Kovacs E, Limperger, Kiprich (Fodor 79), Kozma, Bognar, Lorincz, Kovacs K (Urbanyi 89).

Budapest, 17 October 1990, 24,600
Hungary (1) 1 *(Disztl L 16)*
Italy (0) 1 *(Baggio R 54)*
Hungary: Petry; Monos, Disztl L, Garaba (Fodor 60), Szalma, Bognar, Limperger, Kiprich, Kozma (Urbanyi 87), Lorincz, Kovacs K.
Italy: Zenga; Bergomi, De Agostini, Baresi, Ferri, Marocchi, Donadoni, De Napoli, Schillaci (Serena 80), Giannini (Berti 87), Baggio R.

Budapest, 31 October 1990, 2300
Hungary (3) 4 *(Lorincz 1, 19, Kiprich 20 (pen), 67 (pen))*
Cyprus (1) 2 *(Xiourouppas 13, Tsolakis 89)*
Hungary: Petry; Disztl L, Monos, Garaba, Limperger, Szalma, Kozma (Fischer 56), Bognar, Lorincz, Kiprich (Rugovics 75), Kovacs K.
Cyprus: Onisiforou; Kalotheou, Miamiliotis, Christodolou, Socratous, Yiangudakis, Andreou (Tsolakis 59), Savva, Kastanas, Constantinou C (Orthanides 73), Xiourouppas.

Rome, 3 November 1990, 52,208
Italy (0) 0
USSR (0) 0
Italy: Zenga; Ferrara, Baresi, Ferri, Maldini, De Napoli, Crippa, De Agostini, Mancini, Schillaci (Serena 70), Baggio R.
USSR: Uvarov; Chernishov, Kulkov, Tsveiba, Shalimov, Aleinikov, Mikhailichenko, Kanchelskis, Getsko (Protasov 67), Mostovoi (Tatarchuk 85), Dobrovolski.

Nicosia, 14 November 1990, 2123
Cyprus (0) 0
Norway (1) 3 *(Sorloth 39, Bohinen 50, Brandhaug 64)*
Cyprus: Charitou; Kalotheou (Kantilos 49), Miamiliotis, Kastanas, Socratous, Yiangudakis, Christodolou, Savva, Tsolakis (Constantinou C 74), Nicolaou, Xiourouppas.
Norway: Thorstvedt; Lydersen, Pedersen T, Bratseth, Lohen (Pedersen E 64), Halle, Brandhaug, Leonhardsen, Bohinen, Sorloth, Dahlum (Fjortoft 80).

Nicosia, 22 December 1990, 9185

Cyprus (0) 0

Italy (3) 4 *(Vierchowod 15, Serena 22, 50, Lombardo 44)*

Cyprus: Onisiforou; Kalotheou, Miamiliotis, Christodolou, Socratous, Yiangudakis, Punnas, Savva (Constantinou C 56), Tsolakis, Nicolaou, Papavasiliu (Xiourouppas 64).
Italy: Zenga; Bergomi, Ferrara, Eranio, Vierchowod, Crippa, Lombardo, Berti, Schillaci, Morocchi, Serena.

Limassol, 3 April 1991, 3000

Cyprus (0) 0

Hungary (2) 2 *(Szalma 15, Kiprich 40)*

Cyprus: Marangos; Constantinou G, Pittas (Kasianos 75), Ioannou, Constantinou C, Yiangudakis, Christofi C, Savva (Sotiriu 83), Savvidis, Nicolaou, Tsolakis.
Hungary: Petry; Monos, Disztl L, Szalma, Nagy, Limperger, Kiprich, Bognar, Fischer (Maroszan 72), Lorincz, Kovacs K.

Budapest, 17 April 1991, 40,000

Hungary (0) 0

USSR (1) 1 *(Mikhailichenko 30)*

Hungary: Petry; Disztl L, Garaba, Limperger, Monos, Kozma (Detari 63), Bognar (Vincze 71), Lorincz, Szalma, Kiprich, Kovacs K.
USSR: Uvarov; Chernishov, Kulkov, Tsveiba, Galiamin, Shalimov, Mikhailichenko, Kanchelskis, Youran (Kuznetsov D 86), Kolivanov, Aleinikov.

Salerno, 1 May 1991, 45,000

Italy (2) 3 *(Donadoni 4, 16, Vialli 56)*

Hungary (0) 1 *(Bognar 66)*

Italy: Zenga; Ferrara (Vierchowod 65), Ferri, Baresi, Maldini, Crippa, De Napoli, Giannini, Donadoni (Eranio 36), Vialli, Mancini.
Hungary: Petry; Monos, Disztl L, Palaczky (Kozma 33), Limperger, Garaba, Kiprich (Gregor 46), Lorincz, Bognar, Detari, Kovacs K.

Oslo, 1 May 1991, 7833

Norway (0) 3 *(Lydersen 49 (pen), Dahlum 65, Sorloth 90)*

Cyprus (0) 0

Norway: Thorstvedt; Pedersen T, Bratseth (Ingebrigtsen 46), Lydersen, Halle (Pedersen E), Ahlsen, Brandhaug, Leonhardsen, Bjornbye, Sorloth, Dahlum.
Cyprus: Charitou; Nicolaou (Sotiriu 89), Constantinou C, Ioannou, Costa, Kalotheou (Constantinou G 84), Savva, Yiangudakis, Pittas, Savvidis, Xiourouppas.

Moscow, 29 May 1991, 20,000

USSR (1) 4 *(Mostovoi 20, Mikhailichenko 51, Korneyev 83, Aleinikov 89)*

Cyprus (0) 0

USSR: Uvarov; Chernishov, Kulkov, Mostovoi (Kuznetsov D 74), Galiamin, Shalimov, Mikhailichenko, Kanchelskis, Aleinikov, Kolivanov, Youran (Korneyev 46).
Cyprus: Charitou; Kalotheou, Pittas, Ioannou, Nicolaou, Yiangudakis, Costa, Christofi C, Savvidis, Christodolou (Constantinou G 88), Xiourouppas (Savva 89).

Oslo, 5 June 1991, 27,500

Norway (2) 2 *(Dahlum 4, Bohinen 24)*

Italy (0) 1 *(Schillaci 79)*

Norway: Thorstvedt; Pedersen T, Ahlsen, Bratseth, Lydersen, Dahlum (Pedersen E 46), Bohinen, Lokken, Ingebrigtsen, Jakobsen, Sorloth.
Italy: Zenga; Baresi, Ferrara, Ferri (Bergomi 89), Maldini, Lombardo, Eranio, De Napoli (Schillaci 53), Crippa, Vialli, Mancini.

Oslo, 28 August 1991, 25,427

Norway (0) 0

USSR (0) 1 *(Mostovoi 74)*

Norway: Thorstvedt; Lydersen, Pedersen T, Bratseth, Nilsen R (Riisnes 66), Lokken, Halle, Leonhardsen, Jakobsen (Skammelsrud 80), Sorloth, Fjortoft.
USSR: Cherchesov; Chernishov, Kulkov, Tsveiba, Kuznetsov O, Shalimov, Mikhailichenko, Kanchelskis (Korneev 71), Aleinikov, Kolivanov, Youran (Mostovoi 46).

Moscow, 25 September 1991, 50,000

USSR (1) 2 *(Shalimov 41 (pen), Kanchelskis 48)*

Hungary (1) 2 *(Kiprich 17, 86)*

USSR: Cherchesov; Chernishov, Kulkov, Tsveiba (Kuznetsov O 20), Galiamin, Shalimov, Mikhailichenko, Kanchelskis, Aleinikov, Kolivanov, Mostovoi (Youran 58).
Hungary: Petry; Monos (Kovacs E 30), Disztl L, Szalma, Linchei, Limperger, Kiprich, Lorincz, Kozma (Fischer 58), Detari, Kovacs K.

Moscow, 12 October 1991, 92,000

USSR (0) 0

Italy (0) 0

USSR: Cherchesov; Chernishov, Kulkov, Kuznetsov O (Tsveiba 46), Galiamin, Shalimov, Mikhailichenko, Kanchelskis, Aleinikov, Protasov (Kuznetsov D 69), Kolivanov.
Italy: Zenga; Ferrara, Maldini, Crippa, Vierchowod, Baresi, Lentini (Lombardo 58), De Napoli, Vialli, Giannini (Mancini 69), Rizzitelli.

Szombathely, 30 October 1991, 10,000

Hungary (0) 0

Norway (0) 0

Hungary: Petry; Pinter, Urban, Lorincz, Nagy, Pisont (Eszenyi 83), Lipcsei (Illes 71), Duro, Detari, Fischer, Kovacs K.
Norway: Grodas; Pedersen T, Bratseth, Ahlsen, Bjornebye, Lokken, Bohinen, Rekdal, Leonhardsen (Ingebrigtsen 78), Jakobsen, Sorloth (Fjortoft 46).

Genoa, 13 November 1991, 30,000

Italy (0) 1 *(Rizzitelli 82)*

Norway (0) 1 *(Jakobsen J-I 60)*

Italy: Pagliuca; Costacurta, Maldini, Berti (De Napoli 66), Ferri, Baresi, Baiano (Rizzitelli 55), Ancelotti, Vialli, Zola, Eranio.
Norway: Thorstvedt; Lokken, Ahlsen, Bratseth, Lydersen, Johnsen R (Pedersen J 46), Rekdal, Ingebrigtsen, Fjortoft, Sorloth, Jakobsen (Berg 77).

Larnaca, 13 November 1991, 4000

Cyprus (0) 0

USSR (1) 3 *(Protasov 27, Youran 79, Kanchelskis 82)*

Cyprus: Charitou; Costa, Pittas, Constantinou C, Socratous, Larkou, Koliandris (Hadjilukas 75), Savva, Savvidis (Sotiriou 46), Ioannou, Charalambous.
USSR: Kharin; Chernishov, Kulkov, Tsveiba, Galiamin, Shalimov, Mikhailichenko, Kanchelskis, Kuznetsov O, Protasov (Mostovoi 70), Kolivanov (Youran 46).

Foggia, 21 December 1991, 26,000

Italy (1) 2 *(Vialli 27, Baggio 55)*

Cyprus (0) 0

Italy: Zenga; Baggio D, Costacurta, Baresi, Maldini, Albertini, Berti, Evani, Zola, Baggio R (Casiraghi 65), Vialli (Baiano 66).
Cyprus: Christofi M; Constantinou G, Pittas, Constantinou C, Nicolaou, Michael (Andreou 62), Koliandris, Savva, Sotiriou, Ioannou (Larkou 80), Charalambous.

	P	W	D	L	F	A	Pts
USSR	8	5	3	0	13	2	13
Italy	8	3	4	1	12	5	10
Norway	8	3	3	2	9	5	9
Hungary	8	2	4	2	10	9	8
Cyprus	8	0	0	8	2	25	0

USSR qualified

Group 4

Windsor Park, 12 September 1990, 9008

Northern Ireland (0) 0

Yugoslavia (1) 2 *(Pancev 36, Prosinecki 86)*

Northern Ireland: Kee; Donaghy, Worthington, Taggart, McDonald, Rogan, Dennison (Clarke 66), Wilson D, Dowie, Wilson K, Black.

Yugoslavia: Ivkovic; Spasic, Jozic, Vulic, Hadzibegic, Najdoski, Prosinecki, Savicevic, Pancev (Petrovic 87), Stojkovic, Binic (Stosic 87).

Landskrona, Sweden, 12 September 1990, 1544

Faeroes (0) 1 *(Nielsen 61)*

Austria (0) 0

Faeroes: Knudsen; Jakobsen, Hansen TE, Danielsen, Hansen J, Morkore A, Nielsen, Dam, Hansen A, Reynheim, Morkore K.

Austria: Konsel; Russ, Pecl, Hartmann, Streiter, Peischl, Rodax, Linzmaier, Polster, Herzog (Pacult 63), Reisinger (Wilfurth 63).

Copenhagen, 10 October 1990, 38,500

Denmark (2) 4 *(Laudrup M 8, 48, Elstrup 37, Povlsen 89)*

Faeroes (1) 1 *(Morkore A 21)*

Denmark: Schmeichel; Sivebaek, Nielsen K, Olsen L, Heintze, Bartram, Vilfort, Elstrup (Rasmussen E 73), Povlsen, Laudrup M, Laudrup B.

Faeroes: Knudsen; Jakobsen, Hansen TE, Danielsen, Hansen J, Morkore A (Jarnskor 88), Nielsen, Dam, Hansen A, Reynheim, Morkore K (Mohr 76).

Windsor Park, 17 October 1990, 9079

Northern Ireland (0) 1 *(Clarke 58)*

Denmark (1) 1 *(Bartram 11)*

Northern Ireland: Kee; Donaghy, Worthington, Taggart, McDonald, Rogan, Wilson D, O'Neill C (McBride), Dowie, Clarke, Black.

Denmark: Schmeichel; Sivebaek, Nielsen K, Olsen L, Heintze, Bartram, Larsen J, Vilfort, Povlsen, Laudrup M (Helt 80), Laudrup B (Elstrup 70).

Belgrade, 31 October 1990, 11,422

Yugoslavia (2) 4 *(Pancev 32, 52, 85, Katanec 43)*

Austria (1) 1 *(Ogris A 15)*

Yugoslavia: Ivkovic; Vulic, Spasic, Katanec (Jarni 86), Hadzibegic, Jozic, Prosinecki, Susic (Boban 63), Bazdarevic, Pancev, Vujovic.

Austria: Konsel; Artner, Aigner, Pecl, Streiter, Hortnagl, Schottel, Herzog (Linzmaier 46), Reisinger, Ogris A (Pacult 52), Polster.

Copenhagen, 14 November 1990, 40,000

Denmark (0) 0

Yugoslavia (0) 2 *(Bazdarevic 77, Jarni 84)*

Denmark: Schmeichel; Sivebaek, Nielsen K, Olsen L, Heintze, Vilfort, Molby Jan (Elstrup 72), Laudrup M, Bartram, Laudrup B, Povlsen (Jensen J 46).

Yugoslavia: Ivkovic; Vulic, Spasic, Hadzibegic, Jarni, Katanec, Jozic, Susic, Bazdarevic, Pancev (Boban 12), Vujovic (Najdoski 89).

Vienna, 14 November 1990, 7062
Austria (0) 0
Northern Ireland (0) 0
Austria: Konsel; Schottel, Pecl, Polger, Artner, Willfurth, Reischl, Linzmaier, Hortnagl, Ogris A, Polster (Pacult 67).
Northern Ireland: Kee; Donaghy, Worthington, Taggart, McDonald, Rogan, Dennison, Wilson D, Clarke (Dowie 62), Wilson K, Black (Morrow 82).

Belgrade, 27 March 1991, 10,000
Yugoslavia (1) 4 *(Binic 35, Pancey 46, 60, 61)*
Northern Ireland (1) 1 *(Hill 45)*
Yugoslavia: Ivkovic; Vulic (Najdoski 85), Jozic, Jarni, Bazdarevic, Spasic, Hadzibegic, Prosinecki, Savicevic, Pancev, Binic.
Northern Ireland: Kee; Fleming, Rogan, Donaghy, Morrow, Hill, Dennison (Quinn 70), Magilton, Dowie, Wilson K (Clarke 60), Black.

Belgrade, 1 May 1991, 26,000
Yugoslavia (0) 1 *(Pancev 50)*
Denmark (1) 2 *(Christensen 31, 62)*
Yugoslavia: Ivkovic; Vulic, Jarni (Najdoski 84), Spasic, Hadzibegic, Jozic, Prosinecki, Savicevic, Pancev, Bazdarevic, Binic.
Denmark: Schmeichel; Sivebaek (Larsen H 54), Nielsen K, Olsen L, Kristensen, Bartram, Jensen J (Goldbaek 82), Christofte, Povlsen, Vilfort, Christensen.

Windsor Park, 1 May 1991, 10,000
Northern Ireland (1) 1 *(Clarke 44)*
Faeroes (0) 1 *(Reynheim 65)*
Northern Ireland: Kee; Donaghy, Worthington, Taggart, McDonald, Magilton, Wilson D (Dennison 83), Clarke, Dowie (Williams 83), Wilson K, Black.
Faeroes: Knudsen; Jakobsen, Hansen TE, Danielsen, Muller, Morkore A, Nielsen, Dam, Hansen A, Reynheim (Thomassen 74), Morkore K (Rasmussen 85).

Belgrade, 16 May 1991, 8000
Yugoslavia (2) 7 *(Najdoski 20, Prosinecki 24, Pancev 50, 74, Vulic 66, Boban 70, Suker 86)*
Faeroes (0) 0
Yugoslavia: Ivkovic (Lazic 80); Stanojkovic, Jarni (Suker 67), Vulic, Najdoski, Spasic, Prosinecki, Boban, Pancev, Savicevic, Mihajlovic.
Faeroes: Knudsen; Jakobsen, Hansen TE, Danielsen, Jarnskor, Morkore A, Nielsen, Dam, Hansen A, Reynheim, Morkore K (Muller 49).

Vienna, 22 May 1991, 13,000
Austria (1) 3 *(Pfeifenberger 13, Streiter 48, Wetl 63)*
Faeroes (0) 0
Austria: Konsel (Wohlfahrt 86); Baur, Russ, Pfeifenberger (Hortnagl 24), Hartmann, Stoger, Schottel, Herzog, Streuter, Wetl, Ogris A.
Faeroes: Knudsen; Jakobsen, Morkore A, Danielsen, Hansen TE, Simonsen, Nielsen, Hansen A, Dam (Thomassen 71), Reynheim, Rasmussen (Mohr 85).

Copenhagen, 5 June 1991, 12,521
Denmark (1) 2 *(Christensen 2, 77)*
Austria (0) 1 *(Ogris E 83)*
Denmark: Schmeichel; Hansen, Nielsen K, Olsen L, Bruun, Vilfort, Larsen H, Nielsen BS, Nielsen C (Goldbaek 46), Povlsen (Rasmussen E 78), Christensen.
Austria: Konrad; Russ (Prosenik 72), Baur, Hartmann, Pfeifenberger, Streiter, Ogris E, Schottel (Hortnagl 66), Herzog, Stoger, Westerhaler.

Landskrona, Sweden, 11 September 1991, 1623
Faeroes (0) 0
Northern Ireland (3) 5 *(Wilson K 7, Clarke 13, 49, 70 (pen), McDonald 15)*
Faeroes: Knudsen; Jakobsen J (Morkore K 78), Hansen TE, Danielsen, Thomassen (Muller 51), Morkore A, Nielsen, Dam, Hansen A, Reynheim, Jonsson.
Northern Ireland: Wright; Donaghy, Morrow, Taggart, McDonald, Magilton, Dennison, Wilson K (O'Neill 70), Dowie, Clarke, Black (McBride 70).

Landskrona, Sweden, 25 September 1991, 2589
Faeroes (0) 0
Denmark (2) 4 *(Christofte 2 (pen), Christensen 7, Pingel 69, Vilfort 76)*
Faeroes: Knudsen (Johannesen 46); Jakobsen, Hansen TE, Danielsen, Morkore K, Dam, Jarnskor, Jonsson (Davidsen 83), Hansen A, Reynheim, Muller.
Denmark: Schmeichel; Sivebaek, Nielsen K, Olsen L, Larsen H, Christofte (Molby John 60), Jensen J, Vilfort, Povlsen, Christensen, Elstrup (Pingel 68).

Vienna, 9 October 1991, 10,000
Austria (0) 0
Denmark (3) 3 *(Artner (og) 10, Povlsen 16, Christensen 37)*
Austria: Konrad; Prosenik, Baur, Resch, Kogler, Schottel (Gschneidter 46), Ogris A, Artner, Herzog, Stoger, Pacult.
Denmark: Schmeichel; Sivebaek, Nielsen K, Olsen L, Larsen H (Jensen B 81), Christofte (Molby John 59), Jensen J, Vilfort, Povlsen, Christensen, Elstrup.

Landskrona, Sweden, 16 October 1991, 2485
Faeroes (0) 0
Yugoslavia (1) 2 *(Jugovic 18, Savicevic 79)*
Faeroes: Knudsen; Jakobsen, Hansen TE, Danielsen, Morkore K, Dam, Morkore A, Jonsson (Jarnskor 88), Hansen A, Reynheim, Muller.
Yugoslavia: Omerovic; Spasic, Hadzibegic, Najdovski, Brnovic, Jugovic, Jokanovic, Bazdarevic, Mihajlovic (Mijatovic 63), Lukic (Stanic 80), Savicevic.

Windsor Park, 16 October 1991, 8000
Northern Ireland (2) 2 *(Dowie 17, Black 40)*
Austria (1) 1 *(Lainer 44)*
Northern Ireland: Wright; Donaghy, Hill, Taggart, Worthington, Dennison, Magilton, Wilson K, Black, Dowie, Clarke (Wilson D 46).
Austria: Knaller; Lainer, Rotter, Hartmann, Kogler, Zsak, Ogris A, Artner, Keglevits (Herzog 62), Stoger (Westerthaler 62), Garger.

Odense, 13 November 1991, 10,881
Denmark (2) 2 *(Povlsen 22, 36)*
Northern Ireland (0) 1 *(Taggart 71)*
Denmark: Schmeichel; Sivebaek, Olsen L, Nielsen K, Vilfort, Christofte, Povlsen, Molby John, Larsen H, Piechnik, Elstrup (Pingel 53).
Northern Irleand: Fettis; Donaghy, Hill, Taggart, Worthington, McBride, Hughes, Magilton, Wilson K, Black (Dennison 83), Clarke (Dowie 67).

Vienna, 13 November 1991, 8000
Austria (0) 0
Yugoslavia (2) 2 *(Lukic 19, Savicevic 39)*
Austria: Knaller; Zsak, Garger, Kogler, Artner, Gager, Stoger (Keglevits 53), Herzog, Lainer, Ogris A, Westerthaler (Baur 73).
Yugoslavia: Omerovic; Hadzibegic, Vujacic, Milanic, Novak (Brnovic 81), Jokanovic, Savicevic, Bazdarevic, Mihajlovic, Lukic (Mijatovic 46), Pancev.

	P	W	D	L	F	A	Pts
Yugoslavia	8	7	0	1	24	4	14
Denmark	8	6	1	1	18	7	13
Northern Ireland	8	2	3	3	11	11	7
Austria	8	1	1	6	6	14	3
Faeroes	8	1	1	6	3	26	3

Yugoslavia qualified

Group 5

Cardiff (Ninian Park), 17 October 1990, 12,000
Wales (1) 3 *(Rush 29, Saunders 86, Hughes 88)*
Belgium (1) 1 *(Versavel 24)*
Wales: Southall; Ratcliffe, Blackmore, Young, Aizlewood, Bodin, Horne, Nicholas, Hughes, Rush, Saunders.
Belgium: Preud'homme; Gerets, Grun, Demol, De Wolf, Versavel, Van der Elst, Scifo, Emmers, Ceulemans, Nilis (Wilmots 75).

Luxembourg, 31 October 1990, 9512
Luxembourg (0) 2 *(Girres 57, Langers 65)*
West Germany (2) 3 *(Klinsmann 16, Bein 30, Voller 49)*
Luxembourg: Van Rijswick; Malget, Petry, Bossi, Birsens, Groff, Hellers, Girres, Salbene (Jeitz 85), Weis, Langers.
West Germany: Illgner; Binz, Berthold, Kohler, Strunz, Hassler, Matthaus, Bein (Reinhardt 73), Brehme, Klinsmann, Voller.

Luxembourg, 14 November 1990, 6800
Luxembourg (0) 0
Wales (1) 1 *(Rush 15)*
Luxembourg: Van Rijswick; Malget, Bossi, Birsens, Petry, Morocutti (Krings 60), Hellers, Girres, Salbene, Weis, Langers.
Wales: Southall; Blackmore, Bodin, Aizlewood, Young, Hughes, Ratcliffe, Horne, Nicholas, Rush (Speed 83), Saunders (Allen 88).

Brussels, 27 February 1991, 24,505
Belgium (3) 3 *(Vandenbergh 7, Ceulemans 17, Scifo 36)*
Luxembourg (0) 0
Belgium: Preud'homme; Grun, Albert, Emmers, Versavel, Dauwen, Scifo, Ceulemans, Degryse, Vandenbergh, Wilmots.
Luxembourg: Koch; Malget (Jeitz 46), Bossi, Birsens, Petry, Groff (Scuto 75), Hellers, Girres, Salbene, Weis, Krings.

Brussels, 27 March 1991, 25,000
Belgium (0) 1 *(Degryse 47)*
Wales (0) 1 *(Saunders 58)*
Belgium: Preud'homme; Gerets, Albert, Grun, Clijsters, Versavel, Van der Elst, Scifo, Degryse, Vandenbergh, Wilmots.
Wales: Southall; Phillips, Ratcliffe, Young, Aizlewood, Bodin, Horne, Nicholas, Hughes, Rush, Saunders.

Hanover, 1 May 1991, 56,000
West Germany (1) 1 *(Matthaus 3)*
Belgium (0) 0
West Germany: Illgner; Berthold, Reuter, Beiersdorfer, Brehme, Hassler, Sammer, Matthaus, Doll, Klinsmann (Helmer 77), Voller (Riedle 88).
Belgium: Preud'homme; Emmers, Crasson, Grun, Albert, Van der Elst, Scifo, Vervoort, Versavel, Degryse, Wilmots (Nilis 77).

Cardiff (Arms Park), 5 June 1991, 38,000
Wales (0) 1 *(Rush 69)*
West Germany (0) 0
Wales: Southall; Phillips, Melville, Bodin, Aizlewood, Ratcliffe, Nicholas, Saunders (Speed 89), Rush, Hughes, Horne.
West Germany: Illgner; Reuter, Brehme, Kohler, Berthold, Buchwald, Helmer, Sammer (Effenberg 76), Matthaus (Doll 46), Klinsmann, Voller.

Luxembourg, 11 September 1991, 9000
Luxembourg (0) 0
Belgium (1) 2 *(Scifo 23, Degryse 48)*
Luxembourg: Van Rijswick; Jeitz, Bossi, Petry, Wolf, Mirsens, Girres, Hellers, Groff, Langers (Thome 66), Morocutti (Krings 77).
Belgium: Preud'homme; Grun (Medved 75), Van der Elst, Demol (Dauwen 79), Borkelmans, Emmers, Staelens, Scifo, Vervoort, Degryse, Nilis.

Nuremberg, 16 October 1991, 46,000
West Germany (3) 4 *(Moller 34, Voller 39, Riedle 44, Doll 69)*
Wales (0) 1 *(Bodin 85 (pen))*
West Germany: Illgner; Binz, Reuter, Kohler, Buchwald, Brehme, Matthaus, Moller, Doll (Effenberg 74), Voller, Riedle (Hassler 65).
Wales: Southall; Ratcliffe, Bodin, Young (Giggs 86), Bowen, Hughes, Melville, Maguire (Speed 46), Horne, Rush, Saunders.

Cardiff (Arms Park), 13 November 1991, 20,000
Wales (0) 1 *(Bodin 82 (pen))*
Luxembourg (0) 0
Wales: Southall; Phillips, Bowen (Bodin 72), Aizlewood, Young, Melville (Giggs 62), Horne, Nicholas, Rush, Hughes, Speed.
Luxembourg: Van Rijswick; Bossi, Birsens, Petry, Wolf, Girres (Jeitz 87), Hellers, Weis, Groff, Langers (Krings 69), Malget.

Brussels, 20 November 1991, 26,000
Belgium (0) 0
West Germany (1) 1 *(Voller 15)*
Belgium: Preud'homme; Emmers, Grun, Demol (Medved 46), Albert, Borkelmans, Degryse, Scifo, Walem, Boffin, Wilmots (Nilis 67).
West Germany: Illgner; Reuter, Buchwald, Binz, Kohler, Brehme, Doll, Matthaus, Moller (Effenberg 80), Voller, Riedle.

Leverkusen, 17 December 1991, 24,500
West Germany (2) 4 *(Matthaus 15 (pen), Buchwald 44, Riedle 51, Hassler 62)*
Luxembourg (0) 0
West Germany: Illgner; Kohler, Binz, Buchwald, Reuter, Moller (Bein 70), Matthaus, Doll (Hassler 46), Brehme, Riedle, Voller.
Luxembourg: Van Rijswick; Petry, Bossi, Birsens, Girres (Jeitz 83), Weis, Hellers, Groff (Holtz 76), Wolf, Malget, Langers.

	P	W	D	L	F	A	Pts
West Germany	6	5	0	1	13	4	10
Wales	6	4	1	1	8	6	9
Belgium	6	2	1	3	7	6	5
Luxembourg	6	0	0	6	2	14	0

West Germany qualified

Group 6

Helsinki, 12 September 1990, 10,242

Finland (0) 0

Portugal (0) 0

Finland: Huttunen; Rinne, Holmgren, Europaeus, Heikkinen, Petaja, Tarkkio (Paavola 73), Litmanen, Jarvinen (Myyry 84), Hjelm, Paatelainen.
Portugal: Silvino; Joao Pinto, Veloso, Ferreira, Venancio, Fonseca (Pacheco 63), Paneira, Andre, Jaime Pacheco, Rui Barros, Rui Aguas (Cadete 46).

Oporto, 17 October 1990, 17,198

Portugal (0) 1 *(Rui Aguas 54)*

Holland (0) 0

Portugal: Silvino; Joao Pinto, Veloso, Venancio, Leal, Paneira, Oceano, Semedo (Ferreira 89), Nelo (Carlos Xavier 87), Rui Aguas, Cadete.
Holland: Van Breukelen; De Boer (Gillhaus 75), Blind, Van Tiggelen (Van't Schip 58), Valckx, Rutjes, Vanenburg, Witschge, Bergkamp, Van Basten, Gullit.

Athens, 31 October 1990, 7768

Greece (2) 4 *(Tsiantakis 37, Karapialis 40, Saravakos 59, Borbokis 88)*

Malta (0) 0

Greece: Papadopoulos T; Apostolakis, Papadopoulos Y, Manolas, Kalitzakis, Tsiantakis, Tsalouhidis, Karapialis, Kofidis, Saravakos, Dimitriadis (Borbokis 31).
Malta: Cini; Carabott, Vella S, Galea, Scerri, Buttigieg, Vella R, Suda (Degiorgio 46), Laferla, Zerafa, Busuttil.

Rotterdam, 21 November 1990, 25,430

Holland (2) 2 *(Bergkamp 7, Van Basten 18)*

Greece (0) 0

Holland: Van Breukelen; De Jong, Blind, Rutjes, Vanenburg, Wouters, Bergkamp (Winter 80), Witschge, Van't Schip, Van Basten, Roy.
Greece: Papadopoulos T; Apostolakis, Papadopoulos Y, Manolas, Kalitzakis, Tsalouhidis, Kofidis (Karageorgiou 53), Karapialis, Tsiantakis, Saravakos, Borbokis.

Ta'Quali, 25 November 1990, 7200

Malta (0) 1 *(Suda 74)*

Finland (0) 1 *(Holmgren 87)*

Malta: Cluett; Buttigieg, Vella S, Galea, Scerri, Vella R, Laferla, Degiorgio, Carabott, Busuttil, Zarb (Suda 71).
Finland: Huttunen; Europaeus, Rinne (Petaja 46), Heikkinen, Holmgren, Myyry, Litmanen, Hjelm, Tauriainen, Tarkkio (Tegelberg 79), Paatelainen.

Ta'Qali, 19 December 1990, 10,254

Malta (0) 0

Holland (3) 8 *(Van Basten 9, 20, 23, 64, 80 (pen), Winter 53, Bergkamp 60, 66)*

Malta: Cluett; Camilleri E (Suda 46), Camilleri J, Galea, Laferla, Vella S, Carabott, Degiorgio, Scerri, Busuttil, Vella R.
Holland: Van Breukelen; Blind, De Jong, De Boer, Wouters, Koeman E (Winter 46), Bergkamp (Van den Brom 71), Van't Schip, Gullit, Van Basten, Roy.

Athens, 23 January 1991, 20,000

Greece (1) 3 *(Borbokis 7, Manolas 68, Tsalouhidis 85)*

Portugal (1) 2 *(Rui Aguas 18, Futre 62)*

Greece: Sarganis; Apostolakis, Papadopoulos Y, Manolas, Kalitzakis, Tsalouhidis, Kofidis (Athanassiadis 69), Tursunidis, Tsiantakis, Borbokis (Dimitriadis 65), Saravakos.
Portugal: Vitor Baia; Joao Pinto, Veloso, Leal, Venancio, Paneira, Oceano, Rui Barros (Cadete 71), Futre, Rui Aguas, Sousa.

Ta'Qali, 9 February 1991, 5000
Malta (0) 0
Portugal (1) 1 *(Futre 27)*
Malta: Cluett; Vella S, Azzopardi, Galea, Laferla, Buttigieg, Busuttil, Vella R, Suda, Degiorgio, Zerafa.
Portugal: Vitor Baia; Joao Pinto, Leal, Venancio, Veloso, Oceano, Paneira, Rui Barros (Cadete 67), Rui Aguas, Futre (Sousa 63), Semedo.

Oporto, 20 February 1991, 5303
Portugal (3) 5 *(Rui Aguas 5, Leal 33, Paneira 41 (pen), Futre 48, Cadete 81)*
Malta (0) 0
Portugal: Vitor Baia; Joao Pinto (Cadete 46), Leal, Venancio (Madeira 67), Veloso, Oceano, Peneira, Sousa, Rui Aguas, Futre, Semedo.
Malta: Cluett; Vella S, Azzopardi, Camilleri J (Scerri 38), Laferla, Buttigieg, Busuttil, Vella R, Suda (Carabott 51), Degiorgio, Zerafa.

Rotterdam, 13 March 1991, 40,000
Holland (1) 1 *(Van Basten 31 (pen))*
Malta (0) 0
Holland: Van Breukelen; Blind, Vink, De Boer (Kieft 46), Van't Schip, Wouters, Witschge, Gullit, Bergkamp, Van Basten, Roy (Vanenburg 69).
Malta: Cini; Laferla, Camilleri E, Vella S, Brincat (Suda 86), Camilleri J, Azzopardi (Saliba 89), Scerri, Vella R, Degiorgio, Zerafa.

Rotterdam, 17 April 1991, 25,000
Holland (1) 2 *(Van Basten 9, Gullit 75)*
Finland (0) 0
Holland: Van Breukelen; Blind, Vink, De Jong, Gullit, Wouters, Bergkamp (Kieft 72), Witschge, Van't Schip, Van Basten (Rutjes 76), Huistra.
Finland: Huttunen; Kanerva, Heikkinen, Europaeus, Holmgren, Ukkonen, Petaja, Litmanen (Tegelberg 46), Myyry, Tauriainen (Nyssonen 83), Paatelainen.

Helsinki, 16 May 1991, 5150
Finland (0) 2 *(Jarvinen 51, Litmanen 88)*
Malta (0) 0
Finland: Huttunen; Petaja, Holmgren, Heikkinen, Kanerva, Myyry, Litmanen, Ukkonen, Tarkkio (Tauriainen 87), Paatelainen (Paavola 63), Jarvinen.
Malta: Cini; Buttigieg, Brincat, Vella S, Camilleri E (Zerafa 70), Laferla, Busuttil, Vella R, Degiorgio, Scerri, Suda.

Helsinki, 5 June 1991, 21,207
Finland (0) 1 *(Holmgren 78)*
Holland (0) 1 *(De Boer 60)*
Finland: Huttunen; Petaja, Heikkinen, Ukkonen (Hjelm 81), Holmgren, Paavola, Myyry, Litmanen, Jarvinen, Tarkkio, Paatelainen (Tegelberg 66).
Holland: Hiele, Rutjes, Blind, Wouters, De Boer, Koeman R, Winter, Witschge, Van't Schip, Van Basten, Huistra (Kieft 75).

Oporto, 11 September 1991, 30,000
Portugal (1) 1 *(Cesar Brito 22)*
Finland (0) 0
Portugal: Vitor Baia; Joao Pinto, Samuel, Fernando Couto, Leal, Veloso, Cesar Brito (Cadete 80), Rui Barros, Rui Aguas (Oceano 56), Futre, Manuel Guimaraes.
Finland: Huttunen; Tauriainen (Vuorela 59), Holmgren, Heikkinen, Petaja, Pavola, Myyry, Ukkonen (Litmanen 72), Jarvinen, Tarkkio, Paatelainen.

Helsinki, 9 October 1991, 5225

Finland (0) 1 *(Ukkonen 50)*

Greece (0) 1 *(Tsalouhidis 73)*

Finland: Huttunen; Heikkinen, Holmgren, Petaja, Myyry, Jarvinen (Paatelainen 63), Tarkkio (Tegelberg 82), Ukkonen, Hjelm, Litmanen, Vuorela.
Greece: Sarganis; Apostolakis (Athanassiadis 60), Karageorgiou, Mitsibonas, Kalitzakis, Tsalouhidis, Saravakos, Papaioannou, Borbokis (Tursunidis 70), Karapialis, Tsiantakis.

Rotterdam, 16 October 1991, 50,000

Holland (1) 1 *(Witschge 20)*

Portugal (0) 0

Holland: Van Breukelen; Blind, Koeman R, Van Tiggelen, Koeman E, Wouters, Rijkaard (Winter 70), Witschge (Van't Schip 87), Gullit, Van Basten, Bergkamp.
Portugal: Vitor Baia; Joao Pinto, Leal, Venancio, Fernando Couto, Oceano, Peixe (Cesar Brito 80), Rui Barros, Cadete, Futre, Nelo (Figo 56).

Athens, 30 October 1991, 26,000

Greece (0) 2 *(Saravakos 50, Borbokis 52)*

Finland (0) 0

Greece: Sarganis; Apostolakis, Karageorgiou, Mitsibonas, Tsalouhidis, Kalitzakis, Saravakos, Papaioannou, Athanassiadis (Borbokis 46), Karapialis (Tursunidis 73), Tsiantakis.
Finland: Huttunen; Holmgren, Heikkinen, Petaja, Vuorela (Paatelainen 54), Huhtamaki (Tegelberg 83), Litmanen, Ukkonen, Jarvinen, Tarkkio, Hjelm.

Lisbon, 20 November 1991, 2000

Portugal (1) 1 *(Joao Pinto II 17)*

Greece (0) 0

Portugal: Vitor Baia; Joao Pinto I, Rui Bento, Fernando Couto, Leal, Peixe, Vitor Paneira (Oceano 46), Rui Barros, Joao Pinto II, Semedo (Figo 15), Rui Aguas.
Greece: Sarganis; Apostolakis, Karageorgiou, Mitsibonas, Tsalouhidis, Kalitzakis, Saravakos, Papaioannou (Athanassiadis 64), Borbokis (Dimitriadis 69), Karapiakis, Tsiantakis.

Salonika, 4 December 1991, 32,500

Greece (0) 0

Holland (1) 2 *(Bergkamp 38, Blind 87)*

Greece: Sarganis; Pavlos, Papaioannou (Karageorgiou 46), Lagonidis, Kalitzakis, Mitsibonas, Tsalouhidis, Saravakos, Papadopoulos Y, Tsiantakis, Nioblias, Karapialis (Tursunidis 61).
Holland: Van Breukelen; Blind, Van Tiggelen, Koeman R, Koeman E, Wouters, Rijkaard (Winter 61), Witschge, Bergkamp, Van Basten, Kieft.

Valetta, 22 December 1991, 8000

Malta (1) 1 *(Sultana 42)*

Greece (0) 1 *(Marinakis 67)*

Malta: Cluett; Brincat, Galea, Vella S, Saliba, Laferla, Busuttil, Vella R (Camilleri J 66), Scerri (Sultana 33), Gregory, Degiorgio.
Greece: Plitsis; Papaioannou, Kapouranis, Mitsibonas, Kalitzakis, Tsalouhidis, Thonis (Giotsas 56), Marangos (Marinakis 44), Dimitriadis, Noblias, Tsiantakis.

	P	W	D	L	F	A	Pts
Holland	8	6	1	1	17	2	13
Portugal	8	5	1	2	11	4	11
Greece	8	3	2	3	11	9	8
Finland	8	1	4	3	5	8	6
Malta	8	0	2	6	2	23	2

Holland qualified

Group 7

Wembley, 17 October 1990, 77,040
England (1) 2 *(Lineker 39 (pen), Beardsley 89)*
Poland (0) 0
England: Woods; Dixon, Pearce, Parker, Walker, Wright M, Platt, Gascoigne, Bull (Waddle 56), Lineker (Beardsley 56), Barnes.
Poland: Wandzik; Czachowski, Wdowczyk, Szewczyk, Kaczmarek, Nawrocki, Tarasiewicz, Warzycha R, Furtok (Warzycha K 75), Ziober, Kosecki (Kubicki 85).

Dublin, 17 October 1990, 46,000
Republic of Ireland (2) 5 *(Aldridge 15, 58, 73 (pen), O'Leary 40, Quinn 66)*
Turkey (0) 0
Republic of Ireland: Bonner; Irwin, Staunton, McCarthy, O'Leary, Hughton, Townsend (Moran 73), Houghton, Quinn (Cascarino 66), Aldridge, Sheridan.
Turkey: Engin; Riza, Tugay, Kemal, Gokhan, Erkan (Tanju 46), Bulent, Oguz, Mehmet, Hami, Sercan (Metin 46).

Dublin, 14 November 1990, 45,000
Republic of Ireland (0) 1 *(Cascarino 79)*
England (0) 1 *(Platt 67)*
Republic of Ireland: Bonner; Morris, Staunton, McCarthy, O'Leary, Whelan (McLoughlin 74), McGrath, Houghton, Quinn (Cascarino 62), Aldridge, Townsend.
England: Woods; Dixon, Pearce, Adams, Walker, Wright M, Platt, Cowans, Beardsley, Lineker, McMahon.

Istanbul, 14 November 1990, 4868
Turkey (0) 0
Poland (1) 1 *(Dziekanowski 37)*
Turkey: Engin; Riza, Uiken (Mehmet 67), Bulent, Gokhan, Yusuf, Muhammet (Sercan 67), Unal, Oguz, Tanju, Hami.
Poland: Wandzik; Kubicki, Kaczmarek, Wdowczyk, Warzycha R, Nawrocki, Tarasiewicz, Prusik, Warzycha K, Dziekanowski (Ziober 74), Kosecki.

Wembley, 27 March 1991, 77,753
England (1) 1 *(Dixon 9)*
Republic of Ireland (1) 1 *(Quinn 27)*
England: Seaman; Dixon, Pearce, Adams (Sharpe 46), Walker, Wright M, Robson, Platt, Beardsley, Lineker (Wright I 75), Barnes.
Republic of Ireland: Bonner; Irwin, Staunton, O'Leary, Moran, Townsend, McGrath, Houghton, Quinn, Aldridge (Cascarino 70), Sheedy.

Warsaw, 17 April 1991, 1000
Poland (0) 3 *(Tarasiewicz 75, Urban 81, Kosecki 88)*
Turkey (0) 0
Poland: Wandzik; Kubicki, Kaczmarek (Czachowski 62), Wdowczyk, Jakolcewicz, Warzycha K, Warzycha R, Tarasiewicz, Urban, Kosecki, Ziober (Soczynski 70).
Turkey: Engin; Riza, Tayfun, Gokhan, Kemal, Bulent, Feyyaz (Faruk 80), Muhammet, Mehmet, Tanju, Abdullah (Osman 70).

Dublin, 1 May 1991, 48,000
Republic of Ireland (0) 0
Poland (0) 0
Republic of Ireland: Bonner; Irwin, Staunton, O'Leary, Moran, Townsend, McGrath, Houghton, Quinn (Slaven 70), Aldridge (Cascarino 70), Sheedy.
Poland: Wandzik; Kubicki, Jakolcewicz, Wdowczyk, Soczynski, Warzycha R, Tarasiewicz, Czachowski, Furtok (Kosecki 89), Urban (Warzycha K 88), Szewczyk.

Izmir, 1 May 1991, 20,000
Turkey (0) 0
England (1) 1 *(Wise 32)*

Turkey: Hayrettin; Riza, Ogun, Gokhan, Recap, Muhammet, Unal, Ridvan, Mehmet, Tanju, Ali (Feyyaz 72).
England: Seaman; Dixon; Pearce, Wise, Walker, Pallister, Platt, Thomas G (Hodge 46), Smith, Lineker, Barnes.

Poznan, 16 October 1991, 17,000
Poland (0) 3 *(Czachowski 54, Furtok 76, Urban 87)*
Republic of Ireland (1) 3 *(McGrath 10, Townsend 62, Cascarino 68)*

Poland: Wandzik; Kubicki (Lesiak 32), Czachowski, Soczynski, Wdowczyk, Nawrocki (Skrzypczak 81), Tarasiewicz, Ziober, Urban, Kosecki, Furtok.
Republic of Ireland: Bonner; Morris, Staunton (Phelan 56), Irwin, McGrath, Moran, O'Leary, Sheedy, Keane, Townsend, Cascarino.

Wembley, 16 October 1991, 50,896
England (1) 1 *(Smith 21)*
Turkey (0) 0

England: Woods; Dixon, Pearce, Batty, Walker, Mabbutt, Robson, Platt, Smith, Lineker, Waddle.
Turkey: Hayrettin; Recep, Ogun, Gokhan, Tugay, Turhan, Feyyaz (Hami 76), Riza, Unal, Oguz, Orhan.

Istanbul, 13 November 1991, 42,000
Turkey (1) 1 *(Riza 12 (pen))*
Republic of Ireland (1) 3 *(Byrne 7, 58, Cascarino 55)*

Turkey: Hayrettin; Recep (Bulent 69), Turhan, Gokhan, Tugay, Ogun, Feyyaz (Ridvan 46), Riza, Hami, Oguz, Orhan.
Republic of Ireland: Bonner; Hughton, O'Leary, McCarthy, Phelan, Byrne, McGrath, Staunton, Sheedy, Cascarino, Aldridge.

Poznan, 13 November 1991, 15,000
Poland (1) 1 *(Szewczyk 32)*
England (0) 1 *(Lineker 77)*

Poland: Bako; Warzycha R, Szewczyk (Fedoruk 77), Waldoch, Soczynski, Czachowski, Kosecki, Skrzypczak (Kowalczyk 79), Ziober, Furtok, Urban.
England: Woods; Dixon, Pearce, Gray (Smith 46), Walker, Mabbutt, Platt, Thomas, Rocastle, Lineker, Sinton (Daley 70).

	P	W	D	L	F	A	Pts
England	6	3	3	0	7	3	9
Republic of Ireland	6	2	4	0	13	6	8
Poland	6	2	3	1	8	6	7
Turkey	6	0	0	6	1	14	0

England qualified

EUROPEAN CHAMPIONSHIP 1992

(Final tournament in Sweden)

Denmark's success in the 1992 European Championship blasted a gaping hole through the theory that there has to be endless preparation to achieve victory in an international tournament. Pitchforked into the finals on the exclusion of Yugoslavia, they survived unimpressive performances against England and Sweden before putting their game together against France. Then, despite crippling injuries in the match with Holland they managed to win the resultant penalty shoot-out to reach the final. There they displayed much of the character and determination which has epitomised their football down the years, but above all showed a high skill factor. While this was not as previously revealed in the 1984 European Championship and in the early stages of the 1986 World Cup, it was sufficient to win what was a largely disappointing tournament. The Danish win over Germany in the final was well merited, the Germans being forced to resort to the kind of questionable strong-arm tactics which have sadly risen to the surface in times of stress.

Denmark aside, it was difficult to find anything worth savouring, though Scotland gave everything and fully deserved their one victory over the CIS, who were the least enterprising team in a poor competition. The Scots had in Richard Gough, one of the outstanding players in Sweden.

The Dutch promised much, looked controlled and stylish until unsettled by the swift counter-attacking down the flanks by the Danes. They never recovered their composure and it would have been a travesty of justice had they survived the penalty shoot-out.

For Germany, it was a devastating disappointment to fail in the final. They had lost their inspirational captain and midfield maestro Lothar Matthaus before the tournament began. His successor Rudi Voller lasted one half of the first game before departing with an injured arm and they also suffered injuries to key defenders during the matches in Sweden, but were no more affected than the Danes in this respect.

France, who had been wrongly designated as favourites were clearly well past their peak, but Sweden again showed that the host country has an immense advantage and responded well enough to reach the semi-finals.

For England, it was another failure. Robbed of the services of key players themselves like Paul Gascoigne, John Barnes and Mark Wright, they were never allowed a settled side. Perhaps the saddest sight was the departure from international football of Gary Lineker, withdrawn in the match with Sweden, still one goal short of equalling Bobby Charlton's record of goals.

Group 1

Stockholm, 10 June 1992, 29,860

Sweden (1) 1 *(Ericksson 25)*

France (0) 1 *(Papin 58)*

Sweden: Ravelli; Nilsson R, Eriksson J, Andersson P, Bjorklund, Schwarz, Ingesson, Thern, Limpar, Brolin, Andersson K (Dahlin 74).
France: Martini; Angloma (Fernandez 66), Amoros, Blanc, Casoni, Boli, Deschamps, Sauzee, Vahirua (Perez 46), Papin, Cantona.
Referee: A. Spirin (CIS).

Malmo, 11 June 1992, 26,385

Denmark (0) 0

England (0) 0

Denmark: Schmeichel; Sivebaek, Nielsen, Olsen, Andersen, Christofte, Jensen, Vilfort, Laudrup, Povlsen, Christensen.
England: Woods; Curle (Daley 65), Pearce, Palmer, Keown, Walker, Steven, Platt, Smith, Lineker, Merson (Webb 73).
Referee: J. Blankenstein (Holland).

Malmo, 14 June 1992, 26,535

England (0) 0

France (0) 0

England: Woods; Steven, Pearce, Palmer, Keown, Walker, Batty, Platt, Shearer, Lineker, Sinton.
France: Martini; Amoros, Blanc, Boli, Casoni, Deschamps, Sauzee (Angloma 46), Fernandez (Perez 74), Durand, Cantona, Papin.
Referee: S. Puhl (Hungary).

Stockholm, 14 June 1992, 29,902

Sweden (0) 1 *(Brolin 59)*

Denmark (0) 0

Sweden: Ravelli; Nilsson R, Eriksson J, Andersson P, Bjorklund, Limpar (Erlingmark 89), Thern, Schwarz, Ingesson, Brolin, Dahlin (Ekstrom 75).
Denmark: Schmeichel; Sivebaek, Nielsen, Olsen, Andersen, Christofte, Jensen (Larsen 64), Vilfort, Laudrup, Povlsen, Christensen (Frank 51).
Referee: A. Schmidhuber (Germany).

Malmo, 17 June 1992, 25,763

Denmark (1) 2 *(Larsen 7, Elstrup 77)*

France (0) 1 *(Papin 60)*

Denmark: Schmeichel; Sivebaek, Nielsen (Piechnik 62), Olsen, Christofte, Andersen, Larsen, Jensen, Laudrup (Elstrup 69), Frank, Povlsen.
France: Martini; Boli, Blanc, Casoni, Amoros, Deschamps, Perez (Cocard 81), Divert, Papin, Cantona, Vahirua (Fernandez 46).
Referee: H. Forstinger (Austria).

Stockholm, 17 June 1992, 30,126

Sweden (0) 2 *(Eriksson 51, Brolin 82)*

England (1) 1 *(Platt 3)*

Sweden: Ravelli; Nilsson R, Eriksson J, Andersson P, Bjorklund, Schwarz, Ingesson, Thern, Limpar (Ekstrom 46), Brolin, Dahlin.
England: Woods; Batty, Pearce, Palmer, Keown, Walker, Daley, Webb, Platt, Lineker (Smith 64), Sinton (Merson 79).
Referee: J. Rosa dos Santos (Portugal).

	P	W	D	L	F	A	Pts
Sweden	3	2	1	0	4	2	5
Denmark	3	1	1	1	2	2	3
France	3	0	2	1	2	3	2
England	3	0	2	1	1	2	2

Group 2

Norrkoping, 12 June 1992, 17,410

CIS (0) 1 *(Dobrovolski 62 (pen))*

Germany (0) 1 *(Hassler 90)*

CIS: Kharin; Chernishev, Kuznetsov O, Tsveiba, Kanchelskis, Kuznetsov
D, Mikhailichenko, Shalimov (Ivanov 83), Kolyvanov, Dobrovolski, Lyuty
(Onopko 46).
Germany: Illgner; Reuter (Klinsmann 62), Kohler, Binz, Buchwald, Brehme,
Effenberg, Hassler, Dodd, Voller (Moller 46), Riedle.
Referee: G. Biguet (France).

Gothenburg, 12 June 1992, 35,720

Holland (0) 1 *(Bergkamp 76)*

Scotland (0) 0

Holland: Van Breukelen; Van Aerle, Van Tiggelen, Koeman, Witschge,
Wouters (Jonk 55), Bergkamp (Winter 86), Rijkaard, Van Basten, Gullit,
Roy.
Scotland: Goram; Gough, McKimmie, McStay, Malpas, McPherson, Durie,
McCall, McCoist (Gallacher 75), McClair (Ferguson 79), McAllister.
Referee: B. Karlsson (Sweden).

Gothenburg, 15 June 1992, 34,440

Holland (0) 0

CIS (0) 0

Holland: Van Breukelen; Van Aerle, Van Tiggelen, Koeman, Witschge,
Wouters, Bergkamp, Rijkaard, Van Basten, Gullit (Van't Schip 71), Roy.
CIS: Kharin; Chernishev, Onopko, Tsveiba, Kuznetsov O, Aleinikov
(Kuznetsov D 56), Kanchelskis, Youran (Kiryakov 64), Mikhailichenko,
Dobrovolski, Kolyvanov.
Referee: P. Mikkelsen (Denmark).

Norrkoping, 15 June 1992, 17,638

Scotland (0) 0

Germany (1) 2 *(Riedle 28, Effenberg 47)*

Scotland: Goram; McKimmie, Malpas, Gough, McPherson, McStay, Durie
(Nevin 54), McCall, McClair, McCoist (Gallacher 70), McAllister.
Germany: Illgner; Brehme, Kohler, Binz, Buchwald, Moller, Hassler, Riedle
(Reuter 68) (Schulz 74), Sammer, Effenberg, Klinsmann.

Norrkoping, 18 June 1992, 14,660

Scotland (2) 3 *(McStay 6, McClair 17, McAllister 83 (pen))*

CIS (0) 0

Scotland: Goram; McKimmie, Boyd, Gough, McPherson, McAllister, McStay, McCall, McClair, McCoist (McInally 67), Gallacher (Nevin 78).
CIS: Kharin; Chernisev, Tzhadadze, Kuznetsov O, Mikhailichenko, Aleinikov (Kuznetsov D 46), Dobrovolski, Youran, Kanchelskis, Kiryakov (Korneyev 46), Onopko.
Referee: K. Rothlisberger (Switzerland).

Gothenburg, 18 June 1992, 37,725

Holland (2) 3 *(Rijkaard 3, Witschge 15, Bergkamp 73)*

Germany (0) 1 *(Klinsmann 53)*

Holland: Van Breukelen; De Boer (Winter 62), Van Tiggelen, Koeman, Rijkaard, Witschge, Wouters, Bergkamp (Bosz 87), Van Basten, Gullit, Roy.
Germany: Illgner; Kohler, Binz (Sammer 46), Frontzeck, Brehme, Effenberg, Hassler, Helmer, Moller, Riedle (Doll 76), Klinsmann.
Referee: P. Pairetto (Italy).

	P	W	D	L	F	A	Pts
Holland	3	2	1	0	4	1	5
Germany	3	1	1	1	4	4	3
Scotland	3	1	0	2	3	3	2
CIS	3	0	2	1	1	4	2

Semi-finals

Stockholm, 21 June 1992, 28,827

Sweden (0) 2 *(Brolin 63 (pen), Andersson 89)*

Germany (1) 3 *(Hassler 11, Riedle 58, 88)*

Sweden: Ravelli; Nilsson R, Eriksson J, Bjorklund, Ingesson, Thern, Brolin, Andersson K, Dahlin (Ekstrom 72), Ljung, Nilsson J (Limpar 59).
Germany: Illgner; Reuter, Brehme, Kohler, Buchwald, Hassler, Riedle, Helmer, Sammer, Effenberg, Klinsmann.
Referee: T. Lanese (Italy).

Gothenburg, 22 June 1992, 37,450

Denmark (2) 2 *(Larsen 6, 33)*

Holland (1) 2 *(Bergkamp 23, Rijkaard 86)*

Denmark: Schmeichel; Piechnik, Olsen, Christofte, Sivebaek, Vilfort, Jensen, Laudrup (Elstrup 57), Andersen (Christiansen 70), Larsen, Povlsen.
Holland: Van Breukelen; Van Tiggelen, De Boer (Kieft 46), Koeman, Rijkaard, Witschge, Wouters, Bergkamp, Van Basten, Gullit, Roy (Van't Schip 116).
aet; Denmark won 5-4 on penalties
Referee: S. Aladren (Spain).

Penalty shoot-out: Holland: Koeman (scored), Van Basten (shot saved), Bergkamp, Rijkaard, Witschge (scored); *Denmark:* Larsen, Povlsen, Elstrup, Vilfort, Christofte (scored).

Final

Gothenburg, 26 June 1992, 37,800

Denmark (1) 2 *(Jensen 18, Vilfort 78)*

Germany (0) 0

Denmark: Schmeichel; Sivebaek (Christiansen 65), Nielsen, Olsen, Christofte, Jensen, Povlsen, Laudrup, Piechnik, Larsen, Vilfort.
Germany: Illgner; Reuter, Brehme, Kohler, Buchwald, Hassler, Riedle, Helmer, Sammer (Doll 46), Effenberg (Thon 78), Klinsmann.
Referee: B. Galler *(Switzerland).*

OLYMPIC FOOTBALL

Previous winners

1896	Athens*	1.	Denmark	1956	Melbourne	1.	USSR
		2.	Greece			2.	Yugoslavia
1900	Paris*	1.	England			3.	Bulgaria
		2.	France	1960	Rome	1.	Yugoslavia
1904	St Louis**	1.	Canada			2.	Denmark
		2.	USA			3.	Hungary
1908	London	1.	England	1964	Tokyo	1.	Hungary
		2.	Denmark			2.	Czechoslovakia
		3.	Holland			3.	East Germany
1912	Stockholm	1.	England	1968	Mexico City	1.	Hungary
		2.	Denmark			2.	Bulgaria
		3.	Holland			3.	Japan
1920	Antwerp	1.	Belgium	1972	Munich	1.	Poland
		2.	Spain			2.	Hungary
		3.	Holland			3.	East Germany/
1924	Paris	1.	Uruguay				USSR joint bronze
		2.	Switzerland	1976	Montreal	1.	East Germany
		3.	Sweden			2.	Poland
1928	Amsterdam	1.	Uruguay			3.	USSR
		2.	Argentina	1980	Moscow	1.	Czechoslovakia
		3.	Italy			2.	East Germany
1932	Los Angeles no competition					3.	USSR
1936	Berlin	1.	Italy	1984	Los Angeles	1.	France
		2.	Austria			2.	Brazil
		3.	Norway			3.	Yugoslavia
1948	London	1.	Sweden	1988	Seoul	1.	USSR
		2.	Yugoslavia			2.	Brazil
		3.	Denmark			3.	West Germany
1952	Helsinki	1.	Hungary				
		2.	Yugoslavia				
		3.	Sweden				

*No official tournament
**No official tournament but gold medal later awarded by IOC

THE WORLD CUP FINALS

Uruguay 1930
URUGUAY 4, ARGENTINA 2 (1–2) *Montevideo*
Uruguay: Ballesteros; Nasazzi (capt), Mascheroni, Andrade, Fernandez, Gestido, Dorado, Scarone, Castro, Cea, Iriarte. **Scorers:** Dorado, Cea, Iriarte, Castro.
Argentina: Botasso; Della, Torre, Paternoster, Evaristo, J., Monti, Suarez, Peucelle, Varallo, Stabile, Ferreira (capt), Evaristo, M. **Scorers:** Peucelle, Stabile.
Leading scorer: Stabile (Argentina) 8.

Italy 1934
ITALY 2, CZECHOSLOVAKIA 1 (0–0) (1–1)* *Rome*
Italy: Combi (capt); Monseglio, Allemandi, Ferraris IV, Monti, Bertolini, Guaita, Meazza, Schiavio, Ferrari, Orsi. **Scorers:** Orsi, Schiavio.
Czechoslovakia: Planicka (capt); Zenisek, Ctyroky, Kostalek, Cambal, Krcil, Junek, Svoboda, Sobotka, Nejedly, Puc. **Scorer:** Puc.
Leading scorers: Schiavio (Italy), Nejedly (Czechoslovakia), Conen (Germany) each 4.

France 1938
ITALY 4, HUNGARY 2 (3–1) *Paris*
Italy: Olivieri; Foni, Rava, Serantoni, Andreolo, Locatelli, Biavati, Meassa (capt), Piola, Ferrari, Colaussi. **Scorers:** Colaussi 2, Piola 2.
Hungary: Szabo; Polgar, Biro, Szalay, Szucs, Lazar, Vincze, Sarosi (capt), Szengeller, Titkos. **Scorers:** Titkos, Sarosi.
Leading scorer: Leonidas (Brazil) 8.

Brazil 1950
Final pool (replaced knock-out system)

Uruguay 2, Spain 2	Brazil 6, Spain 1
Brazil 7, Sweden 1	Sweden 3, Spain 1
Uruguay 3, Sweden 2	Uruguay 2, Brazil 1

Final positions	P	W	D	L	F	A	Pts
Uruguay	3	2	1	0	7	5	5
Brazil	3	2	0	1	14	4	4
Sweden	3	1	0	2	6	11	2
Spain	3	0	1	2	4	11	1

Leading scorers: Ademir (Brazil) 7, Schiaffino (Uruguay), Basora (Spain) 5.

Switzerland 1954
WEST GERMANY 3, HUNGARY 2 (2–2) *Berne*
West Germany: Turek; Posipal, Kohlmeyer, Eckel, Liebrich, Rahn, Morlock, Walter, O., Walter, F. (capt), Schaefer. **Scorers:** Morlock, Rahn 2.
Hungary: Grosics; Buzansky, Lantos, Bozsik, Lorant, Zakarias, Czibor, Kocsis, Hidegkuti, Puskas (capt), Toth, J. **Scorers:** Puskas, Czibor.
Leading scorer: Kocsis (Hungary) 11.

Sweden 1958
BRAZIL 5, SWEDEN 2 (2–1) *Stockholm*
Brazil: Gilmar; Santos, D., Santos, N., Zito, Bellini, Orlando, Garrincha, Didi, Vavà, Pelé, Zagalo **Scorers:** Vavà 2, Pelé 2, Zagalo.
Sweden: Svensson; Bergmark, Axbom, Boerjesson, Gustavsson, Parling, Hamrin, Gren, Simonsson, Liedholm, Skoglund. **Scorers:** Liedholm, Simonsson.
Leading scorer: Fontaine (France) 13 (present record total).

Chile 1962
BRAZIL 3, CZECHOSLOVAKIA 1 (1–1) *Santiago*
Brazil: Gilmar; Santos, D., Mauro, Zozimo, Santos, N., Zito, Didi, Garrincha, Vavà, Amarildo, Zagalo. **Scorers:** Amarildo, Zito, Vavà.
Czechoslovakia: Schroiff; Tichy, Novak, Pluskal, Popluhar, Masopust, Pospichal, Scherer, Kvasniak, Kadraba, Jelinek. **Scorer:** Masopust.
Leading scorer: Jerkovic (Yugoslavia) 5.

England 1966
ENGLAND 4, WEST GERMANY 2 (1–1) (2–2)* *Wembley*
England: Banks; Cohen, Wilson, Stiles, Charlton, J., Moore, Ball, Hurst, Hunt, Charlton, R., Peters. **Scorers:** Hurst 3, Peters.
West Germany: Tilkowski; Hottges, Schulz, Weber, Schnellinger, Haller, Beckenbauer, Overath, Seeler, Held, Emmerich. **Scorers:** Haller, Weber.
Leading scorer: Eusebio (Portugal) 9.

Mexico 1970
BRAZIL 4, ITALY 1 (1–1) *Mexico City*
Brazil: Felix; Carlos Alberto, Piazza, Everaldo, Gerson, Clodoaldo, Jairzinho, Pelé, Tostäo, Rivelino. **Scorers:** Pelé, Gerson, Jairzinho, Carlos Alberto.
Italy: Albertosi; Burgnich, Cera, Rosato, Fachetti, Bertini (Juliano), Riva, Domenghini, Mazzola, De Sista, Boninsegna (Rivera). **Scorer:** Boninsegna.
Leading scorer: Müller (West Germany) 10.

West Germany 1974
WEST GERMANY 2, HOLLAND 1 (2–1) *Munich*
West Germany: Maier; Vogts, Schwarzenbeck, Beckenbauer, Breitner, Bonhof, Hoeness, Overath, Grabowski, Müller, Holzenbein. **Scorers:** Breitner (pen), Müller.
Holland: Jongbloed; Suurbier, Rijsbergen (De Jong), Haan, Krol, Jansen, Van Hanegem, Neeskens, Rep (Nanninga), Cruyff, Rensenbrink (Van der Kerkhof, R.) **Scorer:** Nanninga (pen).
Leading scorer: Lato (Poland) 7.

Argentina 1978
ARGENTINA 3, HOLLAND 1 (1–1)* *Buenos Aires*
Argentina: Fillol; Olguin, Passarella, Galvan, Tarantini, Ardiles (Larrosa), Gallego, Ortiz (Houseman), Bertoni, Luque, Kempes. **Scorers:** Kempes 2, Bertoni.
Holland: Jongbloed; Poortvliet, Brandts, Krol, Jansen (Suurbier), Neeskens, Van der Kerkhof, W., Van der Kerkhof, R., Haan, Rep (Nanninga), Rensenbrink. **Scorer:** Nanninga.
Leading scorer: Kempes (Argentina) 6.

Spain 1982
ITALY 3 WEST GERMANY 1 (0–0) *Madrid*
Italy: Zoff; Bergomi, Cabrini, Collovati, Scirea, Gentile, Oriali, Tardelli, Conti, Graziani (Altobelli), Rossi (Causio). **Scorers:** Rossi, Tardelli, Altobelli.
West Germany: Schumacher; Kaltz, Forster, K-H., Stielike, Forster, B. Breitner, Dremmler (Hrubesch), Littbarski, Briegel, Fischer, Rummenigge (Müller). **Scorer:** Breitner.
Leading scorer: Rossi (Italy) 6.

Mexico 1986
ARGENTINA 3, WEST GERMANY 2 (1–0) *Mexico City*
Argentina: Pumpido; Cuciuffo, Olarticoechea, Ruggeri, Brown, Giusti, Burruchaga (Trobbiani), Batista, Valdano, Maradona, Enrique. **Scorers:** Brown, Valdano, Burruchaga.

West Germany: Schumacher; Berthold, Briegel, Jakobs, Forster, Eder, Brehme, Matthaus, Allofs (Voller), Magath (Hoeness), Rummenigge. **Scorers:** Rummenigge, Voller.
Leading scorer: Lineker (England) 6.

Italy 1990
WEST GERMANY 1, ARGENTINA 0 (0–0) *Rome*
West Germany: Illgner; Berthold (Reuter 73), Kohler, Augenthaler, Buchwald, Brehme, Littbarski, Hässler, Matthäus, Völler, Klinsmann. **Scorer:** Brehme (pen).
Argentina: Goycochea; Lorenzo, Serrizuela, Sensini, Ruggeri (Monzon 46), Simon, Basualdo, Burruchaga (Calderon 53), Maradona, Troglio, Dezotti.
Referee: Codesal (Mexico). Monzon and Dezotti sent off.
Leading scorer: Schillaci (Italy) 6.

**After extra time*

QUALIFYING DRAW FOR USA 1994

OCEANIA (Members 8, Entries 7)
Either one or no team qualifies
First Round (League System)
Group 1: Australia, Solomon Islands, Western Samoa; *Group 2:* New Zealand, Fiji, Tahiti, Vanuatu.
Two group winners qualify for the **Second Round**. The winner of this Second Round (cup system) will compete against the runner-up of the Concacaf preliminaries, the winner of which will then play the team coming fourth in South America.

ASIA (Members 36, Entries 29)
Two teams qualify
First Round (League System)
Group A: China PR, Iraq, Jordan, Yemen, Pakistan; *Group B:* Iran, Syria, Oman, Chinese Taipei, Myanmar; *Group C:* Korea (North), Qatar, Singapore, Vietnam, Indonesia; *Group D:* Korea (South), Bahrain, Hong Kong, Lebanon, India; *Group E*: Saudi Arabia, Kuwait, Malaysia, Macao; *Group F:* United Arab Emirates, Japan, Thailand, Sri Lanka, Bangladesh
In the **Second Round** the six group winners will play in one group (league system) home and away games.

CONCACAF (Members 27, Entries 23)
Two or three teams qualify (including USA the hosts)
Preliminary Round (Cup System)
Group North: (A) Bermuda v Haiti; (B) Dominican Republic/Puerto Rico v Jamaica; (C) St Lucia/St Vincent v Cuba; *Group South:* (D) Netherlands Antilles v Antigua; (E) Guyana v Surinam; (F) Barbados v Trinidad and Tobago.
First Round
Central Region: (1) Guatemala v Honduras; (2) Panama v Costa Rica; (3) Nicaragua v El Salvador; *Caribbean Region:* (1) Winner E v Winner C; (2) Winner A v Winner D; (3) Winner F v Winner B.

Second Round (League System)
Group A: Mexico, Winner Central 1, Winner Caribbean 1, Winner Central 2;
Group B: Canada, Winner Caribbean 2, Winner Central 3, Winner Caribbean 3.

Third Round (League System)
N.B. After elimination games Dominican Republic v Puerto Rico and St Lucia v
St Vincent, preliminary round and First Round games according to cup system.
Canada and Mexico automatically qualify for the Second Round in two groups of
four. Third Round in one group of four. The winners will qualify for the final
competition, while the runner-up competes against the winner of the Oceania
tournament, the winner of which will play the fourth team from South America.

SOUTH AMERICA (Members 10, Entries 9)
Three or four teams qualify
First Round (League System)
Group A: Argentina, Colombia, Paraguay, Peru; *Group B:* Brazil, Bolivia,
Uruguay, Ecuador, Venezuela. The winner in Group A and the winner and runner-
up in Group B qualify for the final competition. The runner-up in Group A will
have to play the winner of the elimination match between Oceania and Concacaf.
Whichever team wins this match will also qualify for the World Cup finals.

AFRICA (Members 48, Entries 37)
Three teams qualify
First Round (League System)
Group A: Algeria, Ghana, Uganda, Burundi; *Group B:* Cameroon, Zaire, Liberia,
Swaziland; *Group C:* Egypt, Zimbabwe, Sierra Leone, Angola; *Group D:* Nigeria,
Congo, Libya, Togo/Sao Tome; *Group E:* Ivory Coast, Sudan, Niger, Botswana;
Group F: Morocco, Tunisia, Malawi, Ethiopia; *Group G:* Senegal, Gabon, Mo-
zambique, Mauritania; *Group H:* Zambia, Madagascar, Burkina Faso, Tanzania;
Group I: Kenya, Guinea, Mali, Gambia.
Elimination match Togo v Sao Tome. First Round in nine groups of four. Group
winners to go into **Second Round** in three groups of three. The three group winners
qualify for the World Cup finals.

EUROPE/ISRAEL (Members 38+1, Entries 38+1)
Thirteen teams qualify (including Germany as holders)
Group 1: Italy, Scotland, Portugal, Switzerland, Malta, Estonia; *Group 2:* England,
Holland, Poland, Norway, Turkey, San Marino; *Group 3:* Spain, Republic of
Ireland, Denmark, Northern Ireland, Albania, Lithuania, Latvia; *Group 4:*
Belgium, Czechoslovakia, Romania, Wales, Cyprus, Faeroes; *Group 5:* USSR
(now CIS), Yugoslavia, Hungary, Greece, Iceland, Luxembourg; *Group 6:* France,
Austria, Sweden, Bulgaria, Finland, Israel.
League system with the winner and runner-up of each group plus Germany as
holders qualify.
Withdrawals: Cuba, Western Samoa, Sierra Leone

Preliminary Competition
Europe/Israel (38 + 1 Entries)
13 teams will qualify (including Germany as current champions)

Group 1
(Italy, Scotland, Portugal, Switzerland, Malta, Estonia)
16. 8.92 Estonia v Switzerland
 9. 9.92 Switzerland v Scotland
14.10.92 Italy v Switzerland
14.10.92 Scotland v Portugal
25.10.92 Malta v Estonia
18.11.92 Scotland v Italy
18.11.92 Switzerland v Malta
19.12.92 Malta v Italy
24. 1.93 Malta v Portugal
17. 2.93 Scotland v Malta
24. 2.93 Portugal v Italy
24. 3.93 Italy v Malta
31. 3.93 Switzerland v Portugal
14. 4.93 Italy v Estonia
17. 4.93 Malta v Switzerland
28. 4.93 Portugal v Scotland
 1. 5.93 Switzerland v Italy
12. 5.93 Estonia v Malta
19. 5.93 Estonia v Scotland
 2. 6.93 Scotland v Estonia
19. 6.93 Portugal v Malta
 5. 9.93 Estonia v Portugal
 8. 9.93 Scotland v Switzerland
22. 9.93 Estonia v Italy
13.10.93 Italy v Scotland
13.10.93 Portugal v Switzerland
10.11.93 Portugal v Estonia
17.11.93 Italy v Portugal
17.11.93 Malta v Scotland
17.11.93 Switzerland v Estonia

Group 2
(England, Holland, Poland, Norway, Turkey, San Marino)
 9. 9.92 Norway v San Marino
23. 9.92 Norway v Holland
23. 9.92 Poland v Turkey
 7.10.92 San Marino v Norway
14.10.92 England v Norway
14.10.92 Holland v Poland
28.10.92 Turkey v San Marino
18.11.92 England v Turkey
16.12.92 Turkey v Holland
17. 2.93 England v San Marino
24. 2.93 Holland v Turkey
10. 3.93 San Marino v Turkey
24. 3.93 Holland v San Marino

31. 3.93 Turkey v England
28. 4.93 England v Holland
28. 4.93 Norway v Turkey
28. 4.93 Poland v San Marino
19. 5.93 San Marino v Poland
29. 5.93 Poland v England
 2. 6.93 Norway v England
 9. 6.93 Holland v Norway
 8. 9.93 England v Poland
22. 9.93 Norway v Poland
22. 9.93 San Marino v Holland
13.10.93 Holland v England
13.10.93 Poland v Norway
27.10.93 Turkey v Poland
10.11.93 Turkey v Norway
16.11.93 San Marino v England
17.11.93 Poland v Holland

Group 3
(Spain, Republic of Ireland, Denmark, Northern Ireland, Albania, Lithuania, Latvia)
22. 4.92 Spain v Albania
28. 4.92 Northern Ireland v Lithuania
26. 5.92 Republic of Ireland v Albania
 3. 6.92 Albania v Lithuania
12. 8.92 Latvia v Lithuania
26. 8.92 Latvia v Denmark
 9. 9.92 Northern Ireland v Albania
 9. 9.92 Republic of Ireland v Latvia
23. 9.92 Lithuania v Denmark
23. 9.92 Latvia v Spain
14.10.92 Denmark v Republic of Ireland
14.10.92 Northern Ireland v Spain
28.10.92 Lithuania v Latvia
11.11.92 Albania v Latvia
18.11.92 Northern Ireland v Denmark
18.11.92 Spain v Republic of Ireland
16.12.92 Spain v Latvia
17. 2.93 Albania v Northern Ireland
24. 2.93 Spain v Lithuania
31. 3.93 Denmark v Spain
31. 3.93 Republic of Ireland v Northern Ireland
14. 4.93 Denmark v Latvia
14. 4.93 Lithuania v Albania
28. 4.93 Republic of Ireland v Denmark
28. 4.93 Spain v Northern Ireland
15. 5.93 Latvia v Albania
25. 5.93 Lithuania v Northern Ireland
26. 5.93 Albania v Republic of Ireland
 2. 6.93 Denmark v Albania
 2. 6.93 Lithuania v Spain

 2. 6.93 Latvia v Northern Ireland
 9. 6.93 Latvia v Republic of Ireland
16. 6.93 Lithuania v Republic of Ireland
25. 8.93 Denmark v Lithuania
 8. 9.93 Albania v Denmark
 8. 9.93 Northern Ireland v Latvia
 8. 9.93 Republic of Ireland v Lithuania
22. 9.93 Albania v Spain
13.10.93 Denmark v Northern Ireland
13.10.93 Republic of Ireland v Spain
17.11.93 Northern Ireland v Republic of Ireland
17.11.93 Spain v Denmark

Group 4
(Belgium, Czechoslovakia, Romania, Wales, Cyprus, Faeroes)
22. 4.92 Belgium v Cyprus
 6. 5.92 Romania v Faeroes
20. 5.92 Romania v Wales
 3. 6.92 Faeroes v Belgium
17. 6.92 Faeroes v Cyprus
 2. 9.92 Czechoslovakia v Belgium
 9. 9.92 Wales v Faeroes
23. 9.92 Czechoslovakia v Faeroes
14.10.92 Belgium v Romania
14.10.92 Cyprus v Wales
14.11.92 Romania v Czechoslovakia
18.11.92 Wales v Belgium
29.11.92 Cyprus v Romania
14. 2.92 Cyprus v Belgium
24. 3.93 Cyprus v Czechoslovakia
31. 3.93 Belgium v Wales
14. 4.93 Romania v Cyprus
25. 4.93 Cyprus v Faeroes
28. 4.93 Czechoslovakia v Wales
22. 5.93 Belgium v Faeroes
 2. 6.93 Czechoslovakia v Romania
 6. 6.93 Faeroes v Wales
16. 6.93 Faeroes v Czechoslovakia
 8. 9.93 Wales v Czechoslovakia
 8. 9.93 Faeroes v Romania
13.10.93 Romania v Belgium
13.10.93 Wales v Cyprus
27.10.93 Czechoslovakia v Cyprus
17.11.93 Belgium v Czechoslovakia
17.11.93 Wales v Romania

Group 5
(CIS, Yugoslavia, Hungary, Greece, Iceland, Luxembourg)
13. 5.92 Greece v Iceland
 3. 6.92 Hungary v Iceland
 2. 9.92 Iceland v Yugoslavia
 9. 9.92 Luxembourg v Hungary
23. 9.92 Yugoslavia v CIS
 7.10.92 Iceland v Greece
14.10.92 Hungary v Yugoslavia
14.10.92 CIS v Iceland
28.10.92 CIS v Luxembourg
11.11.92 Greece v Hungary
15.11.92 Luxembourg v Yugoslavia
17. 2.93 Greece v Luxembourg
31. 3.93 Hungary v Greece
31. 3.93 Yugoslavia v Luxembourg
14. 4.93 Luxembourg v CIS
28. 4.93 CIS v Hungary
28. 4.93 Yugoslavia v Greece
20. 5.93 Luxembourg v Iceland
23. 5.93 CIS v Greece
 2. 6.93 Iceland v CIS
16. 6.93 Iceland v Hungary
22. 8.93 Yugoslavia v Iceland
 8. 9.93 Hungary v CIS
 8. 9.93 Iceland v Luxembourg
 6.10.93 CIS v Yugoslavia
12.10.93 Luxembourg v Greece
27.10.93 Greece v Yugoslavia
27.10.93 Hungary v Luxembourg
17.11.93 Greece v CIS
17.11.93 Yugoslavia v Hungary

Group 6
(France, Austria, Sweden, Bulgaria, Finland, Israel)
14. 5.92 Finland v Bulgaria
 9. 9.92 Bulgaria v France
 9. 9.92 Finland v Sweden
 7.10.92 Sweden v Bulgaria
14.10.92 France v Austria
28.10.92 Austria v Israel
11.11.92 Israel v Sweden
14.11.92 France v Finland
 2.12.92 Israel v Bulgaria
17. 2.93 Israel v France
27. 3.93 Austria v France
14. 4.93 Austria v Bulgaria
28. 4.93 Bulgaria v Finland
28. 4.93 France v Sweden
12. 5.93 Bulgaria v Israel
13. 5.93 Finland v Austria
19. 5.93 Sweden v Austria
 2. 6.93 Sweden v Israel
16. 6.93 Finland v Israel
22. 8.93 Sweden v France
25. 8.93 Austria v Finland
 8. 9.93 Bulgaria v Sweden
 8. 9.93 Finland v France
13.10.93 Bulgaria v Austria
13.10.93 France v Israel
13.10.93 Sweden v Finland
27.10.93 Israel v Austria

10.11.93 Austria v Sweden
10.11.93 Israel v Finland
17.11.93 France v Bulgaria

Concacaf
(23 Entries)
2 or 3 teams will qualify (including USA as hosts)

Pre-preliminary Round
21. 3.92 Dominican Rep v Puerto Rico : L Livingston, Jamaica
29. 3.92 Puerto Rico v Dominican Rep : E Forbes, Trinidad & Tobago
22. 3.92 St Lucia v St Vincent/Grenada : W Peleris, Haiti
29. 3.92 St Vincent/Grenada v St Lucia : R Ramesh, Trinidad & Tobago

Oceania
(7 Entries)
0 or 1 team will qualify

Group 1: Australia, Tahiti, Solomon Islands
Group 2: New Zealand, Fiji, Vanuatu

 6. 6.92 New Zealand v Fiji
12. 9.92 Fiji v Vanuatu
19. 9.92 Fiji v New Zealand
26. 9.92 Vanuatu v Fiji

Conmebol (South America)
(9 Entries)
3 or 4 teams will qualify

Group A (Argentina, Colombia, Paraguay, Peru)
 1. 8.93 Colombia v Paraguay
 1. 8.93 Peru v Argentina
 8. 8.93 Paraguay v Argentina
 8. 8.93 Peru v Colombia
15. 8.93 Colombia v Argentina
15. 8.93 Paraguay v Peru
22. 8.93 Argentina v Peru
22. 8.93 Paraguay v Colombia
29. 8.93 Argentina v Paraguay
29. 8.93 Colombia v Peru
 5. 9.93 Argentina v Colombia
 5. 9.93 Peru v Paraguay

Group B (Brazil, Uruguay, Ecuador, Bolivia, Venezuela)
18. 7.93 Ecuador v Brazil
18. 7.93 Venezuela v Bolivia
25. 7.93 Bolivia v Brazil
25. 7.93 Venezuela v Uruguay
 1. 8.93 Uruguay v Ecuador
 1. 8.93 Venezuela v Brazil
 8. 8.93 Bolivia v Uruguay
 8. 8.93 Ecuador v Venezuela
15. 8.93 Bolivia v Ecuador
15. 8.93 Uruguay v Brazil
22. 8.93 Bolivia v Venezuela
22. 8.93 Brazil v Ecuador
29. 8.93 Brazil v Bolivia
29. 8.93 Uruguay v Venezuela
 5. 9.93 Brazil v Venezuela
 5. 9.93 Ecuador v Uruguay
12. 9.93 Uruguay v Bolivia
12. 9.93 Venezuela v Ecuador
19. 9.93 Brazil v Uruguay
19. 9.93 Ecuador v Bolivia

WORLD CUP QUALIFYING GAMES PLAYED TO DATE

Europe

Seville, 22 April 1992, 10,000

Spain (1) 3 *(Michel 2, 66 (pen), Hierro 87)*

Albania (0) 0

Spain: Zubizarreta; Abelardo, Nando, Giner, Michel (Eusebio 85), Amor, Hierro, Vizcaino, Manolo (Bakero 53), Butragueno, Goicoechea.
Albania: Strakosha (Dani 69); Josa (Pegini 55), Kola B, Lekbello, Aya, Abazi, Kushta, Barballushi, Millo, Kola A, Demollari.

Brussels, 22 April 1992, 18,000

Belgium (1) 1 *(Wilmots 24)*

Cyprus (0) 0

Belgium: Preud'homme; Albert, Grun, Van der Elst, Emmers, Scifo, Walem, Boffin (Borkelmans 82), Wilmots (Hofmans 75), Degryse, Oliveira.

Cyprus: Christofi; Costa, Pittas, Constantinou C, Nicolau, Yiangudakis, Ioannou, Larku (Constantinou G 88), Sotiriu, Papavasiliu, Gadjilukas (Panayi 70).

Windsor Park, 28 April 1992, 4500

Northern Ireland (2) 2 *(Wilson 13, Taggart 16)*

Lithuania (1) 2 *(Narberkovas 41, Fridrikas 48)*

Northern Ireland: Fettis; Donaghy (Fleming 46), Taggart, McDonald, Worthington, Black, Magilton, Wilson K, Hughes, Quinn, Dowie (Rogan 80).
Lithuania: Martinkenas; Buzmarkovas, Mika, Janonis, Mazeikis, Tautkas, Urbanas, Fridrikas (Zuta 90), Narbekovas, Baranauskas, Ivanauskas (Danisevicius 89).

Bucharest, 6 May 1992, 10,000

Romania (5) 7 *(Balint 4, 40, 78, Hagi 14, Lacatus 28 (pen), Lupescu 44, Pana 55)*

Faeroes (0) 0

Romania: Stelea; Petrescu, Milhali, Popescu, Munteanu, Pana, Balint, Lupescu (Cheregi 78), Hagi, Lacatus (Gane 63), Rotariu.
Faeroes: Knudsen; Jakobsen, Hansen T, Danielsen, Justiniussen, Morkore A, Jamskor (Nielsen T 50), Dam (Jonsson 60), Hansen A, Reynheim, Muller.

Athens, 13 May 1992, 10,000

Greece (1) 1 *(Sofianidis 28)*

Iceland (0) 0

Greece: Papadopoulos; Apostolakis, Kalitzakis, Manolas, Ntsibonas, Tsaluhidis Y, Tsaluhidis G, Sofianidis, Tursunidis (Noplias 77), Alexandria, Tsdiantakis (Borbokis 60).
Iceland: Kristinsson B; Jonsson Kr, Marteinsson (Magnusson 74), Valsson, Bergsson, Jonsson K, Gudjohnsen, Bjarnasson, Gretarsson, Sverisson, Kristinsson R.

Helsinki, 14 May 1992, 10,000

Finland (0) 0

Bulgaria (2) 3 *(Balakov 16, Kostadinov 25, 85)*

Finland: Huttunen; Pertaja, Holmgren, Heikkinen, Eriksson, Rinne (Huhtamaeki 76), Litmanen, Myyry, Jarvinen, Vanhala (Tegelberg 60), Tarkkio.
Bulgaria: Mikhailov; Ivanov, Tzvetanev, Iliev, Hubchev, Sirakov, Yankov, Stoichkov (Yordanov 69), Peney, Balakov, Kostadinov.

Bucharest, 20 May 1992 23,000

Romania (5) 5 *(Hagi 5, 35, Lupescu 7, 24, Balint 31)*

Wales (0) 1 *(Rush 50)*

Romania: Stelea; Petrescu, Mihali, Belodedici, Munteanu, Sabau (Timofte I 80), Popescu, Lupescu, Hagi (Gerstenmaier 71), Lacatus, Balint.
Wales: Southall; Phillips, Bowen (Blackmore 71), Aizlewood, Melville, Horne, Speed, Pembridge (Giggs 59), Hughes, Rush, Saunders.

Dublin, 26 May 1992, 29,727

Republic of Ireland (0) 2 *(Aldridge 60, McGarth 80)*

Albania (0) 0

Republic of Ireland: Bonner; Irwin, Staunton, O'Leary, McGrath, Townsend, Keane, Houghton, Quinn, Aldridge (Coyne 83), Sheedy (McCarthy 52).

Albania: Dani; Smijani, Qendro (Pali 71), Pegini, Vata, Abazi, Kushta, Vasi, Rrakilli, Zola A (Sokoll 80), Demollari.

Tirana, 3 June 1992, 15,000

Albania (0) 1 *(Abazi 77)*

Lithuania (0) 0

Albania: Dani; Zmijani, Pegini, Lekbello, Vata, Abazi, Kushta, Milori (Rrafi 46), Millo (Fortuzi 89), Vasi, Demollari.
Lithuania: Martinkenas; Buzmarkovas, Sukristovas, Mazekis, Tomas, Danisevicius, Baranauskas, Tautkas (Zuta 82), Urbonas, Ramells (Zadancius 52), Kvitkauskas.

Toftir, 3 June 1992, 5156

Faeroes (0) 0

Belgium (1) 3 *(Albert 30, Wilmosts 65, 71)*

Faeroes: Johannesen; Jakobsen, Hansen T, Danielsen, Jonsson T (Jensen 71), Morkore A (Justinussen 83), Nielsen T, Dam, Hansen A, Reynheim, Muller.
Belgium: Preud'homme; Staelens, Grun, Albert, Emmers, Boffin (Versavel 75), Van der Elst, Denil, Degryse, Scifo, Oliveira (Wilmots 63).

Budapest, 3 June 1992, 10,000

Hungary (1) 1 *(Kiprich 3)*

Iceland (0) 2 *(Orlygsson 51, Magnusson 73)*

Hungary: Petry; Telek, Kovacs E, Lorincz, Simon; Limperger, Pisont (Balog 78), Vincze (Eszenyi 54), Keller, Kiprich, Kovacs K.
Iceland: Kristinsson B; Gretarsson S, (Magnusson 64), Bergsson, Orlygsson, Kristinsson R, Gretarsson A, Valsson, Jonsson Kr, Jonsson K (Bragason 80), Bjarnasson, Marteinsson.

Toftir, 16 June 1992, 4500

Faeroes (0) 0

Cyprus (1) 2 *(Sotiriu 30, Papavasiliu 58)*

Faeroes: Johanen; Jakobsen, Hansen T, Danielsen, Jonsson, Morkore A, Hansen A, Nielsen (Jamskor 62), Rasmussen, Reynheim, Muller (Jensen 66(.
Cyprus: Christofi; Kosta (Larku 46), Pittas, Constantinou C, Nicolau, Yiangudakis, Ioannou Charalambous, Savides, Scotiriu (Panayi 84), Papavasiliu.

Concacaf

Pre-preliminary round
Domincian Republic 1, Puerto Rico 2
Puerto Rico 1, Dominican Republic 1
St Lucia 1, St Vincent 0
St Vincent 3, St Lucia 1

Preliminary round
Bermuda 1, Haiti 0
Haiti 2, Bermuda 1
Jamaica 2, Puerto Rico 1
Puerto Rico 0, Jamaica 3
St Vincent w.o. Cuba withdrew
Netherlands Antilles 1, Antigua 1

Antigua 3, Netherlands Antilles 0
Guyana 1, Surinam 2
Surinam 1, Guyana 1
Barbados 1, Trinidad & Tobago 2
Trinidad & Tobago 3, Barbados 0
Bermuda 3, Antigua 0
Jamaica 1, Puerto Rico 0

Oceania
New Zealand 3, Fiji 0
Vanuatu 1, New Zealand 4
New Zealand 8, Vanuatu 0

OTHER BRITISH AND IRISH INTERNATIONAL MATCHES 1991–92

Wembley, 11 September 1991, 59,493

England (0) 0

Germany (1) 1 *(Riedle 45)*

England: Woods; Dixon, Dorigo, Batty, Pallister, Parker, Platt, Steven (Stewart 67), Smith, Lineker, Salako (Merson 67).
Germany: Illgner; Binz, Brehme, Kohler, Effenberg, Buchwald, Moller, Hassler, Riedle, Matthaus, Doll (Klinsmann 82).

Gyor, 11 September 1991, 4000

Hungary (0) 1 *(Kovacs K 50)*

Republic of Ireland (0) 2 *(Kelly 51, Sheedy 70)*

Hungary: Petry; Monos (Rugovics 73), Disztl, Csehi, Lipcsei, Lorincz, Kozma, Kovacs E (Berczy 53), Vincze (Eszenyi 63), Detari, Kovacs K.
Republic of Ireland: Bonner; Irwin, Phelan (Morris 81), O'Leary, McCarthy, Sheridan (McLoughlin 46), Keane, Houghton, Quinn, Kelly (Aldridge 63), Sheedy.

Cardiff Arms Park, 11 September 1991, 20,000

Wales (0) 1 *(Saunders 58)*

Brazil (0) 0

Wales: Southall; Pembridge, Bodin (Bowen 67), Aizlewood, Melville, Ratcliffe (Maguire 87), Pascoe (Hodges 76), Horne, Saunders, Hughes, Speed.
Brazil: Taffarel; Cafu (Cassio 60), Cieber, Marcio Santos, Mauro Silva, Jorginho, Moacir (Valdir 60), Geovani (Mazino II 74), Careca, Bebeto, Joao Paulo.

Wembley, 19 February 1992, 58,723

England (1) 2 *(Shearer 44, Lineker 73)*

France (0) 0

England: Woods; Jones, Pearce, Keown, Walker, Wright, Webb, Thomas, Clough, Shearer, Hirst (Lineker 46).
France: Rousset; Amoros, Angloma, Boli, Blanc, Casoni, Deschamps, Fernandez (Durand 71), Papin, Perez (Simba 71), Cantona.

Dublin, 19 February 1992, 15,100

Republic of Ireland (0) 0

Wales (0) 1 *(Pembridge 72)*

Republic of Ireland: Bonner; Morris, Irwin, O'Leary, Daish, Townsend (McLoughlin 46), Phelan (Aldridge 55), Byrne, Keane, Cascarino (Quinn 67), Sheedy.
Wales: Southall; Phillips, Bowen, Aizlewood, Young (Bodin 63), Symons, Horne, Speed (Blackmore 46), Saunders (Nielsen 86), Hughes, Pembridge (Hodges 76).

Hampden Park, 19 February 1992, 13,650

Scotland (1) 1 *(McCoist 11)*

Northern Ireland (0) 0

Scotland: Smith; McKimmie (Durie 46), Robertson D, McPherson, Gough, Malpas, Strachan, McClair (Collins 66), McCoist (Gallacher 46), McAllister, Wright (Robertson J 76).
Northern Ireland: Wright; Donaghy, Worthington, Taggart (Morrow 85), McDonald, Magilton, Black, Wilson K (O'Neil 81), Clarke (Dowie 46), Wilson D, Hughes.

Prague, 25 March 1992, 3300

Czechoslovakia (1) 2 *(Skuhravy 20, Chovanec 58)*

England (1) 2 *(Merson 27, Keown 66)*

Czechoslovakia: Miklosko; Hapal, Kadlec, Kula (Frydek 86), Glonek, Nemecek (Memec 82), Bilek, Chovanec, Kubik, Skuhravy, Knoflicek (Siegel 87).
England: Seaman; Keown, Pearce, Rocastle (Dixon 46), Walker, Mabbutt (Lineker 73), Platt, Merson, Clough (Stewart 46), Hateley, Barnes (Dorigo 52).

Dublin, 25 March 1992, 23,601

Republic of Ireland (1) 2 *(Schepull 27 (og), Aldridge 88 (pen))*

Switzerland (1) 1 *(Whelan 25 (og))*

Republic of Ireland: Bonner; Morris, Phelan, O'Leary, McGrath, Keane, Whelan, McGoldrick (O'Brien 46), Coyne (Aldridge 80), Cascarino, Staunton (Sheedy 55).
Switzerland: Brunner (Pascolo 40); Ohrei (Rothenbuhler 51), Gamperle, Schepull, Egli, Geiger, Piffaretti, Bickel (Heldmann 66), Turkyilmaz, Sutter A, Chapuisat (Dietlin 81).

Hampden Park 25 March 1992, 9275

Scotland (1) 1 *(McStay 24)*

Finland (1) 1 *(Litmanen 41)*

Scotland: Goram; McKimmie, Boyd, Bowman, McPherson, Malpas, Strachan (McAllister 65), McStay, Robertson J (McCoist 54), Collins, Durie.
Finland: Huttunen; Rinne (Nyysonnen 88), Heikkinen, Petaja, Eriksson, Remes, Litmanen, Myyry, Jarvinen, Tarkkio (Vahala 69), Paatelainen.

Moscow, 29 April 1992, 25,000

CIS (1) 2 *(Tzhadadze 43, Kiryakov 55)*

England (1) 2 *(Lineker 15, Steven 71)*

CIS: Kharin; Chernishev, Tzhadadze, Tsveiba, Ledyskhov (Kiryakov 46), Shalimov, Mikhailichenko, Kanchelskis (Karpin 63), Kolyvanov (Lyuty 46), Mostovoi, Youran (Onopko 55).
England: Woods (Martyn 79); Stevens, Sinton (Curle 63), Palmer, Walker, Keown, Platt, Steven (Stewart 77), Shearer (Clough 63), Lineker, Daley.

Dublin, 29 April 1992, 27,000

Republic of Ireland (0) 4 *(Townsend 47, Irwin 52, Quinn 68, Cascarino 87)*

USA (0) 1 *(Wynalda 89)*

Republic of Ireland: Peyton; Morris, Irwin (Milligan 62), O'Leary (Carey 72), McGrath, Townsend, McGoldrick, McLoughlin, Quinn (Cascarino 72), Coyne (Aldridge 82), Staunton.
USA: Meola; Balboa, Savage (Ibsen 72), Armstrong, Doyle, Clavijo, Quinn, Perez (Kinnear 69), Harkes, Wynalda, Vernes (Eck 82).

Vienna, 29 April 1992, 53,000

Austria (0) 1 *(Baur 59)*

Wales (0) 1 *(Coleman 83)*

Austria: Konsel; Streiter, Rotter, Flogel, Zsak, Prosenik, Ogris (Hasenhutti 44), Stoger, Polster, Herzog (Schottel 79), Gager (Baur 46).
Wales: Southall; Phillips, Bowen, Aizlewood, Young (Coleman), Blackmore, Goss (Rees 87), Allen (Nogan 75), Roberts, Horne, Hodges (Hall 59).

Budapest, 12 May 1992, 25,000

Hungary (0) 0

England (0) 1 *(Telek 56 (og))*

Hungary: Brochauser; Simon, Telek, Szalma (Kecskes 41), Lorincz, Limperger, Kiprich, Kovacs E, Pisont, Lipcsei, Vincze.
England: Martyn (Seaman 46), Stevens, Dorigo, Curle (Sinton 46), Walker, Keown, Webb (Batty 70), Palmer, Merson (Smith 46), Lineker (Wright 70), Daley.

Wembley, 17 May 1992, 53,428

England (0) 1 *(Platt 49)*

Brazil (1) 1 *(Bebeto 25)*

England: Woods; Stevens, Dorigo (Pearce 72), Palmer, Walker, Keown, Daley (Merson 72), Steven (Webb 46), Platt, Lineker, Sinton (Rocastle 46).
Brazil: Carlos, Winck (Charles 46), Mozer, Ricardo, Mauro Silva, Branco, Bebeto, Henrique (Valdir 74), Renato (Junior 78), Rai, Valdo (Paulo Sergio 72).

Denver, 17 May 1992, 24,157

USA (0) 0

Scotland (1) 1 *(Nevin 7)*

USA: Keller; Balboa, Armstrong, Doyle, Clavijo, Michallik (Gibson 71), Quinn, Henderson, Perez, Kinnear, Wynalda.
Scotland: Marshall; McKimmie, McLaren, McStay (McInally 68), McPherson (Whyte 82), Malpas, Nevin (Ferguson 50), McCall, McClair, McCoist (Bowman 76), McAllister.

Toronto, 21 May 1992, 10,872

Canada (1) 1 *(Catliff 45)*

Scotland (1) 3 *(McAllister 22, 85 (pen), McCoist 68)*

Canada: Forrest; Dasovic, Miller, Samuel, Sarantopoulos, Yallop, Limniatis (Hooper 59), Odinga, Valentine, Catliff (Aunger 78), Mobilio (Bunbury 46).
Scotland: Smith; Boyd, McLaren, McStay, Gough, McPherson, Durie (Malpas 78), McCall (McKimmie 90), Ferguson (McClair 54), McCoist, McAllister.

Utrecht, 30 May 1992, 20,000

Holland (2) 4 *(Gullit 16, 37, Winter 74, Jonk 83)*

Wales (0) 0

Holland: Van Breukelen; Van Aerle, Van Tiggelen (De Boer 17), Blind, Witschge, Wouters (Jonk 74), Bergkamp (Bosz 65), Rijkaard (Winter 46), Van Basten (Kieft 46), Gullit (Van't Schip 46), Roy.
Wales: Southall; Bodin (Phillips 52), Speed, Blackmore (Hughes C 82), Melville, Symons, Horne, Pembridge (Bowen 60), Saunders, Hughes M, Aizlewood.

Washington, 30 May 1992, 35,696

USA (0) 3 *(Perez 54, Balboa 70, Harkes 87)*

Republic of Ireland (0) 1 *(McCarthy 51)*

USA: Meola; Balboa, Doyle, Dooley, Caligiuri, Quinn, Harkes, Ramos (Michallik 78), Murray (Henderson 46) (Clavijo 59), Perez (Stewart 57), Vermes (Wegerle 46).
Republic of Ireland: Peyton; Morris (Irwin 78), Phelan, McGrath, McCarthy, Moran, Houghton, Keane, Quinn, Townsend, Staunton (Coyne 60).

Bremen, 2 June 1992, 24,000

Germany (1) 1 *(Binz 40)*

Northern Ireland (1) 1 *(Hughes 22)*

Germany: Illgner; Reuter, Brehme, Kohler, Binz, Buchwald, Hassler (Doll 46), Voller, Riedle, Sammer (Thom), Effenberg.
Northern Ireland: Wright; Fleming, Worthington, Taggart, McDonald, Donaghy, Black (Morrow 78), Magilton, Clarke (O'Neill 87), Wilson K, Hughes.

Helsinki, 3 June 1992, 16,101

Finland (1) 1 *(Hjelm 27 (pen))*

England (1) 2 *(Platt 45, 62)*

Finland: Huttunen; Rinne (Vanhala 79), Jarvinen, Petaja, Holmgren (Heikkinen 46), Kinnunen, Litmanen (Vurolea 89), Myyry, Hjelm, Tarkkio (Tetelberg 67), Huhtamaki.
England: Woods; Stevens (Palmer 46), Pearce, Keown, Walker, Wright, Platt, Steven (Daley 82), Webb, Lineker, Barnes (Merson 12).

Oslo, 3 June 1992, 8786

Norway (0) 0

Scotland (0) 0

Norway: Grodas; Berg, Bjornebye, Bratseth, Nilsen, Petersen (Mykland 30), Bohinen (Brigtfen 76), Rekdal, Leonhardsen, Dahlum (Flo 73), Strandli.
Scotland: Goram; McLaren, Malpas (McKimmie 68), Gough, McPherson, Boyd, McCall, McStay, McClair (Gallagher 46), McCoist (Durie 46), McAllister (McInally 78).

Continued on Page 280

POST-WAR INTERNATIONAL APPEARANCES
As at June 1992

ENGLAND

A'Court, A. (5) (Liverpool) 1957/8, 1958/9.
Adams, T.A. (19) (Arsenal) 1986/7, 1987/8, 1988/9, 1990/91.
Allen, C. (5) (QPR) 1983/4, 1986/7 (Tottenham Hotspur) 1987/8.
Allen, R. (5) (West Bromwich Albion) 1951/2, 1953/4, 1954/5.
Allen, T. (3) (Stoke City) 1959/60.
Anderson, S. (2) (Sunderland) 1961/2.
Anderson, V. (30) (Nottingham Forest) 1978/9, 1979/80, 1980/1, 1981/2, 1983/84, (Arsenal) 1984/5, 1985/6, 1986/7, (Manchester United).
Angus, J. (1) (Burnley) 1960/1.
Armfield, J. (43) (Blackpool) 1958/9, 1959/60, 1960/1, 1961/2, 1962/3, 1963/4, 1965/6.
Armstrong, D. (3) (Middlesbrough) 1979/80, (Southampton) 1982/3, 1983/4.
Armstrong, K. (1) (Chelsea) 1954/5.
Astall, G. (2) (Birmingham) 1955/6.
Astle, J. (5) (West Bromwich Albion) 1968/9, 1969/70.
Aston, J. (17) (Manchester United) 1948/9, 1949/50, 1950/1.
Atyeo, J. (6) (Bristol City) 1955/6, 1956/7.

Bailey, G.R. (2) Manchester United) 1984/5.
Bailey, M. (2) (Charlton) 1963/4, 1964/5.
Baily, E. (9) (Tottenham Hotspur) 1949/50, 1950/1, 1951/2, 1952/3.
Baker, J. (8) (Hibernian) 1959/60, 1965/6, (Arsenal).
Ball, A. (72) (Blackpool) 1964/5, 1965/6, 1966/7, (Everton) 1967/8, 1968/9, 1969/70, 1970/1, 1971/2 (Arsenal) 1972/3, 1973/4, 1974/5.
Banks, G. (73) (Leicester) 1962/3, 1963/4, 1964/5, 1965/6, 1966/7, 1967/8, (Stoke) 1968/9, 1969/70, 1970/1, 1971/2.
Banks, T. (6) (Bolton Wanderers) 1957/8, 1958/9.
Barham, M. (2) (Norwich City) 1982/3.
Barlow, R. (1) (West Bromwich Albion) 1954/5.
Barnes, J. (67) (Watford) 1982/3, 1983/4, 1984/5, 1985/6, 1986/7, (Liverpool) 1987/8, 1988/9, 1989/90, 1990/91, 1991/2.
Barnes, P. (22) (Manchester City) 1977/8, 1978/9, 1979/80 (West Bromwich Albion) 1980/1, 1981/2 (Leeds United).
Barrass, M. (3) (Bolton Wanderers) 1951/2, 1952/3.
Barrett, E.D. (1) (Oldham Athletic) 1990/91.
Batty, D. (10) (Leeds United) 1990/91, 1991/2.
Baynham, R. (3) (Luton Town) 1955/6.

Beardsley P.A. (49) (Newcastle United) 1985/6, 1986/7 (Liverpool) 1987/8, 1988/9, 1989/90, 1990/1.
Beasant, D.J. (2) (Chelsea), 1989/90.
Beattie, T.K. (9) (Ipswich Town) 1974/5, 1975/6, 1976/7, 1977/8.
Bell, C. (48) (Manchester City) 1967/8, 1968/9, 1969/70, 1971/2, 1972/3, 1973/4, 1974/5, 1975/6.
Bentley, R. (12) (Chelsea) 1948/9, 1949/50, 1952/3, 1954/5.
Berry, J. (4) (Manchester United) 1952/3, 1955/6.
Birtles, G. (3) (Nottingham Forest) 1979/80, 1980/1 (Manchester United).
Blissett, L. (14) (Watford) 1982/3, 1983/4 (AC Milan).
Blockley, J. (1) (Arsenal) 1972/3.
Blunstone, F. (5) (Chelsea) 1954/5, 1956/7.
Bonetti, P. (7) (Chelsea) 1965/6, 1966/7, 1967/8, 1969/70.
Bowles, S. (5) (QPR) 1973/4, 1976/7.
Boyer, P. (1) (Norwich City) 1975/6.
Brabrook, P. (3) (Chelsea) 1957/8, 1959/60.
Bracewell, P.W. (3) (Everton) 1984/5, 1985/6.
Bradford, G. (1) (Bristol Rovers) 1955/6.
Bradley, W. (3) (Manchester United) 1958/9.
Bridges, B. (4) (Chelsea) 1964/5, 1965/6.
Broadbent, P. (7) (Wolverhampton Wanderers) 1957/8, 1958/9, 1959/60.
Broadis, I. (14) (Manchester City) 1951/2, 1952/3 (Newcastle United) 1953/4.
Brooking, T. (47) (West Ham United) 1973/4, 1974/5, 1975/6, 1976/7, 1977/8, 1978/9, 1979/80, 1980/1, 1981/2.
Brooks, J. (3) (Tottenham Hotspur) 1956/7.
Brown, A. (1) (West Bromwich Albion) 1970/1.
Brown, K. (1) (West Ham United) 1959/60.
Bull, S.G. (13) (Wolverhampton Wanderers) 1988/9, 1989/90, 1990/1.
Butcher, T. (77) (Ipswich Town) 1979/80, 1980/1, 1981/2, 1982/3, 1983/4, 1984/5, 1985/6, 1986/7 (Rangers) 1987/8, 1988/9, 1989/90.
Byrne, G. (2) (Liverpool) 1962/3, 1965/6.
Byrne, J. (11) (Crystal Palace) 1961/2, 1962/3, (West Ham United) 1963/4, 1964/5.
Byrne, R. (33) (Manchester United) 1953/4, 1954/5, 1955/6, 1956/7, 1957/8.

Callaghan, I. (4) (Liverpool) 1965/6, 1977/8.
Carter, H. (7) (Derby County) 1946/7.
Chamberlain, M. (8) (Stoke City) 1982/3, 1983/4, 1984/5.
Channon, M. (46) (Southampton) 1972/3, 1973/4, 1974/5, 1975/6, 1976/7, (Manchester City) 1977/8.
Charles, G.A. (2) (Nottingham Forest) 1990/1.

Charlton, J. (35) (Leeds United) 1964/5, 1965/6, 1966/7, 1967/8, 1968/9, 1969/70.
Charlton, R. (106) (Manchester United) 1957/8, 1958/9, 1959/60, 1960/1, 1961/2, 1962/3, 1963/4, 1964/5, 1965/6, 1966/7, 1967/8, 1968/9, 1969/70.
Charnley, R. (1) (Blackpool) 1961/2.
Cherry, T. (27) (Leeds United) 1975/6, 1976/7, 1977/8, 1978/9, 1979/80.
Chilton, A. (2) (Manchester United) 1950/1, 1951/2.
Chivers, M. (24) (Tottenham Hotspur) 1970/1, 1971/2, 1972/3, 1973/4.
Clamp, E. (4) (Wolverhampton Wanderers) 1957/8.
Clapton, D. (1) (Arsenal) 1958/9.
Clarke, A. (19) (Leeds United) 1969/70, 1970/1, 1972/3, 1973/4, 1974/5, 1975/6.
Clarke, H. (1) (Tottenham Hotspur) 1953/4.
Clayton, R. (35) (Blackburn Rovers) 1955/6, 1956/7, 1957/8, 1958/9, 1959/60.
Clemence, R (61) (Liverpool) 1972/3, 1973/4, 1974/5, 1975/6, 1976/7, 1977/8, 1978/9, 1979/80, 1980/1, 1981/2, (Tottenham Hotspur) 1982/3, 1983/4.
Clement, D. (5) (QPR) 1975/6, 1976/7.
Clough, B. (2) (Middlesbrough) 1959/60.
Clough, N.H. (7) (Nottingham Forest) 1988/9, 1990/91, 1991/2.
Coates, R. (4) (Burnley) 1969/70, 1970/1, (Tottenham Hotspur).
Cockburn, H. (13) (Manchester United) 1946/7, 1947/8, 1948/9, 1950/1, 1951/2.
Cohen, G. (37) (Fulham) 1963/4, 1964/5, 1965/6, 1966/7, 1967/8.
Compton, L. (2) (Arsenal) 1950/1.
Connelly J. (20) (Burnley) 1959/60, 1961/2, 1962/3, 1964/5 (Manchester United) 1965/6.
Cooper, T. (20) (Leeds United) 1968/9, 1969/70, 1970/1, 1971/2, 1974/5.
Coppell, S. (42) (Manchester United) 1977/8, 1978/9, 1979/80, 1980/1, 1981/2, 1982/3.
Corrigan J. (9) (Manchester City) 1975/6, 1977/8, 1978/9, 1979/80, 1980/1, 1981/2.
Cottee, A.R. (7) (West Ham United) 1986/7, 1987/8, (Everton) 1988/9.
Cowans, G. (10) (Aston Villa) 1982/3, 1985/6 (Bari) 1990/1 (Aston Villa).
Crawford, R. (2) (Ipswich Town) 1961/2.
Crowe, C. (1) (Wolverhampton Wanderers) 1962/3.
Cunningham, L. (6) (West Bromwich Albion) 1978/9 (Real Madrid) 1979/80, 1980/1.
Curle, K. (3) (Manchester City) 1991/2.

Currie, A. (17) (Sheffield United) 1971/2, 1972/3, 1973/4, 1975/6 (Leeds United) 1977/8, 1978/9.

Daley, A.M. (7) (Aston Villa) 1991/2.
Davenport, P. (1) (Nottingham Forest) 1984/5.
Deane, B.C. (2) (Sheffield United) 1990/91.
Deeley, N. (2) (Wolverhampton Wanderers) 1958/9.
Devonshire, A. (8) (West Ham United) 1979/80, 1981/2, 1982/3, 1983/4.
Dickinson, J. (48) (Portsmouth) 1948/9, 1949/50, 1950/1, 1951/2, 1952/3, 1953/4, 1954/5, 1955/6, 1956/7.
Ditchburn, E. (6) (Tottenham Hotspur) 1948/9, 1952/3, 1956/7.
Dixon, K.M. (8) (Chelsea) 1984/5, 1985/6, 1986/7.
Dixon, L.M. (12) (Arsenal) 1989/90, 1990/1, 1991/2.
Dobson, M. (5) (Burnley) 1973/4, 1974/5 (Everton).
Dorigo, A.R. (10) (Chelsea) 1989/90, 1990/1, (Leeds United) 1991/2.
Douglas, B. (36) (Blackburn Rovers) 1957/8, 1958/9, 1959/60, 1960/1, 1961/2, 1962/3.
Doyle, M. (5) (Manchester City) 1975/6, 1976/7.
Duxbury, M. (10) (Manchester United) 1983/4, 1984/5.

Eastham, G. (19) (Arsenal) 1962/3, 1963/4, 1964/5, 1965/6.
Eckersley, W. (17) (Blackburn Rovers) 1949/50, 1950/1, 1951/2, 1952/3, 1953/4.
Edwards, D. (18) (Manchester United) 1954/5, 1955/6, 1956/7, 1957/8.
Ellerington, W. (2) (Southampton) 1948/9.
Elliott, W. H. (5) (Burnley) 1951/2, 1952/3.

Fantham, J. (1) (Sheffield Wednesday) 1961/2.
Fashanu, J. (2) (Wimbledon) 1988/9.
Fenwick, T. (20) (QPR) 1983/4, 1984/5, 1985/6 (Tottenham Hotspur) 1987/8.
Finney, T. (76) (Preston) 1946/7, 1947/8, 1948/9, 1949/50, 1950/1, 1951/2, 1952/3, 1953/4, 1954/5, 1955/6, 1956/7, 1957/8, 1958/9.
Flowers R. (49) (Wolverhampton Wanderers) 1954/5, 1958/9, 1959/60, 1960/1, 1961/2, 1962/3, 1963/4, 1964/5, 1965/6.
Foster, S. (3) (Brighton) 1981/2.
Foulkes, W. (1) (Manchester United) 1954/5.
Francis, G. (12) (QPR) 1974/5, 1975/6.
Francis, T. (52) (Birmingham City) 1976/7, 1977/8 (Nottingham Forest) 1978/9, 1979/80, 1980/1, 1981/2 (Manchester City) 1982/3, (Sampdoria) 1983/4, 1984/5, 1985/6.
Franklin, N. (27) (Stoke City) 1946/7, 1947/8, 1948/9, 1949/50.
Froggatt, J. (13) (Portsmouth) 1949/50, 1950/1, 1951/2, 1952/3.
Froggatt, R. (4) (Sheffield Wednesday) 1952/3.

Garrett, T. (3) (Blackpool) 1951/2, 1953/4.
Gascoigne, P.J. (20) (Tottenham Hotspur) 1988/9, 1989/90, 1990/1.
Gates, E. (2) (Ipswich Town) 1980/1.
George, F.C. (1) (Derby County) 1976/7.
Gidman, J. (1) (Aston Villa) 1976/7.
Gillard, I. (3) (QPR) 1974/5, 1975/6.
Goddard, P. (1) (West Ham United) 1981/2.
Grainger, C. (7) (Sheffield United) 1955/6, 1956/7 (Sunderland).
Gray, A.A. (1) (Crystal Palace) 1991/2.
Greaves, J. (57) (Chelsea) 1958/9, 1959/60, 1960/1, 1961/2
(Tottenham Hotspur) 1962/3, 1963/4, 1964/5, 1965/6, 1966/7.
Greenhoff, B. (18) (Manchester United) 1975/6, 1976/7, 1977/8,
1979/80.
Gregory, J. (6) (QPR) 1982/3, 1983/4.

Hagan, J. (1) (Sheffield United) 1948/9.
Haines, J. (1) (West Bromwich Albion) 1948/9.
Hall, J. (17) (Birmingham City) 1955/6, 1956/7.
Hancocks, J. (3) (Wolverhampton Wanderers) 1948/9, 1949/50,
1950/1.
Hardwick, G. (13) (Middlesbrough) 1946/7, 1947/8.
Harford, M.G. (2) (Luton Town) 1987/8, 1988/9.
Harris, G. (1) (Burnley) 1965/6.
Harris, P. (2) (Portsmouth) 1949/50, 1953/4.
Harvey, C. (1) (Everton) 1970/1.
Hassall, H. (5) (Huddersfield Town) 1950/1, 1951/2 (Bolton
Wanderers) 1953/4.
Hateley, M. (32) (Portsmouth) 1983/4, 1984/5, (AC Milan) 1985/6,
1986/7, (Monaco) 1987/8, (Rangers) 1991/2.
Haynes, J. (56) (Fulham) 1954/5, 1955/6, 1956/7, 1957/8, 1958/9,
1959/60, 1960/1, 1961/2.
Hector, K. (2) (Derby County) 1973/4.
Hellawell, M. (2) (Birmingham City) 1962/3.
Henry, R. (1) (Tottenham Hotspur) 1962/3.
Hill, F. (2) (Bolton Wanderers) 1962/3.
Hill, G. (6) (Manchester United) 1975/6, 1976/7, 1977/8.
Hill, R. (3) (Luton Town) 1982/3, 1985/6.
Hinton A. (3) (Wolverhampton Wanderers) 1962/3, 1964/5
(Nottingham Forest).
Hirst, D.E. (3) (Sheffield Wednesday) 1990/91, 1991/2.
Hitchens, G. (7) (Aston Villa) 1960/1, (Inter Milan) 1961/2.
Hoddle, G. (53) (Tottenham Hotspur) 1979/80, 1980/1, 1981/2,
1982/3, 1983/4, 1984/5, 1985/6, 1986/7 (Monaco) 1987/8.
Hodge, S.B. (24) (Aston Villa) 1985/6, 1986/7, (Tottenham
Hotspur), (Nottingham Forest) 1988/9, 1989/90, 1990/1.
Hodgkinson, A. (5) (Sheffield United) 1956/7, 1960/1.

Holden, D. (5) (Bolton Wanderers) 1958/9.
Holliday, E. (3) (Middlesbrough) 1959/60.
Hollins, J. (1) (Chelsea) 1966/7.
Hopkinson, E. (14) (Bolton Wanderers) 1957/8, 1958/9, 1959/60.
Howe, D. (23) (West Bromwich Albion) 1957/8, 1958/9, 1959/60.
Howe, J. (3) (Derby County) 1947/8, 1948/9.
Hudson, A. (2) (Stoke City) 1974/5.
Hughes, E. (62) (Liverpool) 1969/70, 1970/1, 1971/2, 1972/3,
1973/4, 1974/5, 1976/7, 1977/8, 1978/9 (Wolverhampton Wanderers)
1979/80.
Hughes, L. (3) (Liverpool) 1949/50.
Hunt, R. (34) (Liverpool) 1961/2, 1962/3, 1963/4, 1964/5, 1965/6,
1966/7, 1967/8, 1968/9.
Hunt, S. (2) (West Bromwich Albion) 1983/4.
Hunter, N. (28) (Leeds United) 1965/6, 1966/7, 1967/8, 1968/9,
1969/70, 1970/1, 1971/2, 1972/3, 1973/4, 1974/5.
Hurst, G. (49) (West Ham United) 1965/6, 1966/7, 1967/8, 1968/9,
1969/70, 1970/1, 1971/2.

Jezzard, B. (2) (Fulham) 1953/4, 1955/6.
Johnson, D. (8) (Ipswich Town) 1974/5, 1975/6, (Liverpool)
1979/80.
Johnston, H. (10) (Blackpool) 1946/7, 1950/1, 1952/3, 1953/4.
Jones, M. (3) (Sheffield United) 1964/5 (Leeds United) 1969/70.
Jones, R. (1) (Liverpool) 1991/2.
Jones, W.H. (2) (Liverpool) 1949/50.

Kay, A. (1) (Everton) 1962/3.
Keegan, K. (63) (Liverpool) 1972/3, 1973/4, 1974/5, 1975/6, 1976/7
(SV Hamburg) 1977/8, 1978/9, 1979/80 (Southampton) 1980/1,
1981/2.
Kennedy, A. (2) (Liverpool) 1983/4.
Kennedy, R. (17) (Liverpool) 1975/6, 1977/8, 1979/80.
Keown, M.R. (9) (Everton) 1991/2.
Kevan, D. (14) (West Bromwich Albion) 1956/7, 1957/8, 1958/9,
1960/1.
Kidd, B. (2) (Manchester United) 1969/70.
Knowles, C. (4) (Tottenham Hotspur) 1967/8.

Labone, B. (26) (Everton) 1962/3, 1966/7, 1967/8, 1968/9, 1969/70.
Lampard, F. (2) (West Ham United) 1972/3, 1979/80.
Langley, J. (3) (Fulham) 1957/8.
Langton, R. (11) (Blackburn Rovers) 1946/7, 1947/8, 1948/9,
(Preston North End) 1949/50, (Bolton Wanderers) 1950/1.
Latchford, R. (12) (Everton) 1977/8, 1978/9.
Lawler, C. (4) (Liverpool) 1970/1, 1971/2.

Lawton, T. (15) (Chelsea) 1946/7, 1947/8, (Notts County) 1948/9.
Lee, F. (27) (Manchester City) 1968/9, 1969/70, 1970/1, 1971/2.
Lee, J. (1) (Derby County) 1950/1.
Lee, S. (14) (Liverpool) 1982/3, 1983/4.
Lindsay, A. (4) (Liverpool) 1973/4.
Lineker, G. (80) (Leicester City) 1983/4, 1984/5 (Everton) 1985/6, 1986/7, (Barcelona) 1987/8, 1988/9 (Tottenham H) 1989/90, 1990/1, 1991/2.
Little, B. (1) (Aston Villa) 1974/5.
Lloyd, L. (4) (Liverpool) 1970/1, 1971/2, (Nottingham Forest) 1979/80.
Lofthouse, N. (33) (Bolton Wanderers) 1950/1, 1951/2, 1952/3, 1953/4, 1954/5, 1955/6, 1958/9.
Lowe, E. (3) (Aston Villa) 1946/7.

Mabbutt, G. (16) (Tottenham Hotspur) 1982/3, 1983/4, 1986/7, 1987/8, 1991/2.
Macdonald, M. (14) (Newcastle United) 1971/2, 1972/3, 1973/4, 1974/5, (Arsenal) 1975/6.
Madeley, P. (24) (Leeds United) 1970/1, 1971/2, 1972/3, 1973/4, 1974/5, 1975/6, 1976/7.
Mannion, W. (26) (Middlesbrough) 1946/7, 1947/8, 1948/9, 1949/50, 1950/1, 1951/2.
Mariner, P. (35) (Ipswich Town) 1976/7, 1977/8, 1979/80, 1980/1, 1981/2, 1982/3, 1983/4, 1984/5 (Arsenal)
Marsh, R. (9) (QPR) 1971/2 (Manchester City) 1972/3.
Martin, A. (17) (West Ham United) 1980/1, 1981/2, 1982/3, 1983/4, 1984/5, 1985/6, 1986/7.
Marwood, B. (1) (Arsenal) 1988/9.
Matthews, R. (5) (Coventry City) 1955/6, 1956/7.
Matthews, S. (37) (Stoke City) 1946/7, (Blackpool) 1947/8, 1948/9, 1949/50, 1950/1, 1953/4, 1954/5, 1955/6, 1956/7.
McDermott, T. (25) (Liverpool) 1977/8, 1978/9, 1979/80, 1980/1, 1981/2.
McDonald, C. (8) (Burnley) 1957/8, 1958/9.
McFarland, R. (28) (Derby County) 1970/1, 1971/2, 1972/3, 1973/4, 1975/6, 1976/7.
McGarry, W. (4) (Huddersfield Town) 1953/4, 1955/6.
McGuinness, W. (2) (Manchester United) 1958/9.
McMahon, S. (17) (Liverpool) 1987/8, 1988/9, 1989/90, 1990/1.
McNab, R. (4) (Arsenal) 1968/9.
McNeil, M. (9) (Middlesbrough) 1960/1, 1961/2.
Martyn, A.N. (2) (Crystal Palace) 1991/2.
Meadows, J. (1) (Manchester City) 1954/5.
Medley, L. (Tottenham Hotspur) 1950/1, 1951/2.
Melia, J. (2) (Liverpool) 1962/3.

Merrick, G. (23) (Birmingham City) 1951/2, 1952/3, 1953/4.
Merson, P.C. (7) (Arsenal) 1991/2.
Metcalfe, V. (2) (Huddersfield Town) 1950/1.
Milburn, J. (13) (Newcastle United) 1948/9, 1949/50, 1950/1, 1951/2, 1955/6.
Miller, B. (1) (Burnley) 1960/1.
Mills, M. (42) (Ipswich Town) 1972/3, 1975/6, 1976/7, 1977/8, 1978/9, 1979/80, 1980/1, 1981/2.
Milne, G. (14) (Liverpool) 1962/3, 1963/4, 1964/5.
Milton, C.A. (1) (Arsenal) 1951/2.
Moore, R. (108) (West Ham United) 1961/2, 1962/3, 1963/4, 1964/5, 1965/6, 1966/7, 1967/8, 1968/9, 1969/70, 1970/1, 1971/2, 1972/3, 1973/4.
Morley, A. (6) (Aston Villa) 1981/2, 1982/3.
Morris, J. (3) (Derby County) 1948/9, 1949/50.
Mortensen, S. (25) (Blackpool) 1946/7, 1947/8, 1948/9, 1949/50, 1950/1, 1953/4.
Mozley, B. (3) (Derby County) 1949/50.
Mullen, J. (12) (Wolverhampton Wanderers) 1946/7, 1948/9, 1949/50, 1953/4.
Mullery, A. (35) (Tottenham Hotspur) 1964/5, 1966/7, 1967/8, 1968/9, 1969/70, 1970/1, 1971/2.

Neal, P. (50) (Liverpool) 1975/6, 1976/7, 1977/8, 1978/9, 1979/80, 1980/1, 1981/2, 1982/3, 1983/4.
Newton, K. (27) (Blackburn Rovers) 1965/6, 1966/7, 1967/8, 1968/9, 1969/70, (Everton).
Nicholls, J. (2) (West Bromwich Albion) 1953/4.
Nicholson W. (1) (Tottenham Hotspur) 1950/1.
Nish, D. (5) (Derby County) 1972/3, 1973/4.
Norman, M. (23) (Tottenham Hotspur) 1961/2, 1962/3, 1963/4, 1964/5.

O'Grady, M. (2) (Huddersfield Town) 1962/3, 1968/9 (Leeds United).
Osgood, P. (4) (Chelsea) 1969/70, 1973/4.
Osman, R. (11) (Ipswich Town) 1979/80, 1980/1, 1981/2, 1982/3, 1983/4.
Owen, S. (3) (Luton Town) 1953/4.

Paine, T. (19) (Southampton) 1962/3, 1963/4, 1964/5, 1965/6.
Pallister, G. (5) (Middlesbrough) 1987/8, 1990/91 (Manchester United), 1991/2.
Palmer, C.L. (7) (Sheffield Wednesday) 1991/2.
Parker, P.A. (17) (QPR) 1988/9, 1989/90, 1990/1, (Manchester United) 1991/2.

Parkes, P. (1) (QPR) 1973/4.
Parry, R. (2) (Bolton Wanderers) 1959/60.
Peacock, A. (6) (Middlesbrough) 1961/2, 1962/3, 1965/6 (Leeds United).
Pearce, S. (50) (Nottingham Forest) 1986/7, 1987/8, 1988/9, 1989/90, 1990/1, 1991/2.
Person, Stan (8) (Manchester United) 1947/8, 1948/9, 1949/50, 1950/1, 1951/2.
Pearson, Stuart (15) (Manchester United) 1975/6, 1976/7, 1977/8.
Pegg, D. (1) (Manchester United) 1956/7.
Pejic, M. (4) (Stoke City) 1973/4.
Perry, W. (3) (Blackpool) 1955/6.
Perryman, S. (1) (Tottenham Hotspur) 1981/2.
Peters, M. (67) (West Ham United) 1965/6, 1966/7, 1967/8, 1968/9, 1969/70, (Tottenham Hotspur) 1970/1, 1971/2, 1972/3, 1973/4.
Phelan, M.C. (1) (Manchester United) 1989/90.
Phillips, L. (3) (Portsmouth) 1951/2, 1954/5.
Pickering, F. (3) (Everton) 1963/4, 1964/5.
Pickering, N. (1) (Sunderland) 1982/3.
Pilkington, B. (1) (Burnley) 1954/5.
Platt, D. (32) (Aston Villa) 1989/90, 1990/1, (Bari) 1991/2.
Pointer, R. (3) (Burnley) 1961/2.
Pye, J. (1) (Wolverhampton Wanderers) 1949/50.

Quixall, A. (5) (Sheffield Wednesday) 1953/4, 1954/5.

Radford, J. (2) (Arsenal) 1968/9, 1971/2.
Ramsey, A. (32) (Southampton) 1948/9, 1949/50, (Tottenham Hotspur) 1950/1, 1951/2, 1952/3, 1953/4.
Reaney, P. (3) (Leeds United) 1968/9, 1969/70, 1970/1.
Reeves, K. (2) (Norwich City) 1979/80.
Regis, C. (5) (West Bromwich Albion) 1981/2, 1982/3, (Coventry City).
Reid, P. (13) (Everton) 1984/5, 1985/6, 1986/7.
Revie, D. (6) (Manchester City) 1954/5, 1955/6, 1956/7.
Richards, J. (1) (Wolverhampton Wanderers) 1972/3.
Rickaby, S. (1) (West Bromwich Albion) 1953/4.
Rimmer, J. (1) (Arsenal) 1975/6.
Rix, G. (17) (Arsenal) 1980/1, 1981/2, 1982/3, 1983/4.
Robb, G. (1) (Tottenham Hotspur) 1953/4.
Roberts, G. (6) (Tottenham Hotspur) 1982/3, 1983/4.
Robson, B.(90) (West Bromwich Albion) 1979/80, 1980/1, 1981/2, (Manchester United) 1982/3, 1983/4, 1984/5, 1985/6, 1986/7, 1987/8, 1988/9, 1989/90, 1990/1, 1991/2.
Robson, R. (20) (West Bromwich Albion) 1957/8, 1959/60, 1960/1, 1961/2.

Rocastle, D. (14) (Arsenal) 1988/9, 1989/90, 1991/2.
Rowley, J. (6) (Manchester United) 1948/9, 1949/50, 1951/2.
Royle, J. (6) (Everton) 1970/1, 1972/3, (Manchester City) 1975/6, 1976/7.

Sadler, D. (4) (Manchester United) 1967/8, 1969/70, 1970/1.
Salako, J.A. (5) (Crystal Palace) 1990/91, 1991/2.
Sansom, K. (86) (Crystal Palace) 1978/9, 1979/80, 1980/1, (Arsenal) 1981/2, 1982/3, 1983/4, 1984/5, 1985/6, 1986/7, 1987/8.
Scott, L. (17) (Arsenal) 1946/7, 1947/8. 1948/9.
Seaman, D.A. (9) (QPR) 1988/9, 1989/90, 1990/1 (Arsenal), 1991/2.
Sewell, J. (6) (Sheffield Wednesday) 1951/2, 1952/3, 1953/4.
Shackleton, L. (5) (Sunderland) 1948/9, 1949/50, 1954/5.
Sharpe, L.S. (1) (Manchester United) 1990/1.
Shaw, G. (5) (Sheffield United) 1958/9, 1962/3.
Shearer, A. (3) (Southampton) 1991/2.
Shellito, K. (1) (Chelsea) 1962/3.
Shilton, P. (125) (Leicester City) 1970/1, 1971/2, 1972/3, 1973/4, 1974/5, (Stoke City) 1976/7, (Nottingham Forest) 1977/8, 1978/9, 1979/80, 1980/1, 1981/2, (Southampton) 1982/3, 1983/4, 1984/5, 1985/6, 1986/7, (Derby County) 1987/8, 1988/9, 1989/90.
Shimwell, E. (1) (Blackpool) 1948/9.
Sillett, P. (3) (Chelsea) 1954/5.
Sinton, A. (5) (QPR) 1991/2.
Slater, W. (12) (Wolverhampton Wanderers) 1954/5, 1957/8, 1958/9, 1959/60.
Smith, A.M. (13) (Arsenal) 1988/9, 1990/1, 1991/2.
Smith, L. (6) (Arsenal) 1950/1, 1951/2, 1952/3.
Smith, R. (15) (Tottenham Hotspur) 1960/1, 1961/2, 1962/3, 1963/4.
Smith, Tom (1) (Liverpool) 1970/1.
Smith, Trevor (2) (Birmingham City) 1959/60.
Spink, N. (1) (Aston Villa) 1982/3.
Springett, R. (33) (Sheffield Wednesday) 1959/60, 1960/1, 1961/2, 1962/3, 1965/6.
Staniforth, R. (8) (Huddersfield Town) 1953/4, 1954/5.
Statham, D. (3) (West Bromwich Albion) 1982/3.
Stein, B. (1) (Luton Town) 1983/4.
Stepney, A. (1) (Manchester United) 1967/8.
Sterland, M. (1) (Sheffield Wednesday) 1988/9.
Steven, T.M. (36) (Everton) 1984/5, 1985/6, 1986/7, 1987/8, 1988/9 (Glasgow Rangers) 1989/90, 1990/1, (Marseille) 1991/2.
Stevens, G.A. (7) (Tottenham Hotspur) 1984/5, 1985/6.
Stevens, M.G. (46) (Everton) 1984/5, 1985/6, 1986/7, 1987/8 (Rangers) 1988/9, 1989/90, 1990/1, 1991/2.
Stewart, P.A. (3) (Tottenham Hotspur) 1991/2.

Stiles, N. (28) (Manchester United) 1964/5, 1965/6, 1966/7, 1967/8, 1968/9, 1969/70.
Storey-Moore, I. (1) (Nottingham Forest) 1969/70.
Storey, P. (19) (Arsenal) 1970/1, 1971/2, 1972/3.
Streten, B. (1) (Luton Town) 1949/50.
Summerbee, M. (8) (Manchester City) 1967/8, 1971/2, 1972/3.
Sunderland, A. (1) (Arsenal) 1979/80.
Swan, P. (19) (Sheffield Wednesday) 1959/60, 1960/1, 1961/2.
Swift, F. (19) (Manchester City) 1946/7, 1947/8, 1948/9.

Talbot, B. (6) (Ipswich Town) 1976/7, 1979/80.
Tambling, R. (3) (Chelsea) 1962/3, 1965/6.
Taylor, E. (1) (Blackpool) 1953/4.
Taylor, J. (2) (Fulham) 1950/1.
Taylor, P.H. (3) (Liverpool) 1947/8.
Taylor, P.J. (4) (Crystal Palace) 1975/6.
Taylor, T. (19) (Manchester United) 1952/3, 1953/4, 1955/6, 1956/7, 1958/9.
Temple, D. (1) (Everton) 1964/5.
Thomas, Danny (2) (Coventry City) 1982/3.
Thomas, Dave (8) (QPR) 1974/5, 1975/6.
Thomas, G.R. (9) (Crystal Palace) 1990/1, 1991/2.
Thomas, M.L. (2) (Arsenal) 1988/9, 1989/90.
Thompson, P. (16) (Liverpool) 1963/4, 1964/5, 1965/6, 1967/8, 1969/70.
Thompson, P.B. (42) (Liverpool) 1975/6, 1976/7, 1978/9, 1979/80, 1980/1, 1981/2, 1982/3.
Thompson, T. (2) (Aston Villa) 1951/2, (Preston North End) 1956/7.
Thomson, R. (8) (Wolverhampton Wanderers) 1963/4, 1964/5.
Todd, C. (27) (Derby County) 1971/2, 1973/4, 1974/5, 1975/6, 1976/7.
Towers, T. (3) (Sunderland) 1975/6.
Tueart, D. (6) (Manchester City) 1974/5, 1976/7.

Ufton, D. (1) (Charlton Athletic) 1953/4.

Venables, T. (2) (Chelsea) 1964/5.
Viljoen, C. (2) (Ipswich Town) 1974/5.
Viollet, D. (2) (Manchester United) 1959/60, 1961/2.

Waddle, C.R. (62) (Newcastle United) 1984/5, (Tottenham Hotspur) 1985/6, 1986/7, 1987/8, 1988/9, (Marseille) 1989/90, 1990/1, 1991/2.
Waiters, A. (5) (Blackpool) 1963/4, 1964/5.

Walker, D.S. (47) (Nottingham Forest) 1988/9, 1989/90, 1990/1, 1991/2.
Wallace, D.L. (1) (Southampton) 1985/6.
Walsh, P. (5) (Luton Town) 1982/3, 1983/4.
Walters, K.M. (1) (Rangers) 1990/91.
Ward, P. (1) (Brighton) 1979/80.
Ward, T. (2) (Derby County) 1947/8, 1948/9.
Watson, D. (12) (Norwich City) 1983/4, 1984/5, 1985/6, 1986/7 (Everton) 1987/8.
Watson D.V. (65) (Sunderland) 1973/4, 1974/5, 1975/6 (Manchester City) 1976/7, 1977/8, (Southampton) 1978/9 (Werder Bremen), 1979/80, (Southampton) 1980/1 , 1981/2, (Stoke City).
Watson, W. (4) (Sunderland) 1949/50, 1950/1.
Webb, N. (26) (Nottingham Forest) 1987/8, 1988/9 (Manchester United) 1989/90, 1991/2.
Weller, K. (4) (Leicester City) 1973/4.
West, G. (3) (Everton) 1968/9.
Wheeler, J. (1) (Bolton Wanderers) 1954/5.
Whitworth, S. (7) (Leicester City) 1974/5, 1975/6.
Whymark, T. (1) (Ipswich Town) 1977/8.
Wignall, F. (2) (Nottingham Forest) 1964/5.
Wilkins, R. (84) (Chelsea) 1975/6, 1976/7, 1977/8, 1978/9, (Manchester United) 1979/80, 1980/1, 1981/2, 1982/3, 1983/4, 1984/5, (AC Milan) 1985/6, 1986/7.
Williams, B. (24) (Wolverhampton Wanderers) 1948/9, 1949/50, 1950/1, 1951/2, 1954/5, 1955/6.
Williams, S. (6) (Southampton) 1982/3, 1983/4, 1984/5.
Willis, A. (1) (Tottenham Hotspur) 1951/2.
Wilshaw, D. (12) (Wolverhampton Wanderers) 1953/4, 1954/5, 1955/6, 1956/7.
Wilson, R. (63) (Huddersfield Town) 1959/60, 1961/2, 1962/3, 1963/4, 1964/5, (Everton) 1965/6, 1966/7, 1967/8.
Winterburn, N. (1) (Arsenal) 1989/90.
Wise, D.F. (5) (Chelsea) 1990/91.
Withe, P. (11) (Aston Villa) 1980/1, 1981/2, 1982/3, 1983/4, 1984/5.
Wood, R. (3) (Manchester United) 1954/5, 1955/6.
Woodcock, A. (42) (Nottingham Forest) 1977/8, 1978/9, 1979/80 (FC Cologne) 1980/1, 1981/2, (Arsenal) 1982/3, 1983/4, 1984/5, 1985/6.
Woods, C.C.E. (34) (Norwich City) 1984/5, 1985/6, 1986/7, (Rangers) 1987/8, 1988/9, 1989/90, 1990/1, (Sheffield Wednesday) 1991/2.
Worthington, F. (8) (Leicester City) 1973/4, 1974/5.
Wright, I.E. (5) (Crystal Palace) 1990/1, 1991/2.
Wright M. (42) (Southampton) 1983/4, 1984/5, 1985/6, 1986/7, (Derby County) 1987/8, 1988/9, 1989/90, 1990/1, (Liverpool) 1991/2.

Wright, T. (11) (Everton) 1967/8, 1968/9, 1969/70.
Wright, W. (105) (Wolverhampton Wanderers) 1946/7, 1947/8, 1948/9, 1949/50, 1950/1, 1951/2, 1952/3, 1953/4, 1954/5, 1955/6, 1956/7, 1957/8, 1958/9.

Young, G. (1) (Sheffield Wednesday) 1964/5.

NORTHERN IRELAND

Aherne, T. (4) (Belfast Celtic) 1946/7, 1947/8, 1948/9, 1949/50 (Luton Town).
Anderson, T. (22) (Manchester United) 1972/3, 1973/4, 1974/5, (Swindon Town) 1975/6, 1976/7, 1977/8, (Peterborough United) 1978/9.
Armstrong, G. (63) (Tottenham Hotspur) 1976/7, 1977/8, 1978/9, 1979/80, 1980/1, (Watford) 1981/2, 1982/3, (Real Mallorca) 1983/4, 1984/5, (West Bromwich Albion) 1985/6 (Chesterfield).

Barr, H. (3) (Linfield) 1961/2, 1962/3, (Coventry City).
Best, G. (37) (Manchester United) 1963/4, 1964/5, 1965/6, 1966/7, 1967/8, 1968/9, 1969/70, 1970/1 , 1971/2, 1972/3, 1973/4 (Fulham) 1976/7, 1977/8.
Bingham, W. (56) (Sunderland) 1950/1, 1951/2, 1952/3, 1953/4, 1954/5, 1955/6, 1956/7, 1957/8, 1958/9 (Luton Town) 1959/60, 1960/1 (Everton) 1961/2, 1962/3, 1963/4 (Port Vale).
Black, K. (22) (Luton Town) 1987/8, 1988/9, 1989/90, 1990/1, (Nottingham Forest) 1991/2.
Blair, R. (5) (Oldham Athletic) 1974/5, 1975/6.
Blanchflower, D. (54) (Barnsley) 1949/50, 1950/1 (Aston Villa) 1951/2, 1952/3, 1953/4, 1954/5, (Tottenham Hotspur) 1955/6, 1956/7, 1957/8, 1958/9, 1959/60, 1960/1, 1961/2, 1962/3.
Blanchflower, J. (12) (Manchester United) 1953/4, 1954/5, 1955/6, 1956/7, 1957/8.
Bowler, G. (3) (Hull City) 1949/50.
Braithwaite, R. (10) (Linfield) 1961/2, 1962/3 (Middlesbrough) 1963/4, 1964/5.
Brennan, R. (5) (Luton Town) 1948/9, 1949/50 (Birmingham City) (Fulham), 1950/1.
Briggs, R. (2) (Manchester United) 1961/2, 1964/5 (Swansea).
Brotherston, N. (27) (Blackburn Rovers) 1979/80, 1980/1, 1981/2, 1982/3, 1983/4, 1984/5.
Bruce, W. (2) (Glentoran) 1960/1, 1966/7.

Campbell, A. (2) (Crusaders) 1962/3, 1964/5.
Campbell, D.A. (10) (Nottingham Forest) 1985/6, 1986/7, 1987/8 (Charlton Athletic).

Campbell, J. (2) (Fulham) 1950/1.
Campbell, R.M. (2) (Bradford City) 1981/2.
Campbell, W. (6) (Dundee) 1967/8, 1968/9, 1969/70.
Carey, J. (7) (Manchester United) 1946/7, 1947/8, 1948/9.
Casey, T. (12) (Newcastle United) 1954/5, 1955/6, 1956/7, 1957/8, 1958/9, (Portsmouth).
Caskey, A. (7) (Derby County) 1978/9, 1979/80, 1981/2 (Tulsa Roughnecks).
Cassidy, T. (24) (Newcastle United) 1970/1, 1971/2, 1973/4, 1974/5, 1975/6, 1976/7, 1979/80 (Burnley) 1980/1, 1981/2.
Caughey, M. (2) (Linfield) 1985/6.
Clarke, C.J. (35) (Bournemouth) 1985/6, 1986/7 (Southampton) 1987/8, 1988/9, 1989/90, 1990/1 (Portsmouth), 1991/2.
Cleary, J. (5) (Glentoran) 1981/2, 1982/3, 1983/4, 1984/5.
Clements, D. (48) (Coventry City) 1964/5, 1965/6, 1966/7, 1967/8, 1968/9, 1969/70, 1970/1, 1971/2 (Sheffield Wednesday) 1972/3 (Everton) 1973/4, 1974/5, 1975/6 (New York Cosmos).
Cochrane, D. (10) (Leeds United) 1946/7, 1947/8, 1948/9, 1949/50.
Cochrane, T. (26) (Coleraine) 1975/6, (Burnley) 1977/8, 1978/9, (Middlesbrough) 1979/80, 1980/1, 1981/2, (Gillingham) 1983/4.
Cowan, J. (1) (Newcastle United) 1969/70.
Coyle, F. (4) (Coleraine) 1955/6, 1956/7, 1957/8 (Nottingham Forest).
Coyle, L. (1) (Derry C) 1988/9.
Coyle, R. (5) (Sheffield Wednesday) 1972/3, 1973/4.
Craig, D. (25) (Newcastle United) 1966/7, 1967/8, 1968/9, 1969/70, 1970/1, 1971/2, 1972/3, 1973/4, 1974/5.
Crossan, E. (3) (Blackburn Rovers) 1949/50, 1950/1, 1954/5.
Crossan, J. (23) (Rotterdam Sparta) 1959/60, 1962/3 (Sunderland), 1963/4, 1964/5, (Manchester City) 1965/6, 1966/7, 1967/8 (Middlesbrough).
Cunningham, W. (30) (St Mirren) 1950/1, 1952/3, 1953/4, 1954/5, 1955/6, 1956/7, (Leicester City) 1957/8, 1958/9, 1959/60, 1960/1 (Dunfermline Athletic) 1961/2.
Cush, W. (26) (Glentoran) 1950/1, 1953/4, 1956/7, 1957/8 (Leeds United) 1958/9, 1959/60, 1960/1 (Portadown) 1961/2.

D'Arcy, S. (5) (Chelsea) 1951/2, 1952/3 (Brentford).
Dennison, R. (15) (Wolverhampton Wanderers) 1987/8, 1988/9, 1989/90, 1990/1, 1991/2.
Devine, J. (1) (Glentoran) 1989/90.
Dickson, D. (4) (Coleraine) 1969/70, 1972/3.
Dickson, T. (1) (Linfield) 1956/7.
Dickson, W. (12) (Chelsea) 1950/1, 1951/2, 1952/3 (Arsenal) 1953/4, 1954/5.
Doherty, L. (2) (Linfield) 1984/5, 1987/8.

Doherty P. (6) (Derby County) 1946/7, (Huddersfield Town) 1947/8, 1948/9, (Doncaster Rovers) 1950/1.

Donaghy, M. (76) (Luton Town) 1979/80, 1980/1, 1981/2, 1982/3, 1983/4, 1984/5, 1985/6, 1986/7, 1987/8, (Manchester United) 1988/9, 1989/90, 1990/1, 1991/2.

Dougan D. (43) (Portsmouth) 1957/8, 1959/60, (Blackburn Rovers), 1960/1, 1962/3 (Aston Villa) 1965/6 (Leicester City), 1966/7 (Wolverhampton Wanderers) 1967/8, 1968/9, 1969/70, 1970/1, 1971/2, 1972/3.

Douglas, J.P. (1) (Belfast Celtic) 1946/7.

Dowd, H. (3) (Glentoran) 1972/3, 1974/5 (Sheffield Wednesday).

Dowie, I. (12) (Luton Town) 1989/90, 1990/1, (Southampton) 1991/ 2.

Dunlop, G. (4) (Linfield) 1984/5, 1986/7.

Eglington T. (6) (Everton) 1946/7, 1947/8, 1948/9.

Elder, A. (40) (Burnley) 1959/60, 1960/1, 1961/2, 1962/3, 1963/4, 1964/5, 1965/6, 1966/7, (Stoke City) 1967/8, 1968/9, 1969/70.

Farrell, P. (7) (Everton) 1946/7, 1947/8, 1948/9.

Feeney, J. (2) (Linfield) 1946/7 (Swansea City) 1949/50.

Feeney, W. (1) (Glentoran) 1975/6.

Ferguson, W. (2) (Linfield) 1965/6, 1966/7.

Ferris, R. (3) (Birmingham City) 1949/50, 1950/1, 1951/2.

Fettis, A. (2) (Hull City) 1991/2.

Finney, T. (14) (Sunderland) 1974/5, 1975/6 (Cambridge United), 1979/80.

Fleming, J.G. (14) (Nottingham Forest) 1986/7, 1987/8, 1988/9 (Manchester City) 1989/90, 1990/1 (Barnsley), 1991/2.

Forde, T. (4) (Ards) 1958/9, 1960/1.

Gallogly, C. (2) (Huddersfield Town) 1950/1.

Garton, R. (1) (Oxford United) 1968/9.

Gorman, W. (4) (Brentford) 1946/7, 1947/8.

Graham, W. (14) (Doncaster Rovers) 1950/1, 1951/2, 1952/3, 1953/4, 1954/5, 1955/6, 1958/9.

Gregg, H. (25) (Doncaster Rovers) 1953/4, 1956/7, 1957/8, (Manchester United) 1958/9, 1959/60, 1960/1, 1961/2, 1963/4.

Hamilton, B. (50) (Linfield) 1968/9, 1970/1, 1971/2 (Ipswich Town), 1972/3, 1973/4, 1974/5, 1975/6 (Everton) 1976/7, 1977/8, (Millwall), 1978/9, (Swindon Town).

Hamilton, W. (41) (QPR) 1977/8, 1979/80 (Burnley) 1980/1, 1981/2, 1982/3, 1983/4, 1984/5, (Oxford United) 1985/6.

Harkin, T. (5) (Southport) 1967/8, 1968/9 (Shrewsbury Town), 1969/70, 1970/1.

Harvey, M. (34) (Sunderland) 1960/1, 1961/2, 1962/3, 1963/4, 1964/5, 1965/6, 1966/7, 1967/8, 1968/9, 1969/70, 1970/1.

Hatton, S. (2) (Linfield) 1962/3.
Healy, F. (4) (Coleraine) 1981/2 (Glentoran) 1982/3.
Hegan, D. (7) (West Bromwich Albion) 1969/70, 1971/2
(Wolverhampton Wanderers) 1972/3.
Hill, C.F. (6) (Sheffield U), 1989/90, 1990/1, 1991/2.
Hill, J. (7) (Norwich City) 1958/9, 1959/60, 1960/1, (Everton)
1961/2, 1963/4.
Hinton, E. (7) (Fulham) 1946/7, 1947/8 (Millwall) 1950/1.
Hughes, M.E. (4) (Manchester City) 1991/2.
Hughes, P. (3) (Bury) 1986/7.
Hughes, W. (1) (Bolton Wanderers) 1950/1.
Humphries, W. (14) (Ards) 1961/2 (Coventry City) 1962/3, 1963/4,
1964/5 (Swansea Town).
Hunter, A. (53) (Blackburn Rovers) 1969/70, 1970/1, 1971/2
(Ipswich Town) 1972/3, 1973/4, 1974/5, 1975/6, 1976/7, 1977/8,
1978/9, 1979/80.

Irvine, R. (8) (Linfield) 1961/2, 1962/3 (Stoke City) 1964/5.
Irvine, W. (23) (Burnley) 1962/3, 1964/5, 1965/6, 1966/7, 1967/8,
1968/9 (Preston North End) (Brighton & Hove Albion) 1971/2.

Jackson, T. (35) (Everton) 1968/9, 1969/70, 1970/1 (Nottingham
Forest) 1971/2, 1972/3, 1973/4, 1974/5 (Manchester United) 1975/6,
1976/7.
Jamison, A. (1) (Glentoran) 1975/6.
Jennings, P. (119) (Watford) 1963/4, 1964/5, (Tottenham Hotspur),
1965/6, 1966/7, 1967/8, 1968/9, 1969/70, 1970/1, 1971/2, 1972/3,
1973/4, 1974/5, 1975/6, 1976/7, (Arsenal) 1977/8, 1978/9, 1979/80,
1980/1, 1981/2, 1982/3, 1983/4, 1984/5, (Tottenham Hotspur)
1985/6.
Johnston, W. (1) (Glentoran) 1961/2, (Oldham Athletic) 1965/6.
Jones, J. (3) (Glenavon) 1955/6, 1956/7.

Keane, T. (1) (Swansea Town) 1948/9.
Kee, P.V. (7) (Oxford United), 1989/90, 1990/91.
Keith, R. (23) (Newcastle United) 1957/8, 1958/9, 1959/60, 1960/1,
1961/2.
Kelly, H. (4) (Fulham) 1949/50 (Southampton) 1950/1.
Kelly, P. (1) (Barnsley) 1949/50.

Lawther, I. (4) (Sunderland) 1959/60, 1960/1, 1961/2 (Blackburn
Rovers).
Lockhart, N. (8) (Linfield) 1946/7, 1949/50, (Coventry City) 1950/1,
1951/2, 1953/4, (Aston Villa) 1954/5, 1955/6.
Lutton, B. (6) (Wolverhampton Wanderers) 1969/70, 1972/3 (West
Ham United) 1973/4.

Magill, E. (26) (Arsenal) 1961/2, 1962/3, 1963/4, 1964/5, 1965/6 (Brighton & Hove Albion).
Magilton, J. (9) (Oxford United) 1990/1, 1991/2.
Martin, C. (6) (Glentoran) 1946/7, 1947/8 (Leeds United) 1948/9 (Aston Villa) 1949/50.
McAdams, W. (15) (Manchester City) 1953/4, 1954/5, 1956/7, 1957/8, 1960/1 (Bolton Wanderers) 1961/2 (Leeds United).
McAlinden, J. (2) (Portsmouth) 1946/7, 1948/9, (Southend United).
McBride, S. (4) (Glenavon) 1990/1, 1991/2.
McCabe, J. (6) (Leeds United) 1948/9, 1949/50, 1950/1, 1952/3, 1953/4.
McCavana, T. (3) (Coleraine) 1954/5, 1955/6.
McCleary, J.W. (1) (Cliftonville) 1954/5.
McClelland, J. (6) (Arsenal) 1960/1, 1965/6 (Fulham).
McClelland, J. (53) (Mansfield Town) 1979/80, 1980/1, 1981/2 (Rangers) 1982/3, 1983/4, 1984/5 (Watford) 1985/6, 1986/7, 1987/8, 1988/9 (Leeds U) 1989/90.
McCourt, F. (6) (Manchester City) 1951/2, 1952/3.
McCoy, R. (1) (Coleraine) 1986/7.
McCreery, D. (67) (Manchester United) 1975/6, 1976/7, 1977/8, 1978/9, 1979/80 (QPR) 1980/1 (Tulsa Roughnecks) 1981/2, 1982/3 (Newcastle United), 1983/4, 1984/5, 1985/6, 1986/7, 1987/8, 1988/9 (Hearts) 1989/90.
McCrory, S. (1) (Southend United) 1957/8.
McCullough, W. (10) (Arsenal) 1960/1, 1962/3, 1963/4, 1964/5, 1966/7, (Millwall).
McCurdy, C. (1) (Linfield) 1979/80.
McDonald, A. (33) (QPR) 1985/6, 1986/7, 1987/8, 1988/9, 1990/1, 1991/2.
McElhinney, G. (6) (Bolton Wanderers) 1983/4, 1984/5.
McFaul, I. (6) (Linfield) 1966/7, 1969/70 (Newcastle United) 1970/1, 1971/2, 1972/3, 1973/4.
McGarry, J.K. (3) (Cliftonville) 1950/1.
McGaughey, M. (1) (Linfield) 1984/5.
McGrath, R. (21) (Tottenham Hotspur) 1973/4, 1974/5, 1975/6 (Manchester United) 1976/7, 1977/8, 1978/9.
McIlroy, J. (55) (Burnley) 1951/2, 1952/3, 1953/4, 1954/5, 1955/6, 1956/7, 1957/8, 1958/9, 1959/60, 1960/1, 1961/2, 1962/3, 1965/6 (Stoke City).
McIlroy, S.B. (88) (Manchester United) 1971/2, 1973/4, 1974/5, 1975/6, 1976/7, 1977/8, 1978/9, 1979/80, 1980/1, 1981/2, (Stoke City), 1982/3, 1983/4, 1984/5 (Manchester City) 1985/6, 1986/7.
McKeag, W. (2) (Glentoran) 1967/8.
McKenna, J. (7) (Huddersfield Town) 1949/50, 1950/1, 1951/2.
McKenzie, R. (1) (Airdrieonians) 1966/7.
McKinney, W. (1) (Falkirk) 1965/6.

McKnight, A. (10) (Celtic) 1987/8, (West Ham United) 1988/9.
McLaughlin, J. (12) (Shrewsbury Town) 1961/2, 1962/3 (Swansea City), 1963/4, 1964/5, 1965/6.
McMichael, A. (39) (Newcastle United) 1949/50, 1950/1, 1951/2, 1952/3, 1953/4, 1954/5, 1955/6, 1956/7, 1957/8, 1958/9, 1959/60.
McMillan, S. (2) (Manchester United) 1962/3.
McMordie, E. (21) (Middlesbrough) 1968/9, 1969/70, 1970/1, 1971/2, 1972/3.
McMorran, E. (15) (Belfast Celtic) 1946/7 (Barnsley) 1950/1, 1951/2, 1952/3, (Doncaster Rovers) 1953/4, 1955/6, 1956/7.
McNally, B.A. (5) (Shrewsbury Town) 1985/6, 1986/7, 1987/8.
McParland, P. (34) (Aston Villa) 1953/4, 1954/5, 1955/6, 1956/7, 1957/8, 1958/9, 1959/60, 1960/1, 1961/2 (Wolverhampton Wanderers).
Montgomery, F.J. (1) (Coleraine) 1954/5.
Moore, C. (1) (Glentoran) 1948/9.
Moreland, V. (6) (Derby County) 1978/9, 1979/80.
Morgan, S. (18) (Port Vale) 1971/2, 1972/3, 1973/4 (Aston Villa), 1974/5, 1975/6 (Brighton & Hove Albion) (Sparta Rotterdam) 1978/9.
Morrow, S.J. (7) (Arsenal) 1989/90, 1990/1, 1991/2.
Mullan, G. (4) (Glentoran) 1982/3.

Napier, R. (1) (Bolton Wanderers) 1965/6.
Neill, T. (59) (Arsenal) 1960/1, 1961/2, 1962/3, 1963/4, 1964/5, 1965/6, 1966/7, 1967/8, 1968/9, 1969/70 (Hull City) 1970/1, 1971/2, 1972/3.
Nelson, S. (51) (Arsenal) 1969/70, 1970/1, 1971/2, 1972/3, 1973/4, 1974/5, 1975/6, 1976/7, 1977/8, 1978/9, 1979/80, 1980/1, 1981/2 (Brighton & Hove Albion).
Nicholl, C. (51) (Aston Villa) 1974/5, 1975/6, 1976/7 (Southampton), 1977/8, 1978/9, 1979/80, 1980/1, 1981/2, 1982/3 (Grimsby Town) 1983/4.
Nicholl, J.M. (73) (Manchester United) 1975/6, 1976/7, 1977/8, 1978/9, 1979/80, 1980/1, 1981/2 (Toronto Blizzard) 1982/3 (Sunderland) (Toronto Blizzard) (Rangers) 1983/4 (Toronto Blizzard) 1984/5 (West Bromwich Albion) 1985/6.
Nicholson, J. (41) (Manchester United) 1960/1, 1961/2, 1962/3, 1964/5, (Huddersfield Town) 1965/6, 1966/7, 1967/8, 1968/9, 1969/70, 1970/1, 1971/2.

O'Doherty, A. (2) (Coleraine) 1969/70.
O'Driscoll, J. (3) (Swansea City) 1948/9.
O'Kane, L. (20) (Nottingham Forest) 1969/70, 1970/1, 1971/2, 1972/3, 1973/4, 1974/5.
O'Neill, C. (3) (Motherwell) 1988/9, 1989/90, 1990/91.

O'Neill, H.M. (64) (Distillery) 1971/2 (Nottingham Forest) 1972/3, 1973/4, 1974/5, 1975/6, 1976/7, 1977/8, 1978/9, 1979/80, 1980/1 (Norwich City) 1981/2 (Manchester City) (Norwich City) 1982/3 (Notts County) 1983/4, 1984/5.
O'Neill, J. (1) (Sunderland) 1961/2.
O'Neill, J. (39) (Leicester City) 1979/80, 1980/1, 1981/2, 1982/3, 1983/4, 1984/5, 1985/6.
O'Neill, M.A. (16) (Newcastle United) 1987/8, 1988/9 (Dundee United) 1989/90, 1990/1, 1991/2.

Parke, J. (13) (Linfield) 1963/4 (Hibernian), 1964/5 (Sunderland), 1965/6, 1966/7, 1967/8.
Peacock, R. (31) (Celtic) 1951/2, 1952/3, 1953/4, 1954/5, 1955/6, 1956/7, 1957/8, 1958/9, 1959/60, 1960/1 (Coleraine) 1961/2.
Penney, S. (17) (Brighton & Hove Albion) 1984/5, 1985/6, 1986/7, 1987/8, 1988/9.
Platt, J.A. (23) (Middlesbrough) 1975/6, 1977/8, 1979/80, 1980/1, 1981/2, 1982/3, (Ballymena United) 1983/4 (Coleraine) 1985/6.

Quinn, J.M. (29) (Blackburn Rovers) 1984/5, 1985/6, 1986/7, 1987/8 (Leicester) 1988/9 (Bradford City) 1989/90 (West Ham United), 1990/1, (Bournemouth) 1991/2.

Rafferty, P. (1) (Linfield) 1979/80.
Ramsey, P. (14) (Leicester City) 1983/4, 1984/5, 1985/6, 1986/7, 1987/8, 1988/9.
Rice, P. (49) (Arsenal) 1968/9, 1969/70, 1970/1, 1971/2, 1972/3, 1973/4, 1974/5, 1975/6, 1976/7, 1977/8, 1978/9, 1979/80.
Rogan, A. (17) (Celtic) 1987/8, 1988/9, 1989/90, 1990/1, 1991/2.
Ross, E. (1) (Newcastle United) 1968/9.
Russell, A. (1) (Linfield) 1946/7.
Ryan, R. (1) (West Bromwich Albion) 1949/50.

Sanchez, L.P. (3) (Wimbledon) 1986/7, 1988/9.
Scott, J. (2) (Grimsby Town) 1957/8.
Scott, P. (10) (Everton) 1974/5, 1975/6, (York City) 1977/8, (Aldershot) 1978/9.
Sharkey, P. (1) (Ipswich Town) 1975/6.
Shields, J. (1) (Southampton) 1956/7.
Simpson, W. (12) (Rangers) 1950/1, 1953/4, 1954/5, 1956/7, 1957/8, 1958/9.
Sloan, D. (2) (Oxford) 1968/9, 1970/1.
Sloan, T. (3) (Manchester United) 1978/9.
Sloan, W. (1) (Arsenal) 1946/7.
Smyth, S. (9) (Wolverhampton Wanderers) 1947/8, 1948/9, 1949/50 (Stoke City) 1951/2.
Smyth, W. (4) (Distillery) 1948/9, 1953/4.

Spence, D. (29) (Bury) 1974/5, 1975/6, (Blackpool) 1976/7, 1978/9, 1979/80, (Southend United) 1980/1, 1981/2.
Stevenson, A. (3) (Everton) 1946/7, 1947/8.
Sfewart, A. (7) (Glentoran) 1966/7, 1967/8 (Derby) 1968/9.
Stewart, D. (1) (Hull City) 1977/8.
Stewart, I. (31) (QPR) 1981/2, 1982/3, 1983/4, 1984/5, (Newcastle United) 1985/6, 1986/7.
Stewart, T. (1) (Linfield) 1960/1.

Taggart, G.P. (13) (Barnsley) 1989/90, 1990/1, 1991/2.
Todd, S. (11) (Burnley) 1965/6, 1966/7, 1967/8, 1968/9, 1969/70 (Sheffield Wednesday) 1970/1.
Trainor, D. (1) (Crusaders) 1966/7.
Tully, C. (10) (Celtic) 1948/9, 1949/50, 1951/2, 1952/3, 1953/4, 1955/6, 1958/9.

Uprichard, N. (18) (Swindon Town) 1951/2, 1952/3 (Portsmouth) 1954/5, 1955/6, 1957/8, 1958/9.

Vernon, J. (17) (Belfast Celtic) 1946/7 (West Bromwich Albion) 1947/8, 1948/9, 1949/50, 1950/1 , 1951/2.

Walker, J. (1) (Doncaster Rovers) 1954/5.
Walsh, D. (9) (West Bromwich Albion) 1946/7, 1947/8, 1948/9, 1949/50.
Walsh, W. (5) (Manchester City) 1947/8, 1948/9.
Watson, P. (1) (Distillery) 1970/1.
Welsh, S. (4) (Carlisle United) 1965/6, 1966/7.
Whiteside, N. (38) (Manchester United) 1981/2, 1982/3, 1983/4, 1984/5, 1985/6, 1986/7, 1987/8, (Everton) 1989/90.
Williams, P. (1) (WBA) 1990/1.
Wilson, D.J. (24) (Brighton & Hove Albion) 1986/7 (Luton) 1987/8, 1988/9, 1989/90, 1990/1, (Sheffield Wednesday) 1991/2.
Wilson, K.J. (27) (Ipswich Town) 1986/7 (Chelsea) 1987/8, 1988/9, 1989/90, 1990/1, 1991/2 (Notts County).
Wilson, S. (12) (Glenavon) 1961/2, 1963/4, (Falkirk) 1964/5 (Dundee), 1965/6, 1966/7, 1967/8.
Worthington, N. (37) (Sheffield Wednesday) 1983/4, 1984/5, 1985/6, 1986/7, 1987/8, 1988/9, 1989/90, 1990/1, 1991/2.
Wright, T.J. (8) (Newcastle United) 1988/9, 1989/90, 1991/2.

SCOTLAND

Aird, J. (4) (Burnley) 1953/4.
Aitken, G.G. (8) (East Fife) 1948/9, 1949/50, 1952/3 (Sunderland) 1953/4.

Aitken, R. (57) (Celtic) 1979/80, 1982/3, 1983/4, 1984/5, 1985/6, 1986/7, 1987/8, (Newcastle United) 1989/90, (St Mirren) 1991/2.
Albiston, A. (14) (Manchester United) 1981/2, 1983/4, 1984/5, 1985/6.
Allan, T. (2) (Dundee) 1973/4.
Anderson, J. (1) (Leicester City) 1953/4.
Archibald, S. (27) (Aberdeen) 1979/80 (Tottenham Hotspur) 1980/1, 1981/2, 1982/3, 1983/4, 1984/5, (Barcelona) 1985/6.
Auld, B. (3) (Celtic) 1958/9, 1959/60.

Baird, H. (1) (Airdrieonians) 1955/6.
Baird, S. (7) (Rangers) 1956/7, 1957/8.
Bannon, E. (11) (Dundee United) 1979/80, 1982/3, 1983/4, 1985/6.
Bauld, W. (3) (Heart of Midlothian) 1949/50.
Baxter, J. (34) (Rangers) 1960/1, 1961/2, 1962/3, 1963/4, 1964/5 (Sunderland) 1965/6, 1966/7, 1967/8.
Bell, W. (2) (Leeds United) 1965/6.
Bett, J. (25) (Rangers) 1981/2, 1982/3 (Lokeren) 1983/4, 1984/5 (Aberdeen) 1985/6, 1986/7, 1987/8, 1988/9, 1989/90.
Black, E. (2) (Metz) 1987/8.
Black, I. (1) (Southampton) 1947/8.
Blacklaw, A. (3) (Burnley) 1962/3, 1965/6.
Blackley, J. (7) (Hibernian) 1973/4, 1975/6, 1976/7.
Blair, J. (1) (Blackpool) 1946/7.
Blyth, J. (2) (Coventry City) 1977/8.
Bone, J. (2) (Norwich City) 1971/2, 1972/3.
Bowman, D. (2) (Dundee United) 1991/2.
Boyd, T. (10) (Motherwell) 1990/1 (Chelsea) 1991/2 (Celtic).
Brand, R. (8) (Rangers) 1960/1, 1961/2.
Brazil, A. (13) (Ipswich Town) 1979/80, 1981/2, 1982/3 (Tottenham Hotspur).
Bremner, D. (1) (Hibernian) 1975/6.
Bremner, W. (54) (Leeds United) 1964/5, 1965/6, 1966/7, 1967/8, 1968/9, 1969/70, 1970/1, 1971/2, 1972/3, 1973/4, 1974/5, 1975/6.
Brennan, F. (7) (Newcastle United) 1946/7, 1952/3, 1963/4.
Brogan, J. (4) (Celtic) 1970/1.
Brown, A. (14) (East Fife) 1949/50 (Blackpool) 1951/2, 1952/3, 1953/4.
Brown, H. (3) (Partick Thistle) 1946/7.
Brown, J. (1) (Sheffield United) 1974/5.
Brown, R. (3) (Rangers) 1946/7, 1948/9, 1951/2.
Brown, W. (28) (Dundee) 1957/8, 1958/9, 1959/60 (Tottenham Hotspur) 1961/2, 1962/3, 1963/4, 1964/5, 1965/6.
Brownlie, J. (7) (Hibernian) 1970/1, 1971/2, 1972/3, 1975/6.
Buchan, M. (34) (Aberdeen) 1971/2 (Manchester United), 1972/3, 1973/4, 1974/5, 1975/6, 1976/7, 1977/8, 1978/9.

Buckley, P. (3) (Aberdeen) 1953/4, 1954/5.
Burley, G. (11) (Ipswich Town) 1978/9, 1979/80, 1981/2.
Burns, F. (1) (Manchester United) 1969/70.
Burns, K. (20) (Birmingham City) 1973/4, 1974/5, 1976/7
(Nottingham Forest) 1977/8, 1978/9, 1979/80, 1980/1.
Burns, T. (8) (Celtic) 1980/1, 1981/2, 1982/3, 1987/8.

Caldow, E. (40) (Rangers) 1956/7, 1957/8, 1958/9, 1959/60, 1960/1,
1961/2, 1962/3.
Callaghan, W. (2) (Dunfermline) 1969/70.
Campbell, R. (5) (Falkirk) 1946/7 (Chelsea) 1949/50.
Campbell, W. (5) (Morton) 1946/7, 1947/8.
Carr, W. (6) (Coventry City) 1969/70, 1970/1, 1971/2, 1972/3.
Chalmers, S. (5) (Celtic) 1964/5, 1965/6, 1966/7.
Clark, J. (4) (Celtic) 1965/6, 1966/7.
Clark, R. (17) (Aberdeen) 1967/8, 1969/70, 1970/1, 1971/2, 1972/3.
Clarke, S. (5) (Chelsea) 1987/8.
Collins, J. (8) (Hibernian) 1987/8, 1989/90, 1990/1 (Celtic), 1991/2.
Collins, R. (31) (Celtic) 1950/1, 1954/5, 1955/6, 1956/7, 1957/8,
1958/9, (Everton) 1964/5, (Leeds United).
Colquhoun, E. (9) (Sheffield United) 1971/2, 1972/3.
Colquhoun, J. (1) (Hearts) 1987/8.
Combe, R. (3) (Hibernian) 1947/8.
Conn, A. (1) (Heart of Midlothian) 1955/6.
Conn, A. (2) (Tottenham Hotspur) 1974/5.
Connachan, E. (2) (Dunfermline Athletic) 1961/2.
Connelly, G. (2) (Celtic) 1973/4.
Connolly, J. (1) (Everton) 1972/3.
Connor, R. (4) (Dundee) 1985/6 (Aberdeen) 1987/8, 1988/9,
1990/91.
Cooke, C. (16) (Dundee) 1965/6 (Chelsea) 1967/8, 1968/9, 1969/70,
1970/1, 1974/5.
Cooper, D. (22) (Rangers) 1979/80, 1983/4, 1984/5, 1985/6, 1986/7
(Motherwell) 1989/90.
Cormack, P. (9) (Hibernian) 1965/6, 1969/70 (Nottingham Forest)
1970/1, 1971/2.
Cowan, J. (25) (Morton) 1947/8, 1948/9, 1949/50, 1950/1, 1951/2
(Motherwell).
Cowie, D. (20) (Dundee) 1952/3, 1953/4, 1954/5, 1955/6, 1956/7,
1957/8.
Cox, C. (1) (Hearts) 1947/8.
Cox, S. (25) (Rangers) 1947/8, 1948/9, 1949/50, 1950/1, 1951/2,
1952/3, 1953/4.
Craig, J. (1) (Celtic) 1976/7.
Craig, J.P. (1) (Celtic) 1967/8.
Craig, T. (1) (Newcastle United) 1975/6.

Crerand, P. (16) (Celtic) 1960/1, 1961/2, 1962/3 (Manchester United) 1963/4, 1964/5, 1965/6.
Cropley, A. (2) (Hibernian) 1971/2.
Cruickshank, J. (6) (Heart of Midlothian) 1963/4, 1969/70, 1970/1, 1975/6.
Cullen, M. (1) (Luton Town) 1955/6.
Cumming, J. (9) (Heart of Midlothian) 1954/5, 1959/60.
Cunningham, W. (8) (Preston North End) 1953/4, 1954/5.
Curran, H. (5) (Wolverhampton Wanderers) 1969/70, 1970/1.

Dalglish, K. (102) (Celtic) 1971/2, 1972/3, 1973/4, 1974/5, 1975/6, 1976/7, (Liverpool) 1977/8, 1978/9, 1979/80, 1980/1, 1981/2, 1982/3, 1983/4, 1984/5, 1985/6, 1986/7.
Davidson, J. (8) (Partick Thistle) 1953/4, 1954/5.
Dawson, A. (5) (Rangers) 1979/80, 1982/3.
Deans, D. (2) (Celtic) 1974/5.
Delaney, J. (4) (Manchester United) 1946/7, 1947/8.
Dick, J. (1) (West Ham United) 1958/9.
Dickson, W. (5) (Kilmarnock) 1969/70, 1970/1.
Docherty, T. (25) (Preston North End) 1951/2, 1952/3, 1953/4, 1954/5, 1956/7, 1957/8, 1958/9 (Arsenal).
Dodds, D. (2) (Dundee United) 1983/4.
Donachie, W. (35) (Manchester City) 1971/2, 1972/3, 1973/4, 1975/6, 1976/7, 1977/8, 1978/9.
Dougall, C. (1) (Birmingham City) 1946/7.
Dougan, R. (1) (Heart of Midlothian) 1949/50.
Doyle, J. (1) (Ayr United) 1975/6.
Duncan, A. (6) (Hibernian) 1974/5, 1975/6.
Duncan, D. (3) (East Fife) 1947/8.
Duncanson, J. (1) (Rangers) 1946/7.
Durie, G.S. (21) (Chelsea) 1987/8, 1988/9, 1989/90, 1990/1, (Tottenham Hotspur) 1991/2.
Durrant, I. (5) (Rangers) 1987/8, 1988/9.

Evans, A. (4) (Aston Villa) 1981/2.
Evans, R. (48) (Celtic) 1948/9, 1949/50, 1950/1, 1951/2, 1952/3, 1953/4, 1954/5, 1955/6, 1956/7, 1957/8, 1958/9, 1959/60 (Chelsea).
Ewing, T. (2) (Partick Thistle) 1957/8.

Farm, G. (10) (Blackpool) 1952/3, 1953/4, 1958/9.
Ferguson, D. (2) (Rangers) 1987/8.
Ferguson, D. (3) (Dundee United) 1991/2.
Ferguson, I. (3) (Rangers) 1988/9.
Ferguson, R. (7) (Kilmarnock) 1965/6, 1966/7.
Fernie, W. (12) (Celtic) 1953/4, 1954/5, 1956/7, 1957/8.
Flavell, R. (2) (Airdrieonians) 1946/7.
Fleck, R. (4) (Norwich City) 1989/90, 1990/1.

Fleming, C. (1) (East Fife) 1953/4.
Forbes, A. (14) (Sheffield United) 1946/7, 1947/8 (Arsenal) 1949/50, 1950/1, 1951/2.
Ford, D. (3) (Heart of Midlothian) 1973/4.
Forrest, J. (1) (Motherwell) 1957/8.
Forrest, J. (5) (Rangers) 1965/6 (Aberdeen) 1970/1.
Forsyth, A. (10) (Partick Thistle) 1971/2, 1972/3 (Manchester United) 1974/5, 1975/6.
Forsyth, C. (4) (Kilmarnock) 1963/4, 1964/5.
Forsyth, T. (22) (Motherwell) 1970/1 (Rangers) 1973/4, 1975/6, 1976/7, 1977/8.
Fraser, D. (2) (West Bromwich Albion) 1967/8, 1968/9.
Fraser, W. (2) (Sunderland) 1954/5.

Gabriel, J. (2) (Everton) 1960/1, 1961/2.
Gallacher, K.W. (12) (Dundee United) 1987/8, 1988/9, 1990/91 (Coventry City), 1991/2.
Galloway, M. (1) (Celtic) 1991/2.
Gardiner, W. (1) (Motherwell) 1957/8.
Gemmell, T. (2) (St Mirren) 1954/5.
Gemmell, T. (18) (Celtic) 1965/6, 1966/7, 1967/8, 1968/9, 1969/70, 1970/1.
Gemmill, A. (43) (Derby County) 1970/1, 1971/2, 1975/6, 1976/7, 1977/8 (Nottingham Forest) 1978/9 (Birmingham City) 1979/80, 1980/1.
Gibson, D. (7) (Leicester City) 1962/3, 1963/4, 1964/5.
Gillespie, G.T. (13) (Liverpool) 1987/8, 1988/9, 1989/90, (Celtic) 1990/91.
Gilzean, A. (22) (Dundee) 1963/4, 1964/5 (Tottenham Hotspur) 1965/6, 1967/8, 1968/9, 1969/70, 1970/1.
Glavin, R. (1) (Celtic) 1976/7.
Glen, A. (2) (Aberdeen) 1955/6.
Goram, A.L. (23) (Oldham Athletic) 1985/6, 1986/7, (Hibernian) 1988/9, 1989/90, 1990/1, (Rangers) 1991/2.
Gough, C.R. (59) (Dundee United) 1982/3, 1983/4, 1984/5, 1985/6, 1986/7 (Tottenham Hotspur) 1987/8 (Rangers) 1988/9, 1989/90, 1990/1, 1991/2.
Govan, J. (6) (Hibernian) 1947/8, 1948/9.
Graham, A. (10) (Leeds United) 1977/8, 1978/9, 1979/80, 1980/1.
Graham, G. (13) (Arsenal) 1971/2, 1972/3 (Manchester United).
Grant, J. (2) (Hibernian) 1958/9.
Grant, P. (2) (Celtic) 1988/9.
Gray, A. (20) (Aston Villa) 1975/6, 1976/7, 1978/9 (Wolverhampton Wanderers) 1979/80, 1980/1, 1981/2, 1982/3, 1984/5 (Everton).
Gray, E. (12) (Leeds United) 1968/9, 1969/70, 1970/71, 1971/2, 1975/6, 1976/7.

Gray F. (32) (Leeds United) 1975/6, 1978/9, 1979/80 (Nottingham Forest) 1980/1, (Leeds United) 1981/2, 1982/3.
Green, A. (6) (Blackpool) 1970/1 (Newcastle United) 1971/2.
Greig, J. (44) (Rangers) 1963/4, 1964/5, 1965/6, 1966/7, 1967/8, 1968/9, 1969/70, 1970/1, 1975/6.
Gunn, B. (1) (Norwich C) 1989/90.

Haddock, H. (6) (Clyde) 1954/5, 1957/8.
Haffey, F. (2) (Celtic) 1959/60, 1960/1.
Hamilton, A. (24) (Dundee) 1961/2, 1962/3, 1963/4, 1964/5, 1965/6.
Hamilton, G. (5) (Aberdeen) 1946/7, 1950/1, 1953/4.
Hamilton, W. (1) (Hibernian) 1964/5.
Hansen, A. (26) (Liverpool) 1978/9, 1979/80, 1980/1, 1981/2, 1982/3, 1984/5, 1985/6, 1986/7.
Hansen J. (2) (Partick Thistle) 1971/2.
Harper, J. (4) (Aberdeen) 1972/3, 1975/6, 1978/9.
Hartford, A. (50) (West Bromwich Albion) 1971/2, 1975/6 (Manchester City) 1976/7, 1977/8, 1978/9, 1979/80 (Everton) 1980/1, 1981/2 (Manchester City).
Harvey, D. (16) (Leeds United) 1972/3, 1973/4, 1974/5, 1975/6, 1976/7.
Haughney, M. (1) (Celtic) 1953/4.
Hay, D. (27) (Celtic) 1969/70, 1970/1, 1971/2, 1972/3, 1973/4.
Hegarty, P. (8) (Dundee United) 1978/9, 1979/80, 1982/3.
Henderson, J. (7) (Portsmouth) 1952/3, 1953/4, 1955/6, 1958/9 (Arsenal).
Henderson, W. (29) (Rangers) 1962/3, 1963/4, 1964/5, 1965/6, 1966/7, 1967/8, 1968/9, 1969/70.
Herd, D. (5) (Arsenal) 1958/9, 1960/1.
Herd, G. (5) (Clyde) 1957/8, 1959/60, 1960/1.
Herriot, J. (8) (Birmingham City) 1968/9, 1969/70.
Hewie, J. (19) (Charlton Athletic) 1955/6, 1956/7, 1957/8, 1958/9, 1959/60.
Holt, D. (5) (Heart of Midlothian) 1962/3, 1963/4.
Holton, J. (15) (Manchester United) 1972/3, 1973/4, 1974/5.
Hope, R. (2) (West Bromwich Albion) 1967/8, 1968/9.
Houliston, W. (3) (Queen of the South) 1948/9.
Houston, S. (1) (Manchester United) 1975/6.
Howie, H. (1) (Hibernian) 1948/9.
Hughes, J. (8) (Celtic) 1964/5, 1965/6, 1967/8, 1968/9, 1969/70.
Hughes, W. (1) (Sunderland) 1974/5.
Humphries, W. (1) (Motherwell) 1951/2.
Hunter, A. (4) (Kilmarnock) 1971/2, 1972/3, (Celtic) 1973/4.
Hunter, W. (3) (Motherwell) 1959/60, 1960/1.
Husband, J. (1) (Partick Thistle) 1946/7.
Hutchison, T. (17) (Coventry City) 1973/4, 1974/5, 1975/6.

Imlach, S. (4) (Nottingham Forest) 1957/8.
Irvine, B. (1) (Aberdeen) 1990/1.

Jackson, C. (8) (Rangers) 1974/5, 1975/6.
Jardine, A. (38) (Rangers) 1970/1, 1971/2, 1972/3, 1973/4, 1974/5, 1976/7, 1977/8, 1978/9, 1979/80.
Jarvie, A. (3) (Airdrieonians) 1970/1.
Johnston, M. (38) (Watford) 1983/4, 1984/5 (Celtic) 1985/6, 1986/7, (Nantes) 1987/8, 1988/9 (Rangers) 1989/90, 1991/2.
Johnston, W. (22) (Rangers) 1965/6, 1967/8, 1968/9, 1969/70, 1970/1 (West Bromwich Albion) 1976/7, 1977/8.
Johnstone, D. (14) (Rangers) 1972/3, 1974/5, 1975/6, 1977/8, 1979/80.
Johnstone, J. (23) (Celtic) 1964/5, 1965/6, 1966/7, 1967/8, 1968/9, 1969/70, 1970/1, 1971/2, 1973/4, 1974/5.
Johnstone, L. (2) (Clyde) 1947/8.
Johnstone, R. (17) (Hibernian) 1950/1, 1951/2, 1952/3, 1953/4, 1954/5, (Manchester City) 1955/6.
Jordan, J. (52) (Leeds United) 1972/3, 1973/4, 1974/5, 1975/6, 1976/7, 1977/8, (Manchester United) 1978/9, 1979/80, 1980/1, 1981/2 (AC Milan).

Kelly, H. (1) (Blackpool) 1951/2.
Kelly, J. (2) (Barnsley) 1948/9.
Kennedy, J. (6) (Celtic) 1963/4, 1964/5.
Kennedy, S. (8) (Aberdeen) 1977/8, 1978/9, 1981/2.
Kennedy, S. (5) (Rangers) 1974/5.
Kerr, A. (2) (Partick Thistle) 1954/5.

Law, D. (55) (Huddersfield Town) 1958/9, 1959/60 (Manchester City) 1960/1, 1961/2 (Torino) 1962/3 (Manchester United) 1963/4, 1964/5, 1965/6, 1966/7, 1967/8, 1968/9, 1971/2, 1973/4 (Manchester City).
Lawrence, T. (3) (Liverpool) 1962/3, 1968/9.
Leggat, G. (18) (Aberdeen) 1955/6, 1956/7, 1957/8, 1958/9 (Fulham) 1959/60.
Leighton, J. (58) (Aberdeen) 1982/3, 1983/4, 1984/5, 1985/6, 1986/7, 1987/8, (Manchester United) 1988/9, 1989/90.
Lennox, R. (10) (Celtic) 1966/7, 1967/8, 1968/9.
Leslie, L. (5) Airdrieonians) 1960/1.
Levein, C. (8) (Hearts) 1989/90, 1991/2.
Liddell, W. (28) (Liverpool) 1946/7, 1947/8, 1949/50, 1950/1, 1951/2, 1952/3, 1953/4, 1954/5, 1955/6.
Linwood, A. (1) (Clyde) 1949/50.
Little, A. (1) (Rangers) 1952/3.
Logie, J. (1) (Arsenal) 1952/3.
Long, H. (1) (Clyde) 1946/7.

Lorimer, P. (21) (Leeds United) 1969/70, 1970/1, 1971/2, 1972/3, 1973/4, 1974/5, 1975/6.

Macari, L. (24) (Celtic) 1971/2, 1972/3 (Manchester United) 1974/5, 1976/7, 1977/8, 1978/9.
Macaulay, A. (7) (Brentford) 1946/7 (Arsenal) 1947/8.
MacDougall, E. (7) (Norwich City) 1974/5, 1975/6.
Mackay, D. (22) (Heart of Midlothian) 1956/7, 1957/8, 1958/9 (Tottenham Hotspur) 1959/60, 1960/1, 1962/3, 1963/4, 1965/6.
Mackay, G. (4) (Heart of Midlothian) 1987/8.
Malpas, M. (52) (Dundee United) 1983/4, 1984/5, 1985/6, 1986/7, 1987/8, 1988/9, 1989/90, 1990/1, 1991/2.
Marshall, G. (1) (Celtic) 1991/2.
Martin, F. (6) (Aberdeen) 1953/4, 1954/5.
Martin, N. (3) (Hibernian) 1964/5, 1965/6 (Sunderland).
Martis, J. (1) (Motherwell) 1960/1.
Mason, J. (7) (Third Lanark) 1948/9, 1949/50, 1950/1.
Masson, D. (17) (QPR) 1975/6, 1976/7, 1977/8 (Derby County) 1978/9.
Mathers, D. (1) (Partick Thistle) 1953/4.
McAllister, G. (18) (Leicester City) 1989/90, 1990/1 (Leeds United), 1991/2.
McAvennie, F. (5) (West Ham United) 1985/6 (Celtic) 1987/8.
McBride, J. (2) (Celtic) 1966/7.
McCall, S.M. (20) (Everton) 1989/90, 1990/1, (Rangers) 1991/2.
McCalliog, J. (5) (Sheffield Wednesday) 1966/7, 1967/8, 1968/9, 1970/1 (Wolverhampton Wanderers).
McCann, R. (5) (Motherwell) 1958/9, 1959/60, 1960/1.
McClair, B. (26) (Celtic) 1986/7 (Manchester United) 1987/8, 1988/9, 1989/90, 1990/1, 1991/2.
McCloy, P. (4) (Rangers) 1972/3.
McCoist, A. (41) (Rangers) 1985/6, 1986/7, 1987/8, 1988/9, 1989/90, 1990/1, 1991/2.
McColl, I. (14) (Rangers) 1949/50, 1950/1, 1956/7, 1957/8.
McCreadie, E. (23) (Chelsea) 1964/5, 1965/6, 1966/7, 1967/8, 1968/9.
MacDonald, A. (1) (Rangers) 1975/6.
MacDonald, J. (2) (Sunderland) 1955/6.
McFarlane, W. (1) (Heart of Midlothian) 1946/7.
McGarr, E. (2) (Aberdeen) 1969/70.
McGarvey, F. (7) (Liverpool) 1978/9 (Celtic) 1983/4.
McGhee, M. (4) (Aberdeen) 1982/3, 1983/4.
McGrain, D. (62) (Celtic) 1972/3, 1973/4, 1974/5, 1975/6, 1976/7, 1977/8, 1979/80, 1980/1, 1981/2.
McGrory, J. (3) (Kilmarnock) 1964/5, 1965/6.
McInally, A. (8) (Aston Villa) 1988/9 (Bayern Munich) 1989/90.

McInally, J. (8) (Dundee United) 1986/7, 1987/8, 1990/1, 1991/2.
McKay, D. (14) (Celtic) 1958/9, 1959/60, 1960/1, 1961/2.
McKean, R. (1) (Rangers) 1975/6.
McKenzie, J. (9) (Partick Thistle) 1953/4, 1954/5, 1955/6.
McKimmie, S. (20) (Aberdeen) 1988/9, 1989/90, 1990/1, 1991/2.
McKinnon, R. (28) (Rangers) 1965/6, 1966/7, 1967/8, 1968/9, 1969/70, 1970/1.
McLaren, A. (4) (Preston North End) 1946/7, 1947/8.
McLaren, A. (3) (Heart of Midlothian) 1991/2.
McLean, G. (1) (Dundee) 1967/8.
McLean, T. (6) (Kilmarnock) 1968/9, 1969/70, 1970/1.
McLeish, A. (76) (Aberdeen) 1979/80, 1980/1, 1981/2, 1982/3, 1983/4, 1984/5, 1985/6, 1986/7, 1987/8, 1988/9, 1989/90, 1990/1.
McLeod, J. (4) (Hibernian) 1960/1.
MacLeod, M. (20) (Celtic) 1984/5, 1986/7 (Borussia Dortmund) 1987/8, 1988/9, 1989/90, 1990/1 (Hibernian).
McLintock, F. (9) (Leicester City) 1962/3, 1964/5 (Arsenal) 1966/7, 1969/70, 1970/1.
McMillan, I. (6) (Airdrieonians) 1951/2, 1954/5, 1955/6 (Rangers) 1960/1.
McNaught, W. (5) (Raith Rovers) 1950/1, 1951/2, 1954/5.
McNeill, W. (29) (Celtic) 1960/1, 1961/2, 1962/3, 1963/4, 1964/5, 1965/6, 1966/7, 1967/8, 1968/9, 1969/70, 1971/2.
McPhail, J. (5) (Celtic) 1949/50, 1950/1, 1953/4.
McPherson, D. (23) (Hearts) 1988/9, 1989/90, 1990/1, 1991/2.
McQueen, G. (30) (Leeds United) 1973/4, 1974/5, 1975/6, 1976/7, 1977/8, (Manchester United) 1978/9, 1979/80, 1980/1.
McStay, P. (60) (Celtic) 1983/4, 1984/5, 1985/6, 1986/7, 1987/8, 1988/9, 1989/90, 1990/1, 1991/2.
Millar, J. (2) (Rangers) 1962/3.
Miller, W. (6) (Celtic) 1946/7, 1947/8.
Miller, W. (65) (Aberdeen) 1974/5, 1977/8, 1979/80, 1980/1, 1981/2, 1982/3, 1983/4, 1984/5, 1985/6, 1986/7, 1987/8, 1988/9, 1989/90.
Mitchell, R. (2) (Newcastle United) 1950/1.
Mochan, N. (3) (Celtic) 1953/4.
Moir, W. (1) (Bolton Wanderers) 1949/50.
Moncur, R. (16) (Newcastle United) 1967/8, 1969/70, 1970/1, 1971/2.
Morgan, W. (21) (Burnley) 1967/8 (Manchester United) 1971/2, 1972/3, 1973/4.
Morris, H. (1) (East Fife) 1949/50.
Mudie, J. (17) (Blackpool) 1956/7, 1957/8.
Mulhall, G. (3) (Aberdeen) 1959/60, 1962/3 (Sunderland) 1963/4.
Munro, F. (9) (Wolverhampton Wanderers) 1970/1, 1974/5.
Munro, I. (7) (St Mirren) 1978/9, 1979/80.
Murdoch, R. (12) (Celtic) 1965/6, 1966/7, 1967/8, 1968/9, 1969/70.

Murray, J. (5) (Heart of Midlothian) 1957/8.
Murray, S. (1) (Aberdeen) 1971/2.

Narey, D. (35) (Dundee United) 1976/7, 1978/9, 1979/80, 1980/1, 1981/2, 1982/3, 1985/6, 1986/7, 1988/9.
Nevin, P.K.F. (14) (Chelsea) 1985/6, 1986/7, 1987/8 (Everton) 1988/9, 1990/1, 1991/2.
Nicholas, C. (20) (Celtic) 1982/3, (Arsenal) 1983/4, 1984/5, 1985/6, 1986/7, (Aberdeen) 1988/9.
Nicol, S. (27) (Liverpool) 1984/5, 1985/6, 1987/8, 1988/9, 1989/90, 1990/1, 1991/2.

O'Hare, J. (13) (Derby County) 1969/70, 1970/1, 1971/2.
Ormond, W. (6) (Hibernian) 1953/4, 1958/9.
Orr, T. (2) (Morton) 1951/2.

Parker, A. (15) (Falkirk) 1954/5, 1955/6, 1956/7, 1957/8.
Parlane, D. (12) (Rangers) 1972/3, 1974/5, 1975/6, 1976/7.
Paton, A. (2) (Motherwell) 1951/2.
Pearson, T. (2) (Newcastle United) 1946/7.
Penman, A. (1) (Dundee) 1965/6.
Pettigrew, W. (5) (Motherwell) 1975/6, 1976/7.
Plenderleith, J. (1) (Manchester City) 1960/1.
Provan, D. (5) (Rangers) 1963/4, 1965/6.
Provan, D. (10) (Celtic) 1979/80, 1980/1, 1981/2.

Quinn, P. (4) (Motherwell) 1960/1, 1961/2.

Redpath, W. (9) (Motherwell) 1948/9, 1950/1, 1951/2.
Reilly, L. (38) (Hibernian) 1948/9, 1949/50, 1950/1, 1951/2, 1952/3, 1953/4, 1954/5, 1955/6, 1956/7.
Ring, T. (12) (Clydebank) 1952/3, 1954/5, 1956/7, 1957/8.
Rioch, B. (24) (Derby County) 1974/5, 1975/6, 1976/7, (Everton) 1977/8, (Derby County) 1978/9.
Robb, D. (5) (Aberdeen) 1970/1.
Robertson, A. (5) (Clyde) 1954/5, 1957/8.
Robertson, D. (1) (Rangers) 1991/2.
Robertson, H. (1) (Dundee) 1961/2.
Robertson, J. (1) (Tottenham Hotspur) 1964/5.
Robertson, J. (7) (Heart of Midlothian) 1990/1, 1991/2.
Robertson, J.N. (28) (Nottingham Forest) 1977/8, 1978/9, 1979/80, 1980/1, 1981/2, 1982/3 (Derby County) 1983/4.
Robinson, B. (4) (Dundee) 1973/4, 1974/5.
Rough, A. (53) (Partick Thistle) 1975/6, 1976/7, 1977/8, 1978/9, 1979/80, 1980/1, 1981/2, (Hibernian) 1985/6.
Rougvie, D. (1) (Aberdeen) 1983/4.
Rutherford, E. (1) (Rangers) 1947/8.

St John, I. (21) (Motherwell) 1958/9, 1959/60, 1960/1, 1961/2 (Liverpool) 1962/3, 1963/4, 1964/5.
Schaedler, E. (1) (Hibernian) 1973/4.
Scott, A. (16) (Rangers) 1956/7, 1957/8, 1958/9, 1961/2 (Everton) 1963/4, 1964/5, 1965/6.
Scott, J. (1) (Hibernian) 1965/6.
Scott, J. (2) (Dundee) 1970/1.
Scoular, J. (9) (Portsmouth) 1950/1, 1951/2, 1952/3.
Sharp, G.M. (12) (Everton) 1984/5, 1985/6, 1986/7, 1987/8.
Shaw, D. (8) (Hibernian) 1946/7, 1947/8, 1948/9.
Shaw, J. (4) (Rangers) 1946/7, 1947/8.
Shearer, R. (4) (Rangers) 1960/1.
Simpson, N. (4) (Aberdeen) 1982/3, 1983/4, 1986/7, 1987/8.
Simpson, R. (5) (Celtic) 1966/7, 1967/8, 1968/9.
Sinclair, J. (1) (Leicester City) 1965/6.
Smith, D. (2) (Aberdeen) 1965/6, 1967/8 (Rangers).
Smith, E. (2) (Celtic) 1958/9.
Smith, G. (18) (Hibernian) 1946/7, 1947/8, 1951/2, 1954/5, 1955/6, 1956/7.
Smith, H.G. (3) (Heart of Midlothian) 1987/8, 1991/2.
Smith, J. (4) (Aberdeen) 1967/8, 1973/4 (Newcastle United).
Souness, G. (54) (Middlesbrough) 1974/5 (Liverpool) 1977/8, 1978/9, 1979/80, 1980/1, 1981/2, 1982/3, 1983/4, (Sampdoria) 1984/5, 1985/6.
Speedie, D.R. (10) (Chelsea) 1984/5, 1985/6, (Coventry City) 1988/9.
Stanton, P. (16) (Hibernian) 1965/6, 1968/9, 1969/70, 1970/1, 1971/2, 1972/3, 1973/4.
Steel, W. (30) (Morton) 1946/7, 1947/8 (Derby County) 1948/9, 1949/50, (Dundee) 1950/1, 1951/2, 1952/3.
Stein, C. (21) (Rangers) 1968/9, 1969/70, 1970/1, 1971/2 (Coventry City).
Stephen, J. (2) (Bradford City) 1946/7, 1947/8.
Stewart, D. (1) (Leeds United) 1977/8.
Stewart, J. (2) (Kilmarnock) 1976/7 (Middlesbrough) 1978/9.
Stewart, R. (10) (West Ham United) 1980/1, 1981/2, 1983/4, 1986/7.
Strachan, G. (50) (Aberdeen) 1979/80, 1980/1, 1981/2, 1982/3, 1983/4 (Manchester United) 1984/5, 1985/6, 1986/7, 1987/8, 1988/9 (Leeds United) 1989/90, 1990/1, 1991/2.
Sturrock, P. (20) (Dundee United) 1980/1, 1981/2, 1982/3, 1983/4, 1984/5, 1985/6, 1986/7.

Telfer, W. (1) (St Mirren) 1953/4.
Thomson, W. (7) (St Mirren) 1979/80, 1980/1, 1981/2, 1982/3, 1983/4.
Thornton, W. (7) (Rangers) 1946/7, 1947/8, 1948/9, 1951/2.

Toner, W. (2) (Kilmarnock) 1958/9.
Turnhull, E. (8) (Hibernian) 1947/8, 1950/1, 1957/8.

Ure, I. (11) (Dundee) 1961/2, 1962/3 (Arsenal) 1963/4, 1967/8.

Waddell, W. (17) (Rangers) 1946/7, 1948/9, 1949/50, 1950/1, 1951/2, 1953/4, 1954/5.
Walker, A. (1) (Celtic) 1987/8.
Wallace, L.A. (3) (Coventry City) 1977/8, 1978/9.
Wallace, W.S.B. (7) (Heart of Midlothian) 1964/5, 1965/6, 1966/7 (Celtic) 1967/8, 1968/9.
Wardhaugh, J. (2) (Heart of Midlothian) 1954/5, 1956/7.
Wark, J. (29) (Ipswich Town) 1978/9, 1979/80, 1980/1, 1981/2, 1982/3, 1983/4 (Liverpool) 1984/5.
Watson, J. (2) (Motherwell) 1947/8 (Huddersfield Town) 1953/4.
Watson, R. (1) (Motherwell) 1970/1.
Weir, A. (6) (Motherwell) 1958/9, 1959/60.
Weir, P. (6) (St Mirren) 1979/80, 1982/3, (Aberdeen) 1983/4.
White, J. (22) (Falkirk) 1958/9, 1959/60 (Tottenham Hotspur) 1960/1, 1961/2, 1962/3, 1963/4.
Whyte, D. (4) (Celtic) 1987/8, 1988/9, 1991/2.
Wilson, A. (1) (Portsmouth) 1953/4.
Wilson, D. (22) (Rangers) 1960/1, 1961/2, 1962/3, 1963/4, 1964/5.
Wilson, I.A. (5) (Leicester City) 1986/7, (Everton) 1987/8.
Wilson, P. (1) (Celtic) 1974/5.
Wilson, R. (2) (Arsenal) 1971/2.
Wood, G. (4) (Everton) 1978/9, 1981/2 (Arsenal).
Woodburn, W. (24) (Rangers) 1946/7, 1947/8, 1948/9, 1949/50, 1950/1, 1951/2.
Wright, K. (1) (Hibernian) 1991/2.
Wright, T. (3) (Sunderland) 1952/3.

Yeats, R. (2) (Liverpool) 1964/5, 1965/6.
Yorston, H. (1) (Aberdeen) 1954/5.
Young, A. (9) (Heart of Midlothian) 1959/60. 1960/1 (Everton) 1965/6.
Young, G. (53) (Rangers) 1946/7, 1947/8, 1948/9, 1949/50, 1950/1, 1951/2, 1952/3, 1953/4, 1954/5, 1955/6, 1956/7.
Younger, T. (24) (Hibernian) 1954/5, 1955/6, 1956/7 (Liverpool) 1957/8.

WALES

Aizlewood, M. (33) (Charlton Athletic) 1985/6, 1986/7 (Leeds United) 1987/8, 1988/9 (Bradford City) 1989/90, 1990/1 (Bristol City), 1991/2.

Allchurch, I. (68) (Swansea Town) 1950/1, 1951/2, 1952/3, 1953/4, 1954/5, 1955/6, 1956/7, 1957/8, 1958/9 (Newcastle United) 1959/60, 1960/1, 1961/2, 1962/3 (Cardiff City) 1963/4, 1964/5, 1965/6 (Swansea Town).
Allchurch L. (11) (Swansea Town) 1954/5, 1955/6, 1957/8, 1958/9, 1961/2, (Sheffield United) 1963/4.
Allen, B. (2) (Coventry City) 1950/1.
Allen, M. (12) (Watford) 1985/6, (Norwich City) 1988/9 (Millwall) 1989/90, 1990/1, 1991/2.

Baker, C. (7) (Cardiff City) 1957/8, 1959/60. 1960/1, 1961/2.
Baker, W. (1) (Cardiff City) 1947/8.
Barnes, W. (22) (Arsenal) 1947/8, 1948/9, 1949/50, 1950/1, 1951/2, 1953/4, 1954/5.
Berry, G. (5) (Wolverhampton Wanderers) 1978/9, 1979/80, 1982/3 (Stoke City).
Blackmore, C.G. (33) (Manchester United) 1984/5, 1985/6, 1986/7, 1987/8, 1988/9, 1989/90, 1990/1, 1991/2.
Bowen, D. (19) (Arsenal) 1954/5, 1956/7, 1957/8, 1958/9.
Bowen, M.R. (19) (Tottenham Hotspur) 1985/6 (Norwich City) 1987/8, 1988/9, 1989/90, 1991/2.
Bodin, P.J. (15) (Swindon Town) 1989/90, 1990/1 (Crystal Palace), 1991/2 (Swindon Town).
Boyle, T. (2) (Crystal Palace) 1980/1.
Burgess, R. (32) (Tottenham Hotspur) 1946/7, 1947/8, 1948/9, 1949/50, 1950/1, 1951/2, 1952/3, 1953/4.
Burton, O. (9) (Norwich City) 1962/3 (Newcastle United) 1963/4, 1968/9, 1971/2.

Cartwright, L. (7) (Coventry City) 1973/4, 1975/6, 1976/7 (Wrexham) 1977/8, 1978/9.
Charles, J. (38) (Leeds United) 1949/50, 1950/1, 1952/3, 1953/4, 1954/5, 1955/6, 1956/7 (Juventus) 1957/8, 1959/60, 1961/2, 1962/3, (Leeds United) (Cardiff City) 1963/4, 1964/5.
Charles, J.M. (19) (Swansea Town) 1980/1, 1981/2, 1982/3, 1983/4 (QPR), (Oxford United) 1984/5, 1985/6, 1986/7.
Charles, M. (31) (Swansea Town) 1954/5, 1955/6, 1956/7, 1957/8, 1958/9 (Arsenal) 1960/1, 1961/2 (Cardiff City) 1962/3.
Clarke, R. (22) (Manchester City) 1948/9, 1949/50, 1950/1, 1951/2, 952/3, 1953/4, 1954/5, 1955/6.
Coleman, C. (1) (Crystal Palace) 1991/2.
Crowe, V. (16) (Aston Villa) 1958/9, 1959/60, 1960/1, 1961/2, 1962/3.
Curtis, A. (35) (Swansea City) 1975/6, 1976/7, 1977/8, 1978/9, 1979/80, 1981/2, 1982/3, 1983/4 (Southampton) 1984/5, 1985/6, 1986/7 (Cardiff City).

Daniel, R. (21) (Arsenal) 1950/1, 1951/2, 1952/3, 1953/4
(Sunderland) 1954/5, 1956/7.
Davies, A. (13) (Manchester United) 1982/3, 1983/4, 1984/5,
(Newcastle United) 1985/6 (Swansea City) 1987/8, 1988/9 (Bradford
City) 1989/90.
Davies, D. (52) (Everton) 1974/5, 1975/6, 1976/7, 1977/8,
(Wrexham) 1978/9, 1979/80, 1980/1 (Swansea City) 1981/2, 1982/3.
Davies, G. (16) (Fulham) 1979/80, 1981/2, 1982/3, 1983/4, 1984/5
(Chelsea), (Manchester City) 1985/6.
Davies, R. Wyn (34) (Bolton Wanderers) 1963/4, 1964/5, 1965/6,
1966/7 (Newcastle United) 1967/8, 1968/9, 1969/70, 1970/1, 1971/2
(Manchester City), (Blackpool) 1972/3 (Manchester United) 1973/4.
Davies, Reg (6) (Newcastle United) 1952/3, 1953/4, 1957/8.
Davies, Ron (29) (Norwich City) 1963/4, 1964/5, 1965/6, 1966/7,
(Southampton) 1967/8, 1968/9, 1969/70, 1970/1, 1971/2, 1973/4
(Portsmouth).
Davis, C. (1) (Charlton Athletic) 1971/2.
Davis, G. (4) (Wrexham) 1977/8.
Deacy, N. (11) (PSV Eindhoven) 1976/7, 1977/8 (Beringen) 1978/9.
Derrett, S. (4) (Cardiff City) 1968/9, 1969/70, 1970/1.
Dibble, A. (3) (Luton Town) 1985/6, (Manchester City) 1988/9.
Durban, A. (27) (Derby County) 1965/6, 1966/7, 1967/8, 1968/9,
1969/70, 1970/1, 1971/2.
Dwyer, P. (10) (Cardiff City) 1977/8, 1978/9, 1979/80.

Edwards, I. (4) (Chester) 1977/8, 1978/9, 1979/80.
Edwards, G. (12) (Birmingham City) 1946/7, 1947/8 (Cardiff City)
1948/9, 1949/50.
Edwards, T. (2) (Charlton Athletic) 1956/7.
Emanuel, J. (2) (Bristol City) 1972/3.
England, M. (44) (Blackburn Rovers) 1961/2, 1962/3, 1963/4,
1964/5, 1965/6, 1966/7 (Tottenham Hotspur) 1967/8, 1968/9,
1969/70, 1970/1, 1971/2, 1972/3, 1973/4, 1974/5.
Evans, B. (7) (Swansea City) 1971/2, 1972/3 (Hereford United)
1973/4.
Evans, I. (13) (Crystal Palace) 1975/6, 1976/7, 1977/8.
Evans, R. (1) (Swansea Town) 1963/4.

Felgate, D. (1) (Lincoln City) 1983/4.
Flynn, B. (66) (Burnley) 1974/5, 1975/6, 1976/7, 1977/8 (Leeds
United) 1978/9, 1979/80, 1980/1, 1981/2, 1982/3 (Burnley) 1983/4.
Ford, T. (38) (Swansea City) 1946/7 (Aston Villa) 1947/8, 1948/9,
1949/50, 1950/1 (Sunderland) 1951/2, 1952/3 (Cardiff City) 1953/4,
1954/5, 1955/6, 1956/7.
Foulkes, W. (11) (Newcastle United) 1951/2, 1952/3, 1953/4.

Giggs, R.J. (3) (Manchester United) 1991/2.
Giles, D. (12) (Swansea City) 1979/80, 1980/1, 1981/2 (Crystal Palace) 1982/3.
Godfrey, B. (3) (Preston North End) 1963/4, 1964/5.
Goss, J. (3) (Norwich City) 1990/1, 1991/2.
Green, C. (15) (Birmingham City) 1964/5, 1965/6, 1966/7, 1967/8, 1968/9.
Griffiths, A. (17) (Wrexham) 1970/1, 1974/5, 1975/6, 1976/7.
Griffiths, H. (1) (Swansea Town) 1952/3.
Griffiths, M. (11) (Leicester City) 1946/7, 1948/9, 1949/50, 1950/1, 1953/4.

Hall, G.D. (9) (Chelsea) 1987/8, 1988/9, 1990/91, 1991/2.
Harrington, A. (11) (Cardiff City) 1955/6, 1956/7, 1957/8, 1960/1, 1961/2.
Harris, C. (24) (Leeds United) 1975/6, 1977/8, 1978/9, 1979/80, 1980/1, 1981/2.
Harris, W. (6) (Middlesbrough) 1953/4, 1956/7, 1957/8.
Hennessey, T. (39) (Birmingham City) 1961/2, 1962/3, 1963/4, 1964/5, 1965/6, (Nottingham Forest) 1966/7, 1967/8, 1968/9, 1969/70 (Derby County) 1971/2, 1972/3.
Hewitt, R. (5) (Cardiff City) 1957/8.
Hill, M. (2) (Ipswich Town) 1971/2.
Hockey, T. (9) (Sheffield United) 1971/2, 1972/3 (Norwich City) 1973/4, (Aston Villa).
Hodges, G. (16) (Wimbledon) 1983/4, 1986/7 (Newcastle United) 1987/8, (Watford) 1989/90, (Sheffield United) 1991/2.
Holden, A. (1) (Chester City) 1983/4.
Hole, B. (30) (Cardiff City) 1962/3, 1963/4, 1964/5, 1965/6, 1966/7, (Blackburn Rovers) 1967/8, 1968/9 (Aston Villa) 1969/70 (Swansea Town) 1970/71.
Hollins, D. (11) (Newcastle United) 1961/2, 1962/3, 1963/4, 1964/5, 1965/6.
Hopkins, J. (16) (Fulham) 1982/3, 1983/4, 1984/5 (Crystal P) 1989/90.
Hopkins, M. (34) (Tottenham Hotspur) 1955/6, 1956/7, 1957/8, 1958/9, 1959/60, 1960/1, 1961/2, 1962/3.
Horne, B. (31) (Portsmouth) 1987/8, (Southampton) 1988/9, 1989/90, 1990/1, 1991/2.
Howells, R. (2) (Cardiff City) 1953/4.
Hughes, C.M. (1) (Luton Town) 1991/2.
Hughes, I. (4) (Luton Town) 1950/1.
Hughes, L.M. (43) (Manchester United) 1983/4, 1984/5, 1985/6, 1986/7 (Barcelona) 1987/8, 1988/9 (Manchester United) 1989/90, 1990/1, 1991/2.
Hughes, W. (3) (Birmingham City) 1946/7.

Hughes, W.A. (5) (Blackburn Rovers) 1948/9.
Humphreys, J. (1) (Everton) 1946/7.

Jackett, K. (31) (Watford) 1982/3, 1983/4, 1984/5, 1985/6, 1986/7, 1987/8.
James, G. (9) (Blackpool) 1965/6, 1966/7, 1967/8, 1970/1.
James, L. (54) (Burnley) 1971/2, 1972/3, 1973/4, 1974/5, 1975/6 (Derby County) 1976/7, 1977/8 (QPR) (Burnley) 1978/9, 1979/80 (Swansea City) 1980/1, 1981/2 (Sunderland) 1982/3.
James, R.M. (47) (Swansea City) 1978/9, 1979/80, 1981/2, 1982/3 (Stoke City) 1983/4, 1984/5 (QPR) 1985/6, 1986/7 (Leicester City) 1987/8 (Swansea City).
Jarvis, A. (3) (Hull City) 1966/7.
Johnson, M. (1) (Swansea City) 1963/4.
Jones, A. (6) (Port Vale) 1986/7, 1987/8 (Charlton Athletic) 1989/90.
Jones, Barrie (15) (Swansea Town) 1962/3, 1963/4, 1964/5 (Plymouth Argyle) 1968/9 (Cardiff City).
Jones, Bryn. (4) (Arsenal) 1946/7, 1947/8, 1948/9.
Jones, C. (59) (Swansea Town) 1953/4, 1955/6, 1956/7, 1957/8 (Tottenham Hotspur) 1958/9, 1959/60, 1960/1, 1961/2, 1962/3, 1963/4, 1964/5, 1966/7, 1967/8, 1968/9 (Fulham) 1969/70.
Jones, D. (8) (Norwich City) 1975/6, 1977/8, 1979/80.
Jones, E. (4) (Swansea Town) 1947/8 (Tottenham Hotspur) 1948/9.
Jones, J. (72) (Liverpool) 1975/6, 1976/7, 1977/8 (Wrexham) 1978/9, 1979/80, 1980/1, 1981/2, 1982/3 (Chelsea) 1983/4, 1984/5 (Huddersfield Town) 1985/6.
Jones, K. (1) (Aston Villa) 1949/50.
Jones, T.G. (13) (Everton) 1946/7, 1947/8, 1948/9, 1949/50.
Jones W. (1) (Bristol City) 1970/1.

Kelsey, J. (41) (Arsenal) 1953/4, 1954/5, 1955/6, 1956/7, 1957/8, 1958/9, 1959/60, 1960/1, 1961/2.
King, J. (1) (Swansea Town) 1954/5.
Kinsey, N. (7) (Norwich City) 1950/1, 1951/2, 1953/4 (Birmingham City) 1955/6.
Knill, A.R. (1) (Swansea City) 1988/9.
Krzywicki, R. (West Bromwich Albion) 1969/70 (Huddersfield Town) 1970/1, 1971/2.

Lambert, R. (5) (Liverpool) 1946/7, 1947/8, 1948/9.
Law, B.J. (1) (QPR), 1989/90.
Lea, C. (2) (Ipswich Town) 1964/5.
Leek, K. (13) (Leicester City) 1960/1, 1961/2 (Newcastle United) (Birmingham City) 1962/3, 1964/5.
Lever, A. (1) (Leicester City) 1952/3.
Lewis, D. (1) (Swansea City) 1982/3.

Lloyd, B. (3) (Wrexham) 1975/6.
Lovell, S. (6) (Crystal Palace) 1981/2 (Millwall) 1984/5, 1985/6.
Lowndes, S. (10) (Newport County) 1982/3 (Millwall) 1984/5,
1985/6, 1986/7, (Barnsley) 1987/8.
Lowrie, G. (4) (Coventry City) 1947/8, 1948/9 (Newcastle United).
Lucas, M. (4) (Leyton Orient) 1961/2, 1962/3.
Lucas, W. (7) (Swansea Town) 1948/9, 1949/50, 1950/1.

Maguire, G.T. (7) (Portsmouth) 1989/90, 1991/2.
Mahoney, J. (51) (Stoke City) 1967/8, 1968/9, 1970/1, 1972/3,
1973/4, 1974/5, 1975/6, 1976/7 (Middlesbrough) 1977/8, 1978/9
(Swansea City) 1979/80, 1981/2, 1982/3.
Marustik, C. (6) (Swansea City) 1981/2, 1982/3.
Medwin, T. (30) (Swansea Town) 1952/3, 1956/7 (Tottenham
Hotspur) 1957/8, 1958/9, 1959/60, 1960/1, 1962/3.
**Melville, A.K. (13) (Swansea C), 1989/90, 1990/1 (Oxford United),
1991/2.**
Mielczarek, R. (1) (Rotherham United) 1970/1.
Millington, A. (21) (West Bromwich Albion) 1962/3, 1964/5 (Crystal
Palace) 1965/6 (Peterborough United) 1966/7, 1967/8, 1968/9,
1969/70 (Swansea City) 1970/1, 1971/2.
Moore, G. (21) (Cardiff City) 1959/60, 1960/1, 1961/2 (Chelsea)
1962/3, (Manchester United) 1963/4 (Northampton Town) 1965/6,
1968/9 (Charlton Athletic) 1969/70, 1970/1.
Morris, W. (5) (Burnley) 1946/7, 1948/9, 1951/2.

Nardiello, D. (2) (Coventry City) 1977/8.
Neilson, A.B. (1) (Newcastle United) 1991/2.
Nicholas, P. (73) (Crystal Palace) 1978/9, 1979/80, 1980/1 (Arsenal)
1981/2, 1982/3, 1983/4 (Crystal Palace) 1984/5, (Luton Town)
1985/6, 1986/7, 1987/8 (Aberdeen), (Chelsea) 1988/9, 1989/90,
1990/1 (Watford), 1991/2.
Niedzwiecki, E.A. (2) (Chelsea) 1984/5, 1987/8.
Nogan, L.M. (1) (Watford) 1991/2.
Nurse, E.A. (2) (Chelsea) 1984/5, 1987/8.
Norman, A.J. (5) (Hull City) 1985/6, 1987/8.
Nurse, M. (12) (Swansea Town) 1959/60, 1960/1, 1962/3
(Middlesbrough) 1963/4.

O'Sullivan, P. (3) (Brighton & Hove Albion) 1972/3, 1975/6,
1978/9.

Page, M. (28) (Birmingham City) 1970/1, 1971/2, 1972/3, 1973/4,
1974/5, 1975/6, 1976/7, 1977/8, 1978/9.
Palmer, D. (3) (Swansea Town) 1956/7, 1957/8.
Parry, J. (1) (Swansea Town) 1950/1.

Pascoe, C. (10) (Swansea Town) 1983/4, (Sunderland) 1988/9, 1989/90 1990/91, 1991/2.
Paul, R. (33) (Swansea Town) 1948/9, 1949/50 (Manchester City) 1950/1, 1951/2, 1952/3, 1953/4, 1954/5, 1955/6.
Pembridge, M.A. (5) (Luton Town) 1991/2.
Phillips, D. (39) (Plymouth Argyle) 1983/4 (Manchester City) 1984/5, 1985/6, 1986/7 (Coventry City) 1987/8, 1988/9 (Norwich City) 1989/90, 1990/1, 1991/2.
Phillips, J. (4) (Chelsea) 1972/3, 1973/4, 1974/5, 1977/8.
Phillips, L. (58) (Cardff City) 1970/1, 1971/2, 1972/3, 1973/4, 1974/5, (Aston Villa) 1975/6, 1976/7, 1977/8, 1978/9 (Swansea City) 1979/80, 1980/1, 1981/2 (Charlton Athletic).
Pontin, K. (2) (Cardiff City) 1979/80.
Powell, A. (8) (Leeds United) 1946/7, 1947/8, 1948/9 (Everton) 1949/50, 1950/1 (Birmingham City).
Powell, D. (11) (Wrexham) 1967/8, 1968/9 (Sheffield United) 1969/70, 1970/1.
Powell, I. (8) (QPR) 1946/7, 1947/8, 1948/9 (Aston Villa) 1949/50, 1950/1.
Price, P. (25) (Luton Town) 1979/80, 1980/1, 1981/2 (Tottenham Hotspur) 1982/3, 1983/4.
Pring, K. (3) (Rotherham United) 1965/6, 1966/7.
Pritchard, H.K. (1) (Bristol City) 1984/5.

Rankmore, F. (1 (Peterborough United) 1965/6.
Ratcliffe, K. (58) (Everton) 1980/1, 1981/2, 1982/3, 1983/4, 1984/5, 1985/6, 1986/7, 1987/8, 1988/9, 1989/90, 1990/1, 1991/2.
Reece, G. (29) (Sheffield United) 1965/6, 1966/7, 1969/70, 1970/1, 1971/2, (Cardiff City) 1972/3, 1973/4, 1974/5.
Reed, W. (2) (Ipswich Town) 1954/5.
Rees, A. (1) (Birmingham City) 1983/4.
Rees, J.M. (1) (Luton Town) 1991/2.
Rees, R. (39) (Coventry City) 1964/5, 1965/6, 1966/7, 1967/8 (West Bromwich Albion) 1968/9 (Nottingham Forest) 1969/70, 1970/1, 1971/2.
Rees, W. (4) (Cardiff City) 1948/9 (Tottenham Hotspur) 1949/50.
Richards, S. (1) (Cardiff City) 1946/7.
Roberts, D. (17) (Oxford United) 1972/3, 1973/4, 1974/5 (Hull City) 1975/6, 1976/7, 1977/8.
Roberts, I.W. (4) (Watford) 1989/90, (Huddersfield Town) 1991/2.
Roberts, J.G. (22) (Arsenal) 1970/1, 1971/2, 1972/3, (Birmingham City) 1973/4, 1974/5, 1975/6..
Roberts, J.H. (1) (Bolton Wanderers) 1948/9.
Roberts, P. (4) (Portsmouth) 1973/4, 1974/5.

Rodrigues, P. (40) (Cardiff City) 1964/5, 1965/6 (Leicester City) 1966/7, 1967/8, 1968/9, 1969/70 (Sheffield Wednesday) 1970/1, 1971/2, 1972/3, 1973/4.
Rouse, V. (1) (Crystal Palace) 1958/9.
Rowley, T. (1) (Tranmere Rovers) 1958/9.
Rush, I. (54) (Liverpool) 1979/80, 1980/1, 1981/2, 1982/3, 1983/4, 1984/5, 1985/6, 1986/7 (Juventus) 1987/8, (Liverpool) 1988/9, 1989/90, 1990/1, 1991/2.

Saunders, D. (34) (Brighton & Hove Albion) 1985/6, 1986/7 (Oxford United) 1987/8, (Derby County) 1988/9, 1989/90, 1990/91, (Liverpool) 1991/2.
Sayer, P. (7) (Cardiff City) 1976/7, 1977/8.
Scrine, F. (2) (Swansea Town) 1949/50.
Sear, C. (1) (Manchester City) 1962/3.
Sherwood, A. (41) (Cardiff City) 1946/7, 1947/8, 1948/9, 1949/50, 1950/1, 1951/2, 1952/3, 1953/4, 1954/5, 1955/6, 1956/7 (Newport County).
Shortt, W. (12) (Plymouth Argyle) 1946/7, 1949/50, 1951/2, 1952/3.
Showers, D. (2) (Cardiff City) 1974/5.
Sidlow, C. (7) (Liverpool) 1946/7, 1947/8, 1948/9, 1949/50.
Slatter, N. (22) (Bristol Rovers) 1982/3, 1983/4, 1984/5 (Oxford United) 1985/6, 1986/7, 1987/8, 1988/9.
Smallman, D. (7 (Wrexham) 1973/4 (Everton) 1974/5, 1975/6.
Southall, N. (61) (Everton) 1981/2, 1982/3, 1983/4, 1984/5, 1985/6, 1986/7, 1987/8, 1988/9, 1989/90, 1990/1, 1991/2,
Speed, G.A. (14) (Leeds U), 1989/90, 1990/91, 1991/2.
Sprake, G. (37) (Leeds United) 1963/4, 1964/5, 1965/6, 1966/7, 1967/8, 1968/9, 1969/70, 1970/1, 1971/2, 1972/3, 1973/4 (Birmingham City) 1974/5.
Stansfield, F. (1) (Cardiff City) 1948/9.
Stevenson, B. (15) (Leeds United) 1977/8, 1978/9, 1979/80, 1981/2 (Birmingham City).
Stevenson, N. (4) (Swansea City) 1981/2, 1982/3.
Stitfall, R. (2) (Cardiff City) 1952/3, 1956/7.
Sullivan, D. (17) (Cardiff City) 1952/3, 1953/4, 1954/5, 1956/7, 1957/8, 1958/9, 1959/60.
Symons, C.J. (4) (Potsmouth) 1991/2.

Tapscott, D. (14) (Arsenal) 1953/4, 1954/5, 1955/6, 1956/7, 1958/9 (Cardiff City).
Thomas, D. (2) (Swansea Town) 1956/7, 1957/8.
Thomas, M. (51) (Wrexham) 1976/7, 1977/8, 1978/9 (Manchester United) 1979/80, 1980/1, 1981/2 (Everton) (Brighton) 1982/3 (Stoke City) 1983/4, (Chelsea) 1984/5, 1985/6 (West Bromwich Albion).
Thomas, M.R. (1) (Newcastle United) 1986/7.

Thomas, R. (50) (Swindon Town) 1966/7, 1967/8, 1968/9, 1969/70, 1970/1, 1971/2, 1972/3, 1973/4 (Derby County) 1974/5, 1975/6, 1976/7, 1977/8 (Cardiff City).
Thomas, S. (4) (Fulham) 1947/8, 1948/9.
Toshack, J. (40) (Cardiff City) 1968/9, 1969/70 (Liverpool) 1970/1, 1971/2, 1972/3, 1974/5, 1975/6, 1976/7, 1977/8 (Swansea City) 1978/9, 1979/80.

Van Den Hauwe, P.W.R. (13) (Everton) 1984/5, 1985/6, 1986/7, 1987/8, 1988/9.
Vaughan, N. (10) (Newport County) 1982/3, 1983/4 (Cardiff City) 1984/5.
Vearncombe, G. (2) (Cardiff City) 1957/8, 1960/1.
Vernon, R. (32) (Blackburn Rovers) 1956/7, 1957/8, 1958/9, 1959/60 (Everton) 1960/1, 1961/2, 1962/3, 1963/4, 1964/5 (Stoke City) 1965/6, 1966/7, 1967/8.
Villars, A. (3) (Cardiff City) 1973/4.

Walley, T. (1) (Watford) 1970/1.
Walsh, I. (18) (Crystal Palace) 1979/80, 1980/1, 1981/2 (Swansea City).
Ward, D. (2) (Bristol Rovers) 1958/9, 1961/2 (Cardiff City).
Webster, C. (4) (Manchester United) 1956/7, 1957/8.
Williams, D.G. (11) 1987/8 (Derby County) 1988/9, 1989/90.
Williams, D.M. (5) (Norwich City) 1985/6, 1986/7.
Williams, G. (1) (Cardiff City) 1950/1.
Williams, G.E. (26) (West Bromwich Albion) 1959/60, 1960/1, 1962/3, 1963/4, 1964/5, 1965/6, 1966/7, 1967/8, 1968/9.
Williams, G.G. (5) (Swansea Town) 1960/1, 1961/2.
Williams, H. (4) (Newport County) 1948/9 (Leeds United) 1949/50, 1950/1.
Williams, Herbert (3) (Swansea Town) 1964/5, 1970/1.
Williams, S. (43) (West Bromwich Albion) 1953/4, 1954/5, 1955/6, 1957/8, 1958/9, 1959/60, 1960/1, 1961/2, 1962/3 (Southampton) 1963/4, 1964/5, 1965/6.
Witcomb, D. (3) (West Bromwich Albion) 1946/7 (Sheffield Wednesday).
Woosnam, P. (17) (Leyton Orient) 1958/9 (West Ham United) 1959/60, 1960/1, 1961/2, 1962/3 (Aston Villa).

Yorath, T. (59) (Leeds United) 1969/70, 1970/1, 1971/2, 1972/3, 1973/4, 1974/5, 1975/6 (Coventry City) 1976/7, 1977/8, 1978/9 (Tottenham Hotspur) 1979/80, 1980/1.
Young, E. (10) (Wimbledon) 1989/90, 1990/1 (Crystal Palace), 1991/2.

EIRE

Aherne, T. (16) (Belfast Celtic) 1945/6 (Luton Town) 1949/50, 1950/1, 1951/2, 1952/3, 1953/4.
Aldridge, J.W. (47) (Oxford United) 1985/6, 1986/7 (Liverpool) 1987/8, 1988/9 (Real Sociedad) 1989/90, 1990/1, (Tranmere Rovers) 1991/2.
Ambrose, P. (5) (Shamrock Rovers) 1954/5, 1963/4.
Anderson, J. (16) (Preston North End) 1979/80, 1981/2 (Newcastle United) 1983/4, 1985/6, 1986/7, 1987/8, 1988/9.

Bailham, E. (1) (Shamrock Rovers) 1963/4.
Barber, E. (2) (Shelbourne) 1965/6 (Birmingham City) 1965/6.
Beglin, J. (15) (Liverpool) 1983/4, 1984/5, 1985/6, 1986/7.
Bonner, P. (57) (Celtic) 1980/1, 1981/2, 1983/4, 1984/5, 1985/6, 1986/7, 1987/8, 1988/9, 1989/90, 1990/1, 1991/2.
Braddish, S. (1) (Dundalk) 1977/8.
Brady T.R. (6) (QPR) 1963/4.
Brady, W. L. (72) (Arsenal) 1974/5, 1975/6, 1976/7, 1977/8, 1978/9, 1979/80 (Juventus) 1980/1, 1981/2 (Sampdoria) 1982/3, 1983/4 (Internazionale) 1984/5, 1985/6 (Ascoli) 1986/7 (West Ham United) 1987/8, 1988/9, 1989/90.
Breen, T. (3) (Shamrock Rovers) 1946/7.
Brennan, F. (1) (Drumcondra) 1964/5.
Brennan, S.A. (19) (Manchester United) 1964/5, 1965/6, 1966/7, 1968/9, 1969/70 (Waterford) 1970/1.
Browne, W. (3) (Bohemians) 1963/4.
Buckley, L. (2) (Shamrock Rovers) 1983/4 (Waregem) 1984/5.
Burke, F. (1) (Cork Athletic) 1951/2.
Byrne, A.B. (14) (Southampton) 1969/70, 1970/1, 1972/3, 1973/4.
Byrne, J. (22) (QPR) 1984/5, 1986/7, 1987/8 (Le Havre) 1989/90, 1990/1 (Brighton & Hove Albion), 1991/2 (Sunderland).
Byrne, P. (9) (Shamrock Rovers) 1983/4, 1984/5, 1985/6.

Campbell, A. (3) (Santander) 1984/5.
Campbell, N. (11) (St Patrick's Athletic) 1970/1 (Fortuna Cologne) 1971/2, 1972/3, 1974/5, 1975/6.
Cantwell, N. (36) (West Ham United) 1953/4, 1955/6, 1956/7, 1957/8, 1958/9, 1959/60, 1960/1 (Manchester United) 1960/1, 1961/2, 1962/3, 1963/4, 1964/5, 1965/6, 1966/7.
Carey, B.P. (1) (Manchester United) 1991/2.
Carey, J.J. (21) (Manchester United) 1945/6, 1946/7, 1947/8, 1948/9, 1949/50, 1950/1, 1952/3.
Carolan, J. (2) (Manchester United) 1959/60.
Carroll, B. (2) (Shelbourne) 1948/9, 1949/50.

Carroll, T.R. (17) (Ipswich Town) 1967/8, 1968/9, 1969/70, 1970/1 (Birmingham City) 1971/2, 1972/3.
Cascarino, A.G. (38) (Gillingham) 1985/6 (Millwall) 1987/8, 1988/9, 1989/90 (Aston Villa), 1990/9 (Celtic) 1991/2 (Chelsea).
Chandler, J. (2) (Leeds United) 1979/80.
Clarke, J. (1) (Drogheda United) 1977/8.
Clarke, K. (2) (Drumcondra) 1947/8.
Clarke, M. (1) (Shamrock Rovers) 1949/50.
Clinton, T.J. (3) (Everton) 1950/1, 1953/4.
Coad, P. (11) (Shamrock Rovers) 1946/7, 1947/8, 1948/9, 1950/1, 1951/2.
Coffey, T. (1) (Drumcondra) 1949/50.
Colfer, M.D. (2) (Shelbourne) 1949/50, 1950/1.
Conmy, O.M. (5) (Peterborough United) 1964/5, 1966/7, 1967/8, 1969/70.
Conroy, G.A. (27) (Stoke City) 1969/70, 1970/1, 1972/3, 1973/4, 1974/5, 1975/6, 1976/7.
Conway, J.P. (20) (Fulham) 1966/7, 1967/8, 1968/9, 1969/70, 1970/1, 1973/4, 1974/5, 1975/6 (Manchester City) 1976/7.
Corr, P.J. (4) (Everton) 1948/9.
Courtney, E. (1) (Cork United) 1945/6.
Coyne, L.S. (6) (Celtic) 1991/2.
Cummins, G.P. (19) (Luton Town) 1953/4, 1954/5, 1955/6, 1957/8, 1958/9, 1959/60, 1960/1.
Cuneen, T. (1) (Limerick) 1950/1.
Curtis, D.P. (17) (Shelbourne) 1956/7 (Bristol City) 1956/7, 1957/8, (Ipswich Town) 1958/9, 1959/60, 1960/1, 1961/2, 1962/3 (Exeter City) 1963/4.
Cusack, S. (1) (Limerick) 1952/3.

Daish, L.S. (1) (Cambridge United) 1991/2.
Daly, G.A. (47) (Manchester United) 1972/3, 1973/4, 1974/5, 1976/7 (Derby County) 1977/8, 1978/9, 1979/80 (Coventry City) 1980/1, 1981/2, 1982/3, 1983/4 (Birmingham City) 1984/5, 1985/6 (Shrewsbury Town) 1986/7.
Daly, M. (2) (Wolverhampton Wanderers) 1977/8.
Daly, P. (1) (Shamrock Rovers) 1949/50.
De Mange, K.J.P.P. (2) (Liverpool) 1986/7, (Hull City) 1988/9.
Deacy, E. (4) (Aston Villa) 1981/2.
Dempsey, J.T. (19) (Fulham) 1966/7, 1967/8, 1968/9 (Chelsea) 1968/9, 1969/70, 1970/1, 1971/2.
Dennehy, J. (11) (Cork Hibernian) 1971/2 (Nottingham Forest) 1972/3, 1973/4, 1974/5 (Walsall) 1975/6, 1976/7.
Desmond, P. (4) (Middlesbrough) 1949/50.
Devine, J. (12) (Arsenal) 1979/80, 1980/1, 1981/2, 1982/3 (Norwich City) 1983/4, 1984/5.

Donovan, D.C. (5) (Everton) 1954/5, 1956/7.
Donovan, T. (1) (Aston Villa) 1979/80.
Doyle, C. (1) (Shelbourne) 1958/9.
Duffy, B. (1) (Shamrock Rovers) 1949/50.
Dunne, A.P. (33) (Manchester United) 1961/2, 1962/3, 1963/4, 1964/5, 1965/6, 1966/7, 1968/9, 1969/70, 1970/1 (Bolton Wanderers) 1973/4, 1974/5, 1975/6.
Dunne, J.C. (1) (Fulham) 1970/1.
Dunne, P.A.J. (5) (Manchester United) 1964/5, 1965/6, 1966/7.
Dunne, S. (15) (Luton Town) 1952/3, 1953/4, 1955/6, 1956/7, 1957/8, 1958/9, 1959/60.
Dunne, T. (3) (St Patrick's Athletic) 1955/6, 1956/7.
Dunning, P. (2) (Shelbourne) 1970/1.
Dunphy, E.M. (23) (York City) 1965/6 (Millwall) 1965/6, 1966/7, 1967/8, 1968/9, 1969/70, 1970/1.
Dwyer, N.M. (14) (West Ham United) 1959/60 (Swansea Town) 1960/1, 1961/2, 1963/4, 1964/5.

Eccles, P. (1) (Shamrock Rovers) 1985/6.
Eglington, T.J. (24) (Shamrock Rovers) 1945/6 (Everton) 1946/7, 1947/8, 1948/9, 1950/1, 1951/2, 1952/3, 1953/4, 1954/5, 1955/6.

Fagan, E. (1) (Shamrock Rovers) 1972/3.
Fagan, F. (8) (Manchester City) 1954/5, 1959/60 (Derby County) 1959/60, 1960/1.
Fairclough, M. (2) (Dundalk) 1981/2.
Fallon, S. (8) (Celtic) 1950/1, 1951/2, 1952/3, 1954/5.
Farrell, P.D. (28) (Shamrock Rovers) 1945/6 (Everton) 1946/7, 1947/8, 1948/9, 1949/50, 1950/1, 1951/2, 1952/3, 1953/4, 1954/5, 1955/6, 1956/7.
Finucane, A. (11) (Limerick) 1966/7, 1968/9, 1969/70, 1970/1, 1971/2.
Fitzgerald, F.J. (2) (Waterford) 1954/5, 1955/6.
Fitzgerald, P.J. (5) (Leeds United) 1960/1, 1961/2.
Fitzpatrick, K. (1) (Limerick) 1969/70.
Fitzsimons, A.G. (26) (Middlesbrough) 1949/50, 1951/2, 1952/3, 1953/4, 1954/5, 1955/6, 1956/7, 1957/8, 1958/9 (Lincoln City) 1958/9.
Fogarty, A. (11) (Sunderland) 1959/60, 1960/1, 1961/2, 1962/3, 1963/4, (Hartlepool United) 1963/4.
Foley, T.C. (9) (Northampton Town) 1963/4, 1964/5, 1965/6, 1966/7.
Fullam, J. (Preston North End) 1960/1 (Shamrock Rovers) 1963/4, 1965/6, 1967/8, 1968/9, 1969/70.

Gallagher, C. (2) (Celtic) 1966/7.

Gallagher, M. (1) (Hibernian) 1953/4.
Galvin, A. (29) (Tottenham Hotspur) 1982/3, 1983/4, 1984/5, 1985/6, 1986/7 (Sheffield Wednesday) 1987/8, 1988/9, 1989/90.
Gannon, E. (14) (Notts County) 1948/9 (Sheffield Wednesday) 1948/9, 1949/50, 1950/1, 1951/2, 1953/4, 1954/5 (Shelbourne 1954/5.
Gannon, M. (1) (Shelbourne) 1971/2.
Gavin, J.T. (7) (Norwich City) 1949/50, 1952/3, 1953/4 (Tottenham Hotspur) 1954/5 (Norwich City) 1956/7.
Gibbons, A. (4) (St Patrick's Athletic) 1951/2, 1953/4, 1955/6.
Gilbert, R. (1) (Shamrock Rovers) 1965/6.
Giles, C. (1) (Doncaster Rovers) 1950/1.
Giles, M.J. (60) (Manchester United) 1959/60, 1960/1, 1961/2, 1962/3 (Leeds United) 1963/4, 1964/5, 1965/6, 1966/7, 1968/9, 1969/70, 1970/1, 1972/3, 1973/4, 1974/5 (West Bromwich Albion) 1975/6, 1976/7 (Shamrock Rovers) 1977/8, 1978/9.
Givens, D.J. (56) (Manchester United) 1968/9, 1969/70 (Luton Town) 1969/70, 1970/1, 1971/2 (QPR) 1972/3, 1973/4, 1974/5, 1975/6, 1976/7, 1977/8 (Birmingham City) 1978/9, 1979/80, 1980/1 (Neuchatel Xamax) 1981/2.
Glynn, D. (2) (Drumcondra) 1951/2, 1954/5.
Godwin, T.F. (13) (Shamrock Rovers) 1948/9, 1949/50 (Leicester City) 1949/50, 1950/1 (Bournemouth) 1955/6, 1956/7, 1957/8.
Gorman, W.C. (2) (Brentford) 1946/7.
Grealish, A. (44) (Orient) 1975/6, 1978/9 (Luton Town) 1979/80, 1980/1, (Brighton & Hove Albion) 1981/2, 1982/3, 1983/4 (West Bromwich Albion) 1984/5, 1985/6.
Gregg, E. (9) (Bohemians) 1977/8, 1978/9, 1979/80.
Grimes, A.A. (17) (Manchester United) 1977/8, 1979/80, 1980/1, 1981/2, 1982/3 (Coventry City) 1983/4 (Luton Town) 1987/8.

Hale, A. (13) (Aston Villa) 1961/2 (Doncaster Rovers) 1962/3, 1963/4, (Waterford) 1966/7, 1967/8, 1968/9, 1969/70, 1970/1, 1971/2.
Hamilton, T. (2) (Shamrock Rovers) 1958/9.
Hand, E.K. (20) (Portsmouth) 1968/9, 1969/70, 1970/1, 1972/3, 1973/4, 1974/5, 1975/6.
Hartnett, J.B. (2) (Middlesbrough) 1948/9, 1953/4.
Haverty, J. (32) (Arsenal) 1955/6, 1956/7, 1957/8, 1958/9, 1959/60, 1960/1, (Blackburn Rovers) 1961/2 (Millwall) 1962/3, 1963/4 (Celtic) 1964/5, (Bristol Rovers) 1964/5 (Shelbourne) 1965/6, 1966/7.
Hayes, A.W.P. (1) (Southampton) 1978/9.
Hayes, W.E. (2) (Huddersfield Town) 1946/7.
Hayes, W.J. (1) (Limerick) 1948/9.
Healey, R. (2) (Cardiff City) 1976/7, 1979/80.

Heighway, S.D. (34) (Liverpool) 1970/1, 1972/3, 1974/5, 1975/6, 1976/7, 1977/8, 1978/9, 1979/80, 1980/1 (Minnesota Kicks) 1981/2.
Henderson, B. (2) (Drumcondra) 1947/8.
Hennessy, J. (5) (Shelbourne) 1955/6, 1965/6 (St Patrick's Athletic) 1968/9.
Herrick, J. (3) (Cork Hibernians) 1971/2 (Shamrock Rovers) 1972/3.
Higgins, J. (1) (Birmingham City) 1950/1.
Holmes, J. (Coventry City) 1970/1, 1972/3, 1973/4, 1974/5, 1975/6, 1976/7 (Tottenham Hotspur) 1977/8, 1978/9, 1980/1 (Vancouver Whitecaps) 1980/1.
Houghton, R.J. (46) (Oxford United) 1985/6, 1986/7, 1987/8 (Liverpool) 1987/8, 1988/9, 1989/90, 1990/1, 1991/2.
Howlett, G. (1) (Brighton & Hove Albion) 1983/4.
Hughton, C. (53) (Tottenham Hotspur) 1979/80, 1980/1, 1981/2, 1982/3, 1983/4, 1984/5, 1985/6, 1986/7, 1987/8, 1988/9, 1989/90, 1990/1 (West Ham United), 1991/2.
Hurley, C.J. (40) (Millwall) 1956/7, 1957/8 (Sunderland) 1958/9, 1959/60, 1960/1, 1961/2, 1962/3, 1963/4, 1964/5, 1965/6, 1966/7, 1967/8 (Bolton Wanderers) 1968/9.

Irwin, D.J. (13) (Manchester United) 1990/1, 1991/2.

Keane, R.M. (7) (Nottingham Forest) 1990/1, 1991/2.
Keane, T.R. (4) (Swansea Town) 1948/9.
Kearin, M. (1) (Shamrock Rovers) 1971/2.
Kearns, F.T. (1) (West Ham United) 1953/4.
Kearns, M. (18) (Oxford United) 1969/70 (Walsall) 1973/4, 1975/6, 1976/7, 1977/8, 1978/9 (Wolverhampton Wanderers) 1979/80.
Kelly, D.T. (13) (Walsall) 1987/8 (West Ham) 1988/9 (Leicester City) 1989/90, 1990/1 (Newcastle United) 1991/2.
Kelly J.A. (47) (Drumcondra) 1956/7 (Preston North End) 1961/2, 1962/3, 1963/4, 1964/5, 1965/6, 1966/7, 1967/8, 1969/70, 1970/1, 1971/2, 1972/3.
Kelly, J.P.V. (5) (Wolverhampton Wanderers) 1960/1, 1961/2.
Kelly, M.J. (4) (Portsmouth) 1987/8, 1988/9, 1990/1.
Kelly, N. (1) (Nottingham Forest) 1953/4.
Kennedy, M.F. (2) (Portsmouth) 1985/6.
Keogh, J. (1) (Shamrock Rovers) 1965/6.
Keogh, S. (1) (Shamrock Rovers) 1958/9.
Kiernan, F.W. (5) (Shamrock Rovers) 1950/1 (Southampton) 1951/2.
Kinnear, J.P. (26) (Tottenham Hotspur) 1966/7, 1967/8, 1968/9, 1969/70, 1970/1, 1971/2, 1972/3, 1973/4, 1974/5 (Brighton & Hove Albion) 1975/6.

Langan, D. (25) (Derby County) 1977/8, 1979/80 (Birmingham City) 1980/1, 1981/2 (Oxford United) 1984/5, 1985/6, 1986/7, 1987/8.
Lawler, J.F. (8) (Fulham) 1952/3, 1953/4, 1954/5, 1955/6.

Lawlor, J.C. (3) (Drumcondra) 1948/9 (Doncaster Rovers) 1950/1.
Lawlor, M. (5) (Shamrock Rovers) 1970/1, 1972/3.
Lawrenson, M. (38) (Preston North End) 1976/7 (Brighton & Hove Albion) 1977/8, 1978/9, 1979/80, 1980/1 (Liverpool) 1981/2, 1982/3, 1983/4, 1984/5, 1985/6, 1986/7, 1987/8.
Leech, M. (8) (Shamrock Rovers) 1968/9, 1971/2, 1972/3.
Lowry, D. (1) (St Patrick's Athletic) 1961/2.

McAlinden, J. (2) (Portsmouth) 1945/6.
McCann, J. (1) (Shamrock Rovers) 1956/7.
McCarthy, M. (57) (Manchester City) 1983/4, 1984/5, 1985/6, 1986/7 (Celtic) 1987/8, 1988/9 (Lyon) 1989/90, 1990/1 (Millwall), 1991/2.
McConville, T. (6) (Dundalk) 1971/2 (Waterford) 1972/3.
McDonagh, J. (24) (Everton) 1980/1 (Bolton Wanderers) 1981/2, 1982/3, (Notts County) 1983/4, 1984/5, 1985/6.
McDonagh, Joe (3) (Shamrock Rovers) 1983/4, 1984/5.
McEvoy, M.A. (17) (Blackburn Rovers) 1960/1, 1962/3, 1963/4, 1964/5, 1965/6, 1966/7.
McGee, P. (15) (QPR) 1977/8, 1978/9, 1979/80 (Preston North End) 1980/1.
McGoldrick, E.J. (4) (Crystal Palace) 1991/2.
McGowan, D. (3) (West Ham United) 1948/9.
McGowan, J. (1) (Cork United) 1946/7.
McGrath, M. (22) (Blackburn Rovers) 1957/8, 1958/9, 1959/60, 1960/1, 1961/2, 1962/3, 1963/4, 1964/5, 1965/6 (Bradford Park Avenue) 1965/6, 1966/7.
McGrath, P. (55) (Manchester United) 1984/5, 1985/6, 1986/7, 1987/8, 1988/9 (Aston Villa) 1989/90, 1990/1, 1991/2.
Macken, A. (1) (Derby County) 1976/7.
Mackey, G. (3) (Shamrock Rovers) 1956/7.
McLoughlin, A.F. (12) (Swindon T) 1989/90, 1990/1 (Southampton) 1991/2 (Portsmouth).
McMillan, W. (2) (Belfast Celtic) 1945/6. **McNally, J.B.** (3) (Luton Town) 1958/9, 1960/1, 1962/3.
Malone, G. (1) (Shelbourne) 1948/9.
Mancini, T.J. (5) (QPR) 1973/4 (Arsenal) 1974/5.
Martin, C.J. (30) (Glentoran) 1945/6, 1946/7 (Leeds United) 1946/7, 1947/8, (Aston Villa) 1948/9, 1949/50 1950/1, 1951/2, 1953/4, 1954/5, 1955/6.
Martin, M.P. (51) (Bohemians) 1971/2, 1972/3 (Manchester United) 1972/3, 1973/4, 1974/5 (West Bromwich Albion) 1975/6, 1976/7 (Newcastle United) 1978/9, 1979/80, 1981/2, 1982/3.
Meagan, M.K. (17) (Everton) 1960/1, 1961/2, 1962/3, 1963/4 (Huddersfield Town) 1964/5, 1965/6, 1966/7, 1967/8 (Drogheda) 1969/70.

Milligan, M.J. (1) (Oldham Athletic) 1991/2.
Mooney, J. (2) (Shamrock Rovers) 1964/5.
Moran, K. (62) (Manchester United) 1979/80, 1980/1, 1981/2,
1982/3, 1983/4, 1984/5, 1985/6, 1986/7, 1987/8 (Sporting Gijon)
1988/9 (Blackburn Rovers) 1989/90, 1990/1, 1991/2.
Moroney, T. (12) (West Ham United) 1947/8, 1948/9, 1949/50,
1950/1, 1951/2, 1953/4.
Morris, C.B. (34) (Celtic) 1987/8, 1988/9, 1989/90, 1990/1, 1991/2.
Moulson, G.B. (3) (Lincoln City) 1947/8, 1948/9.
Mucklan, C. (1) (Drogheda) 1977/8.
Mulligan, P.M. (50) (Shamrock Rovers) 1968/9, 1969/70 (Chelsea)
1969/70, 1970/1, 1971/2 (Crystal Palace) 1972/3, 1973/4, 1974/5
(West Bromwich Albion) 1975/6, 1976/7, 1977/8, 1978/9 (Shamrock
Rovers) 1979/80.
Munroe, L. (1) (Shamrock Rovers) 1953/4.
Murphy, A. (1) (Clyde) 1955/6.
Murphy, B. (1) (Bohemians) 1985/6.
Murphy, J. (1) (Crystal Palace) 1979/80.
Murray, T. (1) (Dundalk) 1949/50.

Newman, W. (1) (Shelbourne) 1968/9.
Nolan, R. (10) (Shamrock Rovers) 1956/7, 1957/8, 1959/60, 1961/2,
1962/3.

O'Brien, F. (4) (Philadelphia Fury) 1979/80.
O'Brien, L. (9) (Shamrock Rovers) 1985/6 (Manchester United)
1986/7, 1987/8, (Newcastle United) 1988/9, 1991/2.
O'Brien R. (4) (Notts County) 1975/6, 1976/7.
O'Byrne, L.B. (1) (Shamrock Rovers) 1948/9.
O'Callaghan, B.R. (6) (Stoke City) 1978/9, 1979/80, 1980/1, 1981/2.
O'Callaghan, K. (20) (Ipswich Town) 1980/1, 1981/2, 1982/3,
1983/4, 1984/5, (Portsmouth) 1985/6, 1986/7.
O'Connnell, A. (2) (Dundalk) 1966/7 (Bohemians) 1970/1.
O'Connor, T. (4) (Shamrock Rovers) 1949/50.
O'Connor, T. (7) (Fulham) 1967/8 (Dundalk) 1971/2 (Bohemians)
1972/3.
O'Driscoll, J.F. (3) (Swansea Town) 1948/9.
O'Driscoll, S. (3) (Fulham) 1981/2.
O'Farrell, F. (9) (West Ham United) 1951/2, 1952/3, 1953/4,
1954/5, 1955/6 (Preston North End) 1957/8, 1958/9.
O'Flanagan, K.P. (3) (Arsenal) 1946/7.
O'Flanagan, M. (1) (Bohemians) 1946/7.
O'Hanlon, K.G. (1) (Rotherham United) 1987/8.
O'Keefe, E. (5) (Everton) 1980/1 (Port Vale) 1983/4.
O'Leary, D. (66) Arsenal) 1976/7, 1977/8, 1978/9, 1979/80, 1980/1,
1981/2, 1982/3, 1983/4, 1984/5, 1985/6, 1988/9, 1989/90, 1990/1,
1991/2.

O'Leary, P. (7) (Shamrock Rovers) 1979/80, 1980/1.
O'Neill, F.S. (20) (Shamrock Rovers) 1961/2, 1964/5, 1965/6, 1966/7, 1968/9, 1971/2.
O'Neill, J. (17) (Everton) 1951/2, 1952/3, 1953/4, 1954/5, 1955/6, 1956/7, 1957/8, 1958/9.
O'Neill, J. (1) (Preston North End) 1960/1.
O'Regan, K. (4) (Brighton & Hove Albion) 1983/4, 1984/5.
O'Reilly, J. (2) (Cork United) 1945/6.

Peyton, G. (33) (Fulham) 1976/7, 1977/8, 1978/9, 1979/80, 1980/1, 1981/2, 1984/5, 1985/6 (Bournemouth) 1987/8, 1988/9, 1989/90, 1990/1 (Everton) 1991/2.
Peyton, N. (6) (Shamrock Rovers) 1956/7 (Leeds United) 1959/60, 1960/1, 1962/3.
Phelan, T. (8) (Wimbledon) 1991/2.

Quinn, N.J. (31) (Arsenal) 1985/6, 1986/7, 1987/8, 1988/9 (Manchester City) 1989/90, 1990/1, 1991/2.

Richardson, D.J. (3) (Shamrock Rovers) 1971/2 (Gillingham) 1972/3, 1979/80.
Ringstead, A. (20) (Sheffield United) 1950/1, 1951/2, 1952/3, 1953/4, 1954/5, 1955/6, 1956/7, 1957/8, 1958/9.
Robinson, M. (23) (Brighton & Hove Albion) 1980/1, 1981/2, 1982/3, (Liverpool) 1983/4, 1984/5 (QPR) 1985/6.
Roche, P.J. (8) (Shelbourne) 1971/2 (Manchester United) 1974/5, 1975/6.
Rogers, E. (19) (Blackburn Rovers) 1967/8, 1968/9, 1969/70, 1970/1, (Charlton Athletic) 1971/2, 1972/3.
Ryan, G. (16) (Derby County) 1977/8 (Brighton & Hove Albion) 1978/9, 1979/80, 1980/1, 1981/2, 1983/4, 1984/5.
Ryan, R.A. (16) (West Bromwich Albion) 1949/50, 1950/1, 1951/2, 1952/3, 1953/4, 1954/5 (Derby County) 1955/6.

Saward, P. (18) (Millwall) 1953/4 (Aston Villa) 1956/7, 1957/8, 1958/9, 1959/60, 1960/1 (Huddersfield Town) 1960/1, 1961/2, 1962/3.
Scannell, T. (1) (Southend United) 1953/4.
Scully, P.J. (1) (Arsenal) 1988/9.
Sheedy, K. (43) (Everton) 1983/4, 1984/5, 1985/6, 1986/7, 1987/8, 1988/9, 1989/90, 1990/1 (Newcastle United) 1991/2.
Sheridan, J.J. (14) (Leeds United) 1987/8, 1988/9 (Sheffield Wed) 1989/90, 1990/1, 1991/2.
Slaven, B. (6) (Middlesbrough) 1989/90, 1990/91.
Sloan, J.W. (2) (Arsenal) 1945/6.
Smyth, M. (1) (Shamrock Rovers) 1968/9.

Stapleton, F. (70) (Arsenal) 1976/7, 1977/8, 1978/9, 1979/80, 1980/1 (Manchester United) 1981/2, 1982/3, 1983/4, 1984/5, 1985/6, 1986/7 (Ajax) 1987/8 (Derby County) 1987/8 (Le Havre) 1988/9 (Blackburn Rovers) 1989/90.
Staunton, S. (34) (Liverpool) 1988/9, 1989/90, 1990/1 (Aston Villa) 1991/2.
Stevenson, A.E. (6) (Everton) 1946/7, 1947/8, 1948/9.
Strahan, F. (5) (Shelbourne) 1963/4, 1964/5, 1965/6.
Swan, M.M.G. (1) (Drumcondra) 1959/60.
Synott, N. (3) (Shamrock Rovers) 1977/8, 1978/9.

Thomas, P. (2) (Waterford) 1973/4.
Townsend, A.D. (31) (Norwich City) 1988/9, 1989/90, 1990/1 (Chelsea) 1991/2.
Traynor, T.J. (8) (Southampton) 1953/4, 1961/2, 1962/3, 1963/4.
Treacy, R.C.P. (43) (West Bromwich Albion) 1965/6, 1966/7, 1967/8 (Charlton Athletic) 1967/8, 1968/9, 1969/70, 1970/1 (Swindon Town) 1971/2, 1972/3, 1973/4 (Preston North End) 1973/4, 1974/5, 1975/6 (West Bromwich Albion) 1976/7, 1977/8 (Shamrock Rovers) 1979/80.
Tuohy, L. (8) (Shamrock Rovers) 1955/6, 1958/9 (Newcastle United) 1961/2, 1962/3 (Shamrock Rovers) 1963/4, 1964/5.
Turner, A. (2) (Celtic) 1962/3, 1963/4.

Vernon, J. (2) (Belfast Celtic) 1945/6.

Waddock, G. (20) (QPR) 1979/80, 1980/1, 1981/2, 1982/3, 1983/4, 1984/5, 1985/6 (Millwall) 1989/90.
Walsh, D.J. (20) (West Bromwich Albion) 1945/6, 1946/7, 1947/8, 1948/9, 1949/50, 1950/1 (Aston Villa) 1951/2, 1952/3, 1953/4.
Walsh, J. (1) (Limerick) 1981/2.
Walsh, M. (22) (Blackpool) 1975/6, 1976/7 (Everton) 1978/9 (QPR) 1978/9 (Porto) 1980/1, 1981/2, 1982/3, 1983/4, 1984/5.
Walsh, M. (5) (Everton) 1981/2, 1982/3 (Norwich City) 1982/3.
Walsh, W. (9) (Manchester City) 1946/7, 1947/8, 1948/9, 1949/50.
Waters, J. (2) (Grimsby Town) 1976/7, 1979/80.
Whelan, R. (2) (St Patrick's Athletic) 1963/4.
Whelan, R. (42) (Liverpool) 1980/1, 1981/2, 1982/3, 1983/4, 1984/5, 1985/6, 1986/7, 1987/8, 1988/9, 1989/90, 1990/1, 1991/2.
Whelan, W. (4) (Manchester United) 1955/6, 1956/7.
Whittaker, R. (1) (Chelsea) 1958/9.

British and Irish results continued from Page 231

Gifu (Tokyo), 3 June 1992, 31,000

Argentina (0) 1 *(Batistuta 88)*

Wales (0) 0

Argentina: Islas; Basualdo, Vazquez, Ruggeri, Altamirano, Villarreal, Cagna, Rodriguez (Acosta 55), Franco, Batistuta, Caniggia.
Wales: Southall; Aizlewood, Phillips, Bodin, Blackmore, Symons, Horne, Speed, Saunders, Hughes, Roberts.

Foxboro, 4 June 1992, 34,797

Italy (1) 2 *(Signori 17, Costacurta 67 (pen))*

Republic of Ireland (0) 0

Italy: Zenga; Baresi, Maldine, Costacurta, Bianchi, Galia, Fusi, Carboni, Signori, Mancini (Vialli), Casiraghi.
Republic of Ireland: Bonner; Staunton, Irwin (Peyton), McGrath, O'Leary, McCarthy (McLoughlin), Houghton, McGoldrick (Phelan), Quinn (Coyne), Aldridge (Kelly), Townsend.

Matsuvama, 7 June 1992, 30,000

Japan (0) 0

Wales (1) 1 *(Bowen 40)*

Japan: Maekawa, Meura, Katuya, Horilke, Ahashiratani, Tsunami (Yoshide 60), Ihara, Takeda (Takegi 74), Hirekawi, Moriyasw, Kitazawi.
Wales: Southall; Phillips, Aizlewood (Melville 68), Blackmore, Symons, Bowen, Speed, Horne, Saunders (Pembridge 80), Hughes, Roberts.

Boston, 7 June 1992, 41,227

Portugal (0) 0

Republic of Ireland (1) 2 *(Staunton, Coyne)*

Portugal: Vitor Baia; Leal (Magalhaes), Couto J (Joao Pinto II), Samuel, Couto F, Joao Pinto I, Semedo (Sousa), Filipe, Paneira, Figo (Domingos), Cadete.
Republic of Ireland: Peyton; Staunton, Morris, McGrath, McCarthy, O'Leary, Houghton, McLoughlin, Quinn (Aldridge), Kelly (Coyne), Phelan (McGoldrick).

BRITISH ISLES INTERNATIONAL GOALSCORERS SINCE 1946

ENGLAND

A'Court, A. 1
Adams, T.A. 4
Allen, R. 2
Anderson, V. 2
Astall, G. 1
Atyeo, P.J.W. 5

Baily, E.F. 5
Baker, J.H. 3
Ball, A.J. 8
Barnes, J. 10
Barnes, P.S. 4
Beardsley, P.A. 8
Beattie, I.K. 1
Bell, C. 9
Bentley, R.T.F. 9
Blissett, L. 3
Bowles, S. 1
Bradford, G.R.W. 1
Bradley, W. 2
Bridges, B.J. 1
Broadbent, P.F. 2
Broadis, I.A. 8
Brooking, T.D. 5
Brooks, J. 2
Bull, S.G. 4
Butcher, T. 3
Byrne, J.J. 8

Carter, H.S. 7
(inc. 2 scored pre-war)
Chamberlain, M. 1
Channon, M.R. 21
Charlton, J. 6
Charlton, R. 49
Chivers, M. 13
Clarke, A.J. 10
Connelly, J.M. 7
Coppell, S.J. 7
Cowans, G. 2

Crawford, R. 1
Currie, A.W. 3

Dixon, L.M. 1
Dixon, K.M. 4
Douglas, B. 11

Eastham, G. 2
Edwards, D. 5
Elliott, W.H. 3

Finney, T. 30
Flowers, R. 10
Francis, G.C.J. 3
Francis, T. 12
Froggatt, J. 2
Froggatt, R. 2

Gascoigne, P.J. 2
Goddard, P. 1
Grainger, C. 3
Greaves, J. 44

Haines, J.T.W. 2
Hancocks, J. 2
Hassall, H.W. 4
Hateley, M. 9
Haynes, J.N. 18
Hirst, D.E. 1
Hitchens, G.A. 5
Hoddle, G. 8
Hughes, E.W. 1
Hunt, R. 18
Hunter, N. 2
Hurst, G.C. 24

Johnson, D.E. 6

Kay, A.H. 1
Keegan, J.K. 21
Kennedy, R. 3
Keown, M.R. 1

Kevan, D.T. 8
Kidd, B. 1

Langton, R. 1
Latchford, R.D. 5
Lawler, C. 1
Lawton, T. 22
(inc. 6 scored pre-war)
Lee, F. 10
Lee, J. 1
Lee, S. 2
Lineker, G. 48
Lofthouse, N. 30

Mabbutt, G. 1
McDermott, T. 3
Macdonald, M. 6
Mannion, W.J. 11
Mariner, P. 13
Marsh, R.W. 1
Matthews, S. 11
(inc. 8 scored pre-war)
Medley, L.D. 1
Melia, J. 1
Merson, P.C. 1
Milburn, J.E.T. 10
Moore, R.F. 2
Morris, J. 3
Mortensen, S.H. 23
Mullen, J. 6
Mullery, A.P. 1

Neal, P.G. 5
Nicholls, J. 1
Nicholson, W.E. 1

O'Grady, M. 3
Own goals 23

Paine, T.L. 7
Parry, R.A. 1

Peacock, A.	3	
Pearce, S.	2	
Pearson, J.S.	5	
Pearson, S.C.	5	
Perry, W.	2	
Peters, M.	20	
Pickering, F.	5	
Platt, D.	11	
Pointer, R.	2	
Ramsay, A.E.	3	
Revie, D.G.	4	
Robson, B.	26	
Robson, R.	4	
Rowley, J.F.	6	
Royle, J.	2	
Sansom, K.	1	
Sewell, J.	3	
Shackleton, L.F.	1	
Shearer, A.	1	
Smith, A.M.	2	
Smith, R.	13	
Steven, T.M.	4	
Stiles, N.P.	13	
Summerbee, M.G.	1	
Tambling, R.V.	1	
Taylor, P.J.	2	
Taylor, T.	16	
Thompson, P.B.	1	
Tueart, D.	2	
Viollet, D.S.	1	
Waddle, C.R.	6	
Wallace, D.L.	1	
Walsh, P.	1	
Watson, D.V.	4	
Webb, N.	3	
Weller, K.	1	
Wignall, F.	2	
Wilkins, R.G.	3	
Wilshaw, D.J.	10	
Wise, D.F.	1	
Withe, P.	1	

Woodcock, T.	16
Worthington, F.S.	2
Wright, M.	1
Wright, W.A.	3

SCOTLAND

Aitken, R.	1
Archibald, S.	4
Baird, S.	2
Bannon, E.	1
Bauld, W.	2
Baxter, J.C.	3
Bett, J.	1
Bone, J.	1
Brand, R.	8
Brazil, A.	1
Bremner, W.J.	3
Brown, A.D.	6
Buckley, P.	1
Burns, K.	1
Caldow, E.	4
Campbell, R.	1
Chalmers, S.	3
Collins, J.	2
Collins, R.V.	10
Combe, J.R.	1
Conn, A.	1
Cooper, D.	6
Craig, J.	1
Curran, H.P.	1
Dalglish, K.	30
Davidson, J.A.	1
Docherty, T.H.	1
Dodds, D.	1
Duncan, D.M.	1
Durie, G.S.	4
Fernie, W.	1
Flavell, R.	2
Fleming, C.	2

Gemmell, T. (St Mirren)	1
Gemmell, T. (Celtic)	1
Gemmill, A.	8
Gibson, D.W.	3
Gilzean, A.J.	10
Gough, C.R.	6
Graham, A.	2
Graham, G.	3
Gray, A.	7
Gray, E.	3
Gray, F.	1
Greig, J.	3
Hamilton, G.	4
Harper, J.M.	2
Hartford, R.A.	4
Henderson, J.G.	1
Henderson, W.	5
Herd, D.G.	4
Hewie, J.D.	2
Holton, J.A.	2
Houliston, W.	2
Howie, H.	1
Hughes, J.	1
Hunter, W.	1
Hutchison, T.	1
Jackson, C.	1
Jardine, A.	1
Johnston, L.H.	1
Johnston, M.	14
Johnstone, D.	2
Johnstone, J.	4
Johnstone, R.	9
Jordan, J.	11
Law, D.	30
Leggat, G.	8
Lennox, R.	3
Liddell, W.	6
Linwood, A.B.	1
Lorimer, P.	4
Macari, L.	5

McAllister, G. 4
MacDougall, E.J. 3
MacKay, D.C. 4
Mackay, G. 1
MacKenzie, J.A. 1
MacLeod, M. 1
McAvennie, F. 1
McCall, S.M. 1
McCalliog, J. 1
McCoist, A. 12
McGhee, M. 2
McInally, A. 3
McKimmie, S.I. 1
McKinnon, R. 1
McClair, B. 1
McLaren, A. 4
McLean, T. 1
McLintock, F. 1
McMillan, I.L. 2
McNeill, W. 3
McPhail, J. 3
McQueen, G. 5
McStay, P. 9
Mason, J. 4
Masson, D.S. 5
Miller, W. 1
Mitchell, R.C. 1
Morgan, W. 1
Morris, H. 3
Mudie, J.K. 9
Mulhall, G. 1
Murdoch, R. 5
Murray, J. 1

Narey, D. 1
Nevin, P. 1
Nicholas, C. 5

O'Hare, J. 5
Ormond, W.E. 1
Orr, T. 1
Own goals 7

Parlane, D. 1
Pettigrew, W. 2
Provan, D. 1

Quinn, J. 7
Quinn, P. 1

Reilly, L. 22
Ring, T. 2
Rioch, B.D. 6
Robertson, A. 2
Robertson, J. 2
Robertson, J.N. 8

St John, I. 9
Scott, A.S. 5
Sharp, G. 1
Smith, G. 4
Souness, G.J. 3
Steel, W. 12
Stein, C. 10
Stewart, R. 1
Strachan, G. 5
Sturrock, P. 3

Thornton, W. 1

Waddell, W. 6
Wallace, I.A. 1
Wark, J. 7
Weir, A. 1
White, J.A. 3
Wilson, D. 9

Young, A. 2

WALES

Allchurch, I.J. 23
Allen, M. 3

Barnes, W. 1
Bodin, P.J. 3
Bowen, D.I. 1
Bowen, M. 2
Boyle, T. 1
Burgess, W.A.R. 1

Charles, J. 1
Charles, M. 6

Charles, W.J. 15
Clarke, R.J. 5
Coleman, C. 1
Curtis, A. 6

Davies, G. 2
Davies, R.T. 8
Davies, R.W. 7
Deacy, N. 4
Durban, A. 2
Dwyer, P. 2

Edwards, G. 2
Edwards, R.I. 5
England, H.M. 3
Evans, I. 1

Flynn, B. 6
Ford, T. 23
Foulkes, W.J. 1

Giles, D. 2
Godfrey, B.C. 2
Griffiths, A.T. 6
Griffiths, M.W. 2

Harris, C.S. 1
Hewitt, R. 1
Hockey, T. 1
Hodges, G. 2
Horne, B. 2
Hughes, L.M. 9

James, L. 10
James, R. 7
Jones, A. 1
Jones, B.S. 2
Jones, Cliff 15
Jones, D.E. 1
Jones, J.P. 1

Kryzwicki, R.I. 1

Leek, K. 5
Lovell, S. 1
Lowrie, G. 2

Mahoney, J.F. 1
Medwin, T.C. 6
Moore, G. 1

Nicholas, P. 2

O'Sullivan, P.A. 1
Own goals 5

Palmer, D. 1
Paul, R. 1
Pembridge, M.A. 1
Phillips, D. 1
Powell, A. 1
Powell, D. 1
Price, P. 1

Reece, G.I. 2
Rees, R.R. 3
Roberts, P.S. 1
Rush, I. 20

Saunders, D. 10
Slatter, N. 2
Smallman, D.P. 1

Tapscott, D.R. 4
Thomas, M. 4
Toshack, J.B. 13

Vernon, T.R. 8

Walsh, I. 7
Williams, G.E. 1
Williams, G.G. 1
Woosnam, A.P. 4

Yorath, T.C. 2

NORTHERN IRELAND

Anderson, T. 3
Armstrong, G. 12

Barr, H.H. 1
Best, G. 9
Bingham, W.L. 10
Blanchflower, D. 2
Blanchflower, J. 1
Brennan, R.A. 1
Brotherston, N. 3

Campbell, W.G. 1
Casey, T. 2
Caskey, W. 1
Cassidy, T. 1
Clarke, C.J. 11
Clements, D. 2
Cochrane, T. 1
Crossan, E. 1
Crossan, J.A. 10
Cush, W.W. 5

D'Arcy, S.D. 1
Doherty, I. 1
Doherty, P.D. 3
(inc. 1 scored pre-war)
Dougan, A.D. 8
Dowie, I. 1

Elder, A.R. 1

Ferguson, W. 1
Ferris, R.O. 1
Finney, T. 2

Hamilton, B. 4
Hamilton, W. 5
Harkin, J.T. 2
Harvey, M. 3
Hill, C.F. 1
Humphries, W. 1
Hughes, M.E. 1
Hunter, A. 1

Irvine, W.J. 8

Johnston, W.C. 1
Jones, J. 1

Lockhart, N. 3

Magilton, J. 1
McAdams, W.J. 7
McClelland, J. 1
McCrory, S. 1
McCurdy, C. 1
McDonald, A. 2
McGarry, J.K. 1
McGrath, R.C. 4
McIlroy, J. 10
McIlroy, S.B. 5
McLaughlin, J.C. 6
McMordie, A.S. 3
McMorran, E.J. 4
McParland, P.J. 10
Moreland, V. 1
Morgan, S. 3

Neill, W.J.T. 2
Nelson, S. 1
Nicholl, C.J. 3
Nicholl, J.M. 2
Nicholson, J.J. 6

O'Kane, W.J. 1
O'Neill, J. 1
O'Neill, M. 1
O'Neill, M.H. 8
Own goals 4

Peacock, R. 2
Penney, S. 2

Quinn, J.M. 6

Simpson, W.J. 5
Smyth, S. 5
Spence, D.W. 3
Stewart, I. 2

Taggart, G.P. 4
Tully, C.P. 3

Walker, J. 1
Walsh, D.J. 5

Welsh, E. 1
Whiteside, N. 9
Wilson, D. 1
Wilson, K.J. 4
Wilson, S.J. 7

EIRE

Aldridge, J. 8
Ambrose, P. 1
Anderson, J. 1

Bermingham, P. 1
Bradshaw, P. 4
Brady, L. 9
Brown, D. 1
Byrne, J. *(Bray)* 1
Byrne, J. *(QPR)* 5

Cantwell, J. 14
Carey, J. 3
Carroll, T. 1
Cascarino, A. 10
Coad, P. 3
Conroy, T. 2
Conway, J. 3
Coyne, T. 1
Cummings, G. 5
Curtis, D. 8

Daly, G. 13
Davis, T. 4
Dempsey, J. 1
Dennehy, M. 2
Donnelly, J. 3
Donnelly, T. 1
Duffy, B. 1
Duggan, H. 1
Dunne, J. 12
Dunne, L. 1

Eglinton, T. 2
Ellis, P. 1

Fagan, F. 5

Fallon, S. 2
Fallon, W. 2
Farrell, P. 3
Fitzgerald, J. 1
Fitzgerald, P. 2
Fitzsimons, A. 7
Flood, J.J. 4
Fogarty, A. 3
Fullam, J. 1
Fullam, R. 1

Galvin, A. 1
Gavin, J. 2
Geoghegan, M. 2
Giles, J. 5
Givens, D. 19
Glynn, D. 1
Grealish, T. 8
Grimes, A.A. 1

Hale, A. 2
Hand, E. 2
Haverty, J. 3
Holmes, J. 1
Horlacher, A. 2
Houghton, R. 3
Hughton, C. 1
Hurley, C. 2

Jordan, D. 1

Kelly, D. 7
Kelly, J. 2

Lacey, W. 1
Lawrenson, M. 5
Leech, M. 2

McCann, J. 1
McCarthy, M. 2
McEvoy, A. 6
McGee, P. 4
McGrath, P. 6
Madden, O. 1
Mancini, T. 1
Martin, C. 6

Martin, M. 4
Mooney, J. 1
Moore, P. 7
Moran, K. 6
Moroney, T. 1
Mulligan, P. 1

O'Callaghan, K. 1
O'Connor, T. 2
O'Farrell, F. 2
O'Flanagan, K. 3
O'Keefe, E. 1
O'Leary, D.A. 1
O'Neill, F. 1
O'Reilly, J. 2
O'Reilly, J. 1
Own goals 6

Quinn, N. 8

Ringstead, A. 7
Robinson, M. 4
Rogers, E. 5
Ryan, G. 1
Ryan, R. 3

Sheedy, K. 7
Sheridan, J. 1
Slaven, B. 1
Sloan, W. 1
Squires, J. 1
Stapleton, F. 20
Staunton, S. 2
Strahan, F. 1
Sullivan, J. 1

Townsend, A.D. 2
Treacy, R. 5
Tuohy, L. 4

Waddock, G. 3
Walsh, D. 5
Walsh, M. 3
Waters, J. 1
White, J.J. 2
Whelan, R. 3

SOUTH AMERICAN CHAMPIONSHIP WINNERS

(Copa America)

1916 Uruguay	1935 Uruguay	1957 Argentina
1917 Uruguay	1937 Argentina	1959 Argentina
1919 Brazil	1939 Peru	1959 Uruguay
1920 Uruguay	1941 Argentina	1963 Bolivia
1921 Argentina	1942 Uruguay	1967 Uruguay
1922 Brazil	1945 Argentina	1975 Peru
1923 Uruguay	1946 Argentina	1979 Paraguay
1924 Uruguay	1947 Argentina	1983 Uruguay
1925 Argentina	1949 Brazil	1987 Uruguay
1926 Uruguay	1953 Paraguay	1989 Brazil
1927 Argentina	1955 Argentina	1991 Argentina
1929 Argentina	1956 Uruguay	

SOUTH AMERICAN CUP WINNERS

(Copa Libertadores)

1960 Penarol (Uruguay)	1977 Boca Juniors (Argentina)
1961 Penarol	1978 Boca Juniors
1962 Santos (Brazil)	1979 Olimpia (Paraguay)
1963 Santos	1980 Nacional
1964 Independiente (Argentina)	1981 Flamengo (Brazil)
1965 Independiente	1982 Penarol
1966 Penarol	1983 Gremio Porto Alegre (Brazil)
1967 Racing Club (Argentina)	1984 Independiente
1968 Estudiantes (Argentina)	1985 Argentinos Juniors (Argentina)
1969 Estudiantes	1986 River Plate (Argentina)
1970 Estudiantes	1987 Penarol
1971 Nacional (Uruguay)	1988 Nacional (Uruguay)
1972 Independiente	1989 Nacional (Colombia)
1973 Independiente	1990 Olimpia
1974 Independiente	1991 Colo Colo (Chile)
1975 Independiente	1992 Sao Paulo (Brazil)
1976 Cruzeiro (Brazil)	

8th UEFA UNDER-21 TOURNAMENT 1990–92

Group 1 *(Czechoslovakia, Spain, France, Albania, Iceland)*

Iceland (0) 0, Albania (0) 0
Iceland (0) 0, France (0) 1
Czechoslovakia (5) 7, Iceland (0) 0
Spain (2) 2, Iceland (0) 0
France (1) 1, Czechoslovakia (1) 2
Czechoslovakia (3) 3, Spain (0) 1
Albania (0) 0, France (0) 0
Spain (0) 1, Albania (0) 0
France (0) 0, Spain (0) 1
France (0) 3, Albania (0) 0
Albania (1) 1, Czechoslovakia (2) 5
Albania (0) 2, Iceland (0) 1
Iceland (0) 0, Czechoslovakia (1) 1
Czechoslovakia (1) 1, France (0) 0
Iceland (1) 1, Spain (0) 0
Spain (0) 0, France (0) 0
Czechoslovakia (1) 3, Albania (0) 0
Spain (0) 1, Czechoslovakia (1) 1
France (1) 2, Iceland (0) 1
Albania v Spain not played

Group 2 *(Bulgaria, Scotland, Romania, Switzerland)*

Scotland (1) 2, Romania (0) 0
Switzerland (0) 0, Bulgaria (0) 2
Romania (0) 0, Bulgaria (1) 1
Scotland (2) 4, Switzerland (1) 2
Bulgaria (2) 2, Scotland (0) 0
Scotland (1) 1, Bulgaria (0) 0
Switzerland (0) 0, Romania (1) 2
Bulgaria (1) 1, Switzerland (0) 0
Switzerland (0) 0, Scotland (0) 3
Romania (0) 1, Scotland (1) 3
Romania (1) 1, Switzerland (2) 3
Bulgaria (0) 0, Romania (1) 1

Group 3 *(Norway, Italy, USSR, Hungary)*

USSR (1) 2, Norway (0) 2
Norway (2) 3, Hungary (0) 1
Italy (0) 1, Hungary (0) 0
Hungary (0) 0, USSR (0) 0
Hungary (0) 0, Italy (0) 1
Norway (2) 6, Italy (0) 0
Italy (0) 1, USSR (0) 0
Norway (0) 0, USSR (1) 1
USSR (0) 2, Hungary (0) 0
USSR (0) 1, Italy (0) 1
Hungary (0) 0, Norway (0) 1
Italy (2) 2, Norway (1) 1

Group 4 *(Denmark, Austria, Yugoslavia, San Marino, Liechtenstein)*

Liechtenstein (0) 0, Austria (3) 6
Austria (6) 10, Liechtenstein (0) 0
San Marino (0) 0, Denmark (1) 3
Yugoslavia (0) 1, Austria (0) 0
Denmark (1) 3, Yugoslavia (0) 0
San Marino (0) 0, Austria (2) 2
Yugoslavia (4) 5, San Marino (0) 0
Austria (0) 3, San Marino (0) 0
Denmark (4) 7, San Marino (0) 0
Yugoslavia (0) 2, Denmark (1) 6
Denmark (0) 1, Austria (1) 1
San Marino (0) 0, Yugoslavia (1) 1
Austria (1) 1, Denmark (1) 1
Austria (0) 1, Yugoslavia (0) 2

Group 5 *(Germany, Luxembourg, Belgium)*

Luxembourg (0) 0, Germany (0) 3
Belgium (0) 2, Luxembourg (0) 0
Germany (1) 3, Belgium (1) 1
Luxembourg (0) 0, Belgium (0) 2
Belgium (0) 0, Germany (0) 3
Germany (1) 3, Luxembourg (0) 0

Group 6 *(Portugal, Holland, Finland, Malta)*

Finland (0) 0, Portugal (1) 1
Portugal (0) 0, Holland (0) 0
Malta (1) 1, Holland (2) 4
Malta (0) 1, Portugal (1) 3
Portugal (2) 2, Malta (0) 0
Holland (3) 7, Malta (0) 1
Holland (0) 1, Finland (0) 0
Finland (0) 1, Holland (0) 7
Finland (1) 3, Malta (0) 1
Portugal (1) 2, Finland (0) 0
Holland (0) 1, Portugal (1) 1
Malta (0) 1, Finland (1) 3

Group 7 *(Poland, England, Rep. of Ireland, Turkey*

England (0) 0, Poland (0) 1
Rep. of Ireland (1) 3, Turkey (1) 2
Rep. of Ireland (0) 0, England (1) 3
Turkey (0) 0, Poland (0) 1
England (1) 3, Rep. of Ireland (0) 0
Poland (1) 2, Turkey (0) 0
Rep. of Ireland (0) 1, Poland (0) 2
Turkey (1) 2, England (1) 2
England (0) 2, Turkey (0) 0
Poland (0) 2, Rep. of Ireland (0) 0
Poland (1) 2, England (0) 1
Turkey (1) 2, Rep. of Ireland (0) 1

Group 8 *(Sweden, Israel, Cyprus, Greece)*
Sweden (2) 5, Greece (0) 0
Cyprus (0) 1, Sweden (0) 1
Greece (2) 2, Israel (1) 2
Israel (1) 4, Cyprus (0) 0
Cyprus (1) 1, Greece (0) 0
Sweden (2) 6, Cyprus (0) 0

Sweden (1) 2, Israel (0) 1
Israel (0) 2, Greece (1) 1
Israel (0) 0, Sweden (0) 0
Greece (0) 1, Sweden (1) 3
Cyprus (0) 1, Israel (1) 2
Greece (2) 2, Cyprus (0) 0

Quarter-finals
Germany (1) 1, Scotland (0) 1
Czechoslovakia (0) 1, Italy (1) 2
Denmark (5) 5, Poland (0) 0
Holland (1) 2, Sweden (1) 1

Scotland (1) 4, Germany (2) 3
Italy (2) 2, Czechoslovakia (0) 0
Poland (0) 1, Denmark (1) 1
Sweden (0) 1, Holland (0) 0

Semi-finals
Denmark (0) 0, Italy (1) 1
Italy (0) 2, Denmark (0) 0

Scotland (0) 0, Sweden (0) 0
Sweden (0) 1, Scotland (0) 0

Final
Italy (0) 2, Sweden (0) 0

Sweden (0) 1, Italy (0) 0

8th UEFA UNDER-18 CHAMPIONSHIP 1990–92

Group 1 *(Israel, Greece, Turkey, Switzerland)*
Greece (1) 1, Switzerland (0) 1
Israel (2) 2, Switzerland (0) 0
Turkey (1) 1, Israel (1) 1
Greece (2) 2, Israel (0) 0
Switzerland (0) 0, Israel (1) 1
Turkey (0) 1, Greece (0) 0

Switzerland (0) 0, Turkey (2) 4
Switzerland (2) 2, Greece (0) 1
Greece (0) 0, Turkey (0) 0
Israel (0) 3, Greece (1) 1
Turkey (0) 1, Switzerland (0) 0
Israel (1) 1, Turkey (1) 1

Group 2 *(Cyprus, Romania, Hungary, Bulgaria)*
Hungary (0) 1, Romania (0) 0
Hungary (0) 0, Cyprus (0) 1
Cyprus (1) 3, Bulgaria (1) 1
Romania (0) 3, Cyprus (0) 2
Bulgaria (0) 0, Cyprus (0) 1
Cyprus (0) 0, Hungary (1) 5

Romania (2) 3, Hungary (0) 1
Romania (1) 1, Bulgaria (0) 1
Hungary (1) 2, Bulgaria (0) 1
Bulgaria (1) 1, Hungary (1) 2
Bulgaria (0) 0, Romania (1) 1
Cyprus (1) 3, Romania (0) 0

Group 3 *(Portugal, France, Denmark, Luxembourg)*
Denmark (2) 7, Luxembourg (0) 0
Portugal (0) 0, France (0) 0
France (0) 2, Denmark (0) 0
Luxembourg (0) 0, Portugal (3) 5
France (0) 0, Portugal (2) 3
Portugal (0) 3, Denmark (0) 0

Luxembourg (0) 0, France (3) 5
Denmark (0) 1, France (1) 2
Portugal (3) 7, Luxembourg (0) 1
France (0) 2, Luxembourg (0) 1
Denmark (0) 0, Portugal (0) 0
Luxembourg (0) 0, Denmark (1) 5

Group 4 *(Italy, Spain, Malta, FR Germany)*
Italy (2) 9, Malta (0) 0
Spain (0) 0, Italy (1) 2
Malta (0) 1, Spain (0) 1
Italy (0) 0, Spain (0) 0
Malta (0) 0, Germany (0) 1
Germany (2) 4, Malta (0) 0

Spain (0) 1, Germany (1) 3
Germany (0) 0, Italy (0) 0
Spain (0) 0, Malta (0) 0
Italy (1) 2, Germany (0) 2
Germany (2) 3, Spain (0) 0
Malta (0) 0, Italy (2) 2

Group 5 *(England, Belgium, Iceland, Wales)*

Iceland (1) 2, England (1) 3	Iceland (0) 0, Wales (0) 0
Belgium (1) 1, Iceland (1) 1	Wales (1) 1, Iceland (1) 1
England (0) 0, Belgium (0) 0	England (0) 2, Iceland (0) 1
Walels (0) 1, Belgium (0) 1	Iceland (0) 2, Belgium (1) 1
Wales (0) 0, England (0) 1	Belgium (1) 1, England (0) 0
England (0) 3, Wales (0) 0	Belgium (1) 2, Wales (0) 0

Group 6 *(Poland, Rep. of Ireland, Scotland, N. Ireland)*

N. Ireland (0) 0, Rep. of Ireland (1) 2	Poland (1) 5, Rep. of Ireland (0) 0
Poland (0) 1, Scotland (0) 0	Rep. of Ireland (0) 0, Poland (1) 3
Rep. of Ireland (2) 2, Scotland (0) 1	N. Ireland (0) 0, Poland (1) 1
Poland (1) 3, N. Ireland (0) 0	Scotland (0) 0, Poland (2) 2
Scotland (0) 0, N. Ireland (0) 0	Rep. of Ireland (1) 2, N. Ireland (0) 2
Scotland (1) 1, Rep. of Ireland (1) 3	N. Ireland (2) 2, Scotland (1) 2

Group 7 *(Norway, Finland, Holland, Austria)*

Finland (0) 0, Norway (2) 2	Norway (0) 0, Finland (0) 1
Norway (2) 4, Holland (0) 1	Austria (0) 0, Finland (2) 2
Holland (0) 0, Finland (1) 3	Austria (0) 0, Norway (4) 5
Holland (0) 2, Norway (0) 0	Finland (1) 2, Holland (0) 0
Norway (1) 1, Austria (0) 0	Austria (0) 0, Holland (0) 1
Finland (0) 0, Austria (1) 3	Holland (3) 4, Austria (0) 1

Group 8 *(Yugoslavia, USSR, Sweden, Czechoslovakia)*

Yugoslavia (2) 3, USSR (1) 2	Sweden (0) 1, Czechoslovakia (0) 1
Czechoslovakia (0) 2, Sweden (2) 2	USSR (2) 4, Yugoslavia (1) 2
USSR (2) 3, Czechoslovakia (0) 0	Yugoslavia (2) 6, Sweden (2) 4
Sweden (1) 1, Yugoslavia (0) 1	Yugoslavia (0) 0, Czechoslovakia (0) 0
Sweden (1) 2, USSR (0) 2	USSR (1) 2, Sweden (0) 0
Czechoslovakia (1) 2, Yugoslavia (0) 0	Czechoslovakia (2) 2, USSR (1) 2

Final tournament to be held in Germany July 1992

10th UEFA UNDER-16 CHAMPIONSHIP 1992

Group 1: Wales 1, Rep. of Ireland 0; Rep. of Ireland 2, Wales 0. Rep. of Ireland qualified.
Group 2: Iceland 2, N. Ireland 1; N. Ireland 2, Iceland 1. N. Ireland qualified.
Group 3: Malta 0, Holland 6; Holland 2, Malta 0. Holland qualified.
Group 4: Germany 8, Albania 1. Albania & Germany not played.
Group 5: CIS 1, Yugoslavia 1; Yugoslavia 1, CIS 1. Yugoslavia qualified.
Group 6: Turkey 1, Israel 0; Israel 2, Turkey 0. Israel qualified.
Group 7: Luxembourg 0, Spain 5; Spain 3, Luxembourg 1. Spain qualified.
Group 8: France 1, Austria 0; Austria 2, France 5. France qualified.
Group 9: Finland 3, Belgium 0; Belgium 1, Finland 2. Finland qualified.
Group 10: Poland 2, Switzerland 1; Switzerland 1, Italy 0; Italy 3, Switzerland 1; Italy 0, Poland 0; Poland 1, Italy 2; Switzerland 2, Poland 0. Italy qualified.
Group 11: Norway 2, Hungary 2; Hungary 3, Norway 1. Hungary qualified.
Group 12: Czechoslovakia 2, Romania 1; Romania 1, Czechoslovakia 0. Romania qualified.
Group 13: Greece 4, Denmark 1; Denmark 5, Greece 1. Denmark qualified.
Group 14: Bulgaria 0, Scotland 1; Scotland 2, Bulgaria 1. Scotland qualified.
Group 15: Sweden 2, Portugal 0; Portugal 3, Sweden 0. Portugal qualified.

FINAL TOURNAMENT IN CYPRUS

GROUP A
Finland (0) 0, Denmark (0) 1
Yugoslavia (0) 0, Italy (2) 4
Denmark (0) 0, Italy (0) 2
Finland (0) 0, Yugoslavia (2) 2
Denmark (0) 1, Yugoslavia (1) 2
Finland (0) 2, Italy (1) 1

GROUP B
Rep. of Ireland (0) 0, Holland (0) 2
Romania (0) 1, Spain (3) 3
Romania (0) 0, Rep. of Ireland (0) 0
Spain (0) 2, Holland (0) 0
Romania (0) 0, Holland (2) 4
Spain (0) 1, Rep. of Ireland (0) 1

GROUP C
Germany (2) 3, N. Ireland (1) 1
Scotland (2) 3, Cyprus (0) 0
Germany (1) 1, Scotland (0) 0
N. Ireland (0) 0, Cyprus (0) 0
Germany (1) 2, Cyprus (0) 1
N. Ireland (0) 1, Scotland (2) 3

GROUP D
France (1) 1, Portugal (0) 2
Israel (2) 3, Hungary (2) 2
France (0) 0, Israel (0) 0
Portugal (0) 1, Hungary (1) 1
France (0) 0, Hungary (0) 1
Portugal (1) 1, Israel (0) 0

Semi-finals
Spain (0) 3, Portugal (1) 1
Italy (0) 0, Germany (0) 0
  Germany won on penalties.

Third-place match
Italy (0) 1, Portugal (0) 0

Final
Germany (1) 2, Spain (1) 1

ENGLAND UNDER-21 INTERNATIONALS

10 Sept

England (1) 2 *(Johnson, Ebbrell)*

Germany (0) 1 *(Stadler)* 6984

England: James; Dodd, Vinnicombe, Ebbrell, Tiler, Warhurst, Johnson, Draper (Matthew), Shearer, Williams P, Campbell.

15 Oct

England (0) 2 *(Shearer 2)*

Turkey (0) 0 7489

England: James; Charles, Vinnicombe, Ebbrell, Tiler, Atherton, Johnson, Matthew (Blake), Shearer, Williams P, Campbell.

12 Nov

Poland (1) 2 *(Juskowiak 2)*

England (0) 1 *(Kitson)* 12,000

England: James; Dodd, Vinnicombe (Atkinson), Blake (Olney), Cundy, Lee, Kitson, Draper, Shearer, Williams P, Johnson.

12 May

Hungary (0) 2 *(Hamori, Harvath)*

England (2) 2 *(Allen, Cole)* 1500

England: Walker; Jackson (Ashcroft), Minto, Sutch, Ehiogu, Hendon (Bazeley), Sheron, Parlour, Cole (Hall), Allen, Heaney.

25 May

Mexico (1) 1 *(Pineda)*

England (1) 1 *(Allen)*

England: Marriott; Jackson, Hendon, Ehiogu, Minto, Sutch, Parlour, Heaney, Johnson, Kitson, Allen.

26 May

England (0) 1 *(Kitson)*

Czechoslovakia (1) 2 *(Neumann, Lerch)* 450

England: Walker; Jackson, Hendon, Ehiogu, Minto (Johnson), Parlour, Sutch (Cole), Clark, Kitson, Allen, Heaney.

28 May

France (0) 0

England (0) 0

England: Walker; Jackson, Hendon, Hall, Ehiogu, Sheron, Parlour (Ramage), Clark, Kitson (Cole), Allen, Heaney.

GM VAUXHALL CONFERENCE 1991–92

GM VAUXHALL CONFERENCE TABLE 1991–92

	P	Home			Goals		Away			Goals		Pts
		W	D	L	F	A	W	D	L	F	A	
Colchester United	42	19	1	1	57	11	9	9	3	41	29	94
Wycombe Wanderers	42	18	1	2	49	13	12	3	6	35	22	94
Kettering Town	42	12	6	3	44	23	8	7	6	28	27	73
Merthyr Tydfil	42	14	4	3	40	24	4	10	7	19	32	68
Farnborough Town	42	8	7	6	36	27	10	5	6	32	26	66
Telford United	42	10	4	7	32	31	9	3	9	30	35	64
Redridge Forest	42	12	4	5	42	27	6	5	10	27	29	63
Boston United	42	10	4	7	40	35	8	5	8	31	31	63
Bath City	42	8	6	7	27	22	8	6	7	27	29	60
Witton Albion	42	11	6	4	41	26	5	4	12	22	34	58
Northwich Victoria	42	10	4	7	40	25	6	2	13	23	33	54
Welling United	42	8	6	7	40	38	6	6	9	29	41	54
Macclesfield Town	42	7	7	7	25	21	6	6	9	25	29	52
Gateshead	42	8	5	8	22	22	4	7	10	27	35	48
Yeovil Town	42	8	6	7	22	21	3	8	10	18	28	47
Runcorn	42	5	11	5	26	26	6	2	13	24	37	46
Stafford Rangers	42	7	8	6	25	24	3	8	10	16	35	46
Altrincham	42	5	8	8	33	39	6	4	11	28	43	45
Kidderminster Harriers	42	8	6	7	35	32	4	3	14	21	45	45
Slough Town	42	7	3	11	26	39	6	3	12	30	43	45
Cheltenham Town	42	8	5	8	28	35	2	8	11	28	47	43
Barrow	42	5	8	8	29	23	3	6	12	23	49	38

GM VAUXHALL CONFERENCE LEADING GOALSCORERS 1991–92

GMVC		FA	BL	FT
29	Paul Cavell (Redbridge Forest)	+ 1	1	2
	Terry Robbins (Welling United)	+ —	—	1
27	Gary Jones (Boston United)	+ 2	1	1
26	Roy McDonough (Colchester United)	+ 1	—	2
21	Simon Read (Farnborough Town)	+ 9	2	3
	Karl Thomas (Witton Albion)	+ 3	1	4
20	Steve McGavin (Colchester United)	+ 2	2	4
	Dave Webley (Merthyr Tydfil)	+ —	—	—
19	Gary Abbott (Welling United)	+ 5	—	1
	Ken McKenna (Altrincham)	+ —	1	—
	Malcolm O'Connor (Northwich Victoria)	+ —	2	1
	Paul Randall (Bath City)	+ 3	2	1
18	Jon Graham (Kettering Town)	+ 3	—	—
	Keith Scott (Wycombe Wanderers)	+ —	1	1
16	Gary Bennett (Colchester United)	+ —	—	2
	Richard Hill (Kettering Town)	+ 1	—	2
	Mickey Spencer (Yeovil Town)	+ 1	3	4
	Ceri Williams (Merthyr Tydfil)	+ 1	1	1

FA: FA Cup. *BL:* Bob Lord Trophy. *FT:* FA Challenge Trophy.

GM VAUXHALL CONFERENCE RESULTS 1991–92

	Altrincham	Barrow	Bath City	Boston United	Cheltenham Town	Colchester United	Farnborough Town	Gateshead	Kettering Town	Kidderminster Harriers	Macclesfield Town	Merthyr Tydfil	Northwich Victoria	Redbridge Forest	Runcorn	Slough Town	Stafford Rangers	Telford United	Welling United	Witton Albion	Wycombe Wanderers	Yeovil Town
Altrincham	—	1-1	4-0	2-4	2-1	1-2	1-1	1-1	1-1	1-1	3-1	1-1	0-1	0-3	2-2	3-7	3-0	2-3	1-2	2-2	0-4	2-1
Barrow	0-2	—	2-0	2-2	0-0	1-1	0-1	1-1	0-0	5-1	2-0	2-2	0-2	0-1	2-3	3-4	0-0	3-0	6-1	0-1	0-1	0-0
Bath City	3-2	2-1	—	2-0	5-1	0-0	1-2	0-1	1-1	0-1	1-1	0-0	2-0	0-0	3-1	2-1	0-1	1-2	3-2	0-2	1-1	3-1
Boston United	2-1	4-1	1-0	—	3-3	0-4	0-1	4-0	1-1	1-1	1-5	2-0	0-2	2-1	2-1	3-1	2-2	1-2	5-1	3-2	2-2	1-3
Cheltenham Town	0-2	0-0	1-2	1-1	—	1-1	4-3	3-2	0-3	1-2	2-3	1-2	1-0	0-7	4-1	1-0	0-0	2-1	3-2	0-1	2-1	1-1
Colchester United	3-3	5-0	5-0	1-0	4-0	—	2-3	2-0	3-1	3-0	2-0	2-0	1-0	1-0	2-1	4-0	2-0	2-0	3-1	3-1	3-0	4-0
Farnborough Town	3-0	5-0	1-2	5-0	1-1	0-2	—	3-1	1-3	2-1	4-2	0-0	2-4	1-0	0-2	2-1	1-1	2-2	1-1	1-1	1-3	0-0
Gateshead	5-0	1-1	0-1	2-1	2-1	0-2	0-2	—	0-0	0-3	2-0	0-1	2-0	0-1	1-1	2-1	0-0	0-2	1-1	2-1	2-3	1-0
Kettering Town	5-0	3-2	2-2	1-3	3-0	2-2	1-2	1-1	—	2-1	2-0	3-1	1-0	3-2	3-0	2-3	2-1	3-0	1-1	1-1	1-1	2-0
Kidderminster Harriers	1-0	1-2	0-1	1-3	2-1	2-2	1-1	5-3	2-3	—	1-1	2-2	1-0	5-1	2-1	3-3	2-1	1-2	1-3	0-1	1-0	1-1
Macclesfield Town	1-1	0-1	0-0	0-1	3-3	4-4	1-2	1-0	0-2	0-0	—	3-0	0-0	0-0	3-0	0-1	1-0	2-1	1-2	1-0	3-1	1-2
Merthyr Tydfil	3-1	2-1	1-1	2-0	3-1	2-0	1-0	1-4	4-1	2-1	3-2	—	2-1	2-2	2-0	1-2	1-0	2-2	2-1	1-0	1-2	2-2
Northwich Victoria	1-2	6-1	1-3	1-1	3-1	1-1	1-1	1-1	4-3	3-1	2-1	4-1	—	0-2	3-0	3-0	1-2	0-1	1-2	3-0	0-1	1-0
Redbridge Forest	0-1	2-2	3-1	1-4	1-2	2-1	2-0	2-1	4-0	5-0	0-0	1-1	4-3	—	1-2	4-0	4-3	1-0	2-0	3-1	0-5	0-0
Runcorn	2-2	2-2	0-2	2-2	2-1	1-3	1-1	1-1	0-0	4-1	0-0	1-1	3-1	1-0	—	1-0	0-0	0-2	2-2	0-1	1-2	2-2
Slough Town	2-3	1-0	2-2	3-1	1-3	2-4	0-5	2-0	0-2	3-1	0-3	0-0	0-1	4-0	1-0	—	2-2	0-3	0-3	2-1	0-1	1-4
Stafford Rangers	1-2	0-0	2-0	0-1	2-2	3-3	0-1	1-3	1-2	2-0	1-1	0-0	2-1	3-0	1-0	1-1	—	3-2	0-0	2-1	0-2	0-0
Telford United	2-1	4-2	0-2	1-2	2-1	0-3	1-2	1-1	1-1	3-1	0-1	1-2	1-4	3-3	2-1	2-2	4-1	—	2-1	2-1	1-1	1-0
Welling United	2-2	5-3	0-5	1-3	1-1	4-1	1-0	2-2	2-3	3-2	2-1	1-2	6-1	2-2	1-2	0-2	1-1	3-1	—	1-1	1-3	1-0
Witton Albion	2-0	0-1	2-2	1-0	4-2	2-2	4-1	0-3	1-0	2-1	1-1	3-2	1-1	2-0	1-3	2-1	6-0	1-1	2-2	—	1-2	3-1
Wycombe Wanderers	4-2	3-2	1-0	2-1	2-2	1-2	2-1	2-1	1-0	2-0	0-1	4-0	2-0	1-0	1-0	3-0	3-0	6-1	4-0	4-0	—	1-0
Yeovil Town	2-1	2-0	1-1	1-1	1-1	0-1	2-2	1-0	0-1	1-1	0-1	1-1	2-1	0-1	1-4	1-0	0-1	0-2	3-0	2-1	1-0	—

THE NEVILLE OVENDEN FOOTBALL COMBINATION

	P	W	D	L	F	A	Pts
Southampton	38	22	9	7	73	36	75
Chelsea	38	22	7	9	72	43	73
Arsenal	38	22	6	10	80	49	72
Queens Park Rangers	38	22	5	11	76	43	71
Norwich City	38	21	6	11	75	37	69
Luton Town	38	18	8	12	59	51	62
Swindon Town	38	16	8	14	62	60	56
Wimbledon	38	14	12	12	56	44	54
Crystal Palace	38	15	9	14	63	61	54
Ipswich Town	38	15	9	14	65	68	54
Tottenham Hotspur	38	14	11	13	63	54	53
Portsmouth	38	16	2	20	69	75	50
Watford	38	15	3	20	59	69	48
Charlton Athletic	38	13	9	16	50	60	48
Oxford United	38	13	7	18	54	77	46
West Ham United	38	11	11	16	55	64	44
Millwall	38	10	12	16	67	80	42
Fulham	38	11	8	19	39	58	41
Brighton & Hove Albion	38	8	8	22	46	67	32
Reading	38	5	4	29	48	135	19

PONTIN'S CENTRAL LEAGUE

Division One

	P	W	D	L	F	A	Pts
Nottingham Forest	34	23	7	4	81	34	76
Aston Villa	34	19	10	5	62	31	67
Liverpool	34	18	5	11	64	48	59
Blackburn Rovers	34	17	8	9	58	43	59
Leeds United	34	14	11	9	47	41	53
Barnsley	34	15	7	12	54	49	52
Manchester City	34	15	5	14	57	57	50
Manchester United	34	14	6	14	55	50	48
Sunderland	34	12	9	13	52	58	45
Sheffield United	34	10	13	11	48	52	43
Newcastle United	34	12	7	15	60	43	43
Bolton Wanderers	34	10	11	13	52	56	41
Sheffield Wednesday	34	10	9	15	44	49	39
Rotherham United	34	11	4	19	49	72	37
Everton	34	10	7	17	44	67	37
Coventry City	34	7	14	13	42	46	35
West Bromwich Albion	34	10	5	19	43	70	35
Bradford City	34	9	2	23	46	70	29

	P	W	D	L	F	A	Pts
Stoke City	34	25	5	4	93	30	80
Wolverhampton Wanderers	34	20	8	6	66	32	68
Leicester City	34	18	8	8	57	29	62
Notts County	34	18	7	9	53	37	61
Huddersfield Town	34	16	8	10	61	46	56
Derby County	34	15	10	9	57	43	55
Burnley	34	14	6	14	48	52	48
Middlesbrough	34	14	4	16	41	52	46
Blackpool	34	13	5	16	51	49	44
Wigan Athletic	34	13	5	16	45	57	44
Scunthorpe United	34	11	10	13	50	68	43
Oldham Athletic	34	12	6	16	56	67	42
Grimsby Town	34	10	8	16	39	45	38
Preston North End	34	10	7	17	36	69	37
Port Vale*	34	9	11	14	51	57	36
Mansfield Town	34	8	7	19	39	54	31
York City	34	9	4	21	33	57	31
Hull City	34	7	9	18	27	59	30

*2 points deducted.

HIGHLAND LEAGUE

	P	W	D	L	F	A	Pts
Ross County	34	24	3	7	95	43	75
Caledonian	34	22	6	6	93	34	72
Huntly	34	21	7	6	70	43	70
Cove Rangers	34	18	9	7	62	35	63
Keith	34	18	6	10	67	44	60
Lossiemouth	34	17	7	10	62	42	58
Buckie Thistle	34	17	6	11	58	46	57
Elgin City	34	16	6	12	76	51	54
Peterhead	34	16	6	12	61	59	54
Inverness Thistle	34	14	8	12	54	57	50
Forres Mechanics	34	13	8	13	66	62	47
Clachnacuddin	34	11	6	17	43	51	39
Deveronvale	34	12	3	19	41	58	39
Brora Rangers	34	11	5	18	52	67	38
Fraserburgh	34	11	3	20	43	67	36
Fort William	34	8	4	22	48	83	28
Rothes	34	4	4	26	38	99	16
Nairn County	34	3	3	28	23	111	12

SOUTH EAST COUNTIES LEAGUE

Division One

	P	W	D	L	F	A	Pts
Tottenham Hotspur	30	23	5	2	83	26	51
Arsenal	30	19	5	6	85	48	43
Queens Park Rangers	30	18	3	9	80	51	39
Norwich City	30	16	3	11	56	41	35
Southend United	30	13	8	9	65	56	34
Chelsea	30	15	3	12	52	40	33
Millwall	30	13	6	11	47	41	32
Watford	30	12	6	12	52	47	30
Ipswich Town	30	13	4	13	55	65	30
Fulham	30	11	6	13	47	48	28
West Ham United	30	9	9	12	57	60	27
Leyton Orient	30	11	3	16	55	73	25
Charlton Athletic	30	9	5	16	51	66	23
Gillingham	30	9	2	19	45	82	20
Cambridge United	30	6	4	20	40	85	16
Portsmouth	30	5	4	21	37	78	14

Division Two

	P	W	D	L	F	A	Pts
Crystal Palace	26	18	5	3	69	24	41
Wimbledon	26	16	5	5	71	24	37
Oxford United	26	15	4	7	49	31	34
Luton Town	26	14	6	6	60	45	34
Brentford	26	13	5	8	47	33	31
Southampton	26	11	8	7	32	30	30
Brighton & Hove Albion	26	12	4	10	51	38	28
Bristol City	26	10	5	11	44	45	25
Tottenham Hotspur	26	9	3	14	34	55	21
Swindon Town	26	7	6	13	30	53	20
Reading	26	8	3	15	44	64	19
Bristol Rovers	26	7	2	17	41	86	16
Bournemouth	26	6	3	17	34	50	15
Maidstone United	26	5	3	18	32	60	13

(Aldershot's record has been expunged).

FA CHALLENGE YOUTH CUP 1991–92

First Round Qualifying

Guisborough Town v Netherfield	1-3
Marske U v Hartlepool U	1-3
(*at Hartlepool United FC*)	
Barrow v Preston North End	3-5
Accrington Stanley v Huddersfield Town	0-3
Halifax Town v Wrexham	0-3
Rotherham U v Atherton LR	7-1
Shrewsbury T v Telford U	4-0
Warrington T v Bolton W	0-2
Burton Alb v Kidderminster H	0-1
Willenhall T v Leicester U	3-0
Rothwell Town v Wisbech Town	6-0
Nuneaton Borough v Tamworth	0-0, 0-2
Norwich City v Wivenhoe Town	9-0
Cambridge C v Brantham Ath	6-2
East Thurrock U v Tiptree U	6-3
Hitchin Town v Letchworth Garden City	6-3
Eton Manor v Clapton	0-1
Braintree T v St Albans C	1-1, 2-8
Harefield United v Staines Town	5-1
Maidenhead United v Bedfont	0-1
Kingsbury Town v Wembley	4-4, 1-3
Leyton-Wingate v Cheshunt	0-2
Bracknell T v Wycombe W	2-2, 4-6
Wingate & Finchley v Southall	4-2
Dulwich Hamlet v Three Bridges	6-0
Chatham Town v Bromley	1-4
Kingstonian v Walton & Hersham	1-3
Farnborough Town v Shoreham	5-2
Malden Vale v Havant Town	0-3
Slough Town v Sutton United	2-3
Petersfield U v Basingstoke T	1-6
Thatcham Town v Witney Town	0-2
Newport AFC v Abingdon United	0-0, 1-4
Evesham U v Cheltenham T	2-4
Bristol Rovers v Bashley	3-3, 1-5
Dorchester T v Odd Down	0-0, 1-0

Second Round Qualifying

Netherfield v Hartlepool United	0-3
Preston NE v Huddersfield T	4-1
Wrexham v Rotherham United	0-4
Shrewsbury T v Bolton W	1-0
Kidderminster H v Willenhall T	3-0
Rothwell Town v Tamworth	2-2, 1-2
Norwich City v Cambridge City	5-0
East Thurrock U v Hitchin T	3-2
Clapton v St Albans City	1-3
Harefield United v Bedfont	0-0, 2-1

Wembley v Cheshunt	1-1, 4-3
Wycombe Wanderers v Wingate & Finchley	3-0
Dulwich Hamlet v Bromley	0-1
Walton & Hersham v Farnborough Town	2-1
Havant Town v Sutton United	2-3
Basingstoke Town v Witney Town	0-2
Abingdon U v Cheltenham T	1-9
(*at Cheltenham Town FC*)	
Bashley v Dorchester Town	1-1, 3-0

First Round Proper

York City v Blackburn R	1-1, 3-4
Carlisle U v Rotherham U	0-1
Blackpool v Bradford City	2-2, 3-0
Barnsley v Darlington	3-2
Bury v Sunderland	3-3, 0-2
Burnley v Sheffield United	0-2
Oldham Ath v Wigan Ath	3-2
Tranmere R v Preston NE	4-1
Shrewsbury T v Hartlepool U	2-0
Nottingham Forest v Wolverhampton Wanderers	0-0, 0-0, 0-1
Scunthorpe U v Norwich C	0-2
Northampton Town v Stoke City	1-0
Crewe Alexandra v Port Vale	1-0
Mansfield Town v Aston Villa	0-1
Peterborough U v Derby Co	1-3
Tamworth v Kidderminster H	1-2
Fulham v Bromley	5-0
Walton & Hersham v Cambridge United	2-2, 0-3
Egham Town v Wimbledon	0-7
Luton Town v East Thurrock U	5-0
Reading v Gillingham	3-1
Sutton United v Wembley	4-3
Harefield U v Charlton Ath	0-6
Aldershot v Carshalton Athletic	3-4
Whyteleafe v St Albans City	0-2
Wokingham Town v Brighton & Hove Albion	0-2
Epsom & Ewell v Wycombe W	2-0
Witney Town v Hereford United	1-0
Bashley v Southampton	0-0, 2-1
AFC Bournemouth v Swansea C	2-0
Exeter C v Cheltenham T	2-2, 1-0
Swindon Town v Bristol City	0-4
Oxford United v Cardiff City	1-2

Second Round Proper

Barnsley v Everton	1-2
Doncaster Rovers v Manchester City	1-1, 0-4

Hull City v Crewe Alexandra 1-1, 0-3
Middlesbrough v Newcastle U 4-0
Sunderland v Manchester United 2-4
Liverpool v Tranmere Rovers 1-2
Blackburn R v Rotherham U 0-2
Sheffield United v Blackpool 5-3
Leeds U v Oldham Ath 3-3, 2-3
Shrewsbury T v Sheffield 3-0
West Ham United v Kidderminster Harriers 3-0
Northampton Town v Birmingham City 3-0
Notts Co v Derby Co 0-0, 0-1
Tottenham H v Coventry C 6-1
West Bromwich Albion v Wolverhampton Wanderers 3-1
Witney Town v Southend United 0-3
Luton Town v Aston Villa 1-0
Watford v Leicester City 2-1
Cambridge U v Colchester U 2-3
Norwich City v Leyton Orient 6-3
Walsall v Ipswich Town 1-0
Sutton U v AFC Bournemouth 1-5
Brighton & Hove Albion v Arsenal 2-5
Portsmouth v Bashley 0-1
Fulham v Brentford 2-2, 0-2
Reading v Carshalton Athletic 3-0
Cardiff City v Queens Park Rangers 0-1
Bristol City v Epsom & Ewell 3-2
Wimbledon v Millwall 2-0
Exeter City v Chelsea 0-4
St Albans City v Plymouth Argyle 0-4
Charlton Athletic v Crystal Palace 0-2

Third Round Proper

Tranmere Rovers v Oldham Athletic 0-0, 1-1, 3-1
Rotherham U v Shrewsbury T 3-1
Northampton T v Derby Co 1-7
Manchester United v Walsall 2-1
Crewe Alex v Middlesbrough 3-2
Manchester City v West Bromwich Albion 1-1, 2-0
Everton v Sheffield United 1-1, 3-2
Reading v West Ham United 2-6
Chelsea v Crystal Palace 0-2
Colchester United v Brentford 1-3
Arsenal v Watford 4-0
Tottenham Hotspur v AFC Bournemouth 7-0
Luton Town v Norwich City 1-1, 1-4
Wimbledon v Bashley 6-0
Southend United v Bristol City 3-0
Plymouth Argyle v Queens Park Rangers 1-3

Fourth Round Proper

Queens Park Rangers v Brentford 5-1
Wimbledon v Norwich City 1-1, 4-3
Southend United v West Ham United 3-3, 1-1, 2-3
Arsenal v Everton 1-2
Crystal Palace v Crewe Alexandra 2-0
Manchester C v Manchester U 1-3
Derby Co v Tottenham H 0-1
Rotherham U v Tranmere R 0-1

Fifth Round Proper

Wimbledon v Queens Park Rangers 2-0
Tottenham H v Everton 4-0
Crystal Palace v West Ham U 2-0
Manchester U v Tranmere R 2-0

Semi-finals

Wimbledon v Crystal Palace 1-2, 3-3
Manchester U v Tottenham H 3-0, 2-1

FINAL First Leg

14 Apr

Crystal Palace (0) 1 *(McCall)*

Manchester United (2) 3 *(Butt 2, Beckham)* 7825

Crystal Palace: Glass; Clark, Cutler, Holman, Edwards, McPherson (Sparrow), Hawthorne, Rollison, Thompson (McCall), Watts, Ndah
Manchester United: Pilkington; O'Kane, Switzer, Casper, Neville, Beckham, Butt, Davies, McKee, Savage (Roberts), Thornley

Second Leg

15 May

Manchester United (1) 3 *(Davies, Thornley, McKee)*

Crystal Palace (1) 2 *(McPherson, McCall)* 14,681

Manchester United: Pilkington; O'Kane, Switzer, Casper, Neville, Beckham, Butt, Davies (Gillespie), McKee, Giggs, Thornley (Savage)
Crystal Palace: Glass; Sparrow, Cutler, Holman, Edwards (Watts), McPherson, Hawthorne, Rollison (Daly), McCall, Ndah, Clark

OTHER AWARDS 1991–92

FOOTBALLER OF THE YEAR

The Football Writers' Association Award for the Footballer of the Year went to Gary Lineker of Tottenham Hotspur and England.

Past Winners
1947–48 Stanley Matthews (Blackpool), 1948–49 Johnny Carey (Manchester U), 1949–50 Joe Mercer (Arsenal), 1950–51 Harry Johnston (Blackpool), 1951–52 Billy Wright (Wolverhampton W), 1952–53 Nat Lofthouse (Bolton W), 1953–54 Tom Finney (Preston NE), 1954–55 Don Revie (Manchester C), 1955–56 Bert Trautmann (Manchester C), 1956–57 Tom Finney (Preston NE), 1957–58 Danny Blanchflower (Tottenham H), 1958–59 Syd Owen (Luton T), 1959–60 Bill Slater (Wolverhampton W), 1960–61 Danny Blanchflower (Tottenham H), 1961–62 Jimmy Adamson (Burnley), 1962–63 Stanley Matthews (Stoke C), 1963–64 Bobby Moore (West Ham U), 1964–65 Bobby Collins (Leeds U), 1965–66 Bobby Charlton (Manchester U), 1966–67 Jackie Charlton (Leeds U), 1967–68 George Best (Manchester U), 1968–69 Dave Mackay (Derby Co) shared with Tony Book (Manchester C), 1969–70 Billy Bremner (Leeds U), 1970–71 Frank McLintock (Arsenal), 1971–72 Gordon Banks (Stoke C), 1972–73 Pat Jennings (Tottenham H), 1973–74 Ian Callaghan (Liverpool), 1974–75 Alan Mullery (Fulham), 1975–76 Kevin Keegan (Liverpool), 1976–77 Emlyn Hughes (Liverpool), 1977–78 Kenny Burns (Nottingham F), 1978–79 Kenny Dalglish (Liverpool), 1979–80 Terry McDermott (Liverpool), 1980–81 Frans Thijssen (Ipswich T), 1981–82 Steve Perryman (Tottenham H), 1982–83 Kenny Dalglish (Liverpool), 1983–84 Ian Rush (Liverpool), 1984–85 Neville Southall (Everton), 1985–86 Gary Lineker (Everton), 1986–87 Clive Allen (Tottenham H), 1987–88 John Barnes (Liverpool), 1988–89 Steve Nicol (Liverpool), 1989–90 John Barnes (Liverpool), 1990–91 Gordon Strachan (Leeds U).

THE PFA AWARDS 1992

Player of the Year: Gary Pallister (Manchester U).
Previous Winners: 1974 Norman Hunter (Leeds U); 1975 Colin Todd (Derby Co); 1976 Pat Jennings (Tottenham H); 1977 Andy Gray (Aston Villa); 1978 Peter Shilton (Nottingham F); 1979 Liam Brady (Arsenal); 1980 Terry McDermot (Liverpool); 1981 John Wark (Ipswich T); 1982 Kevin Keegan (Southampton); 1983 Kenny Dalglish (Liverpool); 1984 Ian Rush (Liverpool); 1985 Peter Reid (Everton); 1986 Gary Lineker (Everton); 1987 Clive Allen (Tottenham H); 1988 John Barnes (Liverpool); 1989 Mark Hughes (Manchester U); 1990 David Platt (Aston Villa); 1991 Mark Hughes (Manchester U).

Young Player of the Year: Ryan Giggs (Manchester U).
Previous Winners: 1974 Kevin Beattie (Ipswich T); 1975 Mervyn Day (West Ham U); 1976 Peter Barnes (Manchester C); 1977 Andy Gray (Aston Villa); 1978 Tony Woodcock (Nottingham F); 1979 Cyrille Regis (WBA); 1980 Glenn Hoddle (Tottenham H); 1981 Gary Shaw (Aston Villa); 1982 Steve Moran (Southampton); 1983 Ian Rush (Liverpool); 1984 Paul Walsh (Luton T); 1985 Mark Hughes (Manchester U); 1986 Tony Cottee (West Ham U); 1987 Tony Adams (Arsenal); 1988 Paul Gascoigne (Tottenham H); 1989 Paul Merson (Arsenal); 1990 Matthew Le Tissier (Southampton); 1991 Lee Sharpe (Manchester U).

HOWARD WILKINSON WINS PERSONAL ACCOLADE FOR LEEDS UNITED TITLE TRIUMPH: HE IS NAMED BARCLAYS BANK MANAGER OF THE YEAR 1992

Howard Wilkinson's achievement in taking Leeds United from the nether regions of the Second Division to the Barclays League title in three and a half years won him the Barclays Bank Manager of the Year award for 1992. He was named for this prestigious accolade – the Barclays Trophy and a Barclays Higher Rate Deposit Account cheque for £5,000 – by a panel of 30 leading football journalists and commentators. The presentation was made by Mr Alastair Robinson, executive director of Barclays Bank.

It was Wilkinson's 9th managerial award: – his 6th at Leeds United from October 1989 with a Division Two monthly award, followed by 2nd Division Manager of the Season 1990, and overall Manager of the month prizes for November 1990 and October & November 1991: the first three were at Sheffield Wednesday – Division 2 monthly awards for September and November 1983 and November 1988.

BARCLAYS BANK DIVISIONAL MANAGERS OF THE SEASON 1991–92

Barclays Bank Divisional Managers of the Season – named in conjunction with The Football League were: Division Two – John Lyall, Ipswich Town; Division Three – Phil Holder, Brentford; Division Four – Jimmy Mullen, Burnley.

Each received a Barclays Eagle trophy and a cheque for £1,000.

LEAGUE MANAGERS ACHIEVEMENT AWARD

Barclays Bank announced in May that it had become the official sponsor of the recently-formed League Managers Association in a three year sponsorship deal. To mark the arrangement, the Barclays Bank Achievement Award – to be decided by the votes of members of the LMA – has been introduced to the Barclays Bank Managers Awards portfolio.

"The award is designed to highlight the efforts of the manager who, in the opinion of his peers has worked wonders with the resources available to him" explained LMA chief executive John Camkin.

"It could go to a manager whose team has won a League or Cup trophy. On the other hand, it may go to someone who has performed a near-miracle to keep his club in its present division . . . or even kept the club afloat by recruitment of youngsters and shrewd financial dealings.

"For too long these outstanding achievements have gone unrecognised by the game itself – and the general public. This is an opportunity for managers to honour a colleague whose work they respect and admire."

The first Barclays Bank Achievement Award winner voted by the LMA is Dave Bassett of Sheffield United, whose second-half of the season run – following a disastrous first half – kept his club on course for next season's Premier League. He received a cheque for £1,000 and a Barclays Eagle trophy.

BARCLAYS YOUNG EAGLE OF THE YEAR

Roy Keane of Nottingham Forest and the Republic of Ireland – the 20 year-old £25,000 'snip' from Cobh Ramblers in the Opel League of Ireland – was named the Barclays Young Eagle of the Year by England team manager Graham Taylor, chairman of the voting panel which includes Jack Charlton, Jimmy Armfield, Trevor Cherry, Stan Cullis, Bill Nicholson, Bill Dodgin and Terry Yorath. Roy received a Silver Eagle trophy, a replica and a Barclays Higher Rate Deposit Account cheque for £5,000.

THE SCOTTISH PFA AWARDS 1992

Player of the Year: Premier Division: Ally McCoist (Rangers); First Division: Gordon Dalziel (Falkirk); Second Division: Andy Thomson (Queen of South).

Previous Winners: 1978 Derek Johnstone (Rangers); 1979 Paul Hegarty (Dundee U); 1980 Davie Provan (Celtic); 1981 Sandy Clark (Airdrieonians); 1982 Mark McGhee (Aberdeen); 1983 Charlie Nicholas (Celtic); 1984 Willie Miller (Aberdeen); 1985 Jim Duffy (Morton); 1986 Richard Gough (Dundee U); 1987 Brian McClair (Celtic); 1988 Paul McStay (Celtic); 1989 Theo Snelders (Aberdeen); 1990 Jim Bett (Aberdeen); 1991 Paul Elliott (Celtic).

Young Player of the Year: Phil O'Donnell (Motherwell).

Previous Winners: 1978 Graeme Payne (Dundee U); 1979 Graham Stewart (Dundee U); 1980 John MacDonald (Rangers); 1981 Francis McAvennie (St Mirren); 1982 Charlie Nicholas (Celtic); 1983 Pat Nevin (Clyde); 1984 John Robertson (Hearts); 1985 Craig Levein (Hearts); 1986 Craig Levein (Hearts); 1987 Robert Fleck (Rangers); 1988 John Collins (Hibernian); 1989 Bill McKinlay (Dundee U); 1990 Scott Crabbe (Hearts); 1991 Eoin Jess (Aberdeen).

SCOTTISH FOOTBALL WRITERS' ASSOCIATION

Player of the Year 1992 – Ally McCoist (Rangers)

1965 **Billy McNeill** (Celtic)
1966 **John Greig** (Rangers)
1967 **Ronnie Simpson** (Celtic)
1968 **Gordon Wallace** (Rath R)
1969 **Bobby Murdoch** (Celtic)
1970 **Pat Stanton** (Hibernian)
1971 **Martin Buchan** (Aberdeen)
1972 **Dave Smith** (Rangers)
1973 **George Connelly** (Celtic)
1974 **Scotland's World Cup Squad**
1975 **Sandy Jardine** (Rangers)
1976 **John Greig** (Rangers)
1977 **Danny McGrain** (Celtic)
1978 **Derek Johnstone** (Rangers)
1979 **Andy Ritchie** (Morton)
1980 **Gordon Strachan** (Aberdeen)
1981 **Alan Rough** (Partick Th)
1982 **Paul Sturrock** (Dundee U)
1983 **Charlie Nicholas** (Celtic)
1984 **Willie Miller** (Aberdeen)
1985 **Hamish McAlpine** (Dundee U)
1986 **Sandy Jardine** (Hearts)
1987 **Brian McClair** (Celtic)
1988 **Paul McStay** (Celtic)
1989 **Richard Gough** (Rangers)
1990 **Alex McLeish** (Aberdeen)
1991 **Maurice Malpas** (Dundee U)

EUROPEAN FOOTBALLER OF THE YEAR 1991

French players have never figured very prominently in the annual *France Football* award for the European Footballer of the Year. This year Jean-Pierre Papin of Marseille became the third of his countrymen to achieve the honour following Raymond Kopa in 1958 and Michel Platini three times in succession from 1983–85.

Past winners
1956 **Stanley Matthews** (Blackpool)
1957 **Alfredo Di Stefano** (Real Madrid)
1958 **Raymond Kopa** (Real Madrid)
1959 **Alfredo Di Stefano** (Real Madrid)
1960 **Luis Suarez** (Barcelona)
1961 **Omar Sivori** (Juventus)
1962 **Josef Masopust** (Dukla Prague)

Year	Player (Club)	Year	Player (Club)
1963	**Lev Yashin** (Moscow Dynamo)	1977	**Allan Simonsen** (Borussia Moenchengladbach)

1963 **Lev Yashin** (Moscow Dynamo)
1964 **Denis Law** (Manchester United)
1965 **Eusebio** (Benefica)
1966 **Bobby Charlton** (Manchester United)
1967 **Florian Albert** (Ferencvaros)
1968 **George Best** (Manchester United)
1969 **Gianni Rivera** (AC Milan)
1970 **Gerd Muller** (Bayern Munich)
1971 **Johan Cruyff** (Ajax)
1972 **Franz Beckenbauer** (Bayern Munich)
1973 **Johan Cruyff** (Barcelona)
1974 **Johan Cruyff** (Barcelona)
1975 **Oleg Blokhin** (Dynamo Kiev)
1976 **Franz Beckenbauer** (Bayern Munich)

1977 **Allan Simonsen** (Borussia Moenchengladbach)
1978 **Kevin Keegan** (SV Hamburg)
1979 **Kevin Keegan** (SV Hamburg)
1980 **Karl-Heinz Rummenigge** (Bayern Munich)
1981 **Karl-Heinz Rummenigge** (Bayern Munich)
1982 **Paolo Rossi** (Juventus)
1983 **Michel Platini** (Juventus)
1984 **Michel Platini** (Juventus)
1985 **Michel Platini** (Juventus)
1986 **Igor Belanov** (Dynamo Kiev)
1987 **Ruud Gullit** (AC Milan)
1988 **Marco Van Basten** (AC Milan)
1989 **Marco Van Basten** (AC Milan)
1990 **Lothar Matthaus** (Inter-Milan)

BARCLAYS BANK MANAGER AWARDS 1991–92

AUGUST
Division 1 – **Alex Ferguson** (Manchester United); *Division 2* – **John Beck** (Cambridge United); *Division 3* – **Terry Cooper** (Birmingham City); *Division 4* – **Billy Ayre** (Blackpool).

SEPTEMBER
Division 1 – **Alex Ferguson** (Manchester United); *Division 2* – **Lennie Lawrence** (Middlesbrough); *Division 3* – **Bobby Gould** (West Bromwich Albion); *Division 4* – **Barry Fry** (Barnet).

OCTOBER
Division 1 – **Howard Wilkinson** (Leeds United); *Division 2* – **Alan Curbishley/Steve Gritt** (Charlton Athletic); *Division 3* – **Terry Cooper** (Birmingham City); *Division 4* – **George Foster** (Mansfield Town).

NOVEMBER
Division 1 – **Howard Wilkinson** (Leeds United); *Division 2* – **David Webb** (Southend United); *Division 3* – **Phil Holder** (Brentford); *Division 4* – **Jimmy Mullen** (Burnley).

DECEMBER
Division 1 – **Alex Ferguson** (Manchester United); *Division 2* – **Graham Turner** (Wolverhampton Wanderers); *Division 3* – **Alan Murray** (Hartlepool United); *Division 4* – **Bill Green** (Scunthorpe United).

JANUARY
Division 1 – **Graeme Souness** (Liverpool); *Division 2* – **Malcolm Crosby** (Sunderland); *Division 3* – **Danny Bergara** (Stockport County); *Division 4* – **Brian Flynn** (Wrexham).

FEBRUARY
Division 1 – **Brian Clough** (Nottingham Forest); *Division 2* – **John Lyall** (Ipswich Town); *Division 3* – **Chris Turner** (Peterborough United); *Division 4* – **Dario Gradi** (Crewe Alexandra).

MARCH
Division 1 – **Gerry Francis** (QPR); *Division 2* – **Alan Curbishley/Steve Gritt** (Charlton Athletic); *Division 3* – **David Philpotts** (Wigan Athletic); *Division 4* – **Phil Henson** (Rotherham United).

APRIL
Division 1 – **Trevor Francis** (Sheffield Wednesday); *Division 2* – **Arthur Cox** (Derby County); *Division 3* – **Phil Holder** (Brentford); *Division 4* – **Steve Thompson** (Lincoln City).

BRITISH FOOTBALL RECORDS

HIGHEST SCORES
First class match
Arbroath 36 Bon Accord 0 *Scottish Cup 1st Rd, 12.9.1885.*
International match
England 13 Ireland 0 *Belfast, 18.2.1882.*
Football League
Tranmere R 13, Oldham Ath 4, *Division 3 (N) 26.12.1935*
FA Cup
Preston NE 26 Hyde U 0 *1st Rd, 15.10.1887*
League Cup
West Ham U 10 Bury 0 *2nd Rd, 2nd leg, 25.10.1983*
Liverpool 10 Fulham 0 *2nd Rd, 1st leg, 23.9.1986*
Scottish League
East Fife 13 Edinburgh C 2 *Division 2, 11.12.1937*

MOST GOALS IN A SEASON
Football League
128 in 42 games, Aston Villa *Division 1, 1930–31*
128 in 42 games, Bradford C *Division 3 (N), 1928–29*
134 in 46 games, Peterborough U *Division 4, 1960–61*
Scottish League
142 in 34 games, Raith R *Division 2, 1937–38*

FEWEST GOALS IN A SEASON
Football League *(minimun 42 games)*
24 in 42 games, Stoke C *Division 1, 1984–85*
24 in 42 games, Watford *Division 2, 1971–72*
27 in 46 games, Stockport Co *Division 3, 1969–70*
Scottish League *(minimum 30 games)*
18 in 39 games, Stirling A *Division 1, 1980–81*

MOST GOALS AGAINST IN A SEASON
Football League
141 in 34 games, Darwen *Division 2, 1898–99*
Scottish League
146 in 38 games, Edinburgh C *Division 2, 1931–32*

FEWEST GOALS AGAINST IN A SEASON
Football League *(minimum 42 games)*
16 in 42 games, Liverpool *Division 1, 1978–79*
21 in 46 games, Port Vale *Division 3 (N), 1953–54*
Scottish League *(minimum 30 games)*
14 in 38 games, Celtic *Division 1, 1913–14*

MOST POINTS IN A SEASON
Football League *(2 points for a win)*
72 in 42 games, Doncaster R *Division 3 (N), 1946–47*
74 in 46 games, Lincoln C *Division 4, 1975–76*
Football League *(3 points for a win)*
76 in 38 games, Arsenal *Division 1, 1988–89*
76 in 38 games, Liverpool *Division 1, 1988–89*
90 in 40 games, Liverpool *Division 1, 1987–88*
90 in 42 games, Everton *Division 1, 1984–85*
102 in 46 games, Swindon T *Division 4, 1985–86*

Scottish League
72 in 44 games, Celtic *Premier Division, 1987–88*
72 in 44 games, Rangers *Premier Division 1991–92*
69 in 38 games, Morton *Division 2, 1966–67*
76 in 42 games, Rangers *Division 1, 1920–21*

FEWEST POINTS IN A SEASON
Football League *(minimum 34 games)*
8 in 34 games, Doncaster R *Division 2, 1904–5*
8 in 34 games, Loughborough T *Division 2, 1899–1900*
11 in 40 games, Rochdale *Division 3 (N), 1931–32*
17 in 42 games, Stoke C *Division 1, 1984–85*
19 in 46 games, Workington *Division 4, 1976–77*
Scottish League *(minimum 30 games)*
6 in 30 games, Stirling A *Division 1, 1954–55*
7 in 34 games, Edinburgh C *Division 2, 1936–37*
11 in 36 games, St Johnstone *Premier Division, 1975–76*

MOST WINS IN A SEASON
Football League
33 in 42 games, Doncaster R *Division 3 (N),1946–47*
Scottish League
27 in 36 games, Aberdeen *Premier Division, 1984–85*
33 in 38 games, Morton *Division 2, 1966–67*
33 in 44 games, Rangers *Premier Division, 1991–92*
35 in 42 games, Rangers *Division 1, 1920–21*
Home
Brentford won all 21 games in Division 3(S) in 1929–30
Away
Doncaster R won 18 out of 21 games in Division 3(N) in 1946–47

FEWEST WINS IN A SEASON
Football League *(minimum 34 games)*
1 in 34 games, Loughborough T *Division 2, 1899–1900*
2 in 46 games, Rochdale *Division 3, 1973–74*
Scottish League *(minimum 22 games)*
0 in 22 games, Vale of Leven *Division 1, 1891–92*
1 in 38 games, Forfar Ath *Division 2, 1974–75*

MOST DEFEATS IN A SEASON
Football League
33 in 40 games, Rochdale *Division 3(N), 1931–32*
Scottish League
30 in 36 games, Brechin C *Division 2, 1962–63*
31 in 42 games, St Mirren *Division 1, 1920–21*

FEWEST DEFEATS IN A SEASON
Football League *(minimum 20 games)*
0 in 22 games, Preston NE *Division 1, 1888–89*
0 in 28 games, Liverpool *Division 2, 1893–94*
1 in 38 games, Arsenal *Division 1, 1990–91*
2 in 40 games, Liverpool *Division 1, 1987–88*
2 in 42 games, Leeds U *Division 1, 1968–69*
3 in 46 games, Port Vale *Division 3(N), 1953–54*
Scottish League *(minimum 20 games)*
1 in 42 games, Rangers *Division 1, 1920–21*

MOST DRAWS IN A SEASON
Football League
23 in 42 games, Norwich C *Division 1, 1978–79*
23 in 46 games, Exeter C *Division 4, 1986–87*
Scottish League
19 in 44 games, Hibernian *Premier Division, 1987–88*
21 in 44 games, East Fife *Division 1, 1986–87*

MOST GOALS IN A GAME
Football League
10, Joe Payne, for Luton T v Bristol R *Division 3(S), 13.4.1936*
Scottish League
8, Jimmy McGrory, for Celtic v Dunfermline Ath *Division 1, 14.9.1928*
8, Owen McNally, for Arthurlie v Armadale *Division 2, 1.10.1927*
8, Jim Dyet, for King's Park v Forfar Ath *Division 2, 2.1.1930*
8, John Calder, for Morton v Raith R *Division 2, 18.4.1936*
FA Cup
9, Ted MacDougall, for Bournemouth v Margate *1st Rd, 20.11.1971*
Scottish Cup
13, John Petrie, for Arbroath v Bon Accord *1st Rd, 12.9.1885*

MOST LEAGUE GOALS IN A SEASON
Football League
60 in 39 games, W.R. "Dixie" Dean (Everton) *Division 1, 1927–28*
59 in 37 games, George Camsell (Middlesbrough) *Division 2, 1926–27*
Scottish League
66 in 38 games, Jim Smith (Ayr U) *Division 2, 1927–28*
52 in 34 games, William McFadyen (Motherwell) *Division 1, 1931–32*

MOST LEAGUE GOALS IN A CAREER
Football League
434 in 619 games, Arthur Rowley *(WBA, Fulham, Leicester C, Shrewsbury T, 1946–65)*
Scottish League
410 in 408 games, Jimmy McGrory *(Celtic, Clydebank, Celtic, 1922–38)*

MOST CUP WINNERS' MEDALS
FA Cup
5, James Forrest (Blackburn R) *1884, 1885, 1886, 1890, 1891*
5, Hon. A.F. Kinnaird (Wanderers) *1873, 1877, 1878,* (Old Etonians) *1879, 1882*
5, C.H.R. Wollaston (Wanderers)*1872, 1873, 1876, 1877, 1878*
Scottish Cup
7, Jimmy McMenemy, (Celtic) *1904, 1907, 1908, 1911, 1912, 1914,* (Partick T) *1921*
7, Bob McPhail, (Airdrieonians) *1924,* (Rangers) *1928, 1930, 1932, 1934, 1935, 1936*
7, Billy McNeill (Celtic) *1965, 1967, 1969, 1971, 1972, 1974, 1975*

RECORD ATTENDANCES
Football League
83,260 Manchester U v Arsenal, Maine Road, 17.1.1948
Scottish League
118,567, Rangers v Celtic, Ibrox Stadium, 2.1.1939
FA Cup-tie (other than the final)
84,569, Manchester C v Stoke C, 6th Rd at Maine Road, 3.3.1934 *(a British record for any game outside London or Glasgow)*

FA Cup Final
126,047*, Bolton W v West Ham U, Wembley, 28.4.1923 *The figure stated is the official one. Perhaps as many as 70,000 more got in without paying.*
European Cup
135,826, Celtic v Leeds U, semi-final at Hampden Park, 15.4.1970

TRANSFER MILESTONES
First four-figure transaction
Alf Common: Sunderland to Middlesbrough £1,000, February 1905.
First five-figure transaction
David Jack: Bolton W to Arsenal £10,340, October 1928.
First six-figure transaction
Alan Ball: Blackpool to Everton £112,000, August 1966.
First £200,000 transaction
Martin Peters: West Ham U to Tottenham H £200,000, March 1970.
First seven-figure transaction
Trevor Francis: Birmingham C to Nottingham F £1,000,000, February 1979.
First £2,000,000 transaction
Paul Gascoigne: Newcastle U to Tottenham H £2,000,000, July 1988.
Highest British transaction
David Platt: Aston Villa to Bari £5,500,000, July 1991.
Paul Gascoigne: Tottenham H to Lazio £5,500,000, May 1992.

MOST GOALS IN AN INTERNATIONAL MATCH
England
5, Malcolm Macdonald (Newcastle U) v Cyprus, Wembley, 16.4.1975
5, Willie Hall (Tottenham H) v Ireland, Old Trafford, 16.11.1938
5, G.O. Smith (Corinthians) v Ireland, Sunderland, 18.2.1899
5*, Steve Bloomer (Derby Co) v Wales, Cardiff, 16.3.1896 (*one of which was credited to him in only some sources)*
5, Oliver Vaughton (Aston Villa) v Ireland, Belfast 18.2.1882
Scotland
5, Charles Heggie (Rangers) v Ireland, Belfast, 20.3.1886
Ireland
6, Joe Bambrick (Linfield) v Wales, Belfast, 1.2.1930
Wales
4, James Price (Wrexham) v Ireland, Wrexham, 25.2.1882
4, Mel Charles (Cardiff C) v N. Ireland, Cardiff, 11.4.1962
4, Ian Edwards (Chester) v Malta, Wrexham, 25.10.1978

MOST GOALS IN AN INTERNATIONAL CAREER
England
49 in 106 games, Bobby Charlton *(Manchester U)*
Scotland
30 in 55 games, Denis Law *(Huddersfield T, Manchester C, Torino, Manchester U)*
30 in 102 games, Kenny Dalglish *(Celtic, Liverpool)*
Ireland
12 in 25 games, Billy Gillespie *(Sheffield U)*
12 in 63 games, Gerry Armstrong *(Tottenham H, Watford, Real Mallorca, WBA, Chesterfield)*
12 in 11 games, Joe Bambrick *(Linfield, Chelsea)*
Wales
23 in 38 games, Trevor Ford *(Swansea T, Aston Villa, Sunderland, Cardiff C)*
23 in 68 games, Ivor Allchurch *(Swansea T, Newcastle U, Cardiff C)*
Republic of Ireland
20 in 70 games, Frank Stapleton *(Arsenal, Manchester U, Ajax, Derby Co, Le Havre, Blackburn R)*

THE FOOTBALL ASSOCIATION
FIXTURE PROGRAMME—SEASON 1992–93

August
1 Sat   Official Opening of Season
8 Sat   FA Charity Shield
15 Sat   Premier League & Football League Season
         commences
22 Sat
29 Sat   FA Challenge Cup Preliminary Round
31 Mon   Bank Holiday

September
5 Sat   FA Challenge Vase Extra Preliminary Round
9 Wed   International Date
12 Sat   FA Challenge Cup 1st Round Qualifying
         FA Youth Challenge Cup Preliminary Round*
16 Wed   EC/ECWC/UEFA 1st Round (1st Leg)
19 Sat   FA Challenge Trophy—1st Round Qualifying
26 Sat   FA Challenge Cup 2nd Round Qualifying
30 Wed   EC/ECWC/UEFA 1st Round (2nd Leg)

October
3 Sat   FA Challenge Vase Preliminary Round
         FA Youth Challenge Cup 1st Round Qualifying*
10 Sat   FA Challenge Cup 3rd Round Qualifying
11 Sun   FA Sunday Cup First Round
14 Wed   England v Norway (World Cup)
17 Sat   FA Challenge Trophy 2nd Round Qualifying
         FA Youth Challenge Cup 2nd Round
         Qualifying*
         FA County Youth Challenge Cup 1st Round*
21 Wed   EC/ECWC/UEFA 2nd Round (1st Leg)
24 Sat   FA Challenge Cup 4th Round Qualifying
31 Sat   FA Challenge Vase 1st Round

November
4 Wed   EC/ECWC/UEFA 2nd Round (2nd Leg)
7 Sat
8 Sun   FA Sunday Cup 2nd Round
14 Sat   FA Challenge Cup 1st Round Proper
         FA Youth Challenge Cup 1st Round Proper*
18 Wed   England v Turkey (World Cup)
21 Sat   FA Challenge Vase 2nd Round
25 Wed   UEFA Cup 3rd Round (1st Leg)
         FA Challenge Cup 1st Round Proper (Replay)
28 Sat   FA Challenge Trophy 3rd Round Qualifying
         FA County Youth Challenge Cup 2nd Round*

December
5 Sat   FA Challenge Cup 2nd Round Proper
6 Sun   FA Sunday Cup 3rd Round
9 Wed   UEFA Cup 3rd Round (2nd Leg)
12 Sat   FA Challenge Vase 3rd Round
         FA Youth Challenge Cup 2nd Round Proper*
16 Wed   FA Challenge Cup 2nd Round Proper (Replay)
19 Sat
25 Fri   Christmas Day
26 Sat   Boxing Day
28 Mon   Bank Holiday

January

1 Fri   New Years Day
2 Sat   FA Challenge Cup 3rd Round Proper
9 Sat   FA Challenge Trophy 1st Round Proper
13 Wed FA Challenge Cup 3rd Round Proper (Replay)
16 Sat FA Challenge Vase 4th Round
         FA Youth Challenge Cup 3rd Round Proper*
         FA County Youth Challenge Cup 3rd Round*
17 Sun FA Sunday Cup 4th Round
23 Sat FA Challenge Cup 4th Round Proper
30 Sat FA Challenge Trophy 2nd Round Proper

February

3 Wed FA Challenge Cup 4th Round Proper (Replay)
6 Sat   FA Challenge Vase 5th Round
         FA Youth Challenge Cup 4th Round Proper*
13 Sat FA Challenge Cup 5th Round Proper
14 Sun FA Sunday Cup 5th Round
17 Wed England v San Marino (World Cup)
20 Sat FA Challenge Trophy 3rd Round Proper
         FA County Youth Challenge Cup 4th Round*
24 Wed FA Challenge Cup 5th Round Proper (Replay)
27 Sat FA Challenge Vase Sixth Round

March

3 Wed EC/ECWC/UEFA Quarter Final (1st Leg)
6 Sat   FA Challenge Cup 6th Round Proper
         FA Youth Challenge Cup 5th Round Proper*
13 Sat FA Challenge Trophy 4th Round Proper
17 Wed EC/ECWC/UEFA Quarter Final (2nd Leg)
         FA Challenge Cup 6th Round Proper (Replay)
20 Sat FA Challenge Vase Semi-Final (1st Leg)
         FA County Youth Challenge Cup Semi-Final*
21 Sun FA Sunday Cup Semi-Final
27 Sat FA Challenge Vase Semi-Final (2nd Leg)
31 Wed Turkey v England (World Cup)

April

3 Sat   FA Challenge Trophy Semi-Final (1st Leg)
         FA Youth Challenge Cup Semi-Final*
4 Sun FA Challenge Cup Semi-Final
7 Wed EC/ECWC/UEFA Semi-Final (1st Leg)
9 Fri   Good Friday
10 Sat FA Challenge Trophy Semi-Final (2nd Leg)
12 Mon Easter Monday
14 Wed FA Challenge Cup Semi-Final (Replay)
17 Sat
21 Wed EC/ECWC/UEFA Semi-Final (2nd Leg)
24 Sat FA Challenge Vase Final (Provisional Date)
28 Wed England v Holland (World Cup)

May

1 Sat   Rugby League Final
         FA County Youth Challenge Cup Final*
2 Sun FA Sunday Cup Final
3 Mon Bank Holiday
5 Wed UEFA Cup Final (1st Leg)

May
 8 Sat   FA Challenge Trophy Final (Provisional Date)
          FA Youth Challenge Cup Final*
12 Wed   European Cup Winners Cup Final
15 Sat   FA Challenge Cup Final
18 Tue   International Date
19 Wed   UEFA Cup Final (2nd Leg)
21 Fri   International Date
23 Sun   International Date
26 Wed   European Champion Clubs' Cup Final
29 Sat   Poland v England (World Cup)

June
 2 Wed   Norway v England (World Cup)

Closing dates of rounds

USEFUL ADDRESSES

Football Association: R.H.G. Kelly, FCIS, 16 Lancaster Gate, London W2 3LW.
Scottish FA: J. Farry, 6 Park Gardens, Glasgow G3 7YF.
Irish FA: D. Bowen, 20 Windsor Avenue, Belfast BT9 6EG.
Welsh FA: A.E. Evans, B.Sc., 3 Westgate Street, Cardiff CF1 1JF.
FA of Ireland (Eire): 80 Merrion Square South, Dublin 2.
League of Ireland: E. Morris, 80 Merrion Square, Dublin 2.
Fedération Internationale de Football Association (FIFA): J. Blatter, FIFA House, 11 Hitzigweg, CH-8032 Zurich, Switzerland.
Union des Associations Européenes de Football (UEFA): G. Aigner, Jupiterstrasse 33 PO Box 16, CH-3000 Berne 15, Switzerland.
Football League: J.D. Dent, Lytham St Annes, Lancashire FY8 1JG.
Scottish League: 188 West Regent Street, Glasgow G2 4RY.
Irish League: M. Brown, 87 University Street, Belfast BT7 1HP.
Welsh League: K.J. Tucker, 16 The Parade, Merthyr Tydfil, Mid-Glamorgan CF47 0ET.
GM Vauxhall Conference: P.D. Hunter, 24 Barnehurst Road, Bexley Heath, Kent DA7 6EZ.
Beazer Homes League: D.J. Strudwick, 11 Welland Close, Durrington, Worthing, W. Sussex BN13 3NR.
Northern Premier League: R.D. Bayley, 22 Woburn Drive, Hale, Altrincham, Cheshire WA15 81Z.
Vauxhall League: N. Robinson, 226 Rye Lane, London SE15 4NL.
The Association of Football League Referees and Linesmen: J.B. Goggins, 1 Tewkesbury Drive, Lytham St Annes, Lancs FY8 4LN.
The Football League Executive Staffs Association: P.O. Box 52, Leamington Spa, Warwickshire.
Women's Football Association: Miss L. Whitehead, 448/450, Hanging Ditch, The Corn Exchange, Manchester M4 3ES.
English Schools FA: M.R. Berry, 4a Eastgate Street, Stafford ST16 2NN.
Professional Footballers' Association: G. Taylor, 2 Oxford Court, Bishopsgate, off Lower Mosley Street, Manchester M2 3W2.
The Association of Football Statisticians: R.J. Spiller, 22 Bretons, Basildon, Essex.
England Supporters' Association: David Stacey, 66 Southend Road, Wickford, Essex SS11 8EN.
The Football Programme Directory: Editor, David Stacey, 66 Southend Road, Wickford, Essex SS11 8EN.
National Federation of Football Supporters' Clubs: 24 South St, Loughborough, Leics LE11 3EG.
Football Trust: Second Floor, Walkden House, 10 Melton Street, London NW1 2EJ.

GM VAUXHALL CONFERENCE FIXTURES 1992–93

	Altrincham	Bath C.	Boston U.	Bromsgrove	Dagenham	Farnborough	Gateshead	Kettering T.	Kidderminster
Altrincham	—	6-2	19-9	24-4	14-11	17-10	25-8	26-12	17-11
Bath C.	21-11	—	3-2	20-3	27-3	7-11	30-1	8-12	26-12
Boston U.	13-3	3-10	—	30-11	2-1	23-1	3-4	14-4	29-8
Bromsgrove R.	12-12	2-1	25-8	—	6-2	26-12	20-2	23-1	12-4
Dagenham/Redbridge	27-2	17-4	17-11	29-8	—	25-8	16-1	1-5	13-3
Farnborough T.	1-5	16-1	21-11	10-4	6-3	—	22-8	10-10	5-9
Gateshead	16-9	31-10	6-2	7-11	5-9	5-12	—	27-3	12-12
Kettering T.	10-4	20-2	23-12	21-11	29-9	8-9	28-11	—	24-4
Kidderminster H.	22-8	10-4	16-1	28-12	19-9	27-2	14-11	31-8	—
Macclesfield T.	28-12	5-9	29-9	17-4	10-10	19-9	19-12	31-10	10-10
Merthyr Tydfil	5-12	31-8	7-11	19-1	22-8	3-4	13-2	23-2	2-1
Northwich V.	6-10	3-4	6-3	1-12	24-4	19-12	26-12	19-9	25-8
Runcorn	2-1	1-5	27-3	27-2	23-1	29-8	6-10	7-11	26-9
Slough T.	5-9	2-2	31-10	3-10	31-8	14-11	20-3	22-8	23-1
Stafford R.	10-11	19-9	23-3	5-12	21-11	3-10	10-10	19-12	15-9
Stalybridge Celtic	27-3	22-8	10-10	17-10	12-12	13-3	12-4	17-4	13-2
Telford U.	31-10	27-2	5-12	9-2	20-3	12-9	6-3	15-9	10-10
Welling U.	23-1	12-12	10-4	27-3	28-12	17-4	24-4	6-2	7-11
Witton A.	31-8	13-3	5-9	22-8	7-11	20-2	27-10	3-10	28-11
Woking	3-10	5-12	19-12	31-10	1-12	12-4	21-11	20-3	3-4
Wycombe W.	17-4	17-10	9-3	19-9	15-2	20-3	29-8	5-12	6-2
Yeovil T.	13-2	28-12	24-4	19-2	10-4	30-1	19-9	5-9	6-3

Macclesfield	Merthyr Tydfil	Northwich V.	Runcorn	Slough T.	Stafford R.	Stalybridge C.	Telford U.	Welling U.	Witton A.	Woking	Wycombe W.	Yeovil T.
12-4	29-8	7-11	10-10	16-1	26-9	30-1	20-2	19-12	3-4	6-3	28-11	20-3
6-3	8-9	10-10	28-11	25-8	24-4	19-12	23-1	13-10	29-8	15-9	29-9	12-4
14-11	1-5	12-12	22-8	26-9	2-9	10-2	17-10	26-12	20-3	28-11	9-9	27-2
15-9	28-11	5-9	3-4	13-2	14-11	6-3	3-11	12-9	16-1	1-5	10-10	26-9
17-10	30-1	3-10	31-10	9-2	13-2	20-2	28-11	12-4	19-12	6-10	3-4	26-12
24-4	6-10	28-11	6-2	23-2	27-3	31-10	12-12	3-11	26-9	28-12	31-8	2-1
26-9	17-4	10-4	31-8	27-2	2-1	28-12	3-10	17-10	17-11	23-1	13-3	1-5
29-8	17-10	13-2	30-1	3-11	6-10	3-4	2-1	13-3	27-2	25-8	26-9	12-12
30-1	27-3	1-5	19-12	5-12	20-3	21-11	17-4	3-10	17-10	12-9	31-10	20-2
—	16-1	31-8	13-3	21-11	17-11	10-4	13-2	27-2	5-12	27-3	22-8	23-1
3-10	—	13-3	24-4	10-4	5-9	14-11	28-12	26-9	23-1	10-10	12-9	2-2
13-10	31-10	—	5-12	29-8	23-1	26-9	21-11	14-11	12-4	6-2	27-2	27-3
25-8	20-3	15-9	—	17-10	12-4	13-10	29-9	13-2	26-12	12-12	21-11	12-9
12-12	26-12	20-2	6-3	—	3-4	6-2	19-9	10-11	24-4	2-1	12-4	13-10
6-2	20-2	17-4	28-12	1-5	—	25-8	10-4	29-8	30-3	13-3	30-1	31-10
26-12	19-9	2-1	17-11	7-11	27-2	—	31-8	1-5	2-2	29-8	23-1	28-11
7-11	12-4	30-1	16-1	19-12	26-12	1-12	—	3-4	25-8	26-9	24-4	29-8
28-11	21-11	20-3	19-9	10-10	6-3	5-9	22-8	—	31-10	8-12	2-1	31-8
2-1	6-3	28-12	10-4	27-3	24-11	15-9	1-5	30-1	—	13-2	12-12	10-10
20-2	27-2	17-10	5-9	30-1	22-8	24-4	30-3	16-1	19-9	—	26-12	19-1
1-5	19-12	16-1	20-2	28-12	7-11	3-10	5-9	25-8	24-10	10-4	—	15-9
3-4	25-8	22-8	3-10	17-4	17-10	16-1	13-3	5-12	21-11	7-11	9-2	—

FA PREMIER LEAGUE FIXTURES 1992–93

	Arsenal	Aston Villa	Blackburn R	Chelsea	Coventry C	Crystal Palace	Everton	Ipswich T	Leeds U	Liverpool
Arsenal	—	12.4	12.9	3.10	7.11	8.5	24.10	26.12	9.3	30.1
Aston Villa	28.12	—	19.10	2.9	10.4	5.9	20.2	6.2	19.8	19.9
Blackburn R	18.8	6.3	—	20.2	26.1	6.2	15.9	12.4	26.12	3.4
Chelsea	27.2	13.2	26.8	—	1.5	7.11	10.3	17.10	28.11	10.2
Coventry C	13.3	26.12	29.8	24.10	—	3.10	6.3	5.12	8.5	19.12
Crystal Palace	2.11	9.2	15.8	13.3	27.2	—	9.1	1.5	19.12	23.3
Everton	1.5	25.8	13.2	21.11	17.10	19.9	—	24.3	16.1	7.12
Ipswich T	10.4	15.8	28.12	6.3	20.3	24.10	28.11	—	3.10	25.8
Leeds U	21.11	13.9	10.4	23.3	31.10	17.4	26.9	27.2	—	29.8
Liverpool	23.8	9.1	12.12	5.9	17.4	28.11	20.3	20.2	27.1	—
Manchester C	16.1	19.12	30.1	20.9	10.3	6.3	8.5	3.4	7.11	12.4
Manchester U	24.3	13.3	1.5	17.4	28.12	2.9	19.8	22.8	6.9	18.10
Middlesbrough	17.4	26.9	5.12	12.12	6.2	28.12	10.4	1.9	22.8	13.3
Norwich C	6.2	24.3	27.2	19.8	16.1	27.1	22.8	21.12	14.4	1.5
Nottingham F	17.10	3.4	10.2	16.1	19.9	10.3	7.11	31.10	20.3	16.8
Oldham Ath	20.2	24.10	16.1	6.2	5.9	19.8	4.10	19.9	1.9	26.12
QPR	2.9	8.5	24.3	27.1	20.2	12.12	28.12	5.9	24.10	23.11
Sheffield U	19.9	29.8	17.4	8.5	28.11	20.3	12.12	16.1	7.3	12.9
Sheffield W	27.1	5.12	31.10	22.8	2.9	20.2	6.2	21.11	3.4	27.2
Southampton	5.12	30.1	21.11	10.4	12.12	16.1	17.4	13.3	19.9	13.2
Tottenham H	12.12	21.11	13.3	5.12	19.8	22.8	5.9	26.1	20.2	31.10
Wimbledon	5.9	3.10	19.9	28.12	22.8	10.4	26.1	18.8	6.2	16.1

Manchester C	Manchester U	Middlesbrough	Norwich C	Nottingham F	Oldham Ath	QPR	Sheffield U	Sheffield W	Southampton	Tottenham H	Wimbledon
28.9	28.11	19.12	15.8	6.3	26.8	13.2	9.1	29.8	20.3	3.4	9.2
17.4	7.11	16.1	28.11	12.12	1.5	1.11	27.1	20.3	22.8	10.3	27.2
22.8	24.10	20.3	3.10	5.9	26.9	28.11	19.12	8.5	9.3	7.11	9.1
9.1	19.12	3.4	12.9	26.9	15.8	29.8	31.10	30.1	26.12	20.3	12.4
21.11	12.4	15.8	26.9	9.1	10.2	26.8	24.3	13.2	3.4	14.9	30.1
17.10	13.2	12.4	29.8	21.11	12.9	3.4	5.12	25.8	26.9	30.1	26.12
31.10	12.9	26.12	30.1	13.3	27.2	12.4	3.4	15.8	19.12	10.2	29.8
12.12	30.1	13.2	17.4	8.5	9.1	9.2	26.9	9.3	7.11	30.8	12.9
13.3	9.2	30.1	28.12	5.12	13.2	1.5	17.10	12.12	9.1	25.8	15.8
28.12	6.3	7.11	24.10	6.2	10.4	10.3	19.8	3.10	1.9	8.5	26.9
—	20.3	12.9	26.8	3.10	29.8	17.8	26.12	10.2	24.10	28.11	13.2
5.12	—	27.2	12.12	27.1	21.11	26.9	6.2	10.4	20.2	9.1	31.10
19.8	3.10	—	8.5	20.2	23.3	9.1	7.9	24.10	26.1	6.3	21.11
20.2	3.4	31.10	—	31.8	13.3	17.10	21.11	19.9	5.9	26.12	5.12
27.2	29.8	21.10	13.2	—	30.1	26.12	1.5	12.9	28.11	12.4	20.12
26.1	9.3	28.11	7.11	22.8	—	20.3	12.4	6.3	8.5	19.12	3.4
6.2	16.1	19.9	6.3	10.4	5.12	—	22.8	17.4	19.8	3.10	13.3
10.4	15.8	9.2	10.3	24.10	29.12	30.1	—	8.11	3.10	13.2	25.8
5.9	26.12	1.5	9.1	19.8	17.10	19.12	14.3	—	12.4	27.9	24.3
1.5	24.8	29.8	10.2	24.3	31.10	12.9	27.2	28.12	—	15.8	17.10
23.3	19.9	17.10	9.4	28.12	17.4	27.2	2.9	16.1	6.2	—	1.5
1.9	8.5	9.3	20.3	17.4	12.12	7.11	20.2	28.11	6.3	25.10	—

BARCLAYS LEAGUE FIXTURES 1992–93

DIVISION ONE

	Barnsley	Birmingham C	Brentford	Bristol C	Bristol R	Cambridge	Charlton Ath	Derby Co	Grimsby T	Leicester C	Luton T
Barnsley	—	21.11	24.10	16.1	27.3	9.3	28.11	12.9	10.4	6.3	10.10
Birmingham C	23.3	—	5.12	13.3	24.10	30.1	8.5	6.4	29.8	10.10	9.1
Brentford	1.5	20.3	—	31.10	30.1	14.2	7.11	26.12	21.11	9.1	12.9
Bristol C	26.9	7.11	8.5	—	6.4	24.4	10.10	13.2	27.3	24.10	30.1
Bristol R	3.11	1.5	22.8	12.12	—	17.4	27.1	14.11	19.9	3.4	5.12
Cambridge	14.11	22.8	4.9	17.10	8.12	—	18.8	3.10	16.1	23.3	3.11
Charlton Ath	3.4	31.10	13.3	27.2	25.8	12.9	—	1.5	15.8	3.11	29.8
Derby Co	10.2	12.12	10.4	5.9	10.3	6.3	24.10	—	17.4	27.1	24.4
Grimsby T	26.12	20.2	23.3	14.11	9.1	26.9	6.2	19.12	—	5.12	13.3
Leicester C	3.10	27.2	19.9	1.5	28.11	21.11	27.3	26.8	20.3	—	15.8
Luton T	27.2	19.9	10.2	22.8	20.3	27.3	20.2	17.10	7.11	6.2	—
Millwall	20.2	12.9	16.1	4.11	8.5	10.10	24.4	13.3	12.12	28.12	24.3
Newcastle U	7.4	27.3	6.3	19.9	13.2	28.11	10.3	30.1	24.10	8.5	2.9
Notts Co	5.9	6.2	28.12	3.4	6.3	12.12	10.4	3.11	10.10	22.8	26.9
Oxford U	17.10	3.10	3.4	10.4	15.8	15.9	17.4	27.2	13.2	12.12	14.11
Peterborough U	9.1	9.3	10.10	17.4	21.11	10.4	28.12	15.8	6.3	24.4	24.10
Portsmouth	22.8	5.9	26.1	6.2	26.12	7.11	20.3	12.4	8.5	20.2	6.3
Southend U	19.12	27.1	21.2	10.2	14.4	25.10	6.3	16.1	23.4	5.9	8.5
Sunderland	5.12	10.4	12.12	20.2	26.9	9.1	5.9	23.3	28.12	14.11	17.4
Swindon T	31.10	29.12	3.11	23.3	12.9	29.8	16.1	5.12	29.9	17.4	10.4
Tranmere R	12.4	17.10	14.11	3.10	28.8	15.8	18.9	2.4	12.9	13.3	13.10
Watford	13.3	17.4	24.4	5.12	10.10	28.12	12.12	29.8	30.1	26.9	3.4
West Ham U	6.2	28.11	17.4	27.1	24.4	8.5	22.8	19.9	10.3	10.4	28.12
Wolverhampton W	26.1	16.1	6.2	28.12	7.11	20.3	21.11	31.10	28.11	18.8	12.12

Millwall	Newcastle U	Notts Co	Oxford U	Peterborough U	Portsmouth	Southend U	Sunderland	Swindon T	Tranmere R	Watford	West Ham U	Wolverhampton
29.8	12.12	13.2	24.4	19.9	30.1	17.4	20.3	8.5	28.12	7.11	15.8	1.9
9.2	3.11	15.8	6.3	2.1	13.2	1.9	26.12	12.4	24.4	19.12	3.4	26.9
26.9	3.10	12.4	28.11	27.2	1.9	29.8	6.4	27.3	9.3	7.10	20.12	15.8
9.3	9.1	28.11	26.12	19.12	15.8	12.9	29.8	21.11	6.3	20.3	15.9	12.4
31.10	5.9	3.10	6.2	24.3	10.4	28.12	16.1	19.8	20.2	27.2	17.10	13.3
27.2	3.4	6.4	26.1	26.12	13.3	1.5	19.9	20.2	6.2	13.4	31.10	5.12
17.10	14.11	30.1	19.12	12.4	5.12	3.10	13.2	26.9	9.1	6.4	26.12	23.3
7.11	22.8	27.3	10.10	6.2	28.12	26.9	21.11	20.3	28.11	20.2	9.1	8.5
6.4	1.5	27.2	5.9	3.10	31.10	17.10	12.4	26.1	9.2	22.8	3.11	3.4
13.4	31.10	26.12	7.4	17.10	29.8	13.2	10.3	20.12	7.11	16.1	30.1	12.9
21.11	27.1	16.1	10.3	1.5	3.10	31.10	19.12	26.12	5.9	28.11	13.4	7.4
—	17.4	19.9	22.8	27.1	3.4	5.12	6.3	5.9	10.4	6.2	15.11	24.10
19.12	—	20.3	12.4	16.1	12.9	15.8	25.4	7.11	10.10	21.11	29.8	26.12
9.1	5.12	—	24.10	20.2	17.4	23.3	8.5	24.4	26.1	25.8	13.3	14.11
30.1	28.12	1.5	—	5.12	3.11	13.3	12.9	9.1	26.9	31.10	23.3	29.8
15.9	26.9	29.8	20.3	—	12.12	30.1	7.11	28.11	8.5	27.3	12.9	13.2
28.11	9.2	19.12	27.3	6.4	—	9.1	24.10	10.10	21.11	9.3	26.9	24.4
20.3	20.1	21.11	7.11	22.8	18.9	—	28.11	10.3	26.3	26.12	7.4	10.10
3.0	18.10	31.10	9.2	13.3	1.5	3.4	—	6.2	22.8	26.1	27.2	3.11
13.2	13.3	17.10	19.9	3.4	27.2	14.11	15.8	—	12.12	3.10	1.5	30.1
26.12	27.2	29.9	15.1	30.10	23.3	3.11	30.1	6.4	—	1.5	4.12	19.12
15.8	23.3	12.9	8.5	3.11	14.11	10.4	29.9	6.3	24.10	—	13.2	9.1
27.3	20.2	7.11	21.11	10.2	16.1	12.12	10.10	24.10	20.3	5.9	—	6.3
1.5	10.4	9.3	20.2	5.9	17.10	27.2	27.3	22.8	17.4	19.9	3.10	—

DIVISION TWO

	Blackpool	Bolton W	Bournemouth	Bradford C	Brighton & HA	Burnley	Chester C	Exeter C	Fulham	Hartlepool U	Huddersfield T
Blackpool	—	20.2	15.9	26.12	19.9	24.10	13.4	22.8	19.12	6.3	3.11
Bolton W	1.9	—	19.9	19.12	30.1	28.11	24.4	20.3	27.3	10.10	15.8
Bournemouth	9.1	23.1	—	6.4	3.11	13.4	3.4	6.3	12.9	5.9	26.9
Bradford C	10.4	17.4	12.12	—	29.8	11.10	15.8	10.3	7.11	8.5	14.2
Brighton & HA	23.1	22.8	20.3	27.1	—	26.12	8.5	20.2	28.11	24.10	12.9
Burnley	1.5	23.3	28.12	27.2	10.4	—	13.2	17.4	17.10	3.4	21.11
Chester C	28.12	17.10	9.3	6.2	31.10	5.9	—	27.3	1.5	20.2	17.4
Exeter C	30.1	3.11	3.10	3.4	1.9	19.12	21.11	—	31.10	13.3	1.5
Fulham	17.4	21.11	2.1	13.3	23.3	24.4	24.10	8.5	—	28.12	2.4
Hartlepool U	4.10	27.2	13.2	31.10	1.5	9.3	1.9	7.11	12.4	—	29.8
Huddersfield T	20.3	6.2	16.1	6.9	2.1	27.3	19.12	24.10	10.3	27.1	—
Hull C	28.11	30.4	17.4	3.10	28.12	7.11	22.8	12.12	27.2	10.4	17.10
Leyton O	29.8	3.10	17.10	1.5	15.8	6.4	12.9	23.1	26.12	9.1	1.9
Mansfield T	13.2	3.4	1.9	12.9	12.12	23.1	9.1	24.4	29.8	21.11	13.3
Plymouth Arg	9.3	26.9	28.11	22.8	17.4	20.2	10.10	10.4	23.1	12.12	9.1
Port Vale	31.10	13.3	30.1	13.4	3.10	9.1	26.9	12.9	15.8	23.1	23.3
Preston NE	27.2	31.10	15.8	23.1	13.2	12.9	29.8	28.12	30.1	26.9	10.4
Reading	7.11	27.1	27.3	17.10	16.1	20.3	7.4	28.11	2.10	6.2	27.2
Rotherham U	26.9	12.9	26.2	23.3	17.10	26.1	3.11	6.2	6.4	22.8	3.10
Stockport Co	16.10	11.12	1.5	9.1	13.3	22.8	22.1	5.9	25.9	23.3	30.10
Stoke C	27.3	5.9	7.11	20.2	16.9	8.5	6.3	27.1	20.3	17.4	12.12
Swansea C	12.9	28.12	10.4	26.9	20.11	5.2	13.3	10.10	9.1	24.4	23.1
WBA	15.8	9.1	29.8	21.11	3.4	6.3	26.12	26.9	13.2	4.11	30.1
Wigan Ath	12.12	10.4	31.10	3.11	27.2	26.9	23.3	9.1	1.9	11.9	28.12

Hull C	Leyton O	Mansfield T	Plymouth Arg	Port Vale	Preston NE	Reading	Rotherham U	Stockport Co	Stoke C	Swansea C	WBA	Wigan Ath
23.3	26.1	5.9	3.4	8.5	10.10	13.3	16.1	24.4	21 11	2.1	6.2	6.4
24.10	6.3	9.3	16.1	7.11	8.5	29.8	2.1	6.4	13.2	12.4	15.9	26.12
19.12	24.4	20.2	23.3	22.8	6.2	21.11	10.10	24.10	13.3	26.12	26.1	8.5
6.3	24.10	2.1	30.1	28.12	19.9	24.4	28.11	16.9	2.9	16.1	27.3	20.3
14.4	6.2	7.4	19.12	6.3	5.9	26.9	24.4	7.11	9.1	27.3	10.3	10.10
13.3	12.12	19.9	29.9	15.9	2.1	3.11	29.8	30.1	31.10	15.8	3.10	16.1
30.1	2.1	15.9	27.2	16.1	26.1	12.12	19.3	19.9	3.10	7.11	10.4	27.11
6.4	19.9	17.10	26.12	2 1	12.4	23.3	15.8	13.2	29.8	27.2	16.1	15.9
10.10	10.4	26.1	19.9	6.2	22.8	6.3	12.12	16.1	3.11	15.9	5.9	20.2
26.12	15.9	27.3	6.4	19.9	16.1	15.8	30.1	28.11	20.12	17.10	20.3	2.1
24.4	20.2	7.11	15.9	28.11	26.12	10.10	6.3	8.5	7.4	19.9	22.8	12.4
—	16.1	20.3	28.8	27.3	15.9	13.2	19.9	2.1	15.8	1.9	31.10	9.3
26.9	—	28.11	13.2	20.3	18.12	30.1	9.3	12.4	27.2	31.10	7.11	27.3
3.11	23.3	—	15.8	10.4	24.10	28.12	8.5	10.10	26.9	30.1	17.4	6.3
26.1	5.9	6.2	—	24.4	6.3	8.5	7.11	27.3	12.9	20.3	28.12	24.10
21.11	3.11	26.12	17.10	—	6.4	3.4	1.9	29.8	16.3	13.2	27.2	19.12
9.1	17.4	1.5	3.10	12.12	—	20.10	27.3	20.3	17.10	9.3	28.11	7.11
5.9	22.8	12.4	31.10	10.3	20.2	—	16.9	19.12	26.12	1.5	2.1	19.9
23.1	3.4	31.10	13.3	20.2	21.11	9.1	—	26.12	12.4	18.12	1.5	5.9
12.9	23.12	26.2	20.11	26.1	3.11	16.4	9.4	—	3.4	3.10	20.2	5.2
6.2	10.10	16.1	2.1	24.10	24.4	10.4	28.12	10.3	—	28.11	19.9	22.8
20.2	8.5	22.3	3.11	5.9	3.4	24.10	17.4	5.3	23.3	—	12.12	26.1
8.5	13.3	20.12	12.4	10.10	24.3	9.9	24.10	2.9	23.1	7.4	—	24.4
3.4	21.11	3.10	1.5	17.4	12.3	23.1	13.2	15.8	30.1	29.8	17. 10	—

DIVISION THREE

	Barnet	Bury	Cardiff C	Carlisle U	Chesterfield	Colchester U	Crewe Alex	Darlington	Doncaster R	Gillingham
Barnet	—	2.1	22.11	5.9	6.2	21.8	31.10	23.3	20.2	26.1
Bury	12.9	—	23.3	20.2	26.1	5.9	1.5	13.3	6.2	22.8
Cardiff C	27.3	28.11	—	8.9	20.3	7.11	27.2	15.8	6.4	19.9
Carlisle U	13.2	1.9	9.1	—	23.1	20.3	12.12	10.4	27.3	7.11
Chesterfield	15.8	29.8	3.11	19.9	—	16.1	15.9	1.9	19.12	2.1
Colchester U	29.1	13.2	12.3	3.11	26.9	—	16.10	29.8	8.1	16.4
Crewe Alex	8.5	24.10	10.10	6.4	9.1	24.4	—	13.2	12.9	6.3
Darlington	28.11	7.11	6.2	26.12	20.2	26.1	5.9	—	12.4	27.3
Doncaster R	1.9	15.8	11.12	21.11	17.4	15.9	2.1	28.12	—	10.10
Gillingham	29.8	30.1	23.1	13.3	12.9	18.12	3.10	21.11	27.2	—
Halifax T	9.3	19.12	26.1	6.3	28.11	10.10	20.2	15.9	26.12	24.10
Hereford U	23.1	27.3	13.9	19.12	7.11	28.11	9.3	30.1	1.5	20.3
Lincoln C	24.10	24.4	28.12	26.1	10.4	6.2	27.3	8.5	23.1	28.11
Maidstone	10.10	8.5	24.4	22.8	5.9	9.3	16.1	2.1	20.3	10.4
Northampton T	8.1	6.4	19.2	23.3	13.10	26.12	26.1	3.11	17.10	6.2
Rochdale	6.4	12.4	6.3	10.10	8.5	27.3	7.11	19.9	28.11	15.9
Scarborough	26.12	6.3	3.4	8.5	24.10	13.4	22.8	24.4	26.9	5.9
Scunthorpe U	24.4	9.3	8.5	16.1	6.3	24.10	19.9	17.4	7.11	28.12
Shrewsbury T	6.3	19.9	24.10	3.4	24.4	20.2	28.12	10.10	22.8	12.12
Torquay U	13.4	16.1	5.9	24.10	10.10	6.4	6.2	6.3	26.1	8.5
Walsall	20.3	15.9	22.8	6.2	9.3	2.1	17.4	12.12	31.10	16.1
Wrexham	26.9	10.10	17.4	24.4	28.12	8.5	10.4	2.4	5.9	20.2
York C	7.11	20.3	10.4	2.1	12.12	19.9	28.11	16.1	3.10	9.3

Halifax T	Hereford U	Lincoln C	Maidstone	Northampton T	Rochdale	Scarborough	Scunthorpe U	Shrewsbury T	Torquay U	Walsall	Wrexham	York C
3.4	19.9	1.5	27.2	15.9	12.2	10.4	17.10	3.10	28.12	3.11	16.1	13.3
17.4	21.11	17.10	31.10	12.12	28.12	3.10	3.4	23.1	26.9	9.1	27.2	3.11
29.8	2.1	12.4	17.10	1.9	3.10	9.3	31.10	1.5	13.2	30.1	18.12	26.12
3.10	17.4	29.8	30.1	28.11	27.2	31.10	26.9	9.3	1.5	15.8	17.10	12.9
23.3	13.3	26.12	13.2	30.1	31.10	1.5	3.10	17.10	27.2	3.4	12.4	6.4
26.2	23.3	15.8	3.4	9.4	21.11	29.12	1.5	1.9	11.12	12.9	30.10	22.1
1.9	2.4	21.11	26.9	28.8	12.3	30.1	23.1	12.4	15.8	18.12	26.12	23.3
9.1	21.8	31.10	12.9	20.3	23.1	17.10	19.12	27.2	2.10	6.4	9.3	25.9
10.4	23.10	18.9	3.11	24.4	23.3	16.1	13.3	29.1	29.8	8.5	13.2	5.3
1.5	3.11	23.3	26.12	15.8	8.1	13.2	12.4	6.4	31.10	26.9	1.9	2.4
—	8.5	2.1	6.4	16.1	6.2	19.9	22.8	20.3	7.11	24.4	26.3	12.4
31.10	—	1.9	12.4	13.2	26.9	15.8	6.4	26.12	17.10	29.8	3.10	9.1
12.9	20.2	—	9.1	6.3	17.4	20.3	5.9	26.9	9.3	10.10	7.11	22.8
12.12	28.12	15.9	—	17.4	20.2	27.3	6.2	7.11	28.11	6.3	19.9	24.10
26.9	6.9	3.10	20.12	–	2.4	27.2	12.9	31.10	23.1	12.4	27.4	21.11
15.8	16.1	19.12	1.9	9.3	—	29.8	26.12	13.2	20.3	24.10	30.1	24.4
23.1	6.2	3.11	21.11	10.10	26.1	—	23.3	9.1	12.9	13.3	6.4	19.12
30.1	12.12	13.2	15.8	2.1	10.4	28.11	—	29.8	27.3	1.9	20.3	10.10
3.11	10.4	16.1	13.3	8.5	5.9	15.9	26.1	—	17.4	21.11	2.1	6.2
13.3	24.4	3.4	23.3	19.9	3.11	2.1	21.11	20.12	—	26.12	15.9	20.2
17.10	26.1	27.2	3.10	28.12	1.5	7.11	20.2	27.3	10.4	—	28.11	5.9
21.11	6.3	13.3	23.1	24.10	22.8	12.12	3.11	12.9	9.1	23.3	—	26.1
28.12	15.9	30.1	1.5	26.3	17.10	17.4	27.2	15.8	1.9	13.2	29.8	—